The Hollow Hope

American Politics and Political Economy

A series edited by BENJAMIN I. PAGE

Gerald N. Rosenberg

The Hollow Hope
Can Courts Bring About Social Change?

Second Edition

The University of Chicago Press

Chicago and London

Gerald N. Rosenberg teaches both law and political science at the University of Chicago and is a member of the Washington, D.C., Bar.

The University of Chicago Press, Chicago 60637
The University of Chicago Press, Ltd., London
© 1991, 2008 by The University of Chicago
All rights reserved. Published 2008
Printed in the United States of America

17 16 15 14 13 12 11 10 09 08   1 2 3 4 5

ISBN-13: 978-0-226-72670-0 (cloth)
ISBN-13: 978-0-226-72671-7 (paper)
ISBN-10: 0-226-72670-3 (cloth)
ISBN-10: 0-226-72671-1 (paper)

Library of Congress Cataloging-in-Publication Data

Rosenberg, Gerald N.
  The hollow hope : can courts bring about social change? / Gerald N. Rosenberg. — 2nd ed.
    p. cm.
  Includes bibliographical references and index.
  ISBN-13: 978-0-226-72670-0 (cloth : alk. paper)
  ISBN-13: 978-0-226-72671-7 (pbk. : alk. paper)
  ISBN-10: 0-226-72670-3 (cloth : alk. paper)
  ISBN-10: 0-226-72671-1 (pbk. : alk. paper) 1. Courts—United States. 2. Political questions and judicial power—United States. 3. Sociological jurisprudence. 4. Civil rights—United States. 5. Women's rights—United States. 6. Social change. I. Title.
  KF8700.R66 2008
  340'.115—dc22
                                                                                        2007038915

♾ The paper used in this publication meets the minimum requirements of the American National Standard for Information Sciences—Permanence of Paper for Printed Library Materials, ANSI Z39.48-1992.

To the Memory of My Parents,
MILTON H. AND BEATRICE N. ROSENBERG

and for
BONNIE L. KOENIG

With the breath, smiles, tears, of all my life.
—Browning

Contents

List of Tables and Figures   ix
Preface to the Second Edition   xi
Preface to the First Edition   xiii
Introduction   1

1. The Dynamic and the Constrained Court   9

Part 1 · Civil Rights

Introduction   39
2. Bound for Glory? *Brown* and the Civil Rights
   Revolution   42
3. Constraints, Conditions, and the Courts   72
4. Planting the Seeds of Progress?   107
5. The Current of History   157

Part 2 · Abortion and Women's Rights

Introduction   173
6. Transforming Women's Lives? The Courts and
   Abortion   175
7. Liberating Women? The Courts and Women's Rights   202
8. The Court as Catalyst?   228
9. The Tide of History   247

Part 3 · The Environment, Reapportionment, and Criminal Law

Introduction   269
10. Cleaning House? The Courts, the Environment, and
    Reapportionment   271

11. Judicial Revolution? Litigation to Reform the Criminal
    Law   304

Part 4 · Same-Sex Marriage

Introduction   339
12. You've Got That *Loving* Feeling? The Litigation
    Campaign for Same-Sex Marriage   342
13. Confusing Rights with Reality: Litigation for Same-Sex
    Marriage and the Counter-Mobilization of Law   355
14. Conclusion: The Fly-Paper Court   420

Epilogue   430

Appendices
1. Black Children in Elementary and Secondary School with
   Whites: 1954–72   433
2. Blacks at Predominantly White Public Colleges and
   Universities   436
3. Black Voter Registration in the Southern States: Pre- and
   Post-Voting Rights Act   437
4. Laws and Actions Designed to Preserve Segregation   438
5. Method for Obtaining Information for Table 4.1 and
   Figure 4.1   440
6. Illegal Abortions   441
7. Method for Obtaining Information for Tables 8.1A, 8.1B,
   8.2A, and 8.2B, and for Figures 8.1 and 8.2   444
8. Coding Rules and Methods for Obtaining Information for
   Tables 13.3, 13.4, 13.5, 13.6, and 13.7   446

Case References   449
References   457
Index   513

Tables and Figures

Tables

2.1. Black Children in Elementary and Secondary School with Whites, 1954–72   50

2.2. Desegregated School Districts, by Primary Source of Intervention, and by Year of Greatest Desegregation, 1901–74   53

2.3A. Blacks at Southern, Predominantly White Public Colleges and Universities, 1963, 1965, 1966   56

2.3B. Percentage of Black Enrollment at Southern, Formerly All-White Public Colleges and Universities, by State, 1970 and 1978   56

2.4. Black Voter Registration in the Southern States, 1940–70   61

3.1. Federal Funds for Public Elementary and Secondary Schools in 17 Southern and Border States, 1963–72   98

3.2. Percentage of Public School Budgets Received from Federal Funds in Southern and Border States, 1963–71, and Percentage of Blacks in School with Whites, 1964–65 and 1972–73   99

3.3. Selected Southern School Districts by Extent of Desegregation and Amount of Federal Funds Received, 1967–70   100

4.1. Magazine and Press Coverage of Civil Rights, 1940–65   114

4.2. Civil Rights Demonstrations, 1940–65   134

4.3. Income for Civil Rights Organizations, 1940–65   151

4.4. NAACP and CORE Membership, 1940–65   154

6.1. Legal Abortions, 1966–85   180

6.2. Percentage of Hospital Providers Providing Abortions, 1973–85   190

6.3. Percentage of Women Going Out of State of Residence to Obtain Abortions   192

6.4. Number of Abortion Providers, 1973–85   197

6.5. Facilities That Provide Abortions, 1973–85   197

7.1. The Earnings Gap   209

8.1A.   Magazine and Press Coverage of Abortion, 1940–76   232
8.1B.   Magazine Coverage of U.S. Supreme Court Abortion Decisions,
        1973–76   234
8.2A.   Magazine and Press Coverage of Women's Rights, 1940–76   233
8.2B.   Magazine Coverage of the Women's Liberation Movement, 1968–76   234
  8.3. Membership in the National Organization for Women and the National
        Abortion Rights Action League, 1967–85   243
 10.1. Magazine and Press Coverage of the Environment, 1965–85   289
 13.1. Key Events in the Movement for Same-Sex Marriage, 1993–2007   357
 13.2. *Reader's Guide to Periodical Literature,* 1990–2005   384
 13.3. *New York Times* Entries Mentioning "Same-Sex Marriage, Gay Marriage or
        Homosexual Marriage," by Year, 1980–2004   387
 13.4. *New York Times* Entries Mentioning "Same-Sex Marriage, Gay Marriage or
        Homosexual Marriage," by Month, Selected Years   389
 13.5. *New York Times* Entries Mentioning "Same-Sex Marriage, Gay Marriage or
        Homosexual Marriage," by Year and Content, 1980–2004   392
 13.6. *New York Times* Editorials and Op-Eds Mentioning "Same-Sex Marriage,
        Gay Marriage, Homosexual Marriage, Domestic Partnership or Civil Union,"
        1980–2004   395
 13.7. *Chicago Tribune* Editorials and Op-Eds Mentioning "Same-Sex Marriage,
        Gay Marriage, Homosexual Marriage, Domestic Partnership or Civil Union,"
        1985–2004   399
 13.8. Should Same-Sex Marriages be Recognized by Law?, 1989–2005
        (percentages)   402–3
 13.9. Should Civil Unions be Recognized by Law? Gallup, 2000–2004
        (percentages)   406
13.10. Percentage of Americans Willing to Hire Gay Men and Lesbians for Various
        Occupations, 1977–2005   409
App. 6, A.1.   Estimates of Illegal Abortions   442

Figures

2.1.   Percentage of Southern Black Schoolchildren Attending School with
       Whites   51
2.2.   Black Voter Registration in the Southern States   60
4.1.   Magazine Coverage of Civil Rights, 1940–65   113
4.2.   The Most Important Problem Facing This Country Today: Civil Rights
       Responses   130
4.3.   Civil Rights Demonstrations, 1940–65   135
6.1.   Legal Abortions, 1966–85   179
8.1.   Magazine Coverage of Abortion, 1940–76   230
8.2.   Magazine Coverage of Women's Rights, 1940–76   231

Preface to the Second Edition

I was standing in the ballroom of a hotel at the 1995 meeting of the American Association of Law Schools when a voice boomed out across the room, catching everyone's attention: "Rosenberg," the voice called out excitedly, "I've got you!" The speaker was a professor at Yale Law School from whom I had taken a class. After exchanging pleasantries, I asked him what he meant. He responded with one word: "Hawaii." Expounding on that answer, he explained that the argument of this book was wrong because the Hawaiian courts were on the verge of requiring the state to issue marriage licenses to same-sex couples. Once that happened, he argued, all states would be required to recognize them under the Full Faith and Credit Clause of Article IV of the Constitution. Thus, the right to same-sex marriage was on the verge of being won nationwide through litigation. I knew, then, that I had to investigate the litigation effort to win the right to same-sex marriage.

This second edition has been a long time in coming. In part this is due to the fact that the battle for same-sex marriage is constantly evolving. Each time I thought I was almost done a new event occurred, enriching and sometimes complicating the analysis. It got to the point where I would have to either set an arbitrary cutoff date or never publish. Obviously, I chose the former.

This edition contains a new section, part IV, on same-sex marriage, which includes an introduction and two chapters. Chapter 12 investigates the direct effects of litigation to win the right to same-sex marriage and chapter 13 focuses on indirect effects. The rest of the book is unchanged except, of course, for the conclusion, now chapter 14, which incorporates the lessons learned from same-sex marriage litigation. I have also added a short epilogue.

The rest of the book is unchanged because, pigheaded though I may be, I still think the argument is correct. While there has been no shortage of critics, for the most part I don't find the criticism particularly troubling. As I note in the epilogue, I have responded to criticisms in several publications. However, for the benefit of the reader, I have posted a response to critics as well as a list of reviews on a permanent Web page maintained by the University of Chicago Press. It can be found at http://www.press.uchicago.edu/books/Rosenberg/.

I presented the ideas contained in these new chapters at several scholarly meetings, including the annual meetings of the Midwest Political Science Association and the Law & Society Association. As the project neared completion I presented the main argument at, and received valuable feedback from, the American Politics Workshop at the Harris School of the University of Chicago and the Law and Political Economy Workshop at Northwestern University Law School. I owe many thanks to Will Howell of the Harris School and Lee Epstein and Emerson Tiller of Northwestern. I also received more than a dozen student critiques from the Northwestern Workshop. An earlier draft of the material was read by Steve Teles's seminar at Yale Law School and I am grateful for the feedback I received from both Professor Teles and a couple of his students.

Two colleagues, Ellen Andersen of Indiana University Purdue University Indianapolis and Andy Koppelman of Northwestern University Law School, read the penultimate draft of these new chapters and provided thoughtful and detailed comments. In their own way each pushed me to refine the argument and make it more nuanced.

I was also aided by two terrific research assistants: Chris Rohrbacher at the early stages of the project and Jennifer Esquibel at the later stages, which included the newspaper coding for part IV. Both are fine scholars and I regret not having dissuaded them from practicing law.

Finally, I owe an enormous debt of gratitude to John Tryneski of the University of Chicago Press. Waiting for me to complete this revised edition took the patience of Job. Over the many years I have worked with John, both as one of his authors and as a member of the Faculty Board of the University of Chicago Press, my admiration has only grown. John is not only knowledgeable, he is also patient and wise. He is all an editor and colleague can be.

Finally, I need hardly state that all errors are mine. If the first edition is any indication, there will be many readers who will make the point crystal clear.

Preface to the First Edition

This is a book about the role of courts in producing major political and social change in the middle and late decades of the twentieth century. Growing
up in the 1960s in a liberal New York City household, I naturally looked
to the Supreme Court, identifying it with important liberal decisions in a host
of fields. But study overseas, and a deepening understanding of the role of
courts in other democratic systems, made me curious about the unique role
of U.S. courts. Completion of a law degree further piqued my curiosity, for
the idea that the Supreme Court played a fundamental role in reshaping modern American society was uncritically assumed by all. Curiosity got the best
of me.

In examining the role of the courts I am neither attacking nor praising
them. Rather, my aim is to understand to what extent they helped and can
help produce liberal change. Both supporters and critics of judicial activism
are likely to be disappointed because I do not take sides on the question of
what courts *ought* to do. I do take a position on the usefulness of litigation to
liberal reformers. And my approach is entirely independent of the individual
makeup of the courts. To many in the liberal community, one lasting impact
of the Reagan revolution is the rightward tilt of the judiciary through the
appointment of politically conservative judges and justices. Regardless of the
accuracy of this assertion, I look past individuals to the structure of the judicial system, for it is likely that sometime in the future a politically liberal
president will appoint different judges and justices. And, of course, I want to
understand the role of the courts in the pre-Reagan era.

This is not a book about what caused or causes liberal change. Readers
looking for such a full-blown analysis will be disappointed. It is about
whether the courts can or did produce such change. While I do address the
broader question in two chapters, the analysis is offered to help the reader
understand the role of the courts, not as a theory standing on its own.

A work of this size only comes to fruition with the help of many minds.

My thinking about the courts evolved over several years and benefited enormously from the insight others offered. While many people have helped, I wish to particularly express my appreciation to Christopher Achen, Henry Brady, Annis Cats, Robert Dahl, Michael Denning, Robert M. Eisinger, Richard Gaskins, John Mark Hansen, Milton Heumann, Dan Kelliher, Donald R. Kinder, Bonnie Koenig, Kevin O'Brien, Gary Orfield, John F. Padgett, Adolph Reed, Steven Rosenstone, Martin Shapiro, Stephen J. Schulhofer, Bernard S. Silberman, Rebecca Stone, and Robin Wolpert. I received helpful and thoughtful comments via the mail from Larry Baum, Derrick Bell, Paul Burstein, Patricia K. Geschwent, Susan Hedman, Doug McAdam, Stuart Scheingold, and Lettie Wenner. Mary Becker and Cass Sunstein provided me detailed, extensive, and helpful written comments on several chapters. Several anonymous readers provided useful criticism. To those I have inadvertently omitted, I apologize.

I was extraordinarily fortunate to have worked closely at various times with J. David Greenstone, David Mayhew, and Rogers Smith. They tirelessly read and criticized repeated drafts with an attention to detail and a grasp of abstract ideas that still astounds me. Their advice, although not always followed, was invaluable.

In particular, David Greenstone treated my manuscript as his "special project." He spent hours over lunch, coffee, and the like offering criticisms and suggestions in his brilliant and endearing way. Even when the illness that took his life left him in pain, he somehow found the time and the energy to continue to work with me. Had he lived longer, this would have been a better book. It is with great admiration and a profound sense of loss that I dedicate the book to his memory.

Ray Lodato, Jadie Moore, Mark Nallia-Tone, Jimmie Reed Shiner, Jr., Tom Thress, and Mark Zaleski provided helpful research assistance. In particular, Jimmie Reed Shiner, Jr., worked long and hard hours in the search for the ever-evasive last piece of evidence and the reference I thought I had seen but couldn't quite remember. Without his help, I would still be working on the project.

A Faculty Fellowship from the John M. Olin Foundation permitted me to take time off from teaching and administrative responsibilities, and the University of Chicago Law School provided me with an office and a congenial setting to complete the book.

Finally, I am tempted to take credit for all the good ideas in the following pages and blame the people mentioned above for the bad ones. Alas, honesty compels me to admit that the truth is much closer to the opposite.

Introduction

The Problem

JUSTICE JACKSON: "I suppose that realistically the reason this case is here was that action couldn't be obtained from Congress. Certainly it would be here much stronger from your point of view if Congress did act, wouldn't it?"

MR. RANKIN: "That is true, but . . . if the Court would delegate back to Congress from time to time the question of deciding what should be done about rights . . . the parties [before the Court] would be deprived by that procedure from getting their constitutional rights because of the present membership or approach of Congress to that particular question." (Oral argument in *Briggs* v. *Elliott*, quoted in Friedman 1969, 244)

When Justice Jackson and Assistant U.S. Attorney General J. Lee Rankin exchanged these thoughts during oral argument in a companion case to *Brown*, they acknowledged that the Supreme Court is part of a larger political system. As their colloquy overtly demonstrates, American courts are political institutions. Though unique in their organization and operation, they are a crucial cog in the machinery of government. But this exchange rests on a more interesting premise that is all the more influential because it is implicit and unexamined: court decisions produce change. Specifically, both Jackson and Rankin assumed that it mattered a great deal how the Court decided the issue of school segregation. If their assumption is correct, then one may ask sensibly to what extent and in what ways courts can be consequential in effecting political and social change. To what degree, and under what conditions, can judicial processes be used to produce political and social change? What are the constraints that operate on them? What factors are important and why?

These descriptive or empirical questions are important for understanding the role of any political institution, yet they are seldom asked of courts. Traditionally, most lawyers and legal scholars have focused on a related normative issue: whether courts *ought* to act. From the perspective of democratic theory, that is an important and useful question. Yet since much of politics is about who gets what, when, and how, and how that distribution is maintained, or changed, understanding to what extent, and under what conditions, courts can produce political and social change is of key importance.

The answer to the questions raised above might appear obvious if it rests on Rankin's and Jackson's implied premise that courts produce a great deal of social change. In the last several decades movements and groups advocating what I will shortly define as significant social reform have turned increasingly to the courts. Starting with the famous cases brought by the civil rights movement and spreading to issues raised by women's groups, environmental groups, political reformers, and others, American courts seemingly have become important producers of political and social change. Cases such as *Brown* (school desegregation) and *Roe* (abortion) are heralded as having produced major change. Further, such litigation has often occurred, and appears to have been most successful, when the other branches of government have failed to act. While officious government officials and rigid, unchanging institutions represent a real social force which may frustrate popular opinion, this litigation activity suggests that courts can produce significant social reform even when the other branches of government are inactive or opposed. Indeed, for many, part of what makes American democracy exceptional is that it includes the world's most powerful court system, protecting minorities and defending liberty, in the face of opposition from the democratically elected branches. Americans look to activist courts, then, as fulfilling an important role in the American scheme.[1] This view of the courts, although informed by recent historical experience, is essentially functional. It sees courts as powerful, vigorous, and potent proponents of change. I refer to this view of the role of the courts as the "Dynamic Court" view.

As attractive as the Dynamic Court view may be, one must guard against uncritical acceptance. Indeed, in a political system that gives sovereignty to the popular will and makes economic decisions through the market, it is not obvious why courts should have the effects it asserts. Maybe its attractiveness is based on something more than effects? Could it be that the self-understanding of the judiciary and legal profession leads to an overstatement of the role of the courts, a "mystification" of the judiciary? If judges see themselves as

1. Not everyone, however, thinks such liberal judicial activism is a good thing. It has spawned a wave of attacks on the judiciary ranging from Nathan Glazer's warning of the rise of an "imperial judiciary" to a spate of legislative proposals to remove court jurisdiction over a number of issues. See Glazer (1975); *An Imperial Judiciary* (1979). And, of course, Presidents Nixon and Reagan pledged to end judicial activism by appointing "strict constructionists" to the federal courts.

powerful; if the Bar views itself as influential, and insulated; if professional training in law schools inculcates students with such beliefs, might these factors inflate the self-importance of the judiciary? The Dynamic Court view may be supported, then, because it offers psychological payoffs to key actors by confirming self-images, not because it is correct.[2] And when this "mystification" is added to a normative belief in the courts as the guardian of fundamental rights and liberties—what Scheingold (1974) calls the "myth of rights"—the allure of the Dynamic Court view may grow.

Further, for all its "obviousness," the Dynamic Court view has a well-established functional and historical competitor. In fact, there is a long tradition of legal scholarship that views the federal judiciary, in Alexander Hamilton's famous language, as the "least dangerous" branch of government. Here, too, there is something of a truism about this claim. Courts, we know, lack both budgetary and physical powers. Because, in Hamilton's words, they lack power over either the "sword or the purse," their ability to produce political and social change is limited. In contrast to the first view, the "least dangerous" branch can do little more than point out how actions have fallen short of constitutional or legislative requirements and hope that appropriate action is taken. The strength of this view, of course, is that it leaves Americans free to govern themselves without interference from non-elected officials. I refer to this view of the courts as weak, ineffective, and powerless as the "Constrained Court" view.

The Constrained Court view fully acknowledges the role of popular preferences and social and economic resources in shaping outcomes. Yet it seems to rely excessively on a formal-process understanding of how change occurs in American politics. But the formal process doesn't always work, for social and political forces may be overly responsive to unevenly distributed resources. Bureaucratic inertia, too, can derail orderly, processional change. There is room, then, for courts to effectively correct the pathologies of the political process. Perhaps accurate at the founding of the political system, the Constrained Court view may miss growth and change in the American political system.

Clearly, these two views, and the aspirations they represent, are in conflict on a number of different dimensions. They differ not only on both the desirability and the effectiveness of court action, but also on the nature of American democracy. The Dynamic Court view gives courts an important place in the American political system while the older view sees courts as much less powerful than other more "political" branches and activities. The conflict is more than one of mere definition, for each view captures a very different part of American democracy. We Americans want courts to protect minorities and defend liberties, *and* to defer to elected officials. We want a

2. As McCann (1986, 114) suggests, in the public-interest movement, lawyers are "quite naturally the most ardent spokespersons" for the use of courts to produce change.

robust political life *and* one that is just. Most of the time, these two visions do not clash. American legislatures do not habitually threaten liberties, and courts do not regularly invalidate the acts of elected officials or require certain actions to be taken. But the most interesting and relevant cases, such as *Brown* and *Roe*, occur when activist courts overrule and invalidate the actions of elected officials, or order actions beyond what elected officials are willing to do. What happens then? Are courts effective producers of change, as the Dynamic Court view suggests, or do their decisions do little more than point the way to a brighter, but perhaps unobtainable future? Once again, this conflict between two deeply held views about the role of the courts in the American political system has an obvious normative dimension that is worth debating. But this book has a different aim. Relying heavily on empirical data, I ask under what conditions can courts produce political and social change? When does it make sense for individuals and groups pressing for such change to litigate? What do the answers mean about the nature of the American regime?

Political and social change are broad terms. Specifically, conflict between the two views is more sharply focused when courts become involved in social reform, the broadening and equalizing of the possession and enjoyment of what are commonly perceived as basic goods in American society. What are these basic goods? Rawls (1971, 42) provides a succinct definition: "Rights and liberties, powers and opportunities, income and wealth." Later he adds self-respect (Rawls 1971, 440). Fleshed out, these include political goods such as participation in the political process and freedom of speech and association; legal goods such as equal and non-discriminatory treatment of all people; material goods; and self-respect, the opportunity for every individual to lead a satisfying and worthy life. Contributions to political and social change bring these benefits to people formerly deprived of them.

Yet, so defined, social reform is still too broad a term to capture the essence of the difference between the two views. At the core of the debate lies those specific social reforms that affect large groups of people such as blacks, or workers, or women, or partisans of a particular political persuasion; in other words, *policy change with nationwide impact.* Litigation aimed at changing the way a single bureaucracy functions would not fit this definition, for example, while litigation attempting to change the functioning of a whole set of bureaucracies or institutions nationwide would. Change affecting groups of this size, as well as altering bureaucratic and institutional practice nationwide can be called *significant* social reform. So, for example, in the *Brown* litigation, when civil rights litigators sued to end school segregation nationwide, not just in the school systems in which the complaints arose, they were attempting to use the courts to produce significant social reform. Similarly, when abortion activists mounted a constitutional challenge to restrictive abortion laws, aimed at affecting all women, they were attempting to use the courts to produce significant social reform. Although the relevant boundary line cannot be drawn precisely, there is no doubt that the aim of modern litigation in the areas of civil rights, women's rights, and the like, is to produce significant social reform.[3]

This definition of significant social reform does not take much note of the role of the courts in individual cases. Due process and court procedures offer at least some protection to the individual from arbitrary action. Interposing courts and set procedures between government officials and citizens has been a hard fought-for and great stride forward in human decency.[4] However, the protection of individuals, in individual cases, tells us little about the effectiveness of courts in producing nationwide policy change. In addition, there is no clash between the two views in dealing with individuals.

There is good reason to focus solely on the effectiveness of courts in producing significant social reform. Other possibilities, such as courts acting as obstacles to significant social reform, can be excluded because adequate work has been done on them. Studies of the role of the courts in the late nineteenth and early twentieth centuries, for example, show that courts can effectively block significant social reform.[5] Further, since the mid-twentieth century litigants have petitioned American courts with increasing frequency to produce significant social reform. Reform-minded groups have brought cases and adopted strategies that assumed courts could be consequential in furthering their goals. To narrow the focus is to concentrate on an important aspect of recent political activity.

The attentive reader will have noticed that I have written of courts being consequential in effecting significant social reform, of courts producing significant social reform, or of courts being of help to reformers. All of these formulations suggest that courts can sometimes make a difference. The question, then, is whether, and under what conditions, this occurs. When does it makes sense to litigate to help bring about significant social reform? If the judiciary lacks power, as the Constrained Court view suggests, then courts cannot make much difference. Perhaps only when political, social, and economic forces have already pushed society far along the road to reform will

3. A major study of public-interest law takes a similar "focus on policy-oriented cases, where a decision will affect large numbers of people or advance a major law reform objective" (Council for Public Interest Law 1976, 7).

4. See, for example, Thompson (1975), particularly chapter 10, and Hay et al. (1975). Though the focus of both works is on the role of the criminal law in the eighteenth century in sustaining the hegemony of the English ruling class, both view law as affording some protection to individuals.

5. A simple example is child labor, where the Supreme Court twice overturned congressional legislation prohibiting it, delaying its eventual outlawing for several decades. For a careful study of the ability of courts to effectively block significant social reform, see Paul (1960). However, it should be noted that given the appointment power, and the general dependence of courts on political elites, such blocking cannot continue indefinitely. On this point, see Dahl (1957).

courts have any independent effect. And even then their decisions may be more a reflection of significant social reform already occurring than an independent, important contribution to it. But if the Dynamic Court view is the more accurate, if courts are effective producers of significant social reform, then they will be able to produce change. And if each view is partly right, if courts are effective under some conditions and not others, then I want to know when and where those conditions exist.

There is a danger that I have set up a straw man. Given the incremental nature of change in American politics, one might wonder if there is ever significant social reform in the U.S. In fact, if there is not, then asking whether and under what conditions courts produce it won't tell me anything about courts and change. I run the danger of "finding" that courts don't produce significant social reform because it doesn't exist! Fortunately, there are numerous examples of significant social reform in the U.S.: the introduction of social security, medicaid and medicare; increased minority participation in the electoral process; the increasing racial integration of American institutions and society; the increasing breakdown of gender barriers and discrimination against women; enhanced protection of the environment and reduction of pollution; protection for working men and women who organize to improve their lot; and so on. Clearly, then, there is significant social reform in the U.S. And, of course, proponents of the Dynamic Court view claim that both *Brown* and *Roe* produced significant social reform.

In order to determine whether and under what conditions courts can produce significant social reform, the bulk of this book concentrates on two key areas of significant social reform litigation, civil rights and women's rights. These two movements and their leading, symbolic cases (*Brown* and *Roe*) are generally considered the prime examples of the successful use of a court-based strategy to produce significant social reform. Proponents of the Dynamic Court view generally credit *Brown* with having revolutionized American race relations while *Roe* is understood as having guaranteed legal abortions for all. Defenders of the Constrained Court view, however, might suggest that neither interpretation is correct. Rather, they would point to changes in the broader political system to explain such major social and political changes. Clearly, the two views are in conflict.

It should be emphasized that an examination of civil rights, abortion, and women's rights avoids the pitfalls of simple case studies. Each movement spans a sufficient length of time to allow for variance. Covering decades, the debate over these issues has been affected by political, social, and economic variables. Besides the importance of these cases for politics (and for law and social science), they are cases in which claims about court effectiveness should be most clearly highlighted, cases which should most likely falsify one of the two views. If the constraints and conditions developed in the next chapter hold in these studies, they should illuminate the broader question under what conditions courts are capable of producing significant social reform. And, for those readers who are uncomfortable with only three case studies, in the final chapters I expand the coverage to examine briefly three other modern uses of the courts to produce significant social reform.

In order to proceed, while not ignoring state and lower federal courts, I will concentrate on the U.S. Supreme Court. Like the Congress and the presidency, the Supreme Court, while not the only institution of its kind in the American political system, is the most visible and important one. It sits atop a hierarchical structure, and decisions of lower courts involving significant social reform seldom escape its scrutiny. Also, because it is the most authoritative U.S. court, it is the most concerned with public policy. Hypotheses that concern the courts and social reform must first deal with the Supreme Court and then turn to the ramifications of its decisions elsewhere in the judiciary.

There remains the question of how to deal with complicated issues of causation. Because it is difficult to isolate the effects of court decisions from other events in producing significant social reform, special care is needed in specifying how courts can be effective. On a general level, one can distinguish two types of influence courts could exercise. Court decisions might produce significant social reform through a *judicial* path that relies on the authority of the court. Alternatively, court influence could follow an *extra-judicial* path that invokes court powers of persuasion, legitimacy, and the ability to give salience to issues. Each of these possible paths of influence is different and requires separate analysis.

The *judicial* path of causal influence is straight-forward. It focuses on the direct outcome of judicial decisions and examines whether the change required by the courts was made. In civil rights, for example, if a Supreme Court decision ordering an end to public segregation was the cause of segregation ending, then one should see lower courts ordering local officials to end segregation, those officials acting to end it, the community at large supporting it, and, most important, segregation actually ending. Similarly, with abortion, if the Court's invalidation of state laws restricting or prohibiting abortion produced direct change, it should be seen in the removal of barriers to abortion and the provision of abortion services where requested. Proponents of the Dynamic Court view believe that the courts have powerful direct effects, while partisans of the Constrained Court view deny this. The effects of this *judicial* path of influence are examined in chapters 2 (civil rights), 6 (abortion), and 7 (women's rights). The constraints and conditions generated in chapter 1 are applied to the findings in chapters 3, 6, and 7.

Separate and distinct from judicial effects is the more subtle and complex causal claim of *extra-judicial* effects. Under this conception of causation, courts do more than simply change behavior in the short run. Court decisions may produce significant social reform by inspiring individuals to act or persuading them to examine and change their opinions. Court decisions, particularly Supreme Court decisions, may be powerful symbols, resources for change. They may affect the intellectual climate, the kinds of ideas that are discussed. The mere bringing of legal claims and the hearing of cases may influence ideas. Courts may produce significant social reform by giving salience to issues, in effect placing them on the political agenda. Courts may bring issues to light and keep them in the public eye when other political institutions wish to bury them. Thus, courts may make it difficult for legislators to avoid deciding controversial issues. Indirect effects are an important part of court power in the Dynamic Court view. Evidence for extra-judicial effects might be found in public-opinion data, media coverage, and in public and elite action supporting significant social reform. Both *Brown* and *Roe* are universally credited with producing important extra-judicial effects, from bringing attention to civil rights and sparking the civil rights and women's rights movement to persuading Americans that abortion is acceptable. Thus, in chapters 4 (civil rights) and 8 (abortion and women's rights) I develop a broad range of evidence to test these claims of salience and persuasion. The provocative and counter-intuitive findings of these chapters may surprise the reader.

In addition, I examine the question of whether significant social reform could possibly have occurred without court action. In chapters 5 (civil rights) and 9 (abortion and women's rights), I assess a host of social, political, and economic changes that could plausibly have led to significant social reform independent of court action. Strictly speaking, the question of which view of the Court is correct, of whether the courts can produce significant social reform, does not depend on developing a full-blown theory of change. That belongs in a study of what caused change rather than a study of whether the courts caused change. However, such a logically correct approach may leave the reader cold. Thus, if it turns out that there is little evidence of the courts' causal contributions in civil rights, or abortion, or women's rights, the reader may find solace in these two chapters.

Finally, in chapters 10 and 11, I briefly assess the applicability of the constraints and conditions developed in chapter 1 to environmental litigation, reapportionment, and reform of the criminal law. Chapter 12 summarizes and concludes. The aim of this book, then, is to make sense of competing claims about the role of courts in the American political system. The findings suggest that neither view of the Court is entirely correct and that a more careful and subtle approach is needed. But surprisingly, they also suggest that one of the views of the Court is much more powerful than the other.

1

The Dynamic and the Constrained Court

What is the role of U.S. courts in producing significant social reform? When and under what conditions will U.S. courts be effective producers of significant social reform? When does it make sense for individuals and groups pressing for such change to litigate? What kinds of effects from court victories can they expect? Which view best captures the reality of American politics? Given the alleged success of the social reform litigation of the last four decades, and Americans' attachment to the Dynamic Court view, it is tempting to suggest that it *always* makes sense for groups to litigate. On the other hand, our attachment to the vision of the Constrained Court, as well as a knowledge of legal history, can suggest that courts can *never* be effective producers of significant social reform. But "always" and "never" are claims about frequency, not conditions. To fully understand the role of the courts in producing significant social reform, we must focus on the latter.

Many scholars have turned their attention to the questions this litigation activity raises. However, their findings remain unconnected and not squarely centered on whether, and under what conditions, courts produce significant social reform. Some writing has focused on the determinants of winning court cases rather than on the effects of court decisions. Galanter (1974), for example, asks "why the 'haves' come out ahead" and suggests that the resources and experience available to established and on-going groups provide an advantage in litigation. Similarly, Handler (1978), while exploring outcomes as well as the resources available to litigants, stresses the latter too. While these and similar works provide interesting theories about winning cases, that is a different question from the effects courts have on political and social change.

On the outcome side, there are numerous individual studies. Unfortunately, they tend to focus narrowly on a given issue and refrain from offering hypotheses about courts and change.[1] More self-consciously theoretical case studies have examined admittedly non-controversial areas (Rebell and Block 1982), the need for federal pressure to improve race relations (Hochschild 1984), or have suggested so many hypotheses (one hundred and thirty-five of them) as to be of little practical help (Wasby 1970, 246–66). Finally, the extensive law review literature on institutional reform either lacks evidence or focuses on individual cases with little or no attempt to generate hypotheses.[2] While much of this work is well done, it does not address the larger question.

In the bulk of this chapter, I flesh out the two views. My aim is to make each view plausible, if not enticing. Then, critically examining evidence for their plausibility, I develop a set of constraints and conditions under which courts can produce significant social reform. These suggest that both views oversimplify court effectiveness.

Structural Constraints: The Logic of the Constrained Court View

The view of courts as unable to produce significant social reform has a distinguished pedigree reaching back to the founders. Premised on the institutional structure of the American political system and the procedures and belief systems created by American law, it suggests that the conditions required for courts to produce significant social reform will seldom exist. Unpacked, the Constrained Court view maintains that courts will generally not be effective producers of significant social reform for three reasons: the limited nature of constitutional rights, the lack of judicial independence, and the judiciary's inability to develop appropriate policies and its lack of powers of implementation.

The Limited Nature of Rights

The Constitution, and the set of beliefs that surround it, is not unbounded. Certain rights are enshrined in it and others are rejected. In economic terms, private control over the allocation and distribution of resources, the use of property, is protected (Miller 1968). "Rights" to certain minimums, or equal shares of basic goods, are not. Further, judicial discretion is bound by the norms and expectations of the legal culture. These two parameters, believers in the Constrained Court view suggest, present a problem for litigators pressing the courts for significant social reform because most such

1. For example, see the studies excerpted and compiled in Becker and Feeley (1973). A more theoretical work, although unfortunately not focused on important political and social change, is Johnson and Canon (1984).
2. For representative examples, see Aronow (1980); Eisenberg and Yeazell (1980); Monti (1980); Note (1980); Note (1975).

litigation is based on constitutional claims that rights are being denied.[3] An individual or group comes into a court claiming it is being denied some benefit, or protection from arbitrary and discriminatory action, and that it is *entitled* to this benefit or that protection. Proponents of the Constrained Court view suggest that this has four important consequences for social reformers.

First, they argue, it limits the sorts of claims that can be made, for not all social reform goals can be plausibly presented in the name of constitutional rights. For example, there are no constitutional rights to decent housing, adequate levels of welfare, or clean air, while there are constitutional rights to minimal governmental interference in the use of one's property. This may mean that "practically significant but legally irrelevant policy matters may remain beyond the purview of the court" (Note 1977, 436). Further, as Gordon (1984, 111) suggests, "the legal forms we use set limits on what we can imagine as practical outcomes." Thus, the nature of rights in the U.S. legal system, embedded in the Constitution, may constrain the courts in producing significant social reform by preventing them from hearing many claims.

A second consequence from the Constrained Court perspective is that, even where claims can be made, social reformers must often argue for the establishment of a new right, or the extension of a generally accepted right to a new situation. In welfare rights litigation, for example, the Court was asked to find a constitutional right to welfare (Krislov 1973). This need to push the courts to read the Constitution in an expansive or "liberal" way creates two main difficulties. Underlying these difficulties is judicial awareness of the need for predictability in the law and the politically exposed nature of judges whose decisions go beyond the positions of electorally accountable officials. First, the Constitution, lawyers, judges, and legal academics form a dominant legal culture that at any given time accepts some rights and not others and sets limits on the interpretation and expansion of rights. Judicial discretion is bound by the beliefs and norms of this legal culture, and decisions that stray too far from them are likely to be reversed and severely criticized. Put simply, courts, and the judges that compose them, even if sympathetic to social reform plaintiffs, may be unwilling to risk crossing this nebulous yet real boundary.[4] Second, and perhaps more important, is the role of precedent and what Justice Traynor calls the "continuity scripts of the law" (Traynor 1977, 11). Traynor, a justice of the California Supreme Court for twenty-five years, Chief Justice from 1964 to 1970, and known as a judge open to new ideas, wrote of the "very caution of the judicial process" (1977, 7). Arguing that

3. Sometimes, however, court cases deal not in the language of constitutional rights but in the world of statutory interpretation. While many of the constraints suggested below are applicable here as well, when elected officials have acted to produce significant social reform, the conditions under which courts operate are dramatically changed.

4. As Diver (1979, 104) puts it, a "judge's actions must conform to that narrow band of conduct considered appropriate for so antimajoritarian an institution."

"a judge must plod rather than soar," Traynor saw that the "greatest judges" proceed "at the pace of a tortoise that steadily makes advances though it carries the past on its back" (1977, 7, 6). Constrained by precedent and the beliefs of the dominant legal culture, judges, the Constrained Court view asserts, are not likely to act as crusaders.

Third, supporters of the Constrained Court view note, as Scheingold (1974) points out, that to claim a right in court is to accept the procedures and obligations of the legal system. These procedures are designed, in part, to make it difficult for courts to hear certain kinds of cases. As the Council for Public Interest Law (CPIL) puts it, doctrines of standing and of class actions, the so-called political question doctrine, the need to have a live controversy, and other technical doctrines can "deter courts from deciding cases on the merits" (CPIL 1976, 355) and can result in social reform groups being unable to present their best arguments, or even have their day in court. Once in court, however, the legal process tends to dissipate significant social reform by making appropriate remedies unlikely. This can occur, McCann (1986, 200) points out, because policy-based litigation aimed at significant social reform is usually "disaggregate[d] . . . into discrete conflicts among limited actors over specific individual entitlements." Remedial decrees, it has been noted, "must not confuse what is socially or judicially desirable with what is legally required" (Special Project 1978, 855). Thus, litigation seldom deals with "underlying issues and problems" and is "directed more toward symptoms than causes" (Harris and Spiller 1976, 26).

Finally, it has long been argued that framing issues in legally sound ways robs them of "political and purposive appeal" (Handler 1978, 33). In the narrow sense, the technical nature of legal argument can denude issues of emotional, widespread appeal. More broadly, there is the danger that litigation by the few will replace political action by the many and reduce the democratic nature of the American polity. James Bradley Thayer, writing in 1901, was concerned that reliance on litigation would sap the democratic process of its vitality. He warned that the "tendency of a common and easy resort" to the courts, especially in asking them to invalidate acts of the democratically accountable branches, would "dwarf the political capacity of the people" (Thayer 1901, 107). This view was echoed more recently by McCann, who found that litigation-prone activists' "legal rights approach to expanding democracy has significantly narrowed their conception of political action itself" (McCann 1986, 26). Expanding the point, McCann argued that "legal tactics not only absorb scarce resources that could be used for popular mobilization . . . [but also] make it difficult to develop broadly based, multiissue grassroots associations of sustained citizen allegiance" (McCann 1986, 200). For these reasons, the Constrained Court view suggests that the nature of rights in the U.S. constrains courts from being effective producers of significant social reform. Thus,

Constraint I: The bounded nature of constitutional rights prevents courts from hearing or effectively acting on many significant social reform claims, and lessens the chances of popular mobilization.

Limits on Judicial Independence—The Institutional Factor

As the colloquy between Justice Jackson and U.S. Attorney Rankin illustrates, reformers have often turned to courts when opposition to significant social reform in the other branches has prevented them from acting. Thus, much significant social reform litigation takes place in the context of stalemate within, or opposition from, the other branches. For courts to be effective in such situations, they must, logically, be independent of those other branches. Supporters of the Constrained Court view point to a broad array of evidence that suggests the founders did not thoroughly insulate courts or provide them with unfailing independence.[5]

To start, the appointment process, of course, limits judicial independence. Judges do not select themselves. Rather, they are chosen by politicians, the president and the Senate at the federal level. Presidents, while not clairvoyant, tend to nominate judges who they think will represent their judicial philosophies. Clearly, changing court personnel can bring court decisions into line with prevailing political opinion (and dampen support for significant social reform).[6] Thus, the Constrained Court perspective sees the appointment process as limiting judicial independence.

Judicial independence requires that court decisions, in comparison to legislation, do not invariably reflect public opinion. Supporters of the Constrained Court view note, however, that Supreme Court decisions, historically, have seldom strayed far from what was politically acceptable (McCloskey 1960, 223–24).[7] Rather than suggesting independence, this judicial unwillingness to often blaze its own trail perhaps suggests, in the words of Finley Peter Dunne's Mr. Dooley, that "th' supreme coort follows th' iliction returns" (Dunne 1901, 26).[8]

---

5. For a clear theoretical discussion of the notion of judicial independence, see Shapiro (1981), chapter 1.

6. In terms of producing significant social reform, the appointment process may be overemphasized. To the extent that the Constrained Court view is correct, appointing judges intent upon significant social reform won't lead to greater court contributions to it because the other structural constraints render courts impotent as producers of significant social reform. Thus, the appointment process only serves a negative role.

7. More specifically, comparing the Court's opinions with those of the public on issues in 146 decisions over the years 1935–1986, Marshall found consistency nearly two-thirds of the time (Marshall 1989, chap. 4). In the period 1969–84, all but two of the years of the Burger Court, the Court's opinions were consistent with the public's over 70 percent of the time (Marshall 1985).

8. In the wake of Mr. Dooley's comments, after the Supreme Court abruptly switched sides and upheld New Deal legislation, Felix Frankfurter wrote the following to Justice Stone: "I must confess I am not wholly happy in thinking that Mr. Dooley should, in the course of history turn out to have been one of the most distinguished legal philosophers" (quoted in O'Brien 1985, 22).

In at least two important ways, the Constrained Court view suggests, Congress may constrain court actions. First, in the statutory area, Congress can override decisions, telling the courts they misinterpreted the intent of the law. That is, Congress may rewrite a provision to meet court objections or simply state more clearly what it meant so that the courts' reading of the law is repudiated.[9] Second, although Congress cannot directly reverse decisions based on constitutional interpretations, presumably untouchable by the democratic process, it may be able to constrain them by threatening certain changes in the legal structure. A large part of the reason, of course, is the appointment process. But even without the power of appointment, the Court may be susceptible to credible threats against it. Historical review of the relations of the Court to the other branches of the federal government suggests that the Court cannot for long stand alone against such pressure. From the "Court-packing" plan of FDR to recent bills proposing to remove federal court jurisdiction over certain issues, court-curbing proposals may allow Congress to constrain courts as producers of significant social reform (Nagel 1965; Rosenberg 1985; cf. Lasser 1988).

American courts, proponents of the Constrained Court view claim, are particularly deferential to the positions of the federal government. On the Supreme Court level, the solicitor general is accorded a special role. The office has unusual access to the Court and is often asked by the Court to intervene in cases and present the government's position. When the solicitor general petitions the Court to enter a case, the Court almost invariably grants the request, regardless of the position of the parties.[10] The government is also unusually successful in convincing the Court to hear cases it appeals and to not hear those it opposes.[11] The solicitor general's access to the Court carries over to the winning of cases. Historically, the solicitor general (or the side the government is supporting when it enters a case as *amicus*) wins about 70 percent of the time (Scigliano 1971; Ulmer and Willison 1985). It appears that the federal government has both extraordinary access to and persuasive abilities with the Court (Ducat and Dudley 1985; Dudley and Ducat 1986).

9. Modern examples include *Grove City College* v. *Bell* (1984), which limited the fund cut-off provisions of Title IX. In the spring of 1988 Congress, over President Reagan's veto, enacted the Civil Rights Restoration Act which overturned the decision. A similar case occurred with *General Electric* v. *Gilbert* (1976), where the Supreme Court held that an employer's disability plan that excluded pregnancy from its coverage did not violate Title VII of the 1964 Civil Rights Act. Congress responded in 1978 by amending the law to prohibit such exclusion. More generally, in the period 1944–60, Congress rewrote courts' decisions fifty times (Wasby 1978b).

10. In the years 1969–83, the solicitor general petitioned to enter 130 cases without the consent of the parties. The Court granted access in 126 of those cases (97 percent) (Ulmer and Willison 1985).

11. While the Court agrees to hear, on average, about 7 or 8 percent of cases appealed to it (13 or 14 percent not including petitions from prisoners), the solicitor general's petitions are accepted almost three-quarters of the time. When the solicitor general opposes an appeal, the Court rarely accepts the case, doing so, for example, in only 4 percent of the cases during the 1969–83 period (Ulmer and Willison 1985).

That does not comport with notions of independence and a judicial system able to defy legislative and political majorities. Thus, the Constrained Court view's adherents believe,

> Constraint II: The judiciary lacks the necessary independence from the other branches of the government to produce significant social reform.

Implementation and Institutional Relations

For courts, or any other institution, to effectively produce significant social reform, they must have the ability to develop appropriate policies and the power to implement them. This, in turn, requires a host of tools that courts, according to proponents of the Constrained Court view, lack. In particular, successful implementation requires enforcement powers. Court decisions, requiring people to act, are not self-executing. But as Hamilton pointed out two centuries ago in *The Federalist Papers* (1787–88), courts lack such powers. Indeed, it is for this reason more than any other that Hamilton emphasized the courts' character as the least dangerous branch. Assuaging fears that the federal courts would be a political threat, Hamilton argued in *Federalist 78* that the judiciary "has no influence over either the sword or the purse; no direction either of the strength or of the wealth of the society; and can take no active resolution whatever. It may truly be said to have neither FORCE nor WILL, but merely judgment; and must ultimately depend upon the aid of the executive arm even for the efficacy of its judgments" (*The Federalist Papers* 1961, 465). Unlike Congress and the executive branch, Hamilton argued, the federal courts were utterly dependent on the support of the other branches and elite actors. In other words, for Court orders to be carried out, political elites, electorally accountable, must support them and act to implement them. Proponents of the Constrained Court view point to historical recognition of this structural "fact" of American political life by early Chief Justices John Jay and John Marshall, both of whom were acutely aware of the Court's limits.[12] President Jackson recognized these limits, too, when he reputedly remarked about a decision with which he did not agree, "John Marshall has made his decision, now let him enforce it."[13] More recently, the unwillingness of state authorities to follow court orders, and the need to send federal troops to Little Rock, Arkansas, to carry them out, makes the same point. Without elite support (the federal government in this case), the Court's orders would have been frustrated. While it is clear that courts can stymie change (Paul 1960), though

12. Having been the nation's first Chief Justice, Jay refused the position in 1801, telling President Adams that he lacked faith that the Court could acquire enough "energy, weight and dignity" to play an important role in the nation's affairs (quoted in McCloskey 1960, 31). And *Marbury* v. *Madison*, if nothing else, demonstrates Marshall's acute awareness of the Court's limits.
13. Supposedly made in response to the Supreme Court's decision in *Worcester* v. *Georgia* (1832).

ultimately not prevent it (Dahl 1957; Nagel 1965; Rosenberg 1985), the Constitution, in the eyes of the Constrained Court view, appears to leave the courts few tools to insure that their decisions are carried out.

If the separation of powers, and the placing of the power to enforce court decisions in the executive branch, leaves courts practically powerless to insure that their decisions are supported by elected and administrative officials, then they are heavily dependent on popular support to implement their decisions. If American citizens are aware of Court decisions, and feel duty-bound to carry them out, then Court orders will be implemented. However, proponents of the Constrained Court view point out that survey data suggest that the American public is consistently uninformed of even major Supreme Court decisions and thus not in a position to support them (Adamany 1973; Daniels 1973; Dolbeare 1967; Goldman and Jahnige 1976). If the public or political elites are not ready or willing to make changes, the most elegant legal reasoning will be for nought.

This constraint may be particularly powerful with issues of significant social reform. It is likely that as courts deal with issues involving contested values, as issues of significant social reform do almost by definition, they will generate opposition. In turn, opposition may induce a withdrawal of the elite and public support crucial for implementation. Thus, proponents of the Constrained Court view suggest that the contested nature of issues of significant social reform makes it unlikely that the popular support necessary for implementation will be forthcoming.

A second claim made by proponents of the Constrained Court view about courts effectively implementing decisions is that the legal system is a particular type of bureaucracy that has few of the advantages and many of the disadvantages of the ideal Weberian type. For example, important components of the Weberian bureaucracy include a hierarchical command structure, a clear agenda, little or no discretion at lower levels, stated procedures, job protection, positions filled strictly by merit, area specialization, and the ability to initiate action and follow-up. While on the surface the U.S. judicial system is hierarchical, has stated procedures, and provides job protection, closer examination under a Constrained Court microscope complicates the picture. For example, although orders are handed down from higher courts to lower ones, there is a great deal of discretion at the lower levels. Decisions announced at the appellate level may not be implemented by lower-court judges who disagree with them or who simply misunderstand them. Similarly, procedures designed to prevent arbitrary action may be used for evasion and delay. Further, unlike the ideal bureaucratic type, courts lack a clear agenda and any degree of specialization. Rather, judges and clerks go from case to case in highly disparate fields. This means that area expertise and planning, often crucial in issues involving significant social reform, are seldom present, making it uncertain that the remedy will be appropriate to the problem. In terms of initiation and follow-up, the nature of the legal bureaucracy puts barriers in the way of courts. For example, courts cannot initiate suits but must wait for litigants to approach them. Because stated procedures must be followed, because courts have small staffs, and because the legal system requires individuals rather than courts to initiate proceedings, appellate courts may never know whether their decisions have been implemented. Follow-up is difficult because it may be years by the time appellate judges discover an incident (or pattern) of non-implementation, through a case working its way up to them. Finally, the insulated "above politics" position of courts limits judges in cutting deals and actively politicking in support of a decision. The distance between the ideal Weberian bureaucracy and the American judiciary is so large, proponents of the Constrained Court view might argue, that even if courts actively promote significant social reform, they cannot easily achieve the results their decisions command.[14]

Through the eyes of the Constrained Court view, the decentralized nature of the judicial system may constrain courts from producing significant social reform for several reasons. In a nutshell, the structure of courts opens the possibility for bias and misinterpretation to influence lower-court decisions. Further, the entrepreneurial nature of many lawyers makes it difficult for groups seeking significant social reform through the courts to present a coherent strategy. And the nature of the legal bureaucracy makes delay endemic. These claims merit brief attention.

The American judicial system vests considerable discretion in lower-court judges. Only rarely do appellate courts issue final orders. In almost all cases, they remand to the trial court for issuance of the final order. This leaves lower-court judges with a great deal of discretion. The objective judge will conscientiously attempt to follow the higher court's orders. However, misinterpretation of those orders, especially if they are vague, is possible. Further, the biased judge has a myriad of tools with which to abuse discretion. These include the "delay endemic to legal proceedings" (CPIL 1976, 355), narrow interpretation, and purposeful misinterpretation. In this kind of case, litigants must follow procedure and re-appeal the case to the higher court for help, further delaying change.

This structural aspect of the American judicial system, those in the Constrained Court camp argue, may pose a particular problem for litigants seeking significant social reform. Bias and misinterpretation aside, it may be difficult for groups seeking reform to present a coherent strategy. Access to the legal system can be gained in any one of hundreds of courts (in the federal

14. In an empirical study of four important cases, Horowitz supports this line of reasoning and concludes that effective implementation aimed at reforming institutions requires information and knowledge that judges don't have and political compromises that they ought not to make. See Horowitz (1977), especially chapters 2 and 7. Interestingly, a much less elaborate version of this argument was made in 1963 (Friendly 1963, 791–92). For a critical review of Horowitz, see Wasby (1978a).

system) by any one of hundreds of thousands of lawyers. In particular, as Cowan (1976), Tushnet (1987), and Wasby (1983, 1985) note, interest groups planning a litigation strategy may find themselves faced with a host of cases not of their doing or to their liking. There is no way to prevent other lawyers, individuals, and groups from filing cases. And if these cases are not well-chosen and well-argued, they may result in decisions that wreak havoc with the best-laid plans. Thus, groups are sometimes on the defensive, forced to disassociate themselves from the legal arguments of purported allies and sometimes even to oppose them.

Although in practice federal judges have life tenure, this does not mean they are free from constraints. In asking for significant social reform, litigants are asking judges to reform existing institutions. However, judges may be unwilling to take on this essentially non-judicial task. To the extent that lower-court judges are part of a given community, ordering massive change in their community may isolate them and threaten the respect of the court. Also, the judicial selection process for lower federal court judges, is designed to select people who reflect the mores and beliefs of the community in which the court sits (Chase 1972). Therefore, adherents to the Constrained Court view argue, it is unlikely that lower-court judges will be predisposed to support significant social reform if the community opposes it.

The opportunity for delay that is built into the judicial bureaucracy constrains courts in several ways. First, through constant appeals, motions, and the use of other procedures, parties under court order to implement significant social reform can gain time. For example, when threatened with a lawsuit over prison conditions, a state corrections director replied: "a lawsuit is twenty-six months away. We could buy some time" (Cooper 1988, 259). Second, parties opposed to change can initiate their own lawsuits, using the courts to challenge and invalidate legislative, administrative, or other judicial action. In the environmental field both Wenner (1982, 1988) and Hays (1986) note that industry has systematically relied on courts to delay change. For those opposed to reform, delay can allow for changes in political and economic conditions, leading to reversals of the ordered reform. Thus, the opportunity for delay inherent in the legal bureaucracy, believers in the Constrained Court view argue, makes courts poor institutions for producing significant social reform.

A further obstacle for court effectiveness, assert believers in the Constrained Court view, is that significant social reform often requires large expenditures. Judges, in general prohibited from actively politicking and cutting deals, are not in a particularly powerful position to successfully order the other branches to expend additional funds. "The real problem" in cases of reform, Judge Bazelon wrote, "is one of inadequate resources, which the courts are helpless to remedy" (Bazelon 1969, 676). While there may be exceptions where courts seize financial resources, they are rare precisely because courts are hesitant to issue such orders which violate separation of powers by in effect appropriating public funds. Even without this concern, courts "ultimately lack the power to force state governments [or the federal government] to act" (Frug 1978, 792) because if governments refuse to act, there is little courts can do. They are unlikely to hold governors, legislators, or administrators in contempt or take other dramatic action because such action sets up a battle between the branches that effectively destroys any chance of government cooperation. Thus, judges are unlikely to put themselves in such no-win situations. Further, the "limits on government resources are no less applicable in the courtroom than outside of it" (Frug 1978, 788). As Frug asserts, "the judicial power of the purse will, in the final analysis, extend no further than a democratic decision permits" (Frug 1978, 794).

The claims of the Constrained Court view about the judiciary's lack of tools, and its dependence on others to implement its decisions, can be illustrated by one kind of significant social reform, the wholesale reshaping of bureaucracies. Recent work suggests that courts encounter particular difficulties when they try to reshape highly complicated institutions and bureaucracies.[15] For example, Frug contends that given the number of variables involved, these kind of institutions are "too complex to be administered under court orders" (Frug 1978, 789). Even supporters of the competence of courts note the importance of the complexity of large organizations to court effectiveness (Note 1977), and realize that litigation in such cases requires "some relatively elaborate rearrangement of the institution's mode of operation" (Eisenberg and Yeazell 1980, 468). More specifically, successful reshaping requires the acquiesence, if not the support, of administrators and staff. This presents several problems. First, without the support of political leaders, there is little incentive for administrators to risk their jobs to implement court orders. In the Alabama mental health litigation, for example, the acting superintendent of the Partlow facility was fired for cooperating with the plaintiffs during the remedy hearings (Cooper 1988, 195). In such cases, staff will be especially reluctant to help implement changes. In addition, rigid insistence on conformity to rules such as court orders "breeds distrust, destruction of documents, and an attitude that 'I won't do anything more than I am absolutely required to do'" (Christopher Stone, quoted in McCann 1986, 229–30). In other words, changes required by outsiders, such as courts, may be "strongly resisted" (Special Project 1978, 837) by administrators and staffs, who, as one study suggested, "have a practically limitless capacity to sabotage reform" (Diver 1979, 94). And if administrators and staffs don't act voluntarily, there is little judges can do. While courts do have the power to cite recalcitrant bureaucrats for contempt, the use of such coercive power tends to make martyrs out of resisters and to strengthen the resolve of others

15. Golann and Fremouw (1976); Harris and Spiller (1976); Kalodner and Fishman (1978); Note (1977); Special Project (1978).

to prevent change (Diver 1979, 99; Special Project 1978, 839). Thus, both administrators and staffs have to be won over by the judge for courts to be effective, and judges may not be in a very good position to receive such support. Such rearrangement is difficult for courts, the logic of the Constrained Court view suggests, because they lack the resources to gain adequate understanding of the intricacies of reform and the tools to insure compliance.

Another aspect of the Weberian ideal type involves specialization and expertise. It is plausible that courts' remedial decrees would be more effective if they took into account "the internal and external factors affecting bureaucratic behavior" (Note 1980, 537). Yet, even proponents of court competence realize that "no single judge" has "the resources, inclination, or the time to pursue this sort of detailed and extensive analysis" (Aronow 1980, 759). This analysis has been seconded by several activist judges. Judge Frank M. Johnson, for example, has written that "judges are trained in the law. They are not penologists, psychiatrists, public administrators, or educators" (Johnson 1981, 274). Similarly, Justice Traynor has pointed out that such analysis pulls judges far from their training: "A judge is constrained by training, experience, and the office itself not to undertake responsibilities that belong to the legislature" (Traynor 1977, 8). This means, Constrained Court view supporters claim, that judges often have incomplete knowledge of the resources available or of the power dynamics of the institution or bureaucracy that appears before them. A common result is that judicial reform decrees may lack a realistic sense of available resources. For example, in the *Wyatt* case, one of the principal attorneys for the plaintiffs demanding reform of Alabama's mental health facilities concluded that the standards adopted by the court required "staffing of the institutions with more professionals than there are in the State of Alabama" (Halpern 1976, 85). Similarly, Yudof suggests that "lawyers and judges frequently fail to distinguish between altering the behavior of an individual and altering the behavior of an institution" (Yudof 1981, 444). Thus, it has been suggested that "the realities of the institutional reform suit correspond neither to the talents of most judges nor to the attributes of traditional adjudication" (Kirp and Babcock 1981, 317).

It may also be the case that the effective implementation of significant social reform requires long-term planning and serious consideration of costs. Courts, it has been suggested, are not constituted to be effective at either of these. Judges, McCann suggests, are "largely bound to episodic case-by-case remedies for complex social problems at odds with the long-term supervisory capacities necessary for effective means-oriented planning" (McCann 1986, 226). Further, if "taking political reform seriously requires taking economics seriously as well" (McCann 1986, 164), then litigation may provide little help for two reasons. First, litigation, by its piecemeal nature, "discourages a comprehensive economic orientation" (McCann 1986, 168). Second, of course, judges are not trained economists, and litigators are limited to legal, rights-oriented forms of argument, not economic analysis. Courts, it can be argued, are not structured to produce significant social reform. Thus, proponents of the Constrained Court view propose,

> Constraint III: Courts lack the tools to readily develop appropriate policies and implement decisions ordering significant social reform.

To sum up, the Constrained Court view holds that litigants asking courts for significant social reform are faced with powerful constraints. First, they must convince courts that the rights they are asserting are required by constitutional or statutory language. Given the limited nature of constitutional rights, the constraints of legal culture, and the general caution of the judiciary, this is no easy task. Second, courts are wary of stepping too far out of the political mainstream. Deferential to the federal government and potentially limited by congressional action, courts may be unwilling to take the heat generated by politically unpopular rulings. Third, if these two constraints are overcome and cases are decided favorably, litigants are faced with the task of implementing the decisions. Lacking powerful tools to force implementation, court decisions are often rendered useless given much opposition. Even if litigators seeking significant social reform win major victories in court, in implementation they often turn out to be worth very little. Borrowing the words of Justice Jackson from another context, the Constrained Court view holds that court litigation to produce significant social reform may amount to little more than "a teasing illusion like a munificent bequest in a pauper's will" (*Edwards* v. *California* 1941, 186).

Court Effectiveness: The Logic of the Dynamic Court View

The three constraints just presented are generated from the view of courts as unable to produce significant social reform. That view appears historically grounded and empirically plausible. Yet, on reflection, it has two main difficulties. First, it seems to overstate the limits on courts. After all, since the mid-twentieth century or so courts have been embroiled in controversies over significant social reform. Many lawyers, activists, and scholars have acted or written with the belief that the constraints are weak or non-existent and can easily be overcome. Indeed, the whole modern debate over judicial activism makes no sense if the Constrained Court view is correct. If courts are as impotent as the constraints suggest, then why has there been such political, academic, and judicial concern with the role of courts in modern America? Theory and practice are unaligned if the Constrained Court view is entirely correct. Second, examined carefully, its claim is that courts are *unlikely* to produce significant social reform; it does not deny the possibility. However, that doesn't help us understand when, and under what conditions, courts can produce significant social reform. The Constrained Court view is not the complete answer.

The Dynamic Court view may help. It maintains that courts can be effective producers of significant social reform. Its basic thrust is that not only are courts not as limited as the Constrained Court view suggests, but also, in some cases, they can be more effective than other governmental institutions in producing significant social reform. As Aryeh Neier puts it, "[s]ince the early 1950s, the courts have been the most accessible and, often, the most effective instrument of government for bringing about the changes in public policy sought by social protest movements" (Neier 1982, 9). The constraints of the Constrained Court view, then, may oversimplify reality.

Political, Institutional, and Economic Independence

Proponents of the Dynamic Court view argue that the Constrained Court view entirely misses key advantages of courts. At the most fundamental level, key to the Dynamic Court view is the belief that courts are free from electoral constraints and institutional arrangements that stymie change. Uniquely situated, courts have the capacity to act where other institutions are politically unwilling or structurally unable to proceed. For example, one of the great strengths of courts is the ability to act in the face of public opposition. Elected and appointed officials, fearful of political repercussions, are seldom willing to fight for unpopular causes and protect the rights of disliked minorities. Courts, free of such electoral accountability, are not so constrained. From civil rights to women's rights, from protecting the rights of the physically and mentally challenged to ensuring that criminal defendants are treated constitutionally, the courts have acted where other institutions have refused. Justice Brennan, concurring in a 1981 prison reform case, summarized this view: "Insulated as they are from political pressures, and charged with the duty of enforcing the Constitution, courts are in the strongest position to insist that unconstitutional conditions be remedied, even at significant financial cost" (*Rhodes* v. *Chapman* 1981, 359).

The ability of courts to act is particularly clear with issues of significant social reform. With such issues, entrenched interests often have the institutional base to prevent change in other political bodies. In civil rights in the 1950s, for example, as the colloquy between Justice Jackson and Assistant Attorney General Rankin reflects, the key position of Southern Democrats in Congress virtually insured that no civil rights legislation would be forthcoming. If change was to come, proponents of the Dynamic Court view argue, it could come only from the courts. Similarly, examining school desegregation in the years 1968–72, Hochschild argues that "were it not for the courts, there would be little reduction in racial isolation [in the public schools]" (Hochschild 1984, 134). And with re-apportionment, legislators from malapportioned districts had no incentive to reform the electoral system and vote themselves out of office, until the courts acted. In other words, the Dynamic Court view proposes that courts are free from the obstacles that lead to "a partial failure of executive or legislative government institutions to do their jobs in a satisfactory and legal way" (CPIL 1976, 208).

A similar argument applies to bureaucratic and institutional change. Proponents of the Dynamic Court view suggest that insulation, institutional inertia stemming from routinized procedures, and group pressure make it difficult for non-judicial institutions to reform themselves. Looking at "entrenched bureaucracies," environmental lawyer Victor Yannacone saw "self-perpetuating, self-sufficient, self-serving bureaus [which] are power sources unto themselves, effectively insulated from the people and responsible to no one but themselves" (Yannacone 1970b, 185). Where there is little incentive to change, it is only an outside force such as a court, uninvolved in daily operations, that may have the will to force change. Organizations contemplating reform also must confront the desires of their constituencies. "In the face of pressures from many diverse constituencies and interests," Aronow writes, "it is unlikely that even public institutions headed by cooperative administrators will reform themselves without the outside coercive force of the court providing the impetus for specific change" (Aronow 1980, 751). Courts simply do not face such pressures. Court decisions will not adversely affect the court's ongoing relations with elected officials, interest groups, financial backers, and the like, whose cooperation is essential for getting work done, for the simple reason that courts are not structured to need or maintain such ongoing relations. Courts do not depend on carefully worked out institutional arrangements because they do not specialize in any one area. Unlike bureaucracies and large institutions, the parties they deal with vary from case to case. Here, too, courts are uniquely situated.

The "inadequacy" of the political process is an essential basis for the Dynamic Court view because "policy formulation in our society is too often a one-sided affair—a process in which only the voices of the economically or politically powerful are heard" (CPIL 1976, 8). In the legislative and executive branches, not all affected interests are heard and not all voices carry the same weight. The predictable result of this systematic exclusion of the "public" is that "government agencies cannot adequately represent all facets of the public interest" (CPIL 1976, 172). However, courts, it is contended, can rectify this exclusion because, "unlike the hierarchical statist view of entrenched elite rule, the judicial view guarantees the independence of citizen groups contending for influence within the adversary process" (McCann 1986, 116). Neither access nor influence depends on connections or position. Access to all affected interests is guaranteed by judicial rules, and influence depends on strength of argument, not political position. As William F. Butler of the Environmental Defense Fund put it, "all it takes is one person with a good legal argument that can convince a judge and that's that" (quoted in

McCann 1986, 208). The judiciary, with "no corrupting links to anyone," affords "equality of both access and influence to citizens" more "completely" than any "other institutional form" (McCann 1986, 118, 116). And this means that it is able to respond to social reform claims of ordinary citizens where other institutions are not (Sax 1971, 57, 112, 231). As Justice Neely of West Virginia puts it, American courts alleviate the "more dangerous structural deficiencies of the other institutions of democratic government" and thus are the "central institution in the United States which makes democracy work" (Neely 1981, xiii, xi).

The underlying claim here of the Dynamic Court view is that access and influence are not dependent on economic and political resources. The kind of professional lobbying that is required to be effective in influencing bureaucracies or enacting legislation is not necessary for winning court cases. Groups lacking key resources can use courts not only directly to change the law but also to strengthen their voices within the other branches of government and authoritatively present their positions. Thus, proponents of the Dynamic Court view claim, courts offer the best hope to poor, powerless, and unorganized groups, those most often seeking significant social reform.

The judicial process may also provide a powerful forum for gathering and assessing information. In contrast to legislative and bureaucratic proceedings, wide participation in legal proceedings makes it likely that the full range of relevant information will be brought to bear on the final decree. Where crucial information is being withheld, or is hard to obtain, the judicial process of discovery, supported by the coercive powers of the court, may help bring it to light. Further, the adversarial process insures that information will be rigorously assessed before it takes the status of "fact." Thus, as Chayes points out, the information that the Court has "will not be filtered through the rigid structures and preconceptions of bureaucracies" (Chayes 1976, 1308). Judges, then, are in a strong position to act. As Cavanagh and Sarat put it, it is "difficult to see how any other institutional actor [than the judge] is better equipped to become informed of the ramifications of comparable decisions" (Cavanagh and Sarat 1980, 381–82).

Influence accompanies access in legal proceedings because judges must respond to legal arguments and provide reasons for their opinions. Unlike in other institutions, arguments cannot be ignored or dismissed without discussion. Judges, in contrast to elected or other appointed officials, cannot easily duck the tough issues. Further, judges are limited by the Constitution, statutes, and precedent in the kind of responses they can make. A judge's dislike or disapproval of actions provides insufficient grounds to support a legal decision. This means, of course, that the positions of unpopular and politically weak groups, denied access to and influence with administrative, executive, and legislative branches, must be taken seriously by the courts.

To sum up, proponents of the Dynamic Court view assert that courts have the ability to act when other institutions won't, because judges are electorally unaccountable and serve with life tenure. Unencumbered by electoral commitments and political deal-making, and protected from recrimination, they can act to fulfill the constitutional mandate. Thus, as Fiss puts it, courts can produce significant social reform because the judicial office is "structured by both ideological and institutional factors that enable and perhaps even force the judge to be objective—not to express his preferences or personal beliefs, or those of the citizenry, as to what is right or just, but constantly to strive for the true meaning of the constitutional value" (Fiss 1979, 12–13). Courts, then, can provide an escape from the pathologies of rigid bureaucracies, ossified institutions, and a reluctant or biased citizenry.

Courts as Catalysts—Indirect Effects of the Dynamic Court

In striving for the "true meaning of the constitutional value," courts base decisions on principle. Unlike legislatures or executives, courts do not act out of calculations of partisan preference. This means, proponents of the Dynamic Court view suggest, that courts can point the way to doing what is "right." They can remind Americans of our highest aspirations and chide us for our failings. Courts, Bickel suggests, have the "capacity to appeal to men's better natures, to call forth their aspirations, which may have been forgotten in the moment's hue and cry" (Bickel [1962] 1986, 26). For Rostow, the "Supreme Court is, among other things, an educational body, and the Justices are inevitably teachers in a vital national seminar" (Rostow 1952, 208). Bickel agrees, viewing courts as "a great and highly effective educational institution" (Bickel [1962] 1986, 26). In the Dynamic Court view, the courts have important indirect effects, educating Americans and heightening their understanding of their constitutional duty.

Court decisions also have indirect effects, proponents of the Dynamic Court view suggest, through dramatizing issues and spurring action. Courts can provide publicity for issues and serve as a "catalyst" for change (Halpern 1976, 75). Where the public is ignorant of certain conditions, and political elites do not want to deal with them, court decisions can "politicize issues that otherwise might have remained unattended" (Monti 1980, 237). This may put public pressure on elites to act. Indeed, litigation may "often" be "the best method of attracting public attention to institutional conditions and of publicly documenting abuses" (Neier 1982, 29). By bringing conditions to light, and showing how far from constitutional or statutory aspirations practice has fallen, court cases can provide a "cheap method of pricking powerful consciences" (Note 1977, 463).[16] Thus, litigation "serves as a catalyst, not a usurper, of the legislative process" (Sax 1971, 157). This ability to dramatize may be particularly effective with custodial institutions such as hospitals, pris-

16. A *small sampling* of such claims includes Halpern (1976, 75); Handler (1978, 209); and Scheingold (1974, 9).

ons, and mental institutions where court cases have brought inhumane conditions to light.[17] As Sax puts it, "courts can be used to bring matters to legislative attention, to force them upon the agendas of reluctant and busy representatives" (Sax 1971, xviii).

In addition, court action may invigorate and encourage groups to mobilize and take political action (Scheingold 1974, 131, 148; McCann 1986, 108). In both civil rights and women's rights, for example, the federal courts are often seen as having served this role. As Yannacone told a conference audience:

> Every piece of enlightened social legislation that has come down in the past
> 50 or 60 years has been preceded by a history of litigation (applause) in which
> trial lawyers somewhere around the country have forcibly focussed the atten
> tion of the legislature on the inadequacies of existing legislation (Yannacone
> 1970a, 77).

Thus, proponents of the Dynamic Court view assert that judicial decisions have important extra-judicial effects.

Another way in which courts may indirectly produce significant social reform is by facilitating negotiations. As an external force unbeholden to involved interests, courts are free to act. They can provide a neutral forum where parties can work out their differences. Also, the threat of litigation can serve as a "basic political resource" (Grossman and Sarat 1981, 89). That is, rather than expend money, time, and energy defending against a lawsuit and countering the publicity it generates, parties may find it more palatable to negotiate. Without the threat of lawsuits, Cavanagh and Sarat suggest, many institutions would "never get to the bargaining table" (Cavanagh and Sarat 1980, 405). Where institutions are incapable of internal reform, and there is ineffective public or interest group-pressure, courts may provide a prod.

For the proponents of the Dynamic Court view, then, courts have powerful indirect effects. Their politically neutral position allows them to teach Americans about the meaning of their constitutional obligations. Court decisions can change opinions, generate media coverage, and inspire action. They can provide the necessary nudge to start the reform process. In other words, they have a unique and important kind of potency.

Evolving Procedures

Much of the Constrained Court view's plausibility comes from Constraint III, the courts' supposed lack of implementation powers. Contrary to this view, however, proponents of the Dynamic Court view assert that not only are courts in a unique position to act, but they also have the "demonstrated ability to evolve new mechanisms and procedures" to cope with the complexities of significant social reform litigation (Cavanagh and Sarat 1980, 373).

17. Halpern (1976, 75); Harris (1976, 57); Neier (1982, 29); Note (1975, 1349–50).

One such mechanism is court appointments of special masters to fill in many of the courts' structural weaknesses. Special masters can survey and gather information, talk with interested parties, hold hearings, conduct investigations, draft and float potential remedial decrees, and generally serve as the eyes and the ears of the judge (Aronow 1980). In other words, they can perform many duties helpful to finding an agreeable solution, duties that would appear unseemly if performed by the judge. They are able to do this, Aronow maintains, while retaining "court-like detachment and independence" (Aronow 1980, 766). Aronow and others argue that to the extent that courts have lacked tools to effectively implement remedial decrees in the past, the problem is well on the way to being solved.

Other changes, it is suggested, that have allowed courts to overcome the obstacles suggested by the Constrained Court view include the court's retention of jurisdiction, the creation of monitoring commissions, and the active engagement of the judge (Chayes 1976; Fiss 1979). These steps are designed to allow the court to closely follow the implementation process. If court decrees are not being implemented, or if unforeseen circumstances render parts of decrees inappropriate, these mechanisms allow for speedy correction. For example, if judges retain jurisdiction, then any of the parties can immediately return to court if the decree is not being implemented or if changing circumstances require its modification. Similarly, monitoring commissions can inform the judge of implementation progress and alert the court to the need for further action. And, of course, the mere availability of these tools can influence the behavior of the parties. With these kind of tools readily at hand, possibly recalcitrant parties may think twice before violating remedial decrees. Even with the uncertainties of institutional reform litigation, courts can create effective tools.

Empirical Support

Several recent studies provide empirical support for many of the Dynamic Court view's claims. Hochschild, for example, concludes that in the case of educational institutions, "many criticisms of judges' capacity to reform institutions are unsubstantiated" (Hochschild 1984, 140). A similar defense of judicial competence is reached by Cavanagh and Sarat in their study of cases dealing with debtors and tenants, intimate or ongoing relationships, and reform of large and complex institutions (Cavanagh and Sarat 1980). Understanding the Dynamic Court claim to be that courts are least likely to be successful in such cases, they find courts competent and effective in dealing with them. Similarly, a 1982 study by Rebell and Block examined sixty-five randomly selected federal court cases dealing with education during the years 1970–77 (Rebell and Block 1982). They found that "basic compliance with court orders predominated overwhelmingly over instances of either intentional or unintentional noncompliance" (Rebell and Block 1982, 65). The authors went on to examine educational issues in New York and Colorado in which both courts and state legislatures were active. Comparing the capacity of the two institutions, they found that courts were in many ways better equipped to be effective than were the state legislatures. They concluded: "Our data largely rebutted the criticism that the judiciary lacks the resources, expertise, or comprehensive perspective needed to implement educational reform successfully" (Rebell and Block 1982, 210).[18]

The Dynamic Court view provides a powerful alternative to the view of courts as the "least dangerous branch." Pointing to pathologies in the other branches, it places courts in a unique position to act. Acknowledging, perhaps, that the Constrained Court view was accurate at the Founding and for part of American history, it maintains that great change has occurred over the last few decades and that courts now have the tools to effectively produce significant social reform. Unlike the Constrained Court view, it is congruent with judicial activism and the modern use of the courts to produce significant social reform. While courts cannot solve all problems, the Dynamic Court view does see them as powerful and effective, unconstrained by the concentrations of power and bureaucratic inertia that stymie self-initiated change in the other branches.

Empirical Problems

Yet for all their plausibility and surface appeal, and their seemingly accurate description of recent litigation, attempts to ground the Dynamic Court view empirically are not entirely satisfying. Unfortunately, studies of the sort referred to above neither completely validate it nor are particularly helpful in constructing hypotheses about courts' effectiveness in producing significant social reform. Often, they either focus on unrepresentative time periods, or on unimportant and noncontroversial cases, or they overstate their findings. In addition, many of the studies that support the Dynamic Court view are theoretical rather than empirical. They mistake what conceivably could happen with what actually has happened. Further, the empirical studies tend to examine only one case. The problem here, from the Constrained Court perspective, is that given the constraints on judges imposed by court rules and the legal culture, it is the rare judge who will become so actively engaged. Although the Dynamic Court view may be correct, the empirical evidence offered in its support does not seal the case.

Without going into much detail, there are several problems with the studies mentioned above. Hochschild's study, for example, picks a short and unrepresentative four-year period in which to assess claims of judicial competence (see chapter 2). Cavanagh and Sarat, on the other hand, pick cases that don't address the issue of court effectiveness in reforming institutions.

18. For case-study literature that explicitly tests and rejects Donald Horowitz's argument that was part of Constraint III, see Fair (1981); Reedy (1982); Youngblood and Folse (1981).

Their evidence is based on cases made difficult not by the resistance of complex institutions but by individuals in complex and emotionally difficult situations. When they do discuss institutional reform cases (what they call extended impact cases), their discussion is theoretical rather than factual.

Somewhat similarly, Rebell and Block's often revealing study excludes cases that involved desegregation. As a result, in their words, "many of the remedial tasks presented by our sample of educational policy cases were relatively straightforward" (Rebell and Block 1982, 212). For example, 42 percent of the cases dealt with "[r]egulation of student appearance, speech, and conduct" (Rebell and Block 1982, 21), hardly the kind of issues that require wholesale rearrangement of institutions. Not surprisingly, although they found compliance in most of their cases, those requiring complex and far-reaching decrees were exceptions (Rebell and Block 1982, 66). Even in their skewed sample, courts did not do very well in overcoming Constraint III. In the cases studied, for example, they report that "not all potentially affected groups seek to participate, and even these groups who do participate do not present a broad spectrum of strongly diverse perspectives to the courts" (Rebell and Block 1982, 39–41). Further, they found judges, when faced with issues of analyzing social facts, in most instances utilized "avoidance techniques" so as not to deal with the information (Rebell and Block 1982, 50). Consequently, "in only 19 [of 65 cases] did the courts scrutinize social fact evidence in order to reach their conclusions" (Rebell and Block 1982, 53). Their study, then, tells us little about the competency of courts to address and reform institutions in non-trivial ways.[19]

With special masters, again, actual case studies do not bear out claims on behalf of the Dynamic Court view. For example, introducing an edited compilation of seven studies of school desegregation, Kalodner concludes that "Masters have seldom if ever been effective in the effort to find a solution that is both acceptable and constitutional" (Kalodner 1978, 9). Reviewing the use of masters in six school desegregation cases, Kirp and Babcock explicitly reject Aronow's optimistic conclusions (Kirp and Babcock 1981, 395). Fi-

---

19. Rebell and Block's findings about the comparative role of courts and legislatures are also not entirely on point. Focusing on hearings and debates, they found legislatures' fact-finding and analytic abilities to be limited when compared to the courts. However, unlike in courts, much of the gathering and assessment of evidence, and much of the persuasion and analytic reasoning, does not take place on legislative floors. Often, it occurs in offices, over the telephone, and in meetings with various interested parties. Judges are generalists and all the information they are likely to have comes from briefs and oral argument. Legislators, on the other hand, build up expertise in select areas. Committee members are often equally or better informed about the ramifications of proposed legislation, its factual and legal basis, and alternatives to it, than are witnesses appearing before them. Committee hearings and floor debates are much less attempts at fact-gathering and persuasion than they are forums for position-taking and record-building. In other words, comparing the actual conduct of a court case with a legislative hearing or debate is to misconstrue the nature of the legislative process. Thus, Rebell and Block are ironically correct when they conclude, for example, in their Colorado legislature study, that legislative hearings "primarily served a showcase function" (Rebell and Block 1982, 194).

nally, a lengthy and detailed study of institutional reform litigation points out that under court rules the use of special masters must "be the exception and not the rule. Consequently, there cannot be reference to masters as a matter of course" (Special Project 1978, 808). While special masters may be helpful in some cases, overall their record of use appears of limited effectiveness. And the crucial question of under what conditions special masters will be effective is left unanswered.

The Dynamic Court view, then, though in large part an effective retort to the unbending constraints of the Constrained Court view, does not get us very far in understanding the conditions under which courts can produce significant social reform. While its logic of independence and equal access makes good sense, its lack of generalizable empirical support is unhelpful. In sum, while courts may be more effective in producing significant social reform than the constraints of the Constrained Court view allow, the Dynamic Court view does not definitively demonstrate when, and under what conditions, court efficacy can be found.

Conditions for Court Efficacy

The thrust of the Dynamic Court view is that its competitor oversimplifies reality by *under*stating court effectiveness. However, it appears that the Dynamic Court view likewise oversimplifies, by *over*stating court effectiveness. Further, the views appear to be in conflict. For example, the Dynamic Court view proposes court action in the face of hostile or inert political institutions while the constraints of the Constrained Court view tell us that in such situations success is least likely. Along with conflict, however, each view appears to convey something of the truth. On an intuitive level, opposition from political elites is not conducive to court effectiveness. On the other hand, judicial isolation from many pressures allows courts to act when other institutions wish to but cannot. Surely it is naive to expect courts to be able to solve political and economic problems that the other branches cannot. But it appears equally short-sighted to deny that since mid-century courts have played an important role in producing significant social reform. It may well be that while each view captures part of the truth, neither is fine-grained enough to capture the conditions under which courts can effectively produce significant social reform.

Combining the two views may point the way to finally understanding these conditions. For example, there would be no conflict between the two views if courts were effective producers of significant social reform when there was general political and popular support for change but institutional blockage. That is, there may be conditions under which the constraints of the Constrained Court view, even if generally correct, can be overcome and courts can produce significant social reform. In the remaining part of this chapter, I suggest that this is the case; the constraints of the Constrained Court view generally limit courts, but when political, social, and economic conditions have become supportive of change, courts can effectively produce significant social reform.

Winning court cases is, of course, the first step toward courts producing significant social reform. In order to maximize chances of winning, the rights constraint must be overcome. What this means is that litigation for significant social reform must be gradual. Since judges are gradualists, small changes must be argued for before big ones. Although this requires a lengthy strategy for change, unless litigators can find strong precedents on which to base their claims, Constraint I suggests that cases demanding significant social reform will be losers.

Overcoming the judiciary's unwillingness to step far from the political mainstream is also difficult. When, however, there is political support for significant social reform, litigation may make sense. Unfortunately, there are no hard-and-fast rules for determining the existence of such support. However, there are several circumstances that provide good evidence that court decisions ordering significant social reform will be well received. One such circumstance is when legislation supportive of significant social reform has been enacted and courts are asked to interpret it. Another is when the executive branch is supportive of the claims of reformers. Cases in which the federal government is willing to appear as *amicus* on the side of significant social reform may be good opportunities for litigation. The appearance of the federal government not only reassures the court that the reform demanded has support, but also suggests that the executive is at the very least not opposed to implementing an affirmative decision.[20] A more nebulous bit of evidence is congressional support for interests similar to those reform litigators are suggesting. If legislation is being seriously considered, or debated, dealing with similar issues, courts need not fear adverse reactions from the Congress. At these times legal arguments are most likely to overcome Constraint II and find a receptive judicial audience.[21]

Even if the rights that significant social reform litigators are demanding are well-grounded in precedent, and there is elite support for such outcomes, there still remains the courts' lack of implementation powers (Constraint III). In many ways this is the most difficult constraint to overcome. For court decisions supporting significant social reform to be effective, a myriad of people need to be supportive. If there is political and popular support, Constraint III can be overcome. When there is such support, the people who need to change their behavior to make the decision a reality may be willing to do

20. Government support in litigation does not guarantee such support in implementation. Civil rights is a perfect example. See discussion in chapters 2 and 3.
21. Public opinion surveys most likely do not provide sufficient evidence of elite political support because public support does not necessarily translate into such elite support.

so. Often, many people will be already so acting and all court action does, in effect, is to remove any threat of legal action against them.[22] Somewhat more subtly, it is in these conditions that many of the claims of the Dynamic Court view may be validated. For example, when strong or widespread opposition to court orders is missing, parties to controversies may be more likely to respond to efforts at serious negotiation. Under such conditions, court orders may serve to overcome inertia and prod parties to the bargaining table. Similarly, when elite and public opinion generally supports court decisions, they may be effective in mobilizing people to effectively implement the decision. When public opinion has started to change, or is open to the possibility of change, it is possible that court opinions can help speed that change along. As Rebell and Block put it, "in situations where the parties (and the public) are inclined to cooperate (or at least to avoid strong resistance), courts are capable of fashioning effective relief" (Rebell and Block 1982, 214). Coercive powers won't be necessary, for the willingness to change will predate court action. Courts, then, may be effective producers of significant social reform when their decisions are announced in a political context of broad elite and popular support for the issue or right in controversy. Thus, when there is a general political climate in favor of significant social reform, Constraint III can be overcome.

Overcoming the three constraints will not automatically lead to significant social reform. As proponents of the Dynamic Court view argue, strategically placed elites, inert bureaucracies, and special interests may work to prevent change. Thus, in addition, certain conditions must be present. The first condition under which court decisions requiring significant social reform are likely to be implemented is when incentives are offered along with the decision. If there is some reward for implementation, those whose cooperation is essential may be willing to go along. The type of inducement can vary. One of the oldest, and most effective, inducements is money. Where, for example, on a national level, Congress provides money to those states, institutions, or bureaucracies which implement court decisions, local politicians or bureaucrats may be willing to do what the court orders. When opposition is fierce, of course, money may be of little help. But the less opposed the key parties are, the more the temptation of government dollars may overcome resistance to implementing court opinions.

Money is not the only form of inducement. Both elites and the public may be willing to implement court decisions if the benefits of so doing are clear. Benefits may include actions of private parties. For example, developers or industry may condition new projects or moves to new areas on implementation of court decisions. Here, too, if opposition to court-ordered change

---

22. It is not clear in such cases that the courts are producing significant social reform. Rather, it seems, they are merely allowing reform behavior to continue.

is strong, parties whose cooperation is essential may be willing to forgo the benefits. Again, inducements work only when parties have at least some willingness to go along. Thus,

Condition I: Courts may effectively produce significant social reform when other actors offer positive incentives to induce compliance.

The other side of benefits is, of course, costs. If the refusal to implement court decisions has high costs, implementation will be more likely. In cases of significant social reform, courts, acting alone, may not have sufficient tools to provide benefits, or impose costs, that would serve to induce compliant behavior (Constraint III). However, if the failure to implement decisions results in legislative or administrative action that imposes costs, then court decisions have a better chance of being implemented. This requires political support for the decisions, in the form of action imposing costs for non-compliance, and a belief on the part of key actors that implementing the decision is less objectionable than bearing the costs of non-implementation. Here, too, the loss of money, either public or private, as a result of non-implementation, can be an effective inducement. Thus,

Condition II: Courts may effectively produce significant social reform when other actors impose costs to induce compliance.

Another condition that may allow courts to produce significant social reform is when decisions can effectively be implemented through the market, side-stepping Constraint III. That is, if existing institutions do not have to change for change to occur, such change is more likely. If individuals or groups are both free and able to create their own institutions to implement court decisions, then the inability of courts to effectively reform existing institutions will not prevent change from occurring. In effect there will be two sets of institutions in existence; an older set that refuses to implement the decision and a newer one that does implement it. Court decisions of the significant social reform type will be implemented, in other words, if supporters can create institutions to do so. When the courts either refuse to allow market forces to act, or when, as in school desegregation, there is no realistic market alternative, this condition is not relevant. Thus,

Condition III: Courts may effectively produce significant social reform when judicial decisions can be implemented by the market.

A final condition that allows courts to be effective producers of significant social reform occurs when officials and administrators use court orders as a tool for leveraging additional resources, or as an excuse or cover for acting. One way in which this can be done is by affected officials relying on court orders to request increased funding from the legislature. Court orders, Diver suggests, give a manager "a powerful ally in his unending quest for additional

funds" (Diver 1979, 71; Stickney 1976, 33; Note 1980, 517). While administrators may resent court attempts to challenge their professional judgment
and interfere with the running of their institutions, they may see a silver lining
in the clouds. For example, Dr. Stonewall Stickney, Commissioner of the
Department of Mental Health for the State of Alabama, and the named defendant in a massive suit against the state in Judge Johnson's court (*Wyatt* v.
Stickney), wrote to his counsel: "At present the court appears to be our only
avenue to adequate funding" (Stickney 1976, 36). Similarly, Justice Powell,
concurring in *Milliken* v. *Bradley* (1977, 293), saw that the parties to the case
"have now joined forces apparently for the purpose of extracting funds from
the state treasury." Where defendants are willing to reform their institutions,
they can parlay court orders into demands for additional funding.

In a related way, court orders can be used to leverage other resources.
"It is perhaps the case," a law-review note suggests, that state administrators
can "rely on the courts to pressure the legislatures and impose needed reforms" (Note 1977, 430). While it is of course possible to ignore such pressure, there are costs involved. The appearance of violating a court order is
not one legislators usually relish. Thus, a court order can provide "*sympathetic* operating officials a powerful lever with which to pry loose cooperation
from intransigent policymakers" (Diver 1979, 81, emphasis added). Such
orders can also be used to entice resisting staff members and others to support
reform. In the Alabama mental health litigation, for example, Dr. Stickney
found that the court's orders enabled him to "'stand up' to staff members,
members of the community, and politicians who objected to actions he took
as Superintendent" (Note 1975, 1368). Sympathetic and reform-minded administrators, while nominally the defendants, can use court intervention to
implement reforms they have been unable to convince others to go along
with.[23] Court orders give *administrators who wish to make reforms* an additional tool for obtaining the necessary support and resources.

Finally, court orders can simply provide a shield or cover for administrators fearful of political reaction. This is particularly helpful for elected officials who can implement required reforms *and* protest against them at the
same time. This pattern is often seen in the school desegregation area. Writing
in 1967, one author noted that "a court order is useful in that it leaves the
official no choice and a perfect excuse" (Note 1967, 361). While the history
of court-ordered desegregation unfortunately shows that officials often had
many choices other than implementing court orders, a review of school desegregation cases did find that "many school boards pursue from the outset a
course designed to shift the entire political burden of desegregation on the

23. According to a participant in many school desegregation cases, such a course is often
urged on school administrators to win their support for desegregation. Incorporating reforms in
court orders offers them a chance to make changes they have been unable to win approval for on
their own (author's conversation with Gary Orfield).

courts" (Kalodner 1978, 3). This was also the case in the Alabama mental
health litigation where "the mental health administrators wanted [Judge]
Johnson to take all the political heat associated with specific orders while they
enjoyed the benefits of his action" (Cooper 1988, 186). Thus,

> Condition IV: Courts may effectively produce significant social reform by pro-
> viding leverage, or a shield, cover, or excuse, for persons crucial to implemen-
> tation who are *willing to act*.

Before summing up, it is important to assess what the conditions suggest
about the role of the courts in the American political system. They suggest
that court decisions are neither necessary nor sufficient for producing significant social reform. They are not necessary because much reform takes place
outside of the judicial system and because courts lack independence (Constraint II). They are not sufficient because courts lack effective tools for implementation (Constraint III) and require the existence of particular conditions
(Conditions I-IV). Without the presence of at least one of the conditions,
court decisions will not produce significant social reform. On the other hand,
if Constraints I *and* II *and* III are overcome, and at least one of the conditions
is present, then courts may effectively produce significant social reform.

Returning to the two views of the role of the courts that framed this
chapter, this analysis suggests that the Constrained Court view more closely
approximates the role of the courts in the American political system. While
the conditions suggest that courts can be effective producers of significant
social reform, capturing part of the Dynamic Court view, they also suggest
that this occurs only when a great deal of change has already been made. For
only when there has been political, social, and economic change will Constraints I, II, and III be overcome and at least one of the conditions be present.
Overall, then, the conditions and constraints suggest that U.S. courts, and
their role in the American political system, are much less exceptional than is
generally thought.[24]

To sum up, the discussion suggests that the conditions enabling courts to
produce significant social reform will seldom be present because courts are
limited by three separate constraints built into the structure of the American
political system:

1) The limited nature of constitutional rights (Constraint I);
2) The lack of judicial independence (Constraint II);
3) The judiciary's lack of powers of implementation (Constraint III).

24. In his classic historical study of the Supreme Court, McCloskey, too, concludes that
the Court has been effective only when it has "operated near the margins rather than in the center
of political controversy, when it has nudged and gently tugged the nation, instead of trying to
rule it" (McCloskey 1960, 229). See also Handler (1978); Grossman (1970). Where this work
differs from those cited is that it shows why this is the case.

However, when certain conditions are met, courts can be effective producers of significant social reform. These conditions occur when:

1) Overcoming Constraint I, there is ample legal precedent for change; *and*,
2) Overcoming Constraint II, there is support for change from substantial numbers in Congress and from the executive; *and*,
3) Overcoming Constraint III, there is either support from some citizens, or at least low levels of opposition from all citizens; *and*, either
   a) Positive incentives are offered to induce compliance (Condition I); or,
   b) Costs are imposed to induce compliance (Condition II); or,
   c) Court decisions allow for market implementation (Condition III); or,
   d) Administrators and officials crucial for implementation are willing to act and see court orders as a tool for leveraging additional resources or for hiding behind (Condition IV).

It is now time to turn to the data and see how well the views, constraints, and conditions fare.

PART 1

Civil Rights

Introduction

". . . in the field of public education the doctrine of 'separate but equal' has no place. Separate educational facilities are inherently unequal." (*Brown* v. *Board of Education* 1954, 495)

With these words Chief Justice Earl Warren, speaking for a unanimous Supreme Court, sounded the death knell for legal segregation of the public schools in the United States. *Brown* overturned nearly sixty years of Court-sanctioned segregation, effectively reversing the infamous separate-but-equal doctrine (*Plessy* v. *Ferguson* 1896). In holding that state-enforced segregation on the basis of color deprives individuals of the equal protection of the laws guaranteed by the Fourteenth Amendment, the Supreme Court "quite simply, buried Jim Crow" (Aleinikoff 1982, 923). *Brown* was followed by decisions banning racial segregation in public parks and recreation facilities, in intrastate and interstate commerce, in courtrooms, and in facilities in public buildings.[1] Thus, *Brown* is invariably seen as "a revolutionary statement of race relations law" (Carter 1968, 237) through which the Supreme Court "blazed the trail" of civil rights (Spicer 1964, 176). Being "nothing short of a reconsecration of American ideals" (Kluger 1976, 710), *Brown* "profoundly affected national thinking and has served as the principal ideological engine" of the civil rights movement (Greenberg 1968, 1522). For five de-

1. Public Parks and Recreation facilities: *Mayor and City Council of Baltimore City* v. *Dawson* (1955) (memorandum decision) (public beaches and bathhouses); *Holmes* v. *City of Atlanta* (1955) (memorandum decision) (public golf course); *New Orleans City Park Improvement Association* v. *Detiege* (1958) (memorandum decision) (public golf courses and other facilities); *Wright* v. *Georgia* (1963) (public parks); *Watson* v. *Memphis* (1963) (public parks). Transportation: *Gayle* v. *Browder* (1956) (memorandum decision) (intrastate); *Boynton* v. *Virginia* (1960) (interstate); *Turner* v. *Memphis* (1962) (airports). Courtrooms: *Johnson* v. *Virginia* (1963) (*per curiam*). Facilities in Public Buildings: *Derrington* v. *Plummer* (1956) (cafeteria in courthouse); *Burton* v. *Wilmington Parking Authority* (1961); *Brown* v. *Louisiana* (1966) (libraries). Other cases in which the Supreme Court banned segregation include *McLaughlin* v. *Florida* (1964) (sexual relations); *Loving* v. *Virginia* (1967) (marriage).

cades, *Brown* has been the "symbol" of the courts' ability to produce significant social reform (Neier 1982, 57), the "principal inspiration to others who
seek change through litigation" (Greenberg 1974, 331). As Wilkinson puts
it, "*Brown* may be the most important political, social, and legal event in
America's twentieth-century history" (Wilkinson 1979, 6). It has served,
Robert Cover tells us, as a "paradigmatic event" (Cover 1982, 1316).

It is hard to avoid being caught up in the rhetoric of the Court's words
and the praise it evoked. History, too, seems to bear this out. For ten years
after *Brown* Congress and the executive branch did little to promote civil
rights. The Court spoke alone. Yet words are not action. Although the conventional wisdom, as cited above, and shared by proponents of the Dynamic
Court view, is that the federal courts, through *Brown* and its progeny, played
a crucial role in producing both changes in civil rights and an active civil
rights movement, truth is not thereby assured. With *Brown* as a paradigm for
the Dynamic Court view, it is important to examine *Brown*'s effects.

To do so, I will focus on the consequences of court action in the battle
for civil rights. Proponents of the Dynamic Court view assert that, starting
with *Brown* and continuing through the desegregation decisions, the courts
have been a key institution producing change in civil rights. The Constrained
Court view, of course, denies this assertion and calls attention to the broader
societal change of which court action is only one small part. In order to test
the two views, and the constraints and conditions generated by them, I will
concentrate on the 1964 Civil Rights Act, the 1965 Voting Rights Act, and
the 1965 Elementary and Secondary Education Act and attempt to untangle
their relative impact as compared to that of the courts. If progress has been
made in civil rights,[2] were Congress and the executive branch helpful back-
ups to the powerful thrust of the courts or were they the key institutions effecting change? Which institution made a difference? Did it vary over issue
(school segregation vs. voting rights vs. segregation in transportation vs. segregation in public places)? Or over time? Was the civil rights movement making the best use of scarce resources by relying heavily on a courts-based
strategy?

In charting the influence that court decisions might have, I will examine
both the judicial and extra-judicial paths. Examining both paths is important,

2. It is incontrovertible that much progress has been made in civil rights in the past several
decades. Unfortunately, it is also incontrovertible that racial discrimination is still prevalent in the
United States. In speaking of progress, then, I do not wish to de-emphasize the immensity of the
task that lies ahead. See, for example, the results of a 1983 study showing how little progress
blacks have made in the last twenty years, excerpted in Herbers (1983). Readers should also note
the sad irony that twenty-five years after *Brown*, a desegregation suit was filed in Topeka, Kansas.
The 1979 suit was called *Brown* v. *Board of Education of Topeka, Kansas*. It was brought by
Linda Brown, the original plaintiff, on behalf of her children! And, in December 1989, the U.S.
Court of Appeals for the Tenth Circuit held that Topeka had still not done enough to desegregate
its schools ("Topeka" 1989, 17).

for extra-judicial effects are a key aspect of the Dynamic Court view. With civil rights, for example, it has often been suggested that the federal courts may have served as agenda-setters, as legitimizers of black protest and needlers of white consciences.[3] The role of the courts in the civil rights movement may have been to bring to light the existence of discrimination and keep it prominent, changing public opinion about civil rights and forcing action from Congress. That is, without *Brown* there may never have been a 1964 Civil Rights Act, a 1965 Voting Rights Act, or a 1968 Housing Act.

Chapter 2 summarizes judicial, legislative, and executive action in key areas of civil rights. By bringing together all government action dealing with civil rights, it allows the reader to see the whole picture. The discussion also compares the results of actions of the different branches. Chapter 3 applies the two views and the constraints and conditions to these findings. Chapter 4 examines the Dynamic Court view claim of extra-judicial effects and chapter 5 completes this part by exploring other societal factors that supported civil rights.

3. See Kluger (1976, ix) (book about *Brown* as the "resurrection" of America's inner resources) and generally Carter (1968); Greenberg (1968); Spicer (1964). See, generally, almost any serious discussion of courts and civil rights.

2

Bound for Glory? *Brown* and the Civil Rights Revolution

Education—Elementary and Secondary Schools

Court Action

Brown and its companion case, *Bolling* v. *Sharpe* (1954),[1] were the Court's first modern foray into questions of segregation in the elementary and secondary schools. *Brown* was actually four consolidated cases coming from the states of Kansas (*Brown* v. *Board of Education of Topeka, Kansas* 1951), South Carolina (*Briggs* v. *Elliott* 1952), Virginia (*Davis* v. *County School Board of Prince Edward County, Virginia* 1952), and Delaware (*Gebhardt* v. *Belton* 1952). Its holding, however, was applicable to all public elementary and secondary schools throughout the nation. At the time of the decision (May 17, 1954), seventeen Southern and Border states,[2] plus the District of Columbia, maintained segregated elementary and secondary schools by law and four states outside the region—Arizona, Kansas, New Mexico, and Wyoming—allowed local segregation. Eleven states had no laws on the subject and sixteen states had laws prohibiting segregation, though not all were enforced. Thus, twenty-seven states either prohibited segregated schools outright or had no laws dealing with the question while twenty-one states either required or allowed segregated schools.

Brown had taken several years to decide. Originally argued in 1952, it was re-argued in 1953 before a Court presided over by a new Chief Justice, Earl Warren. The decision was announced in May of 1954. The time delay between initial argument and final decision was due to the complexity of the

---

1. *Bolling* was directed at the schools of the District of Columbia under the control of the federal government. Thus, the holding was based on the Fifth Amendment. In other respects, it was similar to *Brown*.

2. The Southern states: Alabama, Arkansas, Florida, Georgia, Louisiana, Mississippi, North Carolina, South Carolina, Tennessee, Texas, Virginia. The Border states: Delaware, Kentucky, Maryland, Missouri, Oklahoma, West Virginia. These references are used throughout this study.

issues involved and the desire of the new Chief Justice to reach a unanimous decision (Ulmer 1971).[3]

The National Association for the Advancement of Colored People (NAACP) was euphoric over the unanimous decision. Thurgood Marshall, the chief litigator for the black plaintiffs, told reporters that the Supreme Court's interpretation of the law was "very clear." If the decision were violated anywhere "on one morning" Marshall said, "we'll have the responsible authorities in court by the next morning, if not the same afternoon." When asked how long he thought it would take for segregation to be eliminated from public schools, Marshall replied that "it might be 'up to five years' for the entire country." Finally, "he predicted that by the time the 100th anniversary of the Emancipation Proclamation was observed in 1963, segregation in all its forms would have been eliminated from the nation" ("N.A.A.C.P." 1954, 16).

The decision, however, did not include any announcement as to the appropriate relief for the plaintiffs. This was postponed for reargument due to the "considerable complexity" (*Brown* 1954, 495) of the matter. Reargument lasted for four days in April 1955, and the parties to the case, including the United States, were joined by the attorneys general of Arkansas, Florida, Maryland, North Carolina, Oklahoma, and Texas, as *amici curiae* pursuant to the Court's invitation in *Brown* (1954, 495–96).

The remedy was announced on May 31, 1955, slightly more than a year after the initial decision and two and one-half years after the initial argument. The Court in *Brown II* (1955) held that, because local school problems varied, federal courts were in the best position to assure compliance with *Brown I*, an end to legally enforced public-school segregation. The cases were reversed and remanded to the lower courts[4] which were ordered to "take such proceedings and enter such orders and decrees consistent with this opinion as are necessary and proper to admit to public schools on a racially nondiscriminatory basis with all deliberate speed the parties to these cases" (1955, 301). The phrase "with all deliberate speed" was picked up by commentators, lawyers, and judges as the applicable standard. Thus, the end result of the *Brown* litigation was a unanimous Supreme Court clearly and unequivocally holding that state-enforced segregation of public schools was unconstitutional and ordering that it be ended "with all deliberate speed."

During the years from 1955 through the passage of the 1964 Civil Rights Act, the Court issued only three full opinions in the area of segregation of elementary and secondary schools. It routinely refused to hear cases or curtly

---

3. However, Johnson (1979) has found that unanimity does *not* affect the treatment Supreme Court opinions receive in lower courts. Thus, the effort to achieve unanimity in *Brown* may not have been worth it, particularly if it resulted in compromise over the implementation decision.

4. The Delaware case, *Gebhardt* v. *Belton*, was affirmed and remanded to the Delaware Supreme Court for proceedings consistent with *Brown*.

affirmed or reversed lower-court decisions (for a discussion of these cases, see Wasby et al. 1977, 166–73, 192–98). However, in *Cooper* v. *Aaron* (1958), the first case after *Brown*, the Court spoke strongly.

Cooper v. *Aaron* involved the attempt of Governor Faubus and the Arkansas legislature to block the desegregation of Central High School in Little Rock, Arkansas. The Court convened in a special session for only the fifth time in thirty-eight years to hear the case (Peltason 1971, 187). After reviewing the history of attempts to desegregate the public schools in Little Rock, the Court faced the question of whether violence, or threat of violence, in response to desegregation and resulting in turmoil in the school disruptive of the educational process justified the suspension of desegregation efforts for two and one-half years. In answering in the negative, rejecting the school board's claim and reversing the federal district court, the Supreme Court held that the "constitutional rights of respondents [black students] are not to be sacrificed or yielded to the violence and disorder" which was occurring (1958, 16). This was, as the opinion stated, "enough to dispose of the case" (1958, 17), but the Court continued for several pages to underline its determination that *Brown* be followed. It reminded the parties that Article VI of the Constitution makes the Constitution the "supreme law of the land" (1958, 18). Further, the Court unearthed *Marbury* v. *Madison* (1803) and Chief Justice Marshall's words that "[i]t is emphatically the province and duty of the judicial department to say what the law is" (1803, 177, quoted at 1958, 18). The opinion also pointed out that the decision in "*Brown* was unanimously reached by this Court only after the case had been briefed and twice argued and the issues had been given the most serious consideration." Not stopping here, the justices stressed that twelve justices had considered and approved the *Brown* doctrine (the nine who originally agreed to it and the three who had joined the Court since then) (1958, 19). Finally, in an unprecedented move, all nine justices individually signed the opinion. *Cooper* v. *Aaron* was a massive and unswerving affirmation that desegregation was the law and must be implemented.

The next full opinion in the elementary and secondary education field came in *Goss* v. *Board of Education of Knoxville* (1963). At issue was a desegregation plan that included a provision allowing students to transfer from a school where their race was a minority to one where it predominated. This provision was challenged on the ground that since race was the sole criterion of the plan it would perpetuate rather than alleviate racial segregation, denying plaintiffs the right to attend desegregated schools. The Court agreed, unanimously holding the one-way transfer plan to be violative of the Fourteenth Amendment and contrary to *Brown*.

The third decision, *Griffin* v. *Prince Edward County* was handed down in 1964. The case involved the constitutionality of the closing of Prince Edward County public schools to avoid desegregation and the use of state tuition grants and tax credits to support private segregated education for white children. The Court unanimously[5] found both acts unconstitutional, being essentially devices to avoid the constitutional mandate of desegregation, and denying plaintiffs the equal protection of the law.

Brown I and *II* stated the law and stated clearly that steps had to be taken to end state-enforced segregation. *Cooper* v. *Aaron* emphatically re-iterated it. And *Goss* and *Griffin* unanimously held that patent attempts to avoid desegregation were unconstitutional. The Court had spoken clearly and forcefully.

In the first four years after the passage of the 1964 Civil Rights Act, the Supreme Court remained quiet in the education area. However, the lower federal courts, particularly in the Fourth and Fifth Circuits, became increasingly involved in litigation. In 1965, the Fifth Circuit, in a case from Jackson, Mississippi, upheld desegregation guidelines announced by the U.S. Department of Health, Education, and Welfare (HEW) (to be discussed below). The circuit court "attach[ed] great weight to the standards" established by HEW and warned that it would not allow school districts to avoid HEW requirements by obtaining less stringent desegregation orders from local, and friendly, federal district courts (*Singleton* v. *Jackson Municipal Separate School District* 1965, 731). Similarly, in the *Jefferson County* case, in which a three-judge panel had ordered the defendant school systems to desegregate classrooms, facilities, and staffs by the 1967–68 school year, the Fifth Circuit, quoting *Singleton*, reaffirmed its support for the guidelines (*U.S.* v. *Jefferson County Board of Education* 1966, 847, 848, 851). The court reiterated its concern that the courts not be used to avoid strict HEW standards and stressed that "affirmative action" had to be taken to create a "unitary, nonracial system" (1966, 862, 878).

The Supreme Court re-entered the field in 1968 and issued, for the first time since *Brown*, a detailed opinion on remedies. *Green* v. *County School Board of New Kent County, Va.* (1968), involved a freedom-of-choice plan under which no white child had transferred to the "formerly black school" and only about 15 percent of the black children had transferred to the "formerly white school." In a unanimous opinion, written by Justice Brennan, the Court threw out the freedom-of-choice plan and suggested that such plans would be unlikely to meet constitutional standards. Showing a good deal of impatience, the opinion stated that "the burden on a school board today is to come forward with a plan that promises realistically to work, and promises realistically to work *now*" (1968, 439). In the fall of 1969, in *Alexander* v. *Holmes County* (1969), the Court continued with its impatience, reinstating a July 1969 Fifth Circuit order requiring thirty Mississippi school districts to desegregate by the start of school in September in accordance with *Green*. In

---

5. Justices Clark and Harlan dissented from the remedy portions of the opinion.

a terse, two-page *per curiam* ruling in October, the Court rejected a delay until December, holding that "continued operation of segregated schools under a standard of allowing 'all deliberate speed' for desegregation is no longer constitutionally permissible." Further, the Court held that school districts were required to "terminate dual school systems at once and to operate now and hereafter only unitary schools" (1969, 19, 20).

Finally, in *Swann* v. *Charlotte-Mecklenburg Board of Education* (1971), the Court upheld the power of district judges to include busing as part of a remedial decree. Writing for a unanimous Court, Chief Justice Burger held that "once a right and a violation have been shown, the scope of a district court's equitable powers to remedy past wrongs is broad" (1971, 15). This included, Burger noted, busing, because "desegregation plans cannot be limited to the walk-in school" (1971, 30).

From 1954 through 1971, the Court remained steadfast in its commitment to end public-school segregation. Repeatedly, it reminded parties before it, and the nation, that segregation violated the Constitution. And, as shall soon be shown, for many of those years it was the only branch of the federal government that acted.

Congressional and Executive Branch Action

Congressional and executive branch action in the area of public-school desegregation was virtually non-existent until the passage of the 1964 Civil Rights Act. In stark contrast to the actions of the Supreme Court in *Brown*, the other two branches of the federal government remained essentially passive.

In 1957 Congress passed the first civil rights act since 1875. In the education field the act was most notable for its lack of provisions. While an attempt was made to give the Department of Justice the authority to file suits on behalf of individuals alleging segregation in education, it was unsuccessful. The Eisenhower administration opposed the provision because, in the words of Attorney General William P. Rogers, it "might do more harm than good" (quoted in Sarratt 1966, 72).

Congress passed a second civil rights act in 1960. Unlike the 1957 act, this one gave a fair amount of attention to segregation in education, but as with the earlier act, little of substance was enacted. In particular, the Department of Justice was not given the authority to file desegregation suits on behalf of individuals nor was the federal government given the power to cut off funds to school districts refusing to desegregate.[6] The bill's educational

6. In its first report, the U.S. Commission on Civil Rights (USCCR) had split 3–3 in recommending federal power to cut off funds from segregated institutions of higher learning. One member, Commissioner Johnson, supported such power for secondary and elementary schools as well (USCCR 1959, 328–30).

provisions were aimed at violent interference with court-ordered school desegregation and at providing education for children of military personnel stationed in places where the public schools had been closed to avoid desegregation.

The 1964 act was a major departure from its predecessors. The most sweeping civil rights legislation since the Civil War and Reconstruction era, the act touched many fields. In education, Congress finally empowered the attorney general to bring desegregation suits on behalf of individuals.[7] Also, Title VI of the act gave the federal government the power to cut off federal funds to school districts that discriminated on the basis of race.[8] Its key language held:

> No person in the United States shall, on the ground of race, color, or national origin, be excluded from participation in, be denied the benefits of, or be subjected to discrimination under any program or activity receiving Federal financial assistance.

The 1964 act, as I will demonstrate shortly, had a major impact on school desegregation.

Until 1964, executive action was little better. Although the president and the administration can be a "particularly powerful agenda setter" (Kingdon 1984, 208), the power and prestige of the presidency was not employed in support of civil rights until the mid-1960s. Little was done by President Eisenhower in the 1950s and only slowly did Presidents Kennedy and Johnson bring their administrations into the civil rights battle. Their actions, or lack thereof, are highlighted in chapter 3.

In the spring of 1965 Congress enacted the Elementary and Secondary Education Act (ESEA), providing federal aid to school districts with large percentages of low-income children. The act was heavily directed at the South (Orfield 1969, 94), and nearly $1 billion was expended in the first year of operation (Bailey and Mosher 1968, 156). A total of $1.3 billion was authorized for 1966 (Miles 1974, 148) and in fiscal year 1968 alone, $1.5 billion of federal money was sent to the states (USCCR 1970, chapter 1).

Title VI required some kind of government response. The task of formulating procedures fell to HEW and, specifically, to the Office of Education. Action became imperative with the enactment of ESEA in the spring of 1965, because there was now a large pot of federal money available to Southern

7. Empowering the attorney general to bring suits had not only been proposed as early as the 1957 act, but also had been recommended by the U.S. Commission on Civil Rights in its 1961 and 1963 reports (USCCR 1961b: 2, 181; USCCR 1963a, 69).

8. A partial fund cut-off had been officially recommended by the U.S. Commission on Civil Rights (1961b: 2, 181) as early as 1961. Also, amendments to congressional legislation requiring non-discrimination in the distribution of federal funds had been introduced since the 1940s. On this point, see discussion in chapter 4.

school districts. While the details of government actions are both fascinating and complicated, brief summary is possible.[9]

HEW acted slowly to implement Title VI. At first, it asked school districts for assurances of non-discrimination. The first regulations, adopted on December 3, 1964, allowed federal aid to school districts that either submitted assurances that their schools were totally desegregated, that were under court orders to desegregate and agreed to abide by such orders, or that submitted voluntary desegregation plans. Further, state agencies were instructed not to renew programs or to authorize new ones until the commissioner of education certified that local districts were in compliance with Title VI. These regulations, however, were vague on what was an acceptable voluntary desegregation plan. In April 1965, guidelines were issued that required the opening of all grades to freedom of choice by the start of the 1967 school year.[10] These guidelines were upheld by the Fifth Circuit in *Singleton*, discussed above. The guidelines were again revised and tightened in March 1966, setting standards for acceptable freedom-of-choice plans. The March 1966 guidelines established standards based on the percentage increase in students transferring from segregated schools. In most cases, the guidelines required a doubling or tripling of the percentage of blacks in "formerly white schools" for the 1966–67 school year. It was these guidelines that the Fifth Circuit upheld in the *Jefferson County* case discussed above. Regulations were further tightened in March 1968 when school districts were ordered to submit plans for complete desegregation by the fall of 1968, or, in some cases, the fall of 1969. The Supreme Court, in *Green*, essentially seconded these result-oriented standards that went past freedom of choice. Thus, by the end of the Johnson administration, HEW had come to officially require complete desegregation as a requirement for receiving federal funds under Title VI.

The Nixon administration appeared to back off from this strict requirement. In a July, 1969, statement, HEW Secretary Finch and Attorney General Mitchell announced modifications of the guidelines in several important ways (USCCR 1969, Appendix C). Chief among them was rejection of the 1969–70 terminal date for all districts as "arbitrary" and "too rigid to be either workable or equitable." In terms of freedom of choice, a plan that "genuinely promises to achieve a complete end to racial discrimination at the earliest possible date" would be acceptable. In addition, the statement pledged the administration to rely more heavily on "stepped-up enforcement activities of [the Department of] Justice" and to "minimize" the number of HEW fund cut-off proceedings. However, the statement did not purport to change the guidelines. "In general," the administration announced, the "terminal date" for acceptable plans "must be the 1969–70 school year." Also,

9. For more detail, see Orfield (1969, chaps. 2 and 3); Note (1967); USCCR (1970). The summary that follows is based primarily on these sources.
10. Freedom of choice allowed students to attend any school in the district.

the statement pointed to the courts, holding that "policy in this area will be as defined in the latest Supreme Court and Circuit Court decisions." Finally, the statement quoted approvingly the language from *Green*, quoted above, that desegregation plans must work *now*.[11]

Enforcement proceedings and fund terminations under Title VI were uncommon but not unheard-of. Although by the early 1970s the federal government had "investigated, negotiated with, and arm-twisted over 3,000 districts" (Hochschild 1984, 28), only a small percentage of these districts ended up in enforcement proceedings or had their eligibility for federal funds terminated. Of the approximately 2,800 school districts in the eleven Southern states, 320 were involved in enforcement proceedings from September 15, 1965, through June 30, 1967. While few districts suffered from fund terminations, the period from the passage of Title VI to the end of the Johnson administration saw over 200 such terminations, slightly more than 7 percent of all Southern districts. While terminations were unlikely, the threat was real.[12]

Results and Comparison

The decade from 1954 to 1964 provides close to an ideal setting for measuring the contribution of the courts vis-à-vis Congress and the executive branch in desegregating public schools. For ten years the Court spoke forcefully while Congress and the executive did little. Then, in 1964, Congress and the executive branch entered the battle with the most significant piece of civil rights legislation in nearly ninety years. In 1965, the enactment of ESEA made a billion dollars in federal funds available to school districts that, in accord with Title VI, did not discriminate. This history allows one to isolate the contribution of the courts. If the courts were effective in desegregating public schools, the results should show up before 1964. However, if it was Congress and the executive branch, through the 1964 Civil Rights Act and 1965 ESEA, that made the real difference, then change would occur only in the years after 1964 or 1965.

"In the problem of racial discrimination," Judge Brown once remarked, "statistics often tell much" (*Alabama* v. *U.S.* 1962, 586). Due to the herculean efforts of the Southern Education Reporting Service,[13] supplemented by the U.S. Commission on Civil Rights (USCCR), and later, HEW, fairly good statistics on the progress of school desegregation are available. A summary is

11. It must be noted, however, that in August 1969, the administration petitioned the Fifth Circuit to relax the final date for complete desegregation in thirty Mississippi school districts from September 1, 1969, to December 1, 1969. This action led to the Supreme Court decision in *Alexander* v. *Holmes County*, discussed in the text.

12. Edelman (1973, 39 n.29); Orfield (1969, 115); USCCR (1974b 3: 128; 1970, 37).

13. The Southern Education Reporting Service described itself as an impartial fact-finding agency led by a board of directors of Southern newspaper editors and educators, and funded with a grant from the Ford Foundation.

Table 2.1   Black Children in Elementary and Secondary School with Whites,
                 1954–1972, Selected Years

Year	South		South without Texas and Tennessee		Border		Border without D.C.	
	%	#	%	#	%	#	%	#
1954–55	.001	23	.001	20	NA	NA	NA	NA
1955–56	.12	2,782	.002	47	NA	NA	NA	NA
1956–57	.14	3,514	.002	34	39.6	106,878	18.1	35,378
1957–58	.15	3,829	.005	109	41.4	127,677	25.2	57,677
1958–59	.13	3,456	.006	124	44.4	142,352	31.1	73,345
1959–60	.16	4,216	.03	747	45.4	191,114	35.5	117,824
1960–61	.16	4,308	.02	432	49.0	212,895	38.7	131,503
1961–62	.24	6,725	.07	1,558	52.5	240,226	42.8	151,345
1962–63	.45	12,868	.17	4,058	51.8	251,797	43.7	164,048
1963–64	1.2	34,105	.48	11,619	54.8	281,731	46.2	182,918
1964–65	2.3	66,135	1.2	29,846	58.3	313,919	50.1	207,341
1965–66	6.1	184,308	3.8	95,507	68.9	384,992	64.1	275,722
1966–67	16.9	489,900			71.4	456,258		
1968–69	32.0	942,600			74.7	475,700		
1970–71	85.9	2,707,000			76.8	512,000		
1972–73	91.3	2,886,300			77.3	524,800		

SOURCES: Southern Education Reporting Service (1967, 40–44); USCCR (1967); U.S. Department of HEW, Office of Civil Rights (*Directory*, 1968, 1970, 1972).

NOTE: Numbers in the column marked "%" are the percentages of black students, out of all black schoolchildren, attending school with whites.

presented in table 2.1 and figure 2.1 while state breakdowns are in Appendix 1. The table and graph present the number of black children attending public school with whites as well as their percentages out of all black schoolchildren in the seventeen states (and the District of Columbia) which required segregation in public schools at the time of *Brown*. While this way of presenting the numbers does not discriminate between token and substantial integration, and thus suggests more desegregation than actually occurred, it does allow for a time-series comparison.

The Border States and the District of Columbia

The Supreme Court appears to have had an important impact on school desegregation in the six border states and the District of Columbia. Unfortunately, reliable figures are not available until the 1956 school year. However, during the eight school years from the fall of 1956 until the passage of the 1964 act, the number of black children in school with whites rose 15.2 percent (39.6 percent to 54.8 percent) in the region as a whole and 28.1 percent (18.1 percent to 46.2 percent) excluding the District of Columbia. However, the lack of data for the two years immediately following *Brown* may understate

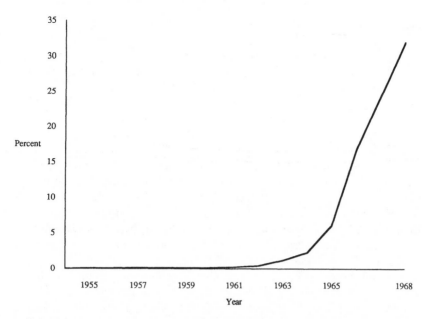

Figure 2.1. Percentage of All Southern Black Schoolchildren Attending School with Whites

the change. That is, the change may have been even greater than these numbers suggest, for substantial change may have taken place in the years 1954–56.[14] Thus, the Supreme Court's actions appear to have had an effect.

The passage of the 1964 Civil Rights Act increased the rate of desegregation. During the two school years after enactment of the 1964 act, there was an increase of 14.1 percentage points (54.8 percent to 68.9 percent) in the number of black children in desegregated schools in the region as a whole, nearly equal to the eight-year increase from 1956–57 through 1963–64. Similarly, excluding the District of Columbia, the increase in just two years was 17.9 percentage points. Looking at the border states and D.C. as a whole, in the eight school years starting in 1963 (before enactment of the 1964 and 1965 acts) and continuing through 1970, the number of black children attending desegregated schools jumped 22.0 percentage points (54.8 percent to 76.8 percent), an even greater increase than that recorded in the eight years prior to congressional and executive action. These numbers suggest two points. First, that the Court made a major contribution to desegregation of the public schools in the border states and, second, that the rate of desegregation noticeably increased after the passage of the 1964 and 1965 acts. The seeming successful contribution of the Supreme Court in the border states and the District of Columbia is explored in chapter 3.

14. For example, there was no desegregation in the District of Columbia prior to 1954.

The Southern States

The statistics from the Southern states are truly amazing. For ten years, 1954–64, virtually *nothing happened*. Ten years after *Brown* only 1.2 percent of black schoolchildren in the South attended school with whites. Excluding Texas and Tennessee,[15] the percent drops to less than one-half of one percent (.48 percent). Despite the unanimity and forcefulness of the *Brown* opinion, the Supreme Court's reiteration of its position and its steadfast refusal to yield, its decree was flagrantly disobeyed. After ten years of Court-ordered desegregation, in the eleven Southern states barely 1 out of every 100 black children attended school with whites. The Court ordered an end to segregation and segregation was not ended. As Judge Wisdom put it, writing in the *Jefferson County* case, "*the courts acting alone have failed*" (1966, 847; emphasis in original). The numbers show that the Supreme Court contributed virtually *nothing* to ending segregation of the public schools in the Southern states in the decade following *Brown*.

The entrance of Congress and the executive branch into the battle changed this. As figure 2.1 graphically demonstrates, desegregation took off after 1964, reaching 91.3 percent in 1972 (not shown). In the first year of the act, 1964–65, nearly as much desegregation was achieved as during all the preceding years of Supreme Court action. In just the few months between the end of the 1964–65 school year and the start of the 1965–66 year, nearly three times as many black students entered desegregated schools as had in the preceding decade of Court action. And the years following showed significant increases. While much segregation still existed, and still exists, the change after 1964 is as extraordinary as is the utter lack of impact of the Supreme Court prior to 1964. The actions of the Supreme Court appear irrelevant to desegregation from *Brown* to the enactment of the 1964 Civil Rights Act and 1965 ESEA. Only after the passage of these acts was there any desegregation of public schools in the South.

What accounts for the phenomenal increase in desegregation in the post-1964 years, particularly the 1968–72 period? Was it the action of HEW? The courts? Local school officials? All three? Part of the answer may be found in the responses of nearly 1,000 school superintendents to a U.S. Commission on Civil Rights survey of school districts containing at least some minorities (USCCR 1977a).[16] When superintendents reported that "substantial steps to desegregate" had been taken, the survey asked, among other questions, "which was the single most important source of pressure for initiation of

15. Tennessee and Texas had the smallest percentage of black enrollment in public schools of any of the eleven Southern states. Thus, resistance to desegregation may have been weaker.
16. The survey covered 47 percent of all school districts with at least 5 percent minority enrollment and enrollments of 1,500 or more. Seventy-seven percent (996) of the superintendents surveyed responded.

Table 2.2   Desegregated School Districts, by Primary Source of Intervention, and by Year of Greatest Desegregation, 1901–1974

	Source of Intervention							
	Courts		HEW		State-Local		Total	
Years	#	%	#	%	#	%	#	%
1901–53	—	—	—	—	6	2	6	1
1954–65	12	6	18	12	52	21	82	13
1966–67	8	4	19	13	45	18	72	12
1968–69	53	26	42	28	34	13	129	21
1970–71	107	52	61	40	46	18	214	35
1972–73	12	6	5	3	38	15	55	9
1974–75	15	7	7	5	31	12	53	9
Total	207	101	152	101	252	99	611	100
Percent of total number of districts	34		25		41			

SOURCE: USCCR (1977a, 26).
NOTE: Percentages do not equal 100 because of rounding.

desegregation?" Table 2.2 presents the results. While the survey's coding rules underestimate the effect of HEW,[17] it can be seen that, overall, state-local pressures were mentioned most often, followed by courts and HEW. It can also be seen that while courts were mentioned in only 20 of 154 districts in the years 1954–67, in the 1968–71 period 160 of 343 districts that initiated desegregation pointed to the courts. Those years also recorded 103 mentions of HEW, suggesting that it was quite active too. The survey suggests that while HEW was active, the courts played an important role in desegregation in the 1968–72 period.

In terms of success, the survey found extremely large decreases in segregation between 1968 and 1972 from both court and HEW action and more moderate decreases with local action. It also found that districts desegregating under HEW pressure were less segregated in 1972 than were districts desegregating under court orders (USCCR 1977a, 66). However, districts desegregating under court orders were more segregated to start with, had, on average, higher percentages of minority students, and achieved a somewhat greater decline in segregation than those desegregating under HEW pressure. Yet perhaps because courts faced a tougher task, desegregation in districts under

17. When there was more than one box checked for "primary" pressure, the survey's coding rule was that "courts took priority over HEW" (Appendix A, 118). The commission also suggests that "many districts that describe their desegregation as locally initiated may have been influenced by HEW" (13).

court orders proceeded less smoothly: "school districts that reported school desegregation by court intervention were far more likely to experience disruptions than those that desegregated under HEW or local pressures" (USCCR 1977a, 84).[18]

These findings were corroborated by Giles in a study of 1,362 Southern school districts. Comparing actual levels of segregation in school districts under HEW and court enforcement in 1968 and 1970, Giles concluded that "districts under H.E.W. enforcement were significantly less segregated than court-ordered districts in both 1968 and 1970" (Giles 1975, 88). He also found greater decline in desegregation in court-ordered districts than in those under HEW enforcement.

In sum, although Hochschild overstated the case in concluding that "were it not for the courts there would be little reduction in racial isolation" (Hochschild 1984, 134), she did pinpoint a period of court efficacy in civil rights. Chapter 3 explores the reasons why, with particular emphasis on why the Constrained Court view seems to explain the first decade after *Brown* while the Dynamic Court view appears to do a better job explaining the post-1964 findings.

Higher Education

The story of Court and governmental action regarding segregation of public colleges and universities is shorter but similar to that of lower education. In the late nineteenth century Congress, in the second Morrill Act, allowed segregation if separate black institutions were maintained (Orfield 1969, 11). Congressional action was followed, of course, by Supreme Court approval of the separate but equal doctrine in *Plessy* v. *Ferguson* (1896). However, the Court began to chip away at that doctrine in a number of cases challenging segregation in graduate and professional education.[19] In these cases, states were ordered to admit black applicants to formerly segregated state universities where the state's practice had been to provide them with out-of-state scholarships (*Missouri ex. rel. Gaines* v. *Canada* 1938), and universities were prohibited from treating black students differently than other students once admitted (*McLaurin* v. *Oklahoma Board of Regents* 1950). Attempts to set up "separate but equal" black institutions were dealt a death blow in *Sweatt* v. *Painter* (1950). Sweatt, a black applicant, had been denied admission to the University of Texas Law School because of his color. The state courts upheld the denial but ordered Texas to build a state law school for blacks. In a unanimous opinion, the Supreme Court ordered Sweatt's admission to the University of Texas Law School, holding, in essence, that although

18. Data on disruptions and violence can be found in USCCR (1977a, 85ff.).
19. The leading cases are *Missouri ex. rel. Gaines* v. *Canada* (1938); *Sipuel* v. *Oklahoma Board of Regents* (1948); *Sweatt* v. *Painter* (1950); *McLaurin* v. *Oklahoma Board of Regents* (1950).

any new law school would certainly be separate, it would hardly be equal. Chief Justice Vinson wrote: "The University of Texas Law School possesses to a far greater degree those qualities which are incapable of objective measurement but which make for greatness in a law school" (1950, 634). Although the separate but equal doctrine was not formally rejected, the clear impact of the holding was that lack of equality would compel admission to the previously segregated institution and that proving equality would be a nearly impossible task. It was not long to *Brown's* declaration that separate educational facilities are inherently unequal.

As with elementary and secondary education, in the years before 1964 Congress and the administration did little to desegregate universities. There was no congressional action until the 1964 Civil Rights Act. President Kennedy, when violence was rampant, did send federal troops to the University of Mississippi in 1963. However, other than utter the occasional platitude, he did little. President Eisenhower had done even less. With the passage of the 1964 Civil Rights Act, however, the executive branch was given the power to bring desegregation suits and cut off federal funds to segregating institutions.

Despite these new powers, the Office of Civil Rights (OCR) did little to enforce the act. Until 1968, for example, there was no compliance review program at all for institutions of higher learning (USCCR 1970, 42). Even after that, there were no clear guidelines or any serious attempt to require compliance (USCCR 1974b: 3, chap. 3). By January 1975, for example, there had been only two fund terminations, involving small schools, Bob Jones University and Freewill Baptist Bible College. However, between January 1969 and February 1970, letters requesting desegregation plans were sent to ten states.[20] Even with that action, it appeared to some that the Nixon administration was dragging its feet in applying the law. Thus, a lawsuit was brought by the Legal Defense and Educational Fund, Inc. of the NAACP to force the government to act. In *Adams* v. *Richardson* (1973), decided in early 1973, OCR was ordered to obtain acceptable desegregation plans or commence enforcement proceedings leading to fund terminations.

Results and Comparison

Unlike with elementary and secondary education, few reliable statistics are available for making the comparison in higher education. This qualification being made, it is clear that there was little movement to desegregate universities prior to the 1964 Civil Rights Act. Tables 2.3A and 2.3B summarize the best information available (for state breakdowns, see Appendix 2). Table 2.3A shows that from 1963 to 1966, from before the passage of the 1964 Act to after it, the number of black students attending predominantly

20. The states were Arkansas, Florida, Georgia, Louisiana, Maryland, Mississippi, North Carolina, Oklahoma, Pennsylvania, and Virginia.

Table 2.3A   **Blacks at Southern, Predominantly White Public Colleges and Universities, 1963, 1965, 1966**

	South		Border	
Year	# of Students	% of Enrollment	# of Students	% of Enrollment
1963	4,639	NA	NA	NA
1965	12,054	1.9	6,607	2.5
1966	20,788	2.6	14,102	4.9

SOURCES: Sarratt (1966, chap. 5); Southern Education Reporting Service (1965, 3–25; 1967, 3).

Table 2.3B   **Percentage of Black Enrollment at Southern, Formerly All-White, Public Colleges and Universities, by State, 1970 and 1978**

States	1970[a]	1978
Southern		
Alabama	3.3	10.0
Arkansas	4.6	10.4
Florida	2.9	6.0
Georgia	3.1	10.5
Louisiana	5.0	11.5
Mississippi	3.5	9.8
North Carolina	2.4	6.6
South Carolina	2.8	9.0
Tennessee	4.1	9.7
Texas	4.3	5.3
Virginia	2.0	5.2
Border		
Delaware	2.3	3.1
Kentucky	3.1	5.1
Maryland	3.9	10.1
Missouri	2.6	4.5
Oklahoma	3.8	5.0
West Virginia	2.3	2.8

SOURCE: Office for Civil Rights data adapted from Ayres (1984, 125).

[a] 1972 data were used for 17 of the 256 traditionally white campuses. They were located in Florida (3), Georgia (2), Maryland (1), Mississippi (1), North Carolina (1), Oklahoma (1), and West Virginia (8).

white universities in the South increased nearly five-fold. In one year alone, from 1965 to 1966, it increased over 70 percent. In the border states, the number of black students in predominantly white institutions more than doubled from 1965 to 1966. These figures suggest that it was the action of Congress and the executive branch, not the Court, that brought at least some desegregation to higher education. Chapter 3 will explore the reasons behind this finding.

On the other hand, as the 1970 and 1978 data presented in table 2.3B show, while there was change, the overall percentages were small. That is, despite congressional and executive action, and despite *Adams*, only some progress was made in bringing more than a token number of black students to formerly white public institutions. The response, for example, to OCR's letters to ten states mentioned above was the submission of unacceptable plans from five states and no plans at all from the other five![21] Other examples of inaction abound. In December 1985, a federal judge in Alabama, in a suit involving Auburn University, found that "the state of Alabama has indeed operated a dual system of education; that in certain aspects, the dual system yet exists" (*U.S.* v. *Alabama* 1985). These findings, too, will be discussed in chapter 3.

Voting

Court Action

The right to vote has long been denied American minorities. Although the Fifteenth Amendment guaranteed blacks the right to vote, the failure of Reconstruction and its replacement by Jim Crow laws and practices put an effective end to black voting in the South. By 1903, every Southern state had passed legislation limiting the vote.[22] Throughout the twentieth century the Supreme Court heard and decided a number of cases in which it held unconstitutional various state attempts to prevent blacks from voting. As early as 1915, the so-called "Grandfather Clause," limiting voters to those who could prove that their ancestors had the right to vote (i.e., whites), was held unconstitutional (*Guinn & Beal* v. *U.S.* 1915).[23] This, of course, was but one of many different ways states attempted (and succeeded) to disenfranchise blacks.

The best-known Supreme Court cases dealing with voting are the Texas Primary Cases. In Texas, as in the rest of the South, the Democratic primary was the real election, with the general election being merely a required procedural formality. The Democratic parties of all eleven Southern states, aware of the realities of political life, banned blacks from voting in Democratic primaries (USCCR 1968, 7). This exclusion was challenged as violative of the Fourteenth Amendment in *Nixon* v. *Herndon* in 1927, and the Supreme Court struck it down. Texas responded by enacting legislation giving the state

21. Florida, Louisiana, Mississippi, North Carolina, and Oklahoma did not submit plans.
22. Kousser (1974, 32). For a good history of state action denying blacks the right to vote, see USCCR (1959, 55–97). For a discussion of some of the state tactics employed in the context of why litigation failed to remedy the discrimination, see chapter 3.
23. A similar case, also from Oklahoma, was *Lane* v. *Wilson* (1939).

executive committee of each party the power to prescribe voting qualifications for its own members. The Democratic Party Executive Committee then required that its members be white. Mr. Nixon again brought suit, challenging this new bar to his ability to vote. In *Nixon* v. *Condon* (1932), the Supreme Court, citing *Nixon* v. *Herndon*, struck down the law, holding that the power to determine membership qualifications resides in the party in convention assembled. Thus, executive committee action was state action violative of the Fourteenth Amendment. Undaunted, and relying on the loophole in the *Condon* opinion, the Texas Democratic party in its convention voted to exclude blacks. This exclusion was upheld by the Supreme Court in *Grovey* v. *Townsend* (1935), where the Court held that since the action had been taken by the "representatives of the party in convention assembled," it was "not state action" (1935, 48) and therefore was constitutional. This position was reversed nine years later in *Smith* v. *Allwright* (1944), where the Court essentially held that primary and general elections are one process and that denying blacks the right to vote in primaries could be held to be state action. The final Texas Primary Case, *Terry* v. *Adams* (1953), involved the Jaybird Democratic Association, purportedly a self-governing voluntary private club whose nominees, it just so happened, "nearly always" (1953, 463) ran unopposed in the Democratic primaries. The Jaybirds, of course, denied membership to blacks. The Court, realizing that the Jaybird election was the real election in Texas (1953, 469), accordingly struck down the exclusion.

The Court also acted to invalidate other blatant attempts to disenfranchise black voters. One case came from Tuskegee, Alabama, where the Alabama legislature had redrawn the city boundaries to exclude nearly all black residents. The local newspapers made much of the "joke" that Tuskegee's blacks had suddenly "moved out of town" (cited in Wasby et al. 1977, 225). In *Gomillion* v. *Lightfoot* (1960), the Court saw past the facially neutral character of the statute and threw out the redistricting plan.

The Court, then, with one exception subsequently reversed, consistently upheld the right of blacks to take part in the electoral process. It continually struck down attempts by state legislatures to prohibit blacks from participating in a meaningful way in the electoral process.

Congressional and Executive Branch Action

Until 1957, congressional and executive branch action in voting discrimination was, as in other civil rights areas, virtually non-existent. As with education, the Supreme Court was left to speak alone.

In 1957, Congress passed its first civil rights act in eighty-two years. The act had several voting rights provisions, the most important of which authorized the Justice Department to initiate suits on behalf of blacks deprived of voting rights. The act also prohibited intimidation of voting in federal elections, including primaries, and established the Civil Rights Commission with power to gather evidence on violations of voting rights.

In 1960, Congress passed its second civil rights act of the century. Among its voting-rights provisions were the requirements that voting records be preserved for twenty-two months and that the attorney general be given access to them. An important provision allowed for judicial appointment of referees to temporarily replace local registrars. However, the process required before such appointments could be made was cumbersome.[24] Thus, both the 1957 and 1960 acts required that courts be a vital part of the process. And little change was made by the 1964 act, which concentrated on other aspects of discrimination.

Finally, in 1965, Congress passed the Voting Rights Act, making a major break with the past. The 1965 act, unlike the prior acts, provided for direct federal action to enable blacks to vote. Federal examiners could be sent to election districts to list eligible voters where tests or devices were required as a precondition for voting or registering and where less than 50 percent of the total voting-age population was registered. The act also suspended all literacy tests in the jurisdictions it covered and directed the attorney general to file suit challenging the constitutionality of the poll tax.[25] The 1965 Voting Rights Act, as will be seen shortly, had a major impact on black registration.

Administration action in voting rights was slight. Eisenhower's reticence in civil rights was noted earlier, and the voting-rights area was no exception. As of 1959, the Eisenhower Justice Department had instituted only three suits under the 1957 act.[26] And while the passage of the 1957 and 1960 acts was important, the Eisenhower administration hardly used them.

The Kennedy administration did make use of the powers it had under the 1957 and 1960 acts by filing scores of voting rights suits. However, it failed to push for major modification of the existing statutes. While its record was a vast improvement over that compiled by the Eisenhower administration, the major effort did not come until the Johnson administration and the 1965 Voting Rights Act.

Until 1957 the Court spoke alone in prohibiting racial discrimination in voting rights. Congress joined in with the 1957, 1960, and 1964 acts with small, but growing, executive support. Finally, Congress and the executive branch forcefully acted to prohibit discrimination in voting with the passage and implementation of the 1965 Voting Rights Act.

24. For a good description, see USCCR (1961b: 1, 77–78).
25. The poll tax had been made unconstitutional in federal elections by the enactment of the Twenty-fourth Amendment in 1964. Subsequently, the poll tax was held unconstitutional in state elections as violative of the equal protection clause of the Fourteenth Amendment in *Harper* v. *Virginia Board Of Elections* (1966).
26. USCCR (1961b: 1, 75). Not surprisingly, the administration lost all three cases.

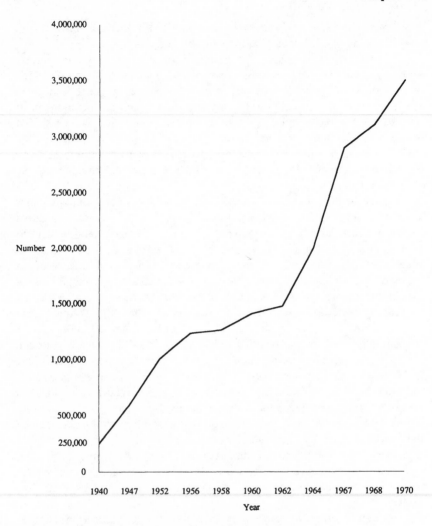

Figure 2.2. Black Voter Registration in the Southern States

Results and Comparison

Voting rights provide a good comparison of the relative contribution of the courts and the other two branches of the government to civil rights. Until 1957, the Court acted alone. It was joined half-heartedly by the other branches in 1957 and strongly in 1965. Figure 2.2 shows the change in the estimated number of black registered voters over the years and table 2.4 contains the raw data. Striking is the large jump in the number and the percentage of blacks registered to vote from just prior to the passage of the 1965 act to

Table 2.4   **Black Voter Registration in the Southern States, 1940–1970, Selected Years**

Year	Estimated # of Black Registered Voters	% of Voting-Age Blacks Registered
1940	250,000	5
1947	595,000	12
1952	1,008,614	20
1956	1,238,038	25
1958	1,266,488	25
1960	1,414,052	28
1962	1,480,720	29.4
1964	2,005,971	40.0
1967	2,903,284	57.6
1968	3,112,000	58.7
1970	3,506,000	66.9

SOURCES: Garrow (1978, 19); Jaynes and Williams (1989, 233); Lawson (1976, 285); Matthews and Prothro (1963a, 27); USCCR (1968, 12, 13, 222, 223).

NOTE: As the U.S. Commission on Civil Rights states: "Registration figures themselves vary widely in their accuracy." For another set of figures which differ, but present the same general pattern, see Voter Education Project (1966); Watters and Cleghorn (1967).

just after it. As table 2.4 records, the number of registered blacks in the eleven Southern states in this period jumped from approximately 2 million to 2.9 million, an increase of nearly 900,000, or 45 percent. In the first few months after the passage of the act more than 300,000 blacks were registered (Rodgers and Bullock 1972, 30). No other time period shows such an increase. Prior to 1957, when only the Court acted, only 1 out of every 4 blacks was registered to vote in the South where nearly 3 out of every 4 whites were. Nearly three-quarters as many blacks registered to vote merely in the two years after passage of the act as had been registered in all the years prior to 1957. The gains in some states were enormous. Mississippi, for example, showed a nine-fold increase in three years (see Appendix 3 for state figures). There can be no doubt that the major increase in the registration of blacks came from the action of Congress and the executive branch through the 1965 Voting Rights Act.

The best case that can be made for Court influence is that the increases from 1940 to 1956 were due to the holdings of the Texas Primary Cases, particularly *Smith* v. *Allwright* in 1944 and *Terry* v. *Adams* in 1953. However, as the U.S. Civil Rights Commission pointed out, the end of World War II brought home many black servicemen who, having risked their lives for America, were determined to exercise the right to vote. Also, the black literacy rate had been continually growing, from 33 percent in 1898 to 82 percent by 1960 (USCCR 1961b: 1, 42). And, as chapter 5 details, blacks had been moving in large numbers from the rural South to the urban South, where registration was sometimes possible, and to the North, where there were few, if any, registration barriers. Although the issue of what accounted for the increase in the percentage of blacks registered to vote between 1940 and 1956 is by no means clear, what is clear is that important societal changes were taking place, independently of the Court, that surely affected registration.[27]

The lack of impact of governmental action prior to the 1965 act can also be seen by the lack of direct results of proceedings initiated with the courts under the 1957 and 1960 acts. In 1963, for example, the U.S. Civil Rights Commission concluded that five years of litigation under the acts had "not provided a prompt or adequate remedy for wide-spread discriminatory denials of the right to vote." It cited the efforts in 100 counties in eight states where, despite the filing of thirty-six voting rights suits by the Department of Justice, registration increased a measly 3.3 percent between 1956 and 1963, from approximately 5 percent to 8.3 percent (USCCR 1963a, 13, 14–15). Another study found that eight years of litigation under the two acts in the forty-six most heavily segregated Southern counties resulted in the registration of only 37,146 blacks out of 548,358 eligibles, a mere 6.8 percent (Note 1966, 1088 n.108). Even administration officials came to the conclusion that litigation was fruitless (Garrow 1978, 34, 67). For example, Deputy Attorney General Katzenbach concluded that the weakness of litigation to produce change "meant essentially that you had to bring a separate lawsuit for each person who was discriminated against, and there were thousands. It would take years to get them registered to vote" (quoted in Hampton 1990, 212). And Attorney General Robert F. Kennedy, testifying before Congress in 1962, noted that the "problem is deep rooted and of long standing. It demands a solution which cannot be provided by lengthy litigation on a piecemeal, county-by-county basis" (U.S. Cong. 1962, 264). These figures and statements provide further evidence that Court action was ineffective in combating discrimination in voting rights.

On the other hand, there is evidence in addition to the figures that suggests the important direct effect of the 1965 act. In July 1966, about one year after the passage of the 1965 act, the Voter Education Project of the Southern Regional Council studied the effects on registration of sending federal examiners to Southern counties. The findings show substantially higher levels of black registration in counties where federal examiners were working than in those where they were not. For example, comparing counties where federal examiners were present to those where they were not, the study found increases in the percentage of blacks registered of 22.6 percent in South Caro-

---

27. This point is expanded upon in chapter 5.

lina (71.4 percent versus 48.8 percent), 18.3 percent in Alabama (63.7 percent versus 45.4 percent), and 17 percent in Mississippi (41.2 percent versus 24.2 percent) (USCCR 1968, 155). Coupled with the huge increase in black registration immediately after the 1965 act, these figures buttress the attribution of those changes to the 1965 Act (see also USCCR 1965).

In sum, the bottom line in voting is that the actions of the Court contributed little to the increase in black registration. When major change did occur, it was clearly attributable to the actions of Congress and the executive.

Transportation

Court Action

Although arguably less important that the right to a desegregated education and the right to vote, racial segregation in transportation deprives individuals of equal treatment. Through a series of cases the Supreme Court strongly reiterated the constitutional prohibition of segregation in interstate and intrastate transportation.

Recent Court history starts in 1941 with *Mitchell* v. *U.S.*, where U.S. Representative Mitchell, a black from Chicago, traveling in Arkansas as part of an interstate trip, was denied equal accommodation in Pullman cars. The Court found this a violation of the separate but equal standard. A similar finding was made in *Henderson* v. *U.S.* (1950), where black interstate travelers received discriminatory treatment in a train's dining car. Through these cases the Court made clear that if segregation was maintained, "substantial equality of treatment" (*Mitchell* 1941, 97) was required. However, by this time the separate but equal standard had been weakened in the transportation field. In 1946, in *Morgan* v. *Virginia*, the Court invalidated as to interstate passengers a Virginia law requiring segregated seating in all passenger motor carriers. By 1960, the Court made clear that this ban on segregation also applied to facilities used in interstate transportation. Specifically, in *Boynton* v. *Virginia* (1960), the Court held that if bus companies made services available to interstate passengers as a regular part of their transportation, then segregation in the use of the facilities was prohibited. Segregation was also prohibited in intrastate transportation. In *Gayle* v. *Browder* (1956), arising out of the Montgomery bus boycott, the Supreme Court affirmed (*per curiam*) the lower court's finding that segregated seating violated the Fourteenth Amendment.[28] Thus, by 1960, if not earlier, the Supreme Court had "clearly established" (Lusky 1963, 1168) that laws requiring segregation in transportation were prohibited. And in 1962 the Court, showing a good deal of exasperation with continuing segregation, cited *Morgan, Gayle,* and *Boynton* for

28. See also *Evers* v. *Dwyer* (1958), involving bus segregation in Memphis.

the proposition that it was "settled beyond question that no State may require racial segregation of interstate or intrastate transportation facilities" (*Bailey* v. *Patterson* 1962, 33 [*per curiam*]).

Congressional and Executive Branch Action

In transportation, Congress did not act. The important actor was the Interstate Commerce Commission (ICC). The ICC, with its members appointed by the president, often reflects the concerns of the administration. Thus, not surprisingly, little action was taken by it until the 1960s. In 1941, for example, the ICC upheld the Arkansas law requiring segregation that the Supreme Court invalidated in *Mitchell*. Throughout the 1940s and 1950s, while the Court was prohibiting segregation, the ICC concerned itself primarily with the carriers' economic woes, confining its anti-discrimination efforts to referring complaints to the Department of Justice (Dixon 1962, 214). "It repeatedly sanctioned the Jim Crow practices of Southern rail lines" (Barnes 1983, 70). While it did issue rail and bus regulations in 1955, rejecting the separate but equal standard, the effort was half-hearted (Dixon 1962, 221–22). This changed, however, with the Kennedy administration and the Freedom Rides. The first Freedom Ride, started in early May 1961, reached bloody heights on Sunday May 14 with the fire-bombing of one of the buses outside of Anniston, Alabama, and the brutal attack on the Freedom Riders in Birmingham. Only then did the Kennedy administration act. Late in May Attorney General Robert Kennedy, supported by other cabinet members (USCCR 1963b, 137) petitioned the ICC to adopt more stringent regulations. In September 1961, the ICC issued new and stronger regulations. Thus, until the September 1961 regulations, the brunt of the battle against segregation in transportation was carried by the Court.

Results and Comparison

Segregation in transportation has not been quantified. Numerical measurements do not exist and comparisons cannot obtain the more precise levels reached in education and voting. Instead, reliance must be placed on the fuzzier measurements of impressions. Yet when impressions are clear, and based on reliable sources, a pattern can emerge. And in transportation, the pattern that emerges is the general ineffectiveness of the Court and the effectiveness of the other branches.

Examining the effectiveness of the Court decisions discussed above, Barnes found that "for the average black rail traveler, *Mitchell* changed nothing" (Barnes 1983, 34). Despite Thurgood Marshall's claim that *Morgan* was "a decisive blow to the evil of segregation and all that it stands for" (quoted in Barnes 1983, 50), Barnes found that "Southern bus travel remained segregated" and that "*Morgan* also made little change in railway Jim Crow practices" though it was extended to them by a later federal circuit court decision

(Barnes 1983, 52, 53). In addition, in 1947 the President's Committee on Civil Rights (PCCR) complained that many states were still enforcing segregation laws in interstate commerce in violation of *Morgan* (PCCR 1947, 170). The effect of the intrastate cases was the same. *Gayle*, the Montgomery bus case, "did not close off even direct local segregation" (Wasby et al. 1977, 268). And despite the 1960 *Boynton* case, "Jim Crow persisted in a majority of Southern bus depots and lunch counters" (Barnes 1983, 150). Throughout the 1950s commentators found that the right to non-segregated transportation, as ordered by the Court, was "systematically frustrated" (Lusky 1963, 1168; Dixon 1962a, 213; Wasby et al. 1977, 268–70). These findings were corroborated by the ICC in its preparatory work for the September 1961 regulations. The Commission found that

> "in a substantial part of the United States many Negro interstate passengers are subjected to racial segregation in several forms. On vehicles they continue to be subjected to segregated seating based on race. In many motor passenger terminals, Negro interstate passengers are compelled to use eating, restroom and other terminal facilities which are segregated . . ." (quoted in Dixon 1962a, 222)

As late as July 1964, the Southern Regional Council complained that "not yet, for example, has the federal government through its prosecution been able to end finally defiance of the ICC ruling of 1961 regarding bus terminal segregation" (Southern Regional Council 1964, 20). The record seems clear that until the ICC, with administration backing, issued strict guidelines and decided to enforce them, little was accomplished in desegregating transportation.

After 1961, and particularly after the passage of the Civil Rights Act of 1964 (public accommodations sections), segregation in transportation essentially was ended. As with the other fields, this comparison shows that desegregation in transportation was the result not of court action but of the action of the other branches of the federal government.

Accommodations and Public Places

Court, Congressional, and Executive Branch Actions

The actions of all branches of the government were limited in ending segregation in accommodations and public places. However, the Court did act early to ban segregation in public places. A series of cases following *Brown* in the 1950s made clear that its command extended to public recreation areas and private restaurants in public buildings such as courthouses.[29] By 1961, this latter holding was extended to apply to virtually any private concern operating on public property. Thus, in *Burton* v. *Wilmington Parking Authority*

29. For case citations, see the introduction to part I.

(1961), segregated service by a private restaurant situated in a public parking garage and operating under a lease from the Parking Authority was held to be state action violative of the Fourteenth Amendment. The Court also banned segregated service for passengers in interstate commerce in *Boynton* (1960). However, these cases did not reach private restaurants and hotels which did not operate in buildings owned by states. The Court entered this area by way of the sit-in cases (discussed in greater detail in chapter 4).

Starting in February 1960 in Greensboro, North Carolina, and quickly spreading throughout the South, sit-ins involved mostly black individuals entering private stores that discriminated against blacks (usually by segregating lunch counters), requesting service, and typically refusing to leave until served. The sit-in demonstrators were often arrested and invariably convicted by state courts. However, the convictions were almost invariably reversed by the Supreme Court.[30] In reversing the convictions in such great numbers the Court made it clear that it would not allow state authorities to aid (by arresting *peaceful* demonstrators) private discrimination. Its decisions allowed the sit-in movement to continue at full force (Carter 1968, 241). Yet the Court did not unequivocally find "state action" in these cases. Such a finding (if implemented) would have made private discrimination in public places illegal by making police action to end the demonstrations state action in violation of the Fourteenth Amendment. As Grossman put it, "perhaps it could be said that never had the Supreme Court used so many cases to make so little law" (Grossman 1967, 436). In the public accommodations field, then, the Court clearly extended *Brown's* prohibition of segregation to public recreation facilities, clearly prohibited segregation in private establishments operating in public places, and clearly prohibited segregation in private restaurants regularly serving interstate travellers.

Congress and the executive branch took no action in this field until 1964. The 1957 and 1960 Civil Rights Acts did not address the issue and executive branch action independent of Congress was lacking. This changed, of course, with the 1964 Civil Rights Act, which banned racial discrimination in restaurants and accommodations affecting interstate commerce in Title II, and in public facilities in Title III. With the 1964 act, Congress made up for its past inactivity.[31]

Results and Comparison

As with transportation, here, too, comparisons must be based on impressions. And the general impression provided by commentators is that in the

30. Eighty-one sit-in cases were appealed to the Supreme Court and review was granted in 61, a whopping 75 percent (the usual rate is under 10 percent). Of these, 57 (93 percent) of the opinions favored the demonstrators or movement in one way or another. For a list of the cases, and a discussion from which the figures above are taken, see Grossman (1967).

31. The public accommodations sections of the 1964 Civil Rights Act were held constitutional in *Heart of Atlanta Motel* v. *U.S.* (1964), and *Katzenbach* v. *McClung* (1964).

areas where segregation was the law prior to court action, little desegregation was achieved until the enactment of the 1964 act. This result may partly be due to the fact that the Court did not address private discrimination in accommodations. But in areas that the Court did address, little changed until Congress acted. Some evidence for this conclusion is provided by recurring cases. For example, despite clear rulings in the few years following *Brown* that segregation of public places was unconstitutional, as late as 1963 the Court was hearing cases challenging segregation in public parks (*Watson* v. *Memphis* 1963; *Wright* v. *Georgia* 1963). That is, its earlier rulings were ignored by state officials, and blacks had been arrested and convicted for entering segregated public parks. In 1956, the Fifth Circuit held it unconstitutional, as violative of the Fourteenth Amendment, for a lunchroom in a courthouse to discriminate on the basis of race (*Derrington* v. *Plummer* 1956). Yet four years later, in the same circuit, sit-ins occurred at the Montgomery County (Alabama) courthouse to protest racial discrimination in services provided in the courthouse (Pollitt 1960, 323). The passage of Title III of the 1964 act finally put an end to most practices of this type.

In public accommodations and restaurants, the Court did not speak directly. Yet when it did so in the interstate travel area, as in *Boynton*, the freedom rides demonstrated the Court's ineffectiveness. And despite the Court's protection of the sit-in demonstrators,[32] segregation continued. In 1961 the U.S. Civil Rights Commission found massive racial discrimination in accommodations and restaurants in the United States (USCCR, State Advisory Commissions 1961; Caldwell 1965). And in *Heart of Atlanta Motel*, the Title II test case, the Court cited evidence from Senate hearings that discrimination remained prevalent and "nationwide" (1964, 252–53). Thus, it again appears that Court action on behalf of blacks challenging segregation was ineffective in ending that segregation. Only when Congress legislated did change occur.

Housing

Court Action

Racial discrimination in housing is one of the most virulent and intractable forms of discrimination. Unfortunately, it is also prevalent throughout America. The Court's first positive contribution to ending housing segregation came in 1948 in the restrictive covenant cases (Vose 1967). Restrictive covenants are clauses in deeds restricting the conveyance of the property to certain groups, usually Caucasians. In the principal case, *Shelley* v. *Kraemer*

32. Sit-in demonstrators still suffered. Lusky estimates that each demonstrator needed about $2,000 in cash for bail and fines if he or she wished to contest the sit-in conviction (Lusky 1963, 1180).

(1948),[33] the Court held that judicial enforcement of restrictive covenants constituted discriminatory "state action" prohibited by the Fourteenth Amendment. *Shelley*, procedurally important for its finding of state action, was followed by *Barrows* v. *Jackson* (1953) where the Court prohibited the granting of damages for the violation of a restrictive covenant, finding that awarding damages for breach of a restrictive covenant would constitute coercion by the state in violation of the Fourteenth Amendment. By 1953 the Court had removed the legal effectiveness of restrictive covenants.

The Court did not hear another housing case until 1967 when it held unconstitutional an amendment to the California constitution, adopted by referendum, prohibiting the state from acting in any way to prevent racial discrimination in the sale, lease, or rental of property. In *Reitman* v. *Mulkey* (1967) the Court affirmed the holding of the California Supreme Court that the amendment, in the California environment of state laws prohibiting such discrimination, would "encourage and significantly involve the State in private racial discrimination contrary to the Fourteenth Amendment" (1967, 376). The Court made clear that state action in support of housing discrimination, broadly construed, would be struck down.

The final Supreme Court case prior to the effective date of Title VIII of the 1968 Civil Rights Act was *Jones* v. *Mayer Co.* (1968). The Joneses were refused the purchase of a house solely on the ground that Mr. Jones was black. The Court held this discriminatory, relying on a law passed in *1866* that barred "*all* racial discrimination, private as well as public, in the sale or rental of property" (1968, 413). In a footnote (1968, 417 n.20) the Court noted the passage of Title VIII but pointed out that for the purposes of the case at hand it did not take effect until 1969.

The Court, then, spoke little in the housing field but did ban state enforcement of restrictive covenants and state action encouraging discrimination. Finally, in 1968, the Court came down firmly in support of open housing.

Congressional and Executive Branch Action

The history of government action in fighting housing discrimination is abysmal.[34] The principal government financial agencies responsible for supervising and regulating home-mortgage lenders "endorsed overt racial and ethnic discrimination in mortgage lending" (USCCR 1975d, 41) until passage of the 1968 Fair Housing Law. And since federal funds and influence "pervade the private housing market" (USCCR 1961b: 4, 4), government policies actively contributed to segregation in housing.

---

33. The second case, *Hurd* v. *Hodge* (1948), involved the District of Columbia.
34. For a brief history of government action in support of segregated housing, see USCCR (1961b: 4, 9–26).

Early action by the executive branch came with the 1947 report of President Truman's Committee on Civil Rights which recommended the outlawing of restrictive covenants (PCCR 1947, 169). The executive branch supported that recommendation and dispatched Solicitor General Perlman to argue in *Shelley* as *amicus curiae*. But little else was done until 1968. For example, in 1958 the administrator of the Housing and Home Finance Agency stated that the federal government "had no responsibility to promote the ending of racial discrimination in residential accommodations" (quoted in USCCR 1959, 459). The Federal Housing Administration maintained as a fundamental principle that builders and lenders should be entirely free to make their own decisions as to who could buy or rent houses, despite the fact that federal money was crucial for their actions (USCCR 1961b: 4, 25).[35] The Veterans Administration maintained roughly similar policies (USCCR 1975d, 40). And the FDIC actually supported racially discriminatory lending practices of insured banks if such practices protected investments. In 1961, the chairman of the FDIC spelled out the corporation's position in a letter to the U.S. Commission on Civil Rights:

> There are circumstances under which a bank in its consideration of a real estate loan application may consider the race of a potential borrower or the racial composition of a neighborhood. There exists a possibility that the financing of a real estate purchase for a member of a minority group might have a serious effect upon values in the neighborhood. If the bank already had a substantial number and dollar volume of mortgage loans in the neighborhood, it would necessarily consider the effect upon these assets. The bank management's important responsibility for safe investment of its depositor's funds may include the consideration of such aspects of any loan. . . . Aside from the moral aspects of racial or other discrimination, every bank has a moral as well as a legal obligation and responsibility toward the economic welfare of its depositors and stockholders. (Reprinted in USCCR 1961b: 4, 49)

The executive branch finally acted in November 1962, when President Kennedy issued Executive Order 11063. The order's broad intent was to prevent racial discrimination in the sale or rental of residential property financed through federal assistance. However, its provisions only covered housing provided through mortgage insurance issued by the FHA or loan guarantees by the VA and federally assisted public housing. Housing financed by mortgage lending institutions (the great bulk of the nation's housing supply) was excluded from the coverage (USCCR 1963a, 102). Further, rather than having federal agencies affirmatively act to prevent discrimination in federally as-

35. See also *Levitt and Sons, Inc.* v. *Division against Discrimination* (1960, 181), where one large builder of suburban tract housing who openly discriminated admitted that he was "100 percent dependent" on government financing.

sisted housing, reliance was placed on the complaint process as the principal means of compliance (USCCR 1975d, 67).

Congress entered the field in both 1964 and 1968. Title VI of the 1964 Civil Rights Act filled in some of the gaps in coverage of the executive order. However, conventionally financed housing was not affected unless it was located in urban areas. In 1968, Congress enacted Title VIII of the 1968 Civil Rights Act. Title VIII prohibited racial discrimination in the sale or rental of all housing, with a few exceptions. Its coverage extended to more than 80 percent of all housing and included conventional mortgages obtained through private lending institutions.

Results and Comparison

It is sad to report that racial segregation in housing has not been eliminated by government action.[36] In fact, by the 1970s it appeared to be getting worse as whites fled to the suburbs where blacks could not afford houses or were not allowed to buy in (USCCR 1975d, 13, 119–36). While a large part of the reason may be the failure of the executive branch to implement the laws it had (USCCR 1975d, 79, 171), it is apparent that Court action has had little effect. As early as 1959 the U.S. Commission on Civil Rights noted that despite the "consistent decisions of the Supreme Court," segregation in housing continued unabated (USCCR 1959, 452–53). Its 1961 report found the same lack of impact from Court action. "What the Supreme Court has declared unconstitutional when attempted through municipal zoning," the report declared, "the private housing industry practiced at will" (USCCR 1961b: 4, 16). Despite the tremendous preparation, time, energy, and money invested in the restrictive covenant cases, as sympathetic a commentator as Clement Vose was forced to conclude that their significance lay in "what went into them rather than in what came out" (Vose 1967, ix). This was corroborated by the Civil Rights Commission, which found that *Shelley* had "little real effect" (USCCR 1975d, 41, 3–4). The point here is that Court decisions prohibiting racial discrimination in housing resulted in no appreciable change in housing discrimination.

Conclusion

The use of the courts in the civil rights movement is considered the paradigm of a successful strategy for social change. The Dynamic Court view is largely based on it. Yet, a closer examination reveals that before Congress and the executive branch acted, courts had virtually *no direct effect* on ending discrimination in the key fields of education, voting, transportation, accom-

36. As recently as February 1985, a nationwide study found massive racial segregation in public housing projects sheltering nearly 10 million people ("Segregation Reported" 1985, 15).

modations and public places, and housing. Courageous and praiseworthy decisions were rendered, and nothing changed. Only when Congress and the executive branch acted in tandem with the courts did change occur in these fields. In terms of judicial effects, then, *Brown* and its progeny stand for the proposition that courts are impotent to produce significant social reform. *Brown* is a paradigm, but for precisely the opposite view.

3

Constraints, Conditions, and the Courts

At first glance, the finding that courts contributed virtually nothing directly to civil rights in the decade when they acted alone is baffling. After all, courts decided so much. It goes against that part of the American belief system captured by the Dynamic Court view to believe that those decisions had no direct effect. In a nation governed by laws, not people, court decisions are legally and morally binding. At second glance, in the late 1960s and early 1970s, it appears that court decisions did have important direct effects. Does this represent the rebirth of the Dynamic Court view in the midst of the Constrained Court view's apparent triumph? In this chapter, I explore these seemingly contradictory findings. In the first part of the chapter I suggest that the constraints of the Constrained Court view handily explain the lack of court efficacy in producing significant social reform in the years when courts acted alone. The second part of the chapter examines the post-1964 years, particularly 1968–72, and suggests that court effectiveness can be explained by the presence of the conditions derived from the Dynamic Court view.[1] Thus, the chapter suggests that a more subtle understanding of the conditions under which litigation aimed at significant social reform will be effective goes far in explaining the success and failure of judicial attempts to end race-based discrimination.

Overcoming the First Constraint

Civil rights litigators were able to overcome the first constraint by slowly building precedent for change. The National Association for the Advancement of Colored People (NAACP) committed itself to a legal strategy for change early in its history. In October 1930, it hired Nathan Margold, a Harvard-educated lawyer and protégé of Felix Frankfurter, to map out a legal

1. For analytical reasons, the experience of the border states is also examined in the second part of the chapter.

strategy for attacking school segregation. His report, covering 218 legal-size pages, urged a direct attack on "the practice of segregation, *as now provided for and administered*" (quoted in Tushnet 1987, 28). In the years following the report, the NAACP slowly put together a brilliant legal staff, including Charles Houston and Thurgood Marshall. Slowly and painstakingly, segregation was attacked. The planning that went into some of the cases was remarkable. The successful legal attack on restrictive covenants, for example, involved a concerted effort to build favorable law-review commentary, garner opinions from respected judges dissenting in losing cases, and arrange for support from various interest groups (Vose 1967). In other cases, the best social science evidence of the day was brought to the courts' attention. While "the press of reality destroyed many possibilities imagined by the planners," and NAACP lawyers were often "doing no more than litigating the cases at the pace imposed by the litigants and the local courts" (Tushnet 1987, 43, 70), a number of precedents were created over the years of the 1930s, 1940s, and early 1950s.[2] The NAACP worked long and hard to create the kind of precedent and beliefs within the broader legal culture that could allow the Court to strike down segregation. And, of course, their efforts were finally vindicated by the Court in *Brown*.[3]

Judicial Independence

The second constraint of the Constrained Court view is the judiciary's lack of independence (Constraint II). Supporters of the Constrained Court view maintain that the judiciary requires elite support, and that strong congressional or executive opposition to court decisions, statutory or constitutional, can result in attacks on the courts which limit what they can accomplish. There is a good deal of evidence that in the years leading up to *Brown* the Court had elite support. After *Brown*, however, that support disintegrated.

In the years leading up to *Brown*, the Court was aided by several factors. The rhetoric of the Cold War, for example (examined in chapter 5), highlighted racial discrimination as a blight on American democracy in its fight against communism. In addition, starting with *Shelley* v. *Kraemer* in 1948, the U.S. entered many of the cases as *amicus curiae*, essentially supporting

2. These include *Missouri ex. rel. Gaines* v. *Canada* (1938)(law school); *Sipuel* v. *Oklahoma Board of Regents* (1948)(law school); *Shelley* v. *Kraemer* (1948) (housing); *Sweatt* v. *Painter* (1950)(law school); *McLaurin* v. *Oklahoma Board of Regents* (1950)(graduate school); *Henderson* v. *U.S.* (1950) (transportation).

3. The NAACP was helped by a number of additional factors. Specifically, starting with *Shelley* v. *Kraemer* in 1948, the U.S. entered many of the cases as *amicus curiae*, essentially supporting the NAACP. Also, in *Brown*, Justice Frankfurter gave Philip Elman, the principal author of the government's brief in the case, confidential information about his views and those of his colleagues. This information allowed Elman to tailor the government's brief (Elman 1987; Taylor 1987, 1, 28, 29).

the NAACP. The government's presence in these cases could have suggested to the Court that decisions ordering an end to segregation would be supported by the federal government. Thus, in the years leading up to *Brown* the Court's lack of meaningful independence was overcome.

The First Decade after *Brown*

In the years following *Brown*, however, that support was withdrawn. Court decisions in free speech and subversion, criminal procedure, and, of course, desegregation, enraged many members of Congress and a concerted attack on the Court was launched. Over fifty Court-curbing bills were introduced into Congress as an alliance of segregationists, cold warriors, and right-to-work advocates teamed up to curb the Court (Murphy 1962). In the summer of 1957, a bill drafted by the Justice Department limiting the Court's opinion in *Jencks* v. *U.S.* (1957) was enacted and a bill removing Supreme Court jurisdiction in five areas dealing with subversion was introduced. With civil rights specifically, there was the Southern Manifesto (discussed below) and the overall lack of administrative support.

Perhaps in response, in the late 1950s and early 1960s, Court action appeared to back away from the kind of decisions that had so angered Congress.[4] In the area of desegregation, the Court appeared to heed these attacks by avoiding major civil rights decisions until well into the 1960s. In education the Court did not issue a full opinion from *Brown* until the Little Rock crisis of 1958. After the crisis passed, there was silence again until 1963. And, of course, despite *Brown*, public schools in the South remained pristinely white, with only one in a hundred black children in elementary and secondary school with whites by 1964, a decade after the ruling. Only after there was a major change in the congressional climate with the passage of the 1964 Civil Rights Act did the Court re-enter the field. As Wasby et al. (1977, 107) put it, after *Brown*, "either overreacting or feeling badly burned by the lesson, the justices beat an unseemly retreat from the public school education field which was to last, with a few exceptions, over a dozen years."

The same pattern appears in other civil rights areas. With housing, de-

4. Important cases include *Beilan* v. *Board of Education* (1958), upholding the discharge of a public school teacher for refusing to tell school authorities whether he had worked for a Communist organization years earlier; *Lerner* v. *Casey* (1958), upholding the firing of a New York City subway conductor for invoking the Fifth Amendment when asked by the city if he was currently a member of the Communist party; *Uphaus* v. *Wyman* (1959), and *Barenblatt* v. *U.S.* (1959), upholding contempt convictions for refusing to answer questions posed by a New Hampshire investigatory committee and the House Un-American Activities Committee, respectively; *Konigsberg* v. *California* (1961) and *In re George Anastaplo* (1961), upholding exclusions from the California and Illinois bars, respectively, for refusing to answer questions about political beliefs. All of these decisions reversed, either explicitly or implicitly, earlier decisions that had angered many members of Congress. For more detail see Murphy (1962); Rosenberg (1985).

spite *Shelley* v. *Kraemer* (1948), from 1953 to 1967 the Court did not hear any housing cases. Some of its refusals to hear cases, such as *Cohen* v. *Public Housing Authority* (1959), and *Barnes* v. *City of Gadsden* (1959), had the effect of upholding segregation. More generally, in *Rice* v. *Sioux City Memorial Park Cemetery* (1954), decided *after Brown*, an equally divided Court issued a *per curiam* opinion upholding a restrictive covenant limiting burial to Caucasians. In *Dawley* v. *City of Norfolk, Virginia* (1959), the Court refused to hear the dismissal of a case challenging segregated restrooms in a state courthouse. The result, of course, was to leave the courthouse restrooms segregated. Another denial of *certiorari, In re Girard College Trusteeship* (1958), had the effect of allowing a segregated school administered by the state to remain segregated by substituting private trustees. And the Court simply avoided any anti-miscegenation cases until the 1960s because, in the words of Philip Elman, a former clerk to Justice Frankfurter and for many years in charge of the solicitor general's civil rights docket in the Supreme Court, "the timing was all wrong" (Elman 1987, 846).

The point this history makes is, I think, accessible. In the wake of congressional hostility the Court did not vigorously follow the logic and power of *Brown*. While not backtracking, and although reiterating the constitutional demand to end segregation in the opinions it did issue, it avoided cases and sidestepped issues. Only after the passage of the 1964 Civil Rights Act did the Court re-enter the field with vigor.

Political Leadership

For courts to effectively produce significant social reform, Constraint III suggested, the active support of political elites was necessary. It was contended that courts, lacking the power of "either the sword or the purse," were uniquely dependent upon the actions of political leaders. Without support from them, the Constrained Court view claimed that little would happen. And that is precisely the case in the decade following *Brown*.

National Leaders

On the executive level, there was little support for the Court until the Johnson presidency. President Eisenhower was one of America's most popular presidents. A World War II hero, he was reputedly offered the presidential nomination of both parties. Yet he steadfastly refused to commit his immense popularity or prestige in support of desegregation in general or *Brown* in particular. Only once in his eight years as president did Eisenhower take executive action to desegregate schools. That was in January 1954 when he issued an executive order banning segregation in schools located on military bases. Further, with the exception of the Little Rock crisis, the president did not involve himself or the executive branch in efforts to achieve compliance with court-ordered desegregation. With one exception,[5] the Eisenhower Justice Department intervened in desegregation suits as a friend of the court only when specifically invited or asked by the court. In general, President Eisenhower did little. As Roy Wilkins, executive secretary of the NAACP put it, "if he had fought World War II the way he fought for civil rights, we would all be speaking German today" (Wilkins 1984, 222).

President Eisenhower never publicly committed himself to support the *Brown* decision.[6] As rumors spread that he opposed the decision, he did nothing to counter them.[7] When asked in a news conference in 1958 if he had endorsed a slower approach to school desegregation than the Court's, he characteristically refused "to give an opinion about my conviction about the Supreme Court decisions." He went on to say:

> I might have said something about "slower," but I do believe that we should— because I do say, as I did yesterday or last week, we have got to have reason and sense and education, and a lot of other developments that go hand in hand as this process—if this process is going to have any real acceptance in the United States. (News conference of August 27, 1958, cited in Peltason 1971, 48)

As Peltason wittily put it, Eisenhower's position was: "Thurgood Marshall got his decision, now let him enforce it" (Peltason 1971, 54). Thus, it is fair to conclude that President Eisenhower and his administration gave little support to school desegregation in particular, and civil rights in general.[8]

President Kennedy was openly and generally supportive of civil rights but took little concrete initiative in school desegregation and other civil rights matters until pressured by events to do so. The administration's "most visible and most significant civil rights activities were responsive, reactive, crisis-managing, violence-avoiding" (Navasky 1977, 97). It did not rank civil rights as a top priority[9] and President Kennedy, like Eisenhower before him, was "unwilling to draw on the moral credit of his office to advance civil rights" (Navasky 1977, 161). For example, the response to the Freedom Rides (discussed in chapter 4) was not to protect American citizens doing nothing more than attempting to sit where they wished on Greyhound and Trailways buses and to use non-segregated terminal facilities, as mandated by Supreme Court rulings. Rather, Attorney General Robert Kennedy asked that the rides be

5. The Justice Department voluntarily intervened on behalf of the local school board in Hoxie, Arkansas, in 1956.

6. In October 1963, nearly three years after he left office, Eisenhower for the first time publicly endorsed *Brown* as "morally and legally correct" (quoted in Sarratt 1966, 50).

7. Burk (1984, 192) reports that during the 1956 campaign Eisenhower told Emmet John Hughes, "I am convinced that the Supreme Court decision set back progress in the South at least fifteen years." He also told Arthur Larson, "I personally think that the decision was wrong."

8. For other examples of Eisenhower's refusal to back civil rights, and for further discussion, see Leuchtenburg (1979, 121–26); Navasky (1977, 294).

9. As late as January 1963, President Kennedy stated that civil rights was not among his top priorities (Harding 1979, 59; Sorensen 1965, 471; Fleming 1965, 930).

halted because the president was going to Europe on "a mission of great importance" and wanted to avoid actions that brought "discredit on our country" (quoted in Goldman 1961, 5). No attempt was made to involve the FBI in the kind of apprehension-and-arrest actions for civil rights violations that was common with other violations of law. Indeed, most civil rights activists in the South came to view the FBI as, at best, passive and, at worst, an ally of racist Southern police forces (Teachout 1965, 59).[10] The only "major" action taken by the Kennedy administration in school desegregation was a decision by the U.S. Department of Health, Education, and Welfare (HEW) to cut off funds to local school districts that forced children living on military bases to attend segregated public schools. The administration refused to extend the ruling to cover students living off military bases (Orfield 1969, 30, 31). And HEW delayed until 1962 before taking any action to ban segregation in programs it financed (Orfield 1969, 52). Although candidate Kennedy had promised that an active president "could integrate all federally assisted housing with a stroke of the Presidential pen," it took over a year and a half and an "Ink for Jack" campaign that flooded the White House with ink bottles before a "watered-down, non-retroactive order" was issued (Navasky 1977, 97). Like the Eisenhower administration, the Kennedy administration rarely went to court in school cases. In 1963, the U.S. Commission on Civil Rights (USCCR) reported the Department of Justice entered only one school desegregation case (USCCR 1967, 42). Caution marked the Kennedy approach.

In terms of legislation, the Kennedy administration's approach to civil rights was marked by caution as well. "The one thing Kennedy did not want," the Whalens report, "was civil rights legislation" (Whalen 1985, 15). The bill Kennedy finally introduced in 1963 was weaker than even Eisenhower's weak 1957 bill, and the administration fought attempts to strengthen the bill. As Dr. Martin Luther King, Jr., told an interviewer, "had he [Kennedy] lived, there would have been continual delays, and attempts to evade it at every point, and water it down at every point" (Branch 1988, 922). It wasn't until the violence at Birmingham and the resulting political pressure that Kennedy became more supportive of civil rights legislation. Until June of 1963 with the proposal that eventually became part of the 1964 Civil Rights Act, President Kennedy acted cautiously in his support of civil rights.[11]

10. It must not be forgotten that Dr. King's phone was tapped and that the FBI attempted to break up his marriage, drive him insane, and destroy his leadership. Eugene Patterson, as editor of the *St. Petersburg Times* (Florida), reports that an FBI agent twice pressured him to print material from FBI wiretaps that allegedly recorded King's involvement in extra-marital sexual affairs. According to Patterson, the FBI approached other Southern editors as well (Patterson in Raines 1977, 368–70). See, generally, Garrow (1981). It turns out, too, that the FBI kept a confidential file on members of the Supreme Court. It wiretapped or monitored conversations involving four justices, including Chief Justice Warren, and employed informants on the Court staff ("F.B.I. Kept Secret File on the Supreme Court" 1988, 14).

11. The Voter Education Project is not an exception to this characterization. Although the administration was instrumental in channelling approximately $870,000 to civil rights groups to

Brown and its progeny were not supported by other national leaders until late in the Kennedy administration. In March 1956, Southern members of Congress, virtually without exception,[12] signed a document entitled a "Declaration of Constitutional Principles," also known as the Southern Manifesto. Its 101 signers attacked the *Brown* decision as an exercise of "naked power" with "no legal basis." They pledged themselves to "use all lawful means to bring about a reversal of this decision which is contrary to the Constitution and to prevent the use of force in its implementation" (*Cong. Rec.* 12 March 1956: 4460 (Senate), 4515–16 (House)). This unprecedented attack on the Court demonstrated to all that pressure from Washington to implement the Court's decisions in civil rights would not be forthcoming.

State Leaders

If national political leaders set the stage for ignoring the courts, local politicians acted their part perfectly. A study of the 250 gubernatorial candidates in the Southern states from 1950 to 1973 revealed that after *Brown* "ambitious politicians, to put it mildly, perceived few incentives to advocate compromise" (Black 1976, 299). This perception was reinforced by Arkansas Governor Orval Faubus's landslide reelection in 1958, after the events in Little Rock, demonstrating the "political rewards of conspicuously defying national authority" (Black 1976, 299). Throughout the South, governors and gubernatorial candidates called for defiance of court orders.[13] Among the most outspoken, although there was no dearth of candidates, was George Wallace of Alabama. In his inaugural address in January 1963, Governor Wallace declared: "I draw the line in the dust and toss the gauntlet before the feet of tyranny and I say segregation now, segregation tomorrow, segregation forever" (quoted in USCCR 1969, 2). On various occasions he characterized federal judges as "a bunch of atheistic pro-Communist bums" and "bearded beatniks and faceless, spineless, power-hungry theorists and black-robed judicial anarchists." Not to be outdone, Governor Ross Barnett of Mississippi pledged that "Ross Barnett will rot in a federal jail before he will let one nigra cross the sacred threshold of our white schools" (quotes from Sarratt 1966, 7). Any individual or institution wishing to end segregation pursuant to court

---

increase black registration in the South, the apparent aim was to end civil rights demonstrations and marches that received publicity and pressured and embarrassed the administration. Indeed, the money was expressly not to be used for direct action, creating great debate among some groups over whether or not to join the project. For confirmation of this interpretation see Branch (1988, 478–79); Carson (1981, 38); Forman (1972, 264–65, 269); Haines (1988, 155, 156); Meier and Rudwick (1973, 173–75); Navasky (1977, 21); Watters and Cleghorn (1967, 46–47).

12. The only Southern senators not to sign the Manifesto were Johnson of Texas and Kefauver and Gore of Tennessee. And two North Carolina congressmen who refused to sign, Charles B. Deane and Thurmond Chatham, lost their seats.

13. For a brief review of their actions, see Sarratt (1966, 1–27). For a state-by-state discussion of candidates and campaigns, illustrated with appropriate quotations, see Black (1976, chapters 4, 5, 7, 8).

order, that is, to obey the law as mandated by the Supreme Court, would incur the wrath of state political leaders and quite possibly national ones. The best they could hope for was a lack of outright condemnation. Political support for desegregation was virtually non-existent.

At the prodding of state leaders, state legislatures throughout the South passed a variety of pro-segregation laws. By 1957, only three years after *Brown*, at least 136 new laws and state constitutional amendments designed to preserve segregation had been enacted (Orfield 1969, 17–18). These laws, and hundreds of similar ones passed after 1957, are categorized and presented in Appendix 4. As the Southern saying went, "as long as we can legislate, we can segregate" (Rodgers and Bullock 1972, 72).

In the field of education, a variety of laws were passed. Virginia, at the behest of the Byrd machine that ran state politics, achieved "some prominence as a showplace for segregation devices" (USCCR 1963c, 41). It closed schools, operated a tuition grant scheme, suspended compulsory attendance laws, and built private segregated schools (Gates 1962; Muse 1961). Other states were not far behind, and their creativity in finding ways to avoid the law was seemingly inexhaustible. In Louisiana a law was passed denying promotion or graduation to any student of a desegregated school. Georgia deprived policemen of their retirement and disability if they failed to enforce the state's segregation laws. Mississippi simply made it illegal to attend a desegregated school (Sarratt 1966, 39). In 1960–61 alone, the Louisiana legislature met in one regular and five extraordinary sessions to pass ninety-two laws and resolutions to maintain segregated public schools (Sarratt 1966, 30). To expect individuals and institutions to follow court orders, even Supreme Court orders, in the face of this kind of hostility is to expect the impossible.[14]

A separate tack taken by state legislatures was to attack the NAACP, seeking to prevent it from operating within the state. Every Southern state except North Carolina adopted anti-NAACP laws (American Jewish Congress 1957). Some states merely went after members, forbidding them to hold state or local government jobs (South Carolina) or to teach (Louisiana). One of the cruder attacks came from Texas, where the state produced documents purporting to be a contract between the NAACP and Sweatt (the plaintiff in *Sweatt* v. *Painter*) binding the NAACP to pay Sweatt $11,500 for the right to use him as the principal plaintiff in a suit against the University of Texas (Murphy 1959b, 376). Other states required the NAACP to turn over its membership lists to state authorities. Still others set up little un-American activities committees and attempted to link the NAACP with communism, as well as obtain membership lists. A final set of attacks involved refurbishing the

---

14. Action was also taken on the local level. A particularly outrageous example comes from Drew, Mississippi, where an ordinance was enacted requiring that all civil rights workers in Drew at dusk be taken into "protective custody" (i.e., jailed) for the night. The ordinance was enacted and implemented during the summer of 1964 (Wilson 1965).

common-law crimes of champerty, barratry, and maintenance.[15] The aim of these laws was to prevent NAACP lawyers from advising clients of their rights and providing free counsel. Action against the NAACP hampered its recruiting and fund-raising and forced it to spend precious funds and energy to defend itself. Alabama, for example, kept the NAACP in court for eight years over its right to operate in the state (Birkby and Murphy 1964, 1019). During the course of the litigation NAACP membership in Alabama dropped from 27,309 to 29, and its estimated loss of revenue, excluding court costs, was $200,000 (Scheingold 1974, 174).

A third type of legislation passed by state legislatures involved statutes non-discriminatory on their face but intended to be administered in a discriminatory fashion. As the first generation of facially discriminatory laws were struck down by the federal courts, Southern legislatures increasingly turned to this tactic (Lusky 1963, 1170–71). While courts might find discrimination here, too, the burden of proving that the law was administered in a discriminatory manner rested on the plaintiff. And if the application of a law was found discriminatory in one jurisdiction within a state, that holding might not be binding on the rest of the state. By passing facially neutral statutes and leaving their administration to local officials, state legislatures could ensure that segregation would be preserved.

One example of this comes from the field of higher education. As was discussed earlier, a series of Supreme Court decisions required that qualified blacks be admitted to graduate and professional schools in their native states. If outright segregation didn't work, the states could rely on segregated elementary and secondary schools to limit the pool of potential qualified black applicants, and on newly established "neutral" health, safety, moral, and age requirements to maintain segregation. Thus, it was easy to create barriers to black applicants through denial of admission based on lack of qualification, or through expulsion after admittance. In this regard, early black applicants such as Gaines (Missouri), Sweatt (Texas), Hawkins (Florida), Frazier (North Carolina), and Lucy (Alabama), all of whom were ordered admitted by the Supreme Court, were either never admitted, admitted and promptly expelled, or admitted and flunked out. Similarly, after six years of "desegregation" at the University of Texas Law School, fewer blacks were enrolled than in the first year of desegregation (Parham 1957, 177).

Voting provides another area where this type of action was successfully employed. Traditionally, good character and literacy tests, neutral on their face, were administered in a discriminatory fashion to ensure that blacks

15. These common-law crimes seek to insure that only parties genuinely aggrieved are involved in litigation. They prohibit, respectively, a "bargain by a stranger with a party to a suit" for money, "frequently exciting and stirring up quarrels and suits," and "officious intermeddling in a suit which in no way belongs to one." See *Black's Law Dictionary* (1979).

could not register. The U.S. Civil Rights Commission also found the following discriminatory applications of non-discriminatory laws in the voting field prevalent: omission of registered blacks from voter lists; exclusion of blacks from precinct meetings; failure to provide sufficient voting facilities in black wards; refusal to assist or permit assistance to illiterate black voters; inadequate or erroneous instructions to black voters; disqualification of blacks' ballots on technical grounds; denial of equal opportunity to vote absentee; discriminatory location of polling places; segregated voting facilities; closing registration offices when blacks tried to register; discriminatory provision of mobile voting units. When blacks attempted to run as candidates, discriminatory administration of neutral laws resulted in the following: abolition of the office; extension of the term of the white incumbent; substitution of appointment for election; increase in filing fees; raising of requirements for independent candidates; increase in property qualifications; withholding information on how to qualify; withholding or delaying required certification of nominating petitions. And finally, of course, there are the time-honored practices of gerrymandering, county consolidation, switching to at-large elections, and the like, which all can act to continue to deprive blacks of any political representation (USCCR 1968, 1975a). As Lawson puts it, "sadly for the blacks who expected political freedom [from court decisions] . . . they found instead the familiar surroundings of second-class citizenship" (Lawson 1976, 115).

The lack of political leadership portrayed in the last few pages makes it no wonder that the courts contributed little directly to civil rights in the years they acted alone. The only way to overcome such opposition is from a change of heart by electors and by national political leaders. Thus, when the Congress passed the 1964 Civil Rights Act and the 1965 Voting Rights Act, and the executive branch intervened, change occurred. Without that intervention, it was an "unfair contest" (Peltason 1971, 45), with black plaintiffs and court decisions destined to be on the losing side. Without leadership at the top, the courts are no match for national, state, and local officials (USCCR 1975b). The tools available to political leaders in the United States system mean that without support from the leaders change will not occur.

This structural constraint on court effectiveness has been rediscovered in recent years. Justice Clark, speaking of the Court, remarked, "we don't have money at the Court for an army and we can't take ads in the newspapers, and we don't want to go out on a picket line in our robes" (quoted in Kluger 1976, 706). An unidentified Justice was reported to have explained the Court's refusal to hear an anti-miscegenation case (*Naim* v. *Naim*) in the year following *Brown* with the following statement: "One bombshell at a time is enough" (quoted in Wasby et al. 1977, 141). Social scientists, too, have rediscovered that Court decisions are not self-implementing (Becker and Feeley 1973;

Johnson and Canon 1984; Wasby 1970). And finally, even some lawyers are beginning to realize that winning a case is only the first step, and often the easiest, in effecting change (Carter 1980, 21–28). The courts depend on the other branches for support. When they don't receive that support, as in civil rights until 1964, their decisions will not be implemented, given any degree of opposition. For a decade after *Brown*, Constraint III prevented the legally victorious litigators from achieving reform.

Social and Cultural Constraints

Another aspect of the Constrained Court claim is that court decisions require popular as well as elite support to be successfully implemented. Law and legal decisions operate in a given cultural environment, and the norms of that environment influence the decisions that are made and the impact they have. In the case of civil rights, decisions were announced in a culture in which slavery had existed and apartheid did exist (Myrdal 1962; Woodward 1974). Institutions and social structures throughout America reflected a history of, if not a present commitment to, racial discrimination. Cultural barriers to civil rights had to be overcome before change could occur. And courts, the Constrained Court view suggests, do not have the tools to do so. This is well illustrated in the decade after *Brown*.

Private Groups

One of the important cultural barriers to civil rights was the existence of private groups supportive of segregation. One type, represented by the Ku Klux Klan, White Citizens Councils, and the like (described in McKay 1956, 1062–63 n.423; Anthony 1957), existed principally to fight civil rights. Either through their own acts, or the atmosphere they helped create, violence against blacks and civil rights workers was commonplace throughout the South. Spectacular cases such as the murder of Medgar Evers, the attacks on the Freedom Riders, the Birmingham church bombing that killed four black girls, and the murder of three civil rights workers near Philadelphia, Mississippi, are well known. But countless bombings and numerous murders occurred throughout the South (Peltason 1971, 5; Southern Regional Council 1964, 7–17). During the summer of 1964 in Mississippi alone there were 35 shootings, 65 bombings (including 35 churches), 80 beatings, and 6 murders (Garrow 1978, 21; McAdam 1988, 257–82). It was a brave soul indeed who worked to end segregation or implement court decisions.

Another tactic used by white groups to fight civil rights was economic coercion. A classic example comes from Yazoo City, Mississippi, in the summer of 1955. There, the White Citizens Council, as a "public service," took out a newspaper advertisement listing the names of the fifty-three blacks who signed a petition supporting desegregation of the city's schools. They also printed their names on placards and posted them in every store in town and in the cotton fields. Of course not all of the South was as severely segregated as the Mississippi delta, but since whites controlled the economy throughout the South, this sort of blacklisting was extraordinarily effective (Sarratt 1966, 301–2; Peltason 1971, 58, 60).[16] In fact, so effective was this sort of intimidation that as late as 1961 *not a single* desegregation suit in education had been filed in Mississippi (Peltason 1971, 99). And economic intimidation and coercion were applied to all kinds of civil rights actions, including, for example, attempting to register to vote (USCCR 1959, 55–106; USCCR 1961b, vol. 1; USCCR 1963a, 15).

More sophisticated forms of intimidation were also practiced by white groups. In Louisiana, for example, the Association of Citizens' Councils published a pamphlet entitled "Voter Qualification Laws In Louisiana, The Key To Victory In The Segregation Struggle." It noted that Louisiana was "in a life and death struggle with the Communists and the NAACP to maintain segregation" and instructed registrars on how to prevent blacks from registering. It was used by state officials to instruct registrars in 1959 (USCCR 1959, 101).

A totally different kind of private group resisted civil rights by simply ignoring court decisions and going about their business as if nothing had changed. Public carriers, for example, even when owned by non-Southerners, looked to the "segregationist milieu" in which they operated and thus took a "narrow view of desegregation decrees, implementing them minimally, if at all" (Barnes 1983, 196, 195). A principal example is real estate brokers and boards. At one point, for example, the National Association of Real Estate Brokers advised its members not to pay any attention to fair-housing laws (Westin 1964, 37). Local organizations, such as the Grosse Pointe Brokers Association (Michigan) refined their discrimination to a complex point system. A broker who violated this system, by following the law, was required to forfeit his commission and was liable to expulsion (USCCR 1961b: 4, 126). Indeed with real estate brokers the U.S. Commission on Civil Rights found that discrimination was "often the rule rather than the exception" (USCCR 1961b: 4, 123) and that the "forces promoting discrimination in housing hold powerful" (USCCR 1975d, 168).

A related example is the tremendous growth of all-white private schools in the South after *Brown* (USCCR 1967, 70–79). In Louisiana, for example, there were sixteen white private schools in existence prior to *Brown*, but in the decade or so after *Brown* fifty-three new all-white schools were opened (USCCR 1967, 71–2).[17] While the creation and existence of all-white private schools does not, in most cases, deny blacks the opportunity to have a deseg-

16. All but two of the fifty-three signers withdrew their names from the petition.
17. I assume these figures do not include Catholic schools.

regated public education, it does add another segregated institution to society. The clear impetus behind the creation of private schools was to preserve segregation.

Finally, and perhaps most poignantly, even the organized legal profession attacked the Court. The attack came not only from the American Bar Association, from which Chief Justice Warren resigned in disgust, but also from both the National Association of State Attorneys General and the Conference of State Chief Justices. Although these attacks on the Court were not limited to its civil rights decisions, as Pollak points out, they were "precipitated by the school segregation decisions" (Pollak 1957, 433). It is clear that there were strong cultural barriers to ending desegregation.[18]

Local Action and Resistance

The cultural biases against civil rights that pervaded private groups also pervaded local governments. Court-ordered action may be fought or ignored on a local level, especially if there is no pressure from higher political leadership to follow the law and pressure from private groups not to. It was common to find that where bus companies followed the law and removed segregation signs in terminals, state and local officials put them back up (Dixon 1962, 213–14). Similarly, little desegregation of public facilities was achieved until pressure was brought to bear, usually through demonstrations (Rodgers and Bullock 1972, 57). In education, as has been demonstrated, local school officials took no action to obey court orders until the pressure from Washington grew strong enough. In fact, in the five Deep South states, as a matter of principle no school-board member or superintendent openly advocated compliance with the Supreme Court decision (Sarratt 1966, 99–100). And despite *Cooper* v. *Aaron*, and the sending of troops to Little Rock in 1957, as of June 1963, only 69 out of 7,700 students at the supposedly desegregated, "formerly" white, junior and senior high schools of Little Rock were black (Brink and Harris 1963, 41).[19]

Local resistance to civil rights has been particularly effective in maintaining segregated housing. Through the use of the power of eminent domain, zoning and re-zoning, local review, and site location, local officials and individuals have been able to continue segregation (USCCR 1975d,

18. The failure of many national leaders supportive of civil rights to recognize this point highlights their naive view of the role of courts. Justice Frankfurter, in a letter to a friend around the time of *Cooper* v. *Aaron* (1958), wrote: "it is the legal profession of the South on which our greatest reliance must be placed . . . because the lawyers of the South will gradually realize that there is a transcending issue, namely respect for law as determined so impressively by a unanimous Court in construing the Constitution of the United States" (letter to C.C. Burlingham, quoted in Yudof 1981, 450).

19. Thirty-two years after Eisenhower acted, problems still remained. In 1989 the predominantly black Little Rock school district settled (for $129 million) its lawsuit against the state and two mostly white suburban school districts. The money is to be used for desegregation programs (Daniels 1989, 4).

70–71; 1961b: 4, 132–38). Even if all these maneuvers fail, the time and cost involved makes the effort not worthwhile for the builder. As one builder testified:

> We as builders are interested in selling homes, but we cannot possibly go through the extraordinarily expensive process of resistance from some local communities in the cases where we indicate that we are willing to sell regardless of race, color, or creed. (USCCR 1961b: 4, 138)

While this may be less true today in terms of housing intended for the general market, it certainly holds for low-cost public housing. Public resistance, supported by local political action, can almost always effectively defeat court-ordered civil rights.

A final cultural barrier to civil rights involves intensity of feeling. The greater the proportion of blacks in a given area, the stronger seems to be the discriminatory intent of white political officials. Orfield found that congressional resistance to civil rights was most bitter among Southern members of Congress whose districts had high proportions of blacks (Orfield 1969, 278). Similarly, Vines (1964) found that the higher the percentage of blacks in federal judicial districts in the South, the less likely were court decisions to support them. These findings suggest that where civil rights violations are massive, as in regions with large black populations, local white resistance will be strong. Where there is more to lose by the coming of civil rights, those who prospered from segregation will fight hard to maintain it. Thus, where segregation and denial of rights is rampant, all the barriers to effective court-ordered change are intensified.

Finally, it is important to note that poverty and low levels of education make individuals less likely to be aware of court-declared rights and to be willing and able to fight for them. Poor blacks, economically dependent on the whites around them, were in no position to assert their court-ordered rights. Only through massive government intervention could such rights be vindicated. For example, Matthews and Prothro found that the low levels of black registration in the South were partly explained by poverty and lack of education (Matthews and Prothro 1963a, 24, 43; 1963b). No court decision striking down discriminatory registration laws could change that. Only political action such as federal intervention and voter registration campaigns made a difference.

In sum, in civil rights, court-ordered change confronted a culture opposed to that change. That being the case, the American judicial system, constrained by the need for both elite and popular support, constrained change.

The Structural Constraints of Courts

In the preceding pages I have discussed political leadership and cultural and social beliefs as obstacles to court-ordered civil rights. The Supreme

Court, acting alone, could not hope to overcome these constraints. However, they are not specific to courts. They exist as barriers to all change, including that produced by segments of state or national government. I turn now to the particular constraints built into the American judicial system, constraints that made courts singularly ineffective institutions for successfully producing direct change in civil rights.

The Constraints of the Legal Bureaucracy

Proponents of the Constrained Court view suggest that specialization, expertise, and political connections are lacking in courts and are crucial for successful implementation of significant social reform. Given the political and social opposition to civil rights, and the complexity of the issue, the need for such knowledge and skills was high. It appears, however, that courts are not equipped to deal with the complex issues involved in areas such as civil rights. On the one hand, many issues involve a sophisticated understanding of a whole range of social processes. In education these might include the learning process itself, the role of families, and the community view of the schools. As one commentator supportive of civil rights has noted, the courts have "lacked an awareness of the complex, multifaceted processes of education" and have "disregarded the development of children and the perspectives of families and communities" (Lightfoot 1980, 4). Court decisions, then, may not have been implemented or, if implemented, may not have worked, because they were not appropriate to the problem.

Similarly, judges may not be aware of, or be able to deal with, the political trade-offs necessary to implement any public policy. Judges are not supposed to telephone politicians, school administrators, local businessmen, or others, and cut a deal. Their decisions, therefore, are likely to overlook political realities that are crucial for implementation. In this regard, the U.S. Commission on Civil Rights found that community preparation and participation in planning, key elements to successful school desegregation, were utterly lacking in court-ordered desegregation plans (USCCR 1959, 309–10). Judge Brown, writing on the record after the issuance of the first HEW guidelines implementing Title VI, summed up these problems:

> These executive standards, perhaps long overdue, are welcome . . . [without them] the Federal judge [was put] in the middle of school administrative problems for which he was not equipped. . . . By the 1964 Act and the action of HEW, administration is largely where it ought to be—in the hands of the Executive and its agencies with the function of the Judiciary confined to those rare cases presenting justiciable, not operational, questions. (*Price* v. *Dennison Independent School District* 1965, 1013–14)[20]

20. Judge Wisdom, writing in 1966, concurred, noting that "most judges do not have sufficient competence—they are not educators or school administrators—to know the right questions, much less the right answers" (*U.S.* v. *Jefferson County Board of Education* 1966, 855).

The record of court attempts at school desegregation before 1964 demonstrates that effective implementation of civil rights decisions requires information and knowledge that judges don't have and political compromises that they ought not to make. Thus, courts were simply not equipped to achieve direct results in civil rights.

Delay

The judiciary, like other large political institutions, is afflicted with many bureaucratic problems. However, as proponents of the Constrained Court view argue, the constraints imposed by the structure and process of the legal bureaucracy make courts a singularly ineffective institution in producing significant social reform. Among these constraints is the inability to respond quickly. The time between the initiation of a suit, the exhaustion of all appeals, and the issuance of a final decree can be years. This is no less the case when judges act in good faith. Delay is built into the judicial system and it serves to limit the effectiveness of courts.

Delay occurs for many reasons. One is overloaded court dockets. During the 1950s and 1960s, the Fifth Circuit, responsible for most of the South, had the nation's most congested dockets (Note 1963, 101). Appeals to that court were naturally delayed. Second, the judicial system allows for many appeals and will bend over backwards to hear a claim.[21] Numerous appeals can serve as a tactic to delay final decision. Another reason for delay is the complicated nature of many civil rights suits. Questions of whether the suit is properly a class action, whether local remedies have been exhausted, or whether a different court is the more appropriate forum can keep cases bouncing around lower courts for years. Even if a lower court enjoins certain actions as discriminatory, it may stay the injunction pending appeal. Fourth, higher courts rarely order action. Normally, they remand to the lower court and order it to act. The time involved here, even assuming good faith, can add up. Finally, if a final order does not have a direct effect, if the discrimination is not remedied, the plaintiff's only judicial remedy is to return to court and re-start the process.

Opponents of civil rights were well aware of the inherent delays of the judicial system. A popular Southern saying, "litigate and legislate," shows awareness of the slowness of judicial proceedings (quoted in Rodgers and Bullock 1972, 72). Soon after *Brown* was decided, the attorney general of Mississippi (later governor), Coleman, remarked: "We could keep the Court busy for years" (quoted in Sarratt 1966, 181). And years later Judge Wisdom's comment that "we shall not permit the courts to be used to destroy or dilute the effectiveness of the Congressional policy expressed in Title VI"

21. The story of Clovis Green is instructive. A prisoner most of his adult life, he claims to have filed over 700 appeals. The Supreme Court acknowledged this aspect of the judicial system by finally refusing to waive his court costs (Greenhouse 1983, 10).

(*U.S.* v. *Jefferson County Board of Education* 1966, 859–60) bears witness to this structural reality. Even if political leaders had no intention of following adverse court decisions, the confrontation could be postponed for years.

Examples of delay in final judgments abound.[22] In higher education, the average case took about two and a half years from initial claim to final judgment (USCCR 1961a, 269). Final judgment, of course, did not guarantee admission or, later, graduation. In elementary and secondary education, delays were legion. Among the most noteworthy were *Briggs* v. *Elliott* and *Davis* v. *Prince Edward County*, two of the original school desegregation cases, commenced in 1951 and 1952 respectively, which were still being litigated in 1963. Other cases noteworthy for seemingly interminable litigation include *Singleton* v. *Jackson Municipal Separate School District*, in which approximately thirty opinions and orders were issued over a seven-year period, and *U.S.* v. *Montgomery County Board of Education* (1969), in which there were seventy-seven docket entries between 1964 and 1969. And the U.S. Commission on Civil Rights found that delay in reaching final decisions in the courts was a major reason for the failure to end discrimination against blacks in the field of voting (USCCR 1963a, 25). Perhaps the most remarkable example is the eight-year effort of Alabama to incapacitate the NAACP. While Alabama eventually lost, it managed to effectively paralyze the NAACP in Alabama for eight crucial years.

In sum, delay is built into the judicial system. Even when all parties act in good faith, judicial proceedings can drag on for years. This structural constraint of courts made them particularly poor institutions for directly affecting civil rights.

Discretion, Interpretation, and Bias

The American judicial system vests considerable discretion in lower-court judges. Only rarely do appellate court judges issue final orders. In almost all cases, they remand to the lower court for issuance of the final decree. This leaves lower-court judges with a great deal of discretion. Review can be gained only on appeal, which further delays final action. This pattern is particularly pronounced in federal-state court relations. Studying this relationship, Beatty found that "one of the most unique characteristics of our dual judiciary is the ability of state courts to avoid, delay or evade the mandates of the Supreme Court" (Beatty 1972, 260). The inability of appellate courts to readily review lower-court action was a principal tool used by some lower courts to delay civil rights (Note 1963, 100).

Discretion is, of course, subjective and it is often difficult to characterize abuses. Different judges react differently to similar cases and this is inevitable. While there is some awareness of the role of discretion in courts, its

22. Note (1963, 94 nn.36–39); Note (1966, 1087–90 nn.107–14); *U.S.* v. *Jefferson County Board of Education* (1966, 860 n.51).

existence is more often denied or hidden. Haines, for example, writes of New York City's efforts to prepare annual comparisons of how different judges handled similar cases in 1914 and 1915: "The results showing to what extent justice is affected by the personality of the judge were so startling and so disconcerting that it seemed advisable to discontinue the comparative tables of the records of the justices" (Haines 1922, 96). Yet at times the abuse of discretion becomes so obvious that there is no hesitancy to so characterize it.

Many lower-court judges systematically and continually abused their discretion to thwart civil rights. At the height of the 1960 New Orleans school crisis, Congressman Otto Passman, addressing the Louisiana legislature, summed up lower-court reactions: "It is not pleasant to contemplate, but it appears to be true that at least some federal judges take their orders directly from the Supreme Court" (quoted in Sarratt 1966, 246). The awareness of the power of discretion, and the use to which some judges would put it, led Southern segregationists to fight to vest control of civil rights in lower-court judges. Arguing for South Carolina in *Brown II*, S. E. Rogers asked for district court control, admitting in response to questions that this would result in no desegregation, "perhaps not until 2015 or 2045" (quoted in Peltason 1971, 16). Another attorney, out of court, commented that "local judges know the local situation and it may be 100 years before . . . [civil rights is] feasible" (quoted in Sarratt 1966, 200). On the state-federal level, state court evasion of Supreme Court mandates was "at least twice as high during the 1960s as in either the 1930s or the 1940s" (Beatty 1972, 283). In areas such as civil rights where feelings run high, the discretion accorded lower-court judges virtually insures its abuse.

There are many ways in which discretion can be abused (Murphy 1959a). One, of course, is delay, referred to earlier. Another is outright refusal to follow the law. Lower-court judges routinely upheld statutes designed to evade compliance with Supreme Court mandates. As late as 1966 Judge Scarlett of the Federal District Court for the Southern District of Georgia attempted to reverse *Brown* by declaring that blacks were not intelligent enough to go to school with whites (discussed in *Stell* v. *Board of Education for City of Savannah* 1967). A third way was to read the cases as narrowly as possible. In *Briggs* v. *Elliott*, for example, the federal district court held: "The Constitution, in other words, does not require integration. It merely forbids discrimination" (1955, 777). While this was a technically correct reading of *Brown*, its impact was to allow segregation to continue as long as defendants could allege that they were not discriminating, that segregation resulted from the "free choice" of all concerned. Another abuse of discretion, discussed above, was to find that local conditions prevented implementation of the law at the present time. One way in which this was done was for private groups to encourage violence, or at least not discourage it, and then use the violence to show that conditions were not appropriate for civil rights (Peltason 1971,

159). Finally, courts could and did refuse to follow the logic of *Brown* into other areas. While this was legally defensible before the Supreme Court so ruled, it was clearly an abuse of discretion after the Court applied *Brown* across the board.

The tools of abuse of discretion—delay, and narrow interpretation (or purposeful misinterpretation)—can be effectively harnessed by biased judges. Unfortunately, throughout the South there were many biased judges (Peltason 1971; USCCR 1969, 39–46; Note 1963). These were judges who made their decisions based on their own segregationist views and not on the law. And given the structure of the judicial system, such judges could delay civil rights for years.

Southern judges were in a difficult position. The "fifty-eight lonely men" (Peltason 1971) who formed the federal judiciary in the Southern states were required to dismantle a social system they had grown up with and were part of. A non-biased judge who felt duty-bound to follow the law could never forget, Peltason concludes, that "any action of his against segregation will threaten his easy and prestigious acceptance by the community" (Peltason 1971, 9). Even as pro-civil-rights a judge as John Minor Wisdom was sympathetic, finding it "not surprising that in a conservative community a federal judge may feel that he cannot jeopardize the respect due the court in all of his cases" by vigorously supporting civil rights (Wisdom 1967, 419). Even with the best of judges, civil rights cases reflected the "customs and mores of the community" (Wisdom 1967, 418). It is no surprise, then, that study of hundreds of cases in Southern federal district courts found judges influenced by their social and political environment (Vines 1964).

The severity of the problem can best be understood by a few examples.[23] Judge Elliott of the Federal District Court for the Middle District of Georgia did not want "pinks, radicals and black voters to outvote those who are trying to preserve our segregation laws" (quoted in Note 1963, 101 n.71). Federal District Judge Cox, of the Southern District of Mississippi, characterized the freedom riders as "counterfeit citizens from other states deliberately seeking to cause trouble here" (Note 1963, 101 n.71). Speaking from the bench in March 1964, he referred repeatedly to black voter-registration applicants as "a bunch of niggers" who were "acting like a bunch of chimpanzees" (quoted in Southern Regional Council 1964, 19–20).[24] Federal Judge Armistead Dobie of the Fourth Circuit saw civil rights as influenced by "a foreign Communistic anthropologist" (quoted in Peltason 1971, 23), an obvious attack on Swedish sociologist Gunnar Myrdal whose classic work on segrega-

---

23. In fairness, it must be remembered that there were some outstanding Southern federal judges such as J. Skelly Wright, John Minor Wisdom, Bryan Simpson, and Frank Johnson. On the particularly aggressive record of Judge Johnson, see Hamilton (1965, 76–84); Kennedy (1978); Note (1975); Yarbrough (1981).

24. Both Judges Elliott and Cox, as well as several other openly and avowedly segregationist judges, were appointed by President Kennedy.

tion in the United States, *An American Dilemma*, was cited in footnote 11 in *Brown*. Judge Dawkins of the Federal District Court in Shreveport, Louisiana, defended his enjoining the U.S. Commission on Civil Rights from holding hearings on alleged voter discrimination in his district in 1959 by stating, "[i]t's all part of the game" (quoted in Peltason 1971, 133). In the Dallas school desegregation case, started in 1955 and still pending in 1960, in which the federal district court was reversed six times, Judge Davidson complained that the "white man has a right to maintain his racial integrity, and it can't be done so easily in integrated schools" (quoted in Sarratt 1966, 201). He also warned against the perils of breaching segregation: "When the President's guard was shot, when the halls of Congress were shot up, they were not from Negroes that were raised in the South. They were from the integrated people of Puerto Rico" (quoted in Peltason 1971, 121).

State judges were, if anything, more biased. Chief Judge J. Edwin Livingston of the Alabama Supreme Court, speaking in 1959 to several hundred students and business leaders, announced: "I'm for segregation in every phase of life and I don't care who knows it. . . . I would close every school from the highest to the lowest before I would go to school with colored people" (quoted in Peltason 1971, 66). Alabama circuit judge Walter B. Jones wrote a column in the *Montgomery Advertiser* which he devoted to the "defense of white supremacy." In those pages in June 1958 he told his readers that in the case against the NAACP, over which he was presiding, he intended to deal the NAACP a "mortal blow" from which it "shall never recover" (quoted in Peltason 1971, 65, 67). It is no wonder, then, that despite clear Supreme Court rulings, Alabama was able to keep the NAACP in litigation for eight years. As Leon Friedman, who talked with scores of civil rights lawyers in the South concluded, "the states' legal institutions were and are the principal enemy" (Friedman 1965, 7).

Biased judges posed a serious obstacle to civil rights in the South. Yet, as the Constrained Court view suggests, the very process by which judges are selected suggests that they will reflect the mores and beliefs of the dominant cultural and political leadership. The existence of biased judges was inevitable. Given the tools of discretion, delay, and interpretation available to judges, resistance to Supreme-Court-ordered civil rights was to be expected. As Judge Wisdom put it, "difficulties in the judicial performance of inferior federal courts are *built into the system* (Wisdom 1967, 419; emphasis added).

Control and Costs

Bringing a civil rights suit is a complicated matter. Not only are there obstacles of coercion and fear, but also most people are unwilling to rock the boat. Although the NAACP and its Legal Defense And Educational Fund, Inc. (Inc. Fund), were often ready to foot the bill, the amount of preparation necessary for a successful suit, especially given the obstacles discussed, was enormous. The result of these facts of life is that until the Justice Department began prosecuting civil rights suits (after 1964), few were brought. Writing in 1968, Jack Greenberg of the Inc. Fund reported that although there are about 3,000 school districts in the South, since 1954 the Inc. Fund had been able to handle only about thirty cases (Greenberg 1968, 1539). By 1964, ten years after *Brown*, the vast majority of Southern school districts had neither desegregated nor been confronted with a court challenge.[25] In a major study of when and why school districts desegregated, the U.S. Commission on Civil Rights found that of 160 school districts that experienced their greatest reduction in segregation before *1968*, only 20 were put under court pressure (USCCR 1977a, 17). And if few cases are brought, the vast majority of jurisdictions will be under no pressure (except the requirement of the law!) to protect civil rights. Indeed, the U.S. Civil Rights Commission found that court cases, limited to the jurisdictions in which they were brought, isolated communities from one another, created little pressure for desegregation elsewhere, and made communities easy targets for segregationist violence (USCCR 1959, 309–10). Thus, the need to bring numerous cases to be effective is an obstacle to court-ordered change.

A further obstacle is that it is virtually impossible to control the selection of cases. Cases come up in more of an ad-hoc basis than many people believe. This means that quality preparation cannot be assumed and cases will be lost,[26] setting bad precedents. For example, James Nabritt III, at one time associate counsel of the Inc. Fund, admitted that the sit-in cases took the Inc. Fund by surprise and that it never developed a long-range strategy for dealing with them (cited in Grossman 1967, 431). And Tushnet, in his study of the NAACP's litigation strategy, noted the trouble the national staff had in controlling local attorneys. The result, often, was lost cases that reflected badly on the NAACP and did the plaintiffs no good (Tushnet 1987, 53–55).

A co-ordinated court strategy has also proved difficult to achieve.[27] Jack Greenberg lamented that seldom do litigators have a substantial ability to influence the development and sequence of cases (Greenberg 1977, 586–87). Thurgood Marshall put it this way: "There's no master plan . . . the cases come to us as they crop up locally. Ha! I wish sometimes we could hand pick them" (quoted in Kraar 1958, 11). Indeed, a study of the Inc. Fund, based on interviews with more than forty attorneys, found that much civil rights litigation was "reflexive," "unplanned," and "impromptu," often based on

---

25. Orfield (1969) 18.

26. Vines (1964) found that in 291 civil rights cases brought in Southern federal district courts between May 1954 and October 1962, blacks barely won half. Outside of education, they won substantially fewer than half the cases. While a good part of the reason is no doubt bias, part is also due to inadequate resources and preparation.

27. In general, see Hakman (1966). O'Connor and Epstein (1982) have updated and criticized the Hakman study. Their new findings, however, do not affect my point.

"fortuitous events." The large number of non-Inc.-Fund civil rights litigators, limited resources, and the need to act "defensively" to prevent bad precedents from being set, were all mentioned prominently as important obstacles to successfully planning long-term strategy (Wasby 1985). Tushnet reached the same conclusion, arguing that the NAACP's choices of forum "were more strongly influenced by internal organizational requirements than by elements in a coherent legal strategy" (Tushnet 1987, 51). In particular, in the pre-*Brown* years, the NAACP focused on the upper South largely because of convenience. Thurgood Marshall, although headquartered in New York, was from Baltimore and Charles Houston lived in the District of Columbia, reducing the expenses of travel and lodging for upper South litigation (Tushnet 1987, 67, 69).

A final obstacle, to be only touched on here, is cost. Litigation is terribly expensive. It is estimated that *Brown* cost "well over $200,000" and Supreme Court cases testing *Brown* averaged between $15,000 and $18,000 (Hakman 1966, 21–22 n.18).[28] And, of course, price-tags went up considerably in the years following *Brown*. As the U.S. Civil Rights Commission found, the high cost of litigation limited the number of suits that could be brought and thus constrained courts from directly affecting civil rights (USCCR 1963a, 15).[29]

In sum, the particular configuration of the legal bureaucracy made it difficult for the courts to effectively produce significant social reform. Asked to end discrimination in areas where it was prevalent, but lacking the tools to do the job, the courts were bound to fail.

Conclusion—The Constrained Court and the First Decade After Brown

The courts were ineffective in producing significant social reform in civil rights in the first decade after *Brown* for three key reasons captured in the constraints of the Constrained Court view. First, political leadership at the national, state, and local levels was arrayed against civil rights, making implementation of judicial decisions virtually impossible. Second, the culture of the South was segregationist, leaving the courts with few public supporters. In response, and after several tries at ordering change, the courts backed off and bided their time, waiting for the political and social climate to change. Third, the American court system itself was designed to lack implementation powers, to move slowly, and to be strongly tied to local concerns. The presence of these constraints made the success of litigation for significant social reform virtually impossible. The fact that little success was achieved should have surprised no one.

28. Hughes (1962, 129) gives a $100,000 figure for the cost of *Brown*.
29. Tushnet (1987, 82) argues that one of the reasons that the NAACP brought *Brown* was that "litigation was draining the NAACP's resources, with increasingly small returns for the effort. The decision to attack the 'separate but equal' doctrine directly was significantly affected by those organizational factors."

The Post–1964 Years

In the years after 1964, particularly from 1968 to 1972, there was a great deal of change in civil rights. The percentage of black children in elementary and secondary school with whites in the South increased from 1.2 percent in the 1963–64 school year to 91.3 percent in the 1972–73 school year (see table 2.1). As chapter 2 detailed, in the years after *Brown* all levels of the federal government became involved in the attempt to end segregation. The question this part of the chapter addresses is what role court action played in bringing about this change. Were courts crucial actors, as proponents of the Dynamic Court view might suggest, or were they peripheral to executive and legislative actions, as Constrained Court view supporters contend? If courts were important, how can the Constrained Court view be powerfully on point in the decade after *Brown* yet be unhelpful in explaining later achievements?

The answer to these questions appears to be that the courts became increasingly more important and effective actors; the political, social, and economic climate changed, allowing the constraints of the Constrained Court view to be overcome. Constraint I was overcome with the victory in *Brown*. In addition, as the political climate changed, and the federal government endorsed civil rights with the passage of legislation in 1964 and 1965, the second constraint was overcome. After 1965 the Court re-entered the civil rights field, upholding congressional action and bringing pressure to bear on recalcitrant institutions.[30] Only Constraint III, the implementation constraint, remained. And here, several of the conditions generated from the Dynamic Court view were present, allowing change to occur. Thus, the theoretical framework developed in the first chapter goes a long way in explaining the changes that occurred.

Political Leadership

The political climate for civil rights in the mid-1960s was quite different than in the first decade after *Brown*. The passage of the 1964 Civil Rights Act, the 1965 Voting Rights Act, and the 1965 Elementary and Secondary Education Act, the tightening of Title VI guidelines by HEW, and the commitment of President Johnson to civil rights propelled the executive branch and Congress into the civil rights battle. The "Great Society" was to be open to all, and the executive branch used its new powers to enforce school desegregation. In 1966 alone the Department of Justice participated in 73 school desegregation cases, up from 1 in 1963 and 2 in 1964 (USCCR 1967, 42).

30. The 1964 Civil Rights Act was upheld in *Heart of Atlanta Motel* v. *U.S.* (1964) and *Katzenbach* v. *McClung* (1964). The 1965 Voting Rights Act withstood constitutional challenge in *South Carolina* v. *Katzenbach* (1966). Pressure was brought to bear on school districts in *Green* v. *County School Board of New Kent County, Virginia* (1968), *Alexander* v. *Holmes County* (1969), and *Swann* v. *Charlotte-Mecklenburg Board of Education* (1971). For additional citations, and case discussion, see chapter 2.

The Johnson administration and the Great Society were committed to ending school segregation. While the Nixon administration backed away from this commitment, it did not do so entirely. Too much bureaucratic structure, and too many expectations, had been created for there to be wholesale reversals in federal pressure to end segregation. Although it took a full ten years after *Brown*, Congress and the executive branch finally came to support civil rights.[31] Constraints II and III were well on the way to being overcome.

In the wake of this commitment at the federal level, state and local leaders weakened in their opposition. Where once leaders had been adamantly opposed to any desegregation, public opposition became more muted and was sometimes replaced by actual public support for desegregation. Southern reaction to the 1965 and 1966 HEW guidelines was "surprisingly moderate." Political leadership throughout the South stayed quiet or counseled support for the law, and most Southern members of Congress "held their fire" (Orfield 1969, 118, 119). This meant that when pressure from either the courts or HEW was applied, political leaders did not automatically rise to oppose implementation. Black, in his study of gubernatorial candidates, noted that the "differences between the governors' pre-1965 and post-1965 campaign stances are remarkable." Pre-1965, nearly three-fifths of the major candidates supported segregation, while from 1966 to 1973 nearly two-thirds took "innovative stances on segregation" (Black 1976, 290, 150, 152). And, by 1970, Governors Holton of Virginia, Scott of North Carolina, and McNair of South Carolina publicly supported desegregation.

Numerous individual studies stress the presence of supportive political leadership in explaining the acceptance of desegregation. In cities ranging from Berkeley to Minneapolis to New Albany (Mississippi) to Tampa, desegregation worked because local leadership came to support it (USCCR 1976b; Winn 1970b, 4, 5). Conversely, in cities ranging from Atlanta to Boston to Jackson (Mississippi) to Mobile (Alabama), leadership opposition is cited as having doomed desegregation (Winn 1970b, 5; USCCR 1976b; Southern Regional Council 1971, 38–49). In Atlanta in 1970, for example, there was a "collapse of public leadership" in which both city and school officials were unprepared to act and Governor Maddox urged a boycott of schools (Winn 1970a, 4). Thus, despite twelve years of litigation and three hundred "legal moves," a commentator concluded that "Atlanta has no more desegregation than Baltimore, which has never experienced anything like the same pressure" (Bowler 1970, 8).

The evidence from school districts under pressure to desegregate is that supportive leadership on all levels is essential. On the local level, a 1976

31. The support was not always as forceful as one might have hoped. As an anonymous author bitterly wrote on the wall of the Council of Federated Civil Rights Organizations (COFO) office in Jackson, Mississippi, in the summer of 1964: "There is a town in Mississippi called Liberty, there is a department in Washington called Justice" (quoted in Burns 1965, 228).

study of twenty-nine school districts by the U.S. Commission on Civil Rights concluded that "perhaps the most important ingredient in successful school desegregation is leadership, both at the community level and in the schools" (USCCR 1976b, 168). A 1969 Southern Regional Council study found local leadership to be a "crucial factor" (Southern Regional Council 1969, 47) and a 1972 report by six groups (including the American Friends Service Committee, the Southern Regional Council, and the Inc. Fund) of forty-three Southern urban school districts elevated these findings to the status of a "truism" ("School Report" 1972, 4). On the state level, the U.S. Commission on Civil Rights found that opposition to local desegregation results in "the encouragement of local officials to act in defiance of the law, and the encouragement of local whites to act to block desegregation themselves" (USCCR 1969, 13). Finally, numerous studies have stressed the importance of national leadership (Southern Regional Council 1969; USCCR 1975b; USCCR 1982). As the U.S. Commission on Civil Rights put it in 1981, "progress in desegregating our nation's schools will not be achieved without the clear support and leadership of government officials at the national, State, and local levels" (USCCR 1981, 1). When there was this leadership support, in the late 1960s and early 1970s, much desegregation occurred.

Social and Cultural Change

Political leaders do not exist in a vacuum. Those who are out of step with large numbers of constituents do not remain in office very long. The fact that political leaders did not oppose desegregation as heartily as before suggests that a change in the social and cultural climate must have taken place. There is a good deal of evidence to suggest that this is the case, particularly in comparison to the actions of private groups discussed in chapter 2.

Throughout the South, successful school desegregation was often accompanied by public support from social and civic groups. In reviewing why some Southern communities desegregated successfully in 1970, Winn noted that in "many cases, loose organizations of business and civic leaders played a vital role" (Winn 1970b, 4). In its review of desegregation attempts in twenty-nine school districts, the U.S. Civil Rights Commission concurred, finding that "affirmative leadership by members of business, religious, and social service organizations has contributed immeasurably to community acceptance of desegregation" (USCCR 1976b, 185). The importance of these activities can be seen in the amount of disruption accompanying desegregation. The U.S. Civil Rights Commission, in comparing districts in which there were no serious disruptions on the issue of school desegregation with those districts that suffered from desegregation violence, found that business leaders differed in their support for desegregation by a margin of 38 percent and religious leaders by a margin of 21 percent (USCCR 1976b, 175).

One reason why there was such support may be that racial barriers in many areas of public life had broken down by the late 1960s and early 1970s. The passage of the 1964 Civil Rights Act put an end to legal and blatant segregation in most forms of public life. Desegregating schools was less of a radical step than it had been earlier. In some cities, desegregation included the work force. In Bogalusa, Louisiana, for example, where school desegregation was achieved, the integrated Crown-Zellerbach plant employed 31 percent of the city's work force. Indeed, the school superintendent pointed to integrated working conditions as being a helpful factor in the general acceptance of school desegregation ("Beautiful Bogalusa" 1970, 8). By the late 1960s and early 1970s there was not as large-scale or as deep-seated a social and cultural aversion to desegregation as there had been in the pre-1964 years. A key constraint limiting court efficacy was removed.[32]

Court Orders and Incentives

The argument developed in chapter 1 suggested that if the constraints of the Constrained Court view could be overcome by changes in the political, social, and economic climate, and certain conditions were present, courts could effectively produce significant social reform. In particular, Conditions I and II suggested that when non-court actors offer incentives to induce compliance with court orders, or impose costs for failure to do so, court efficacy will be enhanced. In the years after 1964, particularly in the period 1968–72, major incentives were offered to induce compliance. The first of these was money from the federal government.

Financial Inducements

When the federal government made money available to local school districts that desegregated, it loosed a powerful and attractive force on segregated schools. This was particularly true in the South because that region spent less on schools, as measured by the percentage of total personal income, than any region in the country ("School Support" 1969). Thus, federal dollars had the potential for the largest impact in just the area where segregation was the greatest, the "desperately poor Southern districts" (Orfield 1969, 97). As Commissioner of Education Francis Keppel noted early on, in a memo to HEW Secretary Celebrezze, "Title VI can become . . . a condition necessary for progress in the future" (Memo of April 13, 1965, quoted in

32. Cultural support should not be overstated. When faced with imminent desegregation of the public schools, many whites fled to new private schools. For example, between the 1961 and 1970 school years, there was an increase of 242 percent in the number of non church-affiliated private schools in the Southeast (Terjen 1972, 50–51). Many, if not most of these, were segregated. In the South, 1969 and 1970 saw the largest increase in the opening of new segregated private schools (Terjen 1972, 50), with Mississippi alone witnessing a threefold increase (USCCR 1977c, 52). By the 1972 school year, there were an estimated 535,000 white students in segregated private schools in the South (Terjen 1972, 50). However, as the text makes clear, there was acceptance of the desegregation process. For further reading on private schools, see "Segregation Academies" (1969); Terjen (1973); Yeates (1970).

Orfield 1969, 94). And that is precisely what happened. Tables 3.1, 3.2, and 3.3 present the data.

The tables dramatically demonstrate that the flow of federal dollars increased markedly to the Southern and Border states in the years after Congress acted. Table 3.1 presents the amount of federal dollars received and table 3.2 calculates that amount as a percentage of state education expenditures. As table 3.2 shows, by 1969 federal funds made up between 11 percent and 21 percent of state budgets for public schools in the Southern states. By the beginning of the 1971 school year, the range was from 12.5 percent to nearly 28 percent. Mississippi, for example, was eligible for more federal money in 1965 than the state had spent on its own for education in 1963! (Orfield 1969, 120). On the district level, as table 3.3 suggests, the increase in federal funding was extraordinary, doubling, tripling, and quadrupling in some districts over just a few short years. In some districts, federal aid amounted to one-third or one-quarter of the school budget (Orfield 1969, 108).

Tables 3.2 and 3.3 also present desegregation data. As can be seen, the changes between the mid-1960s and the early 1970s were huge (the reader

Table 3.1   **Federal Funds (in Millions) for Public Elementary and Secondary Schools in Southern and Border States, 1963–1972, Selected Years**

States	1963–64	1967–68	1969–70	1970–71	1971–72	1972–73
Southern						
Alabama	18.9	78.0	86.5	113.6	117.7	109.0
Arkansas	15.1	45.4	47.8	51.3	64.3	61.6
Florida	37.0	114.8	122.9	141.6	164.1	148.3
Georgia	24.2	87.7	103.0	105.9	132.0	121.2
Louisiana	16.2	67.2	71.0	102.0	110.8	110.6
Mississippi	13.0	56.6	67.0	92.7	98.6	99.4
N. Carolina	24.2	102.1	126.9	133.8	168.8	143.3
S. Carolina	14.5	55.1	67.1	87.5	90.8	100.5
Tennessee	20.5	75.4	79.6	88.9	95.2	100.0
Texas	50.0	159.2	209.9	201.0	290.5	283.3
Virginia	34.0	81.8	117.4	107.2	141.5	133.9
Border						
Delaware	3.1	8.8	10.6	11.7	14.2	14.6
D.C.	12.5	32.9	45.2	27.2	60.2	83.0
Kentucky	14.4	56.0	79.3	88.6	96.3	92.0
Maryland	22.0	64.1	70.1	79.0	90.2	92.6
Missouri	17.6	60.2	61.5	67.5	90.5	91.0
Oklahoma	20.7	48.6	48.7	54.8	65.0	59.4
W. Virginia	7.3	30.7	37.9	50.3	46.4	51.9

SOURCE: U.S. Department of HEW (1973; *Revenues*, 1972–73, 1973–74, 1974–75, 1975–76; *Statistics*, 1963–64, 1965–66, 1967–68, 1969–70, 1971–72).

Table 3.2   Percentage of Public Elementary and Secondary School Budgets Received
from Federal Funds in Southern and Border States, 1963–1971, and
Percentage of Blacks in School With Whites, 1964–65 and 1972–73

	Federal Funds as a % of State School Budgets					% of Blacks in School with Whites	
State	1963–64	1967–68	1969–70	1970–71	1971–72	1964–65	1972–73
Southern							
Alabama	7.6	20.2	18.4	22.5	21.5	.03	83.5
Arkansas	11.1	20.0	18.9	19.0	21.2	.81	98.1
Florida	7.0	12.8	10.7	11.2	12.0	2.7	96.4
Georgia	7.1	13.8	14.3	14.0	15.7	.40	86.8
Louisiana	4.8	12.7	12.0	14.2	14.6	1.1	82.9
Mississippi	8.1	16.8	20.9	28.1	27.8	.02	91.5
N. Carolina	6.1	18.6	16.2	15.8	18.0	1.4	99.4
S. Carolina	7.5	17.5	15.2	19.8	18.7	.10	93.9
Tennessee	8.0	17.8	14.6	15.6	14.7	5.4	80.0
Texas	4.6	11.2	11.5	10.3	12.5	7.8	92.8
Virginia	9.5	12.8	14.1	11.3	14.0	5.2	99.3
Border							
Delaware	4.4	8.6	6.9	7.5	8.4	62.2	98.9
D.C.	15.7	24.4	25.8	16.0	27.1	86.0	64.2
Kentucky	6.5	16.0	17.6	17.2	17.7	68.1	92.6
Maryland	6.0	9.5	8.2	8.0	7.8	50.9	75.9
Missouri	4.3	9.0	7.4	8.0	9.3	42.3	69.4
Oklahoma	10.6	14.6	12.7	12.8	13.5	31.1	100
W. Virginia	5.0	13.6	13.6	16.8	13.7	63.4	98.9

SOURCE: U.S. Department of HEW (1973; *Revenues*, 1972–73, 1973–74, 1974–75, 1975–76; *Statistics*, 1963–64, 1965–66, 1967–68, 1969–70, 1971–72).

NOTE: all figures rounded.

may wish to refer back to table 2.1 and Appendix 1 for the full sweep of the change from 1954 to 1972). Certainly, the increase in federal dollars flowing into the Southern and Border states is highly correlated with the increase in the percentage of black children in school with whites. The question, of course, is whether federal funds caused the increase in desegregation. The answer appears to be a clear yes.

Financially strapped school districts found the lure of federal dollars irresistible. To obtain and keep the money, however, they had to desegregate. And once federal money was received, the thought of losing it the next year, reducing budgets, slashing programs, firing staffs, was excruciating. Thus, along with the lure of federal dollars was the threat of having them taken away. HEW did bring enforcement proceedings and did terminate the eligibility of some school districts. School boards throughout the South, "realiz-

Table 3.3   Selected Southern School Districts by Extent of Desegregation and
              Amount of Federal Funds Received, 1967–1970

	% Blacks in School with Whites			Federal Funds (in Millions)		
District	1967–68	1968–69	1970–71	1967–68	1968–69	1970–71
Jackson, Miss.	—	5.4	98.6	1.4	2.2	4.0
Yazoo County, Miss.	1.7	5.5	28.1	.34	—	.67
Greenville, Miss.	8.7	10.4	100	.69	1.1	1.5
Birmingham City, Ala.	8.9	15.4	66.5	3.6	3.8	5.5
Montgomery City County, Ala.	3.2	5.7	92.8	2.7	3.1	5.3
Pulaski County Special, Ark.	36.8	62.3	100	.92	1.5	2.7
Rapides Parish, La.	10.4	4.1	73.3	.58	1.6	2.5
Jefferson Parish, La.	11.7	20.5	80.5	2.3	2.2	3.1
Caddo Parish, La.	2.7	6.0	55.5	2.6	2.4	3.1
Calcasieu Parish, La.	8.2	9.5	100	1.3	1.4	2.0
Dade County, Fla.	48.1	51.3	87.7	26.5	25.5	32.4
Duval County, Fla.	12.0	23.3	63.0	5.8	5.1	9.3
Orange County, Fla.	15.4	23.0	83.4	3.1	3.9	5.1

SOURCES: U.S. Department of HEW (National Center, 1967, 1968, 1970; Office of Civil Rights, *Directory*, 1967, 1968, 1970).

ing that the loss of monies was intolerable," took some steps to desegregate (Southern Regional Council 1971, 57).[33] As Orfield puts it, "the change [desegregation] would have been *impossible* without the lure of money from the Elementary & Secondary Education Act" (Orfield 1969, 228; emphasis added).

With this background, it should be clear why courts became effective. Put simply, courts could hold up federal funds. While court orders could always be disobeyed, as they were in the first decade after *Brown*, now there were real costs. The federal government was not likely to release federal funds in violation of a court order. Courts, then, because of Title VI and the availability of federal dollars, were in a new position. Provided with non-court-generated incentives, courts had both carrots and sticks to work with. Thus, they were able to contribute to the desegregation of the Southern schools.

33. The quote refers specifically to the school board of Clarke County, Georgia, but it is applicable throughout the South.

Business Inducements

Federal funding was not the only inducement for desegregation in the late 1960s and early 1970s. Another powerful factor at work was the desire of many Southern communities to lure industry and the realization that such moves required good schools and peaceful race relations. A peaceful, desegregated school system was seen as an important component in attracting industry. "Gradually," writes Jacoway, Southern business leaders "came to perceive, dimly at first, that their racism and abdication of leadership were taking a heavy toll; they were losing to other cities the industry they might have had." Thus, she concluded, the "desire to attract new industry and to maintain a progressive image was one very potent force leading to the southern willingness to abandon segregation" (Jacoway 1982, 5, 13). Orfield concurred, writing that, by the late 1960s, Southerners "were coming to see the close relationship between education and continued economic growth." Southern "communities came to realize," Orfield concludes, "that school quality strongly influenced plant locations, and thus local prosperity" (Orfield 1969, 209–10, 210). As Patterson put it, "in case after case the business community in the South found it to *its own interest* to deal with . . . Negro demands" (Patterson 1966, 71; emphasis added).

A few examples illustrate the general pattern. In Yazoo City, Mississippi, first discussed in chapter 2 for the strength of its political, economic, and cultural opposition to desegregation, table 3.3 shows that by the 1970 school year some progress had been made in desegregation. Part of the reason for the change was that the business community came to support desegregation because, in the words of Robert Wheeler, manager of the Chamber of Commerce, "we need good schools if we're going to attract industry" (quoted in Minor 1970, 34). As another report put it, in Yazoo City "pragmatic economics played a leading role in unifying business and civic leaders behind public education" (Winn 1970b, 5). In Louisiana, State School Superintendent William Dodd was told that "it was becoming very difficult to replace employees due to the school situation, and that if the state did not support its public schools, then it would be impossible for large companies to get men with families to move to Louisiana" (Winn 1970b, 5). By the 1972 school year, 83 percent of Louisiana's black students were in school with whites, up from 1.1 percent in 1965 (see table 3.2 and Appendix 1). In Jackson, Mississippi, where by 1970 the amount of federal funds received was nearly triple the amount received in 1967, and 98.6 percent of black students were in school with whites (see table 3.3), business interests switched positions and played a key role in support of desegregation. Part of the reason for the switch were the repeated warnings from Ken Wagner, brought to the city to help plan its economic future, that Jackson faced "financial disaster 'unless' " it improved its schools (Clift 1971, 6). His warnings were repeated in a January 1970 meeting between executives of Allis-Chalmers and the Jackson Chamber of Commerce, in which one company executive told the Mississippians: "I just can't in good conscience ask these people to move from Wisconsin to Mississippi unless you can prove to me what they know about the Jackson schools isn't so" (Clift 1971, 1; Patterson 1966). In Greensboro, North Carolina, change finally came in 1971 when, as a leader of the Chamber of Commerce said, "we're going to do what's good for business . . . It's a question of economics" (quoted in Chafe 1982, 67). Perhaps the new Southern attitude to desegregation was best summed up by the school-board president of a small town: "None of the whites like it, you understand. But they know we are just going to go out of business if we don't have a quality public school system. Nobody will move a plant in here if they know we don't have a school system" (quoted in Winn 1970b, 4).

Given this hunger for new industry by the under-industrialized South, failure to desegregate had costs. Here, too, courts were given a tool not of their making with which to work. Districts that violated court orders risked not only the loss of federal funds but also the inability to attract new industries. On the other hand, districts that did desegregate, maintained their eligibility for the money and could make a stronger pitch for new industry. Courts were effective in the years 1968–72, then, because a set of conditions provided them with useful tools for gaining compliance. When those conditions and tools were lacking, in the first decade after *Brown*, courts were essentially impotent to produce change.[34]

Courts as Cover

The brunt of the discussion in the second part of this chapter has been that by the late 1960s and early 1970s a whole host of factors had changed, removing the constraints from court action and providing the conditions under which they could be effective. With these changes, another condition for court effectiveness came into play: courts as cover (Condition IV). Under this condition, courts, by ordering action, allow officials to do what they believe needs to be done without their taking full responsibility for it. In the South, then, school officials and others could desegregate schools, preserve federal funding, attract new business, *and* still claim that they were forced to act by a distant and uncaring federal bureaucracy. Other changes, too, could be made under the cover of court orders. Courts, in many ways, offered politically exposed officials the best of all possible solutions.

34. An amusing example of an additional incentive that appears to have produced change comes from Columbia, South Carolina, which was on a "perennial quest in the 1950s and 1960s for the *Look* magazine All-American City Award." The city knew that any "disorder or disruption . . . might smear the good name of Columbia." And indeed, "progress in race relations was one of the major points Columbia used to win the All-American City Award in 1964" (Lofton 1982, 71, 81).

Evidence of such behavior is impossible to quantify. However, the overall impression of those who have examined the issue is that such behavior was common. Looking over the history of school desegregation, for example, Kalodner suggests that "many school boards pursue from the outset a course designed to shift the entire political burden of desegregation to the courts" (Kalodner 1978, 3). Similarly, the U.S. Civil Rights Commission, in its review of twenty-nine school districts attempting desegregation, found that overall "school desegregation usually requires revamping of a school system. Administrators often take this opportunity to make needed changes in curriculum, facilities, organization, and teaching methodology" (USCCR 1976b, 130). Finally, the Southern Regional Council discovered that Mississippi school officials understood the protective role of courts well: "at least half of the Mississippi school superintendents revealed in private conversation that their jobs were less difficult when the government was firm in demanding complete desegregation" (Southern Regional Council 1969, 37).

It seems fair to suggest, then, that part of the reason that courts were effective in helping to bring about desegregation in the late 1960s and early 1970s was that many crucial actors were willing to act but fearful of the consequences. Under such conditions, courts can be effective. In earlier years, however, when the willingness to act had not been wetted by government dollars, industrial moves, and general societal change, courts could not serve this protective, blame-taking role.

Education in the Border States

The factors outlined above are nicely illustrated by the progress of the border states in desegregating public schools. As table 2.1 shows, these states did respond positively to *Brown*. While desegregation occurred more rapidly after 1964, there was a good deal of change in the decade following *Brown*.

As in the South after 1965, political leadership in the border states in the 1950s was either supportive of, or not strongly opposed to, desegregation. Throughout the region elected officials either called for adherence to the law or said nothing. In the key cities of Washington, D.C., Baltimore, Wilmington, St. Louis, and Kansas City, the official attitude was supportive (USCCR 1959, 173; McKay 1956, 1012). In none of the border states were any pro-segregation statutes enacted (Sarratt 1966, 41).[35] Maryland even belatedly ratified the Fourteenth Amendment (Sarratt 1966, 41). The contrast between the actions of political leaders in this region and in the eleven Southern states is clear.

Culturally, segregation was breaking down throughout the region. Mu-

---

35. One law was enacted in Delaware providing that no student could transfer from one school district to another without the consent of both school boards. Its obvious intent was to prevent black transfers to white schools.

nicipal facilities were generally, though not completely, desegregated. This included, in various degrees, transportation facilities, parks, auditoriums, libraries, movie houses, and civil service employment. Many private groups and institutions throughout the region, including churches and school officials, pledged co-operation (USCCR 1959, 173–74; McKay 1956, 1012). "Perhaps the greatest state of readiness could be found within several of the school systems themselves" (USCCR 1959, 174). By 1952 Baltimore had a desegregated public school. In Wilmington, teachers' organizations and adult education were desegregated, as were school sports (USCCR 1959, 177, 180). In all the border states, desegregation of higher education had begun before 1954, as far back as the 1930s in Maryland and West Virginia (Sarratt 1966, 131–32; USCCR 1961a, 50). It is no surprise, then, that the Delaware Supreme Court banned segregation in the state's public schools before the U.S. Supreme Court acted (*Gebhardt* v. *Belton*). Finally, all the border states had small percentages of blacks, with only Delaware (14 percent) and Maryland (17 percent) being above ten percent (figures from 1950 census reported by Lasch 1957, 60). In terms of leadership and the political, social, and cultural climate, the constraints had been weakened if not largely neutralized by the time the Court acted in 1954. Added incentives were not necessary, for there was little in the way of large-scale, hard-core opposition.

Higher Education

As chapter 2 showed, no gains were made in ending segregation in higher education until Congress and the executive branch acted. After that action, as table 2.3A illustrates, there were large increases. However, while change did occur, by 1978 the percentage of black enrollment at formerly segregated Southern public colleges and universities remained low (see table 2.3B). And this was true despite the 1973 District of Columbia Circuit Court decision in *Adams* v. *Richardson* ordering the Office of Civil Rights to step up its work in higher education (see chapter 2). The question this poses is why was there initially good progress but then little change? The answer, of course, comes from re-examining this history through the lenses of the constraints and the conditions.

The initial change can be explained by the same set of reasons that fit the other areas of civil rights. With congressional and executive action, political opposition was muted or reversed. By the mid and late 1960s, social and cultural opposition had lost much of its bite. And with the threat of termination of federal funds for higher education through programs ranging from the National Science Foundation to the Higher Education Act of 1965, continuing segregation ran risks.

However, the challenges involved in ending segregation in higher education are of a different magnitude than those faced in elementary and secondary education. Public school education is mandatory throughout the U.S., providing a large pool of students with whom to work. In contrast, the pool of suitably trained minority students is much smaller in higher education. This is due to economic and social forces beyond the control of courts, as well as current racial discrimination and the lingering effects of past discrimination. Courts lack the tools to deal effectively with these "relatively uncontrollable social and environmental factors" (Ayres 1984, 143). Thus, desegregating higher education presented a more complex set of problems.

In addition, however, the federal government appears to lack the necessary commitment to see further progress. This has resulted in little pressure to achieve substantial desegregation. As chapter 2 discussed, few steps have been taken to monitor higher education and almost no proceedings have been initiated. Indeed, in October 1987, a House subcommittee charged that the executive branch had failed to enforce court orders requiring ten states to desegregate their higher education systems (Williams 1987, 11). As one study concluded, "the lack of support for the *Adams* initiative from the Congress, the Presidency, and substantial elements of the vocal and diffuse public, the lack of inducements and sanctions for higher education, and economic and social forces" have combined to constrain continued progress (Paul 1988, 61).

The progress that did occur in the 1970s appears to have been due more to the initiative of individual state and institutional actors than to the federal government. Both Ayres and Paul conclude, for example, in comparing state successes in desegregation, that "states under federal pressure [to desegregate institutions of higher education] were apparently no more successful than other states" not facing such pressure (Ayres 1984, 127). Paul's interviews with Texas officials led her to conclude that the "internal agenda of the higher education institution appears to have played a larger role in determining institutional response to the *Adams* initiative at these schools than any external social agenda, irrespective of the source" (Paul 1988, 56). As Condition IV suggests, administrators and officials willing to act can use court orders to leverage additional resources, institute changes, and make reforms. However, lacking strong federal pressure from the executive branch, and incentives with which to induce behavior, there is little that courts will be able to do. Thus, the changes in desegregation of higher education are well explained by the constraints and conditions.

Conclusion

In explaining the changes that occurred in civil rights in the years after *Brown*, it is clear that paradigms based on court efficacy are simply wrong. It is equally clear that the Constrained Court view captures the key reasons why, despite Supreme Court action, nothing changed in the first decade after *Brown*. These include the lack of political and cultural support for civil rights, the courts' qualified independence, and the judiciary's lack of implementation tools. After Congress and the executive branch became committed to civil rights, however, political and cultural support became stronger. Further, such support provided incentives that helped courts to overcome their lack of implementation tools. In the years after 1964 and 1965, not only were the constraints neutralized, but several of the conditions generated from the Dynamic Court view were present. This meant that courts could be effective agents for significant social reform.

In sum, an examination of the direct effects of courts in producing significant social reform, in this case civil rights, shows that the theoretical framework of the constraints and conditions successfully explains the varying patterns of judicial efficacy. In contrast, neither view of the Court alone, nor the existing paradigm of *Brown* as the symbol of judicial efficacy, works very well. They are too inflexible to take account of the complexity of events. Courts can matter, but only sometimes, and only under limited conditions.

4

Planting the Seeds
of Progress?

The judicial path of influence is not the only way an institution can take in contributing to civil rights. As the Dynamic Court view suggests, by bringing an issue to light courts may put pressure on others to act, sparking change. Thus *Brown* and its progeny may have been the inspiration that eventually led to congressional and executive branch action and some success in civil rights. According to one commentator, "*Brown* set the stage for the ensuing rise in black political activism, for legal challenges to racial discrimination in voting, employment, and education, as well as for the creation of a favorable climate for the passage of the subsequent civil rights legislation and the initiation of the War on Poverty" (Levin 1979, 80). Indeed, most commentators (and I assume most readers) believe this is the case and hold their belief with "little doubt."[1] As C. Herman Pritchett put it, "if the Court had not taken that first giant step in 1954, does anyone think there would now be a Civil Rights Act of 1964?" (Pritchett 1964, 869).

In this chapter I examine these claims. What evidence exists to substantiate them? How can they be measured? Why are they made so automatically and so frequently? How important was *Brown* to the civil rights struggle? Coming to terms with these questions further highlights the applicability of the Dynamic Court view.[2]

Theoretical Difficulties

The path of extra-judicial influence is difficult to trace for two major reasons. First, proponents of the Dynamic Court view have never spelled out

1. Lawrence (1980, 49). See, also, for example, Carter (1968, 247); Greenberg (1968, 1522); Kluger (1976, 749); Stone et al. (1986, 481); Wasby et al. (1977, 5); Wilkinson (1979, 3–7); Woodward (1974, 139).
2. It must be remembered that even if the Dynamic Court view claim is substantiated, the extra-judicial route of influence is less certain and controllable than the judicial one. Lawyers involved in litigation aimed at producing significant social reform may have little ability to lay out and control the causal forces that may be generated.

in any detail exactly how it works. In attempting to come to terms with it then, it must be filled out. Second, and absolutely crucial, is the question of causation. In the social sciences, unlike the natural sciences, the researcher cannot control the environment so as to disentangle all the factors that alone, or in combination, may have led to, caused, created, or influenced a given outcome. Social scientists do not understand well enough the dynamics of influence and causation to state with certainty that the claims of Court influence (or any other causal claims) are right or wrong. Similarly, social scientists do not understand fully the myriad of factors that are involved in an individual's reaching a political decision. Ideas seem to have feet of their own, and tracking their footsteps is an imperfect science. Thus, even if I find little or no evidence of extra-judicial influence, it is simply impossible to state with certainty that the Court did not produce significant social reform in civil rights.

Acknowledging this limitation that all social scientists face is not the end of the assessment. It is a warning that the assessment will remain uncertain, not a barrier to making it. This is so because, at base, the Dynamic Court view claim of extra-judicial influence is empirical. If the Court was consequential in civil rights, then its influence should be identifiable and measurable. The more places in which it can be identified, the stronger the claim is. On the other hand, the fewer places in which it is found, the less likely it is that the effect of the Court is as powerful as the Dynamic Court view contends.

It is worth pausing for a moment to note the resistance that most people exhibit to an argument questioning the contribution of the Court to civil rights. It seems obvious that since the Court ordered an end to segregation, and some time later much segregation was ended, the Court must have been causally responsible for the outcome. It is true, of course, that correlation does not equal causation. Merely because event A preceded event B does not necessarily mean that A caused B. Yet in assessing the influence of the Court on civil rights many assume that it was the crucial agent. To fully understand the contribution of the Court, this seeming uncritical inclination to find causation where none may exist must be overcome. It is of course possible that so doing will lead precisely back to the Dynamic Court view and the generally accepted explanation of the Court's causal influence. But if so, the argument will be strengthened, and will be able to defend itself against the charge of uncritical causal attribution.[3]

This cautionary note, however, does not resolve the problem of how to think about causal influence. Broadly speaking, three types of information must be known. First, the mechanisms or links of influence must be clearly

3. Social psychologists have been intrigued by why people so readily and often incorrectly attribute causation to temporal events. See Jennings et al. (1982, 214); Nisbett and Ross (1980, 117); Tversky and Kahneman (1982a, 128; 1982b, 4).

specified. One needs to be told, for example, that Court decision A influenced President B to win legislation C that improved civil rights. Once the hypothesized links are specified, then, second, the kind of evidence that would substantiate them must be presented. While there are no precise and exact measures that can be applied, there are a number of indicators that can be examined. One is *attribution*. Using the example above, if President B states that action was taken because of Court decision A, that would be good evidence for the link. Similarly, if President B's *actions changed* in such a way as to conform with the Court, regardless of what was said, this might be evidence too. If one of the links involved the public, then *opinion change* would certainly be an important measure. Further, if one of the links involved *salience*, bringing issues to the forefront of elite and public attention, measures of media coverage could be obtained. Third, other possible explanations for the change must be explored and evaluated. This includes examining the evidence mentioned above in the context of other political, social, and economic factors at work. For it is possible that even though President B acted after Court decision A, the action was taken because of pressure from other actors who acted independently of the Court.

In addition, the passage of time plays a critical role, yet one that is difficult to assess. If A orders B to do X, and B immediately does X, it seems reasonable to credit A with influencing B's actions. However, the more time that elapses between the order and the action, the more tenuous is the causal link. This is principally because the longer the time period, the more room there is for other actors to intervene and influence B. While it might be the case that these actors were themselves influenced by A, this would add another step to the causal chain. A chain is only as strong as its weakest link. These kind of determinations can be made only in the context of the data. Thus, the passage of time forms a backdrop to an evaluation of causal claims.

Turning to the specifics, I have tried to delineate the links that are necessary for the Court to have influenced civil rights by the extra-judicial path. The bottom line, the last link, is that the action of the president and Congress resulted in change. That is, the passage of the 1964 Civil Rights Act and the 1965 Voting Rights Act brought about change. This case was made in chapter 2 and it is assumed to be true throughout this chapter. The key question, then, for the Dynamic Court view's extra-judicial influence claim, is the extent to which congressional and presidential action was a product of Court action.

One hypothesized link postulates that Court action gave civil rights prominence, putting it on the political agenda. The Dynamic Court view maintains that when political institutions are unwilling or unable to deal with certain issues, courts can provide an appropriate forum. Elected and appointed officials, the claim goes, find it politically difficult to ignore issues brought out by Court decisions. Media coverage of civil rights over time could provide good evidence to assess this link.

A second link, put quite simply, is that Court action influenced both the president and Congress to act. The Court, in other words, was able to pressure the other branches into dealing with civil rights. With the executive, evidence might be found in what presidents said about civil rights as well as what kinds of bills they had introduced. With members of Congress, one might look to what was said in debates over civil rights legislation and to other indications of congressional concern such as the number of civil rights bills introduced and sponsored. Time, of course, and the general political and social context would overlay this analysis.

A third hypothesized link proposes that the Court favorably influenced white Americans in general about civil rights and they in turn pressured politicians. By bringing the treatment of black Americans to nationwide attention, the Court may have fomented change. Evidence here would include finding that whites knew about what the Court did, that they changed their opinions about blacks, and that changing white opinion affected political elites. The length of time over which any of this occurred and other contextual factors need to be examined too.

A final hypothesized link suggests that the Court influenced black Americans to act in favor of civil rights and that this in turn influenced white political elites either directly or indirectly through influencing whites in general. Evidence for this link might be found in civil rights actions, in the reasons blacks gave for acting, the knowledge they had of the Court's opinions, changes in the size and strength of black civil rights groups, and, as always, the time factor and the political and societal context.

Regardless of the findings of this examination, one additional step is necessary to make believable the causal connection of the Court to congressional and executive action. That, of course, is an examination of the other political, social, and economic factors that could plausibly have influenced the action. While I allude to some of these in this chapter, I postpone the main discussion until chapter 5 and ask the reader to bear with me.

To sum up, in order to assess the claim that the influence of the Court on civil rights followed the Dynamic Court view's extra-judicial path, I have identified necessary links in the causal chain and appropriate places for extra-judicial effects to be found. These include the salience of civil rights as an issue and the actions and attitudes of political elites, of white Americans, and of black Americans. With each of these groups I will look for evidence of the effect of the Court on their attitudes and actions in support of civil rights. If I find such evidence, then the Dynamic Court view will be supported. However, even if I find little or no evidence, this view cannot be totally rejected for the methodological reasons mentioned above. To the extent that I find little or no evidence for the effect, the best I can conclude is that the argument is unproven. But if this is the case, it should serve to shift the burden of proof to the proponents of the claim.

Salience

When the Supreme Court unanimously condemned segregation in 1954, it marked the first time since 1875 that one of the three branches of the federal government spoke strongly in favor of civil rights on a fundamental issue. An important claim of the Dynamic Court view is that the Court's action put civil rights on the political agenda. *"Brown,"* it is claimed, "launched the public debate over racial equality" (Neier 1982, 241–42). One important way in which the political agenda is created is through the press. John Kingdon, in his study of congressional voting decisions, noted that the "printed and broadcast media are capable of the kind of continuous and prominent coverage of a story which makes it virtually impossible for a congressman to ignore." Further, he suggested that the "mass media may be powerful agenda-setters" with a "substantial impact on the determination of which issues will be seriously considered and which will not" (Kingdon 1981, 284, 223; Iyengar and Kinder 1987). Thus, one important way in which the Court may have given salience to civil rights is through inducing increased press coverage of it and balanced treatment of blacks.

Press Coverage

Overall, there is no evidence of such an increase or major change in reporting in the years immediately following *Brown*. In general, newspaper coverage of civil rights was poor until the massive demonstrations of the 1960s. In the South, for example, a study by the Southern Regional Council (SRC) of "representative" white newspapers concluded that they constituted "the greatest single force in perpetuating the popular stereotype of the Negro." The problem, the SRC found, was that "the average white editor believes, rightly or wrongly, that readers want little mention of the Negro which does not fit in with their own concept of colored persons" (SRC n.d., 2). Numerous studies support this conclusion. C. A. McKnight, executive director of the Southern Education Reporting Service, found that in the years following *Brown* Supreme Court treatment of segregation received "minimum coverage" (quoted in Sarratt 1966, 263). In 1956, Ralph McGill, editor of the *Atlanta Constitution*, chided newspapers for failing to do "a good job of presenting and interpreting the segregation controversy" (quoted in Carter 1957, 4, n.4). This was particularly true in the South, where there was a "paucity" of coverage and where the wire services "seldom reported the story in its full dimensions and meaning" (Watters and Cleghorn 1967, 73 n.10). And *Time* magazine criticized Southern newspapers for doing a "patchy, pussyfooting job of covering the region's biggest running story since the end of slavery" ("The Press" 1956, 76).

More specifically, with desegregation, Meyer found "slipshod, lazy handling" of the "Supreme Court's ruling" (Meyer 1960, 37). There was a "failure" to report on the thoughts of blacks and there were "few interviews" with black leaders (Meyer 1960, 38–9). In a study of three national, one regional, and eighteen North Carolina papers, at a time when desegregation was "in the news," Carter concluded that "the most striking aspect of newspaper attention to the desegregation issue in the papers studied was the degree of *inattention*" (Carter 1957, 18, 10). Similarly, a study of five white Mississippi papers for selected months in each of the years 1962, 1963, and 1964 found that the papers "either segregated black news or virtually ignored it." And when they did cover civil rights activities, "there were major flaws, the news columns becoming reflectors, if not alternate outlets, of the editorial columns" (Hooker 1971, 57, 59). A study of 712 papers with 50 million subscribers found that papers with 28 million subscribers gave no coverage to civil rights, while the remaining papers printed "erroneous information" and "committed grievous faults" (cited in Meyer 1960, 52–53). In general, the Southern press did not greatly increase or balance its civil rights coverage in response to the Court.

Part of the reason for this limited coverage of desegregation is the nature of press coverage of the Supreme Court. As late as 1964 most of the reporters covering the Supreme Court lacked training for legal reporting. The Supreme Court assignment was usually joined to a number of others such as the Justice Department and the U.S. Court of Appeals for the District of Columbia Circuit. It was not until 1955, for example, that Anthony Lewis started covering the Supreme Court for the *New York Times*. But even after the training and quality of Court reporters improved, newspaper coverage remained poor. Examining coverage of the reapportionment and prayer decisions of the 1960s, Newland found that headlines were "generally misleading" and that editors had a propensity for "choosing sensational material over more significant cases for reports and blowing up stories to sensational dimensions" (Newland 1964, 29, 33). Newspapers did not appear interested in providing the kind of in-depth and continuous coverage that could have lead to greater public awareness and given civil rights salience. It is no surprise, then, that press coverage of civil rights did not greatly change in the wake of *Brown*.

The most powerful way to determine if there was a sustained increase in press coverage of civil rights in response to *Brown* is to actually count press stories over time. If *Brown* had the impact that the Dynamic Court view predicts, the evidence should show a sustained increase in media coverage of civil rights. The evidence is presented in figure 4.1 and table 4.1. Turning to table 4.1, one can see (column 2) that while press coverage of civil rights, as measured by the number of stories dealing with the issue in the *Reader's Guide To Periodical Literature*, increased moderately in 1954 over the previous year's total, by 1958 and 1959 coverage actually dropped below the level found in several of the years of the late 1940s and early 1950s! The enormous

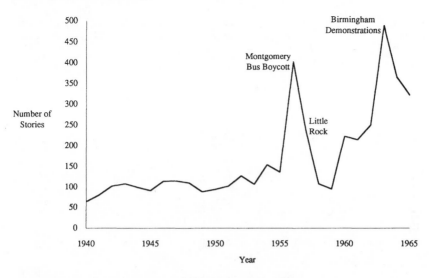

Figure 4.1. Magazine Coverage of Civil Rights, 1940–1965

increases in 1956 and 1957 are most persuasively explained not by Court action but rather by the Montgomery bus boycott, the violence in Clinton, Tennessee, and the presidential election campaign in 1956, as well as the Little Rock crisis in 1957.[4] In addition, if one examines the magazines in America in the 1950s and early 1960s with the largest circulations, *Reader's Digest, Ladies Home Journal, Life*, and the *Saturday Evening Post*, the same general pattern again repeats. And it was not until 1962 that *TV Guide* ran a story having to do with civil rights. Thus, press coverage provides no evidence that the Court's decision gave civil rights salience for most Americans.[5]

It is possible, of course, that the political agenda is formed more by elites than by ordinary citizens. Thus, it may be that the magazines most likely read by elites would provide increased coverage of civil rights in the wake of the Court's decision. But this is not the case. The magazines most likely to be read by political elites, the *New York Times Magazine, Newsweek, Time*, and the *New Republic*, show the same pattern. While most of these magazines did contain more civil rights articles in 1956 and 1957 than in the years prior to *Brown*, this is most plausibly due to the factors identified above. In fact, for each of these magazines there was as much, if not more, coverage of civil rights in several of the years of the 1940s as in 1958 or 1959. The same

4. This conclusion is based on examining the titles to civil rights entries in the *Reader's Guide To Periodical Literature* and *The New York Times Index*, as well as spot-checking articles in several periodicals.

5. The reader should note, too, that Universal Newsreels never mentioned *Brown* (Branch 1988, 113).

Table 4.1   Magazine And Press Coverage Of Civil Rights, 1940–1965

Year	Reader's Guide Entries	# of Journals	NYT Mag.[a]	New Rep.	Newsweek	Time	Reader's Digest	Ladies H.J.	Life	Sat. Eve. Post	TV Guide	NYT Index[b]
1940	64	127	0	5	1	1	1	—	1	2	—	.5
1941	80	118	0	4	2	3	0	1	1	2	—	.4
1942	102		0	5	2	6	2	1	1	2	—	.4
1943	108	115	2	14	0	3	2	0	1	2	—	.6
1944	99		1	8	2	6	3	0	4	0	—	.5
1945	91	127	0	12	1	1	4	0	2	1	—	.6
1946	114		1	7	9	2	2	0	0	2	—	.8
1947	115	133	3	11	5	6	2	1	4	1	—	.4
1948	110		4	7	10	10	4	1	2	5	—	.6
1949	88	122	1	3	4	6	2	0	9	2	—	.5
1950	94		1	16	4	5	1	2	4	2	—	.4
1951	102	119	2	12	6	7	2	1	0	1	—	.3
1952	127		1	19	9	10	3	1	1	6	—	.5
1953	107[c]	122	1	6	6	12	0	0	2	1	0	.3

Year												
1954	154		6	6	6	14	3	0	4	4	0	.3
1955	136	114	1	3	8	13	3	0	1	3	0	.4
1956	402		6	41	15	28	5	0	35	2	0	1.0
1957	235	111	6	11	12	14	2	0	9	2	0	1.0
1958	108		0	3	3	7	0	0	2	1	0	.4
1959	95	110	2	9	1	5	1	1	1	2	0	.6
1960	222		5	19	13	20	3	0	7	1	0	1.1
1961	214[d]	134	11	16	19	13	1	1	4	2	0	1.3
1962	249		6	12	24	12	2	0	3	0	3	1.0
1963	489	129	12	27	49	26	3	2	14	4	1	2.8
1964	365		18	17	17	21	2	1	7	6	2	3.1
1965	322	126	9	14	21	11	4	1	5	3	0[e]	3.0

SOURCE: See Appendix 5.

NOTES:

[a]Repetitions excluded.

[b]Proportion of pages in *New York Times Index* devoted to coverage of civil rights (in percent).

[c]*Negro History Bulletin* first indexed April 1953–February 1955.

[d]*Ebony* first indexed March 1961–February 1963.

[e]For *TV Guide* there was an average of 6.8 stories per year in the years 1966–79.

general pattern holds for civil rights coverage in the *New York Times* (column 12) as measured by the proportion of pages in the *Times Index* devoted to discrimination. In 1952, there was actually more coverage than in 1954 or 1955. Further, coverage in the years 1954, 1955, 1958, and 1959 was barely equal to or actually less than the coverage allotted to civil rights in four of the years of the 1940s! Here again, there is no evidence that the Court's action indirectly affected elites by putting civil rights on the political agenda through the press.

Textbooks

Another way that *Brown* could have influenced perceptions and beliefs is through changing textbook coverage of civil rights. Proponents of the Dynamic Court view claim that Court decisions generally influence the way Americans think about issues. Tracing the path of ideas is difficult, but if in the wake of *Brown* schools presented a different and more positive version of the contributions of black Americans and the need to end all race-based discrimination, this would provide good evidence for the claim. In this way, the Court could help mold the political agenda by influencing beliefs in a direction more supportive of civil rights. Textbook coverage of civil rights, then, might be one way of tracking *Brown*'s subtle but powerful influence on ideas.

Examining textbook coverage of blacks and civil rights in the years prior to *Brown*, several studies have documented how blacks were portrayed as simple, lazy, and content, making few if any contributions to white America (American Council 1949; Carpenter 1941). A major 1949 study of 315 elementary, secondary, and college texts, for example, found that a "very large proportion of the references" to blacks treat them as "slaves or as childlike freedmen." The "little data" that are presented in history and social science textbooks about post Civil War conditions perpetuate the "plantation mammy and Uncle Remus stereotypes" (American Council 1949, 32). The claim is that this changed after *Brown*.

While it is the case that the textbooks of the 1980s correct the racism of earlier presentations, the change was so long in coming that it is difficult to make a case that *Brown* played much of a role. For example, a 1961 study of the 48 "most widely used" secondary-school textbooks found that the "main criticisms" of the 1949 report were still "equally valid." In reaching this conclusion, the study randomly selected one-half of the 48 books. Using the 1949 report as a baseline, the study found that "textbooks continue to present a picture of this group primarily as slaves and as inexperienced, exploited, ignorant freedmen" so that the "impression left with the reader is that Negroes in America have always been, and thus presumably are now, a simple, backward people." Astonishingly, although all the books were published after *Brown*, and almost half (23 of 48) were published in 1960 or 1961, only 12 (of 24) made any reference to *Brown* at all! Of those 12, only 4 made more than incidental mention of it, 2 seeming to blame the Court for stirring up trouble! (Marcus 1961, 7, 38–40, 43). This lack of change was limited to blacks, for the study found positive change since 1949 in the textbook treatment of Jews and other minorities. It is hard to imagine a study less supportive of the Dynamic Court view.

The thrust of these findings was corroborated by a 1970 study of seven texts (six state-approved) being used in elementary and junior high schools in the South. The study found that the "Negro is never portrayed as an actor" and that "there is a deliberate attempt to perpetuate the image of the Negro as an emotional, trusting, lazy child" (McLaurin 1970, 8). If *Brown* supported civil rights by bringing new ideas to public consciousness, there is no evidence that it did so through influencing the textbooks American children read in school.

In sum, neither press coverage of civil rights nor textbook treatment of blacks provides evidence for the Dynamic Court view's extra-judicial-effects claim. This finding is striking since *Brown* is virtually universally credited with having brought civil rights to national attention.

Elites

The extra-judicial-effects argument claims that the actions of the Supreme Court influenced members of Congress, the president, and the executive branch. The argument might be that because of the "deference paid by the other branches of government and by the American public" (Neier 1982, 9) to the Supreme Court, its decisions prodded the other branches of the federal government into action. Further, the argument might run that the Court's actions sensitized elites to the legitimate claims of blacks. As Wilkinson puts it, "*Brown* was the catalyst that shook up Congress" (Wilkinson 1979, 49). Using the approach outlined above, I examine likely places for these effects to be found.

Legislation

A sensible place to look for evidence of indirect effects is in the legislative history and debates over the 1957, 1960, and 1964 civil rights acts, the 1965 Voting Rights Act, and in presidential pronouncements on civil rights legislation. If Court action was crucial to congressional and presidential action, one might reasonably expect to find members of Congress and the president mentioning it as a reason for introducing and supporting civil rights legislation. While it is true that lack of attribution may only mean that the Court's influence was subtle, it would cast doubt on the force, if not the existence, of this extra-judicial effect.

At the outset, the case for influence is supported by the fact that civil rights bills were introduced and, for the first time since 1875, enacted in the years following *Brown*. While this makes it seem likely that *Brown* played an important role, closer examination of the impetus behind the civil rights acts of 1957, 1960, and 1964, and the Voting Rights Act of 1965, does not support this seemingly reasonable inference. While an alternative explanation is suggested below, the discussion is aimed at testing the case for Court influence. A fuller treatment of possible alternative explanations is developed in chapter 5.

Starting with the 1957 bill, the first bill and temporally the closest to *Brown*, students credit it to Attorney General Brownell's pro-civil rights sympathies and to electoral pressures.[6] Conspicuously absent is more than passing mention of *Brown*. As Burk put it, it was the "Montgomery boycott, violent incidents in Mississippi, and the hope of political gain among Northern black voters" that "sparked" "scattered voices within the administration" to press "the case for a stronger official identification with the integration cause" (Burk 1984, 155). Chief among these voices were those of Northern Republican representatives who hoped to appeal to their increasing number of black constituents, and Republican party leaders who saw an opportunity to make inroads on the Democrats post-New Deal strength among black voters. Brownell aside, "Republicans interested in civil rights as a matter of principle," Anderson concluded, were "in the minority" (Anderson 1964, 3).

Eisenhower's position on the bill, and civil rights in general, favors this analysis. His support for the bill was "at best tepid" (Anderson 1964, 45), and the bill was not introduced until April 1956, quite late in a congressional session that faced nominating conventions coming up in the summer and a presidential election looming in the fall. Eisenhower did not speak in support of the bill and "it was only in the heat of the final weeks of the [1956] election campaign, at a moment when the Republican leadership considered the outcome to be hanging in the balance, that the President finally endorsed the Justice Department's program" (Anderson 1964, 45, 135).

The press and political opponents understood the bill as a response to electoral pressures, not to constitutional mandates. Senator Humphrey (D., Minn.) called it "lip service by leap-year liberals" (quoted in Anderson 1964, 39), and a *New York Times* editorial found "the most interesting thing about this series of proposals is that the Administration did not see fit to embody them in legislative form sooner than the spring of this Presidential election year, when they would be calculated to cause maximum embarrassment to the Democratic Party" ("Civil Rights Reports" 1956, 30).[7] Indeed, Anderson

6. See Anderson (1964, 3, 47, 133–35); Burk (1984, 6, 145, 165, 218); Kluger (1976, 754); Lawson (1976, chap. 6); Wilkins (1984, 234).
7. An earlier editorial made the same point, concluding that "the sudden flurry of interest in civil rights legislation so late in the Congressional session is enough to make one wonder" ("Civil Rights at First Base" 1956, 26).

reports that the "civil rights bill was considered by the entire press to be significant only as a gesture and an element in the jockeying between the two parties for advantage in the urban constituencies" (Anderson 1964, 96–97). And, as chapter 2 showed, substantively it accomplished little.

This analysis is strengthened by Eisenhower's extreme reticence to act on civil rights in the years following *Brown*. In a press conference of July 17, 1957, just a few months before Little Rock, Eisenhower stated: "I can't imagine any set of circumstances that would ever induce me to send Federal troops . . . into any area to enforce the order of a federal court" (quoted in Burk 1984, 173). While Eisenhower did send troops to Little Rock, he did so only as a last resort, to prevent violence. Indeed, at Mansfield, Texas, a year earlier, he had done nothing while the governor successfully used the Texas Rangers to remove black students from Mansfield High School and Texarkana Junior College. As Burk points out, 1956 was an election year, Texas was seen as a crucial state, and Eisenhower was on friendly terms with Governor Shivers. These factors were missing at Little Rock (Burk 1984, 167, 185–86). In addition, the administration did not apply the *Brown* decision to funding decisions for segregated Southern institutions. For example, the Library Services Act of 1956 sent $7.5 million to segregated Southern libraries, and Alabama, Georgia, Mississippi, and South Carolina received $5.3 million in National Defense Education Act funds in 1959 despite their lack of compliance with *Brown*. As late as 1960, the Southern states received over $1 billion through the grants-in-aid program to state and local governments (Aptheker 1964, 88). Thus, *Brown* does not appear to have had a positive impact on the Eisenhower administration's activities.

The same general argument can be made for the 1960 Civil Rights Act. Again, electoral pressure was the crucial motivating factor. From the Republican point of view, the apparently successful strategy of courting Northern urban black voters and, at the same time, embarrassing the Democrats, was used again (Berman 1962, 115). On the Democratic side, Senate majority leader Lyndon Johnson (D., Texas) "knew that his party's chances in 1960 might be seriously hurt if the Eighty-Sixth Congress, which the Democrats controlled, failed to pass civil rights legislation." Also, Johnson had his own presidential ambitions and was fearful of being branded a Southern extremist (Berman 1962, 5). Not surprisingly, then, the final product had little substantive content, allowing politicians to play it both ways, taking credit for acting with the black electorate while telling concerned whites that little had changed. Its enactment was of "scant news value" and the bill-signing did not even make the front page of the *New York Times* (Berman 1962, 1). As Thurgood Marshall put it, the bill "isn't worth the paper it's written on" (quoted in Berman 1962, 117). The National Association for the Advancement of Colored People (NAACP) called the bill "a fraud" and Marshall complained to the *New York Times* that " 'it would take two or three years for a good lawyer to get someone registered under this bill.' He emphasized the word 'good' " (Lewis 1960a, 14). Thus, the 1960 Civil Rights Act does not provide evidence for the influence of *Brown*.

The story of the 1964 act is similar in that there is no evidence of Court influence and a great deal of evidence for other factors, in this case the activities of the civil rights movement. The Kennedy administration offered no civil rights bill until February 1963 and the bill it offered then was "a collection of minor changes far more modest than the 1956 Eisenhower program" (Orfield 1969, 24).[8] When a House subcommittee modified and strengthened the bill, Attorney General Robert Kennedy met with the members of the full Judiciary Committee in executive session and "criticized the subcommittee draft in almost every detail" (Berman 1966, 21–22; Whalen 1985, 44–45). The president specifically objected to the prohibition of job discrimination that became Title VII, the provision making the Civil Rights Commission a permanent agency, the provision empowering the attorney general to sue on behalf of individuals alleging racial discrimination, and the provisions mandating no discrimination in federally funded programs and allowing fund cutoffs (Berman 1966, 22; Greenberg 1973, ix). It wasn't until the events of the spring of 1963 that the administration changed its thinking.

In Congress, there is little evidence that *Brown* played any appreciable role. The seemingly endless congressional debates, with some four million words uttered in the Senate alone (Whalen 1985, 193), hardly touched on the case. References to *Brown* can be found on only a few dozen out of many thousands of pages of Senate debate.[9] While much of the focus of the debate was on the constitutionality of the proposed legislation, and on the Fourteenth Amendment, the concern was not with how *Brown* mandated legislative action, or even how *Brown* made such a bill possible. Even in the debates over the fund cut-off provisions, *Brown* was seldom mentioned (Berman 1966; Orfield 1969, 33–45; Whalen 1985; Graham 1990, 82–83). This is particularly surprising since, as Condition IV suggests, it would have been very easy for pressured and uncertain members of Congress to shield their actions behind the constitutional mandate announced by the Court. That they did not credit the Court with affecting their decisions prevents the debates from

8. During the 1960 campaign Kennedy said that he had asked Senator Joseph Clark and Representative Emanuel Celler to prepare civil rights bills. When they introduced these bills in 1961, the administration denied sponsorship and Pierre Salinger, Kennedy's press secretary, stated that the administration did not consider new civil rights legislation "necessary at this time" (quoted in Sarratt 1966, 73).

9. References can be found in the following parts and on the following pages of volume 110 of the *Congressional Record*, 88th Congress, 2nd sess., 1964: Part 4: 4496, 5017, 5087, 5247, 5267, 5342; Part 5: 5695, 5703, 5705, 5935, 6540, 6813, 6814, 6821, 6837, 6838; Part 6: 8052, 8054; Part 7: 8620, 8621; Part 8: 10919, 10921, 10925, 10926, 11194, 11195, 11198; Part 9: 11597, 11875, 12339, 12579, 12580; Part 10: 12683, 13922; Part 11: 14294, 14296, 14447, 14457. Over 40 percent of these references are by Senators opposing the bill.

providing evidence for the indirect-effects thesis. Thus, there does not appear to be evidence for the influence of *Brown* on legislative action.

Finally, there is the question of the 1965 Voting Rights Act. It would make little sense to find major Court influence here, eleven years after *Brown*, not having found evidence for it in the earlier bills. And this is the case, for the impetus and explanation for the enactment of the 1965 Voting Rights Act were the activities in Selma, not Court decisions (Garrow 1978).

Reviewing the public pronouncements of Presidents Eisenhower, Kennedy, and Johnson on civil rights legislation, I do not find the Court mentioned as a reason to act. Neither Eisenhower nor Kennedy committed the moral weight of their office to civil rights. When they did act, it was in response to violence or upcoming elections, not in response to Court decisions. While President Johnson spoke movingly and eloquently about civil rights, he did not mention Court decisions as an important reason for civil rights action. In his moving speeches to Congress and the nation in support of the 1964 Civil Rights Act and the 1965 Voting Rights Act he dwelt on the violence that peaceful black protesters were subjected to, the unfairness of racial discrimination, and the desire to honor the memory of President Kennedy. It was these factors that Johnson highlighted as reasons for supporting civil rights, not Court decisions.

Finally, one can look to the political parties themselves to see if *Brown* induced them to reach out and include more blacks in their organizations. Looking at the number of black convention delegates, as late as 1964 there were only sixty-five black delegates (2.8 percent of the total number) at the Democratic National Convention, the number of black delegates the Republicans achieved in 1912! From 1952 to 1956 the number of black delegates to the Democratic National Convention dropped by nearly one-third. It wasn't until the 1972 Democratic convention that black delegates comprised over 10 percent of the total. On the Republican side, there were actually fewer black delegates in the years 1956–68 than there were in 1952 (Jaynes and Williams 1989, 217). These findings provide no support for *Brown*'s positive influence on political elites.

In sum, I have not found the evidence necessary to make a case of clear attribution for the Court's effects on Congress, the president, or the major political parties. Students of the Civil Rights Acts of 1957, 1960, and 1964, and the 1965 Voting Rights Act, credit their introduction and passage to electoral concerns, or impending violence, not Court decisions. The extrajudicial-effects claim is not supported with Congress or the president.

Title VI

When the 1964 Civil Rights Act became law, it contained a title (Title VI) prohibiting the use of federal funds in programs that discriminated on the basis of race. One claim that is often made is that Title VI stemmed from *Brown*. Without *Brown*, the argument goes, there would not have been the impetus for introducing such legislation. If this is the case, then *Brown* had an important indirect effect.

At first blush it appears that such a case can be made. Starting in 1955, the year after *Brown*, and continuing fairly regularly in the following years, Representative Adam Clayton Powell, Jr., of Harlem, with the support of the NAACP, introduced amendments to federal school-aid bills prohibiting any federal aid to states that maintained segregated schools by law in defiance of *Brown* (Sundquist 1968). If 1955 marked the first appearance of this type of legislative proposal, and if it was inspired by *Brown*, then a case can be made for *Brown*'s influence. However, 1955 was not the first time such amendments had been offered, supported, or taken seriously enough to kill bills. In 1943, for example, Senator Langer of North Dakota had introduced an amendment to the Educational Finance Act of 1943 which read: "there shall be no discrimination in the administration of the benefits and appropriations made under the respective provisions of this act, or in the state funds supplemented thereby on account of race, creed, or color" (quoted in Munger and Fenno 1962, 67–68). While requiring equalization of funding rather than prohibiting it where segregation ruled, the aim was to insure that if federal money was spent, black children would receive their proportionate share.[10]

The equalization strategy changed in 1946 when newly elected Representative Powell himself proposed an amendment to a bill providing for a school-lunch program. The amendment denied lunch program funds "to any state or school if . . . it makes any discrimination because of race, creed, color, or national origin of children" (*Cong. Rec.* 20 February 1946, 1495). While Powell maintained on the House floor that his amendment only required equalization, he describes it in his autobiography as the "first test" of what was later to be called the Powell Amendment (Powell 1971, 81). Other members, particularly Southerners, argued that it prohibited aid to states maintaining segregated schools by law. Making the point clear, Representative Bender of Ohio offered an amendment denying funds to "any State wherein there is maintained under the laws of such State separate schools for the education of children of different color" (*Cong. Rec.* 20 February 1946, 1495). In 1949, Senator Lodge of Massachusetts offered an amendment to a federal education bill prohibiting segregation in districts where federal aid was received. The amendment was supported by the NAACP (Munger and Fenno 1962, 69).[11]

10. The NAACP did not support the Langer Amendment on the ground that it would kill the bill and that federal money, even if unfairly distributed, was better than no money at all (Bendiner 1964, 45).

11. At both its 1950 and 1951 conventions, the NAACP went on record in support of federal aid to education "provided no such federal aid is given to states where racially segregated education is practiced" (quoted in Munger and Fenno 1962, 69).

Also in May of 1949, the NAACP voted to "withhold active support" from federal legislation in "housing, health or education which does not expressly forbid segregation" (quoted in Bernstein 1972, 293).

On the executive level, in 1947 President Truman's Committee on Civil Rights (PCCR) recommended the "conditioning by Congress of all federal grants-in-aid and other forms of federal assistance to public or private agencies for any purpose on the absence of discrimination and segregation based on race, color, creed, or national origin" (PCCR 1947, 166). President Truman, in 1951, without the aid of *Brown*, vetoed a bill containing a provision requiring schools on federal property to conform to local law (Berman 1970, 191). And, as late as April 1963, President Kennedy, when asked at a news conference if he supported such executive branch authority, replied in the negative, finding it "unwise to give the President of the United States that kind of power" (quoted in 110 *Cong. Rec.* 24 March 1964, 6046).

What this brief history demonstrates is that the idea of conditioning federal aid on non-discrimination or non-segregation predated *Brown* in both the legislative and executive branches. Most poignantly, Representative Powell wrote that the inspiration for his amendment came to him in a January 1945 speech in Charlotte, North Carolina. "It was then," he wrote, "that I decided to create the Powell Amendment, forbidding Federal funds to those who sought to preserve segregation, and wherever I thought there was an opportunity that it could be passed . . . there I would introduce it." Nine years before *Brown*, as Powell "thought and prayed, the words came: 'No funds under this Act shall be made available to or paid to any State or school' " (Powell 1971, 81). Thus, it is hard to make a case that *Brown* provided the impetus for Title VI.

It is worth pausing here for a moment to ask what, if not Court action, played a major role in producing congressional and presidential support for civil rights? While chapter 5 is entirely devoted to this question, one key point merits presentation here. The point is that civil rights action, especially in the 1960s, was based in large part on the elite belief that, unless there was federal action on civil rights, mass bloodshed would occur. The avoidance of violence was the linchpin of the Kennedy administration's civil rights program (Navasky 1977). In terms of the 1965 Voting Rights Act, the violence at Selma was crucial in insuring quick passage of a strong bill (Garrow 1978). And in terms of the 1964 Civil Rights Act, Berman, concluding his study of the bill's passage, writes: "First President Kennedy and then President Johnson, as well as the bipartisan leadership in Congress, came to the conclusion that only a strong civil rights bill could possibly prevent widespread bloodshed and utter catastrophe for the nation" (Berman 1966, 139; Graham 1990, 142). The fear of violence, not the inspiration of Court action, was most clearly a major impetus for federal action.

Sponsorship of Civil Rights Legislation

Another potential indicator of Court influence over Congress and the president is sponsorship of civil rights legislation. If *Brown* influenced the other branches, one might reasonably expect to see an increase over time in the number of civil rights bills introduced and in the number of sponsors of civil rights bills. On the surface, the enactment of civil rights bills in 1957, 1960, and 1964 provides evidence for such influence. However, as I suggested above, the introduction and enactment of these bills was based on factors other than Court decisions. Further, there was no increase in the sponsorship of substantive, enforceable equal-opportunity bills. Burstein and MacLeod have identified all such bills introduced, starting in 1941, and counted the number of sponsors. The number grows through the 1940s, reaching thirty-four in the years 1951–52. However, the number of sponsors then drops throughout the 1950s, falling to twenty in 1959–60, before rising to a peak in 1963–64 (Burstein and MacLeod 1979, 27). This pattern, with the number of sponsors actually dropping in the years immediately following *Brown*, does not show evidence of the Court's extra-judicial effects. Rather, it suggests a lessening concern with civil rights.[12]

Time

A final area worth exploring is the passage of time. If Congress and the president had acted immediately after the Court acted, it would seem reasonable to credit the Court with influence. On the other had, the longer the time period between the two acts, the more tenuous the link. Clearly there is a continuum, with a finding of influence more reasonable when the subsequent action is close in time, less reasonable when many years have passed, and somewhat fuzzy in between. But characterizing the passage of time, of course, depends on the circumstances. Turning to the evidence, congressional and executive action was long in coming after Court decisions. In the field of elementary and secondary education, it was a full decade after *Brown* before Congress and the executive branch acted in a forceful manner. With higher education, it was at least a decade and a half from the graduate and professional school cases of the late 1940s until action was taken. In voting, there was more than a decade between the last Texas Primary Case and the 1965 Voting Rights Act. And in housing, *Shelley* v. *Kraemer* preceded the 1968 Fair Housing Act by twenty years. These large time-gaps left opportunities for intervening groups, institutions, and events to exercise influence. While I will have more to say about these intervening factors shortly, they did not gain much publicity until the 1960s, six full years after *Brown*.

One must be cautious in interpreting this data. Taken on their own, the

---

12. The reader should note, too, that between 1937 and the introduction of the 1957 act, the House had passed civil rights bills eight times (Anderson 1964, 47).

time intervals are hard to characterize. Do they represent too long a period to credit the Court with influence or, given the nation's normally glacial response to change, do they illustrate great alacrity? While the characterization is perhaps impossible to make in the abstract, the time intervals can be characterized in the context of the other possible indicators of indirect effects. Given the lack of clear attribution, the lack of changes in legislative initiative, the special role of violence, and the other non-Court related factors, the evidence suggests that the time intervals can be fairly characterized as too long to give the Court much credit. The time concern does not appear to provide strong evidence for the indirect-effects thesis.

In sum, in a number of appropriate places where the Supreme Court would be expected to affect elites, evidence of the effect does not exist. In the areas of clear attribution, legislative action, and time, evidence of the effect on elites is not apparent. I turn now to examine the evidence for the indirect effect on white Americans in general, keeping in mind the possibility that the Court might work its effects on elites through the larger population.

Whites

The extra-judicial-effects thesis reaches white Americans as well as elites. The Dynamic Court view here is that the Supreme Court "pricked the conscience" (Miller 1970, 281) of white America by pointing out both its constitutional duty and its shortcomings. "Except for *Brown*," Aryeh Neier contends, white Americans "would not have known about the plight of blacks under segregation" (Neier 1982, 239). The Supreme Court's contribution to civil rights should be seen as a two-step process: the successful prodding of Americans to change their racial attitudes, resulting in mounting pressures on elites to act.[13] There are a number of places where evidence of this claim should be found.

Public Opinion—General

The extra-judicial-effects thesis of the Dynamic Court claim views courts as playing an important role in alerting Americans to social and political grievances. According to one defender of the claim, "without the dramatic intervention of so dignified an institution as a court, which puts its own prestige and authority on the line, most middle-class Americans would not be informed about such grievances" (Neier 1982, 239). For this claim to hold, in order for courts to affect behavior, directly or indirectly, people must be aware of what the courts do. While this does not seem an onerous responsibility, the Constrained Court view claims that most Americans have little knowledge about U.S. courts and pay little attention to them. This holds true

13. Kingdon argues that "swings in national mood" are an important indicator to elites to give attention to previously low priority items (Kingdon 1984, 207, 153).

even for the Supreme Court, the most visible and important federal court. There is both general and specific evidence to support this claim.

In general, surveys have shown that only about 40 percent of the American public, at best, follows Supreme Court actions, as measured by survey respondents having either read or heard something about the Court (Goldman and Jahnige 1976, 145; Daniels 1973; Kessel 1966). In 1966, for example, nearly 40 percent of the American public could not identify Earl Warren, despite a decade of Court activism in which the Chief Justice was both loudly praised and vilified (Adamany 1973, 808).[14] Also in 1966, despite important Supreme Court decisions on race, religion, criminal justice, and voting rights, 46 percent of a nationwide sample could not recall *anything at all* that the Court had recently done (Murphy et al. 1973, 53). And when prompted with a list of eight "decisions," four of which the Court had recently made and four of which it had never made, and asked to identify which, if any, the Court had made, only 15 percent of a 1966 sample made four or more correct choices (survey cited in Dolbeare 1967, 199–201).

Among Americans who have some awareness of what the Court does, there is little evidence that Court decisions legitimate action. That is, people aware of what the Court does may disagree with it. In fact, the more knowledgeable a person is about the Supreme Court, the more likely he or she is to disagree with it. In reviewing the literature, Adamany writes of the "Court's *incapacity* to legitimize governmental action" (Adamany 1973, 807). Evidence for this conclusion comes from the work of Murphy and Tanenhaus, who found that only 13 percent of the American public has the knowledge and beliefs about the Court necessary for it to legitimate action (Murphy and Tanenhaus 1968a). This includes the belief that the Court is a proper, impartial, and competent interpreter of the Constitution. This means that the potential pool of people who could be spurred into supportive action by a Supreme Court decision is small. The point is that although law may be a powerful legitimating force in American society, courts are weak legitimaters. Generally, then, the social science literature suggests that it would be most unlikely that the courts lit the fire under the civil rights movement.

A possible way in which this general lack of knowledge and barrier to Court effectiveness could be overcome is through heightened press coverage. Winter found that during the years 1948–76 the public's concern over civil rights was more strongly correlated with the amount of press coverage given to the issue than with any other issue he studied, including foreign affairs, the economy, social control, and concerns with the efficiency and integrity of government (Winter 1981, 9). Similarly, Winter and Eyal, focusing on the 1954–76 period, found "evidence of a strong agenda-setting effect" for the media with civil rights (Winter and Eyal 1981, 381). Thus, despite the general

14. Eight percent more Americans correctly identified Charles de Gaulle than the Chief Justice.

findings of the literature, the Supreme Court could have influenced white Americans through the press. Evidence here is important for the thesis, since, as Neier claims, "white Americans discovered black Americans through *Brown*" (Neier 1982, 12). The trouble with this line of reasoning, of course, is that there is no evidence that Supreme Court decisions increased press coverage of civil rights. The point has already been made (see table 4.1 and figure 4.1).

*Public Opinion—*Brown *and Civil Rights*

Another place to look for evidence is responses to survey questions about civil rights in general and support for *Brown* in particular. Surprisingly, and unfortunately, there appear to be no polls addressing knowledge of *Brown*. Two reasons probably explain this. First, until recent decades there was a "tendency" by pollsters to overlook the "race problem" when civil rights issues have been "out of the public eye." Thus, coverage was spotty. Second, it probably never occurred to pollsters, all of whom had presumably heard of *Brown*, to ask how many Americans had too. They probably assumed that all had! (Erskine 1962, 137).

There are, however, polls charting the reaction to *Brown* by Southerners over time (Gallup 1972). In July 1954, just a few months after the decision, 24 percent of *all* Southerners approved of the decision and of integrated schools while 71 percent disapproved. Nearly seven years later, in June 1961, the numbers were virtually identical, with 24 percent approving and 69 percent disapproving. Among white Southerners, in February 1956, only 16 percent approved. When white Southerners were asked in July 1954 whether they would object to sending their children to integrated schools, only 15 percent responded that they would not object. By 1959, support for desegregation actually dropped, with only 8 percent of white Southerners responding that they would not object (AIPO poll in Erskine 1962, 140, 141). Given the lack of positive change over time, it is entirely possible that supportive respondents were supportive before the Court acted. If not, then at most the Court influenced about one-quarter of all Southerners, and about one-sixth of white Southerners. But since there was at least some support for desegregated schools in the South before the Court acted, it seems fair to assume that the actual influence was less.

If there is little evidence that *Brown* changed opinions about school desegregation in the South, perhaps it helped change white opinions more generally. Indeed, a main argument for the indirect-effects thesis is that Court action pricked the conscience of white America and changed racial attitudes, paving the way for the 1964 Civil Rights Act (Wiebe 1979, 153). This is a plausible argument for two reasons. First, Page and Shapiro (1982, 1983) found "considerable congruence between changes in preferences and in policies" (Page and Shapiro 1983, 175). Looking at 357 instances of significant change in the policy preferences of Americans from 1935 to 1979, they found that "when there is an opinion change of 20 percentage points or more, policy change is congruent an overwhelming 90 percent of the time" (Page and Shapiro 1983, 180). Second, it is clear that white Americans underwent a major change of attitude between the early years of the Second World War and the passage of the 1964 act. For example, in 1942 the National Opinion Research Center (NORC) found that a majority of Americans favored segregated transportation (51 percent), restaurants (69 percent), and neighborhoods (84 percent). By 1964, however, two nationwide Gallup polls found that six out of every ten Americans approved of the 1964 Civil Rights Act (Free and Cantril 1967, 121, 122). Is there evidence that this change was the effect of Court action?

Ideally, to answer this question, one would look to time-series data on white opinions about civil rights. Support for the Court's influence would be found if there was a sharp increase in supportive attitudes after *Brown* or if the rate of change of supportive attitudes increased. Unfortunately, the data are not ideal. Questions were not asked regularly and the pre-1954 data are sketchy. That being said, throughout the period from the beginning of the Second World War to the passage of the 1964 act, whites became increasingly supportive of civil rights. Writing in 1956, Hyman and Sheatsley found that the changes in attitude were "solidly based" and "not easily accelerated nor easily reversed" (Hyman and Sheatsley 1956, 39). Reviewing the available data in 1964, they noted the "unbroken trend of the past twenty years" (Hyman and Sheatsley 1964, 23). Further, they found that the changes were not due to any specific event, such as Kennedy's assassination, or a Supreme Court decision. They found that changes in national opinion "represent long-term trends that are not easily modified by specific—even by highly dramatic—events" (Hyman and Sheatsley 1964, 17).

These findings are also supported by various bits of public opinion data. One involves the views whites have of the intelligence of blacks. Here, the belief that blacks are as intelligent and educable as whites has been steadily increasing with no appreciable jump following *Brown* (Erskine 1962, 138; Hyman and Sheatsley 1956, 35; 1964, 20). In the field of job discrimination, by 1947 over 50 percent of Americans felt that Negroes should have an "equal chance" with whites in employment (NORC poll in Strunk 1947, 657). In 1950, 48 percent of Americans thought the federal government should go "all the way" or "part" of the way in requiring employers to hire non-discriminatorily as opposed to 41 percent who thought no action should be taken (AIPO poll in Strunk 1950, 175). These findings suggest that there was a steady trend in changing white opinion. They provide no evidence for the claim that the Court pricked the conscience of white Americans or in some way influenced their views.

Another way of examining the indirect-effects claim on white Americans is to look at how the sensitivity of Americans to civil rights changed generally. According to one proponent of the claim, the "*Brown* decision was central to eliciting the moral outrage that both blacks and whites were to feel and express about segregation" (Levin 1979, 110). If the Court served this role, it would necessarily have increased awareness of the plight of blacks. The evidence, however, shows no sign of such an increase. Survey questions as to whether most blacks were being treated fairly resulted in affirmative responses of 66 percent in 1944, 66 percent in 1946, and 69 percent in 1956 (Hyman and Sheatsley 1956, 39). The variation of 3 percent is virtually meaningless. By 1963, when Gallup asked if any group in America was being treated unfairly, 80 percent said no. Only 5 percent of the sample named "the Negroes" as being unfairly treated while 4 percent named "the whites" (Gallup 1972, 3: 1825). This result, and the change over time, hardly shows an America whose conscience is aroused.

This lack of sensitivity to the plight of blacks can also be seen in views about attempts by blacks to exercise their rights as American citizens. In May 1961, of those respondents (63 percent) who had read or heard something about the freedom rides, nearly two-thirds (64 percent) disapproved while only 24 percent approved. When asked if civil rights demonstrations such as "sit-ins" or "freedom buses" would "hurt or help" the civil rights movement, over half the respondents opined that they would hurt (70 percent of Southerners) (Gallup 1972, 3: 1723, 1724). Former President Harry Truman, who desegregated the army, addressed an NAACP rally, issued a far-reaching civil rights report, and generally did more than any preceding president for civil rights, expressed this lack of sensitivity: "Northerners who go South as Freedom Riders are meddlesome intruders [who] should stay at home and attend to their own business" (quoted in Barnes 1983, 168). Most poignantly, in December 1958, when Gallup asked its usual question about the most admired men in the world, Governor Orval Faubus of Arkansas, who had repeatedly defied court orders a year earlier to prevent the desegregation of Central High School in Little Rock, was among the ten most frequently mentioned (Gallup 1972, 2: 1548). If the Court pricked the conscience of white Americans, the sensitivity disappeared quickly.

Similarly, for years Gallup has been asking its survey respondents their opinion of "the most important problem facing this country today." Figure 4.2 presents results from many of these questions from August 1947 to December 1965. Any response touching on an area of civil rights was counted. There was no change after *Brown*. A jump is recorded in September of 1956. No Court action was going on at the time but the Montgomery bus boycott was in full swing and 600 National Guardsmen patrolled the streets of Clinton, Tennessee, to quell violence over school desegregation. September 1957 shows 10 percent listing civil rights as the most important problem, in response, no doubt, to the crisis at Little Rock. But then the percentage drops,

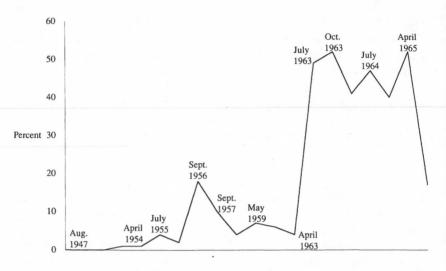

Time (Not to Scale)

Figure 4.2. The Most Important Problem Facing This Country Today: Civil Rights Responses

and remains low, until the explosion in the summer of 1963. Needless to say, the spring and summer of 1963 saw the bloody civil rights protest marches in Birmingham, Alabama, the march on Washington, and the introduction of what became the 1964 Civil Rights Act. And civil rights remained on people's minds through the next two years as Americans marched and died throughout the country. Again, the evidence does not support the claim of the indirect-effects thesis that Court action stirred the conscience of white America.

The jump in the percentage of Americans naming civil rights as the most important problem facing America is startling. While the percentage had stayed at 10 percent or below from 1947 until 1963 (1956 excepted), it remained above 30 percent through the spring of 1965. It is most unlikely that this dramatic change was a result of Court action nearly a decade earlier. More likely, it resulted from the mass media's portrayal of the violence unleashed against peaceful protesters. For example, Garrow (1978) has chronicled the massive and supportive white response to the events in Selma that insured the quick passage of a strong voting-rights bill. One hundred and twenty-two Members of Congress gave 199 speeches supportive of the bill. Sympathy marches were held in Boston, Chicago, Detroit (where Governor Romney and Mayor Cavanaugh led a march of 10,000), and Los Angeles, among other cities. President Johnson, speaking to Congress and an estimated 70 million viewers on all three television networks, gave the first personally delivered special presidential message on domestic legislation in nineteen years. Speaking of the black protester, the President said: "His actions and protests, his courage to risk safety and even to risk his life, have awakened the conscience of this nation" (quoted in Garrow 1978, 107). As will be discussed shortly, there was a virtual explosion of protest activity in the early 1960s, particularly in 1963. Thus, there does not appear to be evidence supporting the claim that the massive change in the opinions of white Americans about civil rights was an effect of Court action. As Burke Marshall, head of the Justice Department's Civil Rights Division put it, "the Negro and his problems were still pretty much invisible to the country . . . until mass demonstrations of the Birmingham type" (quoted in Fairclough 1987, 135).

In sum, in several areas where the Supreme Court would be expected to influence white Americans, evidence of the effect has not been found. Most Americans neither follow Supreme Court decisions nor understand the Court's constitutional role. It is not surprising, then, that change in public opinion appears to be oblivious to the Court. Again, the extra-judicial-effects thesis lacks evidence.

Blacks

The Dynamic Court view's indirect-effects thesis makes claims about the effect of the Supreme Court on black Americans. Here, a plausible claim is that *Brown* was the spark that ignited the black revolution. By recognizing and legitimizing black grievances, the public pronouncement by the Court provided blacks with a new image and encouraged them to act.[15] *Brown* "begot," one legal scholar tells us, "a union of the mightiest and lowliest in America, a mystical, passionate union bound by the pained depths of the black man's cry for justice and the moral authority, unique to the Court, to see that justice realized" (Wilkinson 1979, 5). Thus, *Brown* may have fundamentally re-oriented the views of black Americans by providing hope that the federal government, if made aware of their plight, would help. Black action, in turn, could have changed white opinions and led to elite action and civil rights. If this is the case, then there are a number of places where evidence should be found.

For *Brown* to have played this role, blacks must have known about the decision and approved both of its holdings and of the Court's constitutional role. As discussed earlier, there is little evidence that Americans, black or white, credit the Court with a legitimizing role. Further, it is not entirely clear that knowledge of *Brown* was widespread. For example, during the school desegregation crisis in Clinton, Tennessee, in the fall of 1956, a team of social scientists interviewing people found that "a number" had "never heard of the U.S. Supreme Court decision against segregation" (Robinson 1957, 183).

15. This assumption is virtually universal among lawyers and legal scholars, and representative quotations can be found throughout this and earlier chapters. In addition, see Choper (1980, 92–93); Zanden (1963, 545).

Eldridge Cleaver entered prison one month after the decision without "even the vaguest idea" that *Brown* was anything out of the ordinary (Cleaver 1968, 3). A decade after *Brown*, a volunteer teaching in a Mississippi Freedom School during the summer of 1964 wrote in a letter: "[m]y students are from 13 to 17 years old, and not one of them had heard about the Supreme Court decision of 1954 . . . they are surprised to hear that the law is on their side" (quoted in Sutherland 1965, 93).

Part of the reason for this lack of knowledge is clearly Americans' general ignorance of Supreme Court decisions. Part also is due to poor newspaper coverage, as has been shown. Further, a 1961 survey of Southern blacks found that nearly one-third did not read newspapers or watch TV regularly, over half did not read any magazines regularly, and over 20 percent did not even listen to the radio regularly (Matthews and Prothro 1966, 249). But another possibility is that many blacks did not approve of the decision. In November 1955, a special Gallup poll found that barely half of Southern blacks (53 percent) approved of *Brown* (Gallup 1972, 2: 1402). Although such poll data should be approached cautiously,[16] a poll taken just a few weeks later found that 82 percent of Southern blacks approved of an Interstate Commerce Commission ruling prohibiting segregation in transportation (Gallup 1972, 2: 1402). The large difference between the two approval percentages is striking. Knowledge of, and support for, *Brown* do not appear to have been high.

Brown was not greeted with an outpouring of public support by blacks. Overall, the reaction within the black community to *Brown* was "muted" (Kluger 1976, 710). After *Brown*, "there were no street celebrations in Negro communities" (Branch 1988, 112), and no "grand celebrations" (Williams 1988, 351). Ralph Abernathy understood the lack of public response this way: "most blacks in the Deep South states looked with curiosity at what was going on in the high courts, shrugged their shoulders, and went back to their day-to-day lives. . . . After all, they had waited a lifetime and seen no change at all" (Abernathy 1989, 114). The fact that it was the Supreme Court that had declared an end to segregation made little difference for, as Lawson puts it, blacks were "long accustomed to having favorable court rulings circumvented" (Lawson 1976, 49). Indeed, it was Charles Houston, one of the grand architects of the NAACP's successful litigation strategy, who had remarked years before that "nobody needs to explain to a Negro the difference between the law in books and the law in action" (quoted in Williams 1988, 35). And many Southern blacks had their minds on other matters such as the murder of Emmett Till in 1955 which "shook the foundations of Mississippi" (Myrlie Evers in Hampton and Fayer 1990, 6) and which "without question . . . moved black America in a way the Supreme Court ruling on school desegre-

16. Given the political, social, and economic oppression under which Southern blacks lived, poll results may not reflect honest opinions.

gation could not match" (Williams 1988, 44). This is not an auspicious beginning for a Court-inspired revolution.

Another possible explanation for the generally moderate response may lie with the black press. Its coverage of the cases preceding *Brown* showed "understandable caution" and was sometimes "optimistic, though not ecstatic" (Weaver and Page 1982, 15, 21, 27). After *Brown*, responses varied. In some states, like Texas, the decision was strongly supported (Smallwood 1983). In others, however, the story was different. By 1954, Mississippi had only five black papers, four of which were quite conservative. The *Jackson Advocate*, for example, did not support the efforts of any civil rights organization, including the NAACP. In 1957, it attacked the reform movement in education since *Brown*, and the efforts of the NAACP, as "the greatest mistake in the entire history of the struggles of the American Negro." In 1959 the paper attacked the Montgomery bus boycott for "making matters worse for the masses of Montgomery Negroes" (Thompson 1983, 190, 190–91). While Mississippi is undoubtedly an extreme case, a book-length compilation of studies of the black press in the eleven Southern states and Missouri had only six references to *Brown* (Suggs 1983). Thus, it is possible that the black press did not fill in where the white press failed.

The evidence plainly indicates that civil rights marches and demonstrations affected both white Americans and elites and provided a major impetus for civil rights legislation. A nationwide Harris survey of black Americans revealed their belief that it was the sit-ins, pickets, and marches, not Court action, that "awakened white America" and served as the "torch that set the smoldering civil-rights battle ablaze" (Brink and Harris 1963, 66).[17] Surely, the Dynamic Court view posits that the "historic" action of the Court encouraged and spurred blacks to act. As Wilkinson puts it, "the Court sired the movement, succored it through the early years, [and] encouraged its first taking wing" (Wilkinson 1979, 3). If this were the case, if, in the words of civil rights litigator Jack Greenberg, the direct-action campaign would not have developed "without the legal victories that we'd won earlier" ("Someone" 1975, 111), then there are a number of places where evidence of this effect should be seen.

One such place is the demonstrations. That is, if *Brown* sparked the movement, one would expect to see an increase in the number of demonstrations shortly after the decision. Table 4.2 and figure 4.3 present the data. It can be seen that there is almost no difference in the number of civil rights demonstrations in the years 1953, 1954, and 1955. There was a large jump in 1956, due to Montgomery. But then the numbers drop. For example, 1959 saw fewer civil rights demonstrations than in four of the years of the 1940s! And the number of demonstrations skyrocketed in the 1960s, six or more

---

17. But it should also be noted that a full year after the sit-ins started, nearly one of every six Southern blacks had never heard of them (Matthews and Prothro 1966, 438).

Table 4.2   Civil Rights Demonstrations, 1940–1965

Year	No. of Demonstrations	Year	No. of Demonstrations
1940	5	1953	6
1941	2	1954	10
1942	6	1955	15
1943	15	1956	173
1944	9	1957	13
1945	5	1958	35
1946	19	1959	10
1947	23	1960	414
1948	27	1961	282
1949	7	1962	155
1950	3	1963	685
1951	6	1964	335
1952	1	1965	443

SOURCE: *New York Times* as compiled by Burstein (1979).

NOTE: Demonstration is defined as a "public, manifestly political action by at least five people on behalf of the rights of racial minorities" (Burstein 1979, 168).

years after *Brown*. This pattern does not suggest that the Court played a major role. The time period is too long and the 1960s increases too startling to credit the Court with a meaningful effect.

The Montgomery Bus Boycott

The 1956 Montgomery bus boycott created worldwide attention. Coming just a few years after *Brown*, it is quite plausible that it was sparked by the Court. If this were the case, one might trace the indirect effect of *Brown* to Montgomery to the demonstrations of the 1960s to white opinion to elite action in 1964 and 1965. The problem is that there does not appear to be evidence even for this tortuous causal chain. The immediate crisis in Montgomery was brought about by the arrest, in December 1955, of Mrs. Rosa Parks, a black woman, for refusing to give up her seat to a white person and move to the back of a segregated city bus.[18] Parks was the fourth black woman to be arrested in 1955 for such a refusal (Lewis 1970, 48).[19] It is unclear why

18. Mrs. Parks, who was not feeling well that day, had not planned to be arrested. However, she had been involved in civil rights activities as an active member of the local NAACP since 1943 and as an occasional officer of the organization. Perhaps more important, in July 1955, she spent two weeks at an interracial conference at the Highlander Folk School in Tennessee (Garrow 1986, 11–13).

19. A March 1955 episode involved a fifteen year-old high school student. However, no protest was organized because of the circumstances: the young women was charged with resisting arrest and was unmarried and pregnant (Garrow 1986, 15).

Figure 4.3. Civil Rights Demonstrations, 1940–1965

this particular incident sparked the boycott, although Parks was fairly well-known and commanded respect in the black community. Because the Montgomery bus boycott is mentioned by so many civil rights activists, and because it launched both Dr. King's and Reverend Abernathy's civil rights careers, it is worth examining in greater detail.

In the 1940s and early 1950s there were a number of black civil rights organizations in Montgomery. One of them, the Women's Political Council (WPC), became the "most militant and uncompromising organ of the black community" (Thornton 1980, 173–74).[20] Its president, Jo Ann Robinson, held particularly strong feelings about bus segregation, having suffered a humiliating experience around Christmas, 1949, on her way to the Montgomery airport to fly North for the holiday (Robinson 1987, 15–16). The WPC soon began to focus on bus segregation and, in 1953, received thirty complaints about it (Robinson 1987, 30). Thus, since the early 1950s the WPC had targeted bus segregation. And, as Robinson writes, the "idea [of a bus boycott] itself had been entertained for years" (Robinson 1987, 20; Garrow 1986, 14–16).

In 1953, at the same time as the WPC was preparing to launch a bus boycott, Montgomery elected a racial moderate, Dave Birmingham, to the three-member City Commission. Birmingham's election encouraged black groups to approach the city with their grievances, and Robinson led a WPC delegation to lodge complaints with the city at the end of 1953 and again in the spring of 1954. At the latter meeting, the WPC was joined by a number of other black groups, including "a large group representing black trade union locals." The meeting was evidently quite stormy, for Mayor Gayle subsequently testified that several days later an angry Mrs. Robinson called him and said "they would just show me, they were going in the front door and sitting wherever they pleased" (Thornton 1980, 174, 176–78).

One of the ways in which the WPC had prepared for a boycott was through the preparation of a notice calling on the black community to act and the planning of distribution routes. "On paper, the WPC had already planned for fifty thousand notices calling people to boycott the buses; only the specifics of time and place had to be added" (Robinson 1987, 39). The March 1955 arrest of a student for violating the bus-segregation law was at first seen as providing an opportunity to act, but her personal circumstances mitigated against action. Her conviction, however, was "a bombshell" and following it, "other complaints poured in" to the WPC (Robinson 1987, 42, 43). The arrest of Rosa Parks provided the opportunity the WPC was waiting for, and Robinson and the WPC decided to stage a boycott the day of the Parks trial. Relying on their preparations, and acting on their own, they mimeographed notices announcing a one-day boycott and blanketed black Montgomery with them. By the time of the December 2 meeting of Montgomery's black leadership called by E. D. Nixon to discuss what to do, the forty or so assembled leaders "found themselves faced with a *fait accompli*" (Thornton 1980, 197). Thus, the background of the bus boycott points to many factors, but not to *Brown*.[21]

20. Thornton's article, based in part on extensive interviewing, is by far the most detailed and comprehensive examination of the factors leading to the boycott. See also Garrow (1985), particularly his long note on further reading at 26–27.

21. It is the case that Robinson (1987, viii) wrote a letter to Mayor Gayle four days after the *Brown* decision threatening a boycott, and that King mentioned *Brown* in his December 5

There is another piece of evidence, as well, that suggests that *Brown* was not influential; the nature of the boycotters' initial demands. Despite the efforts of the WPC, and the evident anger of the black community, initially the boycotters did *not* demand an end to bus segregation (Abernathy 1989, 154). Rather, the principal demand called for modified seating by race, with blacks starting at the back and whites at the front. As late as April 1956 King was still willing to settle on these terms (Fairclough 1987, 20).[22] As Thornton describes it, the boycotters were not trying to overturn the segregation law, as *Brown* might have inspired them to do. Instead, they "initially conceived their movement not so much as a direct action against bus segregation itself as rather a search for a means to manipulate the political process" (Thornton 1980, 231). This led the NAACP to withhold support on the grounds that the demands were too "mild" (Wilkins 1984, 228). As Abernathy puts it, "at first we regarded the Montgomery bus boycott as an interruption of our plans rather than as the beginning of their fulfillment" (Abernathy 1989, 169). Again, this suggests that a host of local factors provided the inspiration for the boycott.

Finally, four additional parts of the historical context suggest that *Brown* had little influence. First, the idea of a bus boycott was not new, having been used successfully by blacks in Baton Rouge, Louisiana, during the summer of 1953. Dr. Martin Luther King, Jr., the leader of the Montgomery bus boycott, knew the leader of that boycott, T. J. Jemison, from college days, and spoke with him early in the boycott (Branch 1988, 145). From the Baton Rouge boycott, Abernathy notes, Montgomery's blacks took "considerable inspiration" (Abernathy 1989, 178; Garrow 1986, 26–27).[23] Second, Montgomery's blacks "did know that other cities in the Deep South, notably Mobile and Atlanta, had already conceded the 'first come, first served' principle" (Fairclough 1987, 12). Third, in November 1955, Representative Adam Clayton Powell visited Montgomery and suggested that blacks use their economic power to force change. Characteristically, the flamboyant Powell took credit for instigating the bus boycott (Thornton 1980, 194).[24] Finally, King specifically addressed the influence of *Brown* on the boycott. It was clear, he said, that *Brown* "cannot explain why it happened in Montgomery" and that the

---

speech at the first mass meeting of the boycotters (Garrow 1986, 15) and occasionally in his writing on Montgomery (King 1958, 64, 191). However, when placed in context, these actions provide evidence, at best, of only a small additive influence for *Brown*.

22. Fairclough also points to a similar initial reticence to demand an end to segregation in the Tallahassee, Florida, bus boycott of 1956 (Fairclough 1987, 20).

23. Morris (1984, x) argues that the Montgomery bus boycott was "partly inspired by the Baton Rouge effort and to some extent modeled after it." For the story of the Baton Rouge boycott, see Morris (1984, chap. 2).

24. Powell (1971, 124–25) suggests that it was this speech and a meeting with a group of local black leaders including Nixon, King, and Parks that was decisive. In his visit, just three weeks before Parks acted, he outlined various direct-action nonviolent protests that he had led in New York.

"crisis was not produced by . . . even the Supreme Court" (King 1958, 64, 191–92).[25] Although Montgomery may have inspired blacks, there does not appear to be much evidence that the Court inspired Montgomery.[26]

Little Rock and Frustration

After Montgomery, and the 1956 presidential election, the next major civil rights event to make the news was the Little Rock crisis of September 1957. United States Army troops were sent to Little Rock to control violence and allow nine black children to attend the previously segregated Little Rock Central High School pursuant to a court order. Could it be that the Little Rock crisis and the reaction of the federal government made a difference? That is, perhaps Little Rock suggested to blacks that the federal government would act to help. While this is plausible, equally plausible is the notion that Little Rock suggested how hard it would be to achieve desegregation. It took the U.S. Army's continuing presence to ensure the safety of nine children. And, as the discussion below suggests, Little Rock is not mentioned as a source of inspiration by activists and students of the movement.

A related possibility is that the failure of *Brown* to produce change created a high level of frustration that led to black activism. Stuart Scheingold suggests that "it was not the decisions themselves but the political mobilization spawned by *resistance* to the decisions that brought positive results" (Scheingold 1989, 80). Almost invariably throughout the South, wherever desegregation was tried, it was met with white resistance. Perhaps blacks grew increasingly frustrated by the lack of change and were thus spurred to action. While this again is plausible, it is unlikely to have played more than a minor role, for three reasons. First, frustration was not something new to the black community. The wrongs of segregation had been apparent for a long time. What was new was that blacks were acting to end it. Boycotts in Baton Rouge and Montgomery, demonstrated that blacks, acting on their own, could improve their lives. It did not take *Brown* for blacks to understand that separate but equal was inherently unequal. Second, *Brown* had little meaning for the students who made up the movement. "To these young people," Howard

25. At a news conference in January 1956, King explained the boycott as "part of a world-wide movement. Look at just about any place in the world and the exploited people are rising against their exploiters. This seems to be the outstanding characteristic of our generation" (quoted in Garrow 1986, 54).

26. Morris (1984, 25) credits the Baton Rouge boycott with more importance than the Court. However, the Supreme Court may have played a vital role in the final victory by allowing the city a way out of a boycott that was costly and damaging. In *Gayle* v. *Browder* (1956), the Supreme Court upheld a lower-court decision prohibiting enforcement of Montgomery's bus segregation law. As Condition IV suggests, the Court's decision may have allowed the city to end segregation without "giving in" to the boycotters' demands. On the other hand, without the strength of the boycott, there would have been little pressure on Montgomery to comply. Indeed, as the discussion in chapter 2 showed, court decisions alone were ineffective in ending segregation in transportation.

Zinn wrote in his 1964 study of the Student Non-Violent Coordinating Committee (SNCC), "the Supreme Court decision of 1954 was a childhood memory" only "dimly remembered" (Zinn 1964, 18). This point is elaborated further below. Third, it is not often the case that violence and resistance spur people to action. Rather, it tends to deter them. It seems more plausible to suggest that it was the positive actions of black demonstrators that provided the inspiration. This point will be strengthened in the discussion of the motivations of the activists. Thus, while black Americans were certainly frustrated by the lack of equality, it does not seem likely that the Court added very much to the level of frustration.

Sit-Ins and Demonstrations

Another possible way in which *Brown* may have sparked change is through providing the inspiration for the sit-in movement and the demonstrations of the 1960s. The decision might have given blacks new hope that the federal government would work to end discrimination. It might have confirmed their own belief in the unfairness of segregation. Or it might have suggested that white America was changing. In addition, it could have served as a resource or tool for activists, legitimating their own beliefs in the evils of segregation and justifying, in a constitutional manner, their demands for justice. If this were the case, one might plausibly expect to find participants in, and students of the demonstrations talking and writing about the Court's decision as one reason for their actions. A review of biographies, autobiographies, and scholarly studies of the civil rights movement provides the evidence for assessing the claim.

Dr. Martin Luther King, Jr.

One possible way in which *Brown* might have ignited the civil rights movement is by inspiring Dr. King. His ringing denouncements of segregation, his towering oratory, and his ability to inspire and move both blacks and whites appear to have played an indispensable role in creating pressure for government action (Garrow 1986). Was King motivated to act by the Court? From an examination of King's thinking, the answer appears to be no. King rooted his beliefs in Christian theology and Gandhian non-violence, not constitutional doctrine. His attitude to the Court, far from a source of inspiration, was one of strategic disfavor. "Whenever it is possible," he told reporters in early 1957, "we want to avoid court cases in this integration struggle" (quoted in Garrow 1986, 87). He rejected litigation as a major tool of struggle for a number of reasons. He wrote of blacks' lack of faith in it, of its "unsuitability" to the civil rights struggle, and of its "hampering progress to this day" (King 1963, 23, 157). Further, he complained that to "accumulate resources for legal actions imposes intolerable hardships on the already overburdened" (King 1963, 157). In addition to its expense, King saw the legal process as slow. Blacks, he warned, "must not get involved in legalism [and] needless fights in lower courts" because that is "exactly what the white man wants the Negro to do. Then he can draw out the fight" (quoted in Garrow 1986, 91). Perhaps most important, King believed that litigation was an elite strategy for change that did not involve ordinary people. He believed that when the NAACP was the principal civil rights organization, and court cases were relied on, "the ordinary Negro was involved [only] as a passive spectator" and "his energies were unemployed" (quoted in Morris 1984, 123). Montgomery was particularly poignant, he told the 1957 NAACP annual convention, because, in Garrow's paraphrase, it demonstrated that "rank-and-file blacks themselves could act to advance the race's goals, rather than relying exclusively on lawyers and litigation to win incremental legal gains" (Garrow 1986, 78). And, as he told the NAACP Convention on July 5, 1962, "only when the people themselves begin to act are rights on paper given life blood" (quoted in Branch 1988, 598). King's writings and actions do not provide evidence for the Dynamic Court view that he was inspired by the Court.

The Sit-Ins

The sit-in in Greensboro, North Carolina, in February 1960 started the sit-in movement of the 1960s. Organized by four black college students, it does not appear to have been Court-inspired. The four students, before the sit-in, used to meet for bull sessions where they read and discussed the works of Ralph Bunche, Frederick Douglass, W. E. B. Du Bois, Gandhi, Langston Hughes, and Toussaint L'Ouverture, among others. No mention of the Court or *Brown* is recorded (Chafe 1980, 113; Oppenheimer 1963, 57; Raines 1983, 79).[27] Recorded are repeated references to King and the Montgomery bus boycott (Chafe 1980, 113; Wolff 1970, 155). "Montgomery was like a catalyst," one of the four said, that "started a whole lot of things rolling" (quoted in Chafe 1980, 113). Other non-Court factors have often been cited by both the four participants and those trying to explain why the sit-ins occurred. Joseph McNeil, for example, was particulary angered by a December 1959 episode when he returned to Greensboro from New York and was refused food service at the Greensboro Trailways Bus Terminal (Chafe 1980, 114). In a 1973 interview for a TV special on the "Greensboro Four," McNeil recounted that incident, stating that "the impetus for action came from the 'outrage' he felt when he returned home from a trip North and had to reconfront separate facilities" (Ethridge 1973, 4). McNeil also worked in the college library with Eula Hudgens, who had participated in the 1947 Journey of Reconciliation, the Congress of Racial Equality's (CORE) first freedom ride. Hudgens "spoke frequently" with McNeil about her experience and was "not surprised when the young men acted" (Chafe 1980, 113–14). In addition, an eccentric white

27. Franklin McCain (in Raines 1983, 79) and Ezell Blair, Jr. (in Chafe 1980, 114), two of the four students, particularly stressed the importance of Gandhi.

businessman, Ralph Johns, had been encouraging black students since at least 1949 to test segregation at Woolworth's. One of those he encouraged was McNeil, and Johns helped the four plan their action.[28]

After Greensboro, the sit-ins spread quickly throughout the South. Within sixty days of Greensboro, sit-ins had spread to at least sixty-five Southern cities (SRC 1960b, 1).[29] For black students throughout the South, the inspiration was the action of other students, as well as Montgomery and King. Instead of looking to courts for inspiration and support, the demonstrators "appealed to a higher law" because they "weren't sure about the legality" of their actions.[30] When black students from Atlanta joined the sit-ins, they took out a full-page advertisement in Atlanta's newspapers listing their demands and defending their actions. Entitled "An Appeal For Human Rights," the detailed and lengthy list of grievances was supported by six separate justifications of the sit-ins. No mention of the Court, the Constitution, or *Brown* is found anywhere in the text ("An Appeal" 1960, 13). The six-year time interval between *Brown* and the sit-ins, the lack of attribution to the Court, the crediting of several non-Court factors, and the rapidity with which the movement spread, all suggest it was unlikely that *Brown* played much of a role.

The year 1960 was not the first time sit-ins had occurred for civil rights. As early as 1942 James Farmer had organized a CORE sit-in at the Jack Spratt coffee-house in Chicago (Farmer 1985, 106–8), and Howard University students sat-in at segregated Washington, D.C., restaurants in 1943 (Barnes 1983, 58). In the late 1950s, sit-ins had occurred in Wichita, Kansas (1958), Kansas City, Missouri (1958, 1959), Oklahoma City[31] and a few other Oklahoma cities (1958, 1959), and Miami, Florida (1959), with varying levels of success.[32] But the fact that the movement caught on only in 1960, six full years after *Brown*, does not offer much evidence for the indirect-effects thesis.

Why did the sit-ins work? Was it because white business owners, in the wake of *Brown*, saw the constitutional legitimacy of the protestors' claims? The evidence does not support this conclusion. In most places businesses rejected the demands and refused to alter their practices. Constitutional principle did not appear to motivate them. Rather, they tried to outlast the demonstrators. However, as the discussion in chapter 3 indicated, economics played a big role. Sit-ins and ensuing black boycotts took their toll. In Greensboro, for example, Wolff writes of the "tremendous economic pressure put

28. On the role of Ralph Johns, see Chafe (1980, 113); Meier and Rudwick (1973, 102); Wolff (1970, 17–29).

29. For other accounts of the early sit-ins, see Pollitt (1960); SRC (1960a).

30. Remarks of Julian Bond, University of Chicago, 10 January 1990. In 1960 Bond was a student leader of the Atlanta sit-ins.

31. For a short statement by an Oklahoma City sit-in demonstrator, see Posey (1961). Posey, who was "so impressed with Mr. King" (Posey 1961, 9), also mentions Montgomery and Gandhi, but not the Court or *Brown*.

32. For a description of these events, see SRC (1960b, i-xxv).

on the stores by the Negroes' boycott, along with the reticence of whites to trade there because of fear of trouble." The Woolworth's store where the sit-ins started registered a $200,000 drop in sales in 1960 (Wolff 1970, 173, 174). Economic pressure, not constitutional mandate, appears the best explanation for the success of the sit-ins.

The Freedom Ride

The evidence points to the same conclusion with the Freedom Ride, the courageous and electrifying 1961 bus journey organized by CORE through the Deep South. The Freedom Ride, patterned on CORE's 1947 Journey of Reconciliation, was designed to test desegregation in interstate transportation and facilities.[33] Thirteen "Freedom Riders" left Washington, D.C., on May 4, 1961, aboard Greyhound and Trailways buses with a public itinerary taking them through Virginia, North Carolina, South Carolina, Georgia, Alabama, Mississippi, and Louisiana. The well-known story includes severe beatings and the fire-bombing of a Greyhound bus outside of Anniston, Alabama (Farmer 1985, chaps. 17 and 18; Raines 1983, chap. 3; SRC 1961). Yet in the writings by participants and others about the ride there is virtually no mention of *Brown* or of the Court positively inspiring CORE's action. While the ride was in part organized as a reaction to the *Boynton* decision, CORE, as will be developed below, was committed to non-violent direct action and opposed to a legal strategy for change. The riders knew that Court decisions would have little effect. The purpose of the ride was to publicize the denial of rights, to galvanize blacks into action (the riders held rallies every evening), and to garner publicity. The black riders, with the exception of CORE national director James Farmer, were all under thirty and most were veterans of the sit-in movement, while the whites had peace/socialist backgrounds (Meier and Rudwick 1973, 136, 137). And when the original CORE riders were too badly beaten to go on, the ride was continued by students from SNCC. Indeed, the SRC understood the ride as "an extension of the sit-ins . . . sustained by the same enthusiasm and many of the same persons" (SRC 1961, 4). There is no evidence that civil rights litigation inspired this act of bravery.

Black Groups

The founding of SNCC, CORE, and the Southern Christian Leadership Conference (SCLC), the organizations that provided the leadership and the shock troops of the movement, could quite plausibly have been inspired by the Court. Although SNCC was not founded until six years after *Brown*, and CORE was not revitalized until 1961, it may have taken that long for the effect to be felt.

33. In *Morgan* v. *Virginia* (1946), the Supreme Court invalidated as to interstate passengers a Virginia law requiring segregated seating. In *Boynton* v. *Virginia* (1960), the Court also invalidated segregated facilities in interstate transportation.

The SCLC was founded in the winter of 1957. The moving force behind it was not the inspiration of *Brown* but an attempt to capitalize on the success of the Montgomery bus boycott. Four important actors in SCLC's founding made this clear. For Bayard Rustin, who drafted the working papers for the first meeting, the idea was to create "a sustaining mechanism that could translate what we had learned during the bus boycott into a broad strategy of protest in the South" (quoted in Garrow 1986, 85). Stanley Levison, a confidant of King's who collaborated with Rustin, wanted to create an organization "to reproduce that [the Montgomery] pattern of mass action, underscore mass, in other cities and communities" (quoted in Fairclough 1987, 31). And Ella Baker, whose role in creating SNCC is noted below, was in continual dialogue with Rustin and Levison "about the need for developing in the South a mass force that would . . . become a counterbalance, let's call it, to the NAACP" (quoted in Fairclough 1987, 30). The fourth person, of course, is King, around whom most of the discussions revolved. Elected SCLC president, King's view of the courts has already been established. Given this background, and the fact that the SCLC became synonymous with King, its founding does not lend support to the indirect-effects thesis.

The founding of SNCC in 1960 is similar. SNCC was formed, to a large extent, by the efforts of Ella Baker of the SCLC who organized a conference of student sit-in activists at Shaw University in Raleigh, North Carolina, in April of 1960. Baker's aim was to help students engaged in sit-ins create at least some communication and organization network, albeit of their own choosing. Her inspiration, evidently, far from being the Supreme Court, was the actions of the students themselves, for she was becoming "restive under the cautious leadership of King" (Carson 1981, 20).[34] An important conference contributor, the Reverend James Lawson, urged the students to avoid courts and continue direct action: "The legal question is not central" he reportedly told the conference. "Unless we are prepared to create the climate, the law can never bring victory" (quoted in Williams 1988, 137). The organization that emerged and its leaders did not credit *Brown* with inspiring them. John Lewis, long-time Chairman of SNCC, was "inspired by radio reports of the Montgomery bus boycott and its leader King" (Carson 1981, 21), and by a belief in Christian non-violence (Good 1967, 44). Cleveland Sellers, a respected SNCC activist and later leader also pointed to Montgomery (Sellers 1973, 16). The point is that *Brown* is simply not mentioned as a source of inspiration.

The founding and revitalization of CORE provides little evidence for the Dynamic Court view claim. CORE's founding predates *Brown* by a dozen years. Its April 1942 founders, including James Farmer, were "products of the Christian student movement of the 1930s" (Meier and Rudwick 1973, 4),

34. On the role of Ella Baker, see also Garrow (1986, 131ff.), King (1987, 42–46).

principally the Fellowship of Reconciliation (FOR). In a February 19, 1942, memo to A. J. Muste of FOR, Farmer laid out plans for the building of a Gandhian-type movement of mass non-violent direct action (Farmer 1985, Appendix A). While it was not until the 1960s that CORE was able to act, its thinking was always based on such a model. Indeed, in 1947, it launched the first freedom ride, the Journey of Reconciliation, a bus trip through the upper South to demonstrate the "inherent limitations of legalism" (Meier and Rudwick 1973, 34). As Farmer told Roy Wilkins of the NAACP in response to Wilkins's opposition to the Freedom Ride, and preference for litigation, "we've had test cases and we've won them all and the status remains quo" (Farmer 1985, 13). Indeed, in Farmer's 370-page autobiography, there is scarcely mention of *Brown*, and no index entry.[35] The Dynamic Court view finds little supportive evidence with CORE.

This is also the case with the mostly white students who came to Mississippi in the summer of 1964. McAdam reviewed their applications, which contained statements of why they wanted to participate in "Freedom Summer." Well-educated, mostly white, and from wealthy families, these applicants are as likely a group as could be found (lawyers aside) to credit *Brown* with inspiring them to act. While McAdam did find some mention of *Brown*, other factors were mentioned to a much greater extent.[36] These included notions of a new generation, religion, idealism, and a general political commitment (McAdam 1988, 48). "The vast majority of applicants," McAdam found, "credit their parents with being the models for their actions" (McAdam 1988, 49). And a collection of hundreds of letters written from Mississippi by those who went contains only a few references to *Brown* (Sutherland 1965). It does not seem likely that these kinds of people needed a Court decision to inspire them to act.

If *Brown* played a role in inspiring people to act, one might expect it to have found its way into the music that was an important part of the civil rights movement. However, although references to local and national politicians and law enforcement officials were put to music, *Brown* and the courts were seldom, if ever, included. In Seeger and Reiser's (1989) compilation of over three dozen songs from the movement, there is only one mention of the Court, in a song sung by the freedom riders. And, as has been noted, the freedom riders put little faith in courts. The music of the civil rights movement was inspirational, but *Brown* and the courts were not part of it.

If *Brown* is not mentioned by those who sat in, demonstrated, and marched, was anything? The answer is a clear yes. The participants pointed to a number of sources of inspiration for their actions. For some, the emer-

35. The seeming irrelevance of *Brown* to CORE is also found in Meier and Rudwick's (1973) history of CORE with little discussion and only three minor index references.

36. As with other studies of the movement, there is little discussion of *Brown* throughout the book, and only three minor references.

gence of black African nations and the movements that accompanied their liberation had a "profound effect" (Carson 1981, 16; Williams 1965, 11; Zanden 1963, 545; Zinn 1962, 3). Over the twelve months from June 1960 to June 1961, eleven African countries gained independence. "We identified with the blacks in Africa," John Lewis of SNCC said, "and we were thrilled by what was going on" (quoted in Williams 1988, 139). Third-world liberation movements were also prominently mentioned by King in his classic *Letter From Birmingham Jail* ([1963] 1968, 5, 11). For others, the Montgomery bus boycott was an "inspiration" (Zinn 1964, 18). James Forman, a powerful force in SNCC, credits the bus boycott with having a "very significant effect on the consciousness of black people" and a "particularly important effect on young blacks." Montgomery, Forman believed, "helped to generate the student movement of 1960" (Forman 1972, 84, 85).[37] Participants in sit-ins also pointed to other sit-ins as inspiration (Gaither 1960), and to Dr. King, either by his actions or his writings (Gaither 1960; Finch 1981, 205; Oppenheimer 1963, 103; Woodward 1974, 197). *Brown* and the Supreme Court may have played a role in inspiring the activists of the early 1960s but they did not mention it in describing their inspiration for acting.[38] And given the fact that they did point to other factors as inspiring them, the lack of attribution of *Brown* is all the more telling.[39]

Another possibility for the indirect-effects thesis is that the Court influenced traditional black leaders who in turn called blacks to act. At the outset, this claim appears quite plausible. Members of the NAACP reacted with elation to *Brown*. To Roy Wilkins, NAACP executive secretary, "May 17, 1954 [the date of the *Brown* decision] was one of life's sweetest days. We had won a second Emancipation Proclamation" (Wilkins 1984, 214). So inspiring was the victory, that rather than pull out the usual celebratory bottle of Scotch upon hearing the news, the NAACP staff in New York "just sat there looking at one another. The only emotion we felt at that moment was awe—everyone of us felt it" (Wilkins 1984, 214). Among other leaders of the NAACP, similar reactions were recorded. Dr. Benjamin Mays, president of Morehouse College, and a member of the national board of the NAACP, remembers that

37. John Lewis agrees, writing that the Montgomery bus boycott "had the greatest impact on me, more than anything else" (Lewis in Raines 1983, 73).

38. In questionnaires received from 827 students at three black colleges in Greensboro and Raleigh in May 1960, over one-half ranked "resentment against everyday injustices" as the main source of motivation for the sit-ins. "Democratic ideals," a *possible* stand-in for the courts, was ranked first by only one in five (Searles and Williams 1962, 218).

39. For confirmation of this analysis, see, for example, the following works by participants: Abernathy (1989); Farmer (1985); Forman (1972); King (1958, 1963, 1968); King (1987); various participants in Peck (1960); various participants in Raines (1983); Sellers (1973); Sutherland (1965). Studies of the movement that confirm this analysis include Branch (1988); Carson (1981); Chafe (1980); Fairclough (1987); Garrow (1978, 1986); Hampton and Fayer (1990); McAdam (1988); Meier and Rudwick (1973); Oppenheimer (1963); Southern Regional Council (1960a, 1960b, 1961); Seeger and Reiser (1989); Weiss (1989); Williams (1965); Williams (1988); Wolff (1970); Zanden (1963); Zinn (1964).

"people literally got out and danced in the streets . . . the Negro was jubilant" (quoted in Morris 1984, 81). And Thurgood Marshall publicly expressed his pleasure with the decision (see chapter 2). It seems likely, too, that NAACP chapter leaders throughout the South were emboldened by the decision and redoubled their efforts.

While many NAACP officers were obviously excited and invigorated, the earlier parts of this chapter have shown that there is no substantial evidence that this affected the movement as a whole. One reason is that the ferocious reaction of the Southern states to the NAACP hampered its operations in the South. Many Southern states attempted to legislate or adjudicate the NAACP out of existence. For example, Ruby Hurley, who, in the early 1950s, opened the first permanent NAACP office in the South in Birmingham, was forced to leave in 1956 (Raines 1983, 131, 135). But more important, the NAACP and its leaders were committed to a legal strategy, not one of demonstrations, marches, and civil disobedience. For the NAACP, in the words of long-time Executive Secretary Roy Wilkins, *Brown* was a "fitting reward" for its "faith in the basic institutions of the country and for its patient strategy of correcting injustices by taking them to the courts" (Wilkins 1984, 214). When the movement took to the streets, the NAACP was replaced by other, more aggressive groups and individuals who took the lead in the civil rights movement of the 1960s. The sit-ins, for example, which started the demonstration phase of the civil rights movement, were "entirely student-inspired and directed" (Pollitt 1960, 318).[40] All across the South it was black teenagers who were the first to join the movement when a civil rights organizer came to town (Watters 1965, 119). Traditional black leaders and organizations counseled against direct action. Cleveland Sellers remembers being told by the local NAACP in South Carolina that the question of segregation "should be settled in the courts and not in the streets" (Sellers 1973, 26). Thurgood Marshall counseled against non-violent direct action by "well-meaning radical groups" (quoted in Meier and Rudwick 1973, 35).[41] More important, CORE's 1954 plan for a Ride for Freedom fell through because the NAACP refused support (Meier and Rudwick 1973, 72). As the respected Southern author Harry Golden put it in 1960: "If the NAACP and every other do-good organization disappeared from the face of the earth tonight, the movement would not skip a beat" (quoted in Pollitt 1960, 318).

Traditional black leaders and organizations were taken totally by "surprise" by the sit-in movement (Zinn 1964, 29). Roy Wilkins saw the sit-ins as "spontaneous" (Wilkins 1984, 267), and the NAACP's public relations director, Henry Moon, admitted that "the demonstrations are not something

40. The NAACP did not support the Greensboro sit-in and NAACP lawyers did not defend the demonstrators (Morris 1984, 198).
41. The statement, made in November 1946, was in response to plans for CORE's Journey of Reconciliation.

we planned" (quoted in Lomax 1960, 42). The NAACP Legal Defense and
Educational Fund (Inc. Fund), was totally unprepared for the sit-ins and,
while it did defend the demonstrators when asked, it never developed a long-
term strategy for the situation. One result was the creation of new leadership
and organizations which took the lead in promoting direct action (Killian and
Smith 1960; Williams 1965, 19). The late 1950s and early 1960s saw the
emergence of Dr. King and the SCLC, SNCC and its leaders, and the re-
invigoration of the older direct-action group CORE. Older groups were forced
to change their strategy, too. As Sarratt tactfully puts it, "events caused the
NAACP to shift its emphasis toward direct action in order to maintain its
position of leadership in the Negro protest movement" (Sarratt 1966, 323).
The point is that, rather than leading the movement, the established black
leadership found itself following it, trying to catch up with its troops (Pinard
et al. 1969).

This last point requires elaboration. For most of this century, the NAACP
had been the major black civil rights voice. During the post-*Brown* years it
provided key legal support for arrested demonstrators and lobbied the federal
government in support of civil rights. Yet it remained deeply ambivalent, if
not hostile, to the direct-action movement. To the extent, then, that the
NAACP was inspired by *Brown*, such inspiration had little effect on the
movement as a whole.

Part of the NAACP's hostility to direct action came from the kind of
people who joined and led it. The NAACP's leadership was "drawn almost
exclusively from the ranks of black professionals and businessmen" (Wynn
1974, 42). In many parts of the country it was an "organization for social
prestige" to which the "better people belonged" (Wynn 1955, 43). Its demands, in keeping with its membership, were "directed toward the Negro
status" (Wynn 1955, 40; Lomax 1960, 47). As one commentator put it,
"there were good reasons why just plain [black] folks called it the 'National
Association' for the Advancement of *Certain* People'" (Lewis 1986, 11).
Thus, it is quite accurate to characterize it as a "moderate, elitist organization" (Murphy 1959b, 389; Lomax 1963, 116). In the late 1950s and early
1960s, these were not the kinds of people ready and willing to take to the
streets.

Another reason for the hostility stems from organizational needs. The
NAACP was fearful that new civil rights organizations would diminish its
membership, income, and most important, its influence. Throughout its history, the NAACP has been fearful of competition, viewing, in the 1940s and
1950s for example, both the Communists and the Urban League as threats
(Wilkins 1984, 185, 190). By the 1960s, the NAACP saw itself in "full-
fledged competition" with "S.C.L.C., C.O.R.E., and S.N.C.C" (Wilkins
1984, 285). It was "troubled," Garrow reports, by what King and the SCLC
"might mean for the NAACP's own branches in the South" (Garrow 1986,

91).[42] Indeed, CORE's James Farmer believed that "King's mass meetings in churches across the South were draining away dollars that otherwise would have come to the association" (Farmer 1985, 189). Long accustomed to being the authoritative civil rights voice, the NAACP felt threatened.

Most important, the NAACP was committed to working through the courts, believing that civil rights could best be realized through observance of the law (Wynn 1955, 87).[43] For Roy Wilkins, "our faith in law" meant that the "meat and potatoes [of the civil rights struggle] had to be citizenship protected by law" (Wilkins 1984, 269, 270). Throughout the movement, then, the NAACP was opposed to civil disobedience, to demonstrations that violated the law. In the Jim Crow South, however, almost any civil rights demonstration did just that. Thus, as the movement grew and centered on direct action, the NAACP's influence waned.

A few examples will serve to bring home the seriousness of the conflict between the groups. After the founding of SCLC, Wilkins ordered Medgar Evers, the NAACP's Mississippi representative, to keep his distance, because the "NAACP does not wish to cooperate with the ministers [sic] group" (quoted in Garrow 1986, 91). When, in 1957, King proposed a large-scale voter registration drive, the "Crusade for Citizenship," a "furious" Wilkins sent a memo out to all NAACP staffers requiring them to check with national headquarters before participating in any civil rights conferences. The memo stated, in part, "we need only one national organization to speak for Negroes and all other organizations and leadership should rally around the NAACP" (quoted in Garrow 1986, 97, 98).[44] The same testy relations existed with the activists of CORE and SNCC. For example, Wilkins tried to talk CORE out of staging the Freedom Ride, telling Farmer that, in Farmer's words, "all we really need is one good test case so we can fight it out in the courts and put an end to segregated travel in this country" (Farmer 1986, 13). And when the freedom riders asked the Jackson, Mississippi, NAACP branch for help they were turned down on the ground that the branch "would be having its annual Freedom Fund drive at the time and could not afford to divide its energies" (Lomax 1963, 146). With SNCC and student activists, the NAACP often found itself in competition. In Albany, Georgia, for example, the NAACP refused to join with the other groups, believing that the NAACP Youth Council was the "only organizational vehicle needed for student activism" (Garrow 1986, 175, 176–79). Indeed, SCLC's Abernathy writes of NAACP "informers" who kept Albany Police Chief Laurie Pritchett apprised of dem-

42. Morris repeatedly stresses this tension, writing that in the SCLC the NAACP perceived "a threat to . . . local leadership, its financial base, and its patiently cultivated strategy of working within the law" (Morris 1984, 122, 115, 121).

43. See, generally, any study of the NAACP, including Finch (1981), Hughes (1962), Wilkins (1984).

44. Garrow (1986, 103) reports further that in "some" cities "local NAACP representatives were attempting to sandbag SCLC's efforts."

onstration plans in Albany, a civil rights campaign that was widely perceived as a major defeat for the SCLC and King (Abernathy 1989, 227, 228). A final, telling example is that Wilkins initially opposed the 1963 March on Washington in favor of the "quiet, patient lobbying tactics that worked best on Congress" (Wilkins 1984, 291).

There was also a good deal of personal animosity between the NAACP leaders and other civil rights leaders. Attorney General Robert F. Kennedy, for example, told the president that "Roy Wilkins hates Martin Luther King" (Garrow 1986, 674 n.43), and there is evidence that the NAACP tried to diminish King's influence and remove him from his leadership position (Garrow 1986, 687–88 n.6).[45] A few years earlier, Thurgood Marshall reportedly told the Eisenhower administration that King was an "opportunist" and a "first-rate rabble-rouser" (Branch 1988, 217).[46] At times the NAACP red-baited SNCC over such issues as its willingness to work with the National Lawyers Guild (Forman 1972, 220, 380).[47] And in later years Dr. King was attacked by the established groups for publicly opposing the war in Vietnam.

This conflict, of course, ran both ways. To the activists, the NAACP and the other established groups, with their legal strategy, were a source not of inspiration but of irritation. CORE had always been opposed to the NAACP's legal strategy. James Farmer viewed the NAACP as a lifeless organization whose branches "were all too often mere collection agencies" (Farmer 1985, 191). To the Reverend James Lawson, speaking at the Raleigh Conference in 1960 that formed SNCC, the NAACP was a "black bourgeois club" (quoted in Oppenheimer 1963, 70), emphasizing "fund-raising and court action" (quoted in Carson 1981, 23), not change. Cleveland Sellers found its approach "too slow, too courteous, too deferential and too ineffectual" (Sellers 1973, 19). Eldridge Cleaver wrote of its "Uncle Tom's hat-in-hand approach" (Cleaver 1968, 67). Overall, many young blacks who led and peopled the civil rights demonstrations viewed the NAACP as "a legalistic organization dominated by a timid black bourgeoisie" (Meier and Rudwick 1973, 105). Indeed, some students of the civil rights movement have argued that part of the movement was a generational "revolt against the established Negro leadership" (Lomax 1963, xiii). In sum, I can find no evidence for the claim, and a great deal to the contrary, that it was the traditional black leaders, inspired

45. However, Garrow (1986, 362) also reports that Wilkins met privately with high-ranking FBI officials to demand that leaks about King be stopped.
46. The comments were reportedly made in response to King's plan to lead a Prayer Pilgrimage to Washington, D.C., on the third anniversary of *Brown*. Branch's source is an FBI memo of May 9, 1957 (Branch 1988, 945). The pilgrimage was disappointing to its organizers, drawing "only limited attention" from the press and attracting "far fewer than the fifty thousand participants first predicted by the organizers" (Burk 1984, 220).
47. McAdam (1988, 146, 147) reports that at the "height of planning" for the Mississippi Freedom Summer (1964), Jack Greenberg of the Inc. Fund threatened to withdraw support if the National Lawyers Guild was allowed to participate. SNCC stuck to its principles of refusing ideological tests.

by the Court, who led the civil rights demonstrations of the 1960s. When the older groups did act, they did so to preserve their leadership roles and stand up with their young people. As one adult active in the Albany Movement put it, "the kids were going to do it anyway . . . we didn't want them to have to do it alone" (quoted in Zinn 1962, 4).

In exploring the case for the extra-judicial-effects claims of the Dynamic Court view with blacks, I looked for evidence in a variety of places, ranging from the Court's effects on black public opinion, to its ability to inspire black activists, black protest activity, and black leaders. In none of these places was evidence found for the claim and in a number of places the evidence seems to contradict it. Again, the extra-judicial-effects thesis lacks support.

Money and Membership

A last possible measure of extra-judicial influence that I will examine is changes in contributions to and memberships in civil rights groups. Here, the argument might be that Supreme Court action, particularly *Brown*, led to major increases in both categories and laid the foundations that made the marches and demonstrations of the 1960s possible. It seems plausible to expect an increase in contributions from individuals, labor unions, and foundations as well as surges in membership due to the symbolic and legitimating effect of Supreme Court action. By making civil rights groups financially and numerically stronger, then, the Supreme Court could have contributed to the civil rights movement.

There are a number of difficulties with this argument and in making the examination it requires. First, of the major, active civil rights groups, only the NAACP and CORE existed prior to *Brown*, and CORE was generally inactive until 1960. The only group whose income can be fairly examined over a long time-span is the NAACP. Further, as has been suggested earlier, the NAACP was never enthusiastic about the direct-action activities of the 1960s. They were originated and led by SNCC, SCLC, and CORE, often with only the grudging acceptance of the NAACP. To the extent that the demonstrations and marches were crucial to changes in civil rights, increased contributions to the NAACP may not have had a major influence on those changes. Finally, accurate income data are hard to obtain. Figures differ and it is often unclear exactly what is included in different estimates. However, since I am interested in general-trend data, rather than specific numbers, and since the available sources agree on the trend, inexact and differing figures should not be a serious problem.

Table 4.3 presents income data for the NAACP, the Inc. Fund (LDEF), the National Urban League (NUL), SCLC, CORE, and SNCC. As can be seen in column 2 (labeled NAACP), there was a large increase in income available to the NAACP between 1953 and 1954 (19.2 percent), and between 1954 and 1955 (44.2 percent) (percentages not shown in table), the year af-

Table 4.3   Income For Civil Rights Organizations, 1940–1965
(in Thousands of Dollars)

Year	NAACP	LDEF	NUL	SCLC[a]	CORE[a]	SNCC[a]	Total	%[b]
1940	64	—	—	—	—	—	64	
1941	76	—	—	—	—	—	76	18.8
1942	114	—	—	—	—	—	114	50.0
1943	182	—	—	—	—	—	182	59.7
1944	342	—	—	—	—	—	342	87.9
1945	402	—	—	—	—	—	402	17.5
1946	357	—	—	—	—	—	357	−11.2
1947	319	—	—	—	—	—	319	−10.6
1948	300	—	—	—	5	—	305	−4
1949	—	—	—	—	3	—	—	—
1950	—	—	—	—	2	—	—	—
1951	—	—	—	—	3	—	—	—
1952	—	211	—	—	3	—	—	—
1953	391	224	—	—	5	—	620	—
1954	466	200	—	—	8	—	674	8.7
1955	672	—	—	—	11	—	—	—
1956	—	347	265	—	14	—	—	—
1957	727	320	265	10	21	—	1,343	—
1958	822	315	265	10	47	—	1,459	8.6
1959	890	358	265	25	70	—	1,608	10.2
1960	1,041	490	265	60	242	5	2,103	30.8
1961	1,051	561	340	193	456	14	2,615	24.4
1962	1,082[c]	669	670	198	556	120	3,295	26.0
1963	1,114[c]	1,197	1,410	750	733	309	5,513	67.3
1964	1,147	1,425	1,651	626	838	650	6,337	15.0
1965	1,865	1,662	1,930	1,500	625	638	8,220	29.7

SOURCES: For the *NAACP:* National Association for the Advancement of Colored People (1939–41, 1947–61, 1964–66), McAdam (1982, 253); For *CORE:* Meier and Rudwick (1973, 78, 82, 126, 148, 149), McAdam (1982, 253); For *SCLC:* Fairclough (1987, 47, 70, 142, 206, 255), Haines (1988, 84, 193), McAdam (1982, 253); For *SNCC:* Haines (1988, 84, 195), Roberts (1966, 148), McAdam (1982, 253); For *LDEF:* Haines (1988, 84, 190); For *NUL:* Haines (1988, 84), Weiss (1989, 92–93).

NOTES: Income reports from various sources differ. Different reporting and accounting procedures, and varying estimates make it impossible to achieve exactitude across organizations. The data presented here are an amalgamation from the sources listed above. They should be seen as indicative of the trend, not as precise indicators of actual income.

[a] SCLC was founded in 1957, Core in 1942, and SNCC in 1960.
[b] % increase from previous year.
[c] My estimate.

ter *Brown*. At first glance, it seems obvious that the increase is a result of *Brown*. However, examining where the money came from clouds the picture somewhat. At its June 1953 Annual Conference, the NAACP launched the Fight For Freedom (FFF) campaign, designed to raise $1 million annually. Branches set up special committees to coordinate the fund-raising. Also, a "greater emphasis" was placed upon the life-membership campaign (NAACP

1955, 76). In 1954, perhaps because of a late start, only $66,124 was raised by the FFF campaign. In 1955, however, that amount increased to $150,845. Funds from membership increased by about $70,000. The increase in other contributions was small, only about $15,000. The question this leaves is how important the increased fund-raising activity was in comparison to the *Brown* decision as an impetus for increasing contributions. While it is impossible to know, the fact that both were occurring makes it unlikely that the increases were solely due to one. Further, those who have examined the question have not pointed to the Court. Williams, for example, credits the increase to the murder of Emmett Till in Mississippi in the summer of 1955 (Williams 1988, 44). And the NAACP, in its annual report for 1954, did mention the increased fund-raising activities as the reason for its growing income. No mention is made of *Brown* (NAACP 1955, 3, 76).

Another way of examining the increase is to view it in the context of changes in income available to the NAACP over the long term. The 1953–54 and the 1954–55 percentage increases are less than those of 1941–42, 1942–43, and 1943–44. And they are dwarfed by the 1964–65 increase. This suggests that the increases in 1954 and 1955, if indeed "caused" solely or even primarily by the Court, were not without precedent.

The data collected in the table permit analysis of other civil rights groups. Since the Inc. Fund (LDEF) was the litigation arm of the NAACP, one might expect its income to have increased dramatically in 1954. Unfortunately, the data (column 3) are incomplete, but they suggest approximately a 10 percent *decline* in income from 1953 to 1954 with a resumption of growth after that. Its biggest increases came between 1962 and 1963, when income grew a whopping 78.9 percent. Similarly, the SCLC (column 5) did very poorly in the 1950s, as did the NUL (column 4) where Theodore W. Kheel, president during the late 1950s, remembers "payroll-less days and weeks" (Weiss 1989, 90). The income of both groups skyrocketed in the 1960s, with the NUL taking in over $14.5 million by 1970 (Haines 1988, 84, 188). And while CORE (column 6) did increase its income throughout the 1950s, income growth exploded in the 1960s, with 1965 income nearly nine times as high as 1959 income. Overall, total income data for the leading civil rights groups (columns 8 and 9), give little evidence of the Court's effect. Income growth did rise dramatically, but this happened in the 1960s, in the wake of the activist phase of the civil rights movement. Summarizing his detailed examination of the finances of the civil rights movement in the 1950s and 1960s, Haines concluded: "Through the 1950s the trend line for total income remained rather flat. During the early 1960s, however, and especially in 1963, it began to grow rather rapidly" (Haines 1988, 82). The pattern in the overall increase in income to civil rights groups does not support the indirect-effects thesis.

The extra-judicial-effects thesis also suggests that the increase in income would, in part, result from growing contributions from foundations, labor unions, and other predominantly white organizations. The available data, though sketchy, do not support the claim. Foundation grants were not forthcoming to any large extent until the 1960s. For example, the "funds that Rustin and Levison anticipated from foundations and trade unions" when they helped found the SCLC in 1957 "failed to materialize" (Fairclough 1987, 47). The NAACP, too, seemed to obtain most of its funds from its members, reporting for the year 1959 that, "as always, the bulk of the income was raised by the branches from $2, $5 and $10 annual memberships and from special Freedom Fund projects" (NAACP 1960, 13). In addition, the *Foundation News* "reported no grants to the NAACP, CORE, or their respective tax-exempt funds until 1966" (Haines 1988, 115–16). Thus, in the years before the civil rights movement massively took to the streets, foundations and labor unions did not offer support.

This changed in the 1960s. For example, the United Negro College Fund reportedly went from no foundation grants in 1960 to eight grants totalling nearly $5.25 million in 1964 (Haines 1988, 118–19). The Taconic and Field Foundations and the Stern Family Fund contributed $783,000 to the Voter Education Project in the spring of 1962 (Watters and Cleghorn 1967, 49). Also in 1962, the Phelps Stokes Fund gave money for a meeting of civil rights organizations (Forman 1972, 363). Labor unions contributed some funds after 1960 as well. The AFL-CIO put up the money for the October 1960 conference that formalized SNCC (Forman 1972, 219). And union contributions to CORE, amounting to only $695 in 1958 and $1,347 in 1959, averaged about $40,000 each year in the years 1962–64, before dropping in 1965 (Meier and Rudwick 1973, 82, 126, 149, 336).[48] On the macro level, "larger foundation contributions to 'interracial relations' jumped from $2.3 million to $26.7 million during 1964–65," an increase of over eleven-fold (Henry 1979, 179). And the Ford Foundation, a major supporter of civil rights activity, did not commit itself to support the movement until 1967 (McKay 1977).[49]

Large corporations followed the same pattern. A 1970 study of 247 "major urban-based companies," all on "*Fortune*'s list of the largest U.S. financial and industrial corporations," found that 201 had some sort of civil rights program, including donations to civil rights groups, and hiring and training programs. However, of these 201 programs, only 4 were started before 1965 (Cohn 1970, 69). When executives were asked why they initiated programs, the "principal motive" was "enlightened self-interest," with four-fifths mentioning "appearance" and only two-fifths mentioning "compliance" with the

48. Unions were not always helpful. Forman (1972, 323) reports that in the summer of 1963 the UAW refused to contribute to SNCC.

49. See also Ford Foundation (1974); Ford Foundation and American Bar Association (1976). A cynic might note that it was only after riots broke out in America's cities that major foundations became interested in funding civil rights organizations. On the threat of violence as the most important factor in increasing income for mainstream and conservative civil rights groups, see Haines (1988).

Table 4.4   **NAACP And CORE Membership, 1944–1965**

Year	NAACP Membership	*Crisis* Circulation	CORE Associate Membership	CORE Contributors
1944	429,000	12,000[a]	—	—
1945	405,000	45,000[a]	—	—
1946	420,000	49,000[a]	—	—
1947	"leveled off"	45,000	—	—
1948	383,000	41,000	—	—
1949	248,076	34,388	—	—
1950	193,000	22,000	—	—
1951	210,000	24,000	—	—
1952	215,000	28,000	—	—
1953	240,000	30,000	—	—
1954	240,000	28,000[a]	—	—
1955	309,000	35,700	—	—
1956	350,424	45,000	—	—
1957	312,277	64,350	—	—
1958	334,543	61,645	—	4,500
1959	341,935	65,500	12,000 (Feb. 1960)	—
1960	388,347	77,480	20,000 (Dec.)	12,000
1961	380,134	88,850	26,000 (May)	—
1962	—	70,000[a]	52,000 (Dec.)	—
1963	—	90,000[a]	70,000 (Sept.)	—
1964	455,839	114,748	—	—
1965	440,538	111,700	—	—

SOURCES: NAACP: National Association for the Advancement of Colored People (Various years); CORE: Meier and Rudwick (1973, 97, 127, 149).

NOTE:
[a]N. W. Ayer & Son's.

law (Cohn 1970, 70). The point is that contributions to civil rights activity on the part of white organizations do not appear to have increased in the wake of *Brown*. Contributions did not amount to much until after the outbreak of the marches and demonstrations.

A final bit of evidence available to assess the extra-judicial effects of *Brown* on civil rights organizations is changes in membership. Table 4.4 presents data for the NAACP membership from 1944 through 1965. While there was a modest increase from 1954 to 1955, membership had been building for a number of years from a low point in 1950. It wasn't until the 1960s that the membership level recorded in 1944 was again reached. Subscriptions to *The Crisis*, the magazine of the NAACP, also presented in table 4.4, follow roughly the same pattern. For CORE, the only other organization for which I have obtained data, the number of associate members soared in the 1960s. Membership nearly doubled in 1960, doubled in 1962, and increased by nearly 50 percent in 1963 over the previous year's total. The number of contributors almost tripled from 1958 to 1960. Again, the point here is that the changes in membership do not show evidence of increase in reaction to *Brown*. Rather, the major changes appeared to have come in reaction to the direct-action phase of the civil rights movement.

In sum, evidence in support of the claim that the actions of the Supreme Court increased contributions to, and membership in, civil rights organizations is mixed. At best, some of the impetus for the increase in income available to the NAACP can be credited to the Court. But some can be credited to the fund-raising activities of the organizations themselves, the position the NAACP took. Also, larger increases occurred both in years before and in years after *Brown*, particularly in the 1960s. In terms of growing membership, the modest increase immediately after *Brown* is most accurately seen in the context of NAACP membership activity and the long-term trend. Further, major increases occurred in the 1960s. Finally, it appears that contributions from wealthy white organizations and foundations did not increase in the wake of *Brown*. Rather, it was the activism of the 1960s that appears to be the motivating factor. It was these activities, not Court action, that led to major "growth in numbers and financial resources of all civil rights organizations . . . and the renewed interest in civil rights by white liberal organizations of all types" (Oppenheimer 1963, 274). Evidence in support of extra-judicial effects is weak.

Conclusion

Before I sum up the findings of this chapter, I think it is important to note that while there is little evidence that *Brown* helped produce positive change, there is some evidence that it hardened resistance to civil rights among both elites and the white public. I have documented how, throughout the South, white groups intent on using coercion and violence to prevent change grew. Resistance to change increased in all areas, not merely in education but also in voting, transportation, public places, and so on. *Brown* "unleashed a wave of racism that reached hysterical proportions" (Fairclough 1987, 21). On the elite level, *Brown* was used as a club by Southerners to fight any civil rights legislation as a ploy to force school desegregation on the South. Just a few days before *Brown* was decided, for example, a U.S. House committee opened hearings on a bill introduced by Massachusetts Republican John W. Heselton to ban segregation in interstate travel. The bill died and *Brown*, Barnes concludes, "probably contributed to the demise" (Barnes 1983, 94). In hearings and floor debates on the 1957 Civil Rights Act, Southerners repeatedly charged that the bill, aimed at voting rights, was a subterfuge to force school desegregation on the South (U.S. Cong., House 1957, 806, 1187; *Cong. Rec.* 1957, 9627, 10771). When Attorney General Brownell testified before a Senate committee on the 1957 bill, he was queried repeatedly and to his astonishment on whether the bill gave the president the power to use the armed forces to enforce desegregation (U.S. Cong., Senate, Hearings 1957, 214–16). By stiffening resistance and raising fears before the activist phase of the civil rights movement was in place, *Brown* may actually have delayed the achievement of civil rights. Relying on the Dynamic Court view of change, and litigating to produce significant social reform, may have surprising and unfortunate costs.

In the preceding pages I have examined a number of places which reasonably could be expected to yield evidence of extra-judicial effects. Could it be, however, that the method predetermined the result? That is, wouldn't the result have been the same if, instead of tracing the effect of *Brown*, I had tried to trace the effect of, say, presidential action such as the desegregation of the armed forces? And if so, doesn't that mean that the method is faulty? Although it is theoretically possible that the method determined the result, happily this is not the case. This can be stated with confidence because I can point to activities for which the method would find many effects. For example, if I examined the evidence for the effects on civil rights of the events in Birmingham in the spring of 1963, I would find much. The evidence would range from clear attribution and action by elites to heightened press coverage to rapid changes in white opinion to an increase in the number of civil rights demonstrations. A similar argument can be made for the events in Selma in 1965. If the method can find no more evidence of the extra-judicial effect of Court action than of the effect of any number of other decisions and actions of the federal government, it may well be because the Court's actions were as important, but no more so, than those other activities. It may be the result, more than the method, that is troubling.

In sum, the Dynamic Court view's claim that a major contribution of the courts in civil rights was to give the issue salience, press political elites to act, prick the consciences of whites, legitimate the grievances of blacks, and fire blacks up to act is not substantiated. In all the places examined, where evidence supportive of the claim should exist, it does not. The concerns of clear attribution, time, and increased press coverage all cut against the thesis. Public-opinion evidence does not support it and, at times, clearly contradicts it. The emergence of the sit-ins, demonstrations, and marches, does not support it. While it must be the case that Court action influenced some people, I have found no evidence that this influence was widespread or of much importance to the battle for civil rights. The evidence suggests that *Brown*'s major positive impact was limited to reinforcing the belief in a legal strategy for change of those already committed to it. The burden of showing that *Brown* accomplished more now rests squarely on those who for years have written and spoken of its immeasurable importance.

5

The Current of History

I have found little evidence that the judicial system, from the Supreme Court down, produced much of the massive change in civil rights that swept the United States in the 1960s. This runs so counter to the accepted wisdom that one might be tempted to sympathize with a skeptical reader who might say : "But the Court did act, and change did occur—what else could have accounted for it?" In this chapter, I will marshall evidence suggesting that pro-civil-rights forces existed independent of the Supreme Court and could plausibly have accounted for eventual congressional and executive branch action as well as for Court action. While we can never know what would have happened if the Court had not acted as it did (if *Brown* had never been decided or had come out the other way), the existence and strength of pro-civil-rights forces at least suggest that change would have occurred, albeit at a pace unknown.[1] Such change would have included economic change, black migration and the concentration of black voters in key electoral states, international awareness, and, in general, a changing society. The point of this analysis is to suggest what has been implicit throughout: that the courts were of limited relevance to the actual progress of civil rights in America.

Economic Changes and Effects

When the Second World War ended, the U.S. had set itself on a course for change. The military demands and labor shortages created by the war had opened new opportunities for blacks (Blaustein and Zangrando 1968, 355). The heightened demand for labor had prompted wartime concessions, and many formerly segregated workplaces had desegregated under the pressure to perform (Willhelm 1981, 850). This continued into the 1950s and 1960s as rapid economic growth made it in the self-interest of many whites not to

1. For a further treatment of the argument suggested here, see McAdam (1982).

discriminate, at least in some parts of their economic lives (Burkey 1971, 75). For example, Ray Marshall found that tight labor markets and the movement of whites to better-paying jobs provided textile employers a powerful motive to hire blacks (Marshall 1975, 29). Economic growth pressured segregation.

One result of this pressure was to markedly improve the financial condition of blacks. While in 1939 the median wage and salary income of non-white primary families and individuals was 37 percent of what their white counterparts earned, by 1952 that ratio had increased to 57 percent. In subsequent years, the ratio fluctuated between 51 percent and 56 percent (Burgess 1969, 269). This change can also be seen in the growth of the non-white work force employed in white-collar jobs. In 1940 only 10 percent of the non-white work force was employed in professional, managerial, clerical, sales, or craft professions. By 1960, however, the proportion more than doubled, reaching 22.2 percent (Burgess 1969, 266–67). Between 1950 and 1958 the percentage of non-white workers in skilled and white-collar jobs increased as follows: craftsmen, 20 percent; sales workers, 24 percent; clerical and kindred workers, 69 percent; professional and technical workers, 49 percent (Searles and Williams 1962, 216; Burgess 1969, 265–67). While blacks still lagged far behind whites in economic well-being, their situation was improving.

As black employment improved, economists, business owners, and politicians became increasingly aware of the existence of black purchasing power and the loss of income that segregation inflicted. While precise figures are hard to come by, as early as 1953 the secretary of the Department of Health, Education, and Welfare (HEW) stated that "racial bias was costing the United States between 15 and 30 billion dollars annually" (quoted in Hazel 1957, 234).[2] By 1964, the figure appeared to have been about 30 billion dollars annually, equal to Canada's entire consumer market (Burgess 1969, 270). In 1962, the President's Council of Economic Advisers predicted a gain of 2.5 percent in GNP if racial discrimination was ended and an even larger increase if educational achievement was equalized (cited in Southern Regional Council 1962, 3, 4). The federal government was well aware of the real costs of segregation.

Local business and political leaders also became aware of the economic costs of segregation. Continued segregation and the possibility of violence gave communities a bad reputation and made it unlikely that new businesses would move in. Little Rock, for example, averaged five new industrial sites per year during the period from 1950 to 1957. However, between the fall of 1957 and February 1961, not one new industry came in. This led a group of prominent business leaders to organize against the efforts of Governor Faubus to preserve segregation. In New Orleans, business leaders organized against pro-segregation demonstrations on the ground that they were hurting busi-

---

2. Elmo Roper believed that the figure was closer to $30 billion (Hazel 1957, 60).

ness. And in Virginia, while 1951–53 had seen an average increase of 31,400 new industrial jobs per year, the number dwindled to 5,100 per year in the period from 1957 to 1959, at the height of massive resistance. Here, too, business leaders organized to press political leaders to end segregation (Sarratt 1966, 289–95).

Segregation, then, prevented white business owners from collecting black dollars. It hampered black travel and was an inefficient use of labor.[3] Indeed, as early as 1947, President Truman's Committee on Civil Rights stressed the economic cost of segregation, devoting twice as much text to its "economic reason" to act on civil rights as to its "moral reason." Thus, the needs of an expanding economy and the realization that blacks had money to spend, pressured segregation attitudes.

A distinct effect of economic changes was population shift. Blacks moved from the rural South to the cities of the South and the North in record numbers to take advantage of jobs. In the period from 1940 to 1960, for example, the number of black farm operators decreased from approximately 675,000 to 267,000, and over 3 million blacks left the South. Out-migration of blacks from the South increased dramatically in the 1940s and 1950s, running at nearly four times, and three and a half times respectively, the 1930s rate (McAdam 1982, 95, 78). Numerically, this meant that between 1940 and 1950 the black urban population grew by 3.2 million and that by 1950 nearly 4 million more blacks lived in urban areas than in rural areas. Between 1950 and 1960 the urban population grew again, this time by 4.4 million. By 1960 it was close to three times the black rural population (Brink and Harris 1963, 39). A population that was both rural and Southern had become urban and, to a large extent, Northern.

Improvement in the economic position of blacks and migration from the rural South to urban areas increased the pressure for civil rights in a number of ways. One way was to allow for the strengthening of black organizations. Rural Southern blacks, eking out a meager existence, lacked the time, money, education, and communication networks to organize for civil rights. They also feared for their lives. Migration and improved economic conditions changed that. Southern black churches, later to become a crucial institution in the civil rights movement, expanded enormously (McAdam 1982, 99–100).[4] Black colleges came into their own and their enrollments soared. From 1941 to 1961, enrollments doubled, increasing from 37,203 to 84,770. By 1964, their enrollment was 105,495 (McAdam 1982, 101).[5] Black civil rights organizations, particularly the National Association for the Advance-

3. Segregation was also inefficient in small ways. For example, Pollitt points out that if the demands of productivity don't allow workers to go home for lunch, then lack of facilities where blacks can eat will be a pressure point (Pollitt 1960, 364).
4. On the crucial role of black churches in the desegregation struggle, see Morris (1984).
5. Professor McAdam kindly provided me with this these figures.

ment of Colored People (NAACP), also grew. Whereas NAACP membership in the mid-1930s had been under 100,000, by 1946 dues-paying members totalled 420,000.[6] Improved economic conditions and migration produced black organizations insulated from white economic pressures and able to fight for civil rights.

Electoral Changes

The social processes identified here "served to undermine the politico-economic conditions on which the racial status quo had been based" (McAdam 1982, 73). Yet they did so quietly, without public announcements or a great deal of white scrutiny. The same cannot be said, however, for the potential effect on *elections* that these processes contained. By the mid-1950s, if not earlier, the new strategic electoral position of blacks reached the front pages of America's leading newspapers and the back rooms of presidential and congressional campaign organizations.

The dynamic behind this growing white awareness of black electoral power was migration. Approximately 87 percent of all blacks who left the South between 1910 and 1960 settled in the seven key electoral states of California, Illinois, Michigan, New Jersey, New York, Ohio, and Pennsylvania (McAdam 1982, 79–80). These seven states alone accounted for over 70 percent of the electoral votes needed to elect a president. By 1964, one-third of all blacks lived in those seven states (Brink and Harris 1963, 80). While there was some awareness of this potential vote in the 1930s,[7] and further recognition in the late 1940s, full recognition came in the 1950s.

The need for black votes was a prime motivator of President Truman's civil rights activities: "Following the defeat of the Democratic party in the 1946 election, Truman soon realized that in order to win the 1948 presidential election he would need the votes of the many Negroes who lived in the key industrial states of the North and West" (Berman 1970, 77). He acted accordingly. Soon after the 1946 election, Truman established by executive order a civil rights committee and, in June 1947, he condemned discrimination in a speech to a rally of the NAACP in front of the Lincoln Memorial (Berman 1970, 55, 61). Truman also authorized the government to file a brief before the Supreme Court in the *Shelley* case, arguing for the unenforceability of restrictive covenants (Elman 1987, 818; Berman 1970, 74). In February 1948, he sent a civil rights message to Congress, requesting legislation on ten fronts, including the establishment of a permanent commission on civil rights, the provision of federal protection against lynching, the establishment of a Fair Employment Practices Commission, and the prohibition of discrimination in interstate transportation facilities (Berman 1970, 84). After the nomi-

6. See table 4.4. That figure was not reached again until the mid-1960s.
7. "Let Jesus lead you, and Roosevelt feed you" was an FDR slogan from the 1936 presidential campaign (Lewis 1986, 4).

nating conventions in the summer of 1948, Truman issued several executive orders setting up civil rights review boards in each federal agency, and declaring that it was the policy of the president to desegregate the military (Berman 1970, 116). And, it was black votes in California, Illinois, and Ohio that provided Truman's margin of victory (Berman 1970, 129–30).

The 1956 presidential campaign brought the issue into the open. Writing on the front page of the *Wall Street Journal* in the spring of 1956, Alan Otten declared that "many Negro voters are bolting the Democratic camp in favor of the Republicans" and that Democratic officials, in private, admitted "great concern." "The impact on this year's Presidential and Congressional elections," Otten wrote, "could be decisive" (Otten 1956, 1, 4). *Congressional Quarterly* (*CQ*) followed soon after by pointing out that the Republicans only needed to gain two Senate seats and fifteen House seats to control both houses. This was particularly important, *CQ* noted, since blacks held the balance of power in sixty-one districts outside of the South and since it "appears certain that in 1956 Democrats will lose and Republicans will gain Negro votes" ("Where Does Negro Voter Strength Lie?" 1956, 496). This article was brought to the administration's attention by its congressional liaison, Bryce Harlow, in early May 1956 (Burk 1984, 165). Robert Bendiner, writing in the *Reporter*, found it "safe to say" that the 1956 election "would show a very marked swing away from the Democratic party" by black voters (Bendiner 1956, 9; Rowan 1956, 37–39). He also pointed out that Truman's election in 1948 depended on black voters and "less than a fifteen per cent switch in the Negro vote" would have delivered the election to Dewey (Bendiner 1956, 8).[8] Black leaders added to the chorus. NAACP leaders Wilkins and Mitchell publicly suggested that blacks might do better, in Wilkins's words, by "swapping the known devil for the suspected witch" (quoted in Ware 1962, 56). And a "good part of the Negro press" followed suit by "moving away from the Democratic camp" (Bendiner 1956, 10).

The Republicans attempted to capitalize on this apparent shift by courting black votes. Nearly 100,000 copies of a pamphlet entitled "Abe & Ike—In Deed Alike" were distributed, identifying Republicans as the party of civil rights. The Eisenhower administration sent a four-point civil rights program to the Congress designed to "woo colored voters" (Otten 1956, 1). The impetus behind the program was, in large part, electoral. As Garrow points out, "a group of urban Republicans, looking ahead to the 1956 elections and the growing number of votes being cast by Northern blacks, urged Attorney General Herbert Brownell to consider the introduction of some civil rights legislation" (Garrow 1978, 12).

The results of the 1956 election did show a shift in black votes. *CQ* found that in thirty-five non-Southern districts where blacks were more than 10 per-

8. See also "It's 4 Million Negro Votes that the Fight's All About" (1957, 41).

cent of the population, Eisenhower increased his share of the vote over his 1952 total by 5 percent, more than double his increase nationwide. In Harlem, where Representative Adam Clayton Powell campaigned for Eisenhower, his increase was 16.6 percent ("For Whom Did Negroes Vote in 1956?" 1957, 704). In the largest black district in the country, in Illinois, Eisenhower picked up an additional 10.9 percent (Ware 1962, 59). Overall, *U.S. News & World Report* commented that the "Democratic share of the Negro vote slipped from 79 per cent in the presidential election of 1952, to 61 per cent in that of 1956" ("It's 4 Million Negro Votes That The Fight's About" 1957, 41).[9]

The electoral position of blacks, and the 1956 demonstration that their vote could change, provided pressure for civil rights action. The Eisenhower administration attempted to capitalize on the situation by introducing civil rights legislation. The congressional debate over what became the 1957 Civil Rights Act was greatly influenced by the upcoming 1958 congressional elections. As *U.S. News & World Report* commented, the real debate was "for the vote of 4 million Negro voters who hold a balance of political power in 14 Northern and Border States" containing 107 House seats ("It's 4 Million Negro Votes That The Fight's About" 1957, 41). Similarly, the presidential election of 1960 has been seen as essential to the passage of the 1960 Civil Rights Act (Blaustein and Zangrando 1968, 477). And it must be remembered that in the states of Texas, South Carolina, North Carolina, Illinois, New Jersey, Michigan, Missouri, and Pennsylvania, John Kennedy would have lost without the black vote (Lewis 1960b).[10] Thus, by the 1950s the electoral position of blacks brought increasing pressure for civil rights.

In sum, the Second World War and the changes brought about by economic growth and industrialization weakened segregation. The influx of blacks to the urban centers of America, particularly the North, made segregation and its effects harder to ignore, both visually and politically.

International Demands

The Second World War propelled the U.S. into the international arena. Its new role, leader of the "free world," put its own practices in the spotlight. In the Cold War, in the fight for the hearts and minds of people throughout the world, segregation made the American model unappealing. As the Cold War continued, "racial discrimination in the U.S. received increasing attention from other countries" (Dudziak 1988, 62). Time and time again the U.S. government, political leaders, and commentators argued that segregation hampered foreign relations and provided ammunition for Communist propaganda. Blacks clearly benefited from the rhetoric of the Cold War. In the next

9. For a survey of the party distribution of the black votes in sixty-three cities in 1956, see Glantz (1970); Moon (1956; 1957a; 1957b).

10. Presidents Truman, Kennedy, and Carter all failed to carry the white vote.

few pages I give the reader a brief look at the prevalence of the Cold War argument against segregation.

Even before the Cold War, the rhetoric of World War II itself spurred civil rights. C. Vann Woodward notes that an association between Nazism and "white supremacy was inevitably made in the American mind" (Woodward 1974, 130–31). Similarly, the "democratic ideology and rhetoric with which the war was fought" brought American race relations into question (Dalfiume 1970, 247). The onset of the Cold War insured that the questioning would continue.

The location of the nation's capital south of the Mason-Dixon line ensured segregation a prominent place in international discourse. As Dudziak points out, any claim that segregation was a small, regional problem that was nearly eradicated seemed false when foreign diplomats and dignitaries suffered from it daily (Dudziak 1988, 109). And this was recognized; as the United States argued in its *Brown* brief, Washington, D.C., was "the window through which the world looks into our house," and "the treatment of colored persons here is taken as the measure of our attitude toward minorities generally" (Brief for the United States, *Brown* 1954, 4).

Segregation could also embarrass the U.S. in international affairs through the United Nations. With the UN in New York, a forum was available to highlight segregation. In June 1946, for example, the National Negro Congress filed a petition in the UN seeking "relief from oppression" (Streator 1946). Nearly a year and a half later, the NAACP did likewise, with a document entitled "A Statement on the Denial of Human Rights to Minorities in the Case of Citizens of Negro Descent in the United States of America and an Appeal to the United Nations for Redress" (Streator 1947). Denouncing U.S. racial discrimination as "not only indefensible but barbaric," the 155-page document claimed that racism threatened the U.S. more than Communism did: "It is not Russia that threatens the United States so much as Mississippi; not Stalin and Molotov but [Senator] Bilbo and [Representative] Rankin." [11] The statement received "extensive coverage" in both the national and foreign media (Dudziak 1988, 95), and the Soviets proposed that the UN investigate the charges (Berman 1970, 66). A final example came at the height of the UN debate over the Bay of Pigs invasion when Robert Williams, a black leader in North Carolina, sent the following message to the Cuban ambassador, which he read aloud:

> Please convey to [U.S. ambassador to the UN] Mr. Adlai E. Stevenson: Now that the United States has proclaimed military support for the people willing to rebel against oppression, oppressed Negroes in South urgently request tanks, artillery, bombs, money, and the use of American airfields and white mercenaries

---

11. A condensed version of the introduction to the statement and an abstract of its chapters can be found in Du Bois (1947).

to crush the racist tyrants who have betrayed the American revolution and Civil War. We also request prayers for this noble undertaking. (quoted in Forman 1972, 177–78)

As Eric Goldman put it, writing in the *New York Times Magazine*, in 1961, the "existence of segregation in the United States is a tremendous liability to all Americans in the East-West struggle" (Goldman 1961, 12).

The response of some in the federal government was to argue that segregation must be abolished as an aid in the fight against Communism. In 1947, President Truman's Committee On Civil Rights (PCCR) pointed to the "international reason" as one of three reasons to act on civil rights:

> *The United States is not so strong, the final triumph of the democratic ideal is not so inevitable that we can ignore what the world thinks of us or our record.* (PCCR 1947, 148)

The committee also quoted from a May 1946 letter from Dean Acheson, acting secretary of state, presenting the State Department's position that "the existence of discrimination against minority groups in this country has an adverse effect upon our relations with other countries" (PCCR 1947, 146). President Truman made many references to the Cold War imperative to end segregation, as in his 1947 speech to an NAACP rally, his 1948 message to Congress accompanying the administration's civil rights proposals, a campaign speech in Harlem in October 1948, and his last State of the Union Address in January 1952 (Berman 1970, 63, 85, 137, 194–95). In addition, the State Department continually argued that segregation interfered with U.S. foreign policy. In June of 1961, Secretary of State Dean Rusk formally put the State Department on record in support of the Justice Department's proposals that the Interstate Commerce Commission toughen its anti-discrimination rules (Lewis 1961, 21). In September of that year, the State Department took the unusual step of publicly urging the Maryland legislature to pass an anti-discrimination bill pending before it (Garrison 1961). International opinion in the context of the Cold War was an important concern for government officials in assessing civil rights.

Cold War rhetoric was also a concern for the U.S. Commission on Civil Rights (USCCR) and for elected officials. In its 1959 report, the commission argued that voting discrimination "undermines the moral suasion of our national stand in international affairs" (USCCR 1959, 134). It argued against housing discrimination, in part because "not the least effect of the inequalities in housing is the doubt it casts throughout the world on our moral capacity for the leadership expected of us" (USCCR 1959, 393). These arguments were echoed by political leaders. When Tennessee Governor Frank Clement ordered state troopers to quell desegregation violence in Clinton, Tennessee, in the fall of 1956, he commented: "How can we be trusted with the peace of the world if we cannot keep peace among ourselves?" (quoted in Collier

1957, 128). In hearings before the U.S. Commission On Civil Rights in 1959, Senator Javits of New York spoke of the need to end discrimination for international reasons (USCCR 1959, 393). The Eisenhower administration acted out of a similar concern. A few days after the *Brown* decision, the Republican National Committee issued a press release stating that the decision was "appropriately within the Eisenhower Administration's many-frontal attack on global Communism" (quoted in Dudziak 1988, 115). And after Eisenhower sent troops to Little Rock, his speech explaining the decision was translated into forty-three languages and the Voice of America broadcast details of the intervention (Burk 1984, 186).

In the Kennedy administration, the theme continued. Attorney General Robert Kennedy urged the freedom riders to halt their journey to allow the president to hold forthcoming talks with European and Communist heads of state without the vivid reminder of segregation (Lomax 1964, 23; Branch 1988, 472–73; Goldman 1961, 5), and he called their decision to stay in jail "good propaganda for America's enemies" (quoted in Branch 1988, 476). In a speech at the University of Georgia in 1961, he criticized incidents like Little Rock because they "hurt our country in the eyes of the world." Graduation of black students from the University of Georgia, Kennedy said, "will without question aid and assist the fight against Communist political infiltration and guerilla warfare" (quoted in Branch 1988, 414). And lack of progress, the Kennedy administration feared, would have the opposite effect. Intelligence reports to the administration noted that the Soviet Union broadcast 1,420 anti-U.S. commentaries about racism and repression in Birmingham in just the two weeks following the settlement between civil rights demonstrators and city authorities (Branch 1988, 807).[12]

The concern that segregation hurt the U.S. internationally also found its way into U.S. government briefs in civil rights cases (Dudziak 1988, 103–13). In *Shelley* v. *Kraemer* (1948), the restrictive covenant case, the government's *amicus* brief contained the State Department's position that "the U.S. has been embarrassed in the conduct of foreign relations by acts of discrimination taking place in this country" (Brief for the United States, *Shelley* 1948, 19). To bolster this position, the brief quoted extensively from Secretary of State Acheson's 1946 letter discussed above (PCCR 1947, 19–20). In *Henderson* v. *U.S.* (1950), the U.S. devoted four pages of its brief to documenting the ways in which discrimination embarrassed the government in the conduct of foreign policy (Neier 1982, 51). In *Sweatt* (1950) and *McLaurin* (1950), the U.S. urged the Court to view segregation through a Cold War lens: "It is in the context of a world in which freedom and equality must become living realities, if the democratic way of life is to survive, that

12. Branch also notes intelligence reports that this was a seven-fold increase in hostile broadcasts over the height of the Meredith crisis at the University of Mississippi, and a nine-fold increase over the criticism of the freedom rides.

the issues in these cases should be viewed" (quoted in Dudziak 1988, 109). And finally, in the U.S. brief in *Brown* in 1952, the attorney general wrote: "It is in the context of the present world struggle between freedom and tyranny that the problem of racial discrimination must be viewed. . . . Racial discrimination furnishes grist for the Communist propaganda mills" (Brief for the United States, *Brown* 1954, 6).

So natural was the Cold War rhetoric that even civil rights groups used it. The NAACP used it, both in its briefs defending the rights of blacks (Bell 1980, 96), and in praising the *Brown* decision, the day it was issued, for "being very effective in combatting propaganda of Communists" ("N.A.A.C.P. Sets Advanced Goals" 1954, 16). In the final report of an NAACP conference in Atlanta following *Brown*, the decision was celebrated, in part, as "vindication of America's leadership of the free world" (quoted in Wilkins 1984, 216). Similarly, speaking in the early 1950s, Whitney M. Young, Jr., then working for the Omaha National Urban League, and later to become the league's national leader, relied on Cold War arguments to support civil rights (Weiss 1989, 52). Surprisingly, the more activist wing of the civil rights movement used Cold War rhetoric as well. In 1960, the student sit-in movement in Atlanta included international concerns among its six reasons for acting ("An Appeal" 1960, 13). And Dr. King, in his speech at St. John's Church in Birmingham announcing and celebrating the settlement of that campaign, stated:

> The United States is concerned about its image. When things started happening down here, Mr. Kennedy got disturbed. For Mr. Kennedy . . . is battling for the minds and the hearts of men in Asia and Africa—some one billion men in the neutralist sector of the world—and they aren't gonna respect the United States of America if she deprives men and women of the basic rights of life because of the color of their skin. Mr. Kennedy *knows* that. (quoted in Branch 1988, 791)

Judges, too, were not immune from this argument. At a testimonial dinner in his honor in 1962, J. Skelly Wright reminded his audience:

> In the present great struggle between the East and the West for the minds of men, 90 per cent of the people of the world are colored. . . . If we're going to make any progress with that 90 per cent we had better practice what we preach. (quoted in Sarratt 1966, 203)

Finally, the press used the Cold War to support civil rights. The *St. Louis Post-Dispatch* wrote of the *Brown* decision: "Had the decision gone the other way, the loss to the free world in its struggle against Communist encroachment would have been incalculable. Nine men in Washington have given us a victory that no number of divisions, arms, and bombs could ever have won" (quoted in USCCR 1959, 164). The *New York Times* editorialized: "When some hostile propagandist rises in Moscow or Peiping to accuse us of being a class society, we can . . . recite the courageous words of yesterday's opinion" ("All God's Chillun" 1954, 28). And, despite the fact that Universal Newsreels never mentioned *Brown*, the Voice of America immediately translated the opinion into thirty-four languages and broadcast it around the world (Branch 1988, 113).

The Cold War, and the not-hard-to-come-by perception that segregation was a blemish on American democracy, provided an argument for civil rights. As I have shown, it was an argument that was made much of. And like the effect of industrialization and economic growth cited earlier, it was independent of the courts.[13]

A Changing Society

Throughout the post-war years, America was changing rapidly. The demands and opportunities created by the economy, and the rhetoric of the Cold War, gave civil rights a tremendous boost. But the pressure for civil rights had been building for a long time.[14] Starting with the Unemployment Relief Act of 1933, nondiscrimination provisions were enacted in many employment and training programs of the thirties and early forties. Regulations of many federal agencies also prohibited employment discrimination in various federally assisted programs such as the public works program of the 1933 National Industrial Recovery Act. The Ramspeck Act of 1940 barred racial discrimination in the federal civil service and the armed forces. Although these provisions has little practical effect, they did demonstrate a growing awareness of the need to fight discrimination.

This change can also be seen in a number of other ways. In January 1947, an attempt was made to bar a segregationist Senator, Bilbo of Mississippi, from taking his seat in Congress. Bilbo stepped aside voluntarily for an operation, and died before the matter could be resolved (Lawson 1976, 113). Change can also be seen in the number of civil rights bills introduced and sponsors recorded in successive sessions of Congress. As early as 1940 the House passed an anti-lynching bill. It passed anti-poll-tax bills in 1943, 1945, and 1947. In 1944 and 1945, 134 and 179 signatures, respectively, were gained on discharge petitions for civil rights bills in the House (Hazel 1957, 130, 261, 133, 137). Overall, while only ten pro-civil-rights bills were introduced in the Seventy-fifth Congress (1937–38), the number increased steadily, reaching seventy-two in the 1949–50 period (Eighty-first Congress) (Woodward 1974, 127).[15] In the case of equal opportunity legislation, the number of sponsors in both houses of Congress increased gradually over time,

---

13. These factors were often combined: "Negroes are gradually accumulating economic strength, and a democracy competing in a cold war with Moscow must enfranchise them" (T.R.B. 1957, 2).

14. For a brief history of government action, see USCCR (1977c, 65–69).

15. McAdam gives a figure of thirteen bills introduced in the 1937–38 session but agrees with the latter number and the trend (McAdam 1982, 6).

commencing at one in 1941–42 and reaching thirty-four by 1951–52. Interestingly, the latter number was not reached again for a decade, until 1961–62 (Burstein and MacLeod 1979, 27). The growing increase in civil rights activity in Congress suggests a changing society.

Black leaders made good use of this growing awareness. As already mentioned, as far back as 1946 CORE staged a freedom ride. The Journey of Reconciliation, as it was called, took CORE members through Virginia, North Carolina, and Kentucky and demonstrated the extent of segregation that existed. Earlier, under the leadership of A. Philip Randolph, president of the Brotherhood of Sleeping Car Porters, black leaders threatened a massive march on Washington, D.C., for jobs (Randolph 1964). In response to this threat, President Roosevelt, by executive order (8802), established a Fair Employment Practices Committee to guard against discrimination in federal employment and vocational training programs. The Committee lacked enforcement powers and died in 1946, but it did demonstrate that blacks had the power to exert pressure on the government.

President Truman also responded to civil rights through executive orders. In December 1946, he established a Committee On Civil Rights whose report I have cited repeatedly. In many senses the report served as a "blueprint" for civil rights, "urging much of the significant action to be taken against racial discrimination in the next two decades" (Greenberg 1977, 588).[16] Executive Orders 9980 and 9981, issued in July 1948, established a Fair Employment Board within the Civil Service Commission and a presidential commission on segregation in the armed forces. The point of this brief history is to demonstrate that the civil rights movement that burst forth in the 1960s had been growing for three decades. While the pot did not boil over until the 1960s, it had been simmering for a long time.

Another indication of the growing civil rights movement is the number of reported civil rights demonstrations. Thanks to the work of Paul Burstein the growth in civil rights demonstrations has been traced (see table 4.2). In the 1940s, there was a growing number of such demonstrations, rising from two in 1941 to twenty-seven in 1948. In fact, there were more civil rights demonstrations in the years 1943, 1946, 1947, and 1948 than in any year following until 1960 (1956 and 1958 excepted)!

Other signs of change include the steady growth of black literacy rates through the 1940s and 1950s, reaching 82 percent in 1960 (USCCR 1961b, 1: 42). Also, the social and economic variables that combined with political factors to keep blacks unregistered and politically inactive were "declining rapidly" while "every one of the variables positively associated" with the attainment of civil rights was "on the increase" (Matthews and Prothro

16. In 1948 the report was read virtually verbatim to the American public in four radio broadcasts, accompanied by music, over the Mutual Broadcasting System (Siepmann and Reisberg 1949).

1963a, 44). Blacks themselves were increasingly optimistic about the future. In a 1942 Roper survey fully 50 percent of blacks thought their sons would have more opportunity to get ahead than they had, compared to 46 percent of whites. By 1947, however, the black figure jumped to 75 percent while the white figure reached only 62.1 percent (McAdam 1982, 109).[17] The spread of mass communication was having an impact as television and radio brought the talents of black entertainers or sports heroes like Jackie Robinson to all (Kluger 1976, 749). By the 1960s the media coverage of the brutality of segregation had a receptive audience.

The combination of all these factors—growing civil rights pressure from the 1930s, economic changes, the Cold War, population shifts, electoral concerns, the increase in mass communication—created the pressure that led to civil rights. The Court reflected that pressure; it did not create it. Even Jack Greenberg, head of the NAACP Inc. Fund, admits that by the time of *Brown* there "was a current of history and the Court became part of it" (Greenberg 1977, 589). That current was growing in force and, as my analysis has shown, the Court contributed little to it. So strong was the pressure for change, argues Peltason, that "even if the Supreme Court had sustained segregation, such a decision could not have long endured" (Peltason 1971, 249). Reflecting on the growing social, political, and economic forces of the time, the government's civil rights litigator Elman put it this way: "In *Brown* nothing that the lawyers said made a difference. Thurgood Marshall could have stood up there and recited 'Mary had a little lamb,' and the result would have been exactly the same" (Elman 1987, 852). But I need not engage in historical speculation. All I need to show is that there is evidence that the changes in civil rights could plausibly have happened without Supreme Court action. For if they could have, then my finding that the courts contributed little to civil rights does not violate the skeptic's concern for causation. And while there is no way to be certain, the lack of evidence for the contribution of the courts, and the evidence of the strength of social, economic, and political change, go a long way toward establishing causal connections.

17. The two questions differed in wording.

PART 2

Abortion and Women's Rights

Introduction

The women's rights movement, beginning after the civil rights movement, had the potential advantage of hindsight. In selecting strategies for change, the experience of civil rights loomed large. Its successes and failures could provide guideposts, if not a blueprint, for women's rights activists. Making the strategic choice, many women's rights activists sought to emulate the civil rights movement's use of the courts, viewing the test-case method, pioneered by the NAACP Legal Defense and Educational Fund, Inc., as "equally appropriate for women's rights" (Berger 1980, 7). Relying on the civil rights movement as an example of a successful use of the courts to produce significant social reform, and assuming "congruence between civil rights and women's rights" (Berger 1980, 8), groups were formed to litigate women's rights issues. Money, time, and talent were poured into the litigation strategy. What were the results?

At first glance, the results appear spectacular, particularly with abortion. In 1973, in *Roe* v. *Wade* and *Doe* v. *Bolton*, the Supreme Court found restrictive abortion laws unconstitutional. The cases, it is claimed, "sent shock waves" through the country (Friedman 1983, 13). The Court was seen as making "a landmark decision" ("The Supreme Court and Abortion" 1973, 14) with radical effects: "No victory for women's rights since enactment of the 19th Amendment has been greater than the one achieved Monday in the Supreme Court" ("A Woman's Right" 1973, A4). According to one critic, *Roe* and *Doe* "may stand as the most radical decisions ever issued by the Supreme Court" (Noonan 1973, 261). Thus, supporters and critics alike view the Court as having produced significant social reform.

In other areas, major Court victories were also achieved. In 1971, the Supreme Court, for the first time, found a gender-based classification unconstitutional (*Reed* v. *Reed* 1971). Then, in 1973, it came within one vote of holding gender classifications "suspect," according them the same place as race in equal-protection analysis (*Frontiero* v. *Richardson* 1973). This suggested to many people that the Court was on the eve of a judicial revolution. *Roe* and *Doe*, also decided in 1973, further emboldened those who saw in litigation the way to end gender-based discrimination. Cowan, for example, wrote that achieving equality "through the Supreme Court's interpretation of existing constitutional provisions steadily appears more promising" (Cowan 1976, 373). As early as 1971, Sassower had suggested that the Supreme Court was on the verge of extending the Fourteenth Amendment to women (Sassower 1971). And Berger found that reading sex into the Fourteenth Amendment was the "first priority of women's rights advocates" (Berger 1980, 16). There were even some who argued that passage of the Equal Rights Amendment was unnecessary because the Court was going to apply strict scrutiny to gender-based classifications, in effect reading sex into the Fourteenth Amendment.[1] It appeared that here, too, the Court was producing significant social reform.

If this is the case with both abortion and women's rights, then the constraints and conditions developed in chapter 1 are limited to civil rights. The Dynamic Court view, it appears, has triumphed. Before accepting this conclusion, however, I will examine the data more closely, for if the accepted wisdom in civil rights turned out to be wrong, the same might be true here as well. In chapter 6, I examine the *judicial* effects of the Court's abortion decisions, and apply the constraints and conditions to the findings. Chapter 7 presents a similar discussion with women's rights.

There is also, of course, the question of *extra-judicial* effects of the Dynamic Court view. Litigation may have brought abortion and women's rights to the national political agenda. It may have served to quicken change in American public opinion about the issues. In addition, it may have served as a catalyst for the whole movement. Indeed, one student of the movement's use of the courts finds a "consensus" that "until the litigation effort began, the women's rights movement was a topic for conversation, not action" (Berger 1980, 55). The evidence for extra-judicial effects is examined in chapter 8. Finally, chapter 9 explores the women's rights movement as a whole, helping to put the courts' contributions in a larger perspective.

It must be stressed that there is an ongoing debate about the extent of change in the position of women in American society. The analysis presented in the following chapters, while assuming that some change has occurred, does not depend on the extent of that change. Rather, relying on the constraints and conditions, it examines whether the courts have been instrumental in producing whatever change has occurred.

1. The President's Commission on the Status of Women, appointed by President Kennedy in 1961, took this position as early as the 1960s (Hole and Levine 1971, 23).

6

Transforming Women's Lives?
The Courts and Abortion

Court Action

In *Roe* v. *Wade* (1973) and its companion case, *Doe* v. *Bolton* (1973), the Supreme Court held unconstitutional, as violative of the due process clause of the Fourteenth Amendment, Texas and Georgia laws prohibiting abortions except for "the purpose of saving the life of the mother" (Texas) and where "pregnancy would endanger the life of the pregnant mother or would seriously and permanently injure her health" (Georgia).[1] Although responding specifically to the laws of Texas and Georgia, the broad scope of the Court's constitutional interpretation invalidated abortion laws in forty-six states and the District of Columbia.[2] The Court found that a pregnant woman has a fundamental right of privacy in deciding whether or not to bear a child. This right could only be overcome if the state had a "compelling" interest. Such interest was found to be utterly lacking in the first trimester in which the choice of abortion was constitutionally held to be the woman's alone, in consultation with a physician. The "State's important and legitimate interest in the health of the mother" became "compelling" at "approximately the end of the first trimester." At that point the state could "regulate the abortion procedure to the extent that the regulation reasonably relates to preservation and protection of maternal health." Finally, after "viability," in approximately the third trimester, the Court found a compelling state interest in preserving the life of the then possibly viable fetus and held that the Constitution

1. The Texas law was approximately a century old. It made no exception for rape, incest, or birth defects. The Georgia law, a modern statute patterned upon the American Law Institute's Model Penal Code, also allowed abortion where the "fetus would very likely be born with a grave, permanent, and irremediable mental or physical defect" and for rape. At reargument, the state argued that it interpreted the rape exception to include incest (*Doe* v. *Bolton* 1973, 183 n.5).
2. Alaska, Hawaii, New York, and Washington had previously liberalized their laws. The constitutional requirements set forth in *Roe* and *Doe* were basically met by these state laws.

did not forbid state restrictions, except where abortion was necessary to pre-serve the life or health of the woman (*Roe* 1973, 163, 164).

While *Roe* and *Doe* were the Court's first major abortion decisions,[3] they were not its last. In response to the decisions, many states rewrote their abor-tion laws, ostensibly to conform with the Court's constitutional mandate. Cases quickly arose, however, challenging state laws as inconsistent with the Court's ruling, if not openly and clearly hostile to it. In general, the Court's response was to preserve the core holding of *Roe* and *Doe* but defer to legis-lation in areas not explicitly dealt with in those decisions. What these cases show is that although there was a great deal of support for the decisions, there remained intense opposition in many parts of the country. Thus, these cases require mention.

One such area was the degree of participation in the abortion decision constitutionally allowed to the spouse of a pregnant married woman or the parents of a pregnant single minor. In *Planned Parenthood* v. *Danforth* (1976), and *Bellotti* v. *Baird* (1979), Missouri and Massachusetts laws, re-spectively, requiring such consent were held unconstitutional. In *H.L.* v. *Matheson* (1981), however, a Utah law requiring a physician to "notify, if possible" the parents of an unmarried minor upon whom an abortion is to be performed prior to the abortion was upheld. Finally, in *Planned Parenthood* v. *Ashcroft* (1983), *Hodgson* v. *Minnesota* (1990), and *Ohio* v. *Akron Center for Reproductive Health* (1990), Missouri, Minnesota, and Ohio laws, re-spectively, requiring minors to secure parental or judicial consent before ob-taining an abortion were upheld.

A second area that provoked a great deal of litigation involved state and federal funding for abortion. In *Beal* v. *Doe* (1977), the Court held that states accepting Medicaid funding were not required to perform abortions. In *Maher* v. *Roe* (1977), the Court upheld a Connecticut regulation that provided finan-cial assistance for childbirth but not for abortion, unless "medically neces-sary." In 1980, in *Harris* v. *McRae* (1980), the Court upheld the most restrictive version of the Hyde Amendment, barring the use of federal funds for even most medically necessary abortions including those involving preg-nancies due to rape or incest.[4] Finally, in *Webster* v. *Reproductive Health Services* (1989), the Court upheld a ban on the use of public employees and facilities for non-therapeutic abortions.

Another area of litigation involved the procedural requirements that states could impose before allowing an abortion. The bulk of cases in this area appear to have arisen from state attempts to make abortions as difficult as

3. In 1971, the Court heard an abortion case from Washington, D.C. The decision, how-ever, did not settle the legal issues involved in the abortion controversy (*United States* v. *Vuitch* 1971).

4. In a companion case, *Williams* v. *Zbaraz* (1980), the Court upheld an Illinois law pro-hibiting public funding for abortions except where "necessary for the preservation of the life of the woman."

possible to obtain. One approach was to ban abortions in public hospitals. In *Poelker* v. *Doe* (1977), the Court upheld the claim of the City of St. Louis that it could prohibit non-therapeutic abortions in its municipal hospitals. In *City of Akron* v. *Akron Center for Reproductive Health* (1983), the Court struck down a law requiring all post-first-trimester abortions to be performed in hospitals, holding that such a requirement "unreasonably infringes upon a woman's constitutional right to obtain an abortion" (*Akron* 1983, 439). The requirement of the informed, written consent of a woman before an abortion could be performed was upheld by the Supreme Court in *Danforth* (1976) but rejected in *Akron* (1983). A twenty-four hour waiting period before an abortion could be performed was also rejected in *Akron*. In other cases, a statute requiring physicians to preserve the life of viable fetuses was struck down as "void for vagueness" (*Colautti* v. *Franklin* 1979), and restrictions on the disposal of fetal remains were voided (*Akron* 1983). Finally, the Supreme Court upheld provisions requiring a pathology report for each abortion and the presence of a second physician at abortions occurring after potential viability (*Ashcroft* 1983).

While supporters and critics of *Roe* and *Doe* might disagree as to whether the Court's actions since 1973 upheld the spirit and logic of the decisions, it is clear that they did not end efforts to limit the ease and availability of abortion. Ten years later, the Court felt it necessary to acknowledge the continuing conflict over abortion and reaffirm its earlier decisions. In the first page of the 1983 *Akron* decision, Justice Powell noted that "arguments continue to be made . . . that we erred in interpreting the Constitution." "Nonetheless," he continued, "the doctrine of *stare decisis*, while perhaps never entirely persuasive on a constitutional question, is a doctrine that demands respect in a society governed by the rule of law. We respect it today and reaffirm *Roe* v. *Wade*" (*Akron* 1983, 419–20). The unusualness of this presentation is heightened by the footnote attached to it, the first footnote of the decision. Reminiscent of *Cooper* v. *Aaron*, where the Court went to great lengths to stress that *Brown* was not merely a political decision, and along with that opinion unique in modern constitutional law, the note stressed the non-political nature of the right to abortion:

> There are especially compelling reasons for adhering to *stare decisis* in applying the principles of *Roe* v. *Wade*. That case was considered with special care. It was first argued during the 1971 Term, and reargued—with extensive briefing—the following Term. The decision was joined by the Chief Justice and six other Justices. Since *Roe* was decided in January 1973, the Court repeatedly and consistently has accepted and applied the basic principle that a woman has a fundamental right to make the highly personal choice whether or not to terminate her pregnancy. . . . (*Akron* 1983, 420 n.1)

In sum, in finding a fundamental right for a woman to elect a safe and legal abortion, the Supreme Court invalidated laws in most states. Since

1973, the Court continued to reaffirm that basic right while upholding some, but not all, federal and state laws and regulations that made access to safe and legal abortion more difficult, particularly for indigent women.[5] The question that remains is how access to legal and safe abortion changed in the wake of these decisions.

Legal Abortions in the United States—The Numbers

The involvement of the Court in the abortion debate, and the claims that have been made about it, make *Roe* and *Doe* a good test of the explanatory power of the two views and the constraints and conditions derived from them. If, as the Dynamic Court view would predict, Court action was crucial in enabling women to obtain abortions, a steep increase in the number of abortions after January 1973 should be noted. If, however, the Constrained Court view is the more accurate, and the Court was not effective, no such surge should be seen. Finally, if the Court had a limited but noticeable impact, it may well be that the constraints and conditions derived from the two views offer the best explanation of the change that occurred.

Collecting statistics on legal abortion is not an easy task. Record-keeping is not as precise and complete as one would hope. Two organizations, the public Center for Disease Control in Atlanta and the private Alan Guttmacher Institute in New York[6] are the most thorough and reliable collectors of the information. The data they have collected are presented in table 6.1 and figure 6.1.

The numbers are striking. First, they show that after *Roe* the number of legal abortions increased at a strong pace throughout the 1970s. Second, however, they show that the changes after 1973 were part of a trend that started in 1970, three years before the Court acted. Examining column 3 of table 6.1, labeled "Change," it is clear that the largest increase in the number of legal abortions occurs between 1970 and 1971, two years before *Roe*. The increase between 1972 and 1973 is 157,800, a full 134,500 fewer than the 1970–71 increase. It is possible, of course, that the impact of *Roe* was not felt in 1973. Even though the decision was handed down in January, perhaps the 1973–74 comparison gives a more accurate picture. If this is the case, the increase is 154,000, still substantially smaller than the 1970–71 change. And while the number of legal abortions continued to increase in the years after 1974, the rate of increase stabilized and then declined.

Another way of analyzing the data is to look at two- and three-year com-

5. The 1989 *Webster* case, despite the furor that it created, maintained this position.
6. The Alan Guttmacher Institute is the research division of Planned Parenthood. Periodically it takes national surveys of abortion providers. Its abortion rate figures are the "only national count obtained by directly surveying providers" (Forrest et al. 1979a, 15).

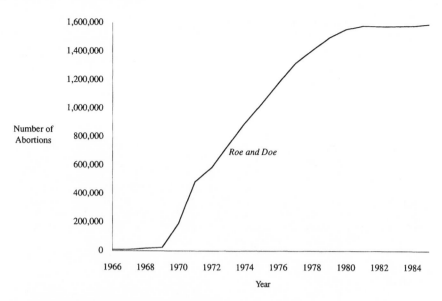

Figure 6.1. Legal Abortions, 1966–1985

parisons. The largest increase over a two-year period is in 1969–71 with an increase of 463,100 legal abortions. Next is 1970–72 with 393,300, about 26 percent higher than the 1972–74 increase of 311,800. The 1971–73 increase is only 258,800. Even the 1973–75 increase is only 289,600. The largest increase over three years comes in the pre-*Roe* 1969–72 period where there were an additional 564,100 legal abortions. The 1972–75 period saw an increase of 447,400 legal abortions, and between 1973 and 1976 the increase was 434,700.

The data presented above show that the largest numerical increases in legal abortions occurred in the years prior to initial Supreme Court action. This holds both for single and multi-year comparisons. There was no steep or unusual increase in the number of legal abortions following *Roe*. While the increases were large and steady, they were smaller than those of previous years. On the one hand, this finding is startling, for it suggests, contradicting the Dynamic Court view, that rather than starting a social revolution, the Supreme Court merely acknowledged one in progress and let it continue. As one commentator put it, with abortion the Supreme Court was "reflecting social change rather than legislating it" (Hansen 1980, 375). On the other hand, it is possible that without constitutional protection for abortion no more states would have liberalized or repealed their restrictive laws and those that did might have overturned their previous efforts. Thus, the fact that the number of legal abortions continued to increase after 1973, contrary to the Constrained Court

Table 6.1   Legal Abortions, 1966–1985

Year	No.	Change	% Change	Period	Change
1966	8,000			1969–71	463,100
1967	9,000	1,000	13	1970–72	393,300
1968	18,000	9,000	100	1971–73	258,800
1969	22,700	4,700	26		
1970	193,500	170,800	752		
1971	485,800	292,300	151		
1972	586,800	101,000	21	1972–74	311,800
1973	744,600	157,800	27	1973–75	289,600
1974	898,600	154,000	21		
1975	1,034,200	135,600	15	1969–72	564,100
1976	1,179,300	145,100	14	1972–75	447,400
1977	1,316,700	137,400	12	1973–76	434,700
1978	1,409,600	92,900	7		
1979	1,497,700	88,100	6		
1980	1,553,900	56,200	4		
1981	1,577,300	23,400	2		
1982	1,573,900	−3,400	−.2		
1983	1,575,000	1,100	.07		
1984	1,577,200	2,200	.1		
1985	1,588,600	11,400	.7		

SOURCES: This table is compiled from estimates by the Alan Guttmacher Institute and the Center for Disease Control found in the following: Alan Guttmacher Institute (1976, 27; 1979, 5–6); Forrest, Sullivan, and Tietze (1979a, 12); Lader (1973, 209); Tietze (1970, 7); Tyler in U.S. Cong. (1974, 1976, 2: 128); U.S. Bureau of the Census (1983, 71); Weinstock et al. (1975, 23); Henshaw, Forrest, and Van Vort (1987, 64).

NOTE: All numbers are rounded. When sources differed I have relied on data from the Alan Guttmacher Institute, since they are based on surveys of all known abortion providers and are generally more complete.

view, suggests that the Court was at least partially effective in easing access to safe and legal abortion.[7] It is the task of the remainder of this chapter to use the constraints and conditions to explore and explain these findings.

Some Explanations

The conclusions of the previous section may appear startling. Much popular and scholarly discussion of abortion is placed in the context of Court action being crucial to change. Yet the data show that the increase in the number of legal abortions can only partly be attributed to the Court. This suggests that neither view of Court effectiveness is correct. It does not, however, rule out the explanatory power of the constraints and conditions derived from them. In the pages following, I explore their applicability to the abortion findings.

7. It appears that the Court may also have been effective in producing change by helping to eliminate *illegal* abortions. Data and a brief discussion on this point are presented in Appendix 6.

Precedent and the Limited Nature of Constitutional Rights

As proponents of the Constrained Court view argue, the Constitution, and the set of beliefs that surround it, is not unbounded. Certain rights are enshrined in it and others are rejected. This means that reformers must often argue for the establishment of a new right, or for the extension of a generally accepted right to a new situation. Courts, however, are not often willing to create "new" rights or extend existing ones. Judicial discretion is bound by both precedent and the norms and expectations of the broader legal culture. This means that litigation for social reform often faces enormous initial barriers. How did abortion reformers overcome this obstacle?

They overcame it by relying on two important Supreme Court decisions in the privacy area, a host of lower federal court and state high court decisions invalidating restrictive abortion laws, and four law-review articles suggesting a supportive legal community. Thus, reformers could plausibly argue that, far from demanding a judicial revolution, all they were asking for was a modest extension of a well-accepted right.

On the Supreme Court level, major reliance was placed on *Griswold* v. *Connecticut* (1965) and *Eisenstadt* v. *Baird* (1972). In *Griswold*, the Supreme Court invalidated a Connecticut law prohibiting the use of contraceptives, finding the law in violation of the "right of privacy" that emanates from the "penumbras" of specific guarantees of the Bill of Rights. *Griswold* established a constitutional right to privacy that protected the use of contraceptives (designed, of course, to prevent pregnancy). In *Eisenstadt*, the Court overturned a conviction for providing a contraceptive to an unmarried person, using broad language to expand the constitutional right of privacy: "If the right of privacy means anything, it is the right of the *individual*, married or single, to be free from unwarranted governmental intrusion into matters so fundamentally affecting a person as the decision whether to bear or beget a child" (*Eisenstadt* 1972, 453).

Reformers were not limited to relying exclusively on Supreme Court precedents. In at least fourteen additional cases, lower federal courts and state supreme courts invalidated restrictive abortion laws, or convictions resulting from them, either as violative of the constitutional right to privacy,[8] as unconstitutionally vague,[9] or for other non-generalizable reasons.[10] Finally, reform-

8. Cases invalidating anti-abortion laws on grounds that they invaded a constitutionally protected zone of privacy include: *People* v. *Belous* (1969); *Babbitz* v. *McCann* (1970); *Roe* v. *Wade* (1970); *Doe* v. *Bolton* (1970); *Doe* v. *Scott* (1971); *Poe* v. *Menghini* (1972); *Abele* v. *Markle* (1972); *YWCA Of Princeton, N.J.* v. *Kugler* (1972); *Klein* v. *Nassau County Medical Center* (1972).

9. Cases voiding anti-abortion statutes on grounds of vagueness include: *People* v. *Belous* (1969); *Doe* v. *Scott* (1971); *YWCA Of Princeton, N.J.* v. *Kugler* (1972); *Florida* v. *Barquet* (1972).

10. Convictions for performing abortions were thrown out in *Doe* v. *Randall* (1970), and *Walsingham* v. *Florida* (1971). Anti-abortion laws were invalidated in *Jacqueline R. and Bee-*

ers made use of four law-review articles that argued for a constitutional right to abortion.[11] The article by former Supreme Court Justice Tom Clark, for example, citing *Griswold*, argued that there was a constitutional right to privacy that included abortion and that until viability the state had no compelling interest in the fetus (Clark 1969, 9). Thus, reformers had a foundation on which to litigate.

It is clear that the Supreme Court made use of this foundation. While it is true that with hindsight disparate and unrelated cases can sometimes be made to appear as coherent precedents, that does not appear to be the case here. The Court's decision is squarely based on the right to privacy as enunciated earlier in *Griswold* and *Eisenstadt*. Also, it is based on the lower-court cases referred to above. Indeed the Court in *Roe* cited many of these cases, taking "note" that "a majority" of "those federal and state courts that have recently considered abortion law challenges . . . have held state laws unconstitutional" (*Roe* 1973, 154). In addition, the Court specifically cited the law-review articles by Clark and Means (*Roe* 1973, 132 n.21, 135 n.26, 140 n.37). Clark's position on when the state's interests become compelling was the standard that the Court adopted. The reformers were able to win in Court in part because the constitutional right they were asking for (or the extension they were asking for) was within the realm of precedent and acceptable legal discourse. Luckily for them, the first factor necessary for Court effectiveness was present.

Political Support

Political support, the constraints suggest, is essential for Court effectiveness. Without such support, as in *Brown*, Court victories provide no reform. How were abortion reformers able to avoid this problem? In order to answer this question, both pre- and post-1973 actions must be examined. In examining them, I make two important arguments. First, by the time the Court reached its decisions in 1973, there was little political opposition to abortion on the federal level, widespread support for it among relevant professional elites and social activists, large-scale use of it (see table 6.1), and growing public support. These positions placed abortion reform in the American mainstream, perhaps suggesting to the Court that giving constitutional protection to abortion was not a radical departure from current American beliefs, practices, and concerns. Second, in the years after 1973, opposition to abortion strengthened and grew. The interesting question this poses is how, given the growing opposition detailed below and referred to in the case discussion, abortion continued to be available.

On the federal level, action evolved from more or less benign neglect to

---

cham v. *Leahy* (1972), and expanded to cover mental health in *Doe* v. *General Hospital of the District of Columbia* (1970).

11. Clark (1969); Lucas (1968); Means (1968; 1971).

an open antipathy to abortion. State action followed a different course. Legislative efforts in the 1960s and early 1970s to reform and repeal abortion laws gave way to efforts to limit access to abortions.

Pre-Roe Support

In the late 1960s, while the abortion-law reform battle was being fought in the states, the federal arena was quiet. Although states with less restrictive laws received Medicaid funds that paid for some abortions, from the enactment of the first state reform law in 1967 to 1973, "not a single bill was introduced, much less considered, in Congress to curtail the use of federal funds for abortion" (Rosoff 1975, 13). The pace quickened in 1968 when the Presidential Advisory Council on the Status of Women, appointed by President Johnson, recommended the repeal of all abortion laws (Lader 1973, 81–82). Abortion was not a major issue in the 1968 presidential campaign. In 1970, the Department of Defense liberalized its abortion policies, permitting abortion in military hospitals for all armed forces personnel and their dependents with the approval of two doctors (Lader 1973, 176; "Judge Rejects Suit" 1971). This policy was further broadened in January of 1971 when the department adopted a policy of paying for abortions in non-military hospitals where legal (Lader 1973, 176). Despite his personal anti-abortion beliefs, President Nixon did not take active steps to limit abortion. While his opponent in the 1972 presidential election, Senator George McGovern, was dubbed by some Republicans the "triple A" candidate (Abortion, Acid, Amnesty), where it mattered the Nixon administration was silent. The U.S. government did not enter Roe nor, after the decision, did it give support to congressional efforts to limit abortion. While it is true that in 1973 and 1974 President Nixon was occupied with other matters, his administration can be characterized as essentially avoiding the abortion issue (O'Connor and Epstein 1984).

In Congress there was virtually no abortion activity prior to 1973. In April 1970, Senator Packwood (R., Ore.) introduced a National Abortion Act designed to "guarantee and protect" the "fundamental constitutional right" of a woman "to control her own fertility" (S. 3746, 91st Cong., 2nd sess., Cong. Rec., 23 Ap. 1970, 12672–73). He also introduced a bill to liberalize the District of Columbia's abortion law (S. 3501, 91st Cong., 2nd sess., Cong. Rec., 24 Feb. 1970, 4538–40). Other than that, Congress remained essentially inactive on the abortion issue.

The story is different in the states. While the full story is told in chapter 9, the essentials are summarized below. Although abortion has always been with us, public discussion did not surface until the 1950s, when medical conferences and publications helped open the question.[12] In the early and mid-

---

12. Luker credits the split in the medical community over abortion with playing a major role in changing it from a purely medical question to a moral and then political one (Luker 1984, chaps. 4 and 5).

1960s, publicity over the infertility drug Thalidomide and over a German-measles epidemic, both of which led to birth defects, gave it increasing urgency. In 1962, the American Law Institute (ALI) published a model penal code on abortion which permitted it in a number of circumstances. By 1965 the American Medical Association's board of trustees urged the code's adoption. Then, in the mid and late 1960s, abortion reform spread from medical and legal professionals to the broader political realm. Groups urging first reform and then repeal of laws prohibiting abortion grew in membership, activities, and willingness to act publicly. Seventy-five leading national groups endorsed the repeal of all abortion laws between 1967 and the end of 1972, including twenty-eight religious and twenty-one medical groups.[13] Among the religious groups support ranged from the American Jewish Congress to the American Baptist Convention. Medical groups included the American Public Health Association, the American Psychiatric Association, the American Medical Association, the National Council of Obstetrics-Gynecology, and the American College of Obstetricians and Gynecologists. Among other groups, support included the American Bar Association and a host of liberal organizations. Even the YWCA supported repeal.

Laws banning abortion were state laws so most of the early abortion-law reform activity was directed at state governments.[14] In the early and mid-1960s action was limited to a few states. In 1967, however, reform bills were introduced in twenty-eight states and by 1968 abortion reform was pending in some thirty states. Finally, in 1970, the four states of Alaska, Hawaii, New York, and Washington essentially repealed their abortion laws.

Another important element in Court efficacy is widespread support from the population at large. By the eve of the Court's decisions in 1973, public opinion had dramatically shifted from opposition to abortion in most cases to substantial, if not majority, support. The data are explored fully in chapter 9. What is important to know here is that by 1973 there was sufficient public support to overcome the constraints.

To sum up, in the five or so years prior to the Supreme Court's decisions, reform and repeal bills had been debated in most states and eighteen had acted to liberalize their laws (Rubin 1982, 164). State action had removed some obstacles to abortion, and safe and legal abortions were available in scattered states. As table 6.1 indicates, in 1972 nearly 600,000 legal abortions were performed. The point of this discussion is to stress the amount of abortion activity taking place prior to the 1973 Court decisions. Activity was widespread, vocal, and effective. Thus, by 1973, there was a great deal of support for the repeal of abortion laws, and the second constraint was overcome.

13. For a list of statements from these groups on their positions, see U.S. Cong. (1976, 4: 53–91).
14. For a thorough history of these laws, see Mohr (1978).

*Post-*Roe *Activity*

On the presidential level, little changed in the immediate years after *Roe*. President Ford, during his short term, said little about abortion until the 1976 presidential campaign in which he took a middle-of-the-road anti-abortion position, supporting local option, the law before *Roe*, and opposing federal funding of abortion (Rubin 1982, 94–95, 149). However, his Justice Department did not enter the *Danforth* case and the Ford administration took no major steps to help the anti-abortion forces.

The Carter administration, unlike its Republican predecessors, did act to limit access to abortion. Candidate Carter opposed federal spending for abortion and President Carter, in a June 1977 press conference, supported the Supreme Court's *Beal* and *Maher* decisions allowing states to refuse Medicaid funding for abortions (Rubin 1982, 107). The Carter administration supported the Hyde Amendment and sent Solicitor General McCree into the Supreme Court to defend it. Clearly, then, the Carter administration put barriers in the way of access to abortion.

Despite the rhetoric of the New Right, the Reagan administration has taken little direct action, an occasional speech aside, to limit abortion. It did enter the *Akron* case, arguing strongly in support of the anti-abortion ordinances, but the Supreme Court did not go along. In addition, as a parting gesture, it filed a brief in the *Webster* case, urging the Court to overturn *Roe*.

On the congressional level, however, there was a great deal of anti-abortion activity after 1973, although almost none of it was successful. From legislation designed to overturn *Roe*, to riders to various spending bills, to constitutional amendments, many members of Congress made their opposition to abortion clear.

Within one week of the Court's decisions, proposals to curtail abortion were flying. One set involved amending the Constitution. Amendments prohibiting abortion in all circumstances were introduced by Representative Lawrence Hogan (R., Md.) in the House and Senator Jesse Helms (R., N.C.) in the Senate. The effect of these amendments, according to the U.S. Commission on Civil Rights (USCCR), would have been to prohibit abortion even to save the life of the woman (USCCR 1975a, 9). A slightly less restrictive constitutional amendment was introduced by Senator Buckley (C-R, N.Y.) and five co-sponsors in the Senate, while a third constitutional amendment, introduced by Representative Whitehurst (R., Va.), would have allowed the states sole discretion in regulating abortion, returning the country to the pre-1973 status quo. In toto, sixty-eight constitutional amendments were proposed in Congress by sixty House members and eight Senators (Rubin 1982, 139).[15]

15. Tatalovich (1988, 201) counts forty-six such amendments.

The 1974 elections removed from Congress a number of staunch anti-abortion leaders including Representative Hogan, who did not seek re-election. However, in the Ninety-fourth Congress, forty House Members (twenty-two Republicans, eighteen Democrats) and seven Senators were identified as strongly anti-abortion. In the first session alone, over fifty constitutional amendments were introduced (Rubin 1982, 139). Amending the Constitution, as supporters of the Equal Rights Amendment have learned, is not a simple task. Since it was not likely that any of the anti-abortion amendments would succeed, another tack was tried. Bills were introduced attaching restrictive anti-abortion riders to seemingly non-abortion-related bills. Here, there was success. An abortion-funding ban was added to the Foreign Assistance Act of 1973, legal services attorneys were prohibited from handling abortion-related cases in the Legal Services Corporation Act of 1974, fetal research was banned in the National Science Foundation Authorization Act of 1974, and a limited ban was included in the National Research Awards and Protection of Human Subjects Act. The Health Programs Extension Act of 1973 was amended to include a "conscience clause" that prohibited the withholding of federal funds from hospitals which refused to perform abortions or sterilizations as a matter of conscience (USCCR 1975a, 11, 12). The initial version of the clause was introduced by Senator Church (D., Idaho) with nineteen Senate co-sponsors and passed the Senate 92 to 1 (Rosoff 1975, 15). But none of these bills had much of an effect on abortions in the United States.

Another approach was tried in 1974: a ban on federal funding of abortion. One bill was defeated in the House nearly 2 to 1 on June 28, 1974, while another was removed in conference committee on November 21, 1974, after the congressional elections (USCCR 1975a, 13–14). Another effort to ban federal funding of abortions was made in 1976. This time the bill was "easily approved" by the House but rejected by the Senate in a 53–35 vote. However, Representative Conte (R., Mass.) eased the bill out of conference by including language allowing the funding of abortion where necessary to save the life of the woman. Thus, the "Hyde Amendment" first became law (Gelb and Palley 1979, 375, 376).[16] It has been staunchly defended by many members of Congress. In *Harris* v. *McRae* 238 members of Congress, "including more than a majority of the members of the House of Representatives," filed an *amicus* brief basically in support of it (Brief of Representative Jim Wright et al., *Harris* 1980, 1). And it has been re-enacted with some variance in language in subsequent years.

Despite the amount of congressional activity,[17] the Hyde Amendment

16. The wording of the Hyde Amendment has varied from year to year. The least restrictive version allowed funding to save the life of the woman, when rape or incest had occurred, or when long-lasting health damage, certified by two physicians, would result from the pregnancy.

17. Overall, the Congressional Research Service reports that Congress enacted thirty restrictive abortion statutes during the 1973–1982 period (Davidson 1983). Tatalovich (1988, 201) reports a slightly smaller figure.

was the only serious piece of anti-abortion legislation passed. While legislation such as the U.S. Civil Rights Extension Act of 1978, which withdrew the Civil Rights Commission's jurisdiction over abortion, and the legislation discussed above, did not further the cause of legal abortion, neither did it do it great harm. Even the Hyde Amendment has had little effect. Although it reduced the annual number of abortions paid for by the federal government from approximately 250,000 prior to 1976 to 2,421 in 1978 (Spencer 1979), it has not greatly affected the number of abortions. According to the Abortion Surveillance Branch of the Center for Disease Control, approximately 94 percent of women who would have been eligible for Medicaid funding before 1976 are still able to obtain some kind of funding. The Center estimates that about 65 percent of these women obtain funding from their states and about 29 percent find other sources. These figures result from the fact that the "vast majority of women seeking abortions live in states that have continued to provide funds for abortions for medically indigent women" (Brody 1981). The point is that Congress was hostile in words but cautious in action with abortion. While not supporting the Court and the right to abortion, congressional action simply did not bar legal abortion.

Prior to 1973 the states had been the main arena for the abortion battle and Court action did not much change that. In the wake of the Court decisions, all but a few states had to rewrite their abortion laws to conform to the Court's constitutional mandate. Their reactions, like those on the federal level, varied enormously. While some states acted to bring their laws into conformity with the Court's ruling, others re-enacted their former restrictive laws or enacted regulations designed to impede access to abortion. Since abortion is a state matter, the potential for state action affecting the availability of legal abortion was high.

At the outset, there was a flurry of legislation. By the end of 1973, Blake reports that 260 abortion-related bills had been introduced in state legislatures and 39 enacted. In 1974, 189 bills were introduced and 19 enacted (Blake 1977b, 46). And state activity continued, with more abortion laws enacted in 1977 than in any year since 1973 (Rubin 1982, 126, 136).

The problem was that many of these laws were hostile to abortion. "Perhaps the major share," Blake discovered, "is obstructive and unconstitutional" (Blake 1977b, 61 n.2). Some of these laws were noted as part of the discussion of the Court's abortion cases. They included spousal and parental consent requirements, tedious written consent forms describing the "horrors" of abortion, funding limitations, waiting periods, hospitalization requirements, elaborate statistical reporting requirements, burdensome medical procedures, and so on. Other state action was simple and directly to the point. North Dakota and Rhode Island responded to the Court's decisions by enacting laws allowing abortion only to preserve the life of the woman (Weinstock et al. 1975, 28; "Rhode Island" 1973). Virginia rejected a bill bringing its statutes into conformity with the Court's order (Brody 1973, 46). Arkansas enforced a state law allowing abortion only if the pregnancy threatened the life or health of the woman ("Abortions Legal for Year" 1973). In Louisiana, the attorney general threatened to take away the license of any physician performing an abortion, and the state medical society declared that any physician who performed an abortion, except to save the woman's life, violated the ethical principles of medicine (Weinstock et al. 1975, 28). The Louisiana State Board of Medical Examiners also pledged to prevent physicians from performing abortions (Brody 1973, 46). In Pennsylvania, the state medical society announced that it did "not condone abortion on demand" and retained its strict standards. And in St. Louis, the city attorney threatened to arrest any physician who performed an abortion (King 1973). Given this kind of activity, it can be concluded that in many states the Court's intent was "widely and purposively frustrated" (Blake 1977b, 60–61).

The years after Court action have also seen the growth of an anti-abortion movement. National groups such as the American Life Lobby, Americans United for Life, the National Right To Life Committee, the Pro-Life Action League, and Operation Rescue, as well as numerous local groups, have adopted some of the tactics of the reformers. They have marched, lobbied, and protested, urging that abortion be made illegal in most or all circumstances. In the last few years, they have adopted more violent tactics. For example, a survey of 1,250 abortion providers in 1985 who served 83 percent of all abortion patients that year found that nearly half (47 percent) had been the target of harassment. Among the group, almost all non-hospital providers performing 400 + abortions per year were harassed. Eighty percent, for example, reported picketing. Illegal activities reported include bomb threats (48 percent), blocking clinic doors (47 percent), trespassing (29 percent), vandalism (28 percent), jamming of telephone lines (22 percent), and death threats (19 percent). As the authors of the survey concluded, "antiabortion harassment in the United States is widespread and frequent" (Forrest and Henshaw 1987, 13).[18]

In terms of public opinion, little has changed since the early 1970s. While differently worded questions produce different results, the American public remains strongly supportive of abortion when the woman's health is endangered by continuing the pregnancy, when there is a strong chance of a serious fetal defect, and when the pregnancy is the result of rape or incest. The public is more divided when abortion is sought for economic reasons, by single unmarried women unwilling to marry, and by married women who do not want more children (Dionne 1989; Lewin 1989; "Average" 1987).

The foregoing discussion suggests two important points about the conditions necessary for the Court to effectively produce significant social reform.

18. See also Sollom and Donovan (1985).

First, by the time of the initial abortion decisions, the conditions for Court effectiveness were present. There was not only sufficient legal precedent for change, but also either indifference to or support for abortion reform from large segments of the political and professional elite. The finding of a constitutional right to abortion appeared to be part of a growing consensus. Second, however, the discussion also suggests that after the decision there was a good deal of opposition to abortion among many political leaders. Congress enacted anti-abortion legislation, as did some of the states. In addition, there was a growing, activist opposition. How this opposition affected the implementation of the decisions, the crucial third constraint, is the focus of the next section.

The Resistance of Local Institutions to Court Orders

On the eve of the abortion decisions, the reformers appeared to have met two necessary conditions for Court effectiveness. First, they had found precedents and scholarly support to argue for a constitutional right of privacy that extended to abortion. Second, they brought their cases with widespread support from critical professional elites, growing public support, successful reform in many states, and indifference from most national politicians. Victory in *Roe* and *Doe*, while perhaps not predictable, was not entirely unexpected. One key constraint remained to be overcome for the Court to be effective—implementation. It is here that reformers were very lucky; one of the conditions necessary for change, a market free to implement, was present.

Abortion is a medical procedure and safe abortion requires trained personnel. But when done properly, first-term and most second-term abortions can be performed on an out-patient basis with less risk of death than with childbirth or with such a routine procedure as tonsillectomy. Following Supreme Court action, however, the medical profession moved with "extreme caution" in making abortion available (Brody 1973, 1). In addition to the hostility of some state legislatures, barriers to legal abortion remained.

The barriers facing access to legal abortion have been strong. Perhaps the strongest barrier has been opposition from hospitals. Table 6.2 tracks the response of hospitals to the Court's decisions. The results are staggering. Despite the relative ease and safety of the abortion procedure, and the unambiguous holding of the Court, both public and private hospitals throughout America refused to perform abortions. In 1973 and the first quarter of 1974, slightly more than three-quarters of public and private non-Catholic short-term general care hospitals did not perform even a single abortion. In the first quarter of 1974, just 17 percent of public short-term general hospitals and 27 percent of comparable non-Catholic private hospitals provided abortion services. As table 6.2 illustrates, the passage of time has not improved the situation. By 1976, three years after the decision, the *vast majority of public and private hospitals had never performed an abortion*! Nationwide, three

Table 6.2   Percentage of Hospital Providers
Providing Abortions, 1973–1985,
Selected Years

Year	Private, Short-Term, Non-Catholic, General	Public
1973	24	
1974	27	17
1975	30	
1976	31	20
1977	31	21
1978	29	
1979	28	
1980	27	17
1982	26	16
1985	23	17

SOURCES: Forrest, Sullivan, and Tietze (1978, 276; 1979a, 12, 46); Henshaw (1986, 253); Henshaw, Forrest, Sullivan, and Tietze (1982, 12); Henshaw, Forrest, and Van Vort (1987, 68); Rubin (1982, 154); Sullivan, Tietze, and Dryfoos (1977, 127); Weinstock et al. (1975, 24, 31).

years after Court action, at least 70 percent of hospitals did not provide any abortion services. In May 1977, Planned Parenthood released figures showing that approximately 80 percent of all public hospitals and 70 percent of non-Catholic private hospitals had *never* performed an abortion (Rubin 1982, 154). And, as recently as 1985, only 17 percent of public and 23 percent of private, non-Catholic, short-term, general hospitals performed any abortions (see table 6.2). Even among hospitals with the capability to perform abortions, only 35 percent performed any in 1985. In only twelve states did a majority of hospitals with such capability actually perform abortions (Tatalovich and Daynes 1989, 82). As Stanley Henshaw concluded, reviewing the data in 1986, "most hospitals have *never* performed abortions" (Henshaw 1986, 253; emphasis added).

These figures mask the fact that even the limited availability of hospital abortions detailed here varied widely across states. In 1973, only 4 percent of all abortions were performed in the eight states that make up the East South-Central and West South-Central census divisions, even though these eight states contained 16 percent of the 1973 U.S. population (Weinstock et al. 1975, 25). Two states, on the other hand, New York and California, home to about 20 percent of U.S. women in 1974, accounted for 37 percent of all abortions that year (Alan Guttmacher Institute 1976, 8). In eleven states, "not a single public hospital reported performance of a single abortion for any purpose whatsoever in all of 1973" (Weinstock et al. 1975, 31). By 1976, three years after Court action, Louisiana, North Dakota, and South Dakota had no hospitals, public or private, which performed abortions (Hansen 1980, 380). In the Dakotas alone, there were thirty public and sixty-two private hospitals. In five other states, with a total of eighty-two public hospitals, not one performed an abortion. In thirteen additional states, less than 10 percent of each state's public hospitals reported performing any abortions (Forrest, Sullivan, and Tietze 1979a, 46). Only in the states of California, Hawaii, New York, and North Carolina, and in the District of Columbia, did more than half the public hospitals perform any abortions in the 1974–75 period (Alan Guttmacher Institute 1976, 30).

These facts did not escape judicial notice. In *Doe* v. *Poelker*, the Eighth Circuit found, in April of 1975, that "not a single abortion has been performed in the St. Louis public hospitals since before the Supreme Court's abortion decisions in January, 1973, to date" (*Doe* v. *Poelker* 1975, 544). And in 1977, three members of the Supreme Court noted that "during 1975 and the first quarter of 1976 only about 18% of all public hospitals in the country provided abortion services, and in 10 states there were no public hospitals providing such services" (*Poelker* v. *Doe* 1977, 523).

This refusal of hospitals to perform abortions means that women seeking them have to travel, often a great distance, to exercise their constitutional rights. In 1973, for example, 150,000 women traveled out of their state of residence to obtain an abortion. By 1982, the numbers had dropped, but over 100,000 women were still forced to travel to another state for abortion services.[19] Table 6.3 lists states in which 10 percent or more of female residents seeking abortions have had to travel to other states to obtain them. As late as 1982, nearly a decade after the Court decisions, over 10 percent of women residing in twenty-two states went to other states to obtain abortions, as did over 20 percent of women residing in twelve states.[20]

Even when women can obtain abortions within their states of residence, they may still have to travel a great distance to obtain them. In 1974 the Guttmacher Institute found that between 300,000 and 400,000 women left their home communities to obtain abortions (Alan Guttmacher Institute 1976, 12). By 1976, matters were no better, and the Guttmacher Institute estimated that 458,000 women had to travel from their homes to another county or state to obtain an abortion (Forrest et al. 1979a, 12). In 1976, the institute estimated that as many as 611,780 women were unable to obtain abortions (Forrest et al. 1979a, 12). In 1980, a study of 300 abortion patients in a clinic in Rapid City, South Dakota, found that half the patients had to travel "more

19. Data from Forrest, Sullivan, and Tietze (1979b, 332); Forrest and Henshaw (1987, 13); Henshaw, Forrest, and Van Vort (1987, 66); Henshaw and O'Reilly (1983, 12); Sullivan, Tietze, and Dryfoos (1977, 124).

20. It is possible, of course, that there are personal reasons for not obtaining an abortion in one's hometown. However, that seems an unlikely explanation as to why in recent years *100,000* women leave their home states to obtain abortions each year.

Table 6.3   Percentage of Women Going Out of State of Residence to
               Obtain Abortions

State of Residence	20% or More				10%–19%			
	1979	1980	1981	1982	1979	1980	1981	1982
Ala.	22							
Ark.		20			10		18	18
Ariz.	25	24	23	22				
Conn.					11			
Del.	23	23					12	19
Idaho	33	26	21					19
Ind.	28	25	26	26				
Iowa			20	20	18	18		
Kan.						10		
Ky.	27	26	33	32				
La.					15	15		15
Me.						11	14	14
Md.	29	26	26	24				
Miss.	45	38	35	36				
Mo.	31	25	27	25				
N.H.	24	24					15	16
N.J.					14	12		
N.M.			25	20				
N.D.	28	24	22					14
Okla.				22	14	13		
Ore.					12			
R.I.					17	14		
S.C.					15	14		14
S.D.	52	52	40	30				
Vt.	21					19		10
Va.					15	15		15
W.Va.	51	52	52	47				
Wyo.	52	54	62	57				
Total no. of states	15	14	13	12	10	10	4	10

SOURCES: 1979 and 1980—Henshaw and O'Reilly (1983, 12)
1981—Henshaw, Binkin, Blaine, and Smith (1985, 96)
1982—Henshaw, Forrest, and Van Vort (1987, 66)

than 100 miles" to obtain their abortions (Henshaw and Wallisch 1984, 180).
While table 6.3 suggests that South Dakota is one of the worst states in the
provision of abortion services, a 1990 survey in Pennsylvania found similar
results: although women residing in all sixty-seven Pennsylvania counties obtained abortions, providers were located in only twenty-five counties, neces-
sitating travel by women residing in forty-two counties (Seelye 1990, 12-A).
In 1980, across the U.S., over one-quarter (27 percent) of all women under-

going abortions did so outside of their home counties (Henshaw and O'Reilly 1983, 5). And, the problem is not merely rural. In 1980, seven years after Court action, there were still fifty-nine metropolitan areas in which *no* facilities could be identified that provided abortions (Henshaw et al. 1982, 5).

Other indicators support these findings. From 1973 on, at least 77 percent of all U.S. counties have been without abortion providers. While rural areas have been the least well served, approximately half of all metropolitan counties have been without abortion providers.[21] It is also the case that almost all legal abortions in the years for which data are available were performed in metropolitan areas. In 1973, 1974, and 1975, the figures were 97 percent, 96 percent, and 95 percent respectively. By 1985, a dozen years after the abortion decisions, 98 percent of all legal abortions still occurred in metropolitan areas.[22] As late as 1985, a full 82 percent of all U.S. counties, with 30 percent of women of reproductive age, had no identified abortion service provider (Henshaw et al. 1987, 64). And between 1985 and 1988, the number of abortion providers in rural areas declined 19 percent (Lewin 1990, A9).

Another bit of evidence for the refusal of hospitals to provide abortion services is the fact that a majority of abortions are performed by a minority of providers. That is, the few providers willing to perform abortions on a regular basis perform the vast majority of them. In the first quarter of 1974, 7 percent of all providers performed 57 percent of all abortions nationwide. In the same period, 3 percent of all hospital providers performed 35 percent of all abortions (Weinstock et al. 1975, 24, 31, 30). In the state of Washington, after it liberalized its abortion laws, only twenty-one physicians performed 66 percent of all abortions (Fujita and Wagner 1973, 247). In terms of numbers, in the years immediately following *Roe*, only 11 percent of providers performed more than two abortions per week (Weinstock et al. 1975, 24, 31). And in the first quarter of 1975, "there were fewer reported hospital abortions than in the first quarter of 1974" (Alan Guttmacher Institute 1976, 11). Further, in 1975 "more than half of hospitals which were classified as providers reported fewer than 100 abortions during the year," or fewer than a minimal two per week (Alan Guttmacher Institute 1976, 29).[23] Across the U.S. between 1974 and 1975 a scant 11 percent of providers accounted for nearly two-thirds of all abortions (Alan Guttmacher Institute 1976, 11). In 1976, 17 percent of providers performed 62 percent of all abortions. In the 1980s, the percentages have remained similar. In 1982, for example, 13 per-

21. Data from Forrest and Henshaw (1987, 13); Henshaw, Forrest, Sullivan, and Tietze (1982, 5, 10); Henshaw, Forrest, and Blaine (1984, 119); Henshaw, Forrest, and Van Vort (1987, 64).

22. Data from Henshaw, Forrest, and Blaine (1984, 120); Henshaw, Forrest, Sullivan, and Tietze (1982, 6); Henshaw, Forrest, and Van Vort (1987, 64).

23. It should be noted that public hospitals account for about 25 percent of all births in the U.S., two and one-half to three times as high as the percentage of abortions (Alan Guttmacher Institute 1976, 12; 1979, 16).

cent of providers performed 56 percent of all abortions and in 1985 15 percent performed 60 percent of all abortions.[24]

Even when abortion service is available, providers have tended to ignore the time periods set out in the Court's opinions. In 1985, a dozen years after the decisions, only 43 percent of all abortion providers performed post-first-trimester procedures. Fewer than half of all hospital providers were willing to perform such abortions. Only with abortion clinics have a majority of providers been willing to perform abortions after the first trimester.[25] Indeed, in 1985 a startling 23 percent of all providers refused to perform abortions past the tenth week of pregnancy, several weeks within the first trimester where the Court has found a woman's constitutional right virtually all-encompassing (Henshaw, Forrest, and Van Vort 1987, 69).

Finally, although abortion is "the most common surgical procedure that women undergo" (Darney et al. 1987, 161), an *increasing* percentage of obstetrics and gynecology residency programs do not provide training for it. A 1985 survey of all such residency programs found that 28 percent of them offer *no* training at all, a nearly fourfold increase since 1976. Approximately one-half of the programs make training available as an option, while only 23 percent include it routinely. And, of course, the percentages that provide training for second trimester abortions are even smaller (figures derived from Darney et al. 1987, 160).

These findings are well illustrated by recent news stories on individual states. In Illinois, the sixth largest state in the Union, abortion is available in only 12 of 102 counties and only 21.6 percent of hospitals with obstetric services perform abortions. Outside of the Chicago area, non-hospital abortion services are available in only four cities (Champaign, Granite City, Peoria, and Rockford). Abortion services are unavailable in the capital, Springfield, a city of 100,000. The result is that "many women have to drive for several hours to find a willing physician" (Lipinski 1989, 1, 12). In Minnesota, there is only one place to obtain an abortion outside of Minneapolis and St. Paul, the Women's Health Center in Duluth. Abortion services are only provided there because a female doctor and long-time abortion activist flies to Duluth from St. Paul once a week (Belkin 1989, 1, 10). In Montana, there are only about a half-dozen doctors in the entire state willing to perform abortions (Belkin 1989, 1). And in North Dakota, the one and only physician performing abortions retired in February 1990. Abortion services are available in North Dakota only because a women's health clinic in Fargo flies physicians in from Minnesota (Wilkerson 1990, 33). As the lead sentence in

24. Data compiled from Henshaw, Forrest, and Blaine (1984, 122, 123, 124); Henshaw, Forrest, and Van Vort (1987, 67); Henshaw and O'Reilly (1983, 11).
25. Data from Henshaw, Forrest, and Blaine (1984, 125); Henshaw, Forrest, and Van Vort (1987, 69).

a July 1989 *New York Times* story put it, "outside of the nation's biggest cities, women who seek abortions must drive for hours and often cross state lines to reach a doctor willing to perform one" (Belkin 1989, 1). Kate Michelman, head of the National Abortion Rights Action League (NARAL), summarized the situation this way: "It's hard to believe we're talking about the United States of America. . . . These women may have the right to an abortion but not the ability to exercise that right" (quoted in Wilkerson 1990, 33).

The bottom line is that hospital administrators, both public and private, refused to change their abortion policies in reaction to the Court decisions. In the years since the Court's decisions, abortion services have remained centered in metropolitan areas and in those states which reformed their abortion laws and regulations prior to the Court's decisions. In 1976, the Alan Guttmacher Institute concluded that "[t]he response of hospitals to the legalization of abortion continues to be so limited . . . as to be tantamount to no response" (Alan Guttmacher Institute 1976, 13). In 1981, Jaffe et al. concluded that "the delivery pattern for abortion services that has emerged since 1973 is *distorted beyond precedent*" (Jaffe et al. 1981, 15; emphasis added). And, reviewing the data in the mid-1980s, Henshaw, Forrest, and Blaine summed up the situation this way: "There is abundant evidence that many women still find it difficult or impossible to obtain abortion services because of the distance of their home to the nearest provider, the cost, a lack of information on where to go, and limitations on the circumstances under which a provider will make abortions available" (Henshaw, Forrest, and Blaine 1984, 122).

The Market as a Condition

The foregoing discussion presents a seeming dilemma. On the one hand, there has been hostility to abortion from politicians, hospital administrators, many doctors, and parts of the public. On the whole, in response to the Court, hospitals did not change their policies to permit abortions. The key constraints that limit Court effectiveness are present. Yet, on the other hand, as table 6.1 demonstrates, the number of legal abortions performed in the U.S. continued to grow after Court action. How is it, for example, that congressional and state hostility seemed to effectively prevent progress in civil rights in the 1950s and early 1960s but did not prevent abortion in the 1970s? Are the constraints of the Constrained Court view simply wrong? The answer to this question not only removes the dilemma but also illustrates why the Court's abortion decisions were effective in making legal abortion more easily available. The answer is that Condition III, a market means of implementation, was present. The Court's decisions allowed the market to implement the decisions. They did so, in a word, with "clinics."

The Court's decisions prohibited the states from interfering with a woman's right to choose an abortion, at least in the first trimester. They did not require hospitalization, and later cases explicitly rejected hospitalization requirements for second trimester abortions (*Akron* 1983; *Ashcroft* 1983).[26] Room was left for abortion reformers, population-control groups, women's groups, and individual physicians to set up clinics to perform abortions. The refusal of many hospitals, then, to perform abortions could be countered by the creation of clinics willing to do the job. And that is exactly what happened.

In the wake of the Court's decisions there was a sharp increase in the number of abortion providers. Table 6.4 presents the data. In the first year after the decisions, the number of providers grew by nearly 25 percent. Over the first three years the percentage increase was 58 percent. The number of providers reached a peak in 1982 and has declined somewhat since then. However, the raw data do not indicate who these providers were. Table 6.5 does.

Table 6.5 clearly shows that the growth in abortion providers came largely from growth in the number of clinics. "To fill the need" that hospitals refused to meet, a 1977 report found, clinics opened in large numbers (Schultz 1977). Between 1973 and 1974 the number of non-hospital abortion providers grew 61 percent. Overall, between 1973 and 1976 the number of non-hospital providers grew 152 percent, nearly five times the rate of growth of hospital providers. In metropolitan areas (not shown), the growth rate was 140 percent between 1973 and 1976, 5 times the rate for hospital providers, while in non-metropolitan areas it was a staggering 304 percent, also about 5 times the growth rate for non-metropolitan hospitals.

The growth in the number of abortion clinics was matched by the increase in the number of abortions performed by them. By 1974, non-hospital clinics were performing approximately 51 percent of all abortions with nearly an additional 3 percent being performed in physicians' offices. Between 1973 and 1974, the number of abortions performed in hospitals rose 5 percent while the number performed in clinics rose 39 percent. By 1975, 55 percent of abortions were performed in non-hospital clinics (Alan Guttmacher Institute 1976, 11, 27), and 60 percent by all non-hospital providers. By 1976, clinics accounted for 62 percent of all reported abortions, despite the fact that they were only 17 percent of all providers (Forrest et al. 1979a, 12, 43). And, the percentages continued to rise, with 87 percent of all abortions performed in non-hospital settings by 1985. In the period 1973–76, the years immediately following Court action, the number of abortions performed in hospitals increased by only 8 percent while the number performed in clinics and physicians' offices increased by a whopping 113 percent (Forrest et al. 1979a,

26. The vast majority of abortions in the U.S. are performed in the first trimester. As early as 1976, the figure was 90 percent (Forrest et al. 1979a, 32).

Table 6.4 **Number of Abortion Providers, 1973–1985**

Year	No.	Change	% Change	Period	Change	% Change
1973	1,627					
		401	24.7			
1974	2,028					
		370	18.3			
1975	2,398					
		169	7.1			
1976	2,567			1973–76	940	57.8
		121	4.7			
1977	2,688			1976–79	167	6.5
		65	2.4			
1978	2,753			1979–82	174	6.4
		−19	−.7			
1979	2,734			1982–85	−228	−7.8*
		24	.9			
1980	2,758					
		138	5.0			
1981	2,896					
		12	.4			
1982	2,908					
1983	u					
1984	2,710					
		−30	−1.1			
1985	2,680					

Source: Compiled from Henshaw, Forrest, and Van Vort (1987, 64).

Notes:
u Data unavailable.
* Because of survey correction, the true % change is reported to be 5%.

Table 6.5 **Facilities that Provide Abortions 1973–1985, Selected Years**

Year	Hospitals		Non-Hospitals*	
	No.	% of Abortions	No.	% of Abortions
1973	1,281	52	346	48
1974	1,471	47	557	54
1975	1,629	40	769	60
1976	1,695	35	872	65
1977	1,654	30	1,055	70
1978	1,626	25	1,127	75
1979	1,526	23	1,208	77
1980	1,504	22	1,254	78
1982	1,405	18	1,503	83
1985	1,191	13	1,489	87

Sources: Forrest, Sullivan, and Tietze (1979a; 1978, 276; 1979b, 329, 338); Henshaw, Forrest, and Blaine (1984, 122, 124, 123); Henshaw, Forrest, Sullivan, and Tietze (1982, 12, 13); Henshaw, Forrest, and Van Vort (1987, 67); Henshaw and O'Reilly (1983, 11); Sullivan, Tietze, and Dryfoos (1977, 127); Weinstock et al. (1975).

*Non-Hospitals include abortion clinics, clinics that provide services in addition to abortion, and physicians' offices.

43).[27] Clinics met the need that hospitals, despite the Court's actions, refused to meet.

In effectively allowing abortions to be performed in clinics as well as hospitals, the Court's decisions allowed a way around the intransigence of existing institutions, notably hospitals. The decisions allowed individuals committed to safe and legal abortion to make use of the market and create their own structures to meet the demand. It also allowed market incentives to operate. At least some clinics were formed solely as money-making ventures. As legal activist Janice Goodman put it, "[s]ome doctors are going to see a very substantial amount of money to be made on this" (Goodman et al. 1973, 31). Even the glacial growth of hospital abortions may be due, in part, to financial considerations. In a study of thirty-six general hospitals in Harris County (Houston), Texas, the need for increased income was found to be an important determinant of whether hospitals performed abortions. Hospitals with low occupancy rates, and therefore low income, the study reported, "saw changing abortion policy as a way to fill beds and raise income" (Kemp et al. 1978, 27).

Although the law of the land was that the choice of an abortion was not to be denied a woman in the first trimester, and regulated only to the extent necessary to preserve a woman's health in the second trimester, American hospitals, on the whole, did not honor the law. However, by allowing the market to meet the need, the Court's decisions resulted in at least a continuation of some availability of safe and legal abortion. While one cannot be sure what might have happened if clinics had not been allowed, if the sole burden for implementing the decisions had been on hospitals, hospital practice suggests that resistance would have been strong. After all, the Court did find abortion constitutionally protected and most hospitals simply refused to accept that decision. Thus, *Roe* and *Doe* offer a clear contrast to *Brown*, where there was no market alternative. Legal activist Nancy Stearns, who filed an *amicus* brief in *Roe* in support of the plaintiffs, put it this way: "In *Brown* the people who were necessary to effect the decision were the very people opposed to the decision. . . . Here [the abortion cases], the people that are necessary to effect the decision are doctors, most of whom are not opposed, probably don't give a damn, and in fact have a whole lot to gain . . . because of the amount of money they can make" (quoted in Goodman et al. 1973, 29). The Court's structural inability to change institutions, as demonstrated by civil rights and hospital abortions, and the unlikeliness of Congress requiring it for abortion, suggests that without clinics the Court's decisions would have been frustrated.

The question that remains is how the Court came to allow the market to

27. The percentage for clinics is not artificially high because of a small number of clinic abortions in the years preceding Court action. In 1973, clinics performed over 330,000 abortions, or about 45 percent of all abortions (Alan Guttmacher Institute 1976, 27).

implement its decision. If, as the data suggest, market implementation was crucial to Court effectiveness, was it a linchpin of the reformers' legal arguments? From a review of all the briefs filed in *Roe* and *Doe*, the oral arguments, and the Court's opinions, it is clear that the issue was hardly touched upon. It was not considered at all in *Roe*. In *Doe*, some attention was paid to it, but it was not of major concern. In other words, the aspect of the abortion decisions that was decisive for their effectiveness was not an important part of the reformers' legal arguments.

In none of the original or supplemental briefs of either party in *Roe*, was there any mention or discussion of the constitutionality of where abortions could be performed.[28] In an *amicus* brief filed on behalf of the Planned Parenthood Federation of America and allied physicians, the issue was referred to or discussed in passing on five of ninety-three pages. Two of the references were to a resolution of the American Medical Association House of Delegates of June 25, 1970, supporting abortion in either "hospitals or approved clinics," and a statement of the Joint Program for the Study of Abortion that there is no increased risk of complications with performance of abortions in free-standing clinics. Two other references were to lower federal court decisions invalidating requirements that abortions be limited to hospitals (Brief for Planned Parenthood Federation of America, *Roe* 1973, 9, 16–17, 17–18). The issue was not discussed in either oral argument.

The issue received somewhat more attention in the appellant's brief in *Doe*, being discussed on five of fifty-seven pages. The brief argued that Georgia's "requirement that abortions be performed in accredited hospitals effectively manipulate[s] out of existence plaintiff's rights." It argued that the statutory limitation of abortions to licensed, accredited hospitals was "irrational" and cited the New York experience since 1970 to demonstrate the safety of non-hospital providers. However, the brief did support licensing of abortion providers and it was not entirely clear if it was opposed to any hospital requirements or only to the particular ones in Georgia (Brief of Appellants, *Doe* 1973, 13, 37, 39, 40). Further, the point was one of many attacks on the Georgia law and it was not given any particular emphasis.

The *amicus* briefs in support of the appellants mentioned the issue as well. One brief cited New York data and argued that health considerations did not support the Georgia accreditation requirement. The discussion was on one of thirty-five pages (Brief of American Ethical Union et al., *Doe* 1973, 23). In the major *amicus* brief, discussion was found on two of ninety-six pages where it was argued that abortion experience did not support the hospital limitation and that there was no sound medical reason to treat abortion differently than any other medical procedure (Brief for The American

28. The appellant's original brief did quote in passing a statement of the Texas Medical Association which limited the performance of abortion to "a duly licensed physician and surgeon in a licensed hospital" (Brief for Appellants, *Roe* 1973, 42–43).

College of Obstetricians and Gynecologists et al., *Doe* 1973, 5, 85). Finally, in a massive four-hundred-and-seventy-seven page supplementary appendix, only the last few articles dealt with the issue at all (Supplementary Appendix, *Doe*, 1973).

The issue came up in oral argument, being mentioned on parts of four of forty-three pages on December 13, 1971, and on six of forty-four pages on October 11, 1972. At the later argument, the Court asked appellant's counsel: "would you think it constitutional to require that the abortion be performed in an accredited hospital?" Mrs. Hames, counsel for the plaintiffs, replied: "I think that abortions should be performed in specialized facilities, regulated by the State . . . clinics are fully capable, by virtue of the New York experience statistics that I was citing, to afford effective and safe abortion services" (Oral Argument, *Doe*, October 11, 1972, 15). The issue was then dropped.

In its opinions, the Court devoted little time to the issue. In *Roe*, the Court cited the positions of the American Medical Association House of Delegates, the American Public Health Association, and the American Bar Association House of Delegates, not opposing the performance of abortions outside of hospitals (*Roe* 1973, 143–44 n.38, 145, 146). In *Doe*, the issue was mentioned on only two pages where the Court held that the "accreditation requirement does not withstand constitutional scrutiny in the present context" (*Doe* 1973, 194).

The scant attention paid to the issue by both the parties and the Court does not mean that its resolution was inevitable. In *People* v. *Barksdale* (1972), decided just two months before *Roe* and *Doe*, the California Supreme Court unanimously upheld that part of the California abortion law that required abortions to be performed in hospitals accredited by the Joint Commission on Accreditation of hospitals.[29] Since not even all hospitals meet this standard, this was a strict limitation. Taking note of the positive New York state experience with clinic abortions, and of the fact that "abortion is the only medical procedure required by criminal sanction to be performed in a hospital" (*Barksdale* 1972, 336, 338), the Court had little trouble upholding the hospital requirement: "Evidence unequivocally points to the risks associated with the performance of abortions in other than a proper surgical environment and supports the requirement that abortions be performed in hospitals" (*Barksdale* 1972, 336). Resolution of the issue was far from inevitable.

The legal record clearly shows that the issue of where abortions could be performed was given little attention. While it was mentioned by several of the *amici*, it was not afforded prominence or even emphasis among a host of issues. It is quite conceivable that the Court could have ignored it completely, and either required abortions to be performed in hospitals or, more likely, left

29. The Court divided on other issues.

states the leeway to decide. Thus, the crucial part of the decision, the holding that allowed the Court to be effective, came more from the Court than the reformers. As Sarah Weddington, who argued in the Supreme Court on behalf of Jane Roe, put it, as far as she knew, allowing abortions to be performed in clinics came entirely from Justice Blackmun, the author of the Court's opinions (author's conversation with Ms. Sarah Weddington, January 22, 1988, University of Chicago Law School). In other words, the reformers got very lucky.

Conclusion

To sum up, detailed examination of the Court's abortion decisions show that the Court has not been the unique actor claimed by proponents of the Dynamic Court view. On the other hand, in refutation of the adherents of the Constrained Court view, the Court has produced some change. Neither view is subtle enough to satisfactorily explain the changes in abortion after Court action. Successful explanation requires a more fine-tuned approach that lays out conditions for Court effectiveness. Such an approach is found in the constraints and conditions derived from the two views. Incorporating pieces of each view, the constraints and conditions highlight the existence of precedent, a supportive legal culture, and the political support necessary for the Court to overcome its structural constraints. Further, they highlight how the availability of a market mechanism for implementation meant that in states where actors were willing to perform abortions change could occur despite the opposition of key institutional actors. As with civil rights, the constraints and conditions offer a powerful explanation of when litigation for significant social reform is likely to succeed and why. And, as with civil rights, the Court is far less responsible for the changes that occurred than most people think.

7

Liberating Women? The Courts and Women's Rights

The Court over the last several decades has been active in promoting, along with civil rights and abortion, women's rights. As suggested in the introduction to Part II, many commentators credited the Court with making major changes in ending gender discrimination. Have the courts played a major role in improving the condition of women? Has litigation been a sensible strategy for producing significant social reform for women? After setting forth the facts of judicial and governmental action, this chapter assesses the judicial contribution in terms of the two views and the constraints and conditions.

Court Action

Until the 1970s, the record of the federal courts in protecting and extending women's rights was abysmal. In the 1870s, despite the recently enacted Fourteenth Amendment, the courts had little trouble in upholding state statutes excluding women from the practice of law (*Bradwell* v. *The State* 1872), from voting (*Minor* v. *Happersett* 1879; *United States* v. *Anthony* 1873), and from jury service.[1] This pattern continued well into the twentieth century. As late as the 1960s, the Supreme Court upheld state statutes excluding women from jury service (*Hoyt* v. *Florida* 1961), and removing the legal capacity of married women to bind themselves personally in contracts (*United States* v. *Yazell* 1966).[2] It was not until 1971 that the Supreme Court first held a state

1. In *Strauder* v. *West Virginia* (1879), the Supreme Court heard a challenge by blacks to a West Virginia statute limiting jury service to white men. In finding the statute constitutionally defective, the Court noted that there is no constitutional problem where states "confine the [jury] selection to males" (1879, 310).
2. *Yazell* is an amazing case. In a nutshell, the Small Business Administration (SBA) moved to foreclose on the Yazell's property after Mr. and Mrs. Yazell defaulted on a SBA disaster loan. Mrs. Yazell's successful defense was that under the Texas law of coverture a married women had no capacity to bind herself personally by contract and thus no foreclosure could be enforced against her separate property.

statute based on gender unconstitutional. After 1971 the Court became more sensitive to gender-based distinctions, examining them with greater scrutiny than most classifications but with explicitly less scrutiny than that afforded race. The result was numerous victories for women's rights litigants. In the paragraphs that follow I briefly highlight some of the more important cases, to give the reader an idea of the volume of litigation and the trend of Court action.

Reed v. *Reed* (1971) was the first Supreme Court case to find a gender-based classification unconstitutional. In *Reed*, the Court found unconstitutional an Idaho law that established an automatic preference for males as executors of wills. Challenges to other types of gender-based classifications followed. In 1976 the Supreme Court threw out an Oklahoma law that allowed eighteen-year-old females to drink beer but required that males be twenty-one (*Craig* v. *Boren*). In *Orr* v. *Orr* (1979), the Court invalidated an Alabama law allowing alimony to be awarded only to women. In several jury-duty cases, automatic gender exemptions, and voluntary exemptions that produced nearly all-male jury venires, were invalidated (*Taylor* v. *Louisiana* 1975; *Duren* v. *Missouri* 1979).

A large number of cases involved issues such as social security benefits, taxes, and pension and disability plans. The first, and perhaps most important case, is *Frontiero* v. *Richardson* (1973) where eight members of the Court held unconstitutional a federal statutory scheme that automatically granted dependency benefits to wives of servicemen without any showing of dependency, but required husbands of servicewomen to make such a showing.[3] In *Weinberger* v. *Wiesenfeld* (1975), the Court found unconstitutional a provision of the Social Security Act that granted benefits to the widow of a wage earner who had primary responsibility for the care of a child but denied benefits to similarly situated men.[4] Similarly, in 1977, the Court held unconstitutional a provision of the Social Security Act requiring widowers but not widows to prove dependency on the deceased spouse before receiving benefits (*Califano* v. *Goldfarb* 1977).[5] In the area of pensions and disability plans, in 1978, in *Los Angeles* v. *Manhart*, the Court found a violation of Title VII in a pension plan requiring larger premiums from women than from men.[6]

In the job area the Court has been consistent in striking down barriers to women's employment, relying on both the Constitution and the action of the

3. Four members of the Court wrote that gender classifications are "inherently suspect and must therefore be subjected to strict judicial scrutiny" (*Frontiero* 1973, 688). It was this language, as mentioned in the introduction to Part II, that suggested to some that the Court would read gender equality into the Fourteenth Amendment.

4. However, in *Kahn* v. *Shevin* (1974), the Court upheld a Florida statute that on its face appeared to favor women by granting a property-tax exemption to widows but not widowers.

5. In *Califano* v. *Webster* (1977), decided the same day, the Court upheld a provision of the Social Security Act giving a higher level of monthly benefits to retired female workers than to retired male workers.

6. In 1974 the Court upheld California's refusal to grant pregnancy disability benefits to female workers against an equal protection challenge (*Gedulding* v. *Aiello* 1974). Two years

other branches of the federal government. In 1973 the Court upheld a prohibition of sex-segregated help-wanted advertisements against a First Amendment challenge (*Pittsburgh Press* v. *Pittsburgh Commission on Human Relations*). The next year a state requirement that teachers leave their positions when five months pregnant was held unconstitutional (*Cleveland Board of Education* v. *LaFleur* 1974).[7] In *Dothard* v. *Rawlinson* (1977), the Court found minimum weight and height requirements for the job of prison guard in violation of Title VII of the 1964 Civil Rights Act.[8] In 1987 the Court upheld an affirmative action plan that took consideration of gender into account in promotions (*Johnson* v. *Transportation Agency, Santa Clara County*). And, in 1986, the Court essentially upheld Equal Employment Opportunity Commission (EEOC) regulations that interpreted Title VII as prohibiting sexual harassment as a form of sex discrimination (*Meritor Savings Bank* v. *Vinson*).

There has also been some Court action in the pay area. In 1981, the Supreme Court gave the green light to comparable-worth litigation, allowing sex-based wage discrimination claims to proceed under Title VII without being limited by the equal-work standard of the Equal Pay Act (*County of Washington* v. *Gunther*). In the wake of *Gunther*, "it was generally assumed that the courts would become the major forum for redressing sex-based wage discrimination" (Clauss 1986, 7). Such litigation took place in Washington state, where an initial victory in federal district court gave credence to this belief (*AFSCME* v. *State of Washington* 1983).

In sum, in the area of women's rights, the Court, in the 1970s, moved to strike down many gender-based distinctions. The defense that the preference for males over females was an administrative convenience was conclusively rejected. While some distinctions were upheld,[9] the clear import of the deci-

---

later, the Court held that an employer's disability plan that excluded pregnancy from its coverage did not violate Title VII of the 1964 Civil Rights Act (*General Electric* v. *Gilbert* 1976). Congress reversed the decision in 1978.

7. In *Turner* v. *Utah* (1975), Utah, presumably on the assumption that all pregnant women are unable to work during an eighteen week period beginning before and extending after childbirth, prohibited such women from receiving unemployment benefits. The Court found this to violate the equal protection clause of the Fourteenth Amendment. At the time, fourteen states had almost identical laws and an additional five had similar ones. In *Nashville Gas Co.* v. *Satty* (1976), the Court found a Title VII violation in a company policy requiring pregnant employees to take pregnancy leaves, denying them sick pay, and depriving them of all accumulated seniority when they returned to work.

8. The Court did, however, uphold the prohibition of women serving as guards in maximum-security prisons. In addition, *Schlesinger* v. *Ballard* (1975) upheld a Navy promotion program that gave women more time than men to obtain their promotions.

9. Two important cases upholding gender-based classifications need mention. In *Michael M.* v. *Superior Court* (1981), California's statutory rape law, which punishes the male involved but not the female, was upheld against a Fourteenth Amendment equal protection clause challenge. In *Rostker* v. *Goldberg* (1981), the Court upheld the Military Selective Service Act against the challenge that, by authorizing the president to require registration of males but not females, the act violated the equal protection component of the Fifth Amendment's due process clause.

sions was that gender-based distinctions would seldom be accepted. In the job area in particular, the Court struck down barriers to equal opportunity for women. Compared to the legal history prior to 1970, the years following were a giant step forward.

Congressional and Executive Branch Action

While the courts can fairly be criticized for hostility to women's rights until the 1970s, Congress and the executive branch took little action, too, to combat sex discrimination until the 1960s. In the 1970s, there was a virtual explosion of executive branch and congressional activity. In the next few pages I highlight the most important steps taken by Congress and the executive branch to combat sex discrimination.

A first important step was the creation of the Women's Bureau within the Department of Labor (USDL) in 1920. The First World War had brought a large number of women into the workforce, and the bureau's function was to protect the welfare of working women (USDL 1971, 84). Perhaps another purpose was an attempt by Congress and the president to appear supportive of women. The Nineteenth Amendment, giving women the right to vote, was officially ratified in August 1920, just two months after President Wilson signed the bill creating the bureau. The next most important date does not come until 1957. It was then that Congress passed a civil rights bill which, in part, made most citizens competent to sit on federal juries. Prior practice had been to use the juror qualifications of the state in which the federal court sat, effectively excluding women (and blacks) in many states.

The 1960s saw a large increase in government interest in women's rights. In the executive branch, in 1961, President Kennedy, reportedly at the behest of the director of the Women's Bureau, Esther Petersen, established the President's Commission on the Status of Women, chaired by Eleanor Roosevelt (Freeman 1973, 797). In early November of 1963, by executive order, President Kennedy also established a Citizen's Advisory Council on the Status of Women and an Interdepartmental Committee on the Status of Women, composed of Cabinet officers. There was also legislative action. In 1963, after years of unsuccessful attempts, Congress finally passed the Equal Pay Act. The act applies to all employees covered by the minimum-wage provisions of the Fair Labor Standards Act. It prohibits employers from paying different wages on the basis of sex for equal work on jobs requiring equal skill, effort, and responsibility, and performed under similar working conditions. The next year saw the passage of the 1964 Civil Rights Act, the most sweeping civil rights bill in American history. Title VII, the all-important job discrimination section, prohibited employment discrimination on the basis of race, color, religion, national origin, and sex. Sex was added as an amendment to the bill late in the House debate and the seriousness of some of its proponents is unclear (see chapter 9). But it did become the law of the land.

The remainder of the 1960s saw much executive action. On the state level, by 1967 all fifty states had created commissions on the status of women (Cowan 1976, 376; Hole and Levine 1971, 24). In 1967, President Johnson said he personally favored the Equal Rights Amendment. Also in 1967, he issued an executive order (11375) prohibiting discrimination by most federal government contractors and subcontractors and by contractors and subcontractors in federally assisted construction. In August 1968, the EEOC, created by the 1964 Civil Rights Act to administer Title VII, issued guidelines banning sex-segregated job advertisements. President Nixon kept in step, supporting the Equal Rights Amendment in the 1968 campaign. Early in his first term he acted to strengthen equal rights within the federal government. Executive Order 11478 (August 9, 1969), superseded Executive Order 11375 by prohibiting sex discrimination in the executive agencies of the federal government, in competitive positions in the legislative and judicial branches, and in the District of Columbia government. It directed all federal agencies and departments to establish and maintain an affirmative action program for all civilian employees and job applicants.

The 1970s saw heightened governmental action. In the executive branch action included the banning of sex discrimination in employment by the Federal Communications Commission (FCC) in 1970, the amending of regulations in the Department of Interior prohibiting sex discrimination in programs assisted by it (1973), and the labeling of sex discrimination by lending institutions as an unacceptable practice by the Federal Home Loan Bank Board (1973).[10] On the legislative side, the Ninety-second Congress "passed a bumper crop of women's rights legislation—considerably more than the sum total of all relevant legislation that had been previously passed in the history of this country" (Freeman 1975, 202). Title VII was amended to include federal, state, and local government employers in the prohibition against sex discrimination. The Equal Pay Act was extended to previously uncovered executives, administrative, and professional workers, including academic personnel. The Education Amendments Act of 1972 included Title IX, which prohibits educational institutions that receive federal funds from discriminating on the basis of sex. The State and Local Federal Assistance Act of 1972, the revenue-sharing act, prohibited discrimination on the grounds of sex in employment or distribution of benefits in any program or activity funded in whole or in part by it. The jurisdiction of the Civil Rights Commission was expanded to include sex discrimination in 1972. And, of course, the Equal Rights Amendment was passed in 1972.

10. For a compilation of U.S. government action prohibiting sex discrimination, see U.S. Commission on Civil Rights (1976a).

The years following this initial burst of legislative activity saw continued action. In 1976–77 legislation was enacted banning sex discrimination in federally funded vocational programs and in credit transactions. It became the norm to include prohibitions against sex discrimination in many federally funded programs. On the executive level, the Citizen's Advisory Council on the Status of Women was renewed, symbolizing the continuing executive branch awareness of discrimination against women. And, in 1985, the EEOC issued guidelines interpreting Title VII to include sexual harassment as a form of prohibited sex discrimination.

In sum, then, after a slow start the federal government continually acted to prohibit gender-based discrimination.

Results and Comparison

Disentangling the contribution of the Court from that of the other branches of the federal government is a well-nigh impossible task with women's rights. All the branches began acting at roughly the same time, the early 1970s. Fine lines would have to be drawn to persuasively credit change to one institution rather than another. Further, in making this assessment, I cannot point to a precise correspondence between Court action and judicial effect, as was done with *Brown* and desegregation in the public schools, or with *Roe* and *Doe* and legal abortion. Nevertheless, by looking at the overall picture of the place of women in American society, and where and how it has changed, I can explore whether significant social reform has occurred and if it has occurred in areas that can plausibly be tied to Court action. And focusing on actual numbers rather than on lofty statements of equality is crucial to assess judicial efficacy. For, as Mary Becker puts it, "in achieving equality for women . . . what matters (to a very large extent) is numbers—results—not abstract principles" (Becker 1989, 274).

Fortunately for the analysis, but unfortunately for America, there has been uneven improvement in the position of American women in the key areas of income and jobs. Despite Court and government action prohibiting sex discrimination, there has been "little discernible progress in the relative labor market status of women" (Johnson and Solon 1986, 183). And in the places where change has occurred, students trace it to congressional and executive branch action, not Court action.

A particularly depressing measure of the lack of progress is the difference between the salaries of men and women. Table 7.1 presents the figures of the "earnings gap." As can be seen clearly from the table, year-round full-time women workers made a smaller percentage of their male counterparts' salaries in 1980 than they did in 1955! Even by 1987, after nearly two decades of Court and government action, the relative position of men and women in terms of income was about the same as it was over thirty years earlier.[11] "Even when adjustments are made for education and occupation," the U.S. Commission on Civil Rights (USCCR) found in 1978, "women earn less than men" (USCCR 1978, 9).[12] Other studies, controlling for factors such as age, work experience, and education still find a large gap (Reskin and Hartmann 1986, 10–11, 70–73, 123; Blau 1984, 133–39). In terms of education, the Women's Bureau found that "in 1974 women with 4 years of College had lower incomes than men who had only completed the 8th grade" and "fully employed women high school graduates (no college) had less income on the average than fully employed men who had not completed elementary school" (USDL 1976b, 2–3). By the 1980s, little had changed, with one study concluding that in 1984, among all workers, "male high school graduates have median incomes one and one-half times greater than women with college and graduate degrees" (Tarr-Whelan 1984, 3). With full-time workers, in 1985 female college graduates made less than male high school graduates and women with graduate education made less than male college dropouts! (*The American Woman* 1988, 389). And a recent study by the Rand Corporation found that if "current trends continued women would earn only 74 percent of men's income by the year 2000" ("Women's Pay" 1984, 16). Any contribution of the Court to ending sex discrimination is not found in the area of wage discrimination.

The lack of Court efficacy also holds in the area of comparable worth. Despite litigation, where comparable worth policies have been instituted, they have been the result of collective bargaining and state government action, not litigation. From California and Washington to Minnesota, comparative worth policies have been instituted "through the legislatures and private negotiation," not courts (Clauss 1986, 8). Blumrosen found that "long before the courts" became involved, "state and local governments began identifying and attacking the problem of wage discrimination against women" (Blumrosen 1984, 111 n.5). In other words, "even before *Gunther* there had been considerable activity in the states, which themselves were under pressure from unions and women's groups" (Blumrosen 1984, 111). As of September, 1983, about a dozen and a half states had conducted, or were conducting, job evaluation studies, the first step in ending wage discrimination.[13] And "these studies have taken place through collective bargaining, executive order, legislation or personnel and civil service department action" (Tarr-Whelan 1984,

11. A 1984 study by a senior official of the Census Bureau found that the wages of white women entering the job market in 1980 were further behind the wages of comparable white men than they were in 1970 (Pear 1984).
12. This 1978 study corroborated one done by the commission in 1974 which found the gap remaining large even when age, skill level, race, and part-time work were controlled for (USCCR 1974c, 5).
13. Counting in 1984, Rothchild (1984, 120) found fifteen states with a comparable pay standard in their equal pay acts.

Table 7.1   The Earnings Gap: Women's Earnings as a
             Percentage of Men's Earnings, Median and
             Mean Earnings of Full-Time Year-Round
             Workers, 1955–1987

Year	Women's Earnings as a % of Men's Earnings (Mean)	Women's Earnings as a % of Men's Earnings (Median)
1955	60.2	64.5
1956	57.7	63.3
1957	57.7	63.7
1958	58.0	62.7
1959	57.1	61.2
1960	55.4	60.7
1961	54.6	59.0
1962	54.8	59.3
1963	55.5	58.6
1964	55.9	59.0
1965	54.0	57.8
1966	53.8	57.9
1967	55.0	57.6
1968	54.2	58.5
1969	55.5	58.6
1970	56.8	59.2
1971	56.4	59.2
1972	55.3	57.4
1973	54.8	56.6
1974	55.9	59.0
1975	56.2	59.7
1976	57.0	60.0
1977	56.3	58.5
1978	56.8	60.0
1979	57.4	60.2
1980	59.4	60.5
1981	59.7	60.2
1982	61.0	63.1
1983	62.2	64.4
1984	62.7	64.2
1985	62.9	65.0
1986	62.8	65.0
1987	63.7	65.5

SOURCE: USBC (Series P-60 1988, 24; 1984, 122).

23). Thus, the change that has occurred does not appear to be a result of judicial action (Special Issue 1984; Symposium 1986; USCCR 1984).

A crucial area of sex discrimination has been employment, and both Court and congressional/executive branch action has been taken to end it. The results, however, are not encouraging. While more women are working outside of the home than ever before, they are generally employed in low-paying work traditionally assigned to women. In 1978 the Bureau of Labor Statistics reported that women were 99 percent of all secretaries, 99 percent of all pre-kindergarten and kindergarten teachers, 97 percent of all housekeepers, 95 percent of all telephone operators, dressmakers, and seamstresses, 93 percent of all keypunch operators, and 90 percent of all book-keepers, waitresses, and cashiers (Ross and Barcher 1983, 18). By 1980 women were also 96.5 percent of all registered nurses, 85 percent of all librarians, and 83.7 percent of elementary school teachers (Deckard 1983, 117). By 1987, nearly a decade later, little had changed. Women still remained 99 percent of all secretaries, 98 percent of all pre-kindergarten and kindergarten teachers, 96 percent of all housekeepers,[14] 92 percent of all telephone operators, 85 percent of all waiters and waitresses, 83 percent of all cashiers, 95.1 percent of all registered nurses, and 85.3 percent of elementary school teachers (USDL 1988, 673–92; 1982, I: 651–67). Needless to say, all of these jobs are on the lower end of the pay-and-prestige scale. As Berger concludes, "if current job profiles continue, the typical female worker who is entering the job force in such great numbers will always work at a sex-segregated job, and will accordingly be paid poorly" (Berger 1980, 13).[15]

In the professional-technical categories the data do show some change, although the numbers remain small. Between 1950 and 1976 women's participation rose slightly less than 2 percent, from 40.1 percent to 42 percent. By 1976 women were only 1.8 percent of all engineers (up 0.6 percent from 1950), 9.2 percent of all lawyers and judges (up 5.1 percent), 12.8 percent of all physicians-osteopaths (up 6.3 percent), 26.9 percent of all accountants (up 12 percent), 31.3 percent of all college and university teachers (up 8.5 percent), 13.6 percent of all technicians, excluding medical-dental (down 7 percent), and 34.7 percent of all writers-artists-entertainers (down 5.6 percent) (USDL 1977, 9). By 1987, while some change had occurred, women comprised only 6.9 percent of engineers, 19.6 percent of lawyers, and 19.5 percent of physicians (USDL 1988, 673–92).[16] Even in these professional fields, a woman holding a job is likely to be paid less than her male counterpart. In 1987 female attorneys' salaries were only 75.6 percent of male attorneys' salaries, female physicians made only 78.8 percent of what their

14. The reported category is "Cleaners & Servants." The category "Housekeepers" appears to end in 1981.

15. For studies exploring the structural reasons for this, see Roos and Reskin (1984, especially 248–55); O'Farrell and Harlan (1984, especially 275–79).

16. The 19.6 percent of U.S. lawyers who were women in 1987 compares unfavorably to the following *1961* percentages of women lawyers: Denmark, 50 percent; U.S.S.R., 36 percent. The 19.5 percent of all U.S. physicians who were women in 1987 compares unfavorably to the following *1965* percentages of women physicians: Philippines, 24.7 percent; Finland, 24.2 percent; Israel, 24 percent; Thailand, 23.8 percent (Murray 1971, 245 n.22).

male counterparts made, and female college and university teachers made only 74.7 percent of their male colleagues' salaries.[17] In academics, the U.S. Commission on Civil Rights found that in "1975–76, the salary gap between men and women faculty increased at every level, women faculty earning on the average $3,096 less than faculty men" (USCCR 1979c, 5). By 1987, the difference in the mean earnings of full-time male and female academics was over $9,000![18] The sex-segregated nature of most employment, the growing but still small numbers of women in professional categories, and the discrimination they suffer within them, all point to the lack of much progress for courts to claim credit for.

The treatment of women in the job market is perhaps symbolized by the treatment provided female nominees to the federal courts by the American Bar Association's (ABA) Committee on Judicial Selection. Given Supreme Court action in defense of women's rights, one might expect a heightened awareness of sex discrimination on the part of ABA lawyers scrutinizing nominees. However, in the 1976–79 period, the ABA committee rated 54 percent of the men nominated to the federal district courts qualified but only 8 percent of the women. With the federal circuit courts, the figures were 70 percent and 40 percent respectively (Deckard 1983, 133).

Litigation has failed to end discrimination. In a study for the Ford Foundation of litigation on behalf of women, Berger concluded that litigation "has not been able to achieve substantial gain for the great majority of women who work in sex-segregated jobs." The litigation effort "has not been able to reach the wage structure for traditional female work," Berger found, and blue-collar women "have barely been touched by the litigation effort" (Berger 1980, 51). In the pay equity area, Gertner concurs, finding that "Title VII is too costly and too lengthy a process to provide continuing pressure on an employer to effect pay equity" (Gertner 1986, 178). Further, Berger found that in most women's rights victories the "winners have been men, and . . . women have won only when it was not at the expense of a man." Putting the results in stark terms, Berger concludes: "Women have fared badly when a victory would not confer a corresponding benefit on a male and/or when the issues presented to the Court were unique to women" (Berger 1980, 19, 22).

The underlying reality of litigation attempts to end job discrimination against women is, as the U.S. Commission on Civil Rights puts it, that women are discriminated against everywhere in the job market. "The only evidence of substantial change," the commission found in 1979, "has come from federally-required affirmative action plans" (USCCR 1979b, 18). The

17. Percentages derived from the median weekly earnings of full-time workers found in USDL (1988, 748–67).
18. Figure derived from the mean weekly earnings of full-time workers found in USDL (1988, 748–67).

changes documented by the data have been small and "almost exclusively the result of women's moving into traditionally male fields, while the traditionally female-dominated fields remain segregated" (McLaughlin et al. 1988, 39). Because uneven progress in ending job discrimination based on sex has been made, and because the change that has occurred has come from congressional and executive action, little credit can be given to the Court.

In the end, then, Court action contributed little to eliminating discrimination against women. Cases were argued and won but, litigants aside, little was accomplished. While doors were open to some women, those holding them open were not judges.

Explaining the Results

Advocates of women's rights have "won" quite a number of legal cases. However, as the first part of this chapter demonstrated, there is little evidence that these Court victories have much changed the position of women in American society. Why might this be the case? For the question of Court efficacy in producing significant social reform in women's rights, three approaches are available: the Dynamic Court, the Constrained Court, and the constraints and conditions derived from them. The Dynamic Court view predicts that Court victories would have an important effect in furthering women's rights and improving the condition of women. The Constrained Court view, on the other hand, would expect little change. The constraints and conditions would also predict little change, but for more subtle and fine-tuned reasons.

At the outset, the first part of this chapter shows that for women's rights, the Dynamic Court view is simply wrong. Further, the civil rights and abortion cases have suggested that the constraints and conditions may be most helpful in explaining the lack of judicial efficacy in producing significant social reform. With civil rights it was only after Congress and the Department of Health, Education, and Welfare combined to offer incentives for desegregation and to impose costs for failing to desegregate that courts were helpful in producing change.[19] With abortion, it was the availability of a market mechanism for implementation that allowed the Court's decisions to have at least some efficacy.

Are any of these conditions present with women's rights? If so, Court decisions removing discriminatory laws will result in changes. For example, if gender discrimination is enforced by law, against the beliefs of actors, then changing the law will produce change by allowing actors to do as they wish.

19. By the late 1960s it was also the case that officials necessary for implementation were willing to act, as long as they could assert that they were forced to act by the courts or the federal government.

Once laws requiring gender discrimination are removed, employers will be free to act in a gender-neutral way, and women will be free to make formerly proscribed choices. In other words, removing biased laws will allow the market to correct the discrimination. However, if gender discrimination is largely based on stereotypes and deep-seated beliefs about the role of men and women in American society, then judicial decisions mandating formal equality will produce little amelioration. The market will not respond since laws are not holding it back. If actors are unwilling to respond, and if cultural stereotypes and social pressure continue to direct men and women into different career paths, then favorable Court decisions are likely to be ignored. That is, if the laws are only one of several factors involved in the discriminatory treatment of women, then court decisions may not amount to much.

If this is the case, in order for courts to produce change in the area of women's rights, then one of the remaining three conditions must be present. Have non-court actors either provided incentives or imposed costs? Have officials key to implementation been willing to use courts as cover? If not, the constraints of the Constrained Court view predict that courts will have little effect in producing change in women's rights. In the rest of this chapter, I will argue that this is indeed the case: that none of the conditions allowing for Court effectiveness are regularly present with women's rights. That is, on the whole non-court actors have neither offered incentives nor imposed penalties to end discrimination, and those in a position to act have, on the whole, chosen not to. Thus, Court decisions did not open up the market, as with abortion, nor provide political cover to well-meaning but politically insecure office-holders, as with civil rights. The change that has occurred has been independent of Court activity.

Part of the reason for court inefficacy, it has been argued, is that the Court has adopted an equality standard, treating men and women as similarly situated and prohibiting gender discrimination in such cases. According to one line of thinking, however, sex discrimination is so pervasive in American society and culture that men and women seldom have the same opportunities. For MacKinnon, "gender neutrality is thus simply the male standard" (MacKinnon 1987, 34), and the only women who have a chance to benefit from it are those very few who through class, wealth, or luck are helped to neutralize some of the barriers women face. As Mary Becker puts it, "women and men are too differently situated for women's status to be significantly changed for the better by focusing only on instances in which similarly-situated women and men are treated differently" (Becker letter to author). In addition, while it may be the case that the current equality standard is flawed, a different standard would still face the necessity of overcoming the constraints and meeting the conditions. The problem is not merely the Court's standard but the fact that it is the *courts* that are pronouncing it. For once, perhaps, the fault lies not merely with the message but with the messenger itself.[20]

Cultural Barriers

Court decisions do not exist in a vacuum. They are delivered into a society that has definite beliefs, social institutions, and practices. Where court decisions contradict these cultural beliefs and practices, barriers to change are pronounced. Gender discrimination provides an example. Cultural barriers to gender equality can be seen in a number of ways, including patterns of violence, of leisure time, and of political representation. What all these show is that court decisions mandating equality face powerful cultural barriers. In a society whose behavior manifests such strong gender-based discrimination, court decisions will accomplish little.

Violence

Women suffer from violence at the hands of men at frightening levels. At the most deadly end of the violence continuum, the U.S. Department of Justice (USDJ) reports that 31 percent of all female murder victims in 1988 were murdered by husbands or boyfriends.[21] Wives and girlfriends were more than twice as likely to be murdered by husbands and boyfriends than were husbands and boyfriends to be murdered by wives and girlfriends (USDJ 1989b, 13). In terms of rape, there were over 91,000 reported rapes in 1987, a nearly 35 percent increase from 1978 (U.S. Bureau of the Census, *Statistical Abstract* 1989, 166).[22] There is also the issue of the so-called marital-rape exemption which makes it legally impossible for a husband to rape his wife. The exemption is included in the Model Penal Code and, as of the late 1980s, most states retained some form of it. Although about half the states have moved to permit prosecution in some instances, as where the couple has formally separated, over a quarter have *expanded* the exemption to cover cohabitants (Rhode 1989, 251). As a male California state senator put it in 1979, "if you can't rape your wife, who can you rape?" (Freeman 1981, 1).

Other kinds of violence against women in the family are even more prevalent. Men are charged nearly five times as often as women for "offenses against family and children" (USDJ 1989b, 173).[23] A special report from the U.S. Justice Department in 1986 estimated that 2.1 million women were vic-

---

20. This is not to suggest that either MacKinnon or Becker have high hopes for the courts. MacKinnon's work on pornography suggests a belief in legislation, and Becker (1987) explicitly rejects any judicially enforced abstract standard as offering much help.

21. Only 5 percent of all male murder victims were murdered by wives or girlfriends.

22. These figures need to be seen in light of police estimates that only 48.1 percent of rapes were reported in 1986.

23. The offense is defined as "nonsupport, neglect, desertion, or abuse of family and children" (USDJ 1989b, 320).

tims of domestic violence at least once in the previous twelve months (Langan and Innes 1986, 3). Other estimates vary from three to four million women a year (Diehm and Ross 1988), to 34 percent of married women (Browne 1987, 4–5).[24] And a study reported in the *Journal of the American Medical Association* reported that "[b]attering appears to be the single most common cause of injury to women—more common than automobile accidents, muggings, and rapes combined" ("Domestic Violence" 1990, 939). What these figures suggest is that "there is a tacit acceptance of woman-battering" (Martin 1981, 7). Indeed, as Murray A. Strauss puts it, "our society actually has rules and values which make the marriage license also a hitting license" (quoted in Dutton 1988, 16). Finally, working women suffer from sexual harassment. Surveys suggest that between one-third and two-thirds of working women have experienced some form of harassment.[25] The United States Merit Protection Board, reporting in 1988, found that 42 percent of female workers in the federal government had suffered from some form of sexual harassment in the preceding two years (U.S. Merit Systems Protection Board 1988, 2).[26] And other studies have estimated that 85 percent of all working women will be subject to sexual harassment at some point in their working lives (Rhode 1989, 232). The stark reality is that male violence against women remains prevalent, limiting options for women. It is hard to see how court decisions invalidating discriminatory laws can overcome this frightening aspect of gender relations.

Leisure Time and Political Representation

There is mounting evidence that despite the fact that a majority of women work outside of the home, women still do a disproportionate share of the household work. Hochschild examined findings from the major studies on time-use done in the 1960s and 1970s and found that women worked roughly fifteen hours longer each week than men. Her own in-depth interviews suggested that a "second shift" of work for women—one shift out of the home, one shift in the home—still exists (Hochschild 1989, 3, 276).[27] A national poll taken by the *New York Times* in June 1989 found married women working full-time with children under eighteen reporting that they did most of the

24. The latter figure was for Pittsburgh. For a collection of other survey data, see Dutton (1988, particularly chap. 1).

25. Rhode (1989, 232). See also Bureau of National Affairs (1987); MacKinnon (1979).

26. The finding was based on survey responses from a representative cross-section of over 8,000 federal employees. The results corroborated a similar 1980 study. In addition, survey responses from those federal employees who had also worked in the private sector showed that the problem was no worse within the government than outside it (1988, 2). The study also noted (1988, 4) that sexual harassment costs the government an estimated $267 million per year due to the costs of replacing employees who leave to escape the harassment, sick days taken to recover from harassment, and reduced productivity.

27. Hochschild briefly reviews other studies at 3–4, and 271–73.

cooking (64 percent), housecleaning (65 percent), food shopping (62 percent), child-care (56 percent) and bill-paying (61 percent). The data show a "lopsided division of labor that male respondents hardly disputed" (Cowan 1989, 1, 8). Other studies have found that women working full-time outside of the home do twice as much home-oriented work as do similarly situated men (Blank 1988, 150). The belief that household work and child-care are women's work remains strong. Such beliefs limit women's options. And these beliefs, too, are unlikely to be changed by court decree.

A further example of beliefs about the proper role for women is their lack of involvement in political life. There are very few women in elective political office. No woman has ever served as president or vice-president and only one woman has been nominated for vice-president by a major party. The record is only slighter better in Congress. No woman has ever held a leadership position and, in the 101st Congress, there were only twenty-five women in the House (5.8 percent) and two women in the Senate (2.0 percent). Looking to the states, as of 1988, women were only 15.8 percent of state legislators nationwide (U.S. Bureau of the Census, *Statistical Abstract* 1989, 252, 256). The lack of women in public life may reinforce traditional, discriminatory notions of the role of women.

Economic Constraints

Men and women are not similarly situated economically. Women have many fewer opportunities and are in a much more precarious position than men. Thus, many, if not most, women are unable to take advantage of opportunities provided by court decisions prohibiting discrimination against women similarly situated to men. This can be seen by looking at a number of conditions. One is poverty.

Poverty hits women hard. In 1987, the U.S. Bureau of the Census (USBC) reported that over a third of all households headed by women were below the poverty level, a rate nearly three times higher than that for households headed by males. In addition, nearly half of all households with children under eighteen headed by women were below the poverty level, also nearly three times higher than the rate for similar families headed by men (USBC Series P-60 1989, 11–13). And single women over sixty-five living alone constitute 85 percent of all older people whose income falls below the poverty level (Gelb and Palley 1987, 188).

One of the reasons women fair so poorly is that divorce and child support are areas where cultural biases against women remain strong. Despite the fact that by the mid-1980s nearly all the states had no-fault divorce provisions, studies have repeatedly shown that, economically, divorce hurts women more than men. One national study found that divorced women had a 6.7 percent drop in living standards after divorce while men had an increase of 16.5 percent (Espenshade 1979, 617–18).[28] The most dramatic findings come from a multi-decade study in California, where Weitzman found that "just a year after legal divorce, *men experience a 42 percent increase in their postdivorce standard of living, while women experience a 73 percent decline*" (Weitzman 1985, 339).[29] Studies from Connecticut, Ohio, and Vermont have produced similar findings.[30] These findings can be explained, in part, by the discrimination that continues to limit women's employment options. In addition, courts seldom order alimony, and child support, when ordered, is insufficient and seldom paid in full. In 1986 of the 19.2 million ever-divorced or currently divorced women, only about 15 percent were awarded alimony or maintenance payments. Among women due child support, less than half receive the full amount ordered and over a quarter receive nothing. The average amount of child support received in 1985 was only $2,200 (USBC Series P-23 1989a, 5, 1, 2). As McLindon puts it, "by any measure, men emerge from their divorces in far better economic shape than their wives do" (McLindon 1987, 391).

Retirement income is still another area where women fare far worse than men. Because women generally work at sex-segregated employment that pays low wages, "upon retirement women receive lower social security and pension benefits" than men (Reskin and Hartmann 1986, 123). To make matters worse, working women are "less likely to participate in pension plans than working men" (Newton 1988, 265). For the most part this is due to the segregated job market that concentrates working women in situations where pensions are less common, such as small firms, less-unionized industries, and so on. The result is that over two and one-half times as many men receive private pensions as women, and the average payment to men is about 75 percent greater than to women (Gelb and Palley 1987, 188). Even if their spouses are covered, Gelb and Palley report (1987, 188) that only 5 to 10 percent of surviving spouses receive their spouses' pension benefits. Job segregation and interrupted careers also depress social security payments. Gelb and Palley found that the average social security payment to men was about 28 percent greater than the average payment to women.[31]

When women work outside of the home, and a majority now do, they do not, on average, do the same jobs as men. "The majority of women work in a small number of occupations, particularly in occupations in which the work-

28. These data come from the Panel Study of Income Dynamics, an ongoing survey of more than 5,000 American families.
29. See also Rankin (1986); Weitzman (1981).
30. McLindon (1987) (New Haven, Connecticut); McGraw et al. (1982) (Cuyahoga County, Ohio); Wishik (1986) (Vermont). Discussion of, and citations to, additional studies can be found in McLindon (1987, 352).
31. Percentage calculated from figures in Gelb and Palley (1987, 188). The data are for 1983.

ers are predominantly women." Over half of the census bureau's 503 occupational categories are 80 percent or more filled by one sex. While there has been some lessening of sex segregation over the last two decades, "sex segregation continues to characterize the American workplace, despite the changes that have occurred in some occupations" (Reskin and Hartmann 1986, 1, 7, 124). In addition, like the tipping phenomenon with race and housing, when women enter a job category in large numbers, men leave it and its relative income and status-level drop. In 1935, the job of bank teller went from virtually all male and a stepping stone to higher positions to virtually all-female and dead-end by the 1980s (Strober and Arnold 1987). Similar stories can be told about teaching and other occupations (Strober 1984). Even where men and women work in the same area, sex segregation is often preserved. In real estate men are concentrated in the more lucrative commercial property area, and in the field of baking women "tend to operate bakeries within supermarkets, typically a minimum wage job, while male bakers commonly hold the higher paying positions in commercial baking." In corporate America, women hold only 3 percent of the "most coveted top management positions at the country's largest publicly traded corporations" (Cowan 1989, 8). Among U.S. Department of Justice lawyers, while women were 25 percent of the attorney workforce in 1985, women held only eleven of seventy-seven (14.3 percent) positions as section chiefs or branch directors. And among U.S. attorneys, only four chief prosecutors (of ninety-three) are women (Jost 1989, 54, 60, 58).[32] It seems fair to conclude that the "segregation of the sexes is a basic feature of the world of work" (Reskin and Hartmann 1986, 7). There is no evidence that court decisions, without the presence of one of the conditions, can change this. And without change in women's economic opportunities, court decisions mandating equality will have little effect.

Biased Laws

In addition to the pervasive nature of gender discrimination, there is also the question of discriminatory laws. Gender discrimination has not been entirely removed from either federal or state law. On the state level, the U.S. Commission on Civil Rights found in December 1978, that "state laws are replete with provisions that assign women on the basis of their sex to an inferior role" (USCCR 1978, 30). A powerful example is found in unemployment insurance. Based on the notion of a full-time breadwinner temporarily laid off, it provides little or no benefits for low-paying or part-time work, the kind of work that many women do. Workers forced to quit work to care for

---

32. Of the 24 federal agencies surveyed by the U.S. Merit Systems Protection Board for sexual harassment in 1987, the Department of Justice was among the four worst, with 46 percent of its female employees reporting sexual harassment during the preceding two years (U.S. Merit Systems Protection Board 1988, 18).

children, for example, overwhelmingly female workers, are excluded from coverage. Thus, women who "suffer labor market disadvantages . . . will have those disadvantages reinforced and even intensified by unemployment insurance." Given the fact that men and women are not similarly situated, "unemployment insurance is structurally biased against women" (Pearce 1986, 160, 146).

On the federal level, in April 1977 the Civil Rights Commission identified "800 sections of the [U.S.] Code which contained either substantive sex-biased differentials or terminology inconsistent with a national commitment to equal rights, responsibilities, and opportunities" (USCCR 1977b, 13). Two examples make the point. In the vital area of mortgages, the commission has found that "traditional mortgage lending criteria . . . virtually *require* sex discrimination" and that "sex discrimination is part and parcel of official bank policy" (USCCR 1974a, 18, 20). With social security, Becker has found that "in every category, whether collecting as independent covered workers or as dependents of male workers, women received, on average, less than male workers." The social security system, like unemployment insurance, "is designed so that women are at a much greater risk of poverty than are men" (Becker 1989, 278, 283). The problem is, as a Senate report identified it in 1972, that "persistent patterns of sex discrimination permeate our social, cultural and economic life" (U.S. Cong., Senate 1972, 3). Four years later, the Civil Rights Commission basically agreed: "The achievement of equal opportunity for women, however, is still blocked by political, social, economic, and legal barriers, many of which are sanctioned by law" (USCCR 1976a, 3). With such barriers, there is little that a court can accomplish.

Courts

Discriminatory laws and cultural bias make it unlikely that courts can produce much change for women. This remains the case even when laws are rewritten to remove the discrimination. As with civil rights, laws that are gender-neutral on their face may be interpreted in a gender-biased way. Stereotypes and deeply held beliefs about the roles of men and women can defeat the non-discriminatory intent of laws. There is a great deal of evidence that the courts, composed overwhelmingly of men,[33] have had great difficulty taking sex discrimination claims seriously. Bias has been such a consistent and serious problem that it deserves to be highlighted.

Historically, claims of unconstitutional sex discrimination have met short shrift. In *Bradwell* v. *The State* (1872) however, three concurring justices of the U.S. Supreme Court took the time to record why they felt it was constitutionally permissible for Illinois to deny Myra Bradwell the right to practice law solely on the ground of her sex. They wrote, in part:

33. By the late 1980s, women comprised less than 8 percent of both the federal and state judiciaries.

the civil law, as well as nature herself, has always recognized a wide difference in the respective spheres and destinies of man and woman. Man is, or should be, woman's protector and defender. The natural and proper timidity and delicacy which belongs to the female sex evidently unfits it for many of the occupations of civil life. The constitution of the family organization, which is founded in the divine ordinance, as well as in the nature of things, indicates the domestic sphere as that which properly belongs to the domain and functions of womanhood. The harmony, not to say identity, of interests and views which belong, or should belong, to the family institution is repugnant to the idea of a woman adopting a distinct and independent career from that of her husband. . . . The paramount destiny and mission of woman are to fulfil the noble and benign offices of wife and mother. This is the law of the Creator." (1872, 141)[34]

It is of little comfort that the opinion was written over a hundred years ago for, in the words of two law professors who reviewed sex bias in the courts in 1971, "opinions continue to appear in which both the result and the reasoning are virtually indistinguishable from those issued nearly a century ago" (Johnston and Knapp 1971, 737).

Modern instances of sex bias in court opinions abound. One area that has brought these biases out is cases involving the exclusion of women from juries. In 1961 the Supreme Court upheld a Florida law exempting women from jury service unless they volunteered for it. The Court argued that women are "regarded as the center of home and family life" and that Florida could constitutionally conclude that women had their "own special responsibilities" that were inconsistent with their leaving the home for jury duty (*Hoyt* v. *Florida* 1961, 62). More recently, in 1970, the federal district court for the Southern District of New York, generally considered among the best and most prestigious district courts in the country, rejected a challenge to a New York State law permitting women to exempt themselves from jury duty. The court found "sound and reasonable bases" for exempting women because the "great majority constitute the heart of the home, where they are busily engaged in the 24-hour day task of producing and rearing children, providing a home for the entire family, and performing the daily household work" (*Leighton* v. *Goodman* 1970, 1183). A remarkable opinion, also in 1970, comes from a state appeals court in New York. Again, the challenge was to a law that allowed women to exempt themselves from jury duty. The court conscientiously noted that jury "exclusion stemming from racial or class prejudice is offensive." But in this case the judge found that the plaintiff "desires to have the Court declare that women are no different from men. To this, the Legislature has said 'Vive la difference'." In rejecting the plaintiff's claims, the court offered some final advice: "Plaintiff is in the wrong forum. Her

34. See also *Goesaert* v. *Cleary* (1948), where the Supreme Court upheld a Michigan law prohibiting women from obtaining a bartender license unless they were either the wife or the daughter of a male owner of a licensed liquor establishment.

lament should be addressed to the 'Nineteenth Amendment State of Woman-hood' which prefers cleaning and cooking, rearing of children and television soap operas, bridge and canasta, the beauty parlor and shopping, to [serving on juries and] becoming embroiled in plaintiff's problems with her landlord" (*Dekosenko* v. *Brandt* 1970, 830). New York's jury exemption law for women was not removed by the legislature until 1975.

Sex stereotyping has not been confined to jury cases. In a challenge to the draft by a male arguing that the exemption of women was unconstitu-tional, a federal district court noted that "women may constitutionally be afforded 'special recognition' . . . " Citing the "home and family life" lan-guage of *Hoyt* discussed above, the court held that drafting men but not women follows the "teachings of history that if a nation is to survive, men must provide the first line of defense while women keep the home fires burn-ing" (*U.S.* v. *St. Clair* 1968, 125).

In the area of jobs, much stereotyping still remains. In 1971, for ex-ample, the Supreme Court heard a challenge based on Title VII of the 1964 Civil Rights Act to a hiring policy that automatically excluded women with pre-school-age children but not men. In remanding the case, the Court noted that the "existence of such conflicting family obligations . . . could arguably be a basis for distinction" under the act (*Phillips* v. *Martin Marietta Corp.* 1971, 544).[35] In other words, the Court was willing to entertain the presump-tion that all women with pre-school-age children had primary responsibility for child care and thus could automatically be excluded from the job. Writing in 1980, Berger concluded that "there are indications that the federal courts are reacting more unfavorably now than they did when the litigation effort first began" (Berger 1980, 50).

Given the history of blatant gender bias in courts, one might have ex-pected positive change as the women's movement came into being and as women's rights activists increasingly turned to the courts. However, summa-rizing the situation, one study reported that even as late as 1980 "gender bias in the courts was a topic that was not even recognized, let alone considered legitimate for education and reform" (Schafran 1987, 290). Justice Powell well captured this attitude in his *Bakke* opinion where he went out of his way to note that sex discrimination was not "inherently odious" when compared to the "lengthy and tragic history" of racial discrimination (1978, 303). In order to combat sex discrimination in the courts, the National Judicial Edu-cation Program to Promote Equality for Women and Men in the Courts (NJEP) was founded in 1980.[36] In part as a result of its prodding, several

35. In oral argument, the Chief Justice reportedly stated: "Most men hire women as sec-retaries because they are better at it than men" (quoted in Boylan 1971, 11).
36. Not surprisingly, NJEP was founded not by mainstream judicial organizations but by two women's groups, the National Organization for Women's Legal Defense and Education Fund, and the National Association of Women Judges.

states have set up task forces on gender discrimination in the courts and, as of 1988, three had issued reports.[37] The New Jersey task force summarized its findings as follows:

> Although the law as written is for the most part gender neutral, stereotyped myths, beliefs, and biases were found to sometimes affect decision-making in the areas investigated: damages, domestic violence, juvenile justice, matrimonial and sentencing. In addition, there is strong evidence that women and men are sometimes treated differently in courtrooms, chambers and at professional gatherings. ("The First Year Report" 1986, 136)

As part of its research, the task force surveyed New Jersey lawyers. It found that 71 percent of female lawyers had observed judges treat female witnesses in sexist ways, 83 percent had observed other lawyers so treat female witnesses,[38] and 78 percent had themselves been subject to sexist treatment by judges ("The First Year Report" 1986, 129, 137).

The New York State task force has also found gender bias against women a serious problem:

> gender bias against women litigants, attorneys and court employees is a pervasive problem with grave consequences. Women are often denied equal justice, equal treatment and equal opportunity. Cultural stereotypes of women's role in marriage and in society daily distort courts' application of substantive law. Women uniquely, disproportionately, and with unacceptable frequency must endure a climate of condescension, indifference, and hostility. ("Report of the New York Task Force" 1986, 17–18)

And, "none of the problems cited is unique to those states (New York & New Jersey)" (Schafran 1987, 281).

The fact is that women face much bias in American courts. And that barrier may be receding more slowly than many think. Writing in 1971, Johnston and Knapp concluded that "most male American judges faced with issues of sex discrimination have not adequately met those special responsibilities" for "fairness, objectivity and disinterestedness" that is demanded of judges, particularly in the area of significant social reform (Johnston and Knapp 1971, 747). In 1978, litigators "were still expressing the same assessment" (Berger 1980, 38). And, in the words of a 1986 study, "sexist attitudes regularly surface in the expressed values and beliefs of many judges and lawyers" (Eich 1986, 339).

37. As of April 1988, the sixteen following states had established task forces: Arizona, California, Connecticut, Florida, Hawaii, Illinois, Maryland, Massachusetts, Michigan, Minnesota, New Jersey, New York, Nevada, Rhode Island, Utah, Washington. In addition, in the following states task force formation was in an exploratory stage: Colorado, the District of Columbia, Kentucky, Montana, North Dakota, Oregon, Wisconsin, Vermont. Task forces in New Jersey, New York, and Rhode Island have issued reports.

38. Tellingly, the corresponding figures for male lawyers observing sexist treatment of women were only 30 percent and 47 percent, respectively.

Control of Litigation

An important barrier to court effectiveness is the enormous difficulty of controlling litigation. Activists for women's rights, like civil rights activists before them, had serious problems in making litigation more than an ad hoc process. Finding the right plaintiffs to initiate suits, having the money and legal talent to argue the suits well, and controlling and coordinating the whole process are problems that all legal activists face. They make the success of a litigation campaign problematic.

An initial set of problems plaguing women legal activists involved lack of the very basics of a litigation campaign. To start, women's organizations "often have found it difficult to find willing plaintiffs" (O'Connor 1980, 14). There are two main reasons for this. First, many victims of discrimination lack the information to accurately assess their situation. That is, job applicants who are "turned down are in no position to judge whether the refusal has been based on their race or their sex, or represents merely a fair judgment on their qualifications" (Bergmann 1986, 158). Similarly, if women do not know about job openings, they won't apply for them and such information can be limited so that it is unlikely that those discriminated against will receive it. Second, however, as with civil rights, it takes a brave person to challenge her employer, university, or other major institution in everyday life on the ground of discrimination. The usual result is loss of job or an intolerable work situation. And since suits drag on for years, plaintiffs invariably have to find another source of support. Unfortunately, most people are unwilling to bring litigation and women are no more immune to the fears and unwillingness than others.[39]

Evidence for the paucity of plaintiffs abounds. One study examined the treatment of sex discrimination in state high courts. In the twelve year period 1971–83, only 126 sex discrimination cases were heard in all the highest state courts. The highest courts of ten states heard no cases at all. While one might expect more sex discrimination cases in federal as opposed to state courts, the tiny numbers found, about two and one-half cases per state court over the entire twelve year period, are striking. Further, 65 percent of these cases were brought by men! (Gryski and Main 1983). Indeed, even in the U.S. Supreme Court, "male plaintiffs have dominated" sex discrimination litigation (Cole 1984, 34). A recent study of unionized public-sector employees characterized filing a complaint as "a rare event." Focusing on complaints alleging sex discrimination, the study reported slightly more filings by men than women! Controlling for the gender make-up of the sample, the study concluded that women "do not appear to be filing more than men, even when suits based

39. Berger, in corroborating this point, also notes the huge emotional toll this kind of litigation takes on plaintiffs, reporting litigators' estimates that "fully 50 percent of their clients suffer some form of legal psychosis" (Berger 1980, 61).

upon sex discrimination are considered alone" (Hoyman and Stallworth 1986, 76, 81). Similarly, in the area of wage discrimination, Clauss reports that few suits have been filed (Clauss 1986, 7–8).

Other problems include the need for well-trained lawyers and for funds. An able and ready group of lawyers is obviously essential for successful litigation. Yet for years the shock troops of a successful litigation campaign, a "cadre of voluntary lawyers," were missing from the movement (Freeman 1975, 242). Women's groups "often have suffered from a paucity of lawyers" and this made it nearly impossible to launch a continuous litigation campaign. Even as late as 1980 O'Connor reports that the NOW Legal Defense and Education Fund depended on "volunteer effort" (O'Connor 1980, 22, 104). In financial terms, during the 1970s there was an "astronomical increase in the cost and complexity of a Title VII action" (Berger 1980, 41). Funds were not available to support the enormous costs of a litigation effort, nor was there much fund-raising capability (Freeman 1975, 242–3). As of 1980, litigation-oriented organizations such as the Women's Equity Action League, the NOW Legal Defense and Education Fund, and the Women's Legal Defense Fund could "appear [in court] only as amicus because of limited funds" (O'Connor 1980, 118; Freeman 1975, 82n.17). It was not until well after the women's movement was established and influential that some of these problems were ameliorated.

Perhaps the most serious problem facing women's rights litigators was the "lack of a coordinated effort" among groups (Cowan 1976, 390; Berger 1980, 61, 63). The inevitable result was that cases were brought on an "ad hoc basis" (Berger 1980, 56), with various degrees of appropriate preparation, timing, and chance of success. "The volume and diverse sponsorship of cases," Cowan reports, "presented the courts with a haphazard collection of women's rights issues" which "threatened effective step-by-step development of the law." There was also the very real danger of bad precedents being set "by unsympathetic and opportunistic plaintiffs" (Cowan 1976, 383, 390). This was a serious problem because, as O'Connor found, "few of the organizations involved in Supreme Court sex-discrimination litigation actually have litigation strategies" (O'Connor 1980, 131). One such example is *Schlesinger* v. *Ballard* (1975), which upheld a naval promotion program giving women more time than men to achieve promotions. To many women's rights legal activists, such seemingly benign holdings actually put obstacles in the way of moving toward strict scrutiny of sex discrimination.

A similar example of lack of control leading to unwanted precedents comes from the Women's Rights Project (WRP) of the American Civil Liberties Union (ACLU). The WRP is among the most important women's rights litigators, handling more sex discrimination cases between 1972 and 1980 than all other women's organizations combined (O'Connor 1980, 123). Despite its having laid out a litigation strategy, and the training and expertise of the ACLU staff, it, too, has been taken by surprise. For example, *Kahn* v. *Shevin* (1974) "got to the Supreme Court before the WRP was even aware of it," despite the fact that it "was brought by one of [the] ACLU's own affiliates" and despite the "ACLU National Board policy requiring that all cases directed toward the Supreme Court be reviewed, and most of them briefed and argued, by the national staff" (Cowan 1976, 390, 390–91). The decision was considered a step backwards by the WRP because the Court upheld a gender-based distinction which gave a property-tax exemption to widows but not widowers.[40]

To sum up, the structure of the legal system, and the opportunities courts provide, such as relative ease of access, make coordination of litigation a difficult task. Without such coordination, cases will be lost and bad precedents set. Further, litigation requires individuals willing to take on employers and colleagues. Finally, it requires specially trained lawyers and a great deal of money. These problems, faced by women's rights litigants as well as by civil rights litigants, are inherent in the legal structure. And they make courts poor forums for producing significant social reform.

Incentives and Costs

Given these obstacles to court effectiveness, it is clear that courts need other actors to pitch in. As I have argued, the market has not been responsive nor have there been many actors willing to implement court decisions. Further, in the women's rights field, non-court actors have neither provided incentives for implementation nor imposed costs for non-implementation. Indeed, the burden of implementation has fallen on individuals. For example, although Title IX prohibits education programs or activities receiving federal funds from discriminating on the basis of sex, the legislation and regulations have no provision for government-initiated investigation. Enforcement depends entirely on individuals filing complaints.

When suits or complaints are filed, the results are, at best, mixed. Examining over 2,000 cases brought under a variety of anti-discrimination laws between 1965 and 1984, Burstein and Monaghan found that plaintiffs won either a "full" or "partial" final victory in only about one-quarter of the cases (Burstein and Monaghan 1986, 372).[41] With the EEOC, only a small fraction of complaints brought to it result in legal action. By 1977, the EEOC had a backlog of 126,000 complaints (Deckard 1983, 398). In fiscal year 1985, of the 72,000 complaints brought to it, only 411 (.55 percent) resulted in lawsuits (Bergmann 1986, 159). Summarizing the achievements of the EEOC in ending gender discrimination, Bergmann concluded: "The operations of the

40. Cole (1984, 65) writes that "women's groups, who regarded *Frontiero* as a major victory, viewed *Kahn* as a major setback." Feminist critics of the equality standard, however, did not share this assessment.
41. The data are not limited to sex discrimination cases.

EEOC have had little effect on the behavior of employers, because employers who disobey the law have little cause to fear that the EEOC will come after them" (Bergmann 1986, 302–3). Lack of either incentives or costs has weighed heavily.

It should be no surprise, then, that court decisions have not helped women. Victories in job discrimination suits, setting new precedents, won't help much, when the entire burden of implementation remains with the plaintiffs. Women, in other words, face many of the same problems as blacks in using the courts to produce reform. The difference is that women's rights litigators lack the non-court incentives that civil rights reformers eventually had. And without such incentives (or the presence of one of the other conditions), little will change. Even winning, however, is not easy when federal statutes are being challenged and the U.S. intervenes in opposition.[42]

In comparison, several studies have found that executive and legislative action has made some difference, particularly government-mandated affirmative-action programs and Title VII of the 1964 Civil Rights Act (USCCR 1979b). Beller, for example, found a 7.1 percent reduction in the "sex differential in earnings" and concluded that "Title VII has proved somewhat effective in narrowing the earnings gap between men and women" (Beller 1983, 75; Bergmann 1986, 147). While enforcement has been "uneven and often inadequate" (Reskin and Hartmann 1986, 91), where it has succeeded Reskin points to leadership and incentives. Without them, little will change. The "interventions that were least effective lacked either incentives for compliance or the support of those charged with their implementation" (Reskin and Hartmann 1986, 129). And this, of course, is the constraint that renders courts ineffective.

Conclusion

Women's rights activists have asked courts to change the way American institutions act and citizens behave. Sometimes courts have ordered such change but, unfortunately, it has not occurred on a large scale. The fault lies not with lack of effort by women's rights litigators nor with lack of earnestness

---

42. As was noted in chapter 1, in cases where the federal government appears through the solicitor general, the government's position prevails, generally speaking. This pattern has held with important Supreme Court cases on women's rights in the 1970s. When the solicitor general has argued in support of women's rights' litigants in these cases, they have lost only one, *General Electric* v. *Gilbert*, and won four, *Cleveland Board of Education* v. *Lafleur*, *Corning Glass* v. *Brennan*, *Los Angeles* v. *Manhart*, and *University of Chicago* v. *Cannon*. When the solicitor general argued against them, they won three, *Frontiero* v. *Richardson*, *Califano* v. *Goldfarb*, and *Califano* v. *Westcott*, and lost three, *Kahn* v. *Shevin*, *Schlesinger* v. *Ballard*, and *Califano* v. *Webster* (O'Connor 1980, 132). Overall, of the twenty-one sex discrimination cases in which the solicitor general filed *amicus* briefs between 1971 and 1984, the Supreme Court's decision supported the outcome the solicitor general argued for sixteen times (76 percent). Figures derived from Segal and Reedy (1988, 562).

by judges and justices in requiring that their orders be implemented. It runs deeper than that. It is inherent in the place courts hold in the American political system. Precedent-setting decisions in women's rights have produced little because courts lack all the essential tools required of any institution hoping to implement change. Without the presence of non-court actors offering incentives, or imposing costs, without a market mechanism for change, and without willing actors, court-ordered change in women's rights has changed little. As with civil rights in the years before congressional and executive branch action, women's rights litigators could not overcome the constraints of the Constrained Court view.

8

The Court as Catalyst?

The last two chapters have presented evidence and discussion of why U.S. courts were unable to produce significant social reform through the judicial path of influence. There remains, however, the extra-judicial path. As the Dynamic Court view contends, the courts acted to put sex discrimination on the political agenda. Court decisions served to teach Americans that women are discriminated against. They served to legitimate the actions of women activists and energize others to support them. In other words, the judicial path of influence overlooks a subtle but important path through which the courts exercised influence in women's rights.

In this chapter, I examine these claims. I do so explicitly within the theoretical framework, and with the notes of caution, of chapter 4, the study of the extra-judicial path of influence with civil rights. Rather that repeat it, however, I urge the reader to consult it again, if necessary.

In order to assess the strength of the extra-judicial path of influence, I will identify the links that have to be present for such influence to exist. The underlying claim is that Court action increased concern and interest in women's rights throughout American society and that such concern and interest led to legislative and other change. Following the format of the civil rights discussion in chapter 4, I will examine appropriate places for extra-judicial effects to be found. These include the actions of political leaders in support of women's rights, the beliefs of Americans about sex discrimination, and the actions and beliefs of women's rights activists. It must be stressed that to the extent that I find little or no evidence of Court influence for these links, I can not conclude that the Court had no extra-judicial influence, or that the Dynamic Court view is wrong. I can conclude, however, that lacking evidence in these appropriate places, the Dynamic Court argument for extra-judicial influence is on weak ground.

The 1973 abortion decisions provide a clear-cut line around which to test for extra-judicial effects. With women's rights other than abortion, however, no such clear line is presented. The cases are spread out throughout the 1970s and lack the clear holdings of the abortion cases. To proceed, then, I will first identify when major changes occurred and see where they fit in the Court's chronology. Surely, if no major changes occurred, or if they occurred before Court action, then the question of extra-judicial influence is misplaced. Second, I will assume for the sake of argument, however uncomfortably, that the 1973 abortion decisions were potentially influential not only on abortion but also with issues of women's rights in general. While the connection may be weak, the assumption will provide a demarcation line, if somewhat artificial, that allows for comparison.[1]

Salience

One of the major claims of extra-judicial influence is that Court action made women's rights and abortion public issues. "Publicity generated by adjudication," O'Connor suggests, "places its sponsor in the public eye and can provide a legitimate way for the organization to place its issue on the public agenda" (O'Connor 1980, 5; Berger 1980, 55). If this is the case, then increased press coverage of women's rights and abortion should be seen after 1973. The evidence is presented in figures 8.1 and 8.2, and tables 8.1 and 8.2.

To start with abortion, table 8.1A shows that the major increase in magazine coverage came in 1970 and 1971 (column 2) when the number of entries in the *Reader's Guide* increased from 36 in 1969 to 75 in 1970 and then 81 in 1971. There was actually less coverage in 1973, the year of the Court's decisions, than in the years 1972, 1971, or 1970! Adding an additional category, coverage of U.S. Supreme Court abortion decisions, as shown in table 8.1B, does raise 1973 coverage to the level of 1970, still below the coverage given abortion in 1971. With the large-circulation magazines shown in table 8.1A, there is no large increase in 1973. To the extent there was a change, it also appears to be in 1970 and 1971. And coverage in the *New York Times* is no different.[2] With women's rights, table 8.2A reports a similar pattern. A steep increase is recorded, but it is in 1970 and 1971, prior to any major Court action. This is particularly pronounced in table 8.2B. Large-circulation magazine coverage of women's rights did not change dramatically after major Court decisions. To the extent there is much of an increase, it is in the years 1970 and 1971, before Court action. Again, *New York Times*

1. This assumption is supported by Luker (1984), who argues that the fight over abortion is really a fight about the social role of women.

2. Interestingly, Luker notes that there were sixty-nine stories devoted to abortion in the *New York Times* in 1869! (Luker 1984, 268 n.30).

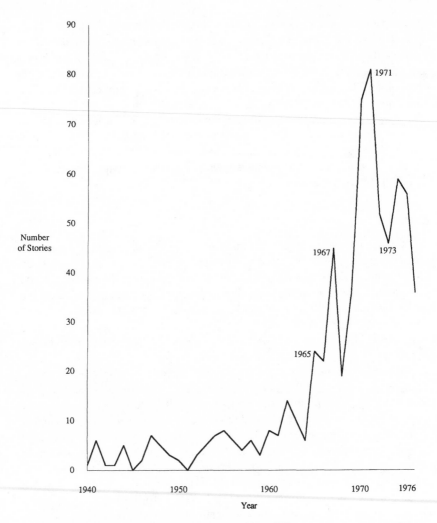

Figure 8.1. Magazine Coverage of Abortion, 1940–1976

coverage is similar. It is fair to conclude, then, that there was no sharp increase in press and magazine coverage of abortion and women's rights after the major Court decisions.

There is still the possibility, however, that there was an increase in coverage in the magazines most likely read by political elites. With abortion, however, as table 8.1A indicates, this was not the case. An examination of coverage in the *New York Times Sunday Magazine*, the *New Republic, Time*, and *Newsweek*—magazines most likely to be read by political elites—shows that the major increase came in 1970 and 1971. There was no increase in

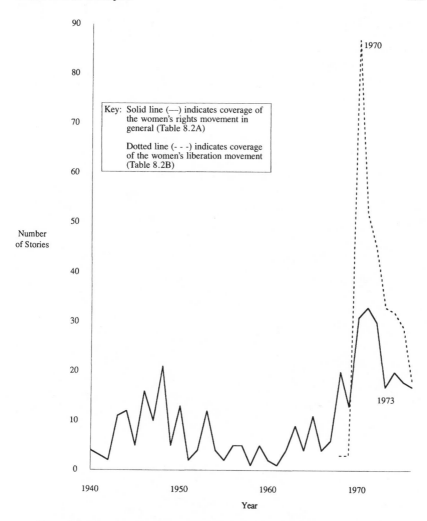

Figure 8.2. Magazine Coverage of Women's Rights, 1940–1976

abortion coverage in 1973, the year of the Court's decisions. In fact, all four magazines had more abortion stories in previous recent years than in 1973. Turning to women's rights, table 8.2A shows no large increase in the years 1973 and beyond. The change that did occur in the coverage accorded women's rights in the four magazines elites would likely read is found in 1970 and 1971. This pattern is particularly pronounced in table 8.2B. The point is clear: Court decisions on abortion and women's rights did *not* result in greater coverage of these issues in the magazines political elites would most likely read. While there was a large increase in coverage, it predated Court action.

Table 8.1A   Magazine And Press Coverage Of Abortion, 1940–1976

Year	Entries	Reader's Guide # of Journals	NYT Mag.[a]	New Rep.	News-week	Time	Reader's Digest	Ladies H.J.	Life	Sat. Eve. Post	NYT Index[b]
1940	1	127									.004
1941	6	118				1	1	1			.003
1942	1										.02
1943	1	115									.01
1944	5					1	1				.01
1945	0	127									.002
1946	2					1					.004
1947	7	133			2	2	1				.004
1948	5				2	1					.01
1949	3	122									.004
1950	2				1						.01
1951	0	119									.01
1952	3							1			.004
1953	5	122			1			2			.01
1954	7				1	1		1			.01
1955	8	114				2					.01
1956	6				1	1	1	1			.01
1957	4	111				2					.001
1958	6				1	1					.002
1959	3	110					1				.003
1960	8				1	1	1	2			.02
1961	7	134						1		3	.001
1962	14				3	2			1		.02
1963	10	129		2	1			1			.01
1964	6					1	1				.02
1965	24	126	1		1	1			1	1	.02
1966	22			1	2		1	1		1	.03
1967	45	128		2	6	4	1	1	1	1	.13
1968	19		1		2	1					.05
1969	36	162	1	1	3	4	1				.15
1970	75		3	1	9	5		2	2		.16
1971	81	157	5		4	5	1	1	1		.12
1972	52		2		3	4					.25
1973	46	161			3	3	3				.18
1974[c]	59			10	2	4					.12
1975	56	160		2	9	4					.13
1976	36				2	1					.15

SOURCE: See Appendix 7.

NOTES:

[a]Repetitions excluded.
[b]Proportion of pages in *New York Times Index* devoted to coverage of abortion (in percent).
[c]*Ms.* first indexed March 1974–February 1975.

Table 8.2A   Magazine And Press Coverage Of Women's Rights, 1940–1976

Year	Reader's Guide # of Entries	Reader's Guide # of Journals	NYT Mag.[a]	New Rep.	News-week	Time	Reader's Digest	Ladies H.J.	Life	Sat. Eve. Post	NYT Index[b]
1940	4	127				1					.25
1941	3	118									.24
1942	2										.25
1943	11	115									.18
1944	12		2				1				.19
1945	5	127		2		1		1			.17
1946	16				1			1			.16
1947	10	133									.17
1948	21		1			1		2		1	.14
1949	5	122									.15
1950	13		1		1	2			1		.13
1951	2	119									.12
1952	4					1					.14
1953	12	122									.14
1954	4										.002
1955	2	114									.06
1956	5										.07
1957	5	111				1					.1
1958	1										.07
1959	5	110									.06
1960	2										.06
1961	1	134									.03
1962	4		1					1			.06
1963	9	129									.06
1964	4		1				1			1	.05
1965	11	126		1	1						.05
1966	4										.05
1967	6	128	1								.05
1968	20		2								.05
1969	13	162		2		1					.05
1970	31		1		2	3		1			.17
1971	33	157		2	4	3	1				.18
1972	30				2	2	2	1			.20
1973	17	161		2				1			.20
1974[c]	20				2	2				1	.22
1975	18	160				1	1				.3
1976	17					1					.19

SOURCE: See Appendix 7.

NOTES:

[a]Repetitions excluded.
[b]Proportion of pages in *New York Times Index* devoted to coverage of women's rights (in percent).
[c]*Ms.* first indexed March 1974–February 1975.

Table 8.1B   Magazine Coverage Of U.S. Supreme Court Abortion Decisions, 1973–1976

Year	Reader's Guide Entries	# of Journals	NYT Mag.	New Rep.	News-week	Time	Reader's Digest	Ladies H.J.	Life	Sat. Eve. Post
1973	30	161	0	2	1	1	0	0	0	0
1974	7		0	0	0	1	0	0	0	0
1975	2	160	0	0	0	0	0	0	0	0
1976	6		0	0	1	0	0	0	0	0

SOURCE: See Appendix 7.

NOTE: Repetitions are *not* excluded.

Table 8.2B   Magazine Coverage Of The Women's Liberation Movement, 1968–1976

Year	Reader's Guide Entries	# of Journals	NYT Mag.[a]	New Rep.	News-week	Time	Reader's Digest	Ladies H.J.	Life	Sat. Eve. Post
1968	3		2	0	0	0	0	0	0	0
1969	3	162	0	0	0	1	0	0	1	0
1970	87		5	2	9	7	1	3	3	0
1971	52	157	4	0	2	4	1	0	3	0
1972	45		6	1	2	7	0	0	1	0
1973	33	161	2	2	3	2	0	0	0	1
1974[b]	32		1	1	4	0	0	0	0	0
1975	29	160	0	0	0	2	0	0	0	0
1976	18		2	1	1	0	1	0	0	0

SOURCE: See Appendix 7.

NOTES:

[a]Repetitions are excluded.
[b]*Ms.* first indexed March 1974–February 1975.

The argument that Court action gave women's rights and abortion salience lacks evidence.[3]

Political Leaders

An important place to look for evidence of extra-judicial influence is the reaction of political leaders to Court action. If the Court exerted influence, reminding elected leaders of the demands of the Constitution, one might expect to see increased executive branch and legislative action on behalf of women's rights after major Court action. If, however, there is little or no

3. Is it possible, though, that without Court action, there would have been even less coverage? This seems unlikely because titles of abortion stories in both 1970 and 1973 rarely mentioned the Court.

change, the claim of extra-judicial influence lacks evidence in an important place.

The Court's abortion decisions were indeed followed by executive branch and congressional action in the years following their issuance. Rather than acting to protect and enlarge the constitutional rights enunciated by the Court, however, political action was aimed at undermining them. As I have detailed in past chapters, a large number of constitutional amendments were introduced to overturn the Court's decisions. While none passed, the Congress did pass some restrictive abortion legislation, most notably the Hyde Amendment. The executive branch, as well, did not show a heightened awareness of the need to protect a woman's constitutional right to abortion. Like Congress, presidents after 1973 moved with some hostility to abortion, certainly more than their predecessors before the Court's action. Thus, there is little evidence for the positive influence of the courts in heightening political leaders' interest in protecting the right to abortion.

In areas other than abortion, the evidence does not clearly support Court influence. While there was a great deal of political activity on behalf of women after the first major women's rights cases, there was also a great deal before them. I have detailed some of this activity in chapter 7. A massive increase in the passage of women's rights legislation did take place in Congress but it was in the Ninety-second Congress, 1971–72, before the major Court cases. The Equal Rights Amendment was sponsored by 81 Senators and 273 members of the House, a majority in both bodies, in the Ninety-first Congress in 1970 (U.S. Cong., Senate 1970a, 70). It was passed in 1972. At the 1972 major party conventions, the percentage of female delegates showed a dramatic gain over 1968, increasing from 13 percent to 40 percent at the Democratic convention and from 17 percent to about one-third at the Republican convention (Freeman 1975, 160; Wayne 1980, 91, 93). While the pace of legislative activity remained high, there was no large change or increase after the major Court cases. The dramatic rise came earlier, before the Court was active. Again, the evidence for the extra-judicial influence of the Court is not there.

In sum, with the crucial target group of political leaders, in appropriate places to find evidence of Court influence, the evidence is not found. While there was an increase in political activity in support of women's rights, it predated major Court action. The extra-judicial path of influence is not supported with political leaders.

Public Opinion

One of the major claims of the Dynamic Court view is that Court action can prick the conscience of Americans and heighten their awareness of discrimination. It is entirely possible that litigation in abortion and women's rights changed perceptions of the position of women in American society, smoothing the way for change. Indeed, many groups involved in women's rights litigation believe that "litigation, because it attracts television, newspaper, and magazine attention, is critical in raising the consciousness of the American public" (O'Connor 1980, 120). A good place to look for evidence of this is in changes in public opinion. One might reasonably suggest that, for the Court to have an influence on the opinions of Americans, a large number need to know that the Court acted and what it did. However, as was shown in chapter 4, Americans do not much follow Supreme Court activity. Fortunately, there are some data available. Judith Blake commissioned two questions on knowledge of the Supreme Court's abortion decisions from Gallup in April 1975. Although the questions were asked only a little more than two years after the decisions, Blake found that "less than half of American adult respondents were informed about the 1973 decisions" (Blake 1977b, 57–59). That is, fewer than half of the "public of voting age has heard of the Court's decisions *and* is correctly apprised of their general intent" (Blake 1977a, 54). By 1982, almost a decade after the decisions, little had changed. When a national sample was asked whether the Supreme Court forbids or permits a woman to obtain an abortion during the first three months of pregnancy, 59 percent of the respondents replied "no" or "don't know" ("Americans Evaluate" 1982, 25). These findings may appear startling to many. But they are in line with what students have learned about the Supreme Court and public opinion. While I lack data for other women's rights issues, it seems likely that if more than half the American public didn't know about *Roe*, then at least that percentage wouldn't know about other, less famous, Court decisions. In this important place for evidence of extra-judicial effects, the evidence cuts against the claim.

Public opinion is crucial for the claim for extra-judicial influence. Starting with abortion, the claim of extra-judicial influence must be that the Court greatly influenced public opinion in favor of abortion. As Nancy Stearns, a women's rights lawyer put it, courts can be used as "a tool for reaching more women and for educating them on the whole question of abortion and women's rights" (quoted in Goodman et al. 1973, 29). The figures, then, should show a large increase in public support after the Court's decisions. If the increase is small or nonexistent, claims of extra-judicial influence would appear lacking in relevant support. Fortunately, there are a number of polls and numerous commentators examining how opinion changed over the years. Unfortunately, while "systematic consideration of the data on abortion seems to provide encouraging evidence of reliability" (Blake 1977b, 48), differences in question wording and question order turn out to make a difference in responses. One must be careful in evaluating poll results.[4]

4. For example, comparing a 1970 poll in which respondents were asked, *after* a whole list of reasons for allowing abortion, whether "any reason" was sufficient, with a 1971 poll when

Turning to the data, polls done by the National Opinion Research Center (NORC) in 1972 and 1973 show, in the words of Ebaugh and Haney, a "dramatic increase in favorable attitudes" toward legal abortion. The increase in support of legal abortion across six different questions ranges from 6 to 8 percentage points and averages about six and one-third percentage points (Ebaugh and Haney 1980, 492, 493). Using the same data, Arney and Trescher found an average increase of 7.33 percentage points and conclude that "the very fact of the [Supreme Court] decisions apparently caused a rapid shift in abortion attitudes" (Arney and Trescher 1976, 118, 124). Finally, also using the same data, Tedrow and Mahoney found an average increase of 5 percentage points in support of abortion (Tedrow and Mahoney 1979, 183).

Assuming the NORC data are correct, are Arney and Trescher correct in suggesting that the Court "caused" the "rapid shift" in attitudes? Is the Dynamic Court view finally vindicated? One way of examining the question is to place the NORC data in the context of a broader time-scale.[5] Looking at the 1960s as a whole, Blake found a "sharp decline in disapproval" of purely elective abortion (Blake 1973, 450). She noted that opinions on discretionary abortion were "changing rapidly over time" and polls were recording "rapidly growing support" (Blake 1971, 543, 544). Granberg and Granberg, while finding a 5-point increase in the NORC data immediately after Court action, put the data in the context of a longer time-period and found it "compatible with the analysis that the largest part of the change in abortion attitudes occurred before 1970." They pointed to data from the 1965, 1970, and 1975 National Fertility Studies which suggest a spurt in approval in 1970 and a slightly slowed rate of growth after, including the period of Court action. Relying on the NORC data, they concluded that the "growth in approval

---

that question was asked *first*, Jones and Westoff found a difference of approximately 34 percent in responses supportive of abortion (Jones and Westoff 1972, 574). Similarly, in a January 1973 Gallup poll in which half the sample was asked the "any reason" question first and half last, there was a difference of 13 percent in approval of abortion for any reason by men and a 9 percent increase in approval by women. Also, the average of approving responses in all categories for both men and women rose slightly when the order was reversed (Blake 1977a, 61).

5. It should be obvious that one can't make claims about the magnitude of change without knowing what the trend line looks like. This is particularly the case with NORC polls on abortion, which have systematically showed higher proportions approving of abortion than have Gallup polls. "These differences," according to Blake who studied both Gallup and NORC polls, as well as other polls, "are doubtless due to differences in the wording and order of the questions asked" (Blake 1977b, 50). The Gallup survey question was asked fourth, after three questions concerning the mother's health, possible child deformity, and financial problems as reasons for allowing abortion. The NORC question was asked second, following a question about child deformity. In terms of possible wording bias, Gallup asked if abortion should be legal where the "parents *simply* have all the children they want although there would be no major health or financial problems involved in having another child?" (emphasis added). Coming after three previous questions, and with the word "simply," the question does suggest a negative answer. This is particularly true in contrast with the NORC question, which asked if a pregnant woman should be able to obtain a legal abortion if "she is married and does not want any more children?" Given these differences in wording and order, different levels of responses are of little surprise (Blake 1977b, 48).

between 1972 and 1973 was not as spectacular as might have been expected, given the drama and unambiguous nature of the Supreme Court decisions" (Granberg and Granberg 1980, 252).

One of the problems of relying too heavily on the NORC data is that they do not predate 1972. Gallup surveys, however, go back to the 1960s. They show much larger increases prior to Court action than after it. For example, between 1969 and 1970 Gallup recorded a 9-point increase in the percentage of respondents approving of elective abortion. By 1972, an additional 4 percent increase was recorded (Blake 1977b, 49). Another set of Gallup polls recorded a 15-point drop in the percent of respondents disapproving of abortions for financial reasons in only the eight months between October 1969 and June 1970. The same eight months showed a 10-point drop in the percentage disapproving of abortions for discretionary reasons (Blake 1977a, 58). Finally, polls done for Planned Parenthood in January and June of 1972, showed a 7-point increase in the percentage of respondents in favor of allowing a woman and her physician the sole choice in abortion (Pomeroy and Landman 1972, 45).

Putting the NORC changes in context, then, shows change not any greater than in years prior to 1973. In fact, the numbers suggest that the 1972–73 changes were actually smaller than those that preceded them. The Gallup polls make this clear. The poll that recorded a 9 percent increase between 1969 and 1970, for example, showed *no* increase between 1972 and 1973 and only a 4 percent change by 1977 (Blake 1977b, 49). The Gallup-poll question that showed a 15-point drop in the percentage disapproving of abortion for financial reasons between 1969 and 1970 showed *no* change between March 1972 and November 1973. With abortion for purely discretionary reasons, the question resulting in a 10-point drop between 1969 and 1970 also showed *no* change between 1972 and 1973 (Blake 1977a, 58). Finally, Gallup surveys done in September of 1972 and 1974, asking whether there should be no legal restraint on abortion or whether the law should specify circumstances that justify abortion, showed only a 1-point gain for the more pro-choice position (Blake 1977b, 51).

The point of this discussion is that there was clearly no rapid or large change in Americans' support of abortion after the Court's action. "None of our time series on public views regarding abortion indicates that the Supreme Court decisions had an important effect on opinion" (Blake 1977b, 57). Even if the NORC data are accurate, the changes were the same size as, or smaller than, changes in the past. In this crucial area for finding evidence for extra-judicial effects, the evidence is not there.[6] The Dynamic Court view remains unproven.

6. This conclusion is buttressed by the lack of change in the percentage of National Election Study respondents who named abortion as a major national problem. In 1972, 1974, 1976, and 1978, the percentage remained unchanged, at less than one-half of one percent! (Jackson and

Another area to examine for evidence of extra-judicial effects of Court action is the change in public opinion on women's rights issues other than abortion. While there is no firm demarcation line, as with abortion, the 1973 abortion decisions are a rough break-point. If the Dynamic Court view's extra-judicial effects thesis is correct, then major changes in public opinion should occur after these dates, not before them.

There has been substantial change in public opinion about women's rights.[7] In general, Lou Harris found, writing in 1972, "a swing in attitude—and a dramatic one—is taking place among women in America today" (Harris n.d., 1). As the data below will demonstrate, that dramatic swing occurred in the late 1960s and early 1970s, before Court action. One area where it was pronounced was in opinions about the place of women in American society. In 1970, for example, 40 percent of women and 42 percent of a national sample favored efforts to strengthen and change women's status in society. In 1971, there was no change. The next year, however, showed an 8-point gain in the percentage of women supporting efforts for change (48 percent) and a 6-point gain in the percentage of the national sample (48 percent) (Boer 1977, 269; Harris n.d., 2). However, a 1975 survey for the National Commission on the Observance of International Women's Year found little change, with only half of its respondents supporting efforts to strengthen and change women's status in society (Bryant 1977, 43).[8]

The same pattern is found with college-educated women in questions of sex-role beliefs. Using surveys from the 1960s and 1970s, Mason et al. found that the period 1964–70 saw "rather sizable attitude shifts" among these women. By 1970, they found that "large majorities held relatively egalitarian beliefs about women's dependency on men's plans, about the consequences of maternal employment for children's well-being, and about the differential socialization of boys and girls" (Mason et al. 1976, 587). College-educated men also appeared to be changing. In 1972, for the first time fewer than one-half of entering male college freshmen accepted the notion that a woman's place is in the home (Carden 1974, xiii, n.11).[9] Finally, as early as 1962, a Gallup poll found that 90 percent of housewives surveyed did not want their daughters to lead the same type of life they had (cited in Deckard 1983, 319).

Another indication of changing opinion about the appropriate role of

Vinovskis 1983, 68). For an argument that the impact of the Court's decisions was "primarily to increase polarization of groups on the issue, with little or no increase in overall approval," see Franklin and Kosaki (1989, 759).

7. Although time-series data are available, they are spotty. Male poll-takers were not above the sexism of their times. Thus, Erskine notes that "questions on women's role abounded until 1950, fell off to zero in the late 1950s, and only began a slow revival in the 1960s as the women's liberation movement moved into the public eye" (Erskine 1971, 276).

8. Other polls show increases over the years 1972–75, albeit smaller than that of 1971–72 (Boer 1977, 269).

9. The survey, done by the American Council on Education, also found that only about a quarter of women entering college held the notion.

women is found in opinions about married women working. In 1936, only 18 percent of Gallup's respondents said yes to the question "should a married woman earn money if she has a husband capable of supporting her?" A full 82 percent opposed women working (Gallup 1972, 1: 39).[10] In 1938, 22 percent of the sample approved with 81 percent of men and 75 percent of women responding in the negative (Gallup 1972, 1: 131). By 1967, opinions had changed a great deal, with 44 percent of the sample responding positively to a similar Roper question (Erskine 1971, 285). Just two years later, however, the percentage of respondents approving of a married woman earning money increased to 55 percent (McGlen and O'Connor 1983, 217). This 11-point increase in two years was half the increase recorded in the nearly thirty years between 1938 and 1967! And it was recorded before any major Court action.

Feelings about the proper role of men and women in the political world show the same pattern. In 1937, for example, only 33 percent of a national sample expressed a willingness to vote for a woman for president. Support increased gradually over time until the 1969–71 period when the increase was 12 points, over half the increase recorded between 1937 and 1969! The 1969–72 increase was also large, 15 points. Examining the figures by gender shows a 7-point change in men's attitudes between 1969 and 1971 and a whopping 18-point increase in women's attitudes. By 1972, men and women expressed equal levels of support. While the increases in the late 1940s were of approximately the same magnitude, both predate Court activity on behalf of women's rights.[11]

The data are limited for other political offices. As early as 1949, thirty-five years before a woman was selected as the vice-presidential nominee of a major party, a majority of 53 percent told Gallup pollsters they would vote for a qualified woman for vice-president (Gallup 1972, 2: 862). By 1945, a full thirty-six years before a woman was nominated to serve on the Supreme Court, more Americans said they would approve of such a nomination (47 percent) than would disapprove (40 percent) (Gallup 1972, 1: 548). This marked a vast improvement over 1938 when disapproval was selected by 21 percentage points more than approval (Erskine 1971, 279). And by 1949, 54 percent of the sample approved of female ambassadors (Gallup 1972, 2: 837).

One theme that has been touched on repeatedly is whether the country would be better off if women had more say about politics. In 1945, 32 percent of a Gallup sample agreed that not enough capable women were holding important government jobs (Gallup 1972, 1: 548). By 1952, only 39 percent thought the country would be better governed if more women held important

10. A National Education Association study in 1930–31 showed that 77 percent of the 1,500 school systems surveyed refused to hire married women and 63 percent dismissed female teachers if they married (Chafe 1972, 108).
11. Data from Erskine (1971, 275); Ferree (1974, 393); Gallup (1972, 1: 37, 548; 2: 861, 1315, 1576; 3: 1846, 1852, 2066, 2189, 2319).

government jobs (Gallup 1972, 2: 1074). By 1971, however, majorities of both men (51 percent) and women (56 percent) thought so (Harris n.d., 15). In terms of candidates for Congress, in 1946 75 percent of men and 67 percent of women thought that members of Congress should nearly always be men (Erskine 1971, 280). By 1970, however, the numbers had reversed, with 84 percent saying they would vote for a qualified woman (Gallup 1972, 3: 2261).

In sum, in the area of public opinion, abortion, and women's rights, while there were major changes, they pre-dated Court action. With women's rights, public-opinion change did continue to occur in the 1970s, but it "did not occur at a consistently faster pace after 1970 than before" (Mason et al. 1976, 594). Again, evidence for extra-judicial influence is lacking.

The Women's Movement

An important area to find evidence for extra-judicial effects is with women activists and the women's movement. Here, the argument would be that by legitimating the claims of women, Court decisions spurred women to form and join women's rights organizations and to raise large sums of money, empowering the women's rights movement. Many women's rights legal groups believe that litigation is "critical in raising the consciousness of the American public, particularly women" (O'Connor 1980, 120). Nancy Stearns, an activist lawyer, suggests that women can use courts as "one very specific means to assist their organizing other women" (quoted in Goodman et al. 1973, 24). And, as mentioned in the introduction to Part 2, some commentators believe that "until the litigation effort began, the women's rights movement was a topic for conversation, not action" (Berger 1980, 55). Court action may have had important extra-judicial effects in stimulating change on behalf of women.

In the material that follows I will highlight the simple point that the women's movement was moving full blast before Court decisions on behalf of women's rights came to be. Chapter 9 makes this point in detail. To avoid repetition, I will focus on a few key points where Court influence could possibly have been felt. But it should be noted that claims for this influence are predicated on increased media coverage after Court decisions—an increase that I have shown did not occur.

A vital piece of information is simple dates. One might suspect that Court decisions expanding women's rights would spark the creation of women's rights groups, particularly those primarily interested in litigation. However, all the important women's groups were founded before Court action. The National Organization for Women (NOW) was formed in the fall of 1966. The National Association for the Repeal of Abortion Laws (NARAL) was formed in 1969.[12] The National Women's Political Caucus dates from 1971. Even those groups most active in women's rights litigation pre-date Court action. The Women's Rights Project (WRP) was formed in 1971 and *Reed*, the first case in which the Supreme Court found unconstitutional a gender-based distinction, was brought by it. The Women's Equity Action League (WEAL) was formed as a split-off from NOW in 1968 and NOW's Legal Defense and Education Fund was formed in 1971. Thus, it does not appear that Court action helped create important women's rights organizations, including those whose primary focus is litigation.

Another possible place to look for evidence of Court influence is in the growth of feminist periodicals and publications. Court influence might have produced new interest in feminist studies and sparked the growth of magazines, journals, and publishers dedicated to women's rights. While a virtual explosion in such material did take place, it, too, predates Court action. Carden reports that the number of feminist newsletters and journals grew from two in 1968 to sixty in 1971. The 1970–71 increase alone was thirty (Carden 1974, 65). Including feminist newspapers as well as journals, Hole and Levine report "over one hundred" by the beginning of 1971 (Hole and Levine 1971, 271). By the spring of 1973, there were 163 feminist publications of all sorts and 18 feminist pamphlet publishers or printing co-ops in operation (Freeman 1975, 119n.25). *Ms.* magazine was started in July 1972 after a sample run of 300,000 copies sold out in eight days (Deckard 1983, 355). The growth of feminist literature provides no evidence for extra-judicial influence.

Money and Membership

The growth in membership of women's rights organizations is a potential place for evidence of Court influence. Evidence for extra-judicial influence would be large increases in membership after important Court cases. Unfortunately, only NOW and NARAL are large enough to potentially show such change and, like many other interest groups, they jealously guard membership information. Table 8.3 presents the available data. Looking first at NOW, the data suggest that there were large increases in membership in the early years, 1971–72, 1972–73, and 1973–74. Chapter growth was particularly strong in these years, increasing from 150 chapters in 1971 to 365 chapters in February 1973 to 700 chapters in 1974.[13] Since the Supreme Court's abortion decisions came in January 1973, it is quite possible that these numbers reflect Court influence. However, there are several reasons for caution in accepting

12. After the 1973 decisions, NARAL kept its acronym but changed its name to the National Abortion Rights Action League and kept working to improve access to safe and legal abortion.
13. Chapter data from Carden (1974, 105); Deckard (1983, 322); Freeman (1975, 87).

Year	NOW Membership	NARAL Membership
Table 8.3	**Membership In The National Organization For Women and the National Abortion Rights Action League, 1967–1985**	

Table 8.3   **Membership In The National Organization For Women and the National Abortion Rights Action League, 1967–1985**

Year	NOW Membership	NARAL Membership
1967	1,122	—
1968	1,313	—
1969	3,033[a]	—
1970	4,289[a]	—
1971	5,801	—
1972	14,924	—
1973	20,000	—
1974	40,000	—
1975	55,000	10,000
1976	60,000	13,000
1977	70,000	13,000
1978	77,000	32,000
1979[b]	107,500	67,500
1980	130,000	90,000
1981	130,000	130,000
1982	260,000	156,000
1983	260,000	115,000
1984	260,000	115,000
1985	260,000	115,000
1986	260,000	150,000
1987	260,000	250,000

SOURCES: *Encyclopedia of Associations* (1976–88).
Additional figures derived for NOW from:
1967–73: Carden (1974, 105)
1967, 1974: Freeman (1975, 80, 87)
1971, 1973: Deckard (1983, 322)
1970, 1974: Carden (1977, 19)
1975–77: "Lawyer Re-elected" (1975, 8); "NOW Still Growing" (1976, 20); "Women's Movement" (1977, 46)

NOTES: The *Encyclopedia of Associations* compiles its data from the associations surveyed. When no data are available, the previous year's figures are used. Figures are assigned to the copyright year of the publication, not the year in the title.

[a] Estimates.
[b] 1979 figures are the average of data presented in the fourteenth and fifteenth editions of the *Encyclopedia of Associations*, which both have a copyright date of 1980.

this claim. All the early numbers are quite small, with large increases not coming until the late 1970s and mid-1980s. Even if the Court can be credited with producing change, the change was small. However, there are reasons for questioning judicial influence. The growth between 1971 and 1972 suggests that something was going on within the organization or its potential membership. While the 1971 base was small, an increase of two and one-half times the membership in one year does speak to growing interest. In fact, in 1973

NOW opened three national offices and added twelve to fifteen paid staffers. These offices included a legislative office in Washington, D.C., in February, a public information office in New York City in May, and an administrative office in Chicago in November (Freeman 1975, 83). One would expect that this institutional growth gave NOW much greater visibility, encouraging a growth in membership. Also, in 1973 and 1974 NOW launched five direct-mail fund-raising drives (Freeman 1975, 91). Here, too, one would expect such efforts to increase membership. Finally, the Equal Rights Amendment was passed by Congress and sent to the states for ratification in 1972. Indeed Gelb and Palley find that NOW's increase in membership from 1967 to 1978 was "largely owing to its campaign for ERA ratification" (Gelb and Palley 1982, 29). With NARAL, membership data are lacking for the early years. However, since the organization was founded before Court action, and had only 10,000 members in 1975, the Court could not have had much of an effect. NARAL's membership did increase dramatically, but only in the late 1970s and 1980s, long after Court action supportive of abortion. Further, Gelb and Palley credit this growth to a "direct-mail recruiting effort" (Gelb and Palley 1982, 36). While it is impossible to state with certainty how all these factors add up, crediting the influence to one act or one institution is probably misplaced. The change in NOW membership remains a potential but unlikely result of Court action.[14]

A final indicator of potential Court influence is the growth of contributions to women's groups. If the Court made an indirect contribution to the women's movement, then an increase in revenues available to women's organizations would be expected. As with membership, accurate financial data are close to impossible to obtain. The careful scholar is reduced to relying on hazy estimates. These do show, however, a rather large increase in available funds. NOW reportedly increased its revenues from $26,000 in 1970 to $521,000 in 1974 (Carden 1977, 19). Foundation grants to women's rights organizations in the years 1971–74 amounted to about 2 million dollars. By the end of 1975, a total of $4.2 million had been awarded (Carden 1977, 19, 20). These ranged from a small grant from the Stern Foundation in 1971 to help set up the Women's Action Alliance, to "sizable grants" to WEAL and the WRP from the Playboy Foundation in the early 1970s (Freeman 1975, 154; O'Connor 1980, 119; Cowan 1976, 384). Since these figures suggest an increase in the years after some Supreme Court action on behalf of women's rights, it is possible that they reflect the extra-judicial influence of the Court.

The increase in funds available to NOW was huge. However, Carden concludes that the membership increase was "primarily responsible" for the increase in revenues. She notes, too, that "almost all the additional funds went to pay for membership services," suggesting that her analysis is correct

14. None of the studies of the women's movement consulted that examine membership mentions the Court as a contributor to membership growth.

(Carden 1977, 19). Further, in the 1972–73 period, when NOW's membership doubled, its normal fund-raising reportedly only brought in an additional $14,000 (Freeman 1975, 91). Again, this suggests that increased membership provided most of the additional revenue. Finally, a special direct-mail fund-raising campaign asking for money to support work for states' ratification of the Equal Rights Amendment brought in $150,000 in the beginning of 1973 (Carden 1974, 125). All and all, then, it appears unlikely that Court action played a key role in increasing NOW's funds.

It is not difficult to characterize the increase in foundation support. In the 1971–74 period, "only nineteen" feminist groups received foundation support and five of the groups received three-quarters of the money. By 1975 the list of grantees had expanded to thirty-one but nine groups, including the five from the earlier period, received 80 percent of the money. The "great majority of non-establishment feminist groups received no funds" (Carden 1977, 19, 20). Of the nine groups which received the bulk of the funds, all but two were research, publishing, and referral services. Overall, "less than one-fifth of 1 percent" of foundation monies distributed between 1972 and 1974 went to women's groups, with the Ford Foundation alone providing "at least one-half" of the funds (Berger 1980, 7). As with civil rights before the activist phase of the movement, foundation support for women's rights was "disappointing" (Berger 1980, 7). Reviewing the literature in the early 1980s, Gelb and Palley found that "numerous studies have documented the relatively impoverished state of feminist groups." Feminist groups, they reported, are "disadvantaged in their ability to raise funds from foundations" (Gelb and Palley 1982, 47, 48). It is hard to see how this pattern of giving reflects Court influence.

To sum up, the extra-judicial effects of Court action might have influenced the women's movement, but there is little evidence that can plausibly be said to support this assertion. The creation of women's groups does not support it nor does the large growth in feminist publishing. It is possible but unlikely that the growth in membership and in funds available to the movement are a result of Court action. Evidence for extra-judicial influence is not found with the women's movement.

Conclusion

Proponents of the Dynamic Court view argue that Court action, if stymied in judicial effect, has large and important extra-judicial effects. In the area of abortion and women's rights, both students and activists have claimed that the Court put women's rights issues on the national agenda, changed public opinion, and energized women's groups. They have pointed, too, to the symbolic importance of the Court finding a constitutional right to abortion. In examining these claims, I have looked at sensible and appropriate places to find evidence for them. The evidence is not there. With political leaders and government action, the increase in sensitivity to women's rights predates Court action. With abortion, government officials were actually more hostile after Court action than before it. Press and magazine coverage of abortion and women's rights does not appear responsive to Court action. Public opinion, while changing, seems to have acted independently of any Court decisions, with the sharpest changes pre-dating Court action. Finally, there is no clear evidence that the growth of women's organizations and the women's movement as a whole were influenced in any important way by the Court. Thus, the conclusion the data suggest is that, if Court influence exists, it is of the subtlest nature. And while subtlety has its virtues, relying on it may not be the best use of scarce resources in important battles for significant social reform.

9

The Tide of History

In the preceding chapters of this part I have found little evidence that Court action was of help in ending discrimination against women. Since this cuts against the prevailing wisdom, in this chapter I will suggest a number of factors that together may plausibly account for the changes that have occurred. These include massive economic and technological changes that brought women out of the home, the formation of women's groups, and the growth of communication. I must caution the reader that I am not presenting a theory of social change and this discussion should not be read as offering one. Rather, it is designed for the skeptical reader whose reaction to the chapters of this part may be, "What else could have possibly caused changes other than Court action?" In the following pages I will highlight possible answers, thus putting Court action in its proper historical setting. For as with civil rights, the Court in women's rights was falling in line with the changes happening around it.

Economic Changes and Effects

The changes in the economic position of American women in the three or four decades preceding the 1970s have been phenomenal. From a group predominantly at home, American women entered the labor force in increasing numbers. Such a major disruption in life patterns quite likely challenged existing beliefs about appropriate roles as it opened a new life for tens of millions of American women. However, these changes did not come about suddenly. Rather, they "have been unfolding gradually, as a result of long-standing tendencies in the economy and society" (Bergmann 1986, 6).

In 1940, before the start of the Second World War, only about one-quarter of American women held jobs outside of the home. Among married women, only 15.2 percent worked outside of the home in 1940, representing a small change since 1910. Work outside of the home by women, particularly married women, was frowned upon. Such work by wives, Chafe reports, "often testified to family poverty," and in 1930 over 57 percent of women workers were foreign-born whites, or blacks (Chafe 1972, 55, 56, 57). However, this was soon to change.

World War II "radically transformed the economic outlook of women" (Chafe 1972, 135). As men left jobs to go to war, and weapons manufacturers needed workers, women stepped in. By the end of the war, 6.5 million women had joined the work force, an increase of 57 percent (Chafe 1972, 148). Twice as many wives went to work outside of the home as ever before (Deckard 1983, 297). While nearly one million women went to work for the federal government, other women took traditionally male jobs. The number of women operatives in heavy industry increased from 340,000 at the beginning of the war to over 2 million in four years (Chafe 1972, 140, 141). By the end of the war, women accounted for 40 percent of the workers in aircraft plants (McGlen and O'Connor 1983, 165). Other examples abound:

> Women maneuvered giant overhead traveling cranes and cleaned out blast furnaces. Elsewhere, women ran lathes, cut dies, read blueprints, and serviced airplanes. They maintained roadbeds, greased locomotives, and took the place of lumberjacks in toppling giant red-woods. As stevedores, blacksmiths, foundry helpers, and drill-press operators, they demonstrated that they could fill almost any job, no matter how difficult or arduous. (Chafe 1972, 137–38)

The war simply marked a "watershed in the history of women at work" (Chafe 1972, 136).

There were other effects of the war as well. The number of women union members rose from 800,000 in 1939 to over 3 million by 1945 (Deckard 1983, 299; Chafe 1972, 144). More than 7 million women changed their county of residence during the first three and a half years of the war (Chafe 1972, 139–40). The government, anxious to encourage women workers, took steps to fight discrimination. Sixty percent of the women hired by the War Department had children of school and pre-school age (Chafe 1972, 145). The federal government, for the first time, endorsed in principle the idea of equal pay for equal work in 1942 with the issuance of a joint statement supporting the principle by the War, Navy, and Labor departments. And the National War Labor Board applied it on a mandatory basis in war disputes coming before it (Freeman 1975, 175–76).[1] In a related action, the image of a happy, healthy, female worker, "Rosie the Riveter," was created as a role model for women. There was also an effort to point out that one of the dangers

---

1. The motivation behind these actions is not entirely clear. As far back as 1879, President Strasser of the International Cigarmakers Union stated: "We cannot drive the females out of the trade but we can restrict this daily quota of labor through factory laws" (Freeman 1971, 214). Chafe (1972, 124–25) traces such attitudes as far back as 1836. Equal pay requirements remove wage incentives for employers to keep women employed when men are available. Thus, by

of fascism was that it kept women at home, viewing them only as baby machines (Deckard 1983, 299). Polls reflected the new set of beliefs. In 1938 only 22 percent of Americans approved of married women working outside of the home (Gallup 1972, 1: 131). By 1942, however, a nationwide poll reported that 60 percent of Americans favored married women working in war industries (Erskine 1971, 284). The switch in opportunities, benefits, and pressures for working women challenged former views. As the Women's Bureau put it, the increase in female employment and the changes accompanying it represent "one of the most fundamental social and economic changes in our time" (quoted in Chafe 1972, 148–49).

After the war, many women, either voluntarily or involuntarily, left their jobs and returned home. Within two months of the end of the war, for example, almost 800,000 women lost their jobs in the aircraft industry alone (McGlen and O'Connor 1983, 166). Between 1945 and 1947 the number of women at work outside the home reportedly declined by 4 million (Deckard 1983, 299). Whereas between 36 and 38 percent of all women were working outside of the home in 1945, in 1947 the figure had dropped to 32 percent (Deckard 1983, 298; Chafe 1972, 148). Public opinion turned against female employment and, by the 1950s, the cult of the happy housewife and "momism" was firmly entrenched. But women did not disappear from the labor market or return to their pre-war levels of work-force participation. Indeed, by 1949, as compared to 1940, "the female labor force had increased by over 5.25 million—more than twice the increase which might have been expected without the war" (Chafe 1972, 181–82). And by 1950, the U.S. Department of Labor (USDL) reported that the percentage of women in the labor force out of all women had risen again, to 34 percent (USDL 1977, 5).

There are a number of possible explanations for the continued employment of women. In general, women's ability to earn money made remaining in the home costly. As Bergmann puts it, women's time, "in the eyes of family members, [became] too valuable to be spent entirely in the home" (Bergmann 1986, 17). Specifically, between 1945 and 1947, inflation soared. Meat prices alone rose 122 percent in the two-year period, and the rash of strikes that broke out after the war sent the cost of basics skyrocketing. If the war legitimized women working outside of the home by making it a question of national necessity, after the war "inflation and rising consumer demand served much the same purpose" (Chafe 1972, 189, 193; McLaughlin et al. 1988, 25). But perhaps more important, the war experience had broken the myths surround-

---

requiring equal pay, the federal government may have been trying to insure that women would be fired when men returned. Freeman (1975, 175) traces the origins of the Equal Pay Act to the fear that women workers in World War I would depress wages for returning veterans. And when the act was finally passed in 1963, male-dominated unions considered it innocuous since it "*increased job security for men* by discouraging the replacement of men with lower paid women" (Berger 1971, 326).

ing women's role. Women had shown men as well as themselves that they could work outside the home. And once the cultural barrier was broken, change ensued.

Between 1950 and 1970 there was steady but large growth in the percentage of women working outside the home. The changes, of course, continued after 1970, but that date provides the crucial break-point, since Court action commenced in the early 1970s.[2] By the end of the 1960s, a *majority* of women between eighteen and sixty-four were in the labor force (Deckard 1983, 317). In terms of numbers, between 1950 and 1970 over 13 million women joined the labor force, an increase of 71.4 percent. Among married women, increases in labor-force participation were "particularly pronounced" (USDL 1976a, 1). While only 15.2 percent of married women were employed outside of the home before World War II, by 1950 the figure was 24.6 percent. By 1970, however, the number of married women working outside the home increased nearly two and a half times, resulting in 43.9 percent of all married women being part of the labor force (USDL 1977, 22). Finally, there have been huge increases in the percentage of married, working women with children under eighteen. While in 1950 only 18.4 percent of such women worked outside the home, by 1970 about 40 percent did (USDL 1977, 22). The number of working women with children under eighteen years of age increased more than threefold between 1950 and 1976 (USDL 1976c, 3). Excluding children under six, while only 28 percent of mothers with children under eighteen worked outside the home in 1950, by 1972 *over half did*. And even with children under six, the increase was two and a half times, from 11.9 percent in 1950 to 30.3 percent in 1970 (USDL 1977, 22).[3] Thus, the challenge put in motion during the Second World War continued strongly, radically widening opportunities for women.

Decreasing Fertility

Along with increasing economic opportunities for women, fertility rates have been decreasing. In 1900, for example, white women, on average, had slightly fewer than four births over the course of their fertile years. By 1970, that average had been nearly halved, to about two births per white woman. Improved methods of contraception, a decreasing economic benefit derived

2. For easily accessible data on more recent years, see the yearly reports of *The American Woman*.

3. In 1985, half of all married women with a child under one year of age worked outside of the home. By 1980 there was virtually no difference in the labor-force participation rate of married women with preschool children compared to married women with no children, the ratio being .98 (McLaughlin et al. 1988, 96). And, by 1988, the U.S. Bureau of the Census (USBC) reported that 50.9 percent of women eighteen to forty-four who had a child in the preceding twelve months were working outside of the home (USBC 1989b, 17).

from large families, and increasing job opportunities for women all inter-
acted. Regardless of which way the causal arrows flow, a result of this smaller
family size was that child care, traditionally performed by women, became
increasingly less time-consuming. In turn, this freed women to participate
more actively in the labor force.

Education

Leaving the home is an important step in expanding opportunities. Another step is education. Here, much progress occurred in the 1960s as both
the number and percent of degrees awarded to women rose. In 1940, women
received 42 percent of all B.A.'s, 38 percent of all M.A.'s, and 13 percent of
all Ph.D.'s. By 1950, however, the post-war reaction had reduced the percentage of female B.A.-degree recipients 18 points, to 24 percent.[4] The percent of women earning masters degrees dropped 9 points, to 29 percent of all
such degrees, and only 10 percent of all Ph.D's went to women (Deckard
1983, 315).[5]

After the 1950s, however, progress resumed. Between 1960 and 1968 the
percentage of female high school graduates increased 11 points, to 78 per
100 females aged seventeen and over (U.S. Cong., Senate 1970b, 518). In
the first five years of the 1960s, the number of academic degrees earned by
women increased at more than twice the rate achieved by men (57 percent to
25 percent) (Freeman 1975, 29). By 1970 women had reached the percentages
of academic degrees received in 1940, with a slight increase in the percentage
of masters degrees (Deckard 1983, 315). This time, women's presence was
felt in higher education. In the 1971–72 academic year there were over
1,000 college-level women's studies courses. By the next year, at least 70 colleges and universities had formal programs in women's studies, including five
M.A. programs (Carden 1974, 198n.19). And, as of 1971, almost 100 universities had official committees on the status of women (Freeman 1975, 169).

By 1970, women were working and studying in record proportions. Summarizing these changes, McLaughlin et al. concluded that they have been
"driven by economic, technological, and cultural developments that have permitted women greater control over their lives" (McLaughlin et al. 1988, 5).
These changes, accelerating in the 1950s and 1960s, could have provided a

---

4. This drop also reflects the large post-war influx of men into college under the GI bill.
5. This massive step backwards can perhaps be understood by the example of Lynn White,
president of Mills College in California. In speeches and books, he urged that women's education
be oriented to their "sexual aptitudes." Instead of a course in post-Kantian philosophy, for example, White suggested women study the "theory and preparation of a Basque paella" (quoted
in Chafe 1972, 208). So widespread was the backlash against women having careers that two out
of five Barnard graduates urged greater preparation for the responsibilities of family life (Chafe
1972, 209).

base on which to form a modern women's movement. It is of little surprise, then, that the movement was started in the 1960s. I turn now to a brief discussion of its origins and early history.

The Modern Women's Movement: Formation and Early History

The 1960s witnessed the formation of the modern women's movement. A number of factors, including the economic and educational changes previously noted, the emergence of the civil rights and New Left movements, and growing political liberalization all contributed to building the movement. In the pages that follow I highlight some of these factors.

Issues Other Than Abortion

An important impetus for the formation of one wing of the women's movement was the inclusion of sex as a prohibited ground for discrimination in Title VII of the 1964 Civil Rights Act. The inclusion of the sex prohibition appears to have resulted in large part from the failure of a tactical move by opponents of the civil rights bill.[6] Introduced as "my amendment" by Representative Howard W. Smith (D., Va.), chairman of the House Rules Committee and an implacable opponent of civil rights and women's rights, the amendment caused many liberal supporters of civil rights to fear that its inclusion would result in the defeat of Title VII.[7] An attempt by them to move it to Title X, Miscellaneous, where it could safely be voted down, failed, and the amendment was approved. Fortunately, the fears of civil rights supporters proved erroneous and the bill, sex amendment and all, did become law.[8]

The enforcement mechanism for Title VII was the Equal Employment Opportunity Commission (EEOC) created by the act. To put it mildly, its concerns were not with sex discrimination. Herman Edelsberg, its first executive director, publicly stated that the sex amendment was a "fluke" that was "conceived out of wedlock." He stated that he and others at the EEOC be-

6. The discussion is based on my reading of the House debate and on the full-chapter treatment given the passage of the sex amendment by Bird (1968). DeCrow (1974) agrees that the amendment was designed to defeat the bill while Berger (1971, 336–37) denies it. While many of the women in the House did speak in support of the amendment, the overwhelming nature of the evidence in the text and in the next two notes supports the interpretation presented.

7. The amendment was opposed by liberals such as Lindsay (R., N.Y.), Thompson (D., N.J.), and Green (D., Ore.), author of the Equal Pay Act. It was supported by a host of Southern members distinguished by their historic opposition to civil rights and women's rights. Indeed, Anderson notes that a similar attempt to include women in a civil rights bill in order to defeat it was used by opponents of the 1957 Civil Rights Act. That proposal, to instruct the proposed U.S. Commission on Civil Rights to study discrimination against women, was defeated (Anderson 1964, 93).

8. It seems quite clear that Smith's intention was to defeat Title VII. His opposition to women's rights was well known and he had continually voted against bills guaranteeing equal pay

lieved that men were "entitled" to female secretaries (quoted in Griffiths 1966, 13689). In a similar vein, an EEOC member attending a White House conference on equal opportunity in August 1965, said it was unclear if the law would require Playboy clubs to hire male bunnies. The *New York Times* got into the act, labeling a Commission official the "Deputy Counsel on Bunnies." The *Times* editorialized: "Better if Congress had just abolished sex itself. . . . A maid can now become a man. Girl Friday is an intolerable offense. . . . The classic beginning of many wondrous careers in the Horatio Alger fashion—Boy Wanted—has reached its last chapter" ("De-Sexing" 1965, 20).[9] Summing up the first few years of EEOC action on sex discrimination, Representative Martha Griffiths (D., Mich.) speaking on the floor of the House, said that the EEOC had "started out by casting disrespect and ridicule on the law" but that its "unprofessional" and "wholly negative attitude" had "changed for the worse" (Griffiths 1966, 13689).

The importance of the passage of Title VII and the EEOC's subsequent inaction was that it first elated but then angered many politically active women. Some of them, as delegates to the Third National Conference of Commissions on the Status of Women, were in a position to act. The participants at this conference, representing the state commissions on the status of women, had all received copies of Representative Griffiths' speech criticizing the EEOC (Freeman 1973, 798). A resolution was prepared which, in effect, urged implementation of laws prohibiting sex discrimination. However, the resolution was ruled out of order and no vote was taken. In response, twenty-eight participants, and activists, including Betty Friedan, met together at lunch on June 30, 1966, the last day of the conference, and founded the National Organization for Women (NOW). Its official launching came at a press conference on October 29, 1966, at its first conference.

NOW was the first of what became a large number of women's rights groups. As Betty Friedan put it: "The absolute necessity of a civil rights movement for women had reached such a point of subterranean explosive urgency by 1966, that it only took a few of us to get together to ignite the spark—and it spread like a nuclear chain-reaction" (quoted in Hole and Levine 1971, 81). Both as a model and as a creator of friction, NOW pioneered the way. In 1968, for example, a group of "conservatives" who disagreed with NOW's newly adopted pro-choice abortion position left and formed the

---

for equal work. He was also vehemently opposed to the civil rights bill. In support of his amendment, Smith read a letter to the House from a woman complaining that there were 2,661,000 more women than men and asking Congress to do something about it. "I read that letter," Smith said on the floor of the House, "just to illustrate that women have some real grievances." After this action that, Bird reports, "brought down the House," Smith opposed transferring the amendment to Title X, Miscellaneous, because, as he put it, "women are entitled to more dignity than that." The debate can be found in *Cong. Rec.*, 8 Feb. 1964, 2577–84. See also Bird (1968, chap. 1).

9. See also Bird (1968, 15, 16, 17).

Women's Equity Action League (WEAL). Also in that year two NOW lawyers who had been trying to get NOW to set up a legal defense fund left and started their own, Human Rights For Women. Federally Employed Women (FEW) was founded in 1968 while 1970 witnessed the founding of the Professional Women's Caucus and the Interstate Association of Commissions on the Status of Women. In 1971, the Women's Rights Project of the American Civil Liberties Union (ACLU), the National Women's Political Caucus, the Women's Legal Defense Fund, the Women's Action Alliance, the NOW Legal Defense and Education Fund, and the Network for Economic Rights were started. This latter group, organized by the Women's Department of the United Auto Workers, has been given credit for winning reversal of the AFL-CIO's long-standing opposition to the Equal Rights Amendment (Freeman 1975, 165–66). By the end of 1971, a women's caucus existed in nearly every professional association (Deckard 1983, 403). Opening doors in 1972 were the Women's Lobby, Equal Rights Advocates, and the Women's Rights Project of the Center for Law and Social Policy. And these are just a few of the many women's groups that were formed.

At the same time as these groups were being formed, a different but vitally important set of organizations was also being created. Referred to as the "younger branch," or the "radicals," or "women's liberation" groups (in contrast to women's rights groups like NOW), their members were "drawn primarily from the civil rights movement, counterculture, and student protest movements" (McGlen and O'Connor 1983, 25).[10] The experience of women in the civil rights and New Left movements provided them with political training and organizing skills. It also showed them that sex discrimination was a political issue and that eliminating it was a full-time job.

The civil rights movement had a profound effect on many Americans, including, of course, women. "For a while," Freeman reports, "'woman as nigger' was one of the most popular short ways of describing how women's position in society was perceived" (Freeman 1975, 28). This was forcefully brought home to female civil rights workers at a 1964 Student Nonviolent Coordinating Committee (SNCC) retreat when two SNCC workers, Mary King and Casey Hayden, anonymously circulated a paper raising the issue of the position of women in the movement (King 1987, 445). The paper was met with "crushing criticism" and "ridicule" (King 1987, 450).[11]

On the left, the same sorts of actions and reactions were taking place. In the fall of 1965, Hayden and King circulated another paper on issues of sex

10. In general, see Echols (1989).
11. According to most accounts, Stokely Carmichael cut off all debate on sex discrimination at the retreat by stating "the only position for women in SNCC is prone." King (1987, 452) refutes this. She and Hayden felt that Carmichael was one of the most responsive men to their paper. Carmichael's comment was made well after the paper was discussed, as part of a comedy routine in front of King and a few others, and was clearly intended to break the tension and poke fun at his own attitudes. The paper is reprinted in King (1987, 567–69).

discrimination (King 1987, 456–58; 571–74). The issues they raised, however, were "laughed off the floor" at the 1965 convention of Students for a Democratic Society (SDS) (Freeman 1975, 57–58).[12] At the 1966 SDS convention, Carden records, women demanding support for a women's rights plank were "pelted with tomatoes and thrown out of the convention" (Carden 1974, 57). Interest in women's rights by women and hostility by men wasn't limited to just the civil rights movement and SDS. Freeman cites as a "typical example" of sexism an August 1967 National Conference on New Politics where debate on a women's rights resolution was refused with the comment, "Cool down, little girl, we have more important things to talk about than women's problems."[13] And, during the 1968 Columbia University student rebellion, a male student leader in occupied Fayerweather Hall demanded that all the cooking be done by the women (DeMott 1970, 116).[14]

The experience of women in the civil rights and New Left movements was radicalizing both in the political skills and new awareness developed and in the level of male hostility encountered. How long the tension might have endured without causing a split is unclear. However, by 1967 there developed a "lack of available opportunities for political work" for women. As Freeman put it: "The year 1967 was the one in which the blacks kicked the whites out of the civil rights movement, student power had been discredited by SDS, and the organized New Left was on the wane. . . . Only draft resistance activities were on the increase, and this movement more than any other exemplified the social inequities of the sexes: Men could resist the draft; women could only counsel resistance" (Freeman 1973, 800). The response was the creation of a loosely organized, highly motivated, and intensely serious set of women's groups.

The first groups sprung up independently in 1967 and 1968 in Chicago, Toronto, Detroit, Seattle, and Gainesville. They were started by women "who had become exasperated by the New Left males' refusal to treat seriously their complaints about being treated as inferiors" (Carden 1974, 32). One of their organizing techniques was "consciousness-raising," a term coined by Kathie Sarachild, a former civil rights worker in Mississippi (Echols 1989, 83). The inspiration for "consciousness-raising" came from the civil rights movement: "[w]e were applying to women and to ourselves as women's liberation organizers the practice a number of us had learned in the civil rights movement in the South in the early 1960s" (Sarachild quoted in Echols 1989, 84).

12. The paper was entitled "A Kind of Memo" and was later published under the title "Sex and Caste" (1966). It can also be found in King (1987, 571–74). Surprisingly, given the reaction it received, it raises the issue of sexism in a mild manner.

13. Freeman (1975, 59, 60); Hole and Levine (1971, 113–14); Echols (1989, 49). The "little girl" was Shulamith Firestone, who went on to write an important book in the feminist movement.

14. For other examples of sexist responses to feminist demands on the left, see Hole and Levine (1971, 133–34).

Consciousness-raising groups spread quickly and by 1969 such groups had been established in "at least forty American cities" (Carden 1974, 64). In the "majority" of cities, "former [1964 freedom summer] volunteers were in the forefront of the initial organizing efforts" (McAdam 1988, 182).[15] This movement also spawned the creation of many centers focused on women. By 1973, the *New Woman's Survival Catalog* counted 23 rape squads, 5 film co-ops, 116 women's centers, 35 health clinics or projects, 6 legal services clinics, 6 feminist theater groups, 12 liberation schools, 18 employment services, 12 bookstores, and 3 craft stores (Freeman 1975, 119n.25). In just the three years between 1970 and 1973 the reported number of women's liberation groups grew from several hundred to several thousand (Freeman 1975, 147). The members of these groups tended to be young, politically on the left, and highly critical of organizational structure. By the end of 1969, this branch of the movement was firmly established "with its own ideology, a growing membership, and an informal but defined organizational structure" (Carden 1974, 70).

The women who joined both types of women's groups in the 1960s learned about them almost exclusively from their friends and acquaintances. After 1969, however, when media coverage improved, about one-half of one sample said they were influenced by the media as well, with about one-fourth crediting the media alone with their decision to join a group. Interestingly, about half of one sample of group members said they had read Betty Friedan's *The Feminine Mystique* when it was first published in 1963. And half of these women said they were seriously influenced by Friedan's ideas (Carden 1974, 32, 33, 154, 155).[16]

As women's groups grew, they began to act. Some worked privately to help their members understand the discrimination they faced and to change opinions of friends and colleagues. Some pressed for political changes and for the implementation of existing laws. As was discussed in chapter 7, the latter was a serious problem. Not until 1970 did the Justice Department file its first sex discrimination suit. The reason for this inaction, a Justice Department lawyer told the President's Task Force on the Status of Women, was that the Justice Department responds to "social turmoil" and "the fact that women have not gone into the streets is indicative that they do not take employment

15. McAdam (1988, 185) suggests that the emphasis on consciousness-raising may have come from the freedom schools in Mississippi in which many of the volunteers taught, and from the meeting-style of SNCC.

16. Carden interviewed members of women's groups of both branches in the summers of 1969 and 1970, and from November 1970 to July 1971. The responses to questions about *The Feminine Mystique*, which sold more than 1 million copies (Chafe 1972, 232), support the claims of writers such as Epstein and Freeman that Friedan's book provided an ideological underpinning for the women's movement and was of much significance. See Epstein (1975, 169); Freeman (1975, 53). However, King (1987, 78) found Friedan's concerns "irrelevant" and "marginal." For King, Hayden, and other female SNCC workers, Simone de Beauvoir and Doris Lessing were of much greater importance (King 1987, 76–77).

discrimination too seriously" (quoted in Freeman 1975, 79). But this was soon to change, for other women marched and demonstrated for equal rights.

A few examples of public demonstrations give a good idea of what happened. In September 1968, in one of the first public demonstrations, the Miss America Pageant was picketed. Later that fall, the Women's International Conspiracy From Hell (WITCH) put a "hex" on Wall Street through guerilla theater presentations. Other WITCH groups demonstrated at the phone company (Women Incensed at Telephone Company Harassment), and at an insurance company (Women Indentured to Traveler's Corporate Hell). Feminists in San Francisco and New York disrupted bridal fairs and others demonstrated at Playboy Clubs (Carden 1974, 63). In September of 1969 the Miss America Pageant in Atlantic City was again picketed. In 1970 there was a variety of actions. NOW initiated and largely organized a women's strike on August 26 to commemorate the fiftieth anniversary of the Nineteenth Amendment (Freeman 1975, 84).[17] On March 18, one hundred women held a sit-in at the office of the publisher of the *Ladies Home Journal*, protesting its lack of coverage of the movement (Freeman 1975, 231; Hole and Levine 1971, 255–58). The protesters won, as the *Journal* agreed to include an insert on the movement in the August 1970 edition. "Invasions" also occurred at a CBS stockholders' meeting in April and at the offices of the *San Francisco Chronicle* in June. And earlier that spring, "roughly two dozen NOW members" disrupted Senate hearings on the constitutional amendment giving eighteen-year-olds the vote, to demand hearings on the Equal Rights Amendment (Freeman 1975, 213).[18] By 1970, then, public action in support of women's rights was firmly established.

The story of congressional passage of the Equal Rights Amendment (ERA) illustrates an area where women's activity appears to have paid off. The ERA was first introduced into Congress by Representative Daniel Anthony (R., Kan.), a nephew of Susan B. Anthony, in 1923. It was introduced repeatedly until passage in 1972. It was endorsed by a House subcommittee in 1936 and reported to the floor by the Senate Judiciary Committee in 1938. In 1940 the Republican party put ERA support in its platform. The Senate Judiciary Committee reported favorable resolutions in the Eightieth to Eighty-fourth and Eighty-sixth to Eighty-eighth Congresses. In 1950 and 1953, the Senate passed the ERA with a rider exempting "protective" labor legislation. Finally, in 1972 it was passed by both houses by large majorities.

The number and power of supporters of the ERA grew considerably. In 1963, for example, the President's Commission on the Status of Women, the

17. Both Freeman (1975, 85) and Carden (1974, 33) report that the strike greatly swelled NOW's membership.

18. The committee agreed and hearings were held in May. According to Hole and Levine (1971, 56), Senator Bayh (D., Ind.), chair of the relevant committee, admitted that the hearings were a direct result of the disruption.

Women's Bureau, the League of Women Voters, the United Auto Workers, and the AFL-CIO all opposed it. Supporters included the National Women's Party and the National Federation of Business and Professional Women's Clubs. As the 1960s progressed, however, support grew. President Johnson said he personally favored it in late 1967 and candidate Nixon supported it in 1968. The next year, President Nixon's Task Force on Women's Rights and Responsibilities endorsed the ERA, arguing in part that it would deter "accelerating militancy" by women (quoted in Freeman 1975, 208). The Nixon-appointed Citizen's Advisory Council on the Status of Women also endorsed it in February 1970. By 1970, fifty-two governmental, labor, lay, and professional groups supported the ERA,[19] including two that reversed past opposition, the United Auto Workers and the Women's Bureau. By the time of passage in 1972, with one major exception (the AFL-CIO), the only nationally known opponents were right-wing groups such as the John Birch Society, the Ku Klux Klan, the White Citizens Councils, the States' Rights Party, Young Americans For Freedom, and the organization headed by Phyllis Schlafly. While the AFL-CIO opposed it until 1974, the UAW, the Teamsters, the Communication Workers, and many AFL-CIO affiliates supported it.

When the ERA was finally passed, then, it had tremendous support. In Congress it had been introduced by 81 senators and 273 House members. Its final House passage, however, required the use of a discharge petition to get it past Chairman Cellar (D., N.Y.) of the House Judiciary Committee. This success is particularly noteworthy because prior to 1972 only twenty-four bills had successfully been discharged from any House committee since 1910 (Deckard 1983, 443). And the ERA had public support, with 74 percent of Americans supporting it in 1974 (McGlen and O'Connor 1983, 380).

The point of this discussion is that by 1972, if not 1970, there was a powerful women's movement in America. As I have noted, it was a diverse movement of many separate groups—"small, large, structured, unstructured, radical, and conservative" (Carden 1977, 6). It was active and visible and had won the support of many established institutions and groups on issues such as the ERA. And through the communications network discussed below, it reached virtually all Americans.

Abortion

At the same time that the women's movement was coming into being, the battle to reform abortion laws was being fought. Support for reform grew steadily throughout the 1960s, enabling much pressure to be brought to bear. In the material that follows I will focus on the background to the movement as a whole.

Abortion is an ancient practice. In recent times, however, public discus-

---

19. For a list of supporters, see U.S. Cong., Senate (1970a, 393–94).

sion did not surface until the 1950s, and when it did its initial progress was slow. In 1954, Planned Parenthood and the New York Academy of Medicine sponsored a conference that dealt with abortion. A collection of essays on abortion was published in 1954 and Kinsey published his abortion data in 1958. Discussion picked up in the 1960s. In 1962 the American Law Institute (ALI) published its Model Penal Code on abortion, permitting abortion if continuing the pregnancy would adversely affect the physical or mental health of the woman, or if there was risk of birth defects, or if the pregnancy resulted from rape or incest. An important event in 1962 was the publicity over Thalidomide, a drug prescribed by doctors to cure infertility. It turned out that the risk of birth defects among women taking the drug was very high. Sherri Finkbine, a Phoenix host of a popular children's TV show who had taken Thalidomide, attempted to obtain an abortion in her home state of Arizona. Turned down, and with much publicity, she flew to Sweden where the abortion was performed. A Gallup poll found that by a 52 to 32 percent margin, the American public felt that she did the right thing (Gallup 1972, 3: 1784).

Another health related factor that brought abortion into the public domain was a German measles epidemic in the years 1962–65. While normally not dangerous, German measles can cause birth defects if contracted during pregnancy. About 82,000 pregnant women contracted German measles and many unsuccessfully sought abortions (Rubin 1982, 21). By November 1965, the American Medical Association Board of Trustees approved a report urging adoption of the ALI law (Lader 1966, 145).

In 1966 abortion-reform activity was picking up.[20] Lawrence Lader, an eventual founder of the National Association for the Repeal of Abortion Laws (NARAL), and author of a book urging abortion law reform, went on a coast-to-coast tour, making numerous radio and TV appearances. In San Francisco, Patricia Maginnis held a conference which adopted an abortion-on-demand position. She then traveled cross-country, giving lectures on abortion in Ohio, Wisconsin, and Washington, D.C. By 1966 there were several pro-choice groups including the Society for Humane Abortion in California, organized by Maginnis, and the Association for the Study of Abortion in New York, a prestigious board of doctors and lawyers. In 1966 the Illinois Committee For Medical Control of Abortion was formed. Advocating repeal of all abortion laws, it built a reported membership of 10,000. Groups were formed in many states including Washington and Wisconsin.

Abortion referral services were also started. Previously, pro-choice activists like Lader, Maginnis, and Bill Baird would furtively make referrals to competent doctors in the U.S. and Mexico, who would perform abortions. By the late 1960s, abortion referral groups publicly operated. In New York City, in 1967, 22 clergy announced the formation of their group, gaining

20. The following discussion, except where noted, is based on Lader (1973).

front-page coverage in the *New York Times* (Fiske 1967). The Chicago referral service took out a full-page add in the *Sun-Times* announcing its services. In Los Angeles, the referral service was serving over 1,000 women per month. Thus, by the late 1960s pro-abortion organizations, including abortion-referral services, were operating in many major U.S. cities. And by 1971, the clergy referral service operated publicly in eighteen states with a staff of about 700 clergy and lay people (Hole and Levine 1971, 299).

State authorities sometimes intervened to stop abortions. When they did, their actions met with public protest. In 1966, for example, when nine San Francisco doctors were charged with unprofessional conduct for performing abortions on pregnant women with rubella, 200 of the nation's leading physicians, including 127 deans of medical schools, filed a brief in their support. Both major San Francisco papers editorialized in support of the doctors. When in 1967 an eminent Los Angeles physician, Leon Belous, was arrested for making an abortion referral, 178 medical school deans and professors filed a brief in his support. And by 1967, the *New York Times* editorially supported abortion law reform ("Start on Abortion Reform" 1967).

In order to tap this emerging support, NARAL was founded in 1968 by Lader and fellow activists. Protesting in the streets, presenting lectures, and organizing "days of anger" began to have an effect. Women who had undergone illegal abortions spoke and wrote openly about them.[21] As noted in chapter 6, seventy-five leading national groups endorsed the repeal of all abortion laws between 1967 and the end of 1972, including 28 religious and 21 medical groups.[22]

Public Opinion

Much of the reason for the growth in major organization support for abortion repeal may have come from changes in American public opinion. By the eve of the Court's decisions in 1973, public opinion had dramatically shifted from opposition to abortion in most cases to substantial, if not majority, support.

Looking at the 1960s as a whole, Blake found a decline in disapproval of economic justifications for abortion (Blake 1973, 449–50). She noted that opinions on discretionary abortion were "changing rapidly over time" and polls were recording "rapidly growing support" (Blake 1971, 543, 544). Relying on Gallup data, Blake found that support for elective abortion increased approximately two and one-half times from 1968 to 1972 (Blake 1977b, 49). Relying on data from the National Opinion Research Center (NORC), and averaging responses to six abortion questions, Granberg and Granberg found

21. For example, see the collection of testimony in Schulder and Kennedy (1971).
22. For a list of statements from these groups on their positions, see U.S. Cong., Senate (1976, 4: 53–91).

an increase of over 50 percent between 1965 and 1972 in supportive responses, with an average of 41 percent approving of abortion in 1965 and 63 percent approving in 1972. By 1972, at least 40 percent or more of NORC respondents approved of abortion in each of six circumstances, including abortion for "discretionary" reasons such as a single woman not wishing to marry the man and married women not wishing to have more children (Granberg and Granberg 1980, 252). Examining Gallup polls in the years 1962–69, and National Fertility Study polls in 1965 and 1970, Jones and Westoff found a "substantial shift toward more permissive attitudes" in the late 1960s (Jones and Westoff 1972, 576). On the state level, in California, 73 percent of the population supported the liberalization of abortion laws in 1967, the year California acted to liberalize its law. In New York in 1968, a poll done by the Quayle organization, with a sample size of 1,200, found that 75 percent of New Yorkers supported liberalized abortion laws (Schanberg 1968, 23). And polls done by members of the New York State legislature showed large support for reform (Schanberg 1969, 22).

This generally supportive trend quickened its pace in the late 1960s and early 1970s. Between 1969 and 1970, Blake noted a "sharp decline in disapproval" of purely elective abortion (Blake 1973, 450). Gallup surveys between 1969 and 1970 record a 9-point increase in the percentage of respondents approving of elective abortion. By 1972, an additional 4 percent increase was recorded (Blake 1977b, 49). Another set of Gallup polls recorded a 15-point drop in the percent of respondents disapproving of abortions for financial reasons in only the eight months between October 1969 and June 1970. The same eight months showed a 10-point drop in the percentage disapproving of abortions for discretionary reasons (Blake 1977a, 58). A 1970 poll by the American Council of Education of 180,000 college freshmen found that 83 percent favored the legalization of abortion (Currivan 1970, 42). In 1971, a national poll taken for the Commission on Population Growth and the American Future found 50 percent of its respondents agreeing with the statement that the abortion "decision should be left up to persons involved and their doctor" (Rosenthal 1971, 1). Finally, polls done for Planned Parenthood in January and June of 1972 showed a 7-point increase in the percentage of respondents in favor of allowing a woman and her physician the sole choice in abortion (Pomeroy and Landman 1972, 45). Thus, in the words of one study, "[b]y the time the Supreme Court made its ruling, there was strong public support behind the legalization of abortion" (Ebaugh and Haney 1980, 493).

Much of the reason for the growth in both public and major organization support for repeal of restrictive abortion laws may have come from changes in elite, professional opinion. Polls throughout the late 1960s reported that important sub-groups of the American population were increasingly supportive of abortion-law reform and repeal. As early as 1964, the *San Francisco*

Chronicle found that 70 percent of doctors at the 1964 American Medical Association annual conference wanted abortion laws liberalized. In 1967, magazine coupons mailed by 40,000 doctors showed that 87 percent favored more liberal laws (Schmeck 1967, 82). By 1969, a poll in *Modern Medicine* reported that 51 percent of U.S. physicians supported abortion on request. While none of these polls is particularly scientific, they do at least suggest a growing level of support for abortion reform among relevant professional elites. In addition, a poll of nearly 13,000 respondents in nursing, medical, and social work schools in the autumn and winter of 1971 showed strong support for repeal of restrictive abortion laws. The poll found split opinions among nursing students and faculty, but found that 69 percent of medical students, 71 percent of medical faculty, 76 percent of social work students, and 75 percent of social work faculty supported "freely accessible abortion" (Rosen et al. 1974, 165). It is evident that public opinion changed very quickly, to the surprise of many experts in the public health field (Rosenthal 1971, 22).

Legislative Reform

Legislative action to reform abortion laws dates from the 1960s. Laws banning abortion were state laws, so most of the early abortion-law reform activity was directed at state governments. In the early and mid-part of the decade action was limited to a few states. Committee hearings were first held in New York in 1966 and reform bills were introduced in the California legislature as early as 1961 (Lader 1973, 57, 67). In New Hampshire, the state legislature passed a reform bill in 1961 only to have it vetoed by Governor Powell (Tatalovich and Daynes 1981, 43–44; Lader 1966, 111–16). In 1967 there was an outbreak of legislative activity to liberalize abortion laws. Reform bills were introduced in twenty-eight states including California, Colorado, Delaware, Florida, Georgia, Maryland, Oklahoma, New Jersey, New York, North Carolina, and Pennsylvania (Rubin 1982, 22). The first successful liberalization drive was in Colorado in the late winter and early spring of 1967. The reform bill, modeled on the ALI's Model Penal Code, permitted abortion if there was "substantial risk" that continuing the pregnancy would "gravely impair the physical or mental health of the mother." It also permitted abortion in cases of rape or incest or where there was a substantial risk that the child would be born with a "grave physical or mental defect." [23]

At about the same time a similar bill was being maneuvered through the North Carolina legislature. In a state with a Catholic population of only 1 percent, there was little public opposition and the bill was passed on May 8 (Lader 1973, 65–66).

___

23. The bill was introduced by a then unknown first-term state representative, Richard Lamm, and became law on April 25, 1967. Lamm later became governor of Colorado. For a brief discussion of the successful effort, see Lader (1973, 62–65).

Opposition was intense in California, where State Senator Beilenson successfully steered a reform bill through the legislature. Despite eleventh-hour tactics by Governor Reagan suggesting he might not sign the bill, in mid-June of 1967 California joined the ranks of abortion reform (Lader 1973, 66–70). These three victories further propelled the reform movement. In 1968, abortion reform was pending in some thirty states (Monroe 1968), and in the 1968–69 period the seven states of Arkansas, Delaware, Georgia, Kansas, Maryland, New Mexico, and Oregon enacted reform laws based on or similar to the ALI model (Lader 1973, 84). To many abortion reformers, however, the ALI model, although an improvement over existing laws, was still unduly restrictive. While the mental health standard did liberalize considerably the grounds for abortion, its interpretation was sometimes tricky. Not surprisingly, then, an increasing number of activists began to push for total repeal of abortion laws.

In 1970 this push had major success. The first state to act was Hawaii, where the coalition pressing for repeal included such new allies as the Chamber of Commerce, the AFL-CIO, and the International Longshore and Warehouse Workers Union. The bill was passed by the legislature in late February 1970 and became law on March 13. The law permitted free choice in abortion of a "nonviable" fetus, required that abortions be done in a hospital, and had a ninety-day residency requirement (Lader 1973, 115–17; Steinhoff and Diamond 1977).

In the West, Alaska also acted. Supported by the Alaska Medical Association and the Alaska Council of Churches, among others, a bill based on the Hawaii law was passed in early April. Despite the veto of Alaska Governor Keith Miller, the legislature mustered the two-thirds vote necessary to overturn the veto and Alaska became the third repeal state (Lader 1973, 117–20). The second state to repeal the prohibition on abortion was New York. With an estimated Catholic population of 40 percent, a vocal and organized opposition, and failed attempts at reform in the past, repeal did not seem likely. Yet with strong coalition support, a bill removing all restrictions on abortions in the first twenty-four weeks of pregnancy was enacted (Lader 1973, 122–48).

The final state to repeal its abortion laws in 1970 was Washington, which enacted legislation allowing abortion in the first seventeen weeks of pregnancy in early February 1970. The bill, however, contained a referendum provision, requiring approval of the state's voters. In November, repeal won, 56 percent to 44 percent (Fujita and Wagner 1973).

There was also national and international activity. In 1968 the United Kingdom reformed its abortion law, allowing abortion to preserve total family health. Also in 1968, President Johnson's Advisory Council on the Status of Women recommended the repeal of all abortion laws. Two years later, Senator Packwood introduced a bill to liberalize the District of Columbia's abortion law. In addition, there was also a growing awareness of the danger of population explosion (Rosenthal 1971, 1). The U.S. Postal Service even issued a family-planning postage stamp in 1972! (Sarvis and Rodman 1973, 145). The point of this discussion is to stress the amount of abortion activity taking place prior to the 1973 Court decisions. Activity was wide-spread, vocal, and effective.

Communication

A final area to be stressed is the expansion of the ability of women's rights activists to communicate with each other and the American public in the years prior to Court action. Individual activists and local groups can feel isolated if unaware that others are active too. Knowing that others feel the same way can be an important morale booster. Spreading information also allows more people to be reached. Thus, the ability of feminists to effectively communicate was important.

In the 1960s both the national and local press either ignored women's rights activists or treated them with a "mixture of humor, ridicule, and disbelief" (Freeman 1975, 111). As coverage began to pick up in the late 1960s, the "press and other media had a field day" making fun of the movement (Carden 1974, 1). To the predominantly male reporters and editors, the women's activities were baffling. "Older male editors," North reports, "find it hard to be charming about women's anger" (North 1970, 106). Perhaps the best example was the endlessly reported, and patently untrue, stories that feminists had burned bras.[24] Originating as the misreporting of a symbolic action at the 1968 Miss America Pageant where demonstrators threw women's underwear into a barrel to symbolize their shedding of sexist rolls, the myth of bra-burning was "repeated constantly by the media." Despite the fact that the media has never "documented a specific case in which a women's liberation group was involved in a bra destruction" (Martin 1971, 11; Freeman 1975, 112), Martin found that "every time women's liberation is mentioned, bras are mentioned too, and vice versa." Its appeal to male editors, Martin argued, was that it confirmed their stereotyped views of women as "silly, trivial and sexy" (Martin 1971, 11). Unfortunately, the myth of bra-burning was just "one example of trivial news coverage linked to women's liberation."[25]

Starting in 1969, the coverage of the women's rights movement began to change. In August 1969, the executive director of NOW " 'went crazy' trying

24. The following discussion is based on Martin (1971). See, also, Hole and Levine (1971, 229–31).

25. A mid-nineteenth-century attempt by some feminists to escape restrictive women's clothing was also ridiculed by the press (who referred to the women and their clothes as the "bloomers") and abandoned (Hole and Levine 1971, 9). According to Echols (1989, 94), however, the Atlantic City protesters had planned to burn what they considered sexist clothing, including bras.

to answer inquiries from periodicals, newspapers, radio stations, and TV stations" (Carden 1974, 32). The months of January through March of 1970 were a "grand press blitz" on the women's movement (Freeman 1975, 148). As tables 8.1 and 8.2 (particularly 8.2B) show, press coverage took off in 1970. It also changed in tone. The reporting of the August 26, 1970, strike, for example, was the "first time the press gave a feminist demonstration purely straight coverage" (Freeman 1975, 84). And while many of the problems of press coverage still remained, at least the women's movement was being reported with some attempt at fairness.

Among the most important effects of this increased coverage was that of spreading the message to a larger audience. Previously, as I have discussed, there had been a large growth in feminist newsletters, journals, pamphlets, and so on. But these tended to travel in relatively small circles of committed activists and their friends. Coverage in the "straight" press brought some inkling of the women's movement to nearly all Americans. A CBS News poll conducted after the August 26, 1970, strike found that "four out of every five people over eighteen had read or heard about women's liberation" (Hole and Levine 1971, 269). "The women's liberation movement 'took off' in 1970" (Freeman 1975, 148), and press coverage played a big part.

Conclusion

American women in the 1970s faced a much brighter set of prospects than their mothers and grandmothers had faced. From at least the Second World War on, forces were working to change the opportunities they had and the opinions Americans, both male and female, expressed about women's roles. Starting in 1966, a women's movement came into being. By 1970, seemingly all of a sudden, it was recognized. For reasons that may be impossible to understand or state precisely, press coverage, opinions on abortion, and legislative action all changed rapidly. Yet two points are clear. First, the economic changes brought about by the Second World War were gradually providing momentum that changed women's lives. Second, and crucial for assessing the impact of the Court, all these activities occurred before any important Court decisions and, in some areas, in spite of them. I cannot conclude, of course, that this means that Court action was entirely without effect for change that occurred later. But it does remind us that Court opinions were delivered into a political, economic, and social system in which powerful forces were pushing for change. Court decisions joined a current of social change and a tide of history; they did not create it. Viewed in this context, then, the lack of judicial and extra-judicial effects of Court decisions on women's rights may not appear so startling.

PART 3

The Environment, Reapportionment, and Criminal Law

Introduction

Civil rights, abortion, and women's rights are perhaps the most visible areas in which courts have been asked to produce significant social reform. They are not, however, the only ones. In the next two chapters, I briefly examine three additional areas (the environment, reapportionment, criminal law) where courts are usually credited with having played a crucial role in producing reform. The aim is to determine if a plausible case can be made for one of the views or for the constraints and conditions in explaining the role of the courts in producing change. Because the constraints and conditions have done so well in both civil rights and abortion and women's rights, they are the focus of the chapters. The argument for their analytic power will be strengthened if a plausible case can be made that they explain courts' contributions in these three areas as well.

In examining the contribution of Court decisions (or of any institution) to producing significant social reform, there must be a clear standard for what counts as change. Usually, the standard is obvious. The Court sets out goals to be achieved and the evidence is examined to determine if those goals were achieved. Was race-based school segregation ended? Do women have easy and safe access to legal abortion? In other cases, where the Court sets out a procedure designed to achieve a goal, the standard is more complicated. The first question is whether the procedure was implemented. If it is not, then clearly the Court has not been effective. If the procedure was implemented, however, the analysis is not over. In cases where there are procedural changes, the next question is whether the substantive changes intended by the Court occurred. Changing procedure for its own sake without producing the intended substantive change cannot count as significant social reform. The procedure can fail because of the way it was implemented or because it was incapable of producing the desired change. In either case, one can not credit the Court with producing reform. In criminal law, for example, Court-ordered changes in criminal procedure can fail to produce reform because the procedure is not implemented, or because it is implemented in such a way as to negate its effect, or because it is misguided. Similarly, the implementation of Court decisions mandating lengthy evaluations of projects to determine their environmental impact will produce reform, in this case a cleaner and healthier environment, only if such outcomes follow. Thus, careful examination of the Court's ability to produce significant social reform requires standards flexible enough to change with the Court's aims.

Chapter 10 examines both the environment and reapportionment while chapter 11 deals with criminal law. In the space of a single chapter, neither of these analyses can approach the detail or rigor of the rest of the book. Such a project would entail a book of its own. Thus, much of the argument is an overview, and conclusions can only be tentative.

10

Cleaning House? The Courts, The Environment, and Reapportionment

The Environment

The decades of the 1960s and 1970s witnessed attempts to change much of American society. Among these attempts was a movement to protect the environment. Part of that movement, viewing courts as the crucial institution capable of producing change, focused on litigation. Making explicit analogies from the civil rights movement's use of the courts, early environmental litigators explicitly aimed to constitutionalize a right to a healthy environment. In later years, after a great deal of congressional legislation, environmental litigators went to court aiming to broadly interpret and strictly apply these legislative attempts to protect the environment. In this overview, I argue that while the attempt to constitutionalize a right to a healthy environment could not overcome the constraints of the judicial system, once the other branches acted, litigation was able to contribute to environmental protection when one of the four conditions was present. That is, when other actors added incentives or costs, courts were effective. Similarly, when market forces supported court decisions, litigation helped. Finally, litigation made a difference when those officials necessary for implementation were willing to act and use courts as cover.

The Attempt to Constitutionalize a Right to a Healthy Environment

Speaking at an Earth Day gathering in April 1970, attorney Victor Yannacone told his audience that "only by asserting the fundamental constitutional right of all the people to the cleanest environment modern technology can provide, and asserting this right on behalf of all the people in courts of equity throughout the nation, can we defend the environment" (Yannacone 1970b, 192). Roderick Cameron, the executive director of the Environmental Defense Fund (EDF), also speaking at an Earth Day event, concurred: "the judiciary is the one social institution already structured to provide the wise responses that may enable us to avert ecological disaster" (Cameron 1970, 175). Legislation and political action to protect the environment, even if possible, was seen as too slow in coming by these environmentally conscious attorneys. As Yannacone put it, "we must knock on the door of courthouses throughout this nation and seek equitable protection for our environment. We must not wait for Congress or state legislatures or local government to pass laws" (Yannacone 1970b, 192). Indeed Roberts was prepared to elevate environmental protection to the same constitutional level as the First Amendment, "anticipating a moment when the environment deteriorates to such a point that the Court is compelled to confirm that, along with free speech and religion, there exists a right to an environment fit for human habitation" (Roberts 1970a, 682).

Why were these and other environmental activists so ready to adopt a litigation strategy for change? One reason is that they saw an analogy with civil rights, particularly *Brown*. Esposito (1970, 51), for example, believed that the creation by the Supreme Court of a constitutional right to a clean environment would "result in a decision which would stand alongside *Brown v. Board* in the history of constitutional law." Environmental litigator David Sive suggested that by arguing for a constitutional right to a clean environment lawyers could play "as great a role in this dominant struggle [environmental] of the '70's as they did in the civil rights struggles of the '60's" (Sive 1970b, 3; 1970c, 613). And Stone (1974, 53), in a widely read piece, suggested that winning a constitutional right to a clean environment could serve the same purpose as *Brown*, which "awakened us to moral needs which, when made visible, could not be denied."

A second reason why environmentalists looked to the courts is that they adopted the Dynamic Court view, seeing courts as a more responsive, less biased forum than either the legislative or executive branches. Courts, they argued, in contrast to other institutions, were independent, "largely free of the economic and political pressures of vested interests" (Cameron 1970, 175). Being independent, courts could respond to the demands of environmentalists. Courts, Esposito argued, "provide an arena in which industry lobbyists and indifferent bureaucrats are least able to exercise their powers of dead-center inertia" (Esposito 1970, 33). Echoing this Dynamic Court view in 1988, Rick Sutherland, co-founder of the Los Angeles-based Center for Law and the Public Interest, and executive director of the Sierra Club Legal Defense Fund, argued that environmental litigation "means power for people who don't have economic power. It's one way to fight the political fight" (quoted in Turner 1988, 31). Environmentalists also argued that litigation, compared to other forms of political behavior, is relatively simple: "All it takes to start a lawsuit is a typewriter and a lawyer" (Yannacone 1970a, 90). And even if the environmentalists could gain access to legislatures, the problem remained, Roberts wrote in 1969, that the "legislature has ceased to be an effective originator of ideas" (Roberts 1970b, 157).[1] In other words, there was nowhere else for environmentalists to go. Thus, environmentalists believed courts would be most receptive to their claims.

Environmentalists also believed they had growing precedent and constitutional provisions on their side. In two key cases, *Scenic Hudson Preservation Conference* v. *FPC* (1965), and *Sierra Club* v. *Morton* (1972), courts broadened the notion of legally recognizable harm, giving heightened attention to harm to the environment. While it is true that the Constitution does not mention a right to a clean environment, this did not dampen the enthusiasm. Environmentalists pointed to *Griswold* v. *Connecticut*, a 1965 case where the Supreme Court had found a right to privacy in the "penumbras" of the Bill of Rights. Citing *Griswold*, a law-review note writer summarized the general feeling that "specific textual reference in the Constitution to an environmental right is not a prerequisite to the bestowal of constitutional protection" (Note 1970, 459).[2] Such protection could be found, environmentalists urged, in the Fifth, Ninth, Tenth, and Fourteenth Amendments.[3] In addition, the Court's special role as protector of minorities was called for, with environmentalists finding a minority interest in the right of future generations to enjoy a healthy environment (Note 1970, 483).

Finally, environmentalists believed that protecting the environment was so important, and that the Court played such a special role in American society, that it simply had to act. Environmentalists spoke of the irrevocable nature of environmental harm, of the need to "save the whole society" (Roberts 1970b, 164; Sive 1970b, 3; Note 1970, 486). And here, they believed, the Court was at its best: "the Court may be at its best not in its work of handing down decrees, but at the very task that is called for: of summoning up from the human spirit the kindest and most generous and worthy ideas that abound there, giving them shape and reality and legitimacy" (Stone 1974, 53). Throughout the early 1970s, environmental advocates "argued for the existence of a fundamental right to a non-hazardous environment" (Kirchick 1975, 515).

Despite the rhetoric, environmentalists failed to create a constitutional right to a healthy environment. In a number of cases, federal courts explicitly declined the invitation to elevate environmental concerns to the constitutional level.[4] The first constraint could not be overcome.

1. The reader should note that the National Environmental Policy Act was enacted shortly after Roberts's comments. And, in the 1970s, Congress enacted a slew of environmental laws.
2. See also, for example, Roberts (1970b); Sive (1970b, 3).
3. Esposito (1970, 47–48) pointed to the "life" and "liberty" guarantees of the Fifth and Fourteenth Amendments while Roberts (1970b, 162–63), stressed the Ninth Amendment. Sive (1970b, 3), included the due process and just compensation clauses of the Fifth Amendment, the Ninth and Tenth Amendments, and the due process, equal protection, and privileges and immunities clauses of the Fourteenth Amendment.
4. See, for example, *EDF* v. *Corps of Engineers* (1971); *Ely* v. *Velde* (1971); *Tanner* v. *Armco Steel Corp.* (1972); *Pinkney* v. *Ohio EPA* (1974).

Environmental Legislation and the Courts

While environmentalists did not succeed in constitutionalizing a right to
a healthy environment, they did help pressure Congress into passing a great
deal of legislation designed to protect the environment. President Nixon ushered in the "Environmental Decade" when he signed the National Environmental Policy Act (NEPA) into law as his first official act of 1970. NEPA was
followed by a number of major pieces of federal environmental legislation,
including the Clean Air Act Amendments (1970), the Resources Recovery
Act (1970), the Federal Water Pollution Control Act Amendments (1970), the
Federal Environmental Pesticide Control Act (1972), the Noise Control Act
(1972), the Marine Protection Act (1972), the Coastal Zone Management
Act (1972), the Endangered Species Act (1973), the Safe Drinking Water Act
(1974), the Federal Land Policy and Management Act (1976), the National
Forest Management Act (1976), the Toxic Substances Control Act (1976), the
Resource Conservation and Recovery Act (1976), the Clean Air Act Amendments (1977)[5], the Clean Water Act Amendments (1977)[6], the Surface Min-
ing Control and Reclamation Act (1977), the Alaska National Interest Lands
Conservation Act (1980), and the Comprehensive Environmental Response,
Compensation, and Liability Act (Superfund) (1980). Environmental protection became an important political issue and the public came to support it in
large numbers. This litany of legislation and environmental sensitivity poses
two questions: 1. How important were the courts in furthering the goals of
environmental legislation? 2. What role did the courts play in furthering the
environmental movement, enacting environmental legislation, and producing
a cleaner and healthier environment? I start with the first question.

Litigation and Environmental Legislation

Environmentalists had great hopes that the courts would become an ally
in furthering environmental protection. I have shown the faith that was put in
courts in the absence of legislation. However, even with legislation in place,
environmentalists, in keeping with the beliefs of the Dynamic Court view,
were fearful that administrative agencies would fail to enforce the legislative
mandate. Many looked to the courts to force reluctant agencies to do their
job. Much of the earlier discussion conveyed the distrust environmentalists
placed in government bureaucracies. Even some courts reflected this view. In
the oft-cited case of *Calvert Cliffs' Coordinating Committee* v. *AEC*, Judge
Skelly Wright noted that "our duty, in short, is to see that important legislative purposes, heralded in the halls of Congress, are not lost or misdirected in
the vast hallways of the federal bureaucracy" (1971, 1111). In this NEPA

5. Part of these amendments delayed deadlines for compliance with auto-emission and air-
quality standards.
6. Part of these amendments delayed deadlines for compliance with treatment standards.

case, the District of Columbia Circuit Court warned "footdragging agencies" that the court would neither allow NEPA to be a "paper tiger" nor accept an agency's "crabbed interpretation" that "makes a mockery of the Act" (1971, 1114, 1117). Thus, environmentalists placed high hopes in the courts.

Looking to the courts, environmentalists brought a great deal of litigation. On the Supreme Court level, 143 environmental cases were filed in the 1970s by all parties and the Court accepted a remarkable 55 (39 percent) (Wenner 1982, 147–49).

Who won? According to environmental litigator Sutherland, "litigation is the most important thing the environmental movement has done over the past fifteen years" (quoted in Turner 1988, 27). Is he right? Although coding cases for outcomes can be tricky, overall it is clear from Wenner's work that in the 1970s the government won more than half its cases and won substantially more often than either environmentalists or industry. Specifically, the Supreme Court's record was "primarily antienvironmental" (Wenner 1982, 151). These figures suggest that if litigation is the most important contribution the environmental movement has made over the past fifteen years, then its contribution has been modest indeed.

Won-lost rates, while providing the big picture, are not the whole story. Where environmentalists won court victories, were the holdings implemented and did implementation make a difference? As President Nixon said in signing NEPA, "we are most interested in results" ("Text" 1970, 12). To assess the impact of the Court, one must first know something about changes in environmental quality to see if there has been any progress to assign credit for. Overall, the results of environmental action in the 1970s and 1980s are decidedly mixed. In general, attempts to improve the environment "have achieved some substantial successes, but they still have not attained some of the goals established over a decade ago" (Conservation Foundation 1987, xxiv).[7] In terms of air pollution, while there have been "some significant improvements" since 1975, particularly in levels of sulfur dioxide, carbon monoxide, and lead, "significant problems remain," including acid deposition, rising levels of atmospheric carbon dioxide, and the destruction of the ozone layer (Conservation Foundation 1987, xxiv–xxvi, 73). With water, a 1986 Government Accounting Office study concluded that between 1972 and 1982 "the nation's water quality did not significantly change" (cited in Crandall 1987, 70), and the Conservation Foundation found that "while many waters are becoming cleaner, others are degrading" (Conservation Foundation 1987, xxv). In the words of Ingram and Mann, "waters are not cleaner than they were in 1972" (Ingram and Mann 1984, 269). With pesticides, concentrations have been reduced, although pesticides are still widely used (Conservation Foundation

7. The material that follows is general. Readers wishing a more detailed account can find it easily in the various time-series tables in the appendices of the annual reports of the Council on Environmental Quality.

1987, xxvi). And, of course, the problem of toxic waste is far from solved. Overall, then, improvements have been "modest" (Vogel 1987, 51).

How is this general report of modest change to be understood? On the one hand, given the ambitious goals of many environmentalists, and much environmental legislation, disappointment seems most appropriate. In the eyes of environmental activist Barry Commoner, "apart from a few notable exceptions, environmental quality has improved only slightly, and in some cases has become worse" (Commoner 1988, 10195). On the other hand, continuing deterioration of the environment from a wide variety of sources appears to have been stopped, and in some cases rolled back. And since this occurred while the economy grew, it does suggest that progress was made. The question I now turn to is what role courts played in making this modest difference.

The Role of the Courts

The obvious place to start is with NEPA. It was the first piece of environmental legislation in the 1970s and the broadest. More suits were brought under NEPA in the 1970s than under any other environmental statute (Wenner 1982, 5–7).[8] In its key terms, Section 101 required the "Federal Government to use all practical means . . . [to] assure for all Americans safe, healthful, productive, and aesthetically and culturally pleasing surroundings."[9] It required the government, to the "fullest extent possible," to interpret and administer its activities in accordance with the act. And, in what turned out to be its most important provision, Section 102, it required the filing of "Environmental Impact Statements" (EIS's). Finally, NEPA created, in Title II, a Council on Environmental Quality (CEQ) in the executive office of the president to advise and assist the president.

Although the "legislative history is virtually silent on the possibility of judicial enforcement of the Act" (Anderson 1973, 13, 16; Liroff 1976, 31), NEPA was quickly read by environmentalists to create "a judicially cognizable interest in environmental values" (Hanks and Hanks 1970, 265). As two authors suggested, NEPA "could well become our environmental Bill of Rights" (Hanks and Hanks 1970, 269). And environmental litigators took up the challenge. As Handler puts it, "it was environmental lawyers and sympathetic courts that filled the holes in NEPA and added teeth to the vague language" (Handler 1978, 46). The following discussion illustrates the kind of teeth NEPA grew.

On the positive side, litigation under NEPA both forced agencies to file EIS's and delayed many projects. With the help of court decisions such as *Calvert Cliffs'*, noted earlier, the "action-forcing" requirements of the EIS

8. In the 1980s, however, the number of NEPA cases "declined dramatically" with fewer than 20 percent of the cases brought by environmentalists involving it (Wenner 1988, 11, 14).
9. Sections 101 (b) and 101 (b)(2).

were imposed on often recalcitrant and uncooperative government bureaucra-cies. As Hays notes, through NEPA litigation environmentalists were able to "ensure that environmental values were seriously considered" (Hays 1986, 974). One of the results of this general insistence that the EIS procedure be taken seriously was that environmentalists could delay projects. Liroff, for example, found that NEPA's "most readily observed impact was in the tem-porary enjoining of both sizable public works projects and many private proj-ects contingent upon federal action" (Liroff 1976, 142; Wenner 1982, 170, 174).[10] Trubek and Gillen reached the same conclusion in their study of at-tempts by environmentalists to stop numerous water-resource development projects: "environmentalists found they could use litigation to buy time and force agencies to develop more detailed information about projects" (Trubek and Gillen 1978, 211). By challenging EIS's as insufficient, environmentalists were able to gain time while further study was made.

Unfortunately for environmentalists, requiring adherence to procedure is not equivalent to enforcing substance. Despite NEPA's broad language, courts limited the act to its procedural requirements.[11] Procedural consideration, not substantive weight, was the Supreme Court's interpretation. As the Court put it in 1983, "Congress, in enacting NEPA . . . did not require agencies to elevate environmental concerns over other appropriate considerations" (*Bal-timore Gas & Electric Co.* v. *NRDC* 1983, 97).

Overall, then, environmentalists' litigation under NEPA did not achieve the goals sought. There is a virtual consensus that litigation under NEPA did not succeed in forcing the government to take the substantive concerns of NEPA seriously.[12] In other words, NEPA litigation failed to force recalcitrant government agencies to accept environmental criteria. Procedural considera-tion is one thing; substantive acceptance is quite another.

While litigation stemming from NEPA has not been of much substantive help to environmentalists, litigation based on statutes and claims other than NEPA has sometimes helped. With air pollution, the courts provided the ini-tial impetus behind the policy of "non-degradation of existing clean air" (*Sierra Club* v. *Ruckelshaus* 1972, 256), or the prevention of significant de-terioration (PSD). Later, Congress amended the Clean Air Act to incorporate the "core of the judicially developed policy on dispersion and added provi-sions on prevention of significant deterioration (PSD) that were even more demanding than those published by the EPA" (Melnick 1983, 72). Court

10. For a list of wilderness areas protected by Congress after court decisions delayed de-velopment, see Turner (1988, 30).

11. See, for example, *Scenic Hudson Preservation Conference* v. *FPC* (1971, 481); *Ver-mont Yankee Nuclear Power Corp.* v. *NRDC* (1978, 558); *Strycker's Bay Neighborhood Council* v. *Karlen* (1980, 227).

12. Anderson (1973, 288); Caldwell (1985, 38); Goldsmith and Banks (1983, 3, 5); Hays (1986, 974); Macbeth (1975, 14); Rosenbaum (1974, 261); Wenner (forthcoming). Cf., Bardach and Pugliaresi (1977, 22, 23, 37).

decisions helped produce the regulation of lead,[13] limit the emissions of asbestos, beryllium, and mercury (*EDF* v. *Ruckelshaus* 1973), and, by rejecting dispersion of emissions as a way of meeting local clean-air requirements (*NRDC* v. *EPA* 1974), lessen atmospheric loading and thus acid deposition. And with pesticides, the judiciary pushed toward regulation of DDT (*EDF* v. *Ruckelshaus* 1971). Even with these successes, however, the courts have a mixed record. In enforcement, Melnick found that "the pattern of judicial action has been to weaken, not strengthen, environmental regulations" (Melnick 1983, 353). Despite the hopes and aspirations of many environmentalists, and a great deal of legislation, litigation to protect the environment has made only a modest contribution. The question remains as to why.

The Uneven Success of Environmental Litigation

Environmentalists made only modest gains through the courts because of their inability to overcome the constraints of the legal system and because of the uneven presence of the conditions. Where the constraints could be overcome, and where one of the conditions was present, courts did help produce change.

The Failure to Achieve a Constitutional Right to a Clean and Healthy Environment. Environmentalists failed to establish a constitutional right to a clean environment for both general and specific reasons. On a general level, the first constraint of the Constrained Court view is applicable. Judges, constrained by precedent and the beliefs of the dominant legal culture, are unlikely to act as crusaders. Serving an anti-majoritarian, electorally unaccountable institution, federal judges are limited in what they can do. When faced with both constitutional and statutory or regulatory claims, courts traditionally focus on the latter. "Courts by and large do not strain for constitutional imperatives," Brown writes, "if there are more decorous ways to a desired result" (Brown 1970, 2).[14] They are not free to create constitutional rights as they please. To find a constitutional right to a clean environment, courts would have had to make a radical departure from existing law. As the cases cited in the earlier discussion demonstrate, judges were clearly not willing to take such a step.

On the specific level, environmentalists had not built the kind of precedent that might tempt the judiciary to find such a right. Unlike civil rights litigators in 1954, environmentalists did not have decades of precedent behind them. What they did have was imagination. Looking back in 1978, Sive re-

13. In an unreported opinion, EPA was ordered to make a final decision within thirty days on whether lead additives should be regulated for health reasons (*NRDC* v. *EPA* 1973). Subsequent EPA regulations were upheld in *Ethyl Corp.* v. *EPA* (1976, 10), which quoted from the unreported decision. See also *NRDC* v. *Train* (1976).

14. Brown's article is a response to Sive's (1970b) argument for a constitutional right to a clean environment.

alized that environmentalists had "romanticized our concepts of the relationship between man and nature into theories of a constitutional right to a clean and healthy environment" (Sive 1978, 835). Further, environmental concerns touch on most aspects of life. Asking the courts to establish a constitutional right to a clean environment was asking them to become involved in the "entire cycle of production . . . the entire range of our society's output of goods and services" (Hoban and Brooks 1987, 219). Perhaps the only surprise in the courts' refusal to so involve themselves was the fact that anyone asked.

Courts, Legislation, and Administrative Action. Once Congress and the executive had acted, however, environmental litigators attempted to use the courts to enforce compliance and broaden agency interpretations. The results, discussed above, were mixed. There are a number of factors that explain why. I start with those that constrained the courts and show why litigation was mostly unsuccessful.

A basic reason why environmental litigators had little success is that, as the second constraint of the Constrained Court view points out, courts, in important ways, lack meaningful independence from the other branches. Because of their precarious political position, courts tend not to strike out in ways that are likely to raise political ire. Unwilling to branch out very far from the political mainstream, courts traditionally defer to agency interpretations of the statutes they implement. In the environmental field they did so with a vengeance. In one key case, the Supreme Court warned that "although this inquiry into the facts is to be searching and careful, the ultimate standard of review is narrow. The court is not empowered to substitute its judgment for that of the agency" (*Citizens to Preserve Overton Park* v. *Volpe* 1971, 416). In an important lower-court case, Judge Leventhal of the District of Columbia Circuit wrote: "So long as the officials and agencies have taken the 'hard look' at environmental consequences mandated by Congress, the court does not seek to impose unreasonable extremes or to interject itself within the area of discretion of the executive as to the choice of action to be taken" (*NRDC* v. *Morton* 1972, 838). These deferential standards have been repeatedly relied upon by both the Supreme Court and the lower federal courts throughout the 1970s and 1980s.[15] Even off the bench, two judges from the District of Columbia Circuit, the country's most pro-environmental circuit court (Wenner 1982, 110, 112–13), reiterated the judicial belief in deference.[16]

15. Federal circuit court cases include *Connecticut Fund for the Environment* v. *EPA* (1982); *Lead Industries Association* v. *EPA* (1980); *Sierra Club* v. *EPA* (1976); *EDF* v. *Corps of Engineers* (1972); *Scenic Hudson Preservation Conference* v. *FPC* (1971).

Supreme Court cases include *Chevron U.S.A.* v. *NRDC* (1984); *Baltimore Gas & Electric Co.* v. *NRDC* (1983); *Strycker's Bay Neighborhood Council* v. *Karlen* (1980); *Vermont Yankee Nuclear Power Corp.* v. *NRDC* (1978); *Kleppe* v. *Sierra Club* (1976).

16. Bazelon (1981, 209, 211; 1977, 817, 822, 832); Leventhal (1974, 509, 511, 512, 514, 525).

The traditional deference that courts show administrative agencies may be heightened in the environmental field because of the complicated technical and scientific nature of many of the issues. If courts are normally deferential to agencies, they are even more likely to act deferentially when the matter at controversy is highly technical.[17] The Supreme Court made this deference explicit in a case dealing with the Nuclear Regulatory Commission: "the Commission is making predictions, within its area of special expertise, at the frontiers of science. When examining this kind of scientific determination, as opposed to simple findings of fact, a reviewing court must generally be at its most deferential."[18] Off the bench, both Judges Bazelon and Leventhal have noted judges' lack of training and knowledge to assess the merits of scientific arguments.[19] Overall, then, as Hays points out, judges' "lack of sufficient technical training" has reinforced courts' unwillingness to become involved in substantive environmental matters (Hays 1986, 981–82).

The third constraint on courts involves implementation. In the environmental area this constraint is manifested in a number of ways, including the complexity of environmental litigation (*Ohio* v. *Wyandotte Chemicals Corp.* 1971, 504; Wald 1985, 3), the piece-meal picture of the problem that litigation affords (Bowman 1976, 656; Melnick 1983, 345, 366, 367) and courts' lack of resources. Focusing on the latter, courts are not usually aware of the constraints under which implementing agencies operate. Even when courts order agencies to take specific steps or meet certain deadlines, the agencies may lack sufficiently trained personnel, the money, or the political resources necessary to comply. O'Leary, examining over 2,000 environmental decisions in the federal courts found only one instance where Congress provided EPA with additional staff or funds to comply with a court order (O'Leary 1989, 23). In the area of air quality, Melnick notes that the "EPA has missed most of the deadlines set by courts, claiming that Congress has not provided it with enough money or trained personnel." And, as Melnick points out, the "court cannot appropriate more money" (Melnick 1983, 61). In addition, agencies often are forced to make choices about where to invest limited resources. When courts order agencies to invest more resources in a given program,

17. See, *Ethyl Corp.* v. *EPA* (1976, 67, 66–67 n.7); *Lead Industries Association* v. *EPA* (1980, 1146).
18. *Baltimore Gas & Electric Co.* v. *NRDC* (1983, 103). The issue in the case was the validity, for the purposes of NEPA, of the Nuclear Regulatory Commission's decision that the permanent storage of certain nuclear wastes had no significant environmental impact (the "zero-release" assumption). One might think that it does not require a great deal of scientific expertise to find this assumption lacking any rational basis.
19. Bazelon (1981; 1977); Leventhal (1974). Leventhal was so concerned as to recommend "access by an appellate judge to a scientific assistant" (Leventhal 1974, 553). However, it should be noted that a congressionally authorized 1973 study by the Land and Natural Resources Division of the Department of Justice, in which comments were solicited from environmental agencies and groups, found no complaints about judges' ability to handle technical issues. See Smith (1974, 635).

compliance leads to another program being deprived of resources. Thus, the best-intentioned judicial decisions may hurt rather than help the environment.

The decentralized nature of the legal system also means that environmentalists have no control over access to courts. The result, in practice, is that polluters can use the courts the same way environmentalists have, to delay or reverse government decisions and to tie up their opponents. "Litigation," industry discovered, "can delay any real pollution control effort" (Wenner 1982, 72). Reviewing environmental litigation in the 1970s, Wenner found that industry had "set about systematically to challenge every environmental law on the books" (Wenner 1982, 172). By the 1980s, Wenner found "no let-up in industry's strategy that the best defense is a good offense in challenging every government regulation before it can take effect" (Wenner 1988, 7). And comparing the ability of industry to effectively use the courts with that of environmentalists, Hays reached a sobering conclusion: "the relative ability of industry to bring litigation, challenge administrators through lawsuits, and postpone action and neutralize administrative choice, in contrast with the limited capabilities of environmentalists, was striking" (Hays 1986, 976).

One of the main reasons for this last conclusion is that environmentalists, like all social reformers, have limited resources. As environmental attorney Macbeth put it: "there is one brutal necessity for effective participation by the general public in the NEPA procedure: money" (Macbeth 1975, 19). As early as 1970 Sive concluded that when "your defendant is big enough to put on a good defense," as large polluters invariably are, litigation costs will run environmentalists "over $100,000" (Sive 1970a, 87). Writing in 1984, Miller found that the costs of environmental suits ran as high as $200,000, with groups having "difficulty paying 'up front' costs of these cases" (Miller 1984, 10411 n.46). And, of course, these cost estimates assume lawyers work for free or at greatly reduced rates. The result is that environmental lawyers can bring very few suits. Thus, although courts may have offered certain advantages to environmentalists, those advantages were only available to those who made it past the courthouse doors.

Perhaps the most important problem created by the implementation constraint is the courts' inability to insure that their decisions are implemented. "By itself, announcing rights does not protect rights" (Melnick 1983, 297). Courts, as proponents of the Constrained Court view point out, lack most of the necessary tools for implementation. This problem is exacerbated with environmental protection because its effects are widely felt. Courts, as well as the EPA, need political support to implement environmental decisions and regulations. But "standards that seem excessively demanding to state and local administrators, congressmen and presidents, and members of the public directly affected" are hard to enforce (Melnick 1983, 297). This means that agencies, when faced with court decisions requiring action they deem unworkable, "often have better reasons than mere timidity" for dragging their

feet; they may lack the "technical, administrative, and political resources to
carry out" the court order (Melnick 1983, 378). Melnick finds that in the
environmental area the celebrated judicial independence of the Dynamic
Court view is "essentially a negative quality" (Melnick 1983, 372). It leads
courts to ignore the possible in favor of the principled. And, while the enun-
ciation of principles is a noble undertaking, it may produce little in the way
of results. As Melnick cleverly puts it, "one cannot help but wonder whether
state and federal regulators have sometimes thought, 'the NRDC and the
courts have their standard, now let *them* enforce it'" (Melnick 1983, 281).

This last point provides a convenient place to switch from the constraints
of the legal system per se to the broader political system in which courts
operate. For if courts generally defer to the greater expertise of federal agencies, the success of environmental action largely depends on the attitudes
those agencies take. As one commentator put it, the "ultimate impact of
NEPA" depended "to a large extent on the attitude the agencies themselves
took" (Trubek 1978, 170).

In the first few years after NEPA was enacted, the general impression was
that "with few exceptions the agencies have not yet begun to take NEPA's
substantive mandate very seriously."[20] Summarizing the situation in 1976,
Liroff painted "a portrait of agency uncertainty, inertia, and outright hostility" (Liroff 1976, 121). Over time, however, the agency record improved
considerably, with variation replacing outright defiance. By 1985, Holland
could point to "inconsistency" as the best characterization of agency response
(Holland 1985, 745). Although agencies came around to more or less meeting
NEPA's procedural requirements, they did so in part because, they discovered, there was little cost; once they followed the procedure, their plans would
not be invalidated on substantive grounds.

Courts failed to force substantive environmental change because the political and economic system was not ready for such change and because environmentalists did not play politics very well, at least in the early years. Sive,
looking back at those years, noted that environmental activists "viewed as
heresy any claims that the fate of the environment must somehow be determined in the same manner as in other social movements—by the same kind
of bargain-striking in the political process" (Sive 1978, 828). Environmental
litigation, Trubek and Gillen (1978, 214) report, "discouraged direct political
action since it initially looked like the courts would 'take care of things'." By
believing that environmental issues were different, and by divorcing courts
from the political system in which they operate, environmentalists failed to
take politics seriously.

This lack of political activity allowed politicians to take symbolic credit
without imposing large costs (Muskie 1988). When politicians were forced to

20. Anderson (1973, 288). See also Frank (1985); Macbeth (1975, 7, 30, 31, 33).

make hard choices, the environment suffered. On the simple matter of money, for example, despite the large number of environmental laws enacted during the 1970s, the percentage of the federal budget going to environmental protection and natural resources declined by about 20 percent between 1970 and 1984. As the courts began to enforce the procedural requirements of NEPA, and executive agencies and industry began to complain, the politicians' free ride was over and a congressional backlash against NEPA developed. During the 1973–74 oil embargo, rather than investing heavily in conservation, recycling, and renewable energy resources, the president and Congress responded by "relax[ing] scores of costly environmental regulations" (Vogel 1987, 60). As Caldwell concluded, "NEPA's potential remains largely unrealized because no President has yet undertaken to direct the fulfillment of its mandate" (Caldwell 1985, 40).[21]

What many environmentalists overlooked is that "environmental decisions by their very nature must be political" (Hill 1985, 168). So, for example, although environmentalists won the legal battle to stop the Alaska pipeline, Congress promptly overrode the courts and the pipeline was built.[22] Similarly, although the Supreme Court held up the construction of the Tennessee Valley Authority's Tellico Dam project (*Tennessee Valley Authority* v. *Hill* 1978), because of its effect on an endangered species, the Snail Darter, Congress reversed the decision. Agencies that lost court cases to environmentalists over their environmental responsibilities often pressured Congress for change. When the Federal Highway Administration lost a NEPA case in the Second Circuit (*Conservation Society of Southern Vermont* v. *Secretary of Transportation* 1973), it responded by ordering an almost total halt to funding of projects in Connecticut, New York, and Vermont until Congress amended NEPA. When environmentalists won two court victories prohibiting the Forest Service from clear-cutting timber under the 1897 statute that established the service, it successfully lobbied Congress to enact the National Forest Management Act of 1976, which made "clear-cutting legal in many circumstances" (Turner 1988, 37). Political power, not legal argument, is what matters most. NEPA has not succeeded fully because the commitment to it is more symbolic than actual. By 1985, Caldwell had come to understand this: "In retrospect, the substantive provisions of NEPA appear to have been adopted in advance of their becoming politically feasible. . . . What has been lacking in fulfilling NEPA's potential is not the provisions of the Act itself but the political will to act" (Caldwell 1985, 40, 41).

The courts have seldom been able to overcome the constraints of the political and economic system in which they operate. Requiring procedural compliance with congressional acts and forcing delay are only short-term so-

21. See also Bowman (1976, 653); Roisman (1986).
22. *Wilderness Society* v. *Morton* (1973), overturned by the Alaska Pipeline Authorization Act, Pub. L. 93–153 (1973).

lutions to long-term problems. Only when the larger system becomes dedicated to improving environmental quality will courts be able to contribute much to the cause.

Court Successes. On occasion, however, courts have been effective in producing improvements in environmental quality. Aside from random decisions, these instances have in common the overcoming of the constraints by legislative and executive action, and the presence of one of the four conditions. The conditions that have allowed this include agency attitudes, the use of courts for leverage and cover, and the presence of the market.

As I suggested above, agency attitudes and political support play a key role in understanding court efficacy. Where there is agency support for the substance of court orders, implementation is likely. Where agencies are willing to act to protect the environment, and Congress or the executive is willing to support them, the deference of courts will often allow environmental programs to survive opponents' attacks. So, for example, it appears that the varying results of agency compliance with NEPA can best be understood by the attitudes of agency officials about the environment. Where officials share environmentalists' concerns, there is compliance. With the more developmentally oriented agencies, however, compliance has been less prevalent (Macbeth 1975, 33). Courts, on their own, even with a congressional statute to interpret, depend on agency incentive and cost calculations that they can influence only slightly. Thus, the success of environmental legislation depends almost entirely on the political support behind it.

In a similar vein, courts have been effective in helping to produce environmental improvement when there is support within agencies or Congress for change. When political appointees disagree with staff recommendations to implement congressional mandates, courts can clear the way. They can, in effect, allow career staffers to "proceed with their mission of writing regulations and imposing strict limits" (Wenner, forthcoming). In the air-quality area, court decisions backed the already established position of public health advocates within the EPA. Thus, they were able to get the upper hand and tighten regulations (Melnick 1983, 294). Decisions requiring the EPA to reach final decisions on whether to regulate lead additives (*NRDC* v. *EPA* 1973), commence formal administrative procedures on pesticide regulation (*EDF* v. *Ruckelshaus* 1971), and promulgate final emissions standards for certain hazardous pollutants (*EDF* v. *Ruckelshaus* 1973), have all supported large contingents within the EPA who were already committed to change. They helped produce improvements in the environment because there was support for those improvements within the agency and the wider political sphere.

Similarly, courts have provided both leverage and cover for committed agency officials. In battles over priorities and resources, courts can serve as the "gorilla in the closet" that enhances the argument of the side the decisions support (Wenner, forthcoming). In addition to this kind of leverage, courts have been effective where administrators were willing to act but felt the need for political cover. Department of Transportation Secretary Volpe, for example, had demonstrated concern for the environment before the enactment of NEPA. After enactment, however, he would sometimes "rely on the courts to order a project modified or halted [that he wanted modified or halted]. He would then be able to lay on others responsibility for 'meddling' with the project" (Liroff 1976, 127). In other words, when administrators wanted to make pro-environment decisions, courts could help.

Finally, there is also the factor of the market. When market forces favor pro-environment court decisions, courts can make a difference. This was sometimes the outcome of the delay resulting from court orders requiring further research and more thorough EIS's. That is, sometimes the cost of complying was not worth the return and the project was scrapped. Other times the elapsed time between the initial case and the completion of the revised EIS resulted in increases in costs that were too great for the project to bear. Industry and government critics of NEPA, for example, complained bitterly that one result of NEPA was the abandonment of some development projects (Bardach and Pugliaresi 1977; Garrett 1986). The Army Corps of Engineers claimed that by 1975 NEPA had been responsible for modifications, delays, or halts in 350 of its projects (Liroff 1976, 211). But, as a land speculator in Alexandria, Virginia, put it, "money can always wait" (quoted in Sax 1971, 11). Delay is usually only of short-term benefit and if environmentalists do not have the political muscle, they will lose at the final bell.

Conclusion

In sum, environmental activists were confronted with the structural constraints of the legal system. The courts were not willing to create rights nor were they able to take on a political system that was ambivalent about environmental protection. However, given the political rhetoric about protecting the environment, and the array of legislation, courts could act to enforce legislative commitments. When they tried, they met with varying success. When administrative officials were under pressure from other sources to act, they often did comply with court rulings. Similarly, if they wished to act but needed political cover, court decisions were effective. Finally, when market forces supported court decisions protecting the environment, courts were effective too.

Courts and the Environmental Movement

To argue that the courts did not directly produce much in the way of environmental improvement is not necessarily to argue that the courts had little or no positive effect on the environment. It is entirely possible that the courts played an important role in nurturing and supporting the environmental movement. It may well be that the courts had important indirect effects through gaining publicity, mobilizing actors, pressuring politicians, increasing membership in environmental groups, and so on. Indeed, Sive has concluded that the "environmental movement, more than any other social movement in my adult lifetime, has been born and bred in the courts" (Sive 1978, 839). Relying on the theoretical framework of chapter 4, I assess this Dynamic Court view argument.

Many claims have been made about the role courts could and assertedly did play in the environmental movement. Believing in the Dynamic Court view, environmentalists tried to use the courts "for consciousness-raising, for dramatizing the issues, and for arousing political and social concern for environmental issues" (Handler 1978, 63). Litigation was "sometimes sought merely for its symbolic value," or as a "catalyst to stimulate intervention" (Liroff 1976, 151). It was viewed as "a tactic in mobilization politics" (Trubek and Gillen 1978, 204). Finally, it was used to pressure politicians. Sive saw litigation as "one of the greatest ways of serving a political purpose because a lawsuit has inherent drama. When you bring a lawsuit, you can really spur the legislators" (Sive 1970a, 94). Thus, many environmentalists believed that courts had a key role to play in furthering environmental goals.

Public Opinion

One possible way in which litigation could have produced environmental improvement is through changing public opinion about the environment. One of the claims that is made on behalf of the courts' contribution to producing environmental improvement is that court decisions raised the consciousness of Americans about the problems of pollution and the need to build a clean and healthy environment. If this was the case, then public opinion data should show large increases in, and a high rate of, environmentally sensitive responses after courts became active in the environmental field. Since the courts became active in the early 1970s, those years will provide the appropriate cutoff date. A brief look at some national data tests this claim.

One way to track changes in public opinion is through the Gallup "most important problem facing the country" question. Asked repeatedly over the years, and often several times within a year, this open-ended question allows respondents to provide their own answers. Examining these responses over time, no mention of environmentally related issues occurs until 1971 (February) when 7 percent of the sample gave responses that could be categorized as referring to pollution or ecology (Gallup 1972: 3, 2292). And the numbers remained low throughout the 1970s.

Questions focusing on the most important problem facing local communities have also been asked by Gallup and other pollsters. Responses to these questions show a pattern similar to that for the national question. In a Gallup survey of May 1948, for example, 8.5 percent of respondents mentioned issues that could be categorized as dealing with ecology. It was not until 1967 that the 8 percent figure was again reached, and by 1975 only 6.5 percent of respondents mentioned issues relating to ecology (Smith 1985, 406–7).

These findings suggest neither an aroused public nor a sudden and dramatic shift in public opinion. Rather, they show a public not much concerned about environmental matters, at least not at the level of one of the most important national problems. If the courts raised the consciousness of the public about environmental matters, Americans kept it from the pollsters.

This is not to say that Americans were unconcerned about preserving the environment. Indeed, a slew of polls testify to a great deal of concern. They also show, however, that this concern predates environmentalists' use of the courts. As early as February 1965, 64 percent of a national survey thought air pollution control measures were very important and 74 percent thought the same of water pollution control measures. By 1981, these percentages were essentially the same, 62 percent and 75 percent respectively (Gillroy and Shapiro 1986, 274).[23] Major changes in environmental concern appeared to be occurring throughout the late 1960s. A question asking respondents how serious pollution in their part of the country was compared to other places found a steady rise in those saying it was very or somewhat serious, from 28 percent for air and 35 percent for water in 1965 to 69 percent and 74 percent in 1970, respectively (Erskine 1972, 121).

In terms of government action, by 1969 a Harris poll found that 52 percent of respondents thought the government was providing too little attention and financial support to environmental programs, compared to only 5 percent who thought too much was being done (Erskine 1972, 129). As early as 1967, when given a whole list of government activities and programs and asked which they wanted to expand, keep as is, or cut back, 50 percent of the respondents said they wanted to expand air and water pollution programs, a higher percentage than for any of the thirteen other programs on the list (Erskine 1972, 126–27). Similarly, in 1971, when presented with eleven areas of government spending and asked which areas they would cut first, only 3 percent chose pollution control, fewer than for any other area (Erskine 1972, 131).

Despite the claims of environmental litigators that their court-based efforts either could or did sensitize Americans to the dangers of pollution and the need for greater environmental protection, the data show that the public was well aware of these matters before major court action. The claim of court efficacy lacks evidence.

23. The responses did reach their highpoints in August 1972 of 80 percent (air) and 90 percent (water). However, if these are to be credited to court action, the court had little long-lasting effect because by 1974 the responses had declined to the 1965 level.

Media Coverage

Another possibility is that litigation put environmental concerns on the political agenda. That is, increasing media coverage may have helped changed people's minds about the environment and made it difficult for politicians to avoid the issue. If this was the case, then there should be a large increase in environmental coverage in the early 1970s. This Dynamic Court view claim is tested in table 10.1 which tracks magazine and press coverage of the environment from 1965 to 1985. What the table shows (column 2) is that magazine and press coverage of the environment grew slowly in the 1960s and exploded in 1970, with the number of stories increasing approximately seven times over the 1969 total. Thereafter, the number of stories actually dropped before more or less leveling off. An examination of the magazines that elites are likely to read, the *New York Times Sunday Magazine*, the *New Republic*, *Newsweek*, and *Time*, shows a similar pattern, with an explosion of coverage in 1970 and a drop-off to a steady level in the years following. The same pattern is also found in four of the largest-circulation magazines for the period. And, although the measurements are crude, coverage in the *New York Times* (the last column) more than doubled in 1970. In other words, the data provide no support for the claim that environmental litigation led to increasing magazine and press coverage of environmental matters.

Interest-Group Membership

A third possible influence of litigation is on group membership. Perhaps environmental court campaigns encouraged people to join environmental groups which, in turn, pressured politicians to act. If this were the case, one would expect to see a large increase in the number of members in the early and mid-1970s. This, however, is not the case. While many environmental groups did report steady growth in membership throughout the 1970s, there was nothing unusual about the trend. However, in the first few years of the Reagan administration, "membership in environmental organizations grew by leaps and bounds" (Vig and Kraft 1984b, 5). Sierra Club membership nearly doubled between 1980 and 1983, membership in the Wilderness Society nearly tripled (1980–85), and Greenpeace membership more than quadrupled (1980–84).[24] In explaining these enormous changes, most scholars point to the anti-environmental politics of the Reagan administration, particularly the political battles surrounding EPA administrator Anne Burford (Gorsuch) and Secretary of the Interior James Watt. The Sierra Club "led a highly publicized petition drive to replace Watt," collecting more than a

24. See *Encyclopedia of Associations*, various years. This source prints figures as reported to it by the organizations. Since groups have a vested interest in appearing larger than they actually are, the actual numbers may not be reliable. However, the concern here is with the degree of change over time which should be only minimally affected by exaggeration.

Table 10.1 Magazine and Press Coverage of the Environment, 1965–1985

Year	Entries	Reader's Guide # of Journals	NYT Mag.	New Rep.	News-week	Time	Reader's Digest	Ladies H.J.	Life	Sat. Rev.	NYT Index
1965	7	126								1	.005
1966	9	128									.007
1967	27	128	1	1							.005
1968	13	160									.016
1969	42	162				2				1	.036
1970	287	157	2	5	10	12	4		9	17	.08
1971	185	157	2	3	3	6	3		3	5	.05
1972	151	164	1	2	5	5	2			4	.15
1973	124	161		2	1	4	2			1	.02
1974	148	164	1	2	3	2					.03
1975	112	160	1		3	3	1			1	.02
1976	131	162	1	3	3	3	1	2			.03
1977	109	162	1		2	2					.08
1978	123	186			4	3					.07
1979	97	188	5		2						.07
1980	178	183			11	4				1	.08
1981	153	184		2	2	3				1	.11
1982	137	185	1		1	1					.08
1983	101	189	1		1	1					.4
1984	135	197	1	1	5	2					.15
1985	166	189			2	2					.08

SOURCE: The table is based on an examination of the *Reader's Guide To Periodical Literature* from 1960 to 1985. All entries under the index category entitled "Environment" were counted with the exception of those under sub-headings clearly referring to places other than the United States. Since the *Reader's Guide* volumes run from March of one year through February of the next, entries for each year in the table actually lack the first two months of the year and include the first two months of the following year.

NOTES: There was a problem of repetitions. That is, within the larger category, entries were sometimes repeated under different subheadings. Since the number of entries in each year was large, purging repetitions would have been an onerous and time-consuming task. By counting each entry, the actual number of articles has been inflated. However, since the purpose is only to *compare* coverage, and since treatment of the entries was consistent, this should not cause a problem.

Reader's Digest, Ladies Home Journal, Life, and the *Saturday Review* were selected because their circulations were among the largest of any American magazines (Sunday news magazines excluded) over the period in question. The *New York Times Sunday Magazine*, the *New Republic*, *Newsweek*, and *Time* were selected as magazines that political elites would read.

With the *New York Times*, the numbers refer to the proportion of pages in the *New York Times Index* devoted to coverage of the categories "Environment" and "Environmental" (in percentages). They were generated by the rather crude use of a ruler and should be read only as an indication of trends.

million signatures, and "it created direct-mail membership appeal letters featuring attacks on Watt" (Mitchell 1984, 61). Court decisions played no appreciable role.

Legislation

A fourth possible influence is that of litigation on legislation. As suggested by some of the environmentalists quoted at the beginning of this section, litigation may have pressured legislators to act. It is doubtful, however, that this was the case. Much environmental legislation predates major environmental court action. Early legislation included the 1963 Clean Air Act, the 1965 Motor Vehicle Air Pollution Control Act, and the 1967 Air Quality Act. Even with NEPA, the legislation that launched the environmental decade, there is no indication that courts played an initiating role. As noted in the earlier discussion, the legislative history of NEPA is "meager" and virtually no mention is made of courts (Anderson 1973, 275). And while it is possible that courts influenced the array of legislation that followed NEPA, by then, if not earlier, the environmental movement was in full swing, exerting a great deal of pressure. And when court influence on legislation has been expressly noted, its effect has been to pressure Congress to *overturn* pro-environment court decisions. There is little evidence that courts lived up to the high hopes that many environmentalists had for them.

The Environmental Movement

What, then, led to the environmental decade? What, if not courts, produced the level of concern shown by public opinion, by media coverage, by legislation, and by litigation? Logically, having shown that it was not the courts, I need not answer this question. However, the argument may become more convincing if I can point to a plausible cause of change. That cause, I will argue, was an environmental movement galvanized into action by growing knowledge of the harms of pollution and a series of well-covered ecological disasters. And this movement, of course, was independent of court actions.

The modern environmental movement is often seen as starting with the publication of Rachel Carson's *Silent Spring* in 1962. Two other important and widely read books were Paul Ehrlich's *The Population Bomb* (1968) and Meadows et al. 1972 study, *The Limits To Growth*. All three publications warned of the dangers of environmental neglect.

Along with books making the scientific case for cleaning up the environment, the media played a key role by publicizing a series of ecological disasters. Starting with the 1967 wreck of the oil tanker *Torrey Canyon* off the French coast, despoiling British and French beaches, the "news was laden with stories of environmental trauma" (Liroff 1976, 5). The next year the media carried the story of the PCB poisoning of 1,300 Japanese on the island of Kyushu (Vogel 1987, 55). The year 1969 was full of environmental disasters, including the Food and Drug Administration's seizure of 28,000 pounds of Lake Michigan salmon due to high levels of DDT and Dieldrin (Hoban and Brooks 1987, 3), a pesticide spill in the Rhine that killed 40 million fish (Vogel 1987, 55), and the often joked about and dramatic burning of the Cuyahoga River in Cleveland in June. However, by far the most covered environmental event of 1969 was the eleven-day blowout of an oil platform off

Santa Barbara in January and February, covering ocean and beaches with oil. Former U.S. Secretary of the Interior Stewart Udall called the Santa Barbara oil spill the "conservation Bay of Pigs" (quoted in Vogel 1987, 56). The point is that, in the words of environmentalist Rice Odell, "by the time 1969 was over, the environmental revolution was in full swing" (quoted in Vogel 1987, 57).

The events discussed above, showing the presence of both a scientific base and public outrage, lacked only one element for the launching of a full-scale movement; an organizational base. That was present, however, in the existence of a number of conservation groups such as the Sierra Club, the Wilderness Society, the National Audubon Society, and the National Wildlife Federation. While they tended to be relatively small in the early 1960s (National Wildlife Federation excepted), they did command some attention. In 1966 the Sierra Club ran "an emotional and successful campaign to 'save the Grand Canyon' from being damned and flooded."[25] And in the late 1960s, the membership of groups like the Sierra Club and the Wilderness Society doubled and tripled (Goldsmith and Banks 1983, 1n.1).

The different strands of the movement came together publicly, and triumphantly, in 1970. *Time* magazine named "protection of the environment" the issue of the year ("Issue" 1971, 21–22). The year started with President Nixon signing NEPA as his first official act of the decade, on January 1, 1970. In signing the act, he ushered in the "Environmental Decade," declaring that the "nineteen-seventies absolutely must be the years when America pays its debt to the past by reclaiming the purity of its air, its waters and our living environment. It is literally now or never" ("Text" 1970, 12). Later that year, in transmitting the first report of the CEQ, Nixon wrote: "Unless we arrest the depredations that have been inflicted so carelessly on our natural systems—which exist in an intricate set of balances—we face the prospect of ecological disaster" (CEQ 1970, v). The President also created, by executive reorganization, the Environmental Protection Agency, in December. The movement highlight of the year took place on April 22, 1970, "Earth Day," during which "an estimated *20 million* Americans participated in a nationwide program of environmental debates, protests, and parades" (Bowman 1976, 649; emphasis added). Concern with protecting the environment was so great that "both houses of Congress recessed, and legislators joined the popular agitation" (Vogel 1987, 52). Even by the standards of the 1960s and early 1970s, 20 million participants was remarkable. So, too, was the anger and the concern expressed in the speeches.

Given this brief history of the environmental movement, it is no wonder that the 1970s were indeed a time of great environmental activism. Politi-

25. Bowman (1976, 650–51). The fact that any industry could seriously propose to flood the Grand Canyon does suggest that environmental awareness has improved a great deal since the mid-1960s.

cians, ever fearful of a large and aroused constituency, went along with it. President Nixon, initially no great champion of environmental protection, was swept along too. While some activists accused him of using the environment to divert attention from the war in Vietnam, others saw a smart politician riding a wave of popular concern and attempting to steal the thunder of a possible challenger to his re-election, the environmentalist Senator Muskie of Maine. Wherever the truth may lie, the point is that politicians reacted to the power of a political movement, not the command of a court decision.

Conclusion

In sum, then, I have found little evidence that courts had important indirect effects in producing a healthier environment. In terms of public opinion, media coverage, legislation, and interest-group membership, little evidence has been found of court contribution. When this finding is coupled with the earlier conclusion that courts were only of modest help in directly producing environmental improvement, environmentalists' use of the courts looks mostly misplaced.

In the end, by failing to understand the inherently political nature of environmental decisions, litigators substituted legal principles for lobbying, writs of *mandamus* for political mobilization, and brief-writing for button-holing. Even when they won legal cases, they were successful only to the extent that they could find ways of pressuring the defendants to comply. Procedural victories seldom met litigators' goals because, in the end, agencies inevitably met the procedural requirements without reaching the substantive conclusions of the environmentalists. What court decisions could do best was to preserve victories achieved in the political realm from attack. But preservation, while important, is only useful when there are victories to preserve. And environmental litigation, as a strategy for producing a clean and healthy environment, achieved precious few victories.

Reapportionment and the Courts

A second area where the courts are generally considered to have played a key role is in the "Reapportionment Revolution" of the 1960s. In a series of cases in the early and mid-1960s the Supreme Court, at the behest of reformers, required the U.S. House of Representatives and all state legislatures to be apportioned solely on the basis of population. Chief Justice Earl Warren, reflecting on his years of judicial service, considered these reapportionment decisions the most important of his career ("Warren" 1969, 17). Robert McKay, writing in 1963 after the issuance of the first reapportionment decision (*Baker* v. *Carr*), opined that "if asked to identify the two most important cases decided by the Supreme Court of the United States in the twentieth century, informed observers would be likely to name, in whichever order, *Brown* v. *Board of Education* and *Baker* v. *Carr"* (McKay 1963, 645). Is this correct? Did the Court play as key a role as Warren and McKay thought? Is the Dynamic Court view finally vindicated?

The Reformers' Quest for Reapportionment

Looking at the institutional landscape in the 1950s and early 1960s, political reformers saw a host of problems that were not being addressed. From civil rights to social welfare, aid to education to housing, reformers saw little legislative action. A large part of the problem, they believed, was that, although most Americans lived in metropolitan areas, the nation's legislatures were unfairly and undemocratically under the control of rural voters (Elliott 1970, 474–75). This meant, they argued, that the legislatures were unresponsive to the needs of the vast majority of the American people. Necessary reforms were stymied by provincial and anti-urban legislators who served the interests of their rural constituencies and ignored the majority. Lack of equal representation was the problem, and until urban voters were represented according to their numbers, legislatures would fail to solve America's problems. Reapportionment would lead the way to liberal social legislation: "The common assumption was that the cities, once given their proper representation in the councils of government, would be in a position to make significant breakthroughs in various areas of social welfare legislation" (*Representation* 1966, 38). For change to occur, the reformers concluded, the legislatures had to be reapportioned. Thus, reformers pegged their hopes on reapportionment as a necessary step for significant social reform.

The reformers amassed a great deal of data demonstrating the unequal character of legislative representation.[26] From this data, reformers concluded that reapportionment was critical for political reform. In making this argument, they highlighted three distinct aspects of the problem. One position was that democracy required equal representation. It was supported by the U.S. Conference of Mayors (quoted in *Representation* 1966, 11), and the American Political Science Association (Committee 1951, 154), among others (Dixon 1962b, 348). And the U.S. solicitor general, in his *amicus* brief in *Baker*, wrote of "one of the most basic rights in any democracy, the right to fair representation in one's own government" (Brief for the United States, *Baker* 1962, 17).

A second set of concerns was the belief that only through reconstituting the legislatures would urban areas gain the support they needed. In 1955, President Eisenhower's Commission on Intergovernmental Relations (the Kestnbaum Commission) reported that unequal representation often resulted

26. Dixon (1962b); *Representation* (1966); Tyler (1962).

in legislative neglect of urban problems. The National Institute of Municipal Law Officers repeatedly stressed this theme (Brief of the National Institute of Municipal Law Officers, *Baker* 1962, 2, 3, 5–6, 7), as did the plaintiffs in *Baker* (Brief for Appellants, *Baker* 1962, 12). And the United States, in its *amicus* brief in *Baker*, made the point explicitly: "the underrepresentation of urban voters has been a dominant factor in the refusal of state legislatures to meet the growing problems of our urban areas" (Brief for the United States, *Baker* 1962, 18–19).

A third concern was that the lack of state legislative action was forcing municipalities to look to Washington for aid, weakening federalism. In its *Baker* brief, the U.S. argued that "another result of states' neglect of the reapportionment problem is that urban governments now tend to by-pass the states and enter directly into cooperative arrangements with the national government . . . [which] reinforces the debilitation of state governments" (Brief for the United States, *Baker* 1962, 55).[27]

In aiming to produce liberal political outcomes through reapportioning the legislatures, reformers looked not to the legislatures themselves but rather to the courts. They did so because they believed that malapportioned legislatures were not about to reapportion themselves voluntarily. They argued repeatedly that only an outside institution could force legislatures to act. In its *Baker* brief, the United States agreed, arguing that "the only realistic remedy is federal judicial action" (Brief for the United States, *Baker* 1962, 43). And the reformers could point to many states where this position seemed accurate. As Justice Brennan noted in *Baker* (1962, 191), since 1901 "all proposals in both Houses of the [Tennessee] General Assembly for reapportionment have failed to pass."

Court Victory

Despite the earnestness of the reformers, a judicial solution to reapportionment had its obstacles, particularly the 1946 case of *Colegrove* v. *Green* in which the Supreme Court had rejected reapportionment cases as nonjusticiable. Unfortunately for reformers, lower courts followed this precedent. In 1962, however, the Supreme Court re-thought its position and reversed itself. In a case emanating from Tennessee, *Baker* v. *Carr* (1962), the Supreme Court again heard a constitutional challenge to state legislative malapportionment. Although a three-judge federal district court had found that the "legislature of Tennessee is guilty of a clear violation of the state constitution . . . [and that] the evil is a serious one" it felt duty-bound to dismiss

27. Governor J. Howard Edmondson of Oklahoma, who had failed to induce his state legislature to reapportion itself, also submitted a brief in *Baker* supporting reapportionment. In colorful language, the governor argued: "Democracy is engaged in mortal combat throughout the world with atheistic communism, consequently the deterioration of representative government so widespread in the legislatures of our sovereign states must be halted" (Brief of J. Howard Edmondson, *Baker* 1962, 3).

the case (*Baker* v. *Carr* 1959). This time, however, a 6–2 Court held that the federal courts had jurisdiction to hear such claims, that the plaintiffs had standing, and, most important, that "appellants' claim that they are being denied equal protection is justiciable" (1962, 209). The case was reversed and sent back to the lower courts for trial. The "Reapportionment Revolution" had commenced.

In the wake of *Baker*, there was a wave of litigation. In 1962 alone, at least forty-seven reapportionment suits were filed in thirty-four states.[28] The next case to make it to the Supreme Court was *Gray* v. *Sanders* (1963), an attack on Georgia's county unit system as used in statewide and congressional primary elections. With U.S. Attorney General Robert F. Kennedy arguing part of the case for the U.S. in support of the challenge, an 8–1 Court held that because Georgia's system "weights the rural vote more heavily than the urban vote" (1963, 379), it unconstitutionally deprived urban voters of the equal protection of the laws. Writing for the Court, Justice Douglas put it this way: "The conception of political equality from the Declaration of Independence, to Lincoln's Gettysburg Address, to the Fifteenth, Seventeenth, and Nineteenth Amendments can mean only one thing—one person, one vote" (1963, 381).[29] This victory for the reformers was followed by another in *Wesberry* v. *Sanders* (1964), also from Georgia, where the Court held that in state elections "as nearly as is practicable one man's vote in a congressional election is to be worth as much as another's" (1964, 7–8). Finally, in a series of six cases decided on June 15, 1964, the Court required that both houses of state legislatures be apportioned by population. In sweeping language, Chief Justice Warren rejected all other standards: "Legislators represent people, not trees or acres. Legislators are elected by voters, not farms or cities or economic interests" (*Reynolds* 1964, 562). Addressing himself to the concerns of the reformers, Warren held that "the weight of a citizen's vote cannot be made to depend on where he lives" (*Reynolds* v. *Sims* 1964, 567).

In two short years, from 1962 to 1964, the reformers had won a stunning set of Court victories. They had achieved a constitutional mandate to reapportion the state legislatures and the U.S. House of Representatives on the basis of population. And reapportionment did occur, with a *Congressional Quarterly* survey of June 1966 finding substantial compliance with the equal population principle in forty-six states (*Representation* 1966, 23). By 1968, compliance was even better, with Frederickson and Cho (1974, 5) reporting that "all significant malapportionment in state legislatures had virtually disappeared." In Congress, while in 1962 only 9 districts were within 1 percent of the average size in their states, and 236 districts deviated by 10 percent or

28. For a list and a brief description of these cases, see McKay (1963, 706–10).
29. It is telling of our sexist culture that Douglas's language, "one *person*, one vote," was immediately turned into the slogan "one *man*, one vote" (emphases added). In my research I found only one writer who repeatedly used the correct language: Alexander Bickel.

more from the average, by 1972 385 districts deviated by less than 1 percent from the average (McCubbins and Schwartz 1988, 390). This leaves two questions. First, given the constraints of the judicial system that provide the framework for this analysis, and the results of the environmental study, how did the reformers manage to accomplish so much? Second, since the reformers saw reapportionment as only a means, albeit a crucial one, to an end, was that end achieved? The analysis starts with the second question.

The Effects of the "Reapportionment Revolution"

Winning cases, as reformers have learned the hard way (if they have learned it at all), is only the first step in achieving the desired change. The question that some social scientists ask, and that reformers must ask, is what the results of winning actually are. And since for reformers reapportionment was a means to an end and not an end in itself, the question is crucial for addressing their use of the courts.

A number of studies have attempted to assess the effects of reapportionment on a broad array of legislative policy outputs. While many of them demonstrate creativity and sophistication, the task they take on is difficult. One of the more intractable problems is that the world did not stop while reapportionment occurred. In particular, not only did the 1964 Johnson landslide sweep Democrats into elected office all over America, but the turbulent events of the 1960s created all sorts of pressures on elected officials. Deciding which of their actions can be credited to reapportionment and which to other events is close to impossible. In addition, criticisms have been mounted of the choice of variables to study and the lack of comparison to pre-1962 apportionments (Bicker 1971). Given these problems, it is perhaps best to take these studies with a proverbial grain of salt.

One of the first questions that must be answered is whether there was much legislative turnover as a result of the decisions and whether it helped one party or another. The answer seems to be a resounding "yes and no." On the "yes" side, in the California Senate, for example, one of the most malapportioned state houses in the nation, the first election under reapportionment bought twenty-two new senators (out of forty) to Sacramento (Sokolow 1973, 298). Examining six states in depth, O'Rourke found that between 1959 and 1974 "reapportionment in several instances has led to significant gains for one party or to sometimes offsetting gains by both parties" (O'Rourke 1980, 47–48). Shading toward the "no" side, Erikson, examining the partisan distribution of seats in thirty-eight non-Southern legislatures in the 1960s, found that the "overall impact of reapportionment on party strength appears to be slight" (Erikson 1971, 64). Putting the question in historical perspective, Rosenthal found state legislative turnover rates to be quite high regardless of reapportionment. While rates did pick up in the 1967 state elections, after thirty-three senates and thirty-four houses were redistricted, the overall legislative turnover rate for the period 1963–71 appears to be lower than in the 1925–35 period, at least for ten states for which Rosenthal had data. Rosenthal concluded, unsurprisingly, that the crucial explanations for turnover are "electoral factors. The more frequent elections, the higher turnover" (Rosenthal 1974, 615, 616 n.16). Thus, it appears that at least some, but clearly not all, turnover can be credited to the courts.

Assuming that at least some legislative turnover was due to reapportionment is both sensible and allows the analysis to continue. What policy effects did it have? Did the "Reapportionment Revolution" produce the goals its advocates desired? While there are studies both finding[30] and not finding[31] effects, an overall reading seems to be that any effects that can be traced to reapportionment are small. Erikson, for example, writes that "no researcher has been able to show that any amount of tinkering with potential control variables allows state apportionment scores to amount for an appreciable share of the variance in any state policy" (Erikson 1973, 280). Reviewing the case studies in 1980, O'Rourke concluded that "major changes in legislative conflict and policy . . . seem limited to a select category of states" (O'Rourke 1980, 9). As a study that found some effects concluded, the reformers "overstated their case by attributing to malapportionment a host of political ills" (Cho and Frederickson 1973, 267). In general, then, most commentators take the position that the "attribution of 'revolution' to the anticipated effects of the Court's apportionment rule is yet another example of the badly inflated rhetoric of our time" (Sindler 1971, 286).[32] Reflecting on Chief Justice Warren's comments about the decisions, Alexander Bickel concluded, "actually, Chief Justice Warren is quite wrong. His court's apportionment decisions are no significant achievement" (Bickel 1971, 58).

The upshot of this discussion is that the "Reapportionment Revolution," despite stunning court victories, turns out to be a lot like the experience of environmental reformers in court. A procedural victory was won but one that

30. Cantrall and Nagel (1973, 269–79); Cho and Frederickson (1973, 267); Frederickson and Cho (1974); Hanson and Crew (1973, 69).
31. On the side of little or no change, there are a host of studies. Most early studies found no effects. Many of the early studies are discussed in Dixon (1968, 557–81). Later studies have identified limited effects. O'Rourke, for example, stresses the "essential point" that the "effects of apportionment on policy are generally rather weak" (O'Rourke 1980, 141). And several of the studies cited in the preceding note for the proposition that reapportionment had important effects can be read to be making quite narrow claims.
32. See also Dixon (1968); Elliott (1970). A recent study of Congress by McCubbins and Schwartz (1988) argues that the Court's decisions created a large metropolitan majority in Congress that led to some reallocation of governmental benefits from rural to metropolitan areas. Their analysis equates rural areas with farm areas and examines budgetary changes in several national policies, including agricultural policies. There are several problems with this approach. First, their rural areas may be largely suburban. That is, Hansen has found that while in 1950 38 percent of Representatives had over 20 percent of their constituents on farms, by 1960 that percentage had fallen to only 12 percent (Hansen 1987, 243). Also, as this book has documented, there was a sea change in American politics throughout the 1960s that their approach does not appropriately account for.

didn't automatically lead to substantive ends. Legislatures were reapportioned, but the reformers' liberal agenda did not then automatically come to pass. In some states liberal reforms were made, and some of them can be traced to the reapportionment, but the pattern is spotty. How can these results be explained?

Winning in Court—Overcoming Structural Constraints

In order for reformers to win in court, they must convince judges that the relief they are asking for is not beyond precedent and the accepted legal culture. This is a particularly severe problem for reformers asking courts to find a new right, as the reapportionment reformers were doing. Although *Colegrove* v. *Green* appeared as a barrier to that, there were several reasons to believe that the barrier could be overcome.

First, there was a competing set of precedents that suggested, given the importance of the franchise (*United States* v. *Classic* 1941), the Court could involve itself in reapportionment. The Court had long recognized the importance of the right to vote and had upheld congressional action prohibiting the intimidation of voters, dishonest vote counts, and ballot-box stuffing.[33] It had thrown out numerous attempts by Southern legislatures to ban blacks from voting in all elections (*Guinn & Beal* v. *U.S.* 1915; *Lane* v. *Wilson* 1939) and in primaries.[34] As recently as 1960, the Court had overturned a districting plan in Alabama that effectively excluded all black residents of Tuskegee from voting (*Gomillion* v. *Lightfoot* 1960). While it is true that none of these cases spoke directly to the claim of vote dilution through malapportionment, they did provide a bridge to that position.

Second, there was support for finding a constitutional violation in malapportionment from large segments of the academic community and from many political leaders. As noted earlier, a great deal of academic and political writing identified malapportionment as a key ill in American society. As Shapiro put it, "urban political demands had become so powerful that they could no longer be resisted without danger to the entire political system" (Shapiro 1964, 239–40). The lawyer who argued the reform cause in *Baker*, Charles S. Rhyne, was a past president of the American Bar Association. In addition, and perhaps most important, both the Eisenhower and Kennedy administrations urged the Court to act, with the U.S. appearing in all the important reapportionment cases, essentially supporting the reapportionment reformers. Although the solicitor general was in law appearing only as a "friend of the Court," in practice the United States was the "chief advocate" for reform (Dixon 1968, 250). In the six cases headlined by *Reynolds* v. *Sims*, for ex-

---

33. *Ex Parte Yarbrough* (1884); *United States* v. *Mosley* (1915); *United States* v. *Saylor* (1944); *Ex Parte Siebold* (1880).
34. There were a series of cases known as the Texas Primary Cases. They included *Nixon* v. *Herndon* (1927); *Nixon* v. *Condon* (1932); *Smith* v. *Allwright* (1944); *Terry* v. *Adams* (1953).

ample, that held that both houses of the state legislatures had to be apportioned on a population basis, the U.S. filed briefs totalling over 500 pages.
Any fears the justices might have had about stepping out of the mainstream
could easily have been quelled.

Finally, the Court that heard *Baker* had a very different composition from
the one that had heard *Colegrove*. Only three justices remained from the earlier Court, and two, Black and Douglas, had dissented. Given the available
precedents, the political and academic climate, and the growing political liberalism of both the country and the Court, it can be argued that litigators had
at least a fighting chance. While hindsight is a wonderful tool in explaining
Court decisions, it does help highlight the reasons why reformers were able
to surmount the barriers to winning.

Making a Policy Difference—Uneven Results Explained

Winning in Court overcomes only one of the three constraints. The other
two that need to be overcome are the lack of political support and the Court's
lack of implementation powers. While the reformers were able to surmount
the political-support variable, their success with implementation was spotty.
This was the case, I will argue, because of the uneven occurrence of the four
conditions necessary for Court effectiveness.

There was a great deal of political support for reapportionment across
parties and throughout the country. As the *Congressional Quarterly* noted,
"support for federal court scrutiny of state apportionment was bipartisan from
the start" (*Representation* 1966, 27). Much of this support has already been
noted. In addition, reaction to Court decisions was initially supportive. For
example, the chairs of both the Republican and Democratic national party
committees were "quick to offer praise" for the *Reynolds* decision (*Representation* 1966, 30). Although this was soon to change,[35] the breadth and depth
of support allowed the Court to be effective.

Public opinion is an essential aspect of political support. If the public
opposes change, politicians often follow suit. With reapportionment, although the data are scant, the public was generally supportive of, but essentially oblivious to, the "Reapportionment Revolution." A July 1964 Gallup
poll found that 47 percent approved of reapportionment based on equal population while 30 percent disapproved and 23 percent had no opinion. There was
little difference between Democrats and Republicans, and reapportionment
was supported in all sections of the country (Gallup 1972: 3, 1897–98). Five
years later, in June 1969, Gallup asked respondents whether they preferred an

35. A serious attempt to overturn *Reynolds* was made in Congress in 1964 and 1965.
However, at least part of the motivation came from states' rights forces that had tried to curb the
Court in the wake of the civil rights and free-speech decisions of the 1950s. The attempts were
defeated because the Court's decision enjoyed widespread support and because of the effect on
Congress of the 1964 Johnson landslide. For a detailed discussion of these events, see Dixon
(1968, chaps. 15–16).

equal-population basis for state legislatures or "earlier plans" that used non-population criteria. The population basis was favored by 52 percent compared to 23 percent who preferred earlier plans and 23 percent who had no opinion. Again, there was little difference between parties, and regional support for the population basis was better than two-to-one throughout the country (Gallup 1972: 3, 2205–6).

Questions on support do not measure salience. Here, polls have found that the public was only dimly aware of what the Court had done. In a February 1965 survey in Seattle, when asked if they had read or heard anything about the Supreme Court recently, only 8 percent mentioned reapportionment, compared to 42 percent who mentioned civil rights and 20 percent who mentioned school prayer (Kessel 1966, 175).[36] In a 1964 national survey carried out by the Survey Research Center (SRC), only 5 percent of respondents who had likes or dislikes about the Court mentioned reapportionment, compared to 38 percent for civil rights and 30 percent for school prayer (Daniels 1973, 649). A similar 1966 SRC survey found percentages of 8 percent, 25 percent, and 24 percent, respectively (Daniels 1973, 650). As Murphy and Tanenhaus concluded, the Court's reapportionment decisions "were barely visible to the public at large" (Murphy and Tanenhaus 1968b, 35–36).

The remaining obstacle to be overcome was that of implementation. As has been shown, the decisions did lead to reapportionment throughout the country, a good deal of legislative turnover, and some policy change. Why did this pattern appear? It appeared, the conditions suggest, because there were actors independent of the judiciary who had incentives to act, and who used the courts as a tool to win advantages for themselves. As with the environment, the key to understanding the extent of implementation was the political setting. In other words, several of the conditions necessary for court decisions to be effective were present.

Robert Dixon, in his massive study of the Court and reapportionment, reminds the reader that "the political nature and effect of apportionment must be admitted, whatever may be the apportioning agency" (Dixon 1968, 291). But more than being merely "admitted," the political nature was fundamental to the effects of the Court. Overall, O'Rourke, in his six-state case study, concludes that reapportionment's "impact varies according to the state and its political and economic setting" (O'Rourke 1980, 141). And Auerbach points out that the success of the Court depends upon "the result of the struggles between the political parties and within each political party" (Auerbach 1971, 75). These statements appear obvious, and I think they are. But what the reformers evidently forgot is that Court decisions depend upon political elites for their implementation. Placing their hopes in the courts as the route to

---

36. Kessel's sample was better educated, whiter, and wealthier than a random sample, suggesting that it would be more aware of what the Court was doing than were average Americans.

substantive change was straightforwardly to misunderstand what courts can and cannot do. A few examples illustrate the point and the mixed results of Court-ordered reapportionment.

One of the more striking aspects of the reapportionment cases was the speed with which both lower courts and legislatures acted to reapportion. Several reapportionment studies made special note of how different the situation was from both the lower court and the legislative reaction to *Brown* (*Representation* 1966, 18; McKay 1963, 645, 660). The reason is, of course, that there was a set of politically powerful elites ready to act to force compliance. On the cost side, non-court actors put enormous pressure on legislatures to comply. Without that pressure, the courts alone would have been unlikely to induce much compliance. On the incentive side, deals could be cut to preserve the position of former legislators in new, reapportioned legislatures. Thus, conditions one and two were present; there was a set of non-Court actors who could impose costs on legislatures for failing to act and who could offer incentives to those who did act. The presence of these conditions meant that Court decisions were likely to be implemented.

Reapportionment, however, did not always, or even often, achieve the goals the reformers desired. If the fact of implementation depended upon the presence of political elites with incentives and costs to apply, then it should be no surprise that the results of reapportionment depended on what those elites wanted. And that, in large part, was determined by a host of political and economic factors unique to each state and outside the control of courts. In some states, then, reapportionment did result in policy change that reformers wanted. In others, however, it did not. For those who prefer a more quantitative summary, Uslaner and Weber examined eighty-two state legislative chambers and "concluded that the call for reapportionment led party leaders . . . to make concerted efforts to 'gerrymander' legislative districts to insure continued domination of the traditional 'in-party' " (cited in Uslaner 1978, 430). And Frederickson and Cho summed up their forty-eight state analysis that found some policy effects of reapportionment with similar emphasis: "political control variables account for much of the variance in many policy areas" (Frederickson and Cho 1974, 37).

Studies of reapportionment in particular states illustrate these points. In New Jersey Dixon notes that the 1967 election, the first under a new reapportionment plan, turned a near two-to-one Democratic control of both houses into a near three-to-one Republican control. However, he concludes that "the result can be attributed to several causes, none related to the [work of the reapportionment] commission: (1) Vietnam; (2) white backlash from the Newark riot; (3) school busing policy . . . " (Dixon 1968, 339). Similarly, there was an increase in aid to urban areas in New Jersey in the years after reapportionment. O'Rourke, however, concludes that "expanded aid to urban areas in New Jersey appears to be more the result of a general commitment by both parties to address the problems of central cities than of representational changes induced by reapportionment" (O'Rourke 1980, 126). In California, despite the enormous malapportionment of the Senate, and its domination by rural interests, neither Assembly Speaker Unruh nor Governor Brown showed much interest in reapportionment (Dixon 1968, 373). What mattered was politics, not Court orders.

Politics is manifested not only in issue positions but also in the personalities of political leaders and the internal structures of the legislatures and parties. Leadership positions, committee structures, and institutional incentives all effect policy outcomes. As Sokolow points out, "reapportionment must be viewed in the context of internal legislative structure and policymaking" (Sokolow 1973, 291). In other words, the crucial variables in determining policy outputs have a lot more to do with the structures under which politicians operate than with the actions of outside institutions. A legislature is likely to be "change-resistant," Sokolow concluded, "because of such institutional characteristics as policy pluralism, ongoing leadership and leadership control of committee membership, and rapid socialization of new members to the norms of conformity and loyalty" (Sokolow 1973, 308).

These general observations were confirmed by O'Rourke in his six-state study. He found that "in most instances reapportionment has resulted in only slight changes in patterns of leadership selection" (O'Rourke 1980, 81). What this means is that the reformers' goals were unlikely to be achieved as a result of court-ordered change. Addressing the point directly, O'Rourke found that "reapportionment did not necessarily bring about a greater share in committee chairmanships for the constituency categories benefiting from added representation even in states in which redistricting produced profound shifts" (O'Rourke 1980, 81). In addition, reapportionment did not remove economic constraints. That is, even where political incentives combined with Court action to produce both the legislators and the will to change, "revenue limitations, past appropriations, and federal aid stipulations all serve[d] to constrain legislative activity in state budgetary policy" (O'Rourke 1980, 141).

In sum, then, Court reapportionment orders were filtered through the lenses of political actors searching for what was in it for them. When there was something, as often there was, some change did occur. However, it seldom reached the goals for which the reformers had argued. Their mistake was to abstract Court opinions from political reality, and to invest too much time and too many resources in legal battles to the detriment of political ones. Confusing procedural change with substantive change, reformers misunderstood the severe limitations under which courts operate. As Allan Sindler put it, Court-ordered reapportionment did not create "a new ball game for districting, much less a revolution; it has simply tightened up the rules, so that stealing bases has become somewhat more difficult" (Sindler 1971, 287).

Conclusion

In this overview of the environmental movement's use of the courts and the "Reapportionment Revolution," I have shown that neither the Dynamic nor the Constrained Court view is particularly helpful in explaining outcomes. In both cases, litigation accomplished more than the Constrained Court view predicted but decidedly less than the Dynamic Court position predicted. As with civil rights and women's rights, neither view is particularly helpful. But, as with both of these issues, the constraints of the Constrained Court, and the conditions derived from the two views, do explain what happened. The upshot of this overview is to confirm that courts can only sometimes produce significant social reform, and only under unusual conditions.

11

Judicial Revolution? Litigation to Reform the Criminal Law

The Criminal Rights "Revolution"

In a series of cases in the 1960s, the Supreme Court extended a number of procedural rights to criminal defendants. There are essentially four lines of cases that are viewed as the pillars of the criminal rights "revolution." They deal with search and seizure (*Mapp* v. *Ohio* 1961), the rights of criminal defendants (*Gideon* v. *Wainright* 1963; *Miranda* v. *Arizona* 1966), the rights of juvenile defendants (*In re Gault* 1967), and the rights of prison inmates.[1] In the pages that follow, I offer an overview of each area and show how the constraints and conditions explain the outcomes. As an overview, the argument is more suggestive than definitive. However, it should be sufficient to make a plausible case for the analysis offered.

In 1974, a tear-out ballot was placed in the pages of the *American Bar Association Journal* inviting readers to vote for judicial milestones in U.S. history. Responses were ranked by the number of votes received and the top eighteen were discussed in a book celebrating the U.S. Bicentennial (Lieberman 1976). The criminal-law cases that are the subject of the following discussion ranked exceedingly high. For example, *Miranda* v. *Arizona* ranked fourth, one place ahead of *Brown*. *In re Gault* ranked ninth, *Gideon* v. *Wainright* was thirteenth, and *Mapp* v. *Ohio* was sixteenth, all ahead of number 18, *Roe* v. *Wade* (Lieberman 1976, vii).[2] Thus, in the eyes of the *American*

---

1. I have not included the death penalty cases for two reasons. First, although the statutes before the Court were invalidated in *Furman* v. *Georgia* (1972), the penalty was not held unconstitutional, and was explicitly held constitutional in *Gregg* v. *Georgia* (1976). Second, the number of executions dropped throughout the middle part of the twentieth century, from 1,667 in the 1930s to 191 in the 1960s. From 1968 through 1976 there were no executions in the U.S. As final as the death penalty is, it only reaches a fraction of the number of people affected by the other cases (U.S. Bureau of the Census, *Abstract* 1989, 187).

2. However, since "Warren and the Warren Court" ranked second, the high rankings of individual cases should be read more to suggest their importance than their actual rankings vis-à-vis other cases.

Bar Association Journal readers who responded, the criminal-law cases of the Warren Court were "milestones" in American history.

The question this chapter addresses is whether this assessment is correct. Were these decisions milestones, vindicating the Dynamic Court view; lodestones, supporting the Constrained Court view; or a mixed bag, with some change occurring, perhaps because of the presence of the conditions?

The Prisoners' Rights "Revolution"

Over the past several decades there has been a great deal of litigation involving the rights of prison inmates. Prior to the 1960s, the courts had adopted a hands-off policy to prisoner suits, refusing to consider the merits of suits challenging prison conditions, rules, and regulations (Comment 1963). This position changed in the early 1960s when the Court held that section 1983 of the Civil Rights Act of 1871 gave prisoners standing in federal courts to make such challenges (*Cooper* v. *Pate* 1964). By the late 1960s and early 1970s, the Court loosened tight restrictions on prisoners providing legal assistance to each other (*Johnson* v. *Avery*), on mail censorship (*Procunier* v. *Martinez* 1974), on freedom of religion (*Cruz* v. *Beto* 1972), and held that denial of medical care to an inmate can constitute cruel and unusual punishment in violation of the Eighth Amendment (*Estelle* v. *Gamble* 1976). A 1972 case (*Haines* v. *Kerner* 1972), allowed a prisoner to proceed with a suit seeking damages resulting from prison disciplinary regulations, while in 1974 the Court invalidated prison disciplinary proceedings that did not provide any due process protections (*Wolff* v. *McDonnell* 1974). In this latter case, Justice White, writing for the majority, noted that "there is no iron curtain drawn between the Constitution and the prisons of this country" (1974, 555–56). While the Burger Court became increasingly hostile to prisoners' suits, it did not repudiate earlier decisions.[3]

At the same time as the Court was liberalizing prisoners' access to federal courts, the number of prisoners skyrocketed.[4] These increases "created a severe crowding problem"[5] that exacerbated tensions and worsened the already often inadequate delivery of services. Indeed, even before the dramatic rise in prison populations, most of the nations' maximum-security prisons were old, deteriorating, and woefully underfunded, barely able, if at all, to provide even minimal levels of services (Cobb 1985).

In the wake of these occurrences there was a flood of prisoner suits,

---

3. See, for example, *Meachum* v. *Fano* (1976), rejecting a Fourteenth Amendment due process argument that prison transfers require a fact-finding hearing; *Bell* v. *Wolfish* (1979), upholding the "double-bunking" of pre-trial detainees against a Fifth Amendment due process challenge; and *Rhodes* v. *Chapman* (1981), upholding double-celling in an Ohio prison against Eighth and Fourteenth Amendment challenge.

4. See, for example, Finn (1984); Jacobs (1984); Malcolm (1989, 1990, 1991); Selke (1985).

5. Finn (1984, 319). For example, by 1989 the California prison system was "routinely operating" at 175 percent of capacity (Malcolm 1989, 1).

nearly all of which started and ended in the federal district courts. While the first decision invalidating the prison system of an entire state came in 1970 (*Holt* v. *Sarver*), by 1983 prison systems in eight states had been declared unconstitutional (Taggart 1989, 246): By 1986, forty-five states had at least one prison facility involved in litigation and in thirty-seven states correctional administrations or individual prisons were operating under federal court orders (Brakel 1986). What were the results?

Changes in Prisons

The results of prison litigation are not entirely clear. While one school of thought believes that the "collective result of this litigation has been nothing less than the achievement of a legal revolution within a decade" (Orland 1975, 11), the key question is whether this "legal revolution" translated into a revolution in prison conditions. The careful scholar will want to know what changes occurred and whether they can be credited to the courts. In the material that follows I suggest that change varied and that the presence of the constraints and the conditions best explains why litigation worked in some places and not in others.

Overall, the consensus view is that, while some changes have been made, serious problems remain. Although litigation has sometimes succeeded in eliminating the "most severe overcrowding and the most painful and onerous conditions," the contribution of the courts has been "strictly limited" to "only" those achievements (Angelos and Jacobs 1985, 112). Improvements in prisoner health have been reported (Brakel 1986, 64), as has the lessening of the likelihood of "arbitrary abuse" (Turner 1979, 640), but prison over-crowding continues to be a serious problem.[6] One study of four prison reform cases concluded that while "the court orders eliminated the worst abuses and ameliorated the harshest conditions," they failed to deal with "underlying issues and problems" and "were directed more toward symptoms than causes" (Harris and Spiller 1976, 25, 26).[7] As James Jacobs puts it, "there seems to be no agreement on which side is winning" (Jacobs 1980, 430).[8]

There are also the issues of prison construction and the expenditure of funds for the corrections system. Here, the essential argument is that courts have put prison reform on the political agenda and forced states to expend resources to correct constitutionally deficient conditions. The executive director of the American Civil Liberties Union's (ACLU) National Prison Project

6. An example is the Pennsylvania prison riot of October 1989, which occurred in a prison designed for 1,826 inmates but holding 2,607. As of September 30, 1989, the entire Pennsylvania prison system was "about 48 percent over capacity," a situation described as "typical . . . throughout the country" (Hinds 1989, 9).

7. See also Mays and Taggart (1985).

8. When asked if court orders and injunctions were effective in accomplishing the changes intended by the judge, the respondents to a California corrections administrators' survey split fairly evenly (Project 1973, 529).

has argued that prison litigation "exposes the sordid conditions in our prisons to public scrutiny" (Bronstein 1984b, 324).[9] And Justice Brennan, writing in 1981, stated that "the courts have emerged as a critical force behind efforts to ameliorate inhumane conditions." He found it "clear that judicial intervention has been responsible, not only for remedying some of the worst abuses by direct order, but also for 'forcing' the legislative branch of government to reevaluate correction policies and to appropriate funds for upgrading penal systems" (*Rhodes* v. *Chapman* 1981, 359).

Scholars who have closely examined the link between judicial action and prison construction are less sanguine (Finn 1984; Hopper 1985; Peirce 1987). Even ACLU prison litigator Bronstein has noted that "most prison construction is not in response to law suits" but rather "in response to a real need, or at least a perceived need" (Bronstein 1984a, 346). Similarly, studies of the effect of judicial action on expenditures have also found mixed results (Harriman and Straussman 1983; Taggart 1989). A recent study found that "judicial intervention does not ensure a budgetary response" and concluded that "spending is shaped in large measure by forces much more compelling and forceful than a single discrete event such as a court order" (Taggart 1989, 267, 268; cf. Feeley 1989).

Finally, there is the issue of prison violence. Although court-ordered reform is aimed in general at improving the treatment of prisoners, and specifically at reducing arbitrary use of force, there is some evidence suggesting that such reform leads to an increase in prison violence, at least in the short run.[10] Additional factors such as "changes in society" (Project 1973, 494), growing prison populations, and younger, less tractable inmates, have had an effect (Brakel 1986, 6). But overall, as a former Texas prison guard put it, "while prisoners in many institutions now have enhanced civil rights . . . they live in a lawless society at the mercy of aggressive inmates and cliques" (Marquart and Crouch 1985, 584). And by 1986, Brakel concluded that the "contemporary wisdom in corrections is that despite more than a decade of close scrutiny and mandated reforms, many prisons are less safe than they were in the pre-reform days" (Brakel 1986, 6).

In sum, then, it appears that change has been uneven. Many of the worst conditions have been improved to at least minimal standards, but problems still abound. The task that remains is to explain why the change has been so uneven—why there was some change, but only some.

Explaining Judicial Outcomes: Constraints and Conditions

For change to occur as a result of litigation, reformers must overcome the three constraints and then have present at least one of the four conditions.

9. See also Yarbrough (1984, 277).
10. Alpert, Crouch, and Huff (1984, 299); Chilton (1989, 16); Marquart and Crouch (1985, 575, 580); Mays and Taggart (1985, 41–42).

With prison reform, courts overcame only one of the constraints entirely. In individual cases, other constraints were overcome. When this occurred, and when one of the conditions was present, meaningful change occurred. Failure to successfully overcome the constraints, or the lack of at least one of the conditions, meant that court-ordered change was frustrated.

Reformers were able to overcome the problem of lack of precedent. As the brief case discussion indicated, by the early 1970s the Court had essentially opened the court-house doors to prisoner suits. Much of the success here was based on the civil rights litigation of the 1950s and 1960s as well as the reform of criminal procedure initiated by the Warren Court. Once attention was drawn to prison conditions, court action followed.

Political and Social Support. The second constraint on courts' ability to produce significant social reform is the need for political support. Prison reform issues are "essentially political" (Bronstein 1977, 27, 44), and prison reform is "highly dependent upon the political processes" (Resnick 1984, 348). When political leaders are willing to act, this constraint can be overcome. When they do nothing, or oppose court decisions, little change occurs. The reasons for this are relatively straightforward. First, unless prison officials are pushed by political leaders there is "little incentive" for them to "take the risks inherent in changing the current structure" (Note 1979, 1067). Without the support of political leaders, prison officials lack the resources to make many changes and risk their jobs in trying. Ameliorating conditions, improving services, hiring more guards, and building more prisons all cost money, and that money can come only from the legislature and the executive branch. Thus, overcoming the lack of political support was a trickier problem, and one that reformers have not been able to solve uniformly.

Political support for prison reform was based on several factors. In general, a prisoners' rights movement developed that was part of a larger rights movement that swept the U.S. in the 1960s. As one commentator put it, activists "linked the prisoners' cause to the plight of other powerless groups" in the "context of a 'fundamental democratization' which has transformed American society since World War II, and particularly since 1960" (Jacobs 1980, 432).[11] This "social acceptance of civil rights for a variety of 'unconventional' social groups" (Thomas, Keeler, and Harris 1986, 793) made prison reform an issue that politicians could deal with. There was a proliferation of prison support groups ranging from CURE, Citizens United for the Rehabilitation of Errants in Texas (Ekland-Olson and Martin 1988, 368–69), to nationwide, established organizations. In 1970 the American Bar Association created a Commission on Correctional Facilities and Services to advance reform which, with Ford Foundation funding, opened a full-time office in

11. As Jacobs (1980, 436) notes, by the late 1950s and early 1960s, blacks were a majority of prisoners in many Northern prisons and in some state prison systems.

Washington, D.C. (Jacobs 1980, 437–39). The National Institute of Corrections, a federal agency, "played an increasingly important role in the prisoners' rights movement" as did the American Correctional Association, the leading professional association of prison officials (Jacobs 1980, 448). Thus, prison reform moved more toward the political mainstream.

Another important factor in creating political and social support was prison violence. It is an unfortunate fact of American life that it often takes violence to bring an issue to political consciousness. The prison reform movement was unquestionably aided by a series of bloody prison riots and the coming to light of acts of prison violence (Toch 1985, 69). Those acts provided the "critical impetus" (Benton and Silberstein 1983, 122) for reform efforts. In particular, numerous writers point to the riot at New York's Attica prison in September 1971 as having a catalytic effect on the entire prisoners' rights movement.[12] In that riot, described by a state investigating commission as the "bloodiest encounter between Americans since the Civil War" (quoted in Kolbert 1989, 1), forty-three people were killed. And the crucial role of riots and violence in promoting reform has been noted in Mississippi (Hopper 1985, 56), New Mexico (Mays and Taggart 1985, 38, 47), Oklahoma (Giari 1979), and Georgia (Chilton 1989, 10), to cite just a few cases.

Political support for court-ordered prison reform varies enormously. In states like New York and New Mexico, perhaps because of riots and severe overcrowding, Governors Carey, Cuomo, and Anaya have been committed to prison reform and expansion (Jacobs 1984, 216–17 n.19; Mays and Taggart 1985, 48–49). While such political support by no means ensures that reform will occur, it removes the political obstacles found in states such as Oklahoma and Alabama (Giari 1979, 451; Yarbrough 1984). In Alabama, while Lieutenant Governor George McMillen and others supported compliance with court decisions, Attorney General Charles Graddick used opposition to court-ordered reform to bolster his political image (Yarbrough 1984, 287–88, 283). And George Wallace, seldom without a colorful slogan, accused Judge Johnson of creating a "hotel atmosphere" in the state prisons. Wallace's remedy for the problem was simple: "Vote for George Wallace and give a barbed wire enema to a federal judge" (quoted in Yarbrough 1984, 287). It takes no great insight to see that successful prison reform faced major obstacles in many states.

Lack of Implementation Power. The third constraint that must be overcome is the courts' lack of implementation powers. As Bronstein points out, implementation and enforcement of prison reform decrees rests "primarily in the hands of prison officials" (Bronstein 1977, 44) who, like other professionals, do not like having their professional competence challenged. When

12. See, for example, Bronstein (1977, 32); Finn (1984, 320–21); Mullen (1985, 32); Resnick (1984, 348).

courts issue orders requiring prison reform, many administrators see them as doing just that. The problem, of course, is not only that prison officials "often continue to fight for the status quo" (Bronstein 1977, 44), but also that courts lack the tools to insure implementation. Although this is not unusual, the less visible nature of prisons as compared to other governmental agencies which have been the targets of litigation makes implementation even more problematic. Since prison access is regulated for safety reasons, information on conditions and the progress of implementation is difficult to obtain. As Jacobs points out, "even under the best of circumstances," the court "must depend upon the institution's staff for information as to whether a decree is being followed" (Jacobs 1980, 452). The staff, of course, may be uncooperative. Indeed, when California corrections administrators were asked, in a survey, if they could "comply with court orders through changes which meet the letter of the court order, but not its spirit, and thereby frustrate the intent of the court," a whopping 87 percent said yes (Project 1973, 530). As one administrator put it in a follow-up interview, "we can usually get around anything" (Project 1973, 531). Administrators simply play an indispensable role in the success of prison reform. As the assistant attorney general in charge of corrections in Washington state put it, "the key to relief will be commitment by defendants to comply with the letter and the spirit of the order" (Collins 1984, 342). The necessity of support from prison administrators, and their ability to withhold that support, makes overcoming the implementation constraint particularly problematic.[13]

There is also a related issue of staff support below the top administrative level. Since it is the staff who will actually carry out any reform decree, their attitude is vitally important. Yet the staff, operating in a potentially dangerous environment, may have little interest or incentive in reforming their procedures, especially if the reforms are perceived as lessening their authority. A New York study found that the typical corrections officer "opposes prison reform as a threat to his physical security" (New York State 1974, 17). The California correctional administrators' survey just referred to, found "many administrators" stating that the "greatest administrative challenge regarding the effect of change on the staff was having to 'sell' the staff on every new policy" (Project 1973, 502). Indeed, the survey found that "*staff morale* is the operational factor which consistently shows the greatest negative effect" of court-ordered reform (Project 1973, 575).

It makes good sense that staff may feel uneasy about change. Aside from the potential dangers under which they constantly operate, they may also fear for their jobs. Active attempts at implementation may get them into trouble with recalcitrant administrators while active refusal to implement may create similar problems with the court. This attitude can make it doubly hard for

13. For a colorful illustration of this point involving the Texas prison system, see Ekland-Olson and Martin (1988).

courts to find out what prison problems exist, how they are improving and the reasons why. This difficulty in turn limits the courts' ability to mold effective decrees (Note 1979, 1079–80). And when administrators are fighting court-ordered reform, repeated violations of court orders may enhance rather than harm an employee's career.[14] On the other hand, when there is support for the decree on top, staff may be more willing to make a good faith effort.[15]

In sum, the "transformation of the patterns of interaction necessary for prison reform cannot be achieved by decree" (Note 1979, 1073). The active support of administrators and staff is required. And without the presence of factors external to the courts, that support will not be available.

Conditions Necessary for Change

Given the difficulties of implementation that I have laid out, one may wonder why or how reform ever occurs. Clearly, without political support, neither of the first two conditions will be present. It is also clear that there is no market solution. However, there is still room for the fourth condition: administrators willing to make changes who see court decisions as providing cover or a tool for leverage with the legislature and the executive branch. When this condition is present, and the constraints have been overcome, change can occur.

Administrators and staff sometimes believe that changes can be made that will improve life for *everyone* involved in prisons. While, in general, adjudication is "unlikely to be effective because the process remains separate from and foreign to those directly affected" (Note 1979, 1073–74), when administrators and staff are willingly involved in negotiation, change can occur. In the fourteen-year-old Georgia case, for example, as time went on, "key decision makers . . . were comparatively more accepting of the remedial decrees they had to live with, because these orders were the results of their efforts" (Chilton 1989, 14). A similar story can be told of New Mexico and Alabama (Mays and Taggart, 1985; Yarbrough 1984, 282). In Texas, on the other hand, where there was little negotiation, a study concluded that "to the extent that administrators and staff perceive that changes have been imposed, such changes will be resisted and morale among staff will be lowered" (Ekland-Olson and Martin 1988, 378). When prison officials are willing to reform, and take part in the remedial process, reform is more likely.

Much of the argument is highlighted by litigation involving the infamous Parchman Prison in Mississippi. Examining that litigation, one study suggested that "perhaps in no other state has litigation been as fundamentally involved in changing prison conditions." However, the study also identified factors essential to overcoming the constraints and pointed to the conditions

14. For an example from Texas, see Ekland-Olson and Martin (1988, 374).
15. For an argument that this is what happened in New Mexico, see Mays and Taggart (1985, 50).

necessary for change. Prison violence, the result of two inmate guards murdering another prisoner, led to a legislative investigation of prison conditions and the issuance of a report. A "floodtide of prisoners," identified as the "biggest factor operating in corrections in the state," kept the issue in the political spotlight. Within the prison system, much change had been made prior to the filing of the suit. The decline in the profitability of farming made it unattractive for the prison to continue it, and the cruel and exploitative regime that it had fostered was replaced. In the early and mid-1960s, whipping had been stopped and vocational education programs started. By the late 1960s additional education programs were added, including an alcohol and drug rehabilitation center, and a pre-release center staffed with counselors. "In short, Parchman had taken long strides in the changing treatment of inmates by the time the court interceded." Court intervention, then, did not institute change but rather "broadened the scope of the trend" (Hopper 1985, 54, 56–57, 61, 62).

Reform is also more likely where it is seen as involving either a minor issue or as entailing "good correctional policy." [16] This argument is nicely summed up by the Indiana attorney general's comparison of the state's reaction to two cases. In the first, "the federal judge issued a fairly narrow decree dealing with medical care and overcrowding. The state felt that he was right—they were going to comply with it as best they could." However, in the second case, dealing with a reformatory, the judge "issued a very detailed decree telling them how many medical technicians they had to hire, and so on and so forth. They were going to fight this one to the end because they didn't want to be told in detail how to do every single thing in their prison" (as recollected by Bronstein 1984b, 326).

In terms of using court orders as leverage, Herman found that "court orders reducing overcrowding are welcomed by many prison administrators" because such orders give them leverage in the budgetary process (Herman 1984, 308). In other words, the courtroom defendants may actually be secret plaintiffs. The assistant attorney general in charge of corrections for Washington state has noted this too: "sometimes the client wants to lose, since sometimes losing is the only way a correctional administrator can get the money he needs to run a proper program" (Collins 1984, 342). For administrators who wish to make changes but see little hope of obtaining the necessary resources from the legislature, judges may appear as "budgetary saviors" providing the "one possibility for budgetary growth" (Harriman and Straussman 1983, 348, 349).[17] In terms of using courts as cover, administrators can

16. See, for example, Ekland-Olson and Martin (1988, 378); Mays and Taggart (1985, 44, 51); Project (1973, 520, 551).

17. See also *Rhodes* v. *Chapman* (1981, 360) where Justice Brennan noted that "even prison officials have acknowledged that judicial intervention has helped them to obtain support for needed reform."

change rules and then claim that the changes were forced on them by the court. As Jacobs puts it, "rules and practices can be liberalized and then blamed on the courts, thereby blunting criticism from rank and file guards" (Jacobs 1980, 446). For the administrator who is not opposed to at least some changes, court orders can be used as a tool.

Conclusion

Justice Brennan, concurring in a 1981 case (*Rhodes* v. *Chapman*, 359), argued that courts can play a vital role in prison reform. The evidence, however, suggests that despite the good intentions of many prison litigators and judges, courts lack important tools necessary for the successful reform of the American prison system. Justice Powell, for example, has noted that the "problems of prisons in America are complex and intractable, and, more to the point, they are not readily susceptible of resolution by decree" (*Procunier* v. *Martinez* 1974, 404–5). Former Chief Justice Warren Burger agreed, writing in 1985 that "courts are not the primary forum for effective resolution of disputes over prison conditions" (Burger 1985, 9). Clearly, Justice Brennan and proponents of the Dynamic Court view have overstated their case.

On the other hand, courts have made a difference on some issues in some places. If the constraints can be overcome, and one of the conditions is present, litigation can make a difference. The Constrained Court view, then, is also not very helpful. This leaves the conditions. And, as the analysis has shown, they do explain both why change has been uneven and when it has occurred.

Defenders of the use of litigation to improve prison conditions, even if they admit that success is uneven, often argue that there is no other choice. As litigator Turner puts it, "litigation is the clumsiest, most frustrating, costliest way of doing anything, but it's the only game in town because of the default of the other branches of government" (Turner 1984a, 347).[18] Yet there is little evidence that prison reform litigators have put as much time, energy, and resources into political and social change as into litigation. Without that change, litigation will not be effective. Reliance on courts will not bring much change.[19] The political challenge must be faced directly.[20] Litigation, as the

18. See also Comment (1977, 369).

19. Turner's litigation strategy actually recognizes that the ultimate decision must be political. Believing, along with many prison reformers, that a major problem is the excessive use of prison terms in the legal system, he "explicitly" uses litigation to lessen the use of prison terms. Through prison litigation he aims to "improve the conditions of imprisonment and thereby to make it ruinously expensive for the state to continue to incarcerate as many people as they do" (Turner 1984b, 331, 331–32). Yet, as the number of citizens incarcerated has grown enormously, and at an increasing pace, this hardly seems like a sensible strategy.

20. There may be a greater chance of successful implementation when legislatures rather than courts are involved: "Correctional employees understand the legislative process; the Department of Corrections and employee groups are both represented by spokesmen before the legislature" (Project 1973, 554 n.429).

executive director of the ACLU's National Prison Project has come to understand, "is not, of course, the real answer" (Bronstein 1984b, 324).

The Rights of Juvenile Defendants

Traditionally, juvenile justice has lacked the due process protections of "normal" adversarial proceedings. Rather than primarily attempting to ascertain guilt, juvenile courts were based on the rehabilitative notion of helping the juvenile. In *In re Gault* (1967), however, the uncontested facts questioned this noble intention. Gerald Gault, age fifteen, was charged with making a phone call to an older female neighbor of the "irritatingly offensive, adolescent, sex variety" (*In re Gault* 1967, 4). He (his parents) had received very short notice of the proceedings, was not informed of any rights he might have, was not represented by counsel, and was given no opportunity to cross-examine the woman, who was not present at the trial. As a result of the court proceedings, Gault was committed to the State Industrial School until age twenty-one. The decision was upheld throughout the state court system.

In the Supreme Court, the case was used as a vehicle to revamp the juvenile justice system. The Court noted that if Gault had been an adult the maximum sentence that could have been imposed was a $50 fine or imprisonment for not more than two months (1967, 9). "Under our Constitution," Justice Fortas wrote for the Court, "the condition of being a boy does not justify a kangaroo court" (1967, 28). Rather, the Due Process Clause of the Fourteenth Amendment required that when confinement to an institution was a possible outcome of a juvenile proceeding, "the child and his parents must be notified of the child's right to be represented by counsel retained by them, or if they are unable to afford counsel, that counsel will be appointed to represent the child" (1967, 41). In addition, the Constitution required that written notice of charges be sent with sufficient time for preparation, that the privilege against self-incrimination be allowed, and that "absent a valid confession," commitment cannot be sustained without "sworn testimony subjected to the opportunity for cross-examinations" (1967, 33, 55, 57). Entirely revamping judicial proceedings, the "revolutionary dimensions" of the decision are clear (Lefstein, Stapleton and Teitelbaum 1969, 559).

Dimensions, however, are not the same as practice. The question that needs to be answered is how juvenile court procedures changed. While proponents of the Dynamic Court view would be busy popping champagne corks in celebration of the creation of a constitutional juvenile justice system, Constrained Court view supporters would predict little change. In the middle, proponents of the constraints and conditions would suggest that change would be variable, depending on the presence of one of the four specified conditions. What do the data show?

Studies completed in the years immediately following *Gault* found, in the words of the largest study, that "failure to comply with *Gault*'s rules was widespread," resulting in "sometimes flagrant disregard of constitutional rights" (Lefstein et al. 1969, 527, 530).[21] These findings are rather dismal in terms of Court efficacy, but perhaps their time-frame was too short to measure slow but steady change. Recent studies, however, show that time has done little to alter this picture. Reviewing the survey data on the presence of counsel in 1989, Feld concluded that "less than fifty percent of juveniles adjudicated delinquent receive the assistance of counsel to which they are constitutionally entitled" (Feld 1989, 1188–89). In his own Minnesota study, Feld found "enormous county-by-county variations" in the percentage of juveniles represented by counsel, ranging from 90 percent down to 10 percent (Feld 1989, 1200). Similarly, in a six-state study based on 1984 data Feld found that "nearly twenty years after *Gault* held that juveniles are constitutionally entitled to the assistance of counsel, half of the jurisdictions in this study are still not in compliance" (Feld 1988, 416).

There is one additional finding that is so startling that it requires mention. Several studies, including both Feld's Minnesota and six-state study, have found that the presence of counsel actually results in stiffer sentences for juveniles! Holding the offense constant, Feld reported in his six-state study that "youths with lawyers receive more severe dispositions than do those without lawyers" (Feld 1988, 405).[22] The fact that *Gault* has been so unevenly implemented may be a blessing in disguise for juvenile defendants.

The finding that *Gault* has been unevenly implemented leaves both the Dynamic and the Constrained Court views with little analytic power, for each can explain only part of real-world practice. The conditions, however, offer a more powerful explanation. They point to the interests of the main participants in the juvenile justice system. In general, for them, the notion of the juvenile system as rehabilitative rather than adjudicative has remained. Thus, without outside pressure, they have done little to change.

More specifically, three of the four conditions (all but the market) are potentially applicable. However, there have not been outside actors either offering incentives for compliance or imposing costs for non-compliance. Defense lawyers, even when present, have not provided such pressure. This seems to be because they share the rehabilitative ideal of the juvenile system. Horowitz notes that "many lawyers have a marked distaste for helping juveniles to 'beat a case' " (Horowitz 1977, 188).[23] The condition that is left is the interest of the chief official or administrator, the juvenile judge.

That juvenile judges have the power to implement *Gault* is clearly shown by the large variation in its implementation. When judges are supportive of the decision, implementation occurs. Many juvenile judges, however, remain wedded to the rehabilitative ideal rather than the adversarial principle: "the

21. See also Canon and Kolson (1971); Ferster and Courtless (1972).
22. See also Feld (1988, 396; 1989, 1207–9).
23. The same point is made by Feld (1988, 395).

oft-reiterated belief of many judges [is] that the child's best interests are not served by an adversary hearing" (Horowitz 1977, 188). Even when lawyers are present, there is "frequent pressure from juvenile-court judges on lawyers to insist less on their clients' rights and more on what they regard as their welfare" (Horowitz 1977, 190). Not wishing to offend the judge, and thus harm their clients, juvenile defense lawyers might not act as aggressive defenders of their clients' constitutional rights. Indeed, an aggressive lawyer who is not attuned to this atmosphere may actually harm his or her client. It may well be that this widely held attitude explains why juveniles with counsel receive stiffer sentences than those who lack counsel and who thus do not formally fight the rehabilitative ideal.

To sum up, implementation of *Gault* has varied because the Court lacks the tools to enforce its decree and the one condition present that allows for implementation also allows for little or no change. Many juvenile court judges can and do simply ignore the decision or actively discourage juveniles from exercising their rights. Judges, too, can follow the letter but not the spirit of the law. Announcing harsher penalties when counsel is present, or pressuring counsel to act less adversarially, mitigates or vitiates the constitutional rights at stake. As Feld puts it, "organizational pressure to cooperate, judicial hostility toward adversarial litigants, role ambiguity created by the dual goals of rehabilitation and punishment, reluctance to help juveniles 'beat a case,' or an internalization of a court's treatment philosophy" all lead to a "judicial revolution" in the treatment of juvenile defendants that has yet to succeed (Feld 1988, 395). Without a change of philosophy and belief among juvenile court judges, their practice is unlikely to change. And the Court, of course, lacks the ability to bring about such change.

The Exclusionary Rule

The Exclusionary Rule deals with the Fourth Amendment's prohibition of "unreasonable searches and seizures." In 1914 the Court read the prohibition to require the use of search warrants before evidence seized could be introduced in a federal trial (*Weeks* v. *United States* 1914). In 1949, however, in *Wolf* v. *Colorado*, the Court explicitly refused to expand this exclusionary rule to state courts. There was some expansion in 1960 when the Court rejected the "silver platter doctrine" which had allowed evidence illegally seized by *state* officers into federal trials (*Elkins* v. *United States* 1960). Finally, in *Mapp* v. *Ohio*, in 1961, the prohibition was extended to state courts.[24]

The argument behind the exclusionary rule has been enunciated repeatedly by the Court. Justice Stewart, writing for the Court in *Elkins*, put it this

---

24. Federal standards for the determination of what was an unreasonable or illegal search were made mandatory on the states in *Ker* v. *California* (1963), and *Aguilar* v. *Texas* (1964).

way: "Its purpose is to deter—to compel respect for the constitutional guarantee in the only effectively available way—by removing the incentive to disregard it" (*Elkins* 1960, 217). In *Mapp*, the Court noted the "obvious futility of relegating the Fourth Amendment to the protection of other remedies" and approvingly quoted the *Elkins* language above (*Mapp* 1961, 652, 656). In a 1965 case, the Court also quoted the *Elkins* language and stated further that in "rejecting the *Wolf* doctrine as to the exclusionary rule the purpose was to deter the lawless action of the police and to effectively enforce the Fourth Amendment" (*Linkletter* v. *Walker* 1965, 633, 637).[25] And in 1971, Chief Justice Burger, although critical of the exclusionary rule, saw its "objective" as a "remedy to give meaning and teeth to the constitutional guarantees against unlawful conduct by government officials" (*Bivens* v. *Six Unknown Federal Narcotics Agents* 1971, 415). It is clear that the Court intended the exclusionary rule to deter illegal police searches.

The Effects of Mapp

Measuring the effects of *Mapp* is neither simple nor straight-forward. First and foremost, while the cessation of illegal searches and seizures is the aim of *Mapp*, it is not entirely clear what counts as evidence for success or failure. Successful implementation of the exclusionary rule is a non-event; it is the non-observable not carrying out of an illegal search (Critique 1974, 748). The best one can do is to look for proxies such as changes in the arrest rate, the use of search warrants, and the number and percentages of successful motions to suppress evidence. However, there are several problems with these proxy measures. In addition, data from only one city or at only one time, lead to the risk of incorrectly generalizing from a potentially unique occurrence. Yet, if a longer time-series is examined, the indicators can be affected by a variety of factors. Further, knowing police practice today tells us little about the exclusionary rule unless one can compare current practice to pre-rule practice. And given varying state laws at the time of *Mapp*, and the varying seriousness with which they were taken, what counts as an adequate comparison is not straight-forward.

Many of the studies that have been done suffer from these problems, including insufficient data, one-shot data, place-specific non-generalizable data, and data gathered right after the decision that may have been too early to pick up any change that did occur (Canon 1973a, 698–702). Reviewing the data, Canon concluded that they "are sparse and conclusions are not easily wrung from them" (Canon 1977, 59–60). With these warnings in mind, I examine the data.

In general, while a few studies have found some positive effects of *Mapp*

---

25. The langauge was also quoted approvingly in *Tehan* v. *Shott* (1966, 413).

(Canon 1973a, 698; Note 1968), there is a long list of studies that conclude that the exclusionary rule has not deterred illegal searches and seizures to any significant extent. A law-review note writer in 1987 reviewed the empirical literature and concluded that no research has "yet provided persuasive evidence that the rule deters unlawful searches and seizures" (Note 1987, 1017). Various members of the Supreme Court have reached the same conclusion,[26] as have numerous researchers reviewing the literature or publishing studies.[27] As Horowitz put it, "if *Mapp* has deterred police misconduct, the secret has been very well kept" (Horowitz 1977, 223).

There are a number of studies that look to motions to suppress evidence to understand the effect of *Mapp*. However, it is not at all clear that this is helpful. Spiotto argues that if the "exclusionary rule deterred police from making illegal search and seizures, one might expect the number of motions to suppress to have declined" (Spiotto 1973, 248), presumably because there would be fewer illegal searches, but one could just as easily expect an increase regardless of police behavior as *Mapp* made this motion more readily available to defense counsel. Similarly, a drop in the success rate of motions may mean that the police are making fewer illegal searches or that defense counsel are routinely filing motions. There have been a number of studies that have examined this issue. Overall, they find little evidence for the efficacy of the exclusionary rule.[28]

Arrests provide another possible measure of effectiveness. One hypothesized result of *Mapp* is a decline in the rate of arrests for search and seizure offenses. Canon gathered data from nineteen cities and compared arrest rates for narcotics, gambling, and weapons offenses for several years before and after *Mapp*. He found that a little over a third of the cities had rates declining "significantly enough to be adjudged the result of *Mapp*" while nearly two-thirds showed no such pattern. His conclusion: the exclusionary rule "works sometimes" (Canon 1977, 71, 75).

The issuance of search warrants provides another possible indicator of the effect of *Mapp*. If the exclusionary rule was working, presumably police would be more likely to apply for and be granted warrants before initiating searches. And there is some evidence that this has occurred. In Chicago, a 1987 study of the Narcotics Section found a "dramatic, centrally directed increase in warrant use" (Note 1987, 1029). Similarly, former New York City Police Commissioner Murphy noted that while prior to 1961 search warrants were seldom obtained in New York, from the summer of 1961 to 1965 nearly

26. In *Irvine* v. *California* (1954, 135, 136), Justice Jackson found the positive effect of the rule "doubtful" and stated that there was "no reliable evidence" that the rule curtailed illegal searches and seizures. In *Bivens* v. *Six Unknown Federal Narcotics Agents* (1971, 415), Chief Justice Burger found the rule "ineffective" and "hardly more than a wistful dream."

27. Burger (1964); Note (1968); Oaks (1970); Canon (1977); Horowitz (1977).

28. Canon (1973a, 689); Comment (1952, 498); Horowitz (1977, 242); Oaks (1970, 685, 690–95); Spiotto (1973, 247).

18,000 warrants were obtained (Murphy 1966, 941–42).[29] And Canon, in responses to questionnaires received from seventy-four cities, found that nearly 80 percent reported increases of at least 50 percent between 1967–68 and 1972–73 (Canon 1973a, 712).

There are two problems with accepting this as strong evidence of the efficacy of the exclusionary rule. First, over the period of the Canon study there was a large increase in narcotics use. That alone may account for much of the increase in warrant use. Indeed, when Canon asked his respondents to explain the increased use of warrants, 55 percent attributed it to the upsurge in narcotics use while only 24 percent credited judicial rulings, about the same percentage attributing the change to more police and better training. This led Canon to conclude that one "cannot comfortably attribute the increased use of search warrants entirely or even primarily to police reaction to the exclusionary rule" (Canon 1973a, 713). Second, the issuance of warrants may be so routine as to be meaningless. If judges approve warrants without any serious examination, they become a formality without substance. LaFave summarized findings from an American Bar Foundation study of courts in Kansas, Michigan, and Wisconsin this way: "judges often view their warrant-issuing function as merely perfunctory in nature. Warrants are issued by judges, often while they are engaged in trying cases or holding preliminary examinations, with little or no attention to the question of whether the complaint or affidavit meets the requirement of law. . . . Actual inquiry into the grounds for issuance of the warrant was not undertaken [by judges]" (LaFave 1965a, 412). Increases in the use of search warrants may not tell us very much about the efficacy of the exclusionary rule.

There are two bits of final evidence that need to be assessed. They deal with the variation in the rule's efficacy across different locales and the effect of the exclusionary rule in "big cases." In general, numerous studies have noted the wide variation among police departments in their adherence to the exclusionary rule.[30] "Variations exist everywhere" (Critique 1974, 762). The point these studies invariably make is that the local political and legal culture, the organization of the police, and the views of individual police officers make a huge difference. As Horowitz puts it, "the extent to which police behavior is modified by *Mapp* depends on a complex set of local conditions, including, among other things, the extent to which the police are aware of the law of search and seizure and of the exclusionary rule, the type of offense involved, the particular police unit responsible for the specific enforcement tasks, and the way in which local courts and lawyers handle search-and-seizure matters"

29. Increases in the use of warrants were also found in Detroit (from 45 in 1968 to 1,657 in 1972), in Los Angeles (from 207 in 1968 to 999 in 1972), and in St. Paul (from 55 in 1967 to 118 in 1972) (Canon 1973a, 712).

30. Canon (1973a, 689; 1977, 72); Milner (1971a, 467); Traynor (1962, 343); Wasby (1976); Weinstein (1962, 176); Wilson (1968, 83).

(Horowitz 1977, 225). In "big cases," where "conviction is important," numerous studies have noted that the "rules are more likely to be followed," especially where "the police feel avoidance of the rules would limit such prosecution" (Milner 1971a, 478).[31] The variation in police behavior, and the adherence to the exclusionary rule with big cases, suggests, of course, that the police are quite capable of following the exclusionary rule. That leads to the question of why they follow it so unevenly.

Overall, then, the evidence proffered on the efficacy of the exclusionary rule does not make the case that it has deterred illegal search and seizures in any uniform or pervasive way. Rather, there appears to be great variation, but with little in the way of strict compliance.

Explaining the Inefficacy of the Exclusionary Rule. For courts to be effective, at least one of the four conditions has to be present. The first two deal with incentives for compliance and the imposition of costs for non-compliance. The Court apparently thought that having evidence thrown out of court was a sufficient incentive, or imposed a sufficient cost, to induce compliance. For a number of reasons, however, it is largely irrelevant.

The major reason why the exclusion of evidence from trial is irrelevant is that the overwhelming majority of arrests do not eventuate in trial! In the vast majority of cases, defendants plea-bargain and plead guilty. A special report by the U.S. Department of Justice (DOJ) found that approximately eleven times as many defendants plead guilty as request trials, and that only about 5 percent of all felony arrests eventuate in trial (DOJ 1984, 2, 1).[32] It may be the case that good defense attorneys will improve the bargain by threatening to demand a trial where much or all of the evidence is illegally seized, but, as the discussion of effective counsel below will show, this is far from the typical case. The incentive for compliance that the Court built into *Mapp* is unevenly effective because trials play such a minor part in the criminal justice system.

Another reason for the lack of efficacy of the exclusionary rule is that there is a great deal of hostility to it on the part of many state-court judges. While hostility to the rule was well-documented in its early years,[33] as late as 1973 Canon found a "considerable degree of variation in the courts' interpretative responses to *Mapp*" (Canon 1973b, 116), and a great deal of opposition (Canon 1974, 61–76; 1973a, 718 n.108). And, of course, such high-court opposition is not lost on "trial judges and lawyers" who "are quite likely to

31. See also Comment (1952, 498); Skolnick (1975, 224).
32. On the federal level, for the year ending June 30, 1987, over 71 percent of criminal defendants pleaded guilty, about seven and one-half times as many as requested jury trials (DOJ 1989a, 540).
33. Canon (1973a, 694–96); Horowitz (1977, 243); Manwaring (1968, 25); Murphy (1966, 941–42); Specter (1962, 4, 40–42); *State* v. *Louden* (1963, 71).

be aware of the attitudes of their immediate hierarchical superiors" (Canon 1974, 77).

In addition, the police may not care if arrests end in conviction. That is, they may have other goals in mind. Writing in 1968, Chief Justice Warren recognized this point: "Regardless of how effective the rule may be where obtaining convictions is an important objective of the police, it is powerless to deter invasions of constitutionally guaranteed rights where the police either have no interest in prosecution or are willing to forgo successful prosecution in the interest of serving some other goal" (*Terry* v. *Ohio* 1968, 14). Studies of police behavior have highlighted a number of other goals. One is harassment. As one study put it, "where the police believe that a policy of harassment is an effective means of law enforcement, the exclusionary rule will not deter their use of unlawful methods" (Comment 1952, 498). Another goal is confiscation of contraband. Police may "sometimes seize narcotics," for example, "even though they know that the arrests may be thrown out of court, because they are eager to remove the drugs from circulation" (Tybor and Eissman 1986, 13). Still another goal may be the maintenance of law and order and the control of behavior considered anti-social (Horowitz 1977, 223; Oaks 1970, 723). Finally, the police may feel the need to act aggressively to lessen crime regardless of the exclusionary rule where "crime is rampant and the community clamors for strict enforcement" (Note 1968, 103–4). Thus, while the Court may have thought that it had provided incentives for compliance, it did not understand the goals of the police. As the authors of the 1968 Note put it, "some way to encourage the police to make such changes [i.e., observe the exclusionary rule] should be found" (Note 1968, 104).

The organization of the police is a separate factor that mitigates against the efficacy of the exclusionary rule. Police officers have a large degree of discretion in their work. Unlike practically any other organization, police departments have the "special property" that "discretion increases as one moves *down* the hierarchy" (Wilson 1968, 7).[34] This means that for the exclusionary rule to be routinely effective, either police officers must internalize the rule or the command structure must institute incentives for compliance or penalties for noncompliance. Studies suggest that neither has happened to any great extent, nor is likely to soon.

There is no doubt that the police have an exceedingly difficult and dangerous job. Their work experience tends to isolate them from the rest of the community. This leads to a "special ethos: defensiveness, a sense of not being supported by the community, and a distrust of outsiders" (Wilson 1968, 48–49; Milner 1971a, 485). One result is the development of a pragmatic view of crime and the law. As Skolnick puts it, the "policeman, in short, is

34. Others who stress police discretion as a hindrance to the exclusionary rule include Canon (1974, 52); Milner (1971a, 474, 475); Note (1968, 102); Skolnick (1975, iii).

primarily interested in *factual* guilt. Indeed, the idea of *legal* guilt leaves him cold and hostile." If actual guilt is the higher value, than the procedural niceties of criminal procedure will be held in lower esteem. Under the logic of this view, "the demands of apprehension require violation of procedural rules in the name of the 'higher' justification of reducing criminality" (Skolnick 1975, 203, 228).

Supreme Court decisions, then, that impose procedural rules on the police are often seen as aiding criminals and making police work more difficult. Numerous officers and prosecutors echoed this position in the years after *Mapp*. Chicago Police Superintendent Wilson put it this way: "If we followed some of our court decisions literally, the public would be demanding my removal as Superintendent of Police and—I might add—with justification." Chief Parker of Los Angeles noted that "it is anticipated that the police will ignore these legal limitations when the immediate public welfare appears to demand police lawlessness." And Chief Schrotel of Cincinnati put it clearly: "either he [the police officer] abides by the prescribed rules and renders *ineffective* service, or he *violates* or *circumvents* the rules and performs the service *required* of him" (quotes from LaFave 1965a, 444). These views are traceable to the logic of the police officer's position. As Prosecutor Specter summed it up, "[i]t is more important to convict the guilty than to prevent the unconstitutional search and seizure of the innocent which is only unpleasant" (Specter 1962, 41).

The above discussion suggests that given the view of police officers and their commanders, any pressure stemming from *Mapp* would most likely be to circumvent rather than to implement the exclusionary rule. This can be seen in the way many police departments responded to the decision. On the whole, police organizations did not take the steps necessary to increase the likelihood that the exclusionary rule would be implemented and illegal searches and seizures ended.

In particular, studies have revealed that police training remains poor and that there are few organized channels through which police officers are kept informed of the current requirements of the law.[35] Also, police organizations have not created incentives for observing the exclusionary rule, or imposed costs for violating it. At a minimum, police officers need to know when evidence they seize is excluded from trial and why. Also, there must be consequences attached to having evidence thrown out of court. Numerous studies have shown that there are seldom organizational routines for communicating such information, or for evaluating the actions of the police.[36] And even if there is feedback, there appear to be few departments that impose sanctions

35. Burger (1964, 1, 11); LaFave (1965b, 595); Wasby (1973, 1095; 1976, 3, 220).
36. Burger (1964, 11); LaFave (1965a, 396, 402, 403, 415); Note (1968, 101); Spiotto (1973, 276).

for illegally seizing evidence. Nearly a decade after *Mapp*, Oaks reported that "diligent inquiry has failed to reveal a single law enforcement agency where individual sanctions are tied to an application of the exclusionary rule" (Oaks 1970, 710). Thus, police officers will neither be able to easily learn how to change their behavior to conform to the law, nor will they be under any pressure to do so. Wasby sums up the situation well: "If . . . there are no sanctions, or only limited ones, for not knowing the law . . . the police officer is likely to find no reward in following Court-ordered procedure and no punishment for failing to do so; in fact, he may be complimented for trying his hardest *despite* the barriers the Court has established" (Wasby 1973, 1107).

Given the worldview of the police, one might expect that police perjury would not be uncommon. It may make no sense in a police officer's worldview to let a defendant go who was caught red-handed breaking the law, merely because the evidence was not seized in accord with proper procedure. While evidence of such behavior is hard to come by, it does point towards police perjury (Note 1968, 94; Note 1987, 1018, 1051).[37]

For the bulk of this discussion I have focused on the presence of the first two conditions for implementation. The analysis has shown that on the whole there have not been incentives for compliance or costs for non-compliance. However, if police administrators are willing to use court decisions as leverage, to professionalize their departments, for example (Condition IV), there is evidence that they can shape incentives to increase the likelihood of compliance. In other words, leadership in police departments can make a difference. Where incentives or penalties are imposed from within the police organization, police respond. A 1987 examination of the Narcotics Section of the Chicago Police Department found that the department had instituted an "officer rating system" under which having evidence suppressed negatively affected job assignments and promotions. In addition, when evidence is suppressed, the officer who made the seizure is required to file a form explaining why and to take part in an internal review session. The result is that "virtually all of the officers in the Narcotics Section knew when evidence was suppressed and understood why" (Note 1987, 1027–29, 1035–36). Where administrators are willing to use court decisions to further other goals, change has occurred.

In sum, the rights "revolution" brought about by *Mapp* never fully occurred. Lacking the uniform presence of one of the four conditions necessary for change, the Court was only partially effective in producing positive change. When one of the conditions happened to be present, change could

37. There is also documented evidence of illegal and violent police raids. An eight-week investigation by the *New York Times* in 1973 found that "innocent Americans around the country have been subjected to dozens of mistaken, violent and often illegal police raids." These raids, the investigation discovered, were "not isolated incidents" (Malcolm 1973, 1, 22).

and sometimes did occur. But these conditions were not present in any uniform or general way, and certainly their presence was entirely independent of the Court.

Miranda *and* Escobedo—*and Sixth Amendment Rights*

The Court has also extended the Fifth Amendment guarantee against self-incrimination by holding that the police are required to inform custodial suspects of their constitutional rights. In *Escobedo* v. *Illinois* (1964), a Sixth Amendment assistance of counsel case, the Court invalidated the use of an incriminating statement obtained from a suspect in police custody who had requested but been denied an opportunity to consult with his lawyer and who had not been warned by the police of his constitutional right to remain silent and to not answer police questions. Then, in 1966, in *Miranda* v. *Arizona*, the Court heightened the requirements the police were constitutionally required to meet for a suspect's statements to be admissible in court. In language that television police shows made familiar,[38] the Court held that "[p]rior to any questioning, the person must be warned that he has a right to remain silent, that any statement he does make may be used as evidence against him, and that he has a right to the presence of an attorney, either retained or appointed." The Court also held that once the suspect requests an attorney all questioning has to stop, and that the police may not question suspects who indicate they do not wish to talk, even if they have already answered some questions or made some statements (*Miranda* 1966, 444–45). *Miranda* not only incorporated both Fifth and Sixth Amendment protections, but also required the police to inform those in custody of these rights.

There were two major concerns that animated the Court in these cases. The first was police brutality. Chief Justice Warren, writing for the Court, cited examples of police brutality to obtain confessions. Although he surmised that they are "undoubtedly the exception now," he did find police brutality to obtain confessions "sufficiently widespread to be the object of concern" (*Miranda* 1966, 446 n.7, 447). The second, and more major issue, was coercion which, the Court noted, could be "mental as well as physical" (*Miranda* 1966, 448). Quoting and discussing police interrogation manuals (*Miranda* 1966, 448–55), the Court found that "custodial interrogation exacts a heavy toll on individual liberty and trades on the weakness of individuals." Without knowledge of one's rights, the "compulsion inherent in custodial surroundings" means that a suspect "cannot be otherwise than under compulsion to speak" (*Miranda* 1966, 455, 461). To overcome this compulsion, the "accused must be adequately and effectively apprised of his rights." Referring particularly to the right of indigents to have counsel pres-

---

38. As I recall from my childhood, the police on "Dragnet" scrupulously followed *Miranda* requirements.

ent, but applicable more generally to the holding, the Court warned that police warnings "would be hollow if not couched in terms that would convey . . . the knowledge" necessary for suspects to intelligently exercise their rights (*Miranda* 1966, 467, 473). Thus, *Miranda* attempted to remove much of the coercion inherent in police interrogations.

If the police and many politicians were upset by *Mapp*, it was only a warm-up for the reaction to *Escobedo* and *Miranda*. The fear was that the Court's orders would be implemented and would result, in the words of Justice White's *Miranda* dissent, in the inability to convict criminals: "In some unknown number of cases the Court's rule will return a killer, a rapist or other criminal to the streets" (*Miranda* 1966, 542).[39] In particular, along with Justice Harlan, many commentators "expressed little doubt that the Court's new code would markedly decrease the number of confessions" (*Miranda* 1966, 516).[40]

The Findings

Given these predictions and dire warnings, examining the evidence seems the natural thing to do. However, for some critics, like Professor Fred Inbau, author of a police interrogation manual that the Court cited in *Miranda* for its use of psychological coercion, evidence is unnecessary. Proudly proclaiming himself oblivious to empirical testing of ideological beliefs, Inbau argued that "there are some things we can and should accept without demanding statistical proof, and the necessity for police interrogation is one of them" (Inbau 1966, 269). I take a different approach, for it is only the most ideological proponents of the Dynamic Court view who would be so confident that the Court's orders would be strictly followed.

There is a fairly large and fascinating empirical literature on the effect of *Miranda*. In general, the literature concludes that, despite the warnings of critics, *Miranda* has had "little impact" (Schulhofer 1987, 460). While warnings appear to be given routinely, and counsel is provided, "the widely shared perception [is] that *Miranda*'s effect on law enforcement has been negligible" (White 1986, 20).[41] *Miranda*, Schulhofer concludes, has not delivered "even a fraction of what it seems to promise" (Schulhofer 1981, 892).

For *Miranda* to be effective at all, the police must give suspects the warn-

39. See, for example, Clines (1964, 23); Graham (1966b, 9); Justice Harlan (*Miranda* 1966, 504, 517); "Interrogations" (1967, 1610); "Koota" (1966, 1); Milner (1971b, 197); Zion (1965, 39).

40. See also Wehrwein (1966b, 13); Justice White (*Miranda* 1966, 542). The belief these critics shared was that confessions were crucial in obtaining convictions ("The Law" 1966, 52; Ervin 1967, 128; Robertson 1966, 54).

41. See also Faculty Note (1967, 300); Gibbons and Casey (1987, 41); "Interrogations" (1967); Leiken (1970); Milner (1971b); Neubauer (1974); Seeburger and Wettick (1967); Witt (1973); Younger (1966; 1967).

ings. Early studies found that the police were doing a haphazard job but improving over time.[42] In the years following *Miranda* police started carrying cards containing the rights and many departments had suspects sign forms indicating that they had been informed of them. The literature suggests that informing suspects of their rights is now routinely done. Thus, a crucial first step in *Miranda*'s implementation was accomplished.

A second uniform finding is that despite being informed of their rights to silence and to counsel, and that statements they make can be used against them in court, suspects continue to make statements to police and to confess. In general, Pollack has found that "many, if not most suspects . . . frequently make statements to the police even against the advice of their attorneys" (Pollack 1989, 26–27). Numerous studies have repeatedly found that suspects continued to make statements, confessions, and plead guilty at similar rates to the pre-*Miranda* days.[43] This does not necessarily mean that *Miranda* has been ineffective. It is entirely possible that by informing suspects of their rights, the police have removed the unconstitutional coercion and that suspects have acted in intelligent and knowing ways. However, the evidence strongly suggests that this is not the case. The discussion below explains why.

Finally, there is the question of police brutality. Did *Miranda* lessen police brutality as the Court hoped? Evidence is hard to come by but what evidence there is suggests that any reductions that have been achieved in police brutality are independent of the Court and started before *Miranda*. As Caplan points out, "at the time *Miranda* was argued, the worst practices of the 1940's and 1950's . . . were disappearing" (Caplan 1985, 1458). That process, however, has taken a long time. Interviews revealed that until the early 1970s Chicago narcotics police beat suspects with phone books or rubber hoses, or handcuffed them and locked them up for hours or days, until they confessed (Note 1987, 1029 n.63). And police brutality still can be found. As White discovered, "a perusal of the cases . . . indicates that if the 'worst practices' have disappeared, some pretty bad ones are still taking place" (White 1986, 13, 13–14n.73). Again the evidence does not support the argument that *Miranda* has achieved the Court's stated goals.

Explaining Miranda's *Impact.* There are a number of reasons why *Miranda* has not achieved the Court's stated goals even though the police have increasingly given suspects the warnings. They essentially revolve around the imbalance of power between police officer and suspect, and the suspect's lack

42. "Interrogations" (1967, 1536, 1550); Medalie, Zeitz, and Alexander (1968, 1362, 1363).
43. See, for example, Faculty Note (1967); Graham (1966a); Green (1966); "Interrogations" (1967); Leiken (1970); Medalie et al. (1968); Neubauer (1974); "No Shackles" (1966); Seeburger and Wettick (1967); Souris (1966); Witt (1973); Younger (1966).

of usable information.[44] First, there is evidence that while the police may give the warnings, they do so in a way calculated to diminish or disparage their impact. One study found that the typical interrogator "commonly defused the advice by implying that the suspect had better not exercise his rights, or by delivering his statements in a formalized, bureaucratic tone to indicate that his remarks were simply a routine, meaningless legalism" ("Interrogations" 1967, 1552).[45] Similarly, a 1970 study of fifty suspects in Denver found that although the police were in "strict compliance" with *Miranda*'s formal requirements (they read the suspects their rights), they also applied "promises, threats, and the other psychological tactics and strategies which the Court was attempting to neutralize" (Leiken 1970, 47, 46). The mere recitation of the warnings may not do very much to overcome the "compulsion" that *Miranda* found unconstitutional.

There is also evidence that suspects feel under a social or moral obligation to talk, or that they see strategic gain in talking. As the authors of one study put it, "even when we explained the rights to silence and counsel to a group of very bright and extremely willful people, they felt pressed to answer at least some of the questions put to them by the agents" (Faculty Note 1967, 318). One of the reasons they did so, the authors found, was that "interrogation is a social situation, and suspects respond according to the normal rules of social interaction in such situations" (Faculty Note 1967, 315). Other studies have also noted the tendency of well-educated suspects to be cooperative, even to their own detriment (Leiken 1970, 20). In addition, there is the old-fashioned notion of conscience (Younger 1966, 34). Further, suspects may believe that the police have enough evidence to convict them and that their best chance for leniency in what charges are brought and in sentencing is to confess. As one study found, "almost every person arrested . . . had committed the crime for which he was arrested and knew that the police had evidence of this" ("Interrogations" 1967, 1572).

There is an assumption that underlies the above discussion that may be shared by the reader as well. It is that criminal suspects understand the mean-

44. A different explanation of the failure of *Miranda* to achieve the Court's stated goals is that the Court did not intend to drastically alter the police-suspect relationship. For example, Schulhofer suggests that "the Court could have done much better by insisting on the presence of an attorney during interrogation." And, "several" ACLU lawyers involved in the case "objected that *Miranda* had not gone far enough, because it did not mandate the presence of counsel" (Schulhofer 1981, 881, 879 n.65). However, if Supreme Court decisions are the law of the land, then looking to the stated goals of decisions provides a fair measure of substantive intent. In a government of laws and not people, as the Dynamic Court view maintains, court decisions are to be implemented. The discussion of *Miranda* in the text has shown that the Court's stated goals were clear. And, as the following discussion suggests, a "better" solution would still face the barrier of the constraints and the need for the presence of one of the conditions.

45. A 1967 FBI supplement for police on *Miranda* put the "emphasis . . . clearly on ways to maintain pre-*Miranda* procedures and to avoid advising the person of his rights" (Milner 1971a, 483).

ing and importance of their rights as read to them by the police and are in a position to make intelligent use of them. There is evidence that suggests that this assumption is wrong. Even with well-educated political protesters, at a time when there was "widespread publicity" given to the key Supreme Court decisions, one study found that "few of the suspects knew their rights in even the grossest outline" and "did not appreciate the reasons for remaining silent" (Faculty Note 1967, 306, 305–6, 313). And if this is the case with a well-educated, middle-class set of suspects, it may be naive to expect more of the typical criminal defendant who is neither well-educated nor middle-class.

A number of empirical studies highlight how few criminal defendants know or understand their rights and how incapable they are of making intelligent use of them. In terms of knowledge, a study conducted in 1980 found that "a significant portion of adults do not understand their rights when read the *Miranda* warnings" (Grisso 1980, 1165 n.114). Responses to a questionnaire showed that nearly a quarter of the adults had no understanding of at least one of the *Miranda* rights and fewer than half completely understood all of them (Grisso 1980, 1152). Other studies have reported similar, if less precise, findings.[46] Most surprisingly, Grisso found little difference in the use of *Miranda* rights by those arrested several times as compared to people never arrested. In comparing a group of ex-offenders to a group of non-offenders, Grisso found that "ex-offenders' increased exposure to the legal system does not improve their understanding of their *Miranda* rights" (Grisso 1980, 1156).[47] Suspects' knowledge of their rights is low. Thus, they can hardly be expected to use them.

It is also the case the suspects have a great deal of incorrect "information." For example, in the Denver study 60 percent of the suspects believed that "under no circumstances" could their signatures on a waiver form have any legal effect. As the police perhaps intended, they saw the form as "a merely mechanical device—a formality" (Leiken 1970, 33). In 1980, 42.9 percent of a sample of *ex-offenders* believed that they would have to explain their criminal involvement to a judge if questioned in court (Grisso 1980, 1159).

There is one additional factor that needs to be stressed: the opposition of the police to *Miranda* and the incentives of police departments. *Miranda* was "heinous" to the police (Leiken 1970, 45). Thus, interrogators are likely to avoid strict compliance. In addition, they may feel that strict compliance threatens their careers. That is, one of the ways in which police are often evaluated is through the "clearance" rate, the number of unsolved crimes that are finally solved. One of the major ways this occurs is through confessions. Because the "police see the decision as hurting the clearance rate . . . they

46. Faculty Note (1967, 310); "Interrogations" (1967, 1572); Leiken (1970, 16–17, 29, 34); Medalie et al. (1968, 1367); Milner (1971b, 227); Zion (1966, 23).

47. An earlier study found suspects previously convicted of felonies less likely to confess than others. However, 40 percent of them did confess (Neubauer 1974, 107). And Leiken's 1970 study found only a "slightly better performance" by repeat offenders (Leiken 1970, 20–21).

feel *Miranda* threatens their professional standing" ("Interrogations" 1967, 1612). When this is coupled with a hostile attitude on the part of judges and prosecutors, there will be no pressure for compliance ("Koota" 1966, 23; Wasby 1973, 1106; Wehrwein 1966a, 35). Overall, there were few pressures to implement *Miranda*.

Miranda has not done much to rectify the imbalance between interrogators and suspects because the police are in a much more powerful situation:

> The suspect arrested and brought downtown for questioning is in a crisis-laden situation. The stakes are high for him—often his freedom for a few or many years—and his prospects hinge on decisions that must be quickly made: to cooperate and hope for leniency, to try to talk his way out, to stand adamantly on his rights. . . . Warnings help—or at least they might if the police did not geld them of meaning by their tone and manner. . . . ("Interrogations" 1967, 1613–14)

The evidence strongly suggests that the confession rate did not change because the *Miranda* warnings were unable to alter this imbalance. Contrary to the Court's stated goals, those accused are not "adequately and effectively" apprised of their rights.

Given this, the reader may wonder why *Miranda* warnings are given at all. Were any of the conditions necessary for implementation met? There are several answers to this. First and foremost, warnings are given because, as the evidence has shown, they don't affect police work to any large extent. Second, the police found very quickly that they could meet the letter of the law but not its spirit. They could give the warnings in such a way that suspects were unlikely to make use of them. Thus, they could maintain their opposition to them and follow the letter of the law simultaneously. Third, the fourth condition was applicable. Police administrators who wanted to professionalize their departments could use *Miranda* as a tool to do so. Pittsburgh's chief of police, for example, "welcomed *Miranda* because it provided an opportunity to professionalize the police" (quoted in Schulhofer 1987, 458n.59). Finally, it turns out that by giving the warnings and obtaining signed waiver forms, police can insulate themselves from challenges of involuntary confessions. As Leiken found, "one of the latent functions of *Miranda* . . . appears to be to aid the police in overcoming their evidentiary burden with respect to proving the suspect's knowledge and waiver of his constitutional rights" (Leiken 1970, 48).

In the end, then, *Miranda* has failed to end the coercion of interrogation that the Court found unconstitutional. With none of the four conditions present more than randomly, there was little substantive change.

The Right to Counsel

The Court has also dealt with the constitutional guarantee of the right to counsel, based on the Sixth Amendment's guarantee that "[i]n all criminal prosecutions, the accused shall enjoy the right . . . to have the Assistance of counsel for his defence." In *Powell* v. *Alabama* (1932), the "Scottsboro Boys" case, this was interpreted to require court-appointed counsel in capital cases where the defendant is unable to employ counsel and incapable of making his own defence. This right was expanded in 1938 to require the appointment of counsel (unless waived) for indigent defendants in federal courts (*Johnson* v. *Zerbst*). Then, in 1963, in *Gideon* v. *Wainright*, a unanimous Court held that indigent criminal defendants in non-capital cases must be provided with the assistance of counsel. The Court found it an "obvious truth" that the right to counsel was "fundamental and essential to fair trials" (*Gideon* 1963, 344). Finally, in 1972, the Court strengthened *Gideon* in holding that "no person may be imprisoned for any offense . . . unless he was represented by counsel at his trial" (*Argersinger* v. *Hamlin* 1972, 37).[48]

Representation by counsel is a necessary but not a sufficient condition for fulfilling the constitutional mandate. "It has long been recognized," the Court has noted, "that the right to counsel is the right to the effective assistance of counsel" (*McMann* v. *Richardson* 1970, 771 n.14).[49] Mere representation is insufficient, for "if the process loses its character as a confrontation between adversaries, the constitutional guarantee is violated." Thus, along with the Constitution's right to counsel is the "Constitution's guarantee of the effective assistance of counsel" (*United States* v. *Cronic* 1984, 656–57, 655).

The Results

Over the years since *Gideon* there has been a tremendous growth in the number of public defender organizations and lawyers working to defend the indigent. In 1961 there were public defender programs in only 3 percent of U.S. counties; by 1985 there were approximately 1,200 public defender offices nationwide (Lefstein 1986, 8). It is now common practice in American courts to make such counsel available. The practice, however, is not uniform. For example, Lefstein reports that "since 1973 studies have consistently shown that courts do not adequately extend the right to counsel in misdemeanor cases" where incarceration is the outcome, in violation of *Argersinger* (Lefstein 1986, 7). Examining over 1,600 criminal court cases in the late 1970s, Feeley discovered that only half of the defendants were represented by counsel and that "roughly 20 percent of those charged with felonies, and one-third of those receiving jail sentences, were not represented by counsel." Perhaps this is not surprising given the fact that out of the 1,600+ cases, not one defendant requested a trial (Feeley 1979, 9, 9–10). These points being made, it remains clear that access to appointed counsel has grown tremendously.

48. See also *Scott* v. *Illinois* (1979), holding that counsel is required only where the defendant is sentenced to prison.

49. See also *United States* v. *Cronic* (1984, 653–57).

Does this mean that the Court has finally succeeded in substantially reforming criminal rights? Unfortunately, it appears not, because numerous commentators have noted that the mere physical presence of counsel is far from the substantive promise of the effective assistance of counsel. Speaking in 1986, Benjamin Lerner, the president of the National Legal Aid and Defender Association, noted that "as a general rule, the promise of *Powell, Gideon*, and *Argersinger*, with regard to effective assistance of counsel, has not been fulfilled, particularly as concerns indigent criminal defendants" (Lerner 1986b, 101). The editors of a 1986 colloquium concurred, writing that "despite the broadening of the right to legal assistance . . . it is apparent to most observers . . . that we are still far from the *Powell* Court's vision of vigorous, effective representation for indigent criminal defendants" (Preface 1986, 1). In addition, Lefstein pointed out that "anyone who surveys the current delivery of criminal defense services for the poor has to be overwhelmed by the impediments that stand in the way of providing effective legal assistance" (Lefstein 1986, 6). These were noted by Goodpaster, who listed four "generic deficiencies" of court-appointed lawyers in providing effective assistance of counsel: the "failure to . . . develop an effective working relationship with the client . . . to conduct an adequate pre-trial investigation . . . to develop an 'adversarial' or 'fighting' attitude toward the prosecution and its case . . . [and] lack of knowledge or skill" (Goodpaster 1986, 90–91). In general, while the availability of counsel has increased greatly, the legal revolution does not seem to have greatly increased the availability of the *effective* assistance of counsel.

This point is powerfully made in a nearly 400-page 1987 study of criminal defense of the poor in New York City. The very first sentence of the text sets the tone, stating that indigent criminal defendants in New York City "receive ineffective assistance from lawyers who . . . fail to provide competent adversarial representation" (McConville and Mirsky 1987, 582). Overall, the study found that "lawyers for the poor . . . infrequently test the state's case and insufficiently protect defendants' rights" (McConville and Mirsky 1987, 901). In addition, court-appointed lawyers were "usually ignorant of the facts," made pre-trial motions and participated in hearings "only infrequently," did not engage in forms of in-court practice other than seeking adjournments and entering guilty pleas, and "did not develop meaningful lawyer-client relationships, undertake independent factual or legal investigations, engage investigators or experts, or consult with the defendant's family or friends" (McConville and Mirsky 1987, 773, 774). The Court's representation revolution has not achieved the effective assistance of counsel in the nation's largest city.

The Power of the Constraints and the Lack of Conditions Necessary for Change. In examining actual practice to understand why the effective assistance of counsel remains unachieved, the inability of the courts to overcome two of the constraints, and the absence of any of the four conditions, is striking. Although the first constraint was overcome through the long development of a line of cases from *Powell* (1932) on, the other two constraints remained less tractable.

In terms of implementation (the third constraint), as was discussed, the overwhelming majority of arrests do not eventuate in trial. In New York City, of the approximately 259,000 cases in criminal court in 1984, only 0.6 percent involved trials (McConville and Mirsky 1987, 584).[50] While lawyers can certainly help defendants plea-bargain, the major thrust of the Court's decisions was aimed at a very rare event, a criminal trial. Thus, on one level, the relevance of the Court's decisions to actual practice is not clear. But even in terms of plea bargaining, the evidence suggests that appointed counsel are too ill-informed and under-motivated to provide effective assistance.

One reason for this is that lawyers providing counsel to indigent criminal defendants are heavily overworked. Their caseloads are "very high," often unmanageable (Guggenheim 1986, 14). They simply can't be expected to provide even the basic rudiments of effective representation without adequate time to prepare. The U.S. Court of Appeals for the Ninth Circuit took note of this overload in one case where the public defender resigned because she felt that "she was 'actually doing the defendants more harm by just presenting a live body than if they had no representation at all' " (*Cooper* v. *Fitzharris* 1977, 1163 n.1). Summarizing the situation in 1990, Worthington concluded that "overload has resulted in a mockery of 6th Admendment rights to counsel and a fair trial . . . " (Worthington 1990, 1).

Another implementation problem is that the lower federal courts have not taken the Supreme Court's stated definition of the effective assistance of counsel seriously. Reviewing the case law in 1986, Schulhofer concluded that "as the law stands, any investigation, anything more than no investigation at all, is likely to qualify as reasonable" (Schulhofer 1986, 138).[51] As previous chapters have demonstrated, lower-court failure to fully implement Supreme Court decisions is a problem inherent in the legal bureaucracy.

The second constraint points to the courts' need of political support and the corresponding constraint on judicial independence. Insufficient funding is a prime example. There seems to be near-consensus that a "primary reason . . . for the failure to fulfill this promise [of effective assistance of counsel] is a substantial lack of funding." The result is "gross inadequacies" in criminal defense spending, creating "systems throughout the country where effective assistance of counsel is not possible" (Lerner 1986a, 107). Inadequate funds prevent the hiring of a sufficient number of personnel, and the delivery of services to them, to allow for effective assistance of counsel. In addition, "lawyers often resist appointment [to defend indigent criminal defendants] because of inadequate compensation" (Lefstein 1986, 7). Courts, as the second constraint points out, are essentially powerless to successfully order increased funding on a national scale.

There are also a set of factors mitigating against the provision of effective assistance of counsel that can fit under the heading of "to get along you have to go along." From the perspective of the suspect, for example, it may make sense not to ask for counsel because the suspect "does not know if his request for counsel will annoy the police, increasing his chances of prosecution" (Elsen and Rosett 1967, 658). For the providers of criminal defense services, politically it makes more sense to "ally themselves with courts, prosecutors, local government, and the organized bar rather than with indigent defendants" (McConville and Mirsky 1987, 582–83). After all, the former carry political weight with legislatures and the public at large. Criminal defense attorneys may not wish to zealously press every potential claim because they work with "the same cast of characters over an extended period of time" and may need their help from time to time (Guggenheim 1986, 14). Being seen as unreasonable and unyielding may hurt their ability to negotiate cases. For example, a news reporter who stationed himself in New York City criminal court noted a judge rebuking a Legal Aid lawyer for filing a lengthy legal motion. As the lawyer told the reporter, defense lawyers are "frequently treated as irritants. 'The pressure is: You are part of the system, and you should grease the wheels of the system' " (Glaberson 1990, 12). There are pressures structured in the legal system to not press rights as hard as possible, or as hard as the language of the Court's criminal rights decisions required.

Finally, and most importantly, there is a fundamental tension between the constitutional goals the Court enunciated and the practical aims of the criminal justice system. As McConville and Mirsky put it, "those in control of indigent defense want low-cost, efficient processing of criminal defendants through guilty pleas and other non-trial dispositions" (McConville and Mirsky 1987, 582). Trials are expensive. They take the time of many court employees, require investigation and preparation, the empaneling of juries, entail a variety of costs in record-keeping, analysis, and so on. If a substantial number of criminal defendants started demanding trials, the system would have to expand rapidly, requiring massive spending, or it would collapse. Thus, the court-appointed attorney has no incentive to provide adversarial counsel. In addition, where counsel is private, financial reward and future appointment depend "not on the defendant's satisfaction, but on the court's appointment" (McConville and Mirsky 1987, 900). And if these private lawyers are paid by the case, as is normal practice, they have a financial interest in processing as many cases as possible. They become "court functionaries, rather than adversarial representatives of the poor" (McConville and Mirsky 1987, 901).

Thus, there is a "nationwide tension between the adversarial rhetoric of *Gideon* v. *Wainwright* and the cost-effective practices of indigent defense providers" (McConville and Mirsky 1987, 652). From the point of view of those involved in the criminal justice system, the Court decisions challenged the goals of the system. In their view, the system that prevails, where defense lawyers are not able to do much more than plead their clients guilty in exchange for a lenient sentence, is a success. "The method minimizes adversarial advocacy and therefore the cost of criminal defense" (McConville and Mirsky 1987, 877). This is nicely illustrated by the New York City experience where Legal Aid Society staff attorneys struck four times between 1978 and 1982 to protest "excessive caseloads, inadequate resources, and the inability to provide meaningful representation" (McConville and Mirsky 1987, 895). The response was to supplement the legal aid system with another set of lawyers who had the "ability and willingness to assist in efficient case disposal" (McConville and Mirsky 1987, 816). This systemic, institutional rationale puts enormous barriers in the path of achieving the adversarial requirement of the Court's decisions, the effective assistance of counsel.

Although it is possible for Court decisions to overcome barriers, it requires political support and the presence of one of the four conditions. As this discussion has indicated, there were no non-court actors providing either incentives for compliance or imposing costs for non-compliance. There was no market mechanism available for implementation nor were there administrators willing to implement. Instead, there was a realization that lawyers could be appointed, meeting the letter of the Court's decisions, but within a framework that made it unlikely that the effective assistance of counsel would be achieved. Here, too, the "revolution" did not achieve its stated goals.

Conclusion: The Revolution That Wasn't

In the decisions that I have examined in this chapter, reformers attempted to dramatically change police and courtroom practices and prison conditions. They did so by litigating, focusing on rights and arguing that prison officials, the police, and the courts must inform criminal defendants of a wide array of rights and refrain from certain practices. And they won many cases.

The Court, however, was unable to achieve its stated goals because political support was often lacking and seldom were the conditions necessary for change present. What was overlooked was that organizations, be they prison systems, police departments, or lower courts, are often unwilling to change. Watching over 1,600 criminal court cases a decade and a half after the "revolution," Feeley found that "constitutional changes notwithstanding, the lower courts are reluctant to treat formally that which has traditionally been treated informally, and they refuse to consider solemnly that which has usually been taken lightly" (Feeley 1979, 8). For many officials, what the Supreme Court did simply "did not matter much" (Wasby 1976, 221). Of the more than 1,600 cases that Feeley saw, the "overwhelming majority . . . took just a few seconds" and "the courtroom encounter was a ritual in which the judge *ratified* a decision made earlier" (Feeley 1979, 11). While some change has occurred, it depended more on the interests of non-Court actors, especially politicians and administrators, than on the courts. The revolution failed.

PART 4

Same-Sex Marriage

Introduction

Baehr v. Lewin (1993) was "nothing less than a tectonic shift, a fundamental realignment of the landscape, possibly the biggest lesbian and gay rights legal victory ever. . . . A breakthrough case that most might see as gay people's *Loving v. Virginia.*" (Wolfson 1994, 612 n.196) [1]

In 1993, in *Baehr v. Lewin*, the Hawaii Supreme Court held that the state's denial of marriage to gay men and lesbians, absent a compelling justification, violated the state constitution's guarantee of equal protection of the laws. Since it was widely believed that the state could not offer a compelling legal justification for denying lesbians and gay men the right to marry, it appeared that marriage rights were about to be extended as a result of litigation. Evan Wolfson, cocounsel in the case, as well as others, argued that in order to comply with the Full Faith and Credit Clause of the U.S. Constitution, [2] other states would have to recognize same-sex marriages performed in Hawaii. [3] Thus, it appeared to many that through the courts litigators were on the verge of securing for gay men and lesbians throughout the nation an important civil right. If this is the case, then the constraints and conditions identified in the preceding chapters are limited.

The use of litigation to win the right to same-sex marriage fits the definition of significant social reform that I am investigating. Gays are a small minority in the United States that have suffered from, and continue to suffer from,

1. In *Loving v. Virginia* (1967), the United States Supreme Court held that antimiscegenation laws (laws prohibiting interracial marriage) were unconstitutional.

2. "Full Faith and Credit shall be given in each State to the public Acts, Records, and judicial Proceedings of every other State. And the Congress may by general Laws prescribe the Manner in which such Acts, Records and Proceedings shall be proved, and the Effect thereof" (U.S. Const. art. IV, sec. 1).

3. However, Koppelman notes that this is a "fundamental misconception." He points out that states have "always had the power to decline to recognize marriages from other states, and they have been exercising that power for centuries" (Koppelman 2006, 118).

discrimination. Litigation for same-sex marriage is an attempt to broaden and equalize the right to marriage that is enjoyed by heterosexual adults. On a deeper level, it involves a claim for equal respect by lesbians and gay men. Further, it is an attempt to use the courts to produce policy change with nationwide impact.

The litigation campaign for same-sex marriage provides an opportunity to explore a more recent use of litigation to produce significant social reform. Although some litigation was commenced in the 1970s, the litigation movement has made a major push starting in the 1990s and continuing into the twenty-first century. In contrast, the use of litigation to produce significant social reform in civil rights and women's rights largely occurred in the middle decades of the twentieth century. *Brown v. Board of Education* was decided in 1954 and *Roe v. Wade* in 1973. Most of the other decisions discussed in earlier chapters date from the 1950s, 1960s, and 1970s. This leaves open the possibility that the analysis is dated. Perhaps litigants have learned from their experiences and have come to use litigation to produce significant social reform only when the conditions necessary for success exist?

There is a noteworthy distinction between the litigation campaign to win the right to same-sex marriage and the campaigns that preceded it for civil rights and women's rights. The earlier litigation campaigns were based in federal courts while the campaign for same-sex marriage has been based in state courts. That is, same-sex marriage proponents have brought cases in state courts, arguing that prohibiting same-sex couples from marrying violates provisions of state constitutions. In principle, however, there is no reason why the constraints and conditions that limit federal courts from producing significant social reform should not apply to state courts as well. Both federal and state courts are judicial institutions with a great deal in common. In fact, the differences that do exist suggest that state judiciaries are more constrained from producing significant social reform. One obvious reason why is that while U.S. Supreme Court decisions are, in theory, binding on the entire country, state court decisions are only binding on the state in which the court sits. Further, there are good reasons to think that the constraints and conditions apply with greater force to state judiciaries. For example, the second constraint, lack of judicial independence, is stronger in state courts than in federal courts because state judges typically lack life tenure. Likewise, the third constraint, lack of implementation power, might also be stronger in state judicial systems because knowledge of state courts and their decisions is quite low, even in politically salient cases (Lehne and Reynolds 1978). This may make it easier for elected officials to ignore unpopular state-court decisions and make state courts wary of acting. Regardless of these differences, the essential point is that same-sex marriage proponents adopted *litigation* as a main strategy to win the right to marriage. Since the focus of this book is on the use of courts to further significant social reform, the choice of court shouldn't matter.

There is another important distinction between the litigation campaign for same-sex marriage and the earlier campaigns for civil rights and women's rights: the battle for same-sex marriage is ongoing, making it hard to make definitive claims. Also, it was necessary to terminate the analysis at a given date. In general, the analysis goes through the 2004 elections with the caveat that if extraordinary events happened after that date but before publication I include them. This all means that the analysis presented here may be overtaken by events. Having said that, much has transpired in the 1990s and the first decade of the twenty-first century. Thus, although it is perhaps too early to judge the long-term impact of this litigation, this doesn't prevent an assessment of what has been achieved through litigation, and at what costs.

Although *Baehr v. Lewin* was the first major victory for same-sex marriage litigators, it was not the last. In 1999, a second victory was achieved in Vermont. In *Baker v. Vermont* (1999), the Vermont Supreme Court held that the state's refusal to issue marriage licenses to gay men and lesbians violated the Vermont Constitution. Then, on November 18th, 2003, the Supreme Judicial Court of Massachusetts gave same-sex marriage litigators a total victory. In *Goodridge v. Department of Public Health* (2003), the Court held that Massachusetts may not "deny the protections, benefits and obligations conferred by civil marriage to two individuals of the same sex who wish to marry" (*Goodridge* 2003, 312).

At face value, these three legal victories suggest that turning to the courts was a brilliant strategic move by proponents of same-sex marriage. With legal victories in states about as far apart as can be in the United States, change appeared to be in the offing. But did the *Baehr, Baker,* and *Goodridge* victories produce the change for which their proponents hoped? Was litigation the right strategic move at the right time? Were the conditions necessary for judicial efficacy present? Answering these questions is less straightforward than one might think. In answering them, I ask first, in chapter 12, about direct or judicial effects. Did *Baehr* cause the state of Hawaii to change its law and policy regarding same-sex marriage? Did the Vermont legislature's response to *Baker* achieve the goals of the proponents of same-sex marriage? Has the *Goodridge* decision been implemented in Massachusetts? If so, did the Full Faith and Credit Clause of the U.S. Constitution compel other states to recognize same-sex marriages performed in Massachusetts? In chapter 13, I turn to indirect or extra-judicial effects. Following the analysis in earlier chapters, I ask whether the decisions had important indirect effects. Did they indirectly lead to changes in media coverage, public opinion, and political mobilization in favor of same-sex marriage? The chapter also explores other factors that might influence the fight for same-sex marriage.

12

You've Got That *Loving* Feeling?
The Litigation Campaign for
Same-Sex Marriage

In the last several decades of the twentieth century, the legal right to marry became a goal of parts of the gay-rights movement.[1] Beyond the simple practical benefits of marriage,[2] many gay-rights activists argue that same-sex marriage is of enormous symbolic importance (Sullivan 2000). Inclusion of gay men and lesbians in the civil institution of marriage, they argue, would signal their acceptance into mainstream society. Perceiving the difficulty of a legislative fight given the opposition they face,[3] proponents of same-sex marriage have instead turned to the courts.

Litigation over the issue of same-sex marriage dates back to the early 1970s. During this time, gay-rights activists brought suit in Minnesota (*Baker v. Nelson* 1971), Kentucky (*Jones v. Hallahan* 1973), and Washington (*Singer v. Hara* 1974), but their efforts met uniform defeat.[4] After two decades of growing tolerance toward gay men and lesbians (described in chapter 13), proponents of same-sex marriage again turned to the courts. In 1993 in Hawaii, 1999 in Vermont, and 2003 in Massachusetts, they achieved what appeared to be stunning victories. As Evan Wolfson's comment in the introduction to this part of the book suggests, can these decisions be seen as the equivalent of *Loving v. Virginia*, knocking down legal barriers to same-sex marriage?

---

1. For a brief but fascinating history of the growth of marriage as part of the gay-rights agenda, see D'Emilio (2007, 45–52).

2. The General Accounting Office has identified over one thousand, one hundred federal benefits that accrue to married couples (U.S. General Accounting Office 2004).

3. Mucciaroni notes the lack of support for same-sex marriage from powerful groups or interests, pointing out that "stakeholders are relatively scarce in the struggle over gay marriage and partner recognition" (forthcoming, chap. 7, p. 11).

4. A similar fate met a case argued in 1993 in the courts of the District of Columbia (*Dean v. District of Columbia* 1995). Same-sex marriage was also implicated in cases dealing with immigration status in *Adams v. Howerton* (1982) and divorce in *De Santo v. Barnsley* (1984).

The *Baehr* Litigation in Hawaii

In 1990, Nina Baehr and Genora Dancel, along with a male couple and another female couple, applied for marriage licenses in Hawaii, but their applications were denied. The couples sued John Lewin, director of the Department of Health and administrator of the state marriage law, seeking an injunctive order compelling the state to grant them marriage licenses. In 1991, a state court dismissed the suit, finding that Hawaii's marriage statute did not contemplate marriage between members of the same sex. The couples appealed.

In 1993, the Hawaii Supreme Court held in *Baehr v. Lewin* (1993) that Hawaii's refusal to recognize same-sex marriages, absent a compelling justification, violated the state constitution's guarantee of equal protection of the laws. Endorsing a strict scrutiny standard for sex-based classifications, the Court offered the state an opportunity to demonstrate to the trial court on remand that the marriage statute "furthers compelling state interests and is narrowly drawn to avoid unnecessary abridgements of constitutional rights" (*Baehr v. Lewin* 1993, 74). In 1996, the trial court held in *Baehr v. Miike* (1996) that the state had failed to meet this burden and ordered the Department of Health to issue marriage licenses to same-sex couples. Same-sex marriage proponents believed that these two decisions signaled the beginning of a civil rights revolution for gays in American society. However, these two stunning victories proved short-lived.

Winning a court case is one thing but translating that victory into change is quite another. Despite these victories in court, same-sex marriage did not become legal in Hawaii. The decisions were quickly outpaced by subsequent political events. Opposition developed immediately after the 1993 decision. Following the trial court's decision in *Baehr v. Miike* (1996), opponents of same-sex marriage proposed an amendment to the Hawaiian Constitution that would reserve the issue of same-sex marriage for legislative determination, allowing but not requiring the legislature to restrict marriage to opposite sex couples only. Supporters of the amendment mobilized a variety of religious and other opponents of same-sex marriage, including the Mormon Church, the Christian Coalition, the Family Forum, and guitar-strumming Mike Gabbard's Alliance for Traditional Marriage, made up of Hare Krishna–style followers. Proponents of same-sex marriage were outorganized and outspent. As same-sex marriage advocate and lawyer Wolfson noted, "the right wing poured massive resources into Hawai'i" (quoted in Rees 2004). In 1998, following a fierce campaign, Hawaiian voters ratified the amendment by a better than two to one vote (69.2 percent to 28.6 percent), in effect overruling the decisions in *Baehr v. Lewin* (1993) and *Baehr v. Miike* (1996).[5] The constitutional amendment essentially affirmed a 1994 law passed by the legislature during the litigation that defined marriage as limited to heterosexual couples.

Although denied the right to marry, same-sex marriage activists were able to secure a compromise political victory. In order to ensure that the constitutional amendment was placed on the ballot, its sponsors agreed to offer a "reciprocal beneficiaries" law. The bill guaranteed some government and private benefits to registered same-sex couples in Hawaii, including inheritance without a will, ability to sue for the wrongful death of their reciprocal beneficiary, hospital visitation and health care decisions, consent to postmortem exams, loan eligibility, property rights (including joint tenancy), tort liability, and protection under Hawaii domestic violence laws (Dupuis 2002, 73). The state legislature passed the bill and it was signed into law. The law grants any two single adults access to 60 out of the 160 spousal rights available to married heterosexual couples in Hawaii. However the Human Rights Campaign reports that a 1999 State Auditor's Report found that only 435 couples had made use of the law. In addition, some of the benefits have expired. Thus, although they have been denied the right to marry, some same-sex couples in Hawaii came to enjoy somewhat broader rights than they did before the litigation.

The direct effects of the Hawaiian litigation are thus mixed. Despite euphoria over the initial judicial decision, gay men and lesbians still do not have the right to marry in Hawaii. Indeed, state law bans recognition of same-sex marriage. On the other hand, same-sex couples have won extended, albeit limited, rights.

Why was the decision of the Hawaii Supreme Court not effective? The answer is that because same-sex marriage lacked much public or elite support, opponents were able to overturn it, and fairly easily. There was insufficient pressure from either the public or local or national elites to implement it. The majority of the pressure that was brought to bear came from opponents. Without broad support, there was nothing the Hawaii courts could do. Litigators could not overcome the constraints that limit the ability of courts to produce significant social reform.

The Baker Litigation in Vermont

The story in Vermont was different. In *Baker v. Vermont* (1999) the Vermont Supreme Court held that the state's refusal to issue marriage licenses to gay men and lesbians denied them the benefits of civil marriage protected under the Common Benefits Clause of the Vermont Constitution.[6] Rather than impose a

---

5. The amendment added Section 23 to Article I of the Hawaii Constitution: "The legislature shall have the power to reserve marriage to opposite-sex couples."

6. The Common Benefits Clause reads: "That government is, or ought to be, instituted for the common benefit, protection, and security of the people, nation, or community, and not for the

remedy, the Court offered the legislature a short window of time to correct the constitutional violation. The Court suggested that a "domestic partnership" or "registered partnership" law, by which same-sex couples would be granted an alternative marital status that afforded them "all or most of the same rights and obligations provided by the law to married partners," would be constitutionally acceptable (*Baker v. Vermont* 1999, 886).

In response, the legislature held hearings. When the legislature first gave Vermonters a chance to have their opinions heard on January 25, 2000, the Associated Press reported that despite a "raging snowstorm" as many as one thousand, five hundred people came to the Vermont House to express their views (Snyed 2000). After months of difficult debate, in April, 2000, by votes of nineteen to eleven in the Vermont Senate and seventy-nine to sixty-eight in the Vermont House, the legislature passed a bill granting gay men and lesbians the right to form civil unions. Governor Howard Dean, a Democrat, promptly signed it on April 26, 2000. Although the bill did not permit gay men and lesbians to marry, the civil union status it created granted same-sex couples "all the same benefits, protections and responsibilities under law . . . as are granted to spouses in a marriage."[7] The law required same-sex couples seeking civil unions to register with a town and have their unions solemnized by a member of the clergy or a justice of the peace. Partners seeking to dissolve their civil unions were required to petition the Family Court, just as divorcing heterosexual couples are required.

Initial reactions to the civil unions bill among many were supportive. In a July 2, 2000, news story, the day after the law took effect, the *New York Times* reported on the first civil unions. In Brattleboro, Carolyn Conrad and Kathleen Peterson "went to the town clerk's office at midnight and filled out the paperwork. Witnessed by a cheering crowd of about 100 and a handful of protesters, they exchanged vows minutes later before a justice of the peace, making them the first in the country to be civilly united" (Goldberg 2000A). In South Burlington, Lois Farnham and Holly Puterbaugh, two of the original plaintiffs, found that "such a moment was once so unimaginable that they had a soloist sing 'The Impossible Dream' at their church ceremony before about 200 guests" (Goldberg 2000A; see also Mertz 2001). Overall, in the year 2000, there were 1,704 civil unions performed in Vermont, with about 78 percent joining out-of-state partners. For comparison, there were 6,271 marriages in 2000 (State of Vermont 2000).

The euphoria of same-sex marriage proponents was tempered somewhat by public-opinion data showing Vermonters, at best, evenly divided over civil unions, and by a "Take Back Vermont" movement aimed at repealing the civil

---

particular emolument or advantage of any single person, family, or set of persons, who are a part only of that community" (Vt. Const., ch. I, art. 7).

7. 15 V.S.A. Section 1204(a).

unions bill. Signs on barns, yards, and the like made the issue contentious enough that Vermont political leaders, including both U.S. senators, issued a joint statement calling for calm and respectful debate.[8] In January, 2000, after the Vermont legislature commenced debate, a poll showed 52 percent of those surveyed opposed the Supreme Court ruling, while 38 percent agreed and 10 percent said they weren't sure (Snyed 2000).[9]

The November, 2000, elections also tempered the enthusiasm of same-sex marriage supporters. As the *Burlington Free Press* reported, the makeup of the new legislature "changed dramatically" (Remsen 2000). While Governor Dean was reelected, voters "awarded Republicans a 21-seat majority in the Vermont House" (Remsen 2000) and trimmed the Democratic margin in the Vermont Senate to two seats. While civil unions weren't the only issue that produced these results,[10] it was likely the most important one. The House Democratic Leader, John Tracy, said that opposition to the civil union law was an important factor in his party's loss of control of the Vermont House for the first time in fourteen years: "ten of my incumbents who lost were pro-civil union," he said (quoted in Remsen 2000).

The direct effects of the litigation in Vermont appear mostly positive. Although civil unions are not identical to marriage, they carry all of the same rights and responsibilities. Further, they appear to carry a symbolic importance for same-sex couples that not everyone expected. "What surprised a lot of people," said Beth Robinson, a member of the legal team that won the *Baker* case, was "how significant it was to stand before an official and have them say, 'by the power vested in me by the state of Vermont'" (quoted in Remsen 2000). And civil unions appear to have overcome the political backlash, although not without influencing the 2000 elections in a way not supportive of same-sex marriage.

On the other hand, same-sex couples in Vermont have a separate legal status from heterosexual couples. They are not, and can not be, married. While supporters of same-sex marriage won all of the marriage rights accorded to heterosexual couples, civil unions are a "separate but [almost] equal" status. And that status is not recognized by the federal government (see next chapter) and need not be recognized by other states. Same-sex couples in Vermont remain second-class citizens.

Why was the use of litigation to further the right to same-sex marriage

---

8. The idea behind the "Take Back Vermont" movement was that the state was being taken over by outsiders who were imposing changes like civil unions on Vermont. Although quite serious, the movement did have its lighter side when a number of out-of-state tourists mistook the "Take back Vermont" signs for a marketing slogan urging them to buy Vermont products and "Take Back [a bit of] Vermont" to their homes!

9. A March 2 poll, conducted by the *Burlington Free Press*, found Vermonters equally divided (Goldberg 2000B).

10. Other issues included opposition to Act 60 dealing with school funding and an unusually large number of Democratic House retirements.

more successful in Vermont than in Hawaii? The answer is twofold: the constraints limiting judicial action were weaker in Vermont and the Vermont Supreme Court ordered something less than full marriage equality. By allowing civil unions rather than requiring marriage for same-sex couples, the Vermont Supreme Court didn't arouse the depth and breadth of opposition that occurred in Hawaii. Also, there was more support for civil unions among the public and political elites in Vermont than there was support for same-sex marriage in Hawaii. A more modest judicial decision in a more supportive state meant that change occurred, albeit less than same-sex marriage proponents sought.

The Goodridge Litigation in Massachusetts

Judicial victories in Hawaii and Vermont didn't result in same-sex marriages. That took a decision of the Supreme Judicial Court of Massachusetts, announced on November 18, 2003. In *Goodridge v. Department of Public Health* (2003), a case brought by seven same-sex couples, the Court held that Massachusetts may not "deny the protections, benefits and obligations conferred by civil marriage to two individuals of the same sex who wish to marry." In addition, the four to three opinion, authored by Chief Justice Margaret Marshall, held that the "Massachusetts Constitution affirms the dignity and equality of all individuals [and] forbids the creation of second-class citizens" (*Goodridge* 2003, 312). The legislature was given 180 days to change the law to rectify the situation. In both outcome and language the decision was what litigators sought.

The immediate results of the *Goodridge* decision were equally complex.[11] The Massachusetts litigation started on April 11, 2001, when seven same-sex couples, denied marriage licenses, filed suit in Suffolk Superior Court in Boston to challenge the state's prohibition of same-sex marriage. They lost that case in May, 2002, and then appealed to the Supreme Judicial Court. Interestingly, in July of that year the state legislature met in Constitutional Convention in response to a petition signed by one hundred and thirty thousand citizens requesting a constitutional amendment banning same-sex marriage. While the Convention adjourned without voting, it was a harbinger of things to come. The Massachusetts High Court held for the plaintiffs in November, 2003, in the *Goodridge* decision. In response, and after much wrangling in the legislature, on December 11, 2003, the Massachusetts Senate voted to ask the Court if Vermont-style civil unions satisfied the constitutional requirements the Court found applicable in *Goodridge*. On February 4, 2004, the Court said no. It held that the Massachusetts Constitution required equal treatment in both rights and terminology among heterosexual and same-sex couples.

11. For a detailed discussion of events in Massachusetts through 2006, see Pinello (2006, 33–72).

While the state legislature and the Supreme Judicial Court were clarifying the Court's decision, opponents of same-sex marriage were active. Eleven days after the Court's decision was announced the state's four Catholic bishops called the decision a "national tragedy" in a letter read at Sunday masses across the state. The Republican governor of Massachusetts, Mitt Romney, announced his opposition to the decision and stated his determination to use all legal means to prevent the state from legalizing same-sex marriages. A week after the Court rejected civil unions as a constitutionally acceptable response, the Massachusetts Legislature opened a Constitutional Convention to debate a proposed constitutional ban on same-sex marriage.

Under the Massachusetts Constitution, the amendment process is cumbersome. It requires approval by two successive sessions of the legislature sitting together in Constitutional Convention and then approval by the voters. Although the Convention adjourned without acting, it met twice more over the following months. The meetings were characterized by impassioned speeches on all sides of the issue, backroom deals, strategic maneuvers, and large and sometimes boisterous protests outside the building (Klein 2004). A meeting in February, 2004, was described by an observer this way:

> Nineteen hours of debate produced a walkout, a filibuster, a couple of dirty tricks, and a deeply fractured legislature. The members came two votes short of banning gay marriage, then six votes short of establishing civil unions, and then degenerated into a morass of grandstanding, grimacing, and gavel-pounding. (Mulhauser 2004)

Finally, on March 29, 2004, the Constitutional Convention took the first step toward overturning *Goodridge* when it approved, by a vote of 105–92, a constitutional amendment that would ban same-sex marriage but legalize Vermont-style civil unions.

Despite these attempts to overturn the decision, on May 17, 2004, the fiftieth anniversary of *Brown*, the first same-sex marriages were legally performed in the United States. There were euphoric scenes in Boston where ten thousand supporters and onlookers gathered outside of city hall to witness the historic event (Abraham and Klein 2004). Boston Mayor Thomas M. Menino accompanied three of the seven couples who were plaintiffs in *Goodridge* to the registry office at city hall where they applied for their marriage licenses (Abraham and Paulson 2004). Fittingly, Julie and Hillary Goodridge received their marriage license application first. In Cambridge, the city hall opened just after midnight to accept applications for marriage licenses. This special opening time was preceded by a celebration with wedding cake and sparkling cider presided over by Cambridge's mayor. "This is like winning the World Series and the Stanley Cup on the same day," one woman said as she and her partner applied for their marriage license (Abraham and Klein 2004). Across the state, the *Boston Globe* reported that "more than 1,000 gay and lesbian couples" sought marriage licenses (Abraham and Paulson 2004). In the ensuing year, approximately six thousand same-sex couples were legally married (Walker, 2005).

The reaction to the first same-sex marriages was not all positive. In addition to opposition from the governor, the Catholic Church, and conservative groups, President Bush denounced them and called for an amendment to the U.S. Constitution limiting marriage to heterosexuals:

> The sacred institution of marriage should not be redefined by a few activist judges. All Americans have a right to be heard in this debate. I called on the Congress to pass, and to send to the states for ratification, an amendment to our Constitution defining and protecting marriage as a union of a man and a woman as husband and wife. (Quoted in Belluck 2004)

The national reaction to the *Goodridge* decision and the performance of same-sex marriages are explored in greater detail in the next chapter.

Unlike in Vermont there does not appear to have been a legislative backlash in the 2004 election, the one immediately following the *Goodridge* decision (Pinello 2006, 69–70). According to an analysis in the *Boston Globe*, the 2004 elections produced little change. Of the seventeen legislative seats that changed hands in the election, nearly half of the newly elected representatives planned to vote differently on a constitutional amendment banning same-sex marriage than their predecessors. However, the analysis further found that five of the new legislators opposed the amendment, replacing members who supported it, while at least two seats and possibly three changed from opposing to favoring the amendment (Lewis 2004). Also, in September, 2005, the proposed constitutional amendment banning same-sex marriage but establishing civil unions with full marriage rights was defeated.

On the other hand, a coalition of groups, relying on a citizen initiative process, successfully forced the Constitutional Convention to meet to consider a constitutional amendment limiting marriage to heterosexuals. Between September 21 and November 23, 2005, VoteOnMarriage.org collected what it called a "record-breaking 170,000 signatures, the greatest number ever in Massachusetts history" (voteonmarriage.org), to place the amendment on the 2008 ballot. Because the amendment was initiated by citizens and not lawmakers, it only needed support from one-fourth of the Constitutional Convention (fifty votes) in two successive sittings of the legislature.

Initially, the legislature sitting as a Constitutional Convention failed to vote on the amendment, recessing on November 9, 2006. However, in early December VoteOnMarriage.org, joined by Governor Mitt Romney, filed a suit to require the legislature to vote. On December 27, 2006, the Supreme Judicial Court held in a unanimous decision that while it could not order the legislature to vote, state lawmakers had a constitutional duty to do so. Then, on January 2, 2007, the final day of the 2005–6 legislative session, the constitutional amendment won the necessary support in the Constitutional Convention to make it to the next step in the process. The final vote was 62 votes for and 134 against (12 more than needed). However, on June 14, 2007, the amendment garnered only 45 votes, 5 votes shy of the required 50 votes (151 votes were cast against the amendment). Thus, it appears that there will not be a constitutional amendment banning same-sex marriage on the November 2008 ballot.

Summing up the litigation achievements in Massachusetts, as of June, 2007, same-sex marriage in Massachusetts seems secure for the foreseeable future. However, akin to the situation in Vermont, marriages performed between same-sex couples in Massachusetts are not recognized by the federal government and need not be recognized by other states. Nationally, same-sex couples in Massachusetts remain second-class citizens, separate and unequal.

The apparent success of litigation in Massachusetts can be explained by the same constraints that underscore the lack of success in Hawaii and the mixed success in Vermont. Massachusetts is among the most liberal states in the country. In terms of same-sex marriage, this means that there was a good deal of support both among the public at large and among elites. Although the governor opposed them, many local officials, such as the mayors of Boston and Cambridge, noted above, supported them. The state's two major bar associations, the Massachusetts Bar Association and the Boston Bar Association, filed amicus briefs in support of the plaintiffs (Pinello 2006, 42). It also appears that there was a good deal of support from the public. In a statewide poll taken just after the *Goodridge* decision in November, 2003, by the *Boston Globe* and WBZ-TV, half of respondents agreed with the Court's decision. Although the poll had only four hundred respondents, and a correspondingly large error margin of 5 percentage points, it does suggest a strong degree of public support (Frank and Klein 2003). Another poll, taken for the *Boston Herald*, found 49 percent of respondents supporting the legalization of gay marriage (Guarino 2003). These findings were similar to results from an earlier poll by the *Boston Globe* and WBZ-TV in April, 2003, more than half a year before the decision, which again found support for same-sex marriage from 50 percent of respondents (Phillips 2003). Since *Goodridge*, public support for same-sex marriage has held. Two polls taken in 2005 found support for same-sex marriage from more than half of respondents (Andersen 2006, 231). And the results of the 2004 election as well as the defeat of the constitutional amendment banning same-sex marriage also suggest that there is and was a good deal of public support for same-sex marriage. Under such conditions, the constraints on courts can be overcome and litigation can produce change.

It is important to note that if judicial decisions supporting same-sex marriage can survive political backlash then Constraint III, the judiciary's lack of the power of implementation, does not come into play. This is because little or no change is required to implement same-sex marriage. There is already a smoothly functioning bureaucracy that issues marriage licenses. While a form or two might have to be changed in minor ways (for example, if they mention brides and grooms, or husbands and wives), nothing else needs to be done. No new programs are necessary, major additional funds aren't required, and evasion is impossible to disguise. While it is possible that the office personnel who issue marriage licenses in a given state could resign en masse in protest, it would be relatively easy to replace them. Thus, when there is sufficient political support to protect same-sex marriage from backlash, implementation is not problematic.

Post-*Goodridge*

Change has also occurred in seven other states since the *Goodridge* decision. Three states, Connecticut, New Jersey, and New Hampshire, have adopted civil unions. On April 20, 2005, Connecticut adopted civil unions by legislative act. Unlike in Vermont and Massachusetts, Connecticut acted without judicial pressure. Subsequently, on December 21, 2006, the governor of New Jersey, in response to a decision of the New Jersey Supreme Court ordering the legislature to guarantee gay men and lesbians marriage rights (*Lewis v. Harris* 2006), signed a civil unions bill into law.[12] Then, on May 31, 2007, New Hampshire adopted civil unions, also without judicial pressure. In addition, four states have granted same-sex couples various forms of domestic partner benefits that range from full marriage equivalence to substantially less. Starting in 1999, California adopted three progressively broader measures extending rights to same-sex couples. As of January 1, 2005, same-sex couples and some opposite-sex couples over the age of sixty-two may register as domestic partners and receive all of the state-level rights and responsibilities of marriage.[13] Similarly, as of January 1, 2008, Oregon will offer same-sex couples the right to enter into contractual relationships that grant them the same benefits that state law offers to married couples. In Maine (as of July 30, 2004) and Washington State (as of July 22, 2007), same-sex couples have access to a limited number of rights including inheritance and funeral arrangements.

Thus, in the years immediately following the *Goodridge* decision, same-sex partners had won the right to marry in Massachusetts. In Connecticut, New Jersey, and New Hampshire, they won the right to form civil unions with all of the same rights and responsibilities as married couples. In California and Oregon domestic partnerships provide same-sex couples with all of the state-

12. The laws took effect on October 1, 2005, and February 19, 2007, respectively.
13. 2003 Ca. A.B. 205, Section 297.5(a). However, on March 7, 2000, California voters approved Proposition 22 (the "Knight Initiative"), amending the Family Code to state: "Only marriage between a man and a woman is valid and recognized in California." The Proposition was approved with 61 percent of the votes and carried fifty-two of fifty-eight counties, only falling short in six counties in the San Francisco Bay area.

level rights and responsibilities of marriage. Further, limited rights have been granted in Maine and Washington State.

What explains changes in the laws in these post-*Goodridge* states? In large part the answer is that in each of these states there is much broader support and much less opposition to gay rights than in much of the rest of the country. Overall, Lewis and Oh report, based on sixty-nine thousand respondents to fifty-seven surveys on same-sex marriage since 1992, that residents of the states that have acted since Hawaii are "significantly more" supportive of same-sex marriage than residents of other states. The nine states that have extended benefits since Hawaii are among the fourteen states where public opinion is the most supportive of same-sex marriage (Lewis and Oh, forthcoming). Indeed, in all but New Jersey change came about without judicial decisions requiring it. It is likely not an accident that the states are clustered in the Northeast and Pacific Northwest, the two most politically liberal sections of the United States.

There is room for debate on how to characterize these changes and their causes. Before the litigation in Hawaii, Vermont, and Massachusetts, no state provided same-sex couples anything remotely equivalent to marriage rights. In the years following close on the litigation, however, ten states provided either same-sex marriage (Massachusetts), civil unions (Vermont, New Jersey, New Hampshire, Connecticut), domestic partnerships that granted all the rights of marriage (California, Oregon), or limited domestic partner benefits (Hawaii, Maine, Washington). Were these changes the result of litigation? While the legislative changes in Vermont, Massachusetts, and New Jersey were clearly the direct result of litigation, and arguably the result in Hawaii, that is not the case in California, Connecticut, Maine, New Hampshire, Oregon, or Washington State. However, it doesn't follow that litigation played no role in influencing legislation in these states. It is possible, perhaps likely, that changes in these states were spurred on by the litigation campaign. This possibility will be explored in greater detail in the next chapter.

In terms of changes in the law, it can be argued that civil unions, domestic partnerships, and marriage represent a huge step forward in providing expanded rights to same-sex couples. By providing same-sex couples with rights ranging from hospital visitation and medical decision making to health care coverage to inheritance (when a partner dies without a will) to the use of state stepparent adoption procedures, the lives of gay men and lesbians have been dramatically improved. On this characterization, litigation for same-sex marriage has had important, positive effects.

On the other hand, the aim of the litigation was to win same-sex couples equal treatment with heterosexual couples. Nowhere has this been achieved. Even in Massachusetts, where state law provides identical treatment and the name "marriage," same-sex couples are denied over one thousand, one hundred federal rights that accompany marriage (see next chapter). For many litigators, same-sex couples are not even separate but equal; rather they are separate and unequal. Roey Thorpe, executive director of Basic Rights Oregon, a gay-rights group, described civil unions this way: "They are not a goal. They are not what we deserve. They're less than what we deserve . . . we don't believe in them or embrace them, because they are discriminatory" (quoted in Pinello 2006, 140).[14] For Steven Goldstein, director of Garden State Equality, a New Jersey gay-rights advocacy group, "civil unions are nothing like marriage. . . . The cockamamie contraption simply doesn't work. If civil unions were a person, they would be arrested for fraud" (Vestal, 2007A). Indeed Lambda Legal, a self-described "impact litigation" group that has been involved in same-sex marriage litigation, argues that civil unions are "discriminatory" for the following reasons:

> 1. The "only reason to create a separate 'civil union' status for lesbian and gay couples" is "to keep them from entering civil marriages."
> 2. The "'civil union' status labels lesbians and gay men and their relationships as inferior to others. This wrongfully robs lesbian and gay people of dignity and respect."
> 3. "All families should be honored, without some being told they are second class."
> 4. Civil unions violate equal treatment.
> 5. "The name 'marriage' matters. Ask any married couple if they would feel like they lost something if the government told them they were no longer 'married' and instead were in a 'civil union.'"
> 6. "Civil unions are a morally compromised position" that creates "a separate system for a minority of people that the majority wouldn't accept for themselves."

Lambda Legal concludes, "separate and unequal is not the way to go" ("Civil Unions are Discriminatory").

In conclusion, litigation for same-sex marriage led to its creation in Massachusetts and the enactment of civil unions in Vermont and New Jersey. It may have indirectly led to civil unions in Connecticut and New Hampshire, marriage–equivalent domestic partnership legislation in California and Oregon, and the extension of limited benefits in Hawaii, Maine, and Washington. However, while these legal changes can be seen as meaningful, they have only occurred in ten of the fifty states. Further, because of the denial of the federal benefits attendant to marriage, in no state do same-sex couples have the same rights as heterosexual couples. So far, at least, there has been nothing equivalent to *Loving v. Virginia*.

If the analysis were to end here, the conclusion would be mixed. Gay men and lesbians in these states have a broader set of rights than they did before the litigation campaign started, and broader rights than gays in other states. On

---

14. Thorpe does support civil unions for strategic, "practical" purposes, calling them "a step forward" (quoted in Pinello 2006, 140).

the other hand, they are not as well off as if they received equal treatment with heterosexual couples. But the analysis can't end here. It is quite possible that in addition to the direct effects of litigation discussed above, there were indirect effects as well. Litigation for same-sex marriage may have indirectly led to changes in media coverage, public opinion, and political mobilization around same-sex marriage. I now turn to these possibilities.

13

Confusing Rights with Reality: Litigation for Same-Sex Marriage and the Counter-Mobilization of Law

The mixed success of litigation in directly producing the legal right to same-sex marriage doesn't tell the whole story. Proponents of the Dynamic Court model continually claim that court decisions have important extra-judicial or indirect effects in the areas of issue salience, elite action, and public opinion. While neither the *Baehr* (Hawaii) nor the *Baker* (Vermont) litigation succeeded in achieving the legal right of same-sex couples to marry, it is possible that they had substantial indirect effects on political mobilization, elite support, media coverage, and public opinion. What the cases did not do directly, perhaps they achieved indirectly, by raising the issues of same-sex marriage and gay rights more generally in elite and public consciousness, and by mobilizing citizens and legislators sympathetic to the gay cause around these issues. Lawyer Beth Robinson, talking about Vermont, predicted that civil unions would lead to broader acceptance of gay men and lesbians:

> Same-sex couples will be forming civil unions and the state's not going to fall apart. It's just going to be better, and that's going to be the most helpful part of this dialogue. Because the longer we go with the law in effect, the more incredible the claims of our opponents will be exposed as being. (Quoted in Goldberg 2000A)

It is possible, then, that *Baehr* and *Baker* contributed to a climate conducive to significant social reform.

This is even more likely the case with the *Goodridge* decision. Massachusetts, unlike Hawaii and Vermont, is a large, industrial state. According to the 2000 census, Massachusetts had the thirteenth-largest population, compared to Hawaii, ranked forty-second, and tiny Vermont, ranked forty-ninth. Changes in Hawaii and Vermont conceivably could be written off as irrelevant to the mainstream United States, but not Massachusetts. In addition to being one of the largest states in terms of population, Massachusetts also has the second-highest proportion of Catholics of any state, and ranks seventh in the total number of Catholics. Given the Catholic Church's deep opposition to same-sex marriage, the legalization of same-sex marriage in Massachusetts as a constitutional right could likely have a major impact across the United States.

Political Mobilization and Legislative Response

Perhaps litigation is capable of producing significant social reform indirectly by sparking political mobilization. McCann argues that litigation, by providing a forum for protest and a language for grievances, can lead to "building a movement, generating public support for new rights claims, and providing leverage to supplement other political tactics" (McCann 1994, 10). Indeed, McCann argues that "such indirect effects and uses of litigation may be the most important for political struggles by most social movements" (McCann 1994, 10). While I did not find evidence of this indirect mobilization in support of civil rights and women's rights with either *Brown v. Board of Education* or *Roe v. Wade*, perhaps they were unusual. Litigation for same-sex marriage, and the decisions in *Baehr*, *Baker*, and *Goodridge*, might have sparked such mobilization across the country in favor of same-sex marriage and gay rights more generally. On the other hand, like *Brown* and *Roe*, they might have spurred a backlash. It may be that opponents of same-sex marriage were galvanized into action because of judicial victories by same-sex marriage supporters. The next two sections explore these possibilities and table 13.1 presents a timeline of key events.

Same-Sex Marriage Supporters

If the *Baehr*, *Baker*, and *Goodridge* litigation caused increased political mobilization on the issues of same-sex marriage and gay rights more generally, then one place I should see this change reflected is in mobilization aimed at changing state-marriage laws. After the litigation, more states should recognize same-sex marriage and provide protection for the rights of gays and lesbians. I canvassed local, state, and federal legislation to determine if and when any such shift occurred.

There clearly has been an increase in mobilization in support of same-sex marriage, coming from both newly established groups and older gay-rights organizations. Among groups mobilizing in support of gay rights prior to the 1990s same-sex marriage litigation, Lambda Legal, founded in 1973, sponsored a Marriage Project headed by Evan Wolfson. Gay & Lesbian Advocates & Defenders (GLAAD), which dates from 1978, became involved in the Vermont case. The Human Rights Campaign (1980), which claims close to six hundred thousand members and calls itself the largest national gay, lesbian, bisexual, and transgender advocacy organization in the country, became ener-

Table 13.1   Key Events in the Movement for Same-Sex Marriage, 1993–2007

1993
Baehr v. Lewin (Hawaii, May)

1995
Utah bans same-sex marriage (March)

1996
Baehr v. Miike (Hawaii, December)
Thirteen states pass legislation banning same-sex marriage
United States enacts Defense of Marriage Act (September)

1997
Nine states pass legislation banning same-sex marriage

1998
Hawaii adopts constitutional amendment giving legislature power to ban same-sex marriage (November)
Five states pass legislation banning same-sex marriage
Alaska adopts constitutional amendment banning same-sex marriage (November)

1999
Baker v. State (Vermont, December)
Two states pass legislation banning same-sex marriage

2000
Nebraska adopts constitutional amendment banning same-sex marriage
Vermont enacts civil union legislation (April)
3 states pass legislation banning same-sex marriage

2002
Nevada adopts constitutional amendment banning same-sex marriage

2003
Goodridge v. Department of Public Health (Massachusetts, November)

2004
San Francisco starts issuing marriage licenses to same-sex couples (February 12)
Sandoval county, New Mexico issues marriage licenses to same-sex couples (February 20)
New Paltz, New York issues marriage licenses to same-sex couples (February 27)
Portland, Oregon, issues marriage licenses to same-sex couples (March 3)
First same-sex marriages performed in Massachusetts (May 17)
Missouri and Louisiana adopt constitutional amendment banning same-sex marriage (August)

Voters in eleven states (Arkansas, Georgia, Kentucky, Michigan, Mississippi, Montana, North Dakota, Ohio, Oklahoma, Oregon, and Utah) approve constitutional amendments banning same sex marriage

2005
California Domestic Partnership Act goes into effect (January 1)
Connecticut Civil Unions legislation takes effect (October 1)
Kansas adopts constitutional amendment banning same-sex marriage (April)
Texas adopts constitutional amendment banning same-sex marriage (November)

2006
Alabama adopts constitutional amendment banning same-sex marriage (June)
Voters in seven states (Idaho, Colorado, South Dakota, South Carolina, Tennessee, Virginia, and Wisconsin) approve constitutional amendments banning same-sex marriage
Voters in Arizona defeat constitutional amendments banning same-sex marriage
New Jersey Supreme Court holds ban on same-sex marriage unconstitutional (October)
New Jersey adopts civil unions legislation (December)

2007
New Jersey civil unions legislation takes effect (February 19)
Washington State domestic partnership legislation takes effect (July)
Oregon enacts domestic partnership legislation (takes effect January 2008)
New Hampshire enacts civil unions legislation (May)
Massachusetts Constitutional Convention defeats proposed amendment banning same-sex marriage (June)

gized on the issue. More recently, the Alternatives to Marriage Project (1998) was started to promote, as its name states, alternatives to traditional marriage, including same-sex marriage. Finally, Evan Wolfson left Lambda Legal to start Freedom to Marry. Founded on January 1, 2003, the aim of Freedom to Marry is to "win marriage equality nationwide."[1]

These groups have been active and visible. And they have been noticed. For example, every year *Time* magazine selects its *"Time* 100," a list of one hundred people around the world who have "played a critical role in shaping modern society." In 2004, Evan Wolfson of Freedom to Marry was included on the "Heroes and Icons" list of the *"Time* 100" (*"Time* 100/Heroes & Icons" 2004). Others on the list include former President Bill Clinton, Senator Hillary Rodham Clinton, the Dalai Lama, Nelson Mandela, and California Governor Arnold Schwarzenegger. Thus, it appears that same-sex marriage litigation has mobilized some gay-rights activists to organize to win the right to marry.

It also appears that *Goodridge* mobilized same-sex supporters to act. The battle over same-sex marriage took a surprising turn in the winter of 2004. In spite of the fact that marriage law is governed by state legislatures, in locales as varied as San Francisco, California; New Paltz, New York; Portland, Oregon; and Sandoval County, New Mexico, local officials began solemnizing same-sex marriages in the wake of *Goodridge*.

San Francisco, with its large gay population, was the first to act. On February 12, 2004, under the direction of Mayor Gavin Newsom and in defiance of state law, with great fanfare city officials began issuing marriage licenses to same-sex couples. The first couple to receive a marriage license was long-time-gay-rights-activists Phyllis Lyon and Del Martin. Other same-sex couples who wished to marry were euphoric. Long lines formed outside of the San Francisco Clerk's office as couples waited for hours in line to apply for marriage licenses. One sympathetic city attorney described the scene this way:

> The atmosphere was one of elation and love and pride as people were going into the Clerk's office, after standing for many hours in line. . . . Every time a couple came out of the Clerk's office with a license, people cheered. It was just an absolutely amazing experience . . . I literally got chills every time I walked down that hallway. It was like nothing else I've ever experienced. (Quoted in Pinello 2006, 81)

Media coverage of the euphoric scene inspired same-sex marriage supporters throughout the country. One result was a movement, "Flowers from

1. Information on these groups can be found on their Web sites. See Lambda Legal (http://www.lambdalegal.org), Gay & Lesbian Advocates & Defenders (http://www.glaad.org), Human Rights Campaign (http://www.hrc.org), Alternatives to Marriage Project (http://www.unmarried.org), and Freedom to Marry (http://www.freedomtomarry.org).

the Heartland," which raised money from supporters around the country to provide free flowers to same-sex couples married at city hall (Pinello 2006, 85). For approximately one month, until the California Supreme Court issued an injunction ordering the city to stop issuing the licenses on March 11, San Francisco issued 4,037 marriage licenses to same-sex couples. Although approximately 91 percent of the couples were residents of California, couples receiving licenses came from forty-four states and eight foreign countries.

However, on August 12, 2004, the California Supreme Court unanimously held that San Francisco exceeded its authority and violated state law in issuing the marriage licenses to same-sex couples. The Court also held, by a five to two vote, that the same-sex marriages performed were void (*Lockyer v. City and County of San Francisco*, 2004).

A little more than a week after San Francisco acted, marriage licenses were also issued to same-sex couples in New Mexico. On February 20, 2004, Victoria Dunlap, the county clerk of Sandoval County, New Mexico, began to issue same-sex marriage licenses.[2] A total of sixty-four licenses were issued that day until the New Mexico attorney general issued an opinion holding that the licenses were invalid under state law (Pinello 2006, 19).

Not quite a week later, on February 26, 2004, Jason West, the twenty-seven-year-old mayor of the village of New Paltz, New York, seventy-five miles north of New York City, announced that New Paltz would start performing same-sex marriages.[3] The next day, Mayor West apparently performed twenty-four or twenty-five marriages of same-sex couples (Wasserman 2004; "25 New Gay Marriages Conducted in N.Y." 2004). Although Mayor West was banned by court order from continuing to perform same-sex marriages, others stepped in, including six Unitarian Universalist ministers, the deputy mayor, and a village trustee ("25 New Gay Marriages Conducted in N.Y." 2004). Overall, by early June, 2004, 147 marriages of same-sex couples had been performed, and by mid-September, 2004, the number had reached over two hundred ("13 More Gay Couples Wed in New Paltz" 2004; Virtanen 2004).

Portland, Oregon, was next.[4] On March 3, 2004, Multnomah County, Oregon, began issuing marriage licenses to same-sex couples. On that day 422 marriage licenses were issued. By March 9, approximately one thousand, seven hundred marriage licenses had been issued, with all but a handful going to Oregon residents. Until ordered by a judge to stop on April 20, 2004, the county issued 3,022 marriage licenses to same-sex couples. Although Oregon voters amended the state constitution on Election Day, 2004, to limit marriage to heterosexuals, the status of these same-sex marriages was not determined.

---

2. For a discussion of her motivations, and the events of that day, see Pinello (2006, 1–17).
3. For a discussion of these events, see Pinello (2006, 143–48).
4. For a discussion of these and subsequent events in Oregon, see Pinello (2006, 102–42).

That awaited a decision of the Oregon Supreme Court. The Court heard the case in mid-December, 2004, and nullified the purported marriages on April 14, 2005 (*Li v. State* 2005).

Overall, then, it is clear that, in general, same-sex marriage litigation mobilized group support for same-sex marriage. Specifically, the victory in *Goodridge* mobilized some supporters of same-sex marriage who held elective office to issue marriage licenses to same-sex couples. It also mobilized many same-sex couples. Pinello writes that "*Goodridge* brought about enormous social change" and "had a profound inspirational effect for the marriage movement, among elites and the grass roots, at home and abroad" (Pinello 2006, 192). Pinello continues, writing that "the same-sex weddings in San Francisco, Portland, and elsewhere would not have occurred without the example of *Goodridge*" (Pinello 2006, 193). Indeed, he argues that "*Goodridge* radicalized and coalesced the gay community like no other event since the advent of AIDS in the 1980s" (Pinello 2006, 193).

One result of this movement may be the successful efforts in other states, either judicial or legislative, to win the right to same-sex marriage. As noted in chapter 12, in the years immediately following *Goodridge*, Connecticut, New Jersey, and New Hampshire joined Vermont in adopting civil unions. Oregon enacted marriage–equivalent domestic partnerships and Maine and Washington State joined Hawaii in offering limited benefits to same-sex couples. Interestingly, the California legislature passed a same-sex marriage bill only to see it vetoed by Governor Schwarzenegger. However, California did extend its domestic partnership laws to create marriage–equivalent benefits for same-sex couples. In contrast to *Brown*, and especially *Roe*, there is direct evidence that supporters of same-sex marriage were mobilized either directly by litigation or indirectly by events like the performance of marriages in San Francisco, which may have been inspired in turn by previous litigation.

A result of this mobilization may be an increase in contributions to gay-rights groups. To investigate this possibility, I examined contributions to the Human Rights Campaign (HRC), the self-described largest gay-rights group. Fortunately, HRC makes its financial reports going back to 1999 available on its Web site. Unfortunately, the data are contradictory, with different results for the same year found in different reports. Thus, the following analysis must be considered tentative.

The 2006 Report (31) and the 2005 Report (42, 46) each have bar charts that show an "Eight-Year Income Summary" for the years 1999–2006 and 1998–2005, respectively. They report the same data for the years they overlap (1999–2005). If litigation for same-sex marriage spurred contributions to HRC, then I would expect to find a major increase in its 2004 income, the year after the *Goodridge* decision that came in November, 2003. At first blush, the data support this effect. The year 2004 saw an increase in HRC's income of $4.55 million over 2003, a gain of 15.4 percent. The $34.17 million in income in 2004 represented HRC's largest income to date. However, the increase from 2003 to 2004 ranks third in the eight years covered, both numerically and per-centage-wise! The largest increase by far came in 2002 when HRC increased its income by $7.62 million over 2001, an increase of 35.7 percent. In second place was the year 2000, which saw an increase of $4.56 million (27.7 percent) over 1999. It is possible that this large increase was a result of the Vermont Supreme Court decision in December, 1999, and the subsequent enactment of civil unions in the spring of 2000. However, 2000, as well as 2004, was a presi-dential election year. Further, HRC's 2000 Report (22) shows a much smaller increase in income in 2000 of only $1.3 million (8.9 percent) over the income it reports for 1999.

In order to corroborate these data I carefully examined the income tables in each available report and added the figures.[5] Income data for both 2004 and 2005 are reported twice, once in the report for the given year and again in the subsequent year and, unfortunately, they differ. Comparing the figures for 2003 and 2004, income increased by either $3 million (15.9 percent) or $4.2 million (22.2 percent) depending on which income figure for 2004 I used. This compares to an increase of $2.5 million (16.1 percent) in 2002 over 2001. The 2005 and 2004 increases also vary because of different figures. They range from an increase of $2.6 million (11.3 percent) at the low end to $5.8 million (26.5 percent) at the high end.

Taken together, these data suggest that while there was a large increase in HRC's income in 2004, it was neither unprecedented nor the largest yearly increase in HRC's recent past. Thus, the case that litigation increased contribu-tions to HRC is mixed, at best.

Same-Sex Marriage Opponents

Litigation in support of same-sex marriage has also mobilized opponents. Much of the opposition has come from preexisting national groups organized around "traditional values" and a conservative Christian interpretation of the Bible. Leading groups include the Traditional Values Coalition (1980), the American Family Association (1977), Concerned Women for America (1979), the Family Research Council (1983), and Focus on the Family (1977). Many of these groups are large, well organized, and have considerable resources. For example, Focus on the Family, whose mission statement pledges to work to "preserve traditional values and the institution of the family," reported rev-enue of almost $147 million in fiscal year 2004. In addition, a new group, the Alliance for Marriage, was founded by Matt Daniels in 1999 and has had a

5. The income categories sometimes differed from year to year. I included all "Contributions" and "Grants" as well as "Special Events" and "Bequests & Planned Giving." I excluded "Merchandise Sales," "Investment and Other Income," and "Net Assets Released from Restrictions." For each category I included related entries. The data can be found in each report as follows: 2006 (30), 2005 (45), 2004 (17), 2003 (17), 2002 (16), 2001 (16), 2000 (21), 1999 (25).

major impact on the drafting of a constitutional amendment prohibiting same-sex marriage. These groups have poured energy and resources into preventing same-sex marriage.[6]

As the listing of these groups suggests, the political mobilization produced as a direct result of the litigation has been extraordinary. Unfortunately for supporters of same-sex marriage, their opponents have effectively mobilized. Starting chronologically with the *Baehr* litigation in Hawaii, there was a backlash of enormous proportions. As the *Baehr* litigation progressed, opponents of same-sex marriage feared that if Hawaii granted gays and lesbians the right to marry, the Full Faith and Credit Clause of the U.S. Constitution might require the recognition of such marriages in other states.[7] These fears were stoked by the *Goodridge* decision in November, 2003, which seemed to underscore the worst fears of same-sex marriage opponents. In the words of Tim Nashif, a founder and director of the Oregon Family Council (which opposed same-sex marriage):

> Massachusetts was on the verge of legalizing same-sex marriage, not through the people but through the courts. So the question came up, if Massachusetts legalizes same-sex marriage, how do we deal with the fact that [gay and lesbian] Oregonians may be able to go to Massachusetts, get married, come back to Oregon, and then we have a situation in Oregon where there's this debate about whether these marriages should be recognized. (Quoted in Pinello 2006, 107–8)

Determined to contain the spread of same-sex marriage, conservative groups began lobbying efforts on both the state and federal levels, seeking laws defining marriage as a union between one man and one woman and refusing to recognize out-of-state marriages between same-sex couples. These efforts proved extraordinarily successful.[8]

Conservative opponents of same-sex marriage have been particularly successful at the state level, raising money across the country and enacting laws banning same-sex marriage.[9] As of the 2006 election, forty-five states

---

6. Information on these groups can be found on their Web sites. See Alliance for Marriage (http://www.allianceformarriage.org), Traditional Values Coalition (http://www.traditionalvalues. org), American Family Association (http://www.afa.net), Concerned Women for America (http:// www.cwfa.org), Family Research Council (http://www.frc.org), and Focus on the Family (http:// www.family.org).

7. As noted in the introduction, this is not the case (Koppelman 2006, 118). However, the view was either sincerely, if mistakenly, held or used as a rhetorical device.

8. For example, the Oregon Family Council "gathered 244,000 signatures [to place a constitutional amendment on the ballot limiting marriage to heterosexuals] in five and a half weeks, which is the largest number of signatures ever gathered for an initiative in Oregon and in the shortest period of time" (Nashif quoted in Pinello 2006, 122).

9. For example, Roman Catholic, Mormon, and evangelical Christian groups have contributed heavily to a number of state-initiative campaigns. See, for example, Belluck (2000), who describes large out-of-state contributions by religious groups to the campaign for an antigay-marriage initiative in Nebraska.

have adopted measures designed to prevent the recognition of same-sex marriages, with the overwhelming majority of those states acting after the Hawaii Supreme Court decision in 1996. Only five states (Massachusetts, New Jersey, New Mexico, New York, Rhode Island) and the District of Columbia haven't so acted.[10] Because there are fifty states, and because of the changing nature of state laws, it is surprisingly difficult to obtain an exact count of state legislation at any given time. With that caveat in mind, in 1995 Utah became the first post-*Baehr* state to adopt such a measure.[11] In 1996, thirteen more states banned same-sex marriage,[12] and in 1997, nine more states, including liberal Minnesota, followed suit.[13] In 1998, Alabama, Hawaii, Iowa, Kentucky, and Washington State adopted similar measures, and in 1999, Louisiana and Vermont did the same. In 2000, legislators in Colorado, Idaho, and West Virginia banned same-sex marriage, and voters in California ratified an initiative defining marriage as a union between a man and a woman.[14] In addition, during the period from 1990 to 2001, six states—Alaska, California, Colorado, Hawaii, Nebraska, and Nevada—amended their state constitutions or altered existing state laws through a statewide referendum or a statewide initiative to limit marriage to heterosexuals. From 1995 to 2004 at least thirty-nine states adopted statewide "Defense of Marriage Acts." Combined with earlier actions, at least forty-two states have enacted such laws (Vestal 2007B). Overall, between 1990 and Election Day 2004, 436 bills dealing with same-sex marriage were introduced into the fifty state legislatures. While forty-two of these bills supported same-sex marriage, the remaining 91 percent of the bills proscribed it in some manner (Barclay and Fisher 2006, 10).

There has also been activity on the constitutional level. At the state level, a large majority of states have considered amending their constitutions to ban same-sex marriage. Hawaii started the process, amending its constitution in 1998 in the wake of the *Baehr* litigation, reserving the issue of same-sex marriage for legislative determination. Alaska banned same-sex marriage by constitutional amendment in 1998 and Nebraska followed in 2000. In 2002, after

10. These measures typically consist of limiting the definition of marriage to heterosexual couples only and/or refusing to recognize, on public-policy grounds, same-sex marriages from other states. Although Vermont, Connecticut, and New Hampshire allow same-sex couples to form civil unions, they limit marriage to same-sex couples. The data are from the Human Rights Campaign, a gay-rights organization. For more information, see http://www.hrc.org. See also http://www.stateline.org, which has slightly different data.
11. Several state legislatures already proscribed same-sex marriage prior to 1996, including California (1977), Maryland (1973), and Wyoming.
12. Alaska, Arizona, Delaware, Georgia, Illinois, Kansas, Michigan, Oklahoma, North Carolina, Pennsylvania, South Carolina, South Dakota, and Tennessee.
13. Arkansas, Florida, Indiana, Maine, Minnesota, Mississippi, Montana, North Dakota, and Virginia.
14. The legislation in California and Minnesota was especially surprising, as these are two of the most liberal states in the Union. Likewise, the votes in Colorado and Washington State were somewhat unexpected, although both states contain sizeable conservative rural populations.

an initiative petition and the required two ratification votes at the 2000 and 2002 general elections, Nevada limited marriage to heterosexuals. In the summer of 2004, Missouri and Louisiana voters considered constitutional amendments recognizing marriage only as between one man and one woman. In addition, the Louisiana amendment prohibited state judges and officials from recognizing same-sex marriages and civil unions performed in other states. Both amendments were overwhelmingly approved, winning support from nearly 71 percent of Missouri voters and 80 percent of voters in Louisiana. Thus, on the eve of the 2004 election the five states of Alaska, Missouri, Louisiana, Nebraska, and Nevada had amended their constitutions to ban same-sex marriage and Hawaii voters had specifically given the legislature the power to do so.

The 2004 elections brought major changes to the battle over same-sex marriage. Constitutional amendments banning same-sex marriage were on the ballot in eleven states, ranging from Mississippi to Michigan and Oregon to Ohio.[15] In eight of these states (all except Mississippi, Montana, and Oregon), the amendments could be read to ban civil unions as well. Lawmakers in five of those states (Georgia, Kentucky, Mississippi, Oklahoma, and Utah) had acted to put constitutional amendments on the ballot and citizens filed petitions in six states (Arkansas, Michigan, Montana, North Dakota, Ohio, and Oregon) to place gay-marriage amendments on the ballot. These eleven states are home to close to one-fifth of the electorate. On Election Day 2004, all the amendments were adopted, and almost all were adopted by lopsided majorities. Only in Oregon (57 percent) and Michigan (59 percent) was support for the amendments below 60 percent and in more than half of the states support was over 70 percent. As 2004 came to a close, more than one-third of all states, home to close to one-quarter of the American population, had banned same-sex marriage by constitutional amendment.

The efforts of same-sex marriage opponents to pass state constitutional amendments prohibiting same-sex marriage continued after the 2004 election. On Election Day 2006, seven more states added bans on same-sex marriage to their constitutions.[16] In Colorado, voters not only adopted a constitutional ban on same-sex marriage but also defeated an attempt to grant marital rights to same-sex couples through "domestic partnerships." However, for the first time a proposed amendment was defeated, albeit barely (51 percent to 49 percent), in the state of Arizona. Thus, in the wake of the November 2006 election, twenty-seven states, home to 43.4 percent of the U.S. population, prohibit same-sex marriage by constitution.[17] In addition, in at least seventeen of those

15. The other states were Arkansas, Georgia, Kentucky, Montana, North Dakota, Oklahoma, and Utah.

16. Colorado, Idaho, South Carolina, South Dakota, Tennessee, Virginia, and Wisconsin.

17. Calculation based on 2005 U.S. Census Bureau population data available at U.S. Census Bureau 2006. This count includes Hawaii whose constitution gives the state legislature the power

states the constitutional amendment can be read to prohibit civil unions or domestic partnerships as well.[18] Overall, forty-five states prohibit same-sex marriage by state law, by constitution, or by both.

Conservative opponents of same-sex marriage have also been successful at the federal level. In direct response to the Hawaii litigation, in 1996 Representative Bob Barr (Republican, Georgia) and Senator Don Nickles (Republican, Oklahoma) sponsored bills defining marriage as "only a legal union between one man and one woman as husband and wife" and acknowledging the right of each state to refuse recognition of out-of-state-same-sex marriages despite the Full Faith and Credit Clause of the Constitution. This "Defense of Marriage Act" (DOMA), introduced in an election year, passed the House and Senate by lopsided votes, the House vote being on the order of five to one (342–67) and the Senate vote about six to one (85–14). Much to the chagrin of gay activists who had supported him in his 1992 presidential bid, President Clinton signed the bill.[19] As a result of the passage of DOMA, same-sex couples are denied any federal benefits that come with marriage. These range from social security and tax benefits to housing and food stamps to employment benefits to inheritance. Overall, the Government Accounting Office (GAO), in a fifty-eight-page report issued in response to a request from Representative Henry Hyde, the chair of the House Judiciary Committee, found that in 1997 there were 1,049 federal statutory provisions in which benefits, rights, and privileges involved marital status and were thus inapplicable to same-sex couples (U.S. General Accounting Office 1997). In a 2004 update requested by Senate Majority Leader Bill Frist, the GAO updated the list to include 1,138 such provisions (U.S. General Accounting Office 2004).

There was also an attempt to amend the U.S. Constitution to prohibit same-sex marriage. On May 21, 2003, Representative Marilyn Musgrave (Republican, Colorado), and five cosponsors introduced into the House of Representatives H.J. Resolution 56, a resolution to amend the U.S. Constitution to define marriage as between a man and a woman. A companion bill, S.J. Resolution 26, was introduced in the Senate on November 25, 2003, by Senator Wayne Allard (Republican, Colorado). The text of this Federal Marriage Amendment states:

> Marriage in the United States shall consist only of the union of a man and a woman. Neither this Constitution nor the constitution of any state, nor state or federal law, shall be construed to require that marital status or the legal incidents thereof be conferred upon unmarried couples or groups. (H.J. Resolution 56/S.J. Resolution 26)

---

to "reserve marriage to opposite-sex couples." As noted, the legislature did so act.

18. Arkansas, Georgia, Idaho, Kansas, Kentucky, Louisiana, Michigan, Nebraska, North Dakota, Ohio, Oklahoma, South Carolina, South Dakota, Texas, Utah, Virginia, and Wisconsin.

19. Public Law No. 104–1909, Sec. 3(a), 110 Stat. 2419 (1996). President Clinton signaled his distaste for the bill by signing it in private at midnight (Purdum 1996).

President Bush issued a public statement supporting the amendment. In his statement on February 24, 2004, the president noted the overwhelming congressional passage of DOMA and similar actions in over three-quarters of the states. However, he pointed to the *Goodridge* decision in Massachusetts as well as actions taken by some local elected officials, like Mayor Gavin Newsom of San Francisco, to warn that the meaning of marriage was being changed. "After more than two centuries of American jurisprudence and millennia of human experience," the president said, "a few judges and local authorities are presuming to change the most fundamental institution of civilization" ("President Calls for Constitutional Amendment" 2004). DOMA was insufficient to protect traditional marriage, President Bush said, because "activist courts" might strike it down and because it doesn't prevent states and localities from granting marriage licenses to same-sex couples. The only solution was a constitutional amendment:

> If we're to prevent the meaning of marriage from being changed forever, our nation must enact a constitutional amendment to protect marriage in America. . . . I call upon the Congress to promptly pass and to send to the states for ratification an amendment to our Constitution defining and protecting marriage as a union of a man and woman as husband and wife. ("President Calls for Constitutional Amendment" 2004)

The president did leave room for civil unions, stating that the "amendment should fully protect marriage, while leaving the state legislatures free to make their own choices in defining legal arrangements other than marriage" ("President Calls for Constitutional Amendment" 2004). In addition to presidential support for the proposed amendment, at least twenty states considered nonbinding resolutions urging Congress to adopt the amendment. Two states, Alabama and Virginia, adopted such resolutions (http://www.stateline.org).

Under Article V of the Constitution, a proposed constitutional amendment must be approved by two-thirds of each House of Congress before being sent to the states for their consideration. Although the Federal Marriage Amendment was generally thought to lack the two-thirds vote necessary to pass either House of Congress, its introduction was seen as a effort by the Republican Party to create a campaign issue in the 2004 presidential election that would help George W. Bush in his election campaign against the Democratic Party nominees, Senators John Kerry and John Edwards. The Senate took up the proposed amendment first. In part to avoid having Senators Kerry and Edwards vote on the amendment, the Democrats commenced a filibuster. On Wednesday, July 14, 2004, the amendment was in effect defeated in the Senate, garnering forty-eight votes in favor of ending the filibuster and bringing the amendment to a vote and fifty opposed, well short of the sixty votes needed to end debate and the sixty-seven votes needed for approval. On September 30, 2004, the House voted on the amendment. Here, too, the proposed amendment was defeated, garnering 227 votes in favor (186 opposed), well short of the 290 votes needed for approval (Stolberg 2004).

Opposition to same-sex marriage was fueled by the 2004 presidential election. Many in the Republican Party believed that the party could attract conservative voters over the issue. In its 2004 party platform, the Republicans stated, "we strongly support President Bush's call for a Constitutional amendment that fully protects marriage, and we believe that neither federal nor state judges nor bureaucrats should force states to recognize other living arrangements as equivalent to marriage." The platform also urged the Congress to pass the so-called Marriage Protection Act, which removes the jurisdiction of the federal courts to order states to recognize same-sex marriages sanctioned in other states. The platform stated, "activist federal judges cannot [be allowed to] force 49 other states to approve and recognize Massachusetts' attempt to redefine marriage" ("A Safer World and a More Hopeful America" 2004). In contrast, the platform of the Democratic Party barely mentioned the issue. It opposed a constitutional amendment and supported leaving marriage laws to the states ("Strong at Home, Respected in the World" 2004).

The Marriage Protection Act of 2004 did come to a vote in the House. Its purpose was to remove the jurisdiction of the federal courts to hear or decide any case interpreting the language of DOMA. In other words, it provides that the federal courts would not have the power to order a state to give effect to any marriage between persons of the same sex under the laws of any other state. On July 22, 2004, a little more than a week after the Senate failed to approve the Federal Marriage Amendment, the House approved the act by a vote of 233–194.

As with same-sex marriage supporters, it is possible that litigation for same-sex marriage, particularly *Goodridge*, also mobilized opponents to increase their contributions to groups opposing same-sex marriage. In order to investigate this possibility, I examined contributions to, and revenue of, Focus on the Family, a leading "traditional values" group strongly opposed to same-sex marriage. Focus on the Family provides three years of financial reports on its Web site.

The first thing to note about Focus on the Family is that its revenue is roughly four times that of HRC's. In each of the years 2004–6, for example, Focus on the Family received annual contributions of over $130 million and enjoyed revenues of over $140 million. Second, it saw a major increase in both categories between 2003 and 2004. In 2004 its income increased by $15.2 million, an increase of 11.6 percent over its 2003 revenue. Even more impressively, contributions to it increased by over $17 million, an increase of 14.5 percent over 2003. These were the largest increases by far in the years 2003–6. Indeed, the more than $17 million increase in contributions in 2004 is approximately four times as large as the increase in contributions to HRC that year and is more than one-half of HRC's entire 2004 budget! While I can't say for certain that *Goodridge* led to the increase in contributions to Focus on the Family, given the group's strident and forceful opposition to same-sex marriage it seems more likely than not.

Totaling up the negative effects of litigation on political mobilization and legislative action paints a grim portrait for supporters of same-sex marriage. As a result of the litigation, and the political countermobilization that it sparked, forty-five states have legal barriers preventing same-sex marriage and twenty-seven states, home to 43.4 percent of the U.S. population, prohibit same-sex marriage by constitution. In addition, the federal government, through the Defense of Marriage Act, has limited all federal benefits that stem from marriage to heterosexual couples. As a result of litigation, same-sex marriage proponents face legislative and constitutional obstacles on both the state and federal level that did not exist before they turned to litigation.

How can the results of the mobilization of same-sex marriage supporters and opponents be fairly characterized? On the positive side, some might say that they can be characterized as "two steps forward, one step back." Proponents of such a view acknowledge the backlash but point to ten states, home to approximately 23 percent of the 2006 U.S. population, that now offer gay men and lesbians greater benefits than prior to the litigation.[20] In particular, they point to Massachusetts, where gay men and lesbians won the right to marry. They note that civil unions, recently unheard of, are now considered a fallback position, even supported by some conservatives (Zernike 2004). None of this, they argue, likely would have occurred without litigation. Others, however, might characterize the result as "one step forward, two steps back."[21] They agree that ten states have offered gay men and lesbians more rights than previously but they point to the forty-five state laws, twenty-seven constitutional amendments, and the federal DOMA, all of which prohibit same-sex marriage. Further, they note that almost all of these constitutional provisions and laws were created in direct response to litigation for same-sex marriage, litigation that did not have to be brought. Deciding which view to adopt may depend on one's assessment of the goal of same-sex marriage litigation. If the goal is improving the lives of gay men and lesbians, then there is a good deal to celebrate. On the other hand, if the goal of the litigation is marriage equality, then little has been achieved and major obstacles have been created. As a result of the litigation, twenty-seven state constitutions must now be amended and laws in forty-five states and the federal DOMA must be repealed before marriage equality can be achieved. In deciding which viewpoint is more accurate, I look to the litigants and litigators. Because their self-stated goal is marriage equality, the "one step forward, two steps back" view more accurately describes the situation.

20. However, over half of this 23 percent resides in just one state, California.

21. D'Emilio goes further, bluntly concluding that the "marriage campaign has been a disaster" (D'Emilio 2007, 45).

Same-Sex Marriage and Electoral Politics

This issue of same-sex marriage appears to have had electoral effects in many places. Some appear short-lived, such as the backlash in Vermont in the 2000 election. Others are more long-lasting, such as the adoption of constitutional amendments banning same-sex marriage. To the extent that the issue contributed to the election of opponents of same-sex marriage and gay rights more generally, then there were important political costs to the litigation. While it is possible that the issue has played itself out, and whatever political damage that resulted from litigation has already occurred, some of the damage is long-lasting.

The 2004 Election

The same-sex marriage issue appears to have figured in the 2004 election both on the state and federal level. Based on the available data it is hard to know for certain how large a role same-sex marriage played. Most opposed to it claim it was decisive in electing George Bush and like-minded Republicans while most same-sex marriage supporters say it played little or no role. The truth is likely somewhere in the middle. However, it is certainly the case that the Bush campaign and many Republican state campaigns made extensive use of same-sex marriage as a campaign issue. There is some evidence that this resulted in heightened turnout by conservative Republicans, by those who attend church regularly, and by Protestants. And those voters overwhelmingly opposed same-sex marriage and overwhelmingly supported conservative Republicans and George Bush.[22]

"Gay marriage was a key part of [Bush chief strategist] Karl Rove's turnout strategy" *Newsweek* reported (Rosenberg and Breslau 2004). The idea was to play upon what was, for at least some citizens, the "biggest concern: that judges in their states would follow the Massachusetts Supreme Court and force gay marriage on them" (Rosenberg and Breslau 2004). Around the country campaign workers and analysts pointed to Bush's opposition to abortion and his advocacy of a constitutional amendment to ban same-sex marriage as motivating factors for many voters. The Bush campaign "developed a national strategy based on those issues" (Farhi and Grimaldi 2004). Indeed, in postelection interviews Rove said that opposition to gay marriage was one of the most powerful forces in American politics today and that politicians ignored it at their peril. While stating that it was clearly not the only issue that led to Bush's victory, Rove commented that same-sex marriage was "part and parcel of a broader fabric where this year moral values ranked higher than they traditionally do" (Zeleny 2004). As Rove saw the election, the legalization of same-sex

22. For a good review of literature examining the effect of same-sex marriage on the 2004 election, see Smith, DeSantis, and Kassel (2006).

marriage in Massachusetts had "captured and colored the national imagination" throughout the country (Zeleny 2004). A *New York Times* reporter interviewing him wrote that he "appeared to stifle a grin when asked whether he was 'indebted' to Mayor Gavin Newsom of San Francisco, who opened his City Hall to gay marriages until he was blocked by a court, and to the Supreme Judicial Court of Massachusetts, for ruling that gay couples have a right to marriage" (Nagourney 2004).

Exit polls provide some evidence that concern over same-sex marriage was important in some voters' minds on election day.[23] One of the questions that exit pollsters asked was what was the most important issue facing the country. Respondents were given seven choices: taxes, education, Iraq, terrorism, economy/jobs, health care, and moral values. More voters (22 percent) told exit pollsters that moral values were the most important issue facing the country than any other issue! More than the economy or jobs, more than terrorism, and more than the war in Iraq. And among the 22 percent of voters who chose moral values as the most important issue facing the country, a whopping 80 percent voted for George Bush. More specifically, respondents were asked their views of same-sex marriage. While 25 percent supported the right of same-sex couples to marry, 37 percent, or one and one-half times as many respondents, opposed it. Among the more than one-third of the respondents who opposed same-sex marriage, 70 percent voted for Bush.

Who were these voters? Some were people voting for the first time. While John Kerry won a majority among the 11 percent of respondents who said they had never voted before, George Bush increased his vote share among them by 3 percentage points compared to the 2000 election. Some voters held deep religious beliefs. Of these respondents, 23 percent identified themselves as white evangelical/born-again Christians, and they gave 78 percent of their votes to Bush. The 16 percent of respondents who said they attended church more than weekly, and the 26 percent who said they attended weekly, gave 64 percent and 58 percent of their votes, respectively, to Bush. Among those who attended church weekly, Bush increased his 2000 vote share by 7 percentage points (Newport and Moore 2004). Interestingly, while there was no change in Bush's share of the vote from the 2000 election to the 2004 election among respondents who thought abortion should be always or mostly legal, Bush increased his share of the vote among the 26 percent of respondents who thought that abortion should be mostly illegal by 4 percentage points (to 73 percent) and increased his share of the vote among the 16 percent of respondents who thought that abortion should be always illegal by 3 percentage points to 77 percent. Together, these data suggest that there was a massive mobilization of conservative Christians that could, in part, be due to same-sex marriage. This

---

23. The following discussion is based on exit poll data presented by CNN (Exit Polls, 2004; see also Seelye 2004).

"super-charged . . . 'moral minority'" may well have provided Bush with his margin of victory (Froomkin 2004; Ostling 2004).

Additional evidence of the importance of religious voters to the election outcome comes from the Fourth National Survey of Religion and Politics, conducted November–December 2004 by the Bliss Institute at the University of Akron. The survey found that evangelical Protestants increased their support for Bush between 2000 and 2004 by about 4 percentage points and their turnout by 9 percentage points (Green et al. 2004, 8). Further, "a majority of the top four Bush constituencies regarded social issues as very important to their vote" (Green et al. 2004, 10). Overall, 21 percent of the entire sample reported that faith was "more important than other factors" and 26 percent said it was "about as important as other factors" in their voting decisions, for a total of 47 percent (Green et al. 2004, 13).

Are these results an artifact of the way the exit polls were constructed? Some critics believe so. The Pew Research Center conducted a national poll of 1,209 voters on the Friday through the Monday following the election. In contrast to many other polls, Pew used both an open-ended question to probe for the most important issue in deciding how to vote and a list of issues. When voters were given the standard list of seven issues, 27 percent chose moral values as the one issue that mattered most to them in deciding how to vote, placing it first. However, when voters weren't prompted with a list of issues, the percentage listing moral values dropped to 9 percent, tying it as the third most mentioned issue with terrorism/security, behind the war in Iraq and the economy (Pew Research Center 2004; Lester 2004).

Building on this last finding, some commentators dismiss the argument that same-sex marriage played an important role in the election. First, they suggest that the closed-ended question format gave the category "moral values" heightened salience. For example, Humphrey Taylor, the chairman of the Harris Poll, noted that in preelection polls that were open-ended, only 1 percent of respondents mentioned moral values as an important issue (Rutenberg 2004). Second, some argue that the category is unspecific and general, making it impossible to unpack its meaning. Gary Langer, director of polling for ABC News, noted that the category "'moral values' is not the same sort of specific issue that taxes or Iraq are" (Rutenberg 2004). He suggested that "'moral values' became a sort of 'catchall' for Mr. Bush's voters that could include topics as varied as gay marriage and vulgarity on television" (Rutenberg 2004). Third, same-sex marriage proponents noted that Kerry carried states like Oregon and Michigan in which constitutional amendments banning same-sex marriage were on the ballot and were approved. As Mary Bonauto, the civil rights director of the Gay & Lesbian Advocates & Defenders and an attorney in both the Vermont and Massachusetts cases argued, most states that had same-sex marriage constitutional amendments were solidly red states that Bush would have won anyway (Greenberger 2004). For these three reasons some commentators and same-sex marriage supporters conclude the issue had little impact (Langer and Cohen 2005).

There are others, however, who disagree. The notion that "moral values" was a vague and amorphous category was termed "garbage" by Bill McInturff, a Republican pollster. "The people who picked moral values as an issue know what that means . . . it's a code word in surveys for a cluster of issues like gay marriage and abortion," he said (quoted in Rutenberg 2004). To support this claim, McInturff noted that if "moral values" was a "catchall" with a confused meaning, then it would have been selected by Democrats as well as Republicans. However, of those who selected it, 80 percent voted for Bush. He concluded by arguing that this huge margin by which voters concerned about the issue cast their votes for Bush made the difference in the election (quoted in Rutenberg 2004).

It is also the case that additional polls taken after the election highlight the importance of traditional moral values. A Democratic polling firm—Greenberg, Quinlan, Rosner Research— conducted a survey of two thousand voters on the day of the election and the following day. Its results corroborate the findings of other surveys. For example, it gave respondents a choice of eleven issue areas to chose from in responding to the question of which issue was the most important in deciding how to vote, including "none" and "don't know." Of those who responded, 19 percent chose moral values. Only the "situation in Iraq" was chosen by a higher percentage of respondents (20 percent) but that was well within the poll's margin of error. More to the point, the poll asked voters to describe the three "most important issues and best reasons not to vote" for Kerry out of a list of nineteen items including "none" and "don't know." While 36 percent of the respondents selected "flip-flopping on issues," the second most cited issue was "gay marriage," chosen by 22 percent of respondents as a reason not to vote for Kerry (Greenberg 2004).

The Gallup organization also polled after the election, starting Election Day and running through mid-December. Among all voters, when asked an open-ended question about what were the one or two most important issues in their vote choice, 15 percent gave responses that Gallup categorized as involving "morals, values, or religious beliefs." Among Bush voters, when asked why they voted for Bush, responses that Gallup categorized as involving "morals/values/ religious beliefs" were given by 25 percent of Bush voters, more than any other category. In contrast, responses that could be so categorized were not among the eight most frequent issues mentioned by Kerry voters. Overall, 81 percent of Bush voters told Gallup that Bush's policies on moral values issues were either "extremely important" or "very important" in their vote choice, a full 17 percentage points higher than the responses given by Kerry voters. Gallup concluded that "moral values were definitely a key consideration for Bush voters" (Jones 2004).

Even if same-sex marriage played a role in the election, its supporters and some scholars believe that it was mostly limited to states where Bush would have won anyway (Hillygus and Shields 2005). The available evidence doesn't fully support this claim. In Michigan, for example, where a constitutional amendment banning same-sex marriage was approved and Kerry won, the presidential race was much closer than was expected. According to polling done by Ed Sarpolus, a pollster in Lansing, Michigan, 5 percent of Michigan voters said the constitutional amendment was the predominant reason they voted this year. Turnout among Republicans was as high as 72 percent in some counties, many in conservative west Michigan. "Clearly," Sarpolus concluded, "the amendment was a factor in that" (Dao 2004). The heavy turnout in the Republican strongholds of western Michigan, fueled by opposition to same-sex marriage, helped Bush come closer to winning than had been expected (Dao 2004). A county-level study of all eighty-three Michigan counties found "considerable evidence" that support for same-sex marriage ballot measures led to "increased levels of support for Bush" (Smith, DeSantis, and Kassel 2006, 87). Overall, nationwide, Campbell and Monson find that based on county-level data "evangelicals were more likely to vote for Bush in states with a gay marriage ban on the ballot" (Campbell and Monson 2007, 137–39).

In Kentucky, a state that Bush carried easily, there was a tight Senate race between the Republican incumbent, Senator Jim Bunning, and the Democratic challenger, Dr. Daniel Mongiardo. With little presidential campaigning in Kentucky, Republicans were concerned that conservative voters might stay at home on Election Day. In addition, Senator Bunning's behavior on the campaign and some of his statements led many to wonder if he was mentally stable. However, there was also a constitutional amendment banning same-sex marriage on the ballot and the Republicans made use of it. Even though Dr. Mongiardo had endorsed the amendment, the Republicans ran television commercials using the sound of ringing wedding bells to accuse him of being weak on the issue. Supporters of the measure also used extensive church networks to persuade people to vote, particularly rural conservative voters. In one of the closer Senate races of the 2004 election, Senator Bunning was reelected. According to Al Cross, a longtime political reporter in Kentucky and an interim director of the Institute for Rural Journalism and Community Issues at the University of Kentucky, it was the same-sex amendment that made the difference. As Cross put it, "I give this amendment more credit for re-electing Jim Bunning than George Bush's coattails" (quoted in Dao 2004).

Another Senate example of the influence of same-sex marriage on the 2004 election comes from Oklahoma where for much of the campaign there was a tight Senate race for an open seat between two members of the state's congressional delegation, Democrat Brad Carson and Republican Dr. Tom Coburn. Here, too, there was a constitutional amendment on the ballot banning same-sex marriage. Even though Carson supported the amendment, a national group opposed to same-sex marriage ran advertisements against him, charging that his position was open to change. Carson's campaign responded, labeling the advertisements "blatant lies about the congressman's conservative record" (Kirkpatrick 2004B). But Coburn won, and same-sex marriage appears to have played a role. According to candidate Carson himself, the presence of a same-sex marriage amendment on that state's ballot brought out conservatives "in droves" who voted for the amendment and his Republican opponent (Greenberger 2004). Overall, some political analysts suggest that the ballot measures "appear to have acted like magnets for thousands of socially conservative voters in rural and suburban communities who might not otherwise have voted. And in tight races, those voters—who historically have leaned heavily Republican—may have tipped the balance" (Dao 2004). And some scholars agree. Based on analysis of county-level data, Campbell and Monson (2007, 121) conclude that "while gay marriage may not have mattered much to most voters, it mattered a lot to a few voters. And in a close election, that may have been enough to be tip the scales in favor of Bush" and other Republican candidates.

The impact of the issue of same-sex marriage doesn't appear to be limited to states in which there was a constitutional amendment banning it on the ballot. Another important Senate race in which the issue of same-sex marriage may have played a role was South Dakota where Tom Daschle, the Democratic Minority Leader of the U.S. Senate, became the first party leader in the Senate in more than fifty years to lose his seat. According to a Daschle spokesman, the Republican nominee, Tom Thune, an evangelical Christian, made same-sex marriage the "centerpiece of his campaign" (Johnson and Rosenberg 2004). In the days leading up to the U.S. Senate's consideration of a constitutional amendment banning same-sex marriage, Thune focused on the issue: "Barnstorming the state in a twin-prop plane, he crisscrossed South Dakota to warn that gay marriage could be looming" (Johnson and Rosenberg 2004). Although Daschle opposed same-sex marriage, he also opposed the federal constitutional amendment banning it. This brought anti-same-sex marriage activists to the state. Focus on The Family ran a full-page advertisement in South Dakota titled, "Shame on You, Senator Daschle," criticizing Daschle for blocking a Senate vote on the federal constitutional amendment (Gorski 2004). In early October, James Dobson (Focus on the Family), Tony Perkins (Family Research Council), and Gary Bauer (American Values) addressed a rally of more than five thousand in Sioux Falls supporting traditional marriage and criticizing Daschle (Shouse 2004). On Election Day, Thune eked out a close victory over Daschle.

Similarly, in Iowa George Bush became the first Republican since Ronald Reagan in 1984 to carry the state. His campaign succeeded largely because of a massive mobilization of conservative Christians, particularly in the western part of the state. In traditional Democratic areas Bush did better than he did in 2000, picking up additional Catholic votes likely because of his opposition to abortion rights and gay marriage. But his margin of victory "seems to have come from western Iowa, [from] a confluence of heavy Republican registration and conservative values represented by [U.S. Representative Steve] King, one of Congress' most outspoken conservatives" (Beaumont 2004). The Bush campaign aired radio advertisements on Christian stations emphasizing Bush's opposition to abortion rights and gay marriage. In addition, King helped keep the values theme in voters' minds by running ads for his own reelection campaign related to family and marriage (Beaumont 2004). The result was a strong turnout by conservatives. According to the Iowa exit polls, 22 percent of voters identified themselves as white conservative Protestants, and a stunning 87 percent of them voted for Bush. An identical percentage of voters who selected "Moral Values" as the most important issue in the election also voted for Bush. And Bush's largest margin came from the western part of the state where he carried 58 percent of the vote ("Exit Polls" 2004).

These examples all suggest that same-sex marriage played a role in close elections across the country. For many conservative Christians in particular, same-sex marriage evokes a strong response. According to conservative activist Paul Weyrich of the Free Congress Foundation,

> ministers of the Gospel, both evangelical and Catholics and the Orthodox, are saying that this so fundamentally contradicts Scripture that if we permit this, our civilization as we know it is gone. People are saying, 'Oh, my gosh, we had no idea.' It has really grabbed people. Many of them are putting it in apocalyptic terms, that these are 'end times' if this is allowed to happen. (Quoted in Greenberger 2004)

In response, groups and candidates opposed to same-sex marriage mobilized around the issue. For example, an independent organization called Americans United to Preserve Marriage, created by Christian conservative Gary Bauer, ran commercials in Ohio, Michigan, and Pennsylvania and on the Fox News Channel criticizing Kerry for opposing the proposed federal constitutional amendment and voting against the Defense of Marriage Act. The National Republican Congressional Committee ran advertisements accusing Democratic representatives of supporting same-sex unions in Texas, Indiana, and Georgia. Republicans clearly tried to use the issue to win votes, whether in a Republican National Committee mailing with a picture of a man proposing to another man or in millions of phone calls (Tapper and Hassett 2004). According to Terry Nelson, political director of the Bush/Cheney '04 campaign, "in some states, Republican operatives even collected church directories in an effort to identify voters amenable to morality politics" (quoted in Campbell and Monson 2007, 129). Cheryl Jacques, at the time executive director of the Human Rights Campaign, commented that the prevalence of commercials was "the worst we have ever seen" (Kirkpatrick 2004B). Jacques also stated that the 2004 election witnessed the "highest level of intensity and aggression ever" (Kirkpatrick

2004B) against gay rights. "This is being used at every level and on every race" she concluded (Kirkpatrick 2004B).

A study of advertisements confirmed this view. Wilke (2005) found over one hundred advertisements in 2004 on same-sex marriage. Reviewing them, he concluded:

> Over and over again, political candidates running for state or national office—Republican and Democrat, male and female—touted in their ads that they voted against gay marriage or worked to "protect the sanctity of marriage." More negative ads chimed in from anti-gay forces including Focus on the Family and Americans United to Preserve Marriage, a so-called 527 organization from fundamentalist Gary Bauer, against presidential hopeful John Kerry. (Wilke 2005)

The argument that moral values, particularly opposition to same-sex marriage, provided a boost for Bush was vigorously asserted by many opponents to same-sex marriage and acknowledged by some Democrats and gay Republicans. Same-sex marriage "was the great iceberg" (Lochhead 2004; Cooperman 2004) in this election said Robert Knight, director of the Culture & Family Institute, an affiliate of Concerned Women of America and an opponent of same-sex marriage. "A lot of analysts saw the tip but didn't understand the power of the mass underneath. It galvanized millions of Christians to turn out and vote, and George Bush and the GOP got the lion's share of that vote" (Lochhead 2004; Cooperman 2004). "Tongue-in-cheek, Knight said Bush should send a bouquet to Margaret H. Marshall, the chief justice of the Massachusetts court, because she 'did more than any other single person to assure his victory'" (quoted in Cooperman 2004).

Some Democrats, as well as gay Republicans, publicly shared in the assessment that the same-sex marriage issue hurt Kerry. One was Senator Diane Feinstein of California. In response to a question the day after the election about the role of same-sex marriage, Senator Feinstein said, "I believe it did energize a very conservative vote . . . I think that whole issue has been too much, too fast, too soon . . . and people aren't ready for it" (Murphy 2004).[24] Representative Barney Frank, an openly gay Democratic member of the U.S. House of Representatives from Massachusetts, concurred. Pointing particularly to the mass same-sex weddings performed in San Francisco that followed the Massachusetts decision, Representative Frank told the *New York Times* that they helped to galvanize Mr. Bush's conservative supporters by playing into people's fears of same-sex weddings. A supporter of same-sex marriage, Frank had advised Mayor Newsom not to act for fear of the backlash that developed. He told the *Times* that he felt vindicated by the election results. However, even

---

24. Senator Feinstein was responding directly to a question about the electoral impact of San Francisco Mayor Gavin Newsom's issuance of marriage licenses as a response to the Massachusetts court decision.

without the mass weddings, Frank believed that "there would have been some collateral damage" caused by the Massachusetts decision (Murphy 2004). The Log Cabin Republicans, a gay Republican group that refused to endorse Bush, also thought same-sex marriage played an important role. According to Christopher Barron, the group's political director, "it's pretty clear that (Bush political czar) Karl Rove's strategy of using gay and lesbian families as wedge issues in this election worked. It's hard to argue with results" (Lochhead 2004). Even Matt Foreman, executive director of the National Gay and Lesbian Task Force, admitted that "gay marriage" was a "factor" in the election outcome (quoted in Belluck 2004).[25]

Some same-sex marriage supporters responded with equal vigor and with anger. "There's no evidence whatsoever to suggest that gay marriage tipped the scale in any state," said Matt Foreman (quoted in Lochhead 2004). Foreman was particularly concerned that gays were being made scapegoats for Kerry's loss: "To blame gay people for the failure of the Democratic message to motivate people is frankly unfair, and frankly, it's homophobic. Yes, the right wing was energized as never before to turn out for George Bush, but it's energized over a whole range of issues" (quoted in Belluck 2004). Mary Bonauto, speaking, perhaps, in gentler terms, concurred: "it's hard for me to say *Goodridge* tipped everything when these folks were making anti-gay law a centerpiece of their strategy since 1996" (quoted in Lochhead 2004). In an important sense, both Foreman and Bonauto are correct. Same-sex marriage was only one among many issues that motivated Republicans to turnout and individuals to vote for Bush. Using both individual and state-level data Lewis concludes that "other issues mattered much more, but that attitudes toward same-sex marriage had a statistically significant and meaningful impact on both individual voters and state vote totals" (Lewis 2005, 195). In close elections every issue matters. The evidence discussed above suggests that on a national level opponents feel very strongly about the issue. What was different about the 2004 election was the visibility of the issue. That visibility, in turn, was a direct result of the *Goodridge* decision and the same-sex marriages that followed it. Those events also led to the presence of constitutional amendments banning same-sex marriage on eleven state ballots. One of them was Ohio.

Ohio

In assessing the impact of same-sex marriage on the 2004 presidential election it is important to note how close the election was. Nationwide, Bush won by about 3 percent of the vote. As the election night wore on, it became clear that the candidate who carried Ohio would win the election. If John Kerry had carried Ohio he would have become the president, albeit while losing the popular vote (as George Bush had done in 2000). In the end, Bush carried

25. Foreman added that same-sex marriage was a factor, "along with a lot of factors."

Ohio by a slim margin of 51 percent to 49 percent, winning approximately one hundred and nineteen thousand more votes than Kerry when the final vote tally was certified in early December. Did same-sex marriage play any role in this slim Bush victory?

Groups supporting Kerry made a massive push in Ohio. America Coming Together (ACT) "claimed to have knocked on 3.7 million doors and held more than 1.1 million doorstep conversations in the state" (Bai 2004, 69). Steve Bouchard, Ohio state director for ACT, put it this way: "the sheer numbers of doors we knock on and phone calls we make are just astounding" (quoted in Bai 2004, 69). The week before the election Steve Rosenthal, ACT's CEO, told a *New York Times* reporter that he was "just blown away by what I see everywhere I go [in Ohio] . . . I really think we could win by a substantial margin. . . . For the life of me, I can't see how we could lose Ohio" (quoted in Bai 2004, 69). Indeed as vote totals began to come in on Election Day, ACT was ecstatic. It had exceeded the goals it had set for the total Kerry vote in each of its target counties. For example, at the final tally, Kerry exceeded the target vote in Cuyahoga County by 24 percent. In Franklin County (Columbus) Kerry's margin was ten times that of Gore's in 2000 (Farhi and Grimaldi 2004). Overall, Kerry's 2.66 million votes were the most ever received by a Democrat in Ohio (Bai 2004, 73). Kerry received more votes in Ohio in 2004 than Bush did when he carried the state in 2000 (Farhi and Grimaldi 2004). Nearly 70 percent of registered voters cast a ballot, up from 64 percent in 2000.[26]

As impressive as this effort was, it wasn't enough. The massive Democratic turnout was overwhelmed by an even more massive turnout of Republican voters. As the *New York Times* put it, "for Democrats, Election Day in Ohio felt like some kind of horror movie, with conservative voters rising up out of the hills and condo communities in numbers the Kerry forces never knew existed" (quoted in Bai 2004, 72). The ten counties with the highest turnout percentages, all 75 percent or higher, went for Bush (Bai, 2004, 74). In the previous four presidential elections more Democrats had gone to the polls in Ohio than Republicans. In 2004, however, exit polls reported that 5 percentage points more Republicans voted in Ohio than Democrats (Langer 2004; "Exit Polls" 2004). What caused this massive Republican turnout?

There is a good deal of evidence that at least part of the Republican turnout was the result of a constitutional amendment on the Ohio ballot that banned same-sex marriage. The amendment was approved with 62 percent of the vote. That amendment was put on the ballot as a direct response to the *Goodridge* decision. On May 18, 2004, the day after same-sex marriages became legal in Massachusetts, a fateful meeting was held in a Cincinnati suburb. The meeting that some commentators say "doomed" (Greenberger 2004) the

---

26. Turnout and vote data are available at the Web site of the Ohio Secretary of State at http://www.sos.state.oh.us/sos/results/index.html.

Kerry campaign was organized by Phil Burress from a group called Citizens for Community Values. "Shocked by scenes from the Bay State" (quoted in Greenberger 2004), Burress brought together lawyers to discuss how to make sure that same-sex marriages wouldn't happen in Ohio. The group decided to propose and support an amendment to the Ohio Constitution banning same-sex marriage. To place the amendment on the ballot, the group collected five hundred and fifty-seven thousand signatures, registering approximately fifty-four thousand new voters in the process. "We would not have had this on the ballot if they had not started marrying people on May 17," Burress said (quoted in Greenberger 2004). According to Burress, the amendment attracted people to the polls who supported Bush. As he put it, "the Massachusetts Supreme Court cost Kerry the election. . . . If we had not been on the ballot, Bush would not have won Ohio" (quoted in Ring 2004).

Many Democrats in Ohio agreed with this assessment. Raymond F. McGrath, legislative director of the International Brotherhood of Police Officers, volunteered for Kerry and said that Kerry was hurt at the polls in Ohio because of the ballot question on gay marriage (Ring 2004). Greg Hass, a Democratic strategist in Ohio, commented that conservative Republican voters "sure were highly motivated to turn out the vote against gay marriage. . . . That obviously impacted the outcome of the race by at least a couple hundred thousand votes" (quoted in Tapper and Hassett 2004). Haas noted that in "a lot of these small towns and small cities, areas like where I'm from, the turnout was off the charts. It really was you know a very diabolically brilliant move on the part of Karl Rove and others to lay this issue out there" (quoted in Tapper and Hassett 2004). Paul Tipps, a former state Democratic Party chairman and an informal adviser to Kerry, noted that the "evangelicals turned out, and clearly that issue [same-sex marriage] seems to have driven it. I am stunned. I didn't see it. This is a state that has historically voted the pocketbook" (quoted in Farhi and Grimaldi 2004). Examining the vote and a host of variables in all of Ohio's eighty-eight counties, Smith et al. (2006, 84) reported their "most striking" result to be that support for the constitutional amendment "affected the vote for Bush in 2004, even when controlling for his level of support in 2000." As with Michigan, they found "considerable evidence" that support for the amendment led to "increased levels of support for Bush" (Smith, DeSantis, and Kassel 2006, 84, 87).

The fact that Democratic operatives in Ohio, and the national press, were surprised by the mass conservative mobilization was because they weren't looking for it. Instead, they were focused on the registration and mobilization of Democratic voters by groups like ACT and the onslaught of television advertisements. As the *Washington Post* noted after the election, "even close observers of Ohio politics might have missed the Bush campaign's emphasis on social values because much of its outreach efforts occurred away from the mass media" (quoted in Farhi and Grimaldi 2004). According to John Green, a University of Akron professor of religion and politics, Bush's Ohio campaign used targeted mailings, phone calls, and doorstep visits to talk about values like traditional marriage. Robert Knight, director of the Culture & Family Institute, noted the "'massive efforts' by religious groups in Ohio 'to rally pastors and to get Christians out of the pews and into the voting booths'" (Lochhead 2004). Ohio Secretary of State J. Kenneth Blackwell did radio spots and taped a message that was played in 3 million phone calls to voters asking them to turnout and vote for the constitutional amendment banning same-sex marriage (Farhi and Grimaldi 2004). On the Sunday before Election Day, the group founded by Phil Burress to amend the Ohio Constitution had "2.5 million pamphlets inserted into church bulletins. Right before the polls opened, they phoned 850,000 supporters to remind them to vote" (Greenberger 2004). Professor Green described one piece of mail from the Bush campaign that featured a beautiful church and a traditional nuclear family. It was headlined, "George W. Bush shares your values. Marriage. Life. Faith" (quoted in Farhi and Grimaldi 2004). As Professor Green put it, "It could not have been clearer if it had quoted from the Bible" (quoted in Farhi and Grimaldi 2004). Overall, Campbell and Monson report that in Ohio "twenty-five unique pieces of mail linked Bush with opposition to gay marriage, compared to sixteen in Florida" where there was no constitutional amendment (Campbell and Monson 2007, 129).

The result of this mobilization around opposition to same-sex marriage was heightened turnout of conservative voters. "There is plenty of analytical and anecdotal evidence out there over the last couple of days that the Republicans hit the jackpot with the rural folks in Ohio," said Al Cross (quoted in Greenberger 2004). Analysis of the Ohio vote shows that Bush's vote totals and margins of victory soared all across Ohio's Appalachian southeast and its southern and western farm belt compared to the 2000 election (Farhi and Grimaldi 2004; Dao 2004). The *New York Times* reported that Bush's "extra-strong showing in those areas compensated for an extraordinarily large Democratic turnout in Cleveland and in Columbus" (Dao 2004). "I'd be naïve if I didn't say it helped," said Robert T. Bennett, chairman of the Ohio Republican Party. "And it helped most in what we refer to as the Bible Belt area of southeastern and southwestern Ohio, where we had the largest percentage increase in support for the president" (quoted in Dao 2004).

There is additional evidence supporting the claim that the presence of the constitutional amendment banning same-sex marriage increased turnout of conservative voters. That evidence comes from a comparison between the number of votes cast in the presidential race and on the amendment. As is typical, more votes were cast in the presidential race than on the amendment question. The difference is referred to as the drop-off. Revealingly, however, an analysis of several counties showed that the drop-off was much larger in Democratic counties than in Republican ones. For example, in rural Shelby

County in western Ohio, 1.5 percent fewer votes were cast on the constitutional amendment than in the presidential race. In contrast, there was a 6 percentage point drop-off in Cuyahoga County, a Democratic stronghold that includes
Cleveland (Dao 2004). These numbers suggest that at least some Republican
voters turned out to support the constitutional amendment.

Statewide, Professor Green told the *New York Times* that such figures indicated that fervent support for the amendment in conservative areas might have
caused turnout to rise by as much as 3 or 4 percentage points. "If you look
around rural, Appalachian Ohio, you'll see there were many counties that Bush
won by better than 60 percent of the vote," Professor Green said. "Those are
the areas where you'd see increased turnout because of this issue. And I think
that increase was large" (quoted in Dao 2004).

The exit polls tell some of the story. In response to the question of what
was the most important issue facing the country, "moral values" was chosen by 23 percent of Ohio voters, virtually identical to the 24 percent who
chose "economy/jobs." Among the 23 percent who chose "moral values,"
85 percent voted for Bush. Self-described conservatives made up 34 percent of Ohio's voters, and 87 percent of them voted for Bush, an increase
of 5 percentage points over his 2000 vote. White evangelical/born-again
Christians comprised 25 percent of the Ohio electorate and white conservative Protestants comprised 17 percent. They gave 76 percent and a stunning
91 percent of their votes, respectively, to Bush. Among the 14 percent of
voters who attended church more than weekly, 69 percent voted for Bush, as
did 64 percent of the 26 percent of voters who attended weekly. These figures
represented an increase over Bush's 2000 votes of a whopping 17 percentage
points and 5 percentage points, respectively. Interestingly, although Kerry
carried the African American vote overwhelmingly, winning 84 percent of
it, Bush increased his percentage among Ohio's black voters by 7 percentage points from his 2000 showing (nationwide, Bush increased his percentage of the black vote by only 2 percentage points). In contrast, nationwide,
Kerry won 88 percent of the black vote. It is plausible that the constitutional
amendment drew conservative African Americans to the polls. Indeed, in
reviewing public opinion on same-sex marriage, Persily, Egan, and Wallsten
(2008, 247) note that "African-Americans are distinctly opposed to same-sex
marriage, even after controlling for intervening variables such as attendance
at religious services, moral traditionalism, and living in the South." They
are less supportive of same-sex marriage than whites or Hispanics, in some
polls by more than 10 percentage points (Persily, Egan, and Wallsten 2006,
32). Commenting on the black vote, David Bositis, senior research associate
at the Joint Center for Political and Economic Studies, a Washington, D.C.
think tank that focuses on African Americans, noted "if the Supreme Court
put Bush in the White House in 2000, the Massachusetts Supreme Court
probably put him back in the White House in 2004" (quoted in Page 2004).

These data are particularly revealing given the massive mobilization effort by the Democrats in Ohio.

The exit poll data are similar on the constitutional amendment banning same-sex marriage, for which 81 percent of Republicans voted. In addition, 87 percent of conservatives, 89 percent of white conservative Protestants, 86 percent of white evangelical/born-again Christians, 85 percent of those who attend church more than weekly, 72 percent of those who attend church weekly, and 64 percent of monthly churchgoers also voted for the amendment. Geographically, the amendment received its highest level of support from southwest Ohio. The amendment was supported by more than 50 percent of the voters in every age, income, and education group. Interestingly, there was only a 2 percentage point difference in support by race, with 61 percent of African Americans voting in favor of the amendment compared to 63 percent of whites. In terms of actual votes, in over half of the counties in the state the amendment was approved by more than 70 percent of the voters. In contrast, Bush only carried about 14 percent of the counties by that margin.

Thus, analysis of the Ohio vote and informed analysis by both regionally based academics and political activists suggest that same-sex marriage contributed to Bush's slim margin of victory in Ohio.[27] Clearly it was only one among many issues that contributed to Bush's success, but in close elections every issue matters. While this statement is true for a number of issues, including the events of September 11, 2001, same-sex marriage activists had a choice about how to further their cause. By choosing to litigate, they mobilized a powerful opposition. The evidence suggests that if the *Goodridge* case has not been brought, or had come out the other way, John Kerry might well have carried Ohio and thus won the 2004 election.

Media Coverage

The preceding discussion has shown that litigation to further the right to same-sex marriage has had some positive as well as large negative consequences. On the positive side, there are now seven states that offer same-sex couples the same benefits enjoyed by married heterosexual couples, a result that arguably derives from the litigation effort. On the negative side, litigation for same-sex marriage is the direct cause of congressional legislation denying federal rights that accompany marriage to same-sex couples, of constitutional amendments banning it in more than half of the states that are home to nearly half of the population, of state laws limiting marriage to heterosexual couples in forty-five states, and of a political backlash that may have played a role in the 2004 elections. But perhaps there are other positive effects as well? One

27. Rosenthal (2004), the CEO of ACT, believes that the same-sex marriage amendment had no effect and that concern with terrorism was the key factor.

such effect might be in giving salience to the issue of same-sex marriage by increasing media coverage. Increased media coverage, in turn, might lead to increased public support for same-sex marriage (explored in the next section of this chapter) which, in turn, could lead to political and legal change. Thus, by litigating for same-sex marriage, proponents may have brought the issue to national attention. Perhaps there is a silver lining in the dark clouds of backlash?

Reader's Guide to Periodical Literature

In order to assess this claim I first examined the number of entries in the *Reader's Guide to Periodical Literature* dealing with the issue from 1990 to 2005.[28] The data are presented in table 13.2. Surprisingly, from 1990 to 1995 there was no heading for "Same-Sex Marriage" in the *Reader's Guide* despite the Hawaii litigation. The heading "Same-Sex Marriage" first appears in 1996 but refers the reader to the heading "Gay Marriage" under which entries are listed. This treatment of same-sex marriage remains consistent throughout the years examined.

Table 13.2 shows that there are no entries from 1990 to 1992 and only a handful in the years 1993–95. This is quite surprising since in 1993 the Hawaii Supreme Court held in *Baehr v. Lewin* that Hawaii's refusal to recognize same-sex marriages, absent a compelling justification, violated the state constitution's guarantee of equal protection of the laws. In 1996, however, forty-four entries appear in the 256 periodicals cataloged that year. Since 1996 was the year that a Hawaii trial court in *Baehr v. Miike* ordered the Department of Health to issue marriage licenses to same-sex couples, perhaps the increase in the number of entries reflects the litigation. Although this is plausible, the analysis is not so simple. First, while the forty-four entries represent a large increase over the preceding years, it is still quite a small number, especially when compared to the hundreds of entries dealing with civil rights that appeared in each year of the early and mid-1960s (see table 4.1, pp. 114–15). Similarly, it is only slightly more than half the number of entries that appeared about abortion in 1971 despite the fact that there were 63 percent more periodicals cataloged in 1996 than in 1971 (see table 8.1A, p. 232). To complicate matters further, 1996 was also the year the Congress enacted the Defense of Marriage Act. This makes it unclear whether the increase in entries about same-sex marriage was driven by the Hawaii court decision or the negative congressional reaction to it. Indeed, the *Reader's Guide* has a subcategory in 1996 labeled "Hawaii"; it only has seven entries, suggesting the Hawaii litigation was not responsible for many of the 1996 entries. Further, 1996 was a presidential election year.

---

28. See appendix 5 for precautions on interpreting these data in general. In particular, in some cases the *Reader's Guide* counts the same article multiple times under different subheadings. Thus, the absolute numbers may be overstated. This should not effect year-to-year comparisons.

Table 13.2   *Reader's Guide To Periodical Literature,* 1990–2005

# of Journals Catalogued	Year	# Gay Marriage Entries^	#Lesbian Marriage Entries
194	1990	NC	NC
210	1991	NC	NC
254	1992	NC	NC
252	1993	6	NC
248	1994	7	NC
249	1995	6	NC
256	1996	44	1
247	1997	9	3
250	1998	9	3
257	1999	11	3
256	2000	24	5
232	2001	11	1
261	2002	20	NC
244	2003	91	1
234	2004	251	NC
257	2005	63	SA

Key:

NC = No category.

SA = "See also" reference with no entries.

^ = It was not until 1996 that a heading, "same-sex marriage," appeared. From 1996 through 2005 the heading "same-sex marriage" referred the reader to the category "gay marriage."

NOTE: The category "civil unions" did not appear until 2004 when there were seventeen entries. In 2005 there were only five entries.

From 1997 to 1999 there were again very few entries. In late December, 1999, the Vermont Supreme Court issued its decision in *Baker v. Vermont* (1999) and the Vermont legislature enacted the Civil Unions Bill in the spring of 2000. However, there are only twenty-four entries cataloged in 2000, barely half of the 1996 total, although more than in any previous year except 1996. Perhaps the small number of articles is due to the fact that the *Reader's Guide* did not include the category "civil unions" until 2004? This is unlikely since the category "gay marriage" is broad enough to encompass civil unions. Further, one-quarter of the entries did have the words "union" or "unions" in their titles, modified by the words "gay" or "same-sex." This suggests that stories on civil unions were being counted. Similarly, the category "lesbian marriage" recorded its largest numbers of entries in 2000, perhaps reflecting the fact that the lead plaintiffs in Vermont were women. However, there were only five entries. And the following year (2001) saw more than a 50 percent drop in the number of gay marriage entries, with only eleven. This all suggests that the *Reader's Guide* did catalog stories dealing with civil unions; it's just that there weren't very many of them. Finally, again complicating the analysis, 2000 was a presidential election year.

The years 2001 and 2002 saw little coverage of same-sex marriage. However, in 2003 there were ninety-one entries, more than in any previous year. This could conceivably be driven by the Massachusetts Supreme Judicial Court's decision in *Goodridge* in late November, or perhaps by the upcoming presidential primary season. In order to get a better sense of what drove the coverage, I looked first at the dates of publications. Thirty-one of the entries, slightly more than one-third, had dates after the announcement of the *Goodridge* decision on November 18. Interestingly, over a third of those entries (eleven) came from two conservative publications, the *National Review* and the *Weekly Standard*. Subtracting the thirty-one entries published after *Goodridge* still leaves sixty entries prior to *Goodridge*, more than any other year. This suggests that while the *Goodridge* decision may have influenced coverage, there was a good deal of coverage in 2003 prior to it.

In 2004 there were a whopping 251 entries, more than all entries from 1990 to 2003 combined. While this could be due to *Goodridge*, it could also be due to the presidential campaign and the large number of constitutional amendments on state ballots prohibiting same-sex marriage. Without doing a content analysis of each article it is not possible to know for sure. However, it is the case that of the 552 entries cataloged from 1990 to 2005, a full 319 (58 percent) appeared in only the three presidential election years of 1996, 2000, and 2004. And the next year (2005) the number of entries dropped precipitously to sixty-three, fewer than in 2004 and 2003, despite the fact that there was a 10 percent increase in the number of journals cataloged in 2005 compared to 2004.

Overall, then, analysis of the *Reader's Guide* suggests that stories on same-sex marriage appeared infrequently outside of presidential election years and just one year, 2004, accounts for 51 percent of all stories in the fifteen years from 1990 to 2004.

Newspaper Coverage

Newspaper coverage is another important way in which issues are brought to national attention. Perhaps litigation for same-sex marriage led to increased coverage of the issue in newspapers? This, in turn, could influence public opinion. In order to explore this possibility I selected the *New York Times* for study. The *Times* is a good choice for several reasons. First, it is known as an agenda-setter for other newspapers and media outlets around the country. If the *Times* carries a story or covers a topic, it signals that the topic is worthy of attention. Second, the *Times* is widely read by elites and opinion-setters. Increased and positive coverage of same-sex marriage might lead to increased support for it by elites. Third, the *Times* is generally considered a liberal paper and to the extent that it hires correspondents who share its biases, its news coverage is likely to be as or more supportive of same-sex marriage than other major newspapers. Thus, examining coverage of same-sex marriage in the *New York Times* is a reasonable way to explore whether litigation led to increased coverage of the issue.

As a first step in the analysis, I ran a Lexis search for all entries in the *New York Times* from 1980 to 2004 containing the terms "same-sex marriage, gay marriage, or homosexual marriage." The search produced 1,905 hits and they are presented by year in table 13.3.

The first thing to note about the data is that although there was at least one entry in every year of the 1980s, there were never more than seven in any given year. In 1992, there were nineteen entries, the first time the number of entries reached double digits. Surprisingly, there were only nineteen entries in 1993, the year of the Hawaii Supreme Court same-sex marriage decision (*Baehr v. Lewin*) even though the decision was handed down in early May. Nineteen entries is the equivalent of barely one every three weeks, hardly a groundswell of coverage. If court decisions brought the issue of same-sex marriage to the media, the 1993 data don't provide evidence for the claim. The number of entries was a bit larger in 1994 and 1995 but still tiny. However, in 1996 there were 204 entries, 11 percent of the total of the twenty-five-year time span under investigation.

What caused the large increase in the number of entries in 1996? One possibility is that the increase was driven by the Hawaii trial court decision in *Baehr v. Miike* (1996) ordering the Department of Health to issue marriage licenses to same-sex couples. In order to test this hypothesis I broke down the 1996 entries by month. Table 13.4 (p. 389) presents the data.

The data don't provide much support for this hypothesis. Although there were thirty entries in September, 1996, the month in which the trial was conducted, there were more entries in May (thirty-four) and March (thirty-three), well before the trial. Even though the decision was handed down early in December (December 3), there were only fourteen entries that month, fewer entries than in eight other months. Overall, there were 108 entries in the first half of the year (January through June), 12.5 percent more entries than the ninety-six in the second half of the year when the trial was held (September) and the decision announced (early December). These data suggest that the Hawaii same-sex marriage decision isn't responsible for the massive increase in coverage in 1996.

A second possibility is that the increase was due to the 1996 presidential campaign and the passage of the Defense of Marriage Act. The data provide some support for this possibility. The two months of February and March, when the majority of presidential primaries take place, account for 21 percent of the year's entries. In addition, the months of September and October, when the general election campaign was in full swing, account for 24 percent of the year's entries. If entries were distributed evenly throughout the year, those four months should account for one-third of the entries. Instead, they account for 45 percent of the entries. In addition, the Defense of Marriage Act was introduced

Table 13.3   *New York Times* Entries Mentioning "Same-
Sex Marriage, Gay Marriage, or Homosexual
Marriage," by Year, 1980–2004

Year	Entries	% of Total
1980	1	*
1981	2	*
1982	3	*
1983	2	*
1984	6	*
1985	3	*
1986	7	*
1987	2	*
1988	1	*
1989	6	*
1990	2	*
1991	5	*
1992	19	1
1993	19	1
1994	28	1.5
1995	20	1
1996	204	11
1997	61	3.2
1998	56	3
1999	63	3.3
2000	108	5.7
2001	36	1.9
2002	34	1.8
2003	224	11.8
2004	993	52.1

Total: 1,905

* = < 1%

SOURCE: See Appendix 8.

on May 7 and signed by President Clinton on September 21. There were more entries in May than in any other month and September recorded the third largest number of entries. Overall, it appears that the large increase in the number of entries in 1996 was more likely the result of the presidential election and the passage of the Defense of Marriage Act than the Hawaii court decision.

Returning to the yearly data in table 13.3, there is a drop-off in the number of entries in the years 1997, 1998, and 1999. However, in 2000 there is another large increase, to 108 entries. Again, it is possible that this coverage was driven by same-sex marriage litigation. The Vermont Supreme Court issued its decision in *Baker v. Vermont* in December of 1999 and the Vermont legislature debated what to do in the spring of 2000. At first blush, and standing alone, the monthly data in table 13.4 provide support for this causal chain because 51 percent of the entries appearing in 2000 appear in the first four months. However,

2000 was also a presidential election year and the two months of February and March, when most of the presidential primaries were held, alone account for 31 percent of the year's entries. Adding the months of September and October to take note of the presidential election campaign brings the total to 47 percent of the year's entries, just a few entries fewer than the number appearing in the first four months of the year. Further, although Governor Dean signed the bill in April, albeit toward the end of the month, that month saw substantially fewer entries than in March and there were very few entries in the subsequent months of May, June, July, and August. And, of course, there were barely half as many entries overall in 2000 than there were in 1996. This all suggests that the increase in entries from 1999 to 2000 was, at most, only partially driven by the Vermont litigation.

In 2001 and 2002 the yearly data in table 13.3 show very little coverage. Indeed, there are fewer entries in those years than in the years 1997–99. But in 2003 the number of entries jumps again to 224, slightly more than the 204 in 1996 and the most to date. However, that number is dwarfed by the 993 entries that appear in 2004, 52.1 percent of the total number of entries from 1980 to 2004. What can explain this sudden and massive increase?

Again, the analysis is not straightforward. On the one hand, the *Goodridge* decision legalizing same-sex marriage in Massachusetts came down on November 18, 2003. Examining the monthly data in table 13.4 shows that 41 percent of the entries appearing in 2003 appeared in the months of November and December, suggesting that the decision had a large impact on the 2003 coverage. But it is also the case that 40 percent of the coverage appeared in the three months of June, July, and August, powered, I suspect, by the U.S. Supreme Court decision in *Lawrence v. Texas* (2003) striking down sodomy laws. As for 2004, the month of January had fewer entries than any month that year, which would not be expected if *Goodridge* was driving coverage. This may be misleading, however, because the thirty-three entries appearing that month were more than any month in 2003 except for June, November, and December. But, on the other hand, there were many more entries in just the two months of February and March, 2004, when the presidential primary campaign was ongoing, than in all of 2003 (318 to 224). Indeed, February and March, 2004, alone account for 32 percent of the 2004 coverage. Further, when the general campaign months of September and October are added, the four months when campaigning is most intense account for 47 percent of the entries. This suggests that the campaign played an important role in generating entries about same-sex marriage. This finding makes sense since there were eleven constitutional amendments on the 2004 ballot banning same-sex marriage. This may account for the large number of entries in November, 2004.

Overall, it is instructive to note that of the four years with the largest number of entries over the 1980–2004 period, three are presidential election years (1996, 2000, 2004). Indeed, during these years there were 1,305 entries,

Table 13.4   *New York Times* **Entries Mentioning "Same-Sex Marriage, Gay Marriage, or Homosexual Marriage," by Month, Selected Years**

Month	1996 # of Entries	1996 % of Yearly Total	2000 # of Entries	2000 % of Yearly Total	2003 # of Entries	2003 % of Yearly Total	2004 # of Entries	2004 % of Yearly Total
Jan.	0	0	8	7	3	1	33	3
Feb.	10	5	12	11	2	1	152	15
March	33	16	22	20	4	2	166	17
April	12	6	14	13	3	1	42	4
May	34	17	7	7	3	1	86	9
June	19	9	5	5	34	15	46	5
July	18	9	5	5	27	12	84	9
Aug.	12	6	3	3	29	13	81	8
Sept.	30	15	5	5	20	9	60	6
Oct.	18	9	12	11	8	4	91	9
Nov.	4	2	10	9	53	24	114	12
Dec.	14	7	5	5	38	17	38	4
Totals:	204	101*	108	101*	224	100	993	101*

*Percentages sum to greater than 100 percent due to rounding.
SOURCE: See Appendix 8.

approximately 69 percent of all entries appearing over the twenty-five year period. Thus, while it remains possible that same-sex marriage litigation led to increased coverage of same-sex marriage in *The New York Times*, the data suggest that other factors, including presidential elections and the Defense of Marriage Act, played a large role. This is in line with the findings of Franklin and Kosaki (discussed below) that media coverage of issues decided by courts is driven by elite reactions to those decisions. Whatever the cause, it is clear that the *New York Times* is covering same-sex marriage. Indeed, although coverage dropped by slightly more than half in 2005 from the 2004 total, the 438 entries published in 2005 and the 467 published in 2006 (not shown) are the second and third largest entries since 1980, suggesting that same-sex marriage continues to be covered.

The number of entries published, and their distribution over time, only tell part of the story. What they don't tell is the content of the coverage. For media coverage to further the goal of same-sex marriage litigation, that coverage needs to present same-sex marriage in a positive light. If, for example, stories on same-sex marriage talk about public and elite support for it, portray it as a case of equality and justice, show same-sex couples and families as happy, healthy, contributing members of society, as good parents, neighbors, and workers, then it is possible that media coverage can work to create increased support for same-sex marriage. If, on the other hand, stories focus on opposition to it, then the increased coverage is unlikely to further the cause. If they highlight public and elite opposition, efforts to change laws and constitutions to ban it, religious or moral opposition, and claims of pandering to special interests, then increased coverage is of no help. For supporters of a cause, increasing media coverage of their opponents and their arguments is not helpful.

In general, the social science literature finds that most judicial decisions receive little sustained coverage. For example, Franklin and Kosaki find that the U.S. Supreme Court receives substantially less media coverage than the president or the Congress. Finding media coverage of the Court episodic, Franklin and Kosaki report that for Supreme Court cases that receive any media coverage at all "coverage is over a fairly short span of time" (Franklin and Kosaki 1995, 360). Further, they find that "even controversial and unpopular decisions . . . are likely to vanish quickly from the media" (Franklin and Kosaki 1995, 360). If this holds for the U.S. Supreme Court, the most prominent and visible court in the country, then it should hold with even more force for state court opinions. This suggests it is unlikely that the increase in the number of entries on same-sex marriage is driven by litigation.

This, however, is only part of Franklin and Kosaki's findings. They emphasize that although Supreme Court decisions are likely to receive little coverage, and that coverage quickly fades, this can be changed by the action of elites. When Supreme Court decisions provoke "sustained elite reaction," the media covers those reactions. Thus, for example, they find that media coverage of the Supreme Court's 1989 decision overturning a criminal conviction for burning an American flag (*Texas v. Johnson* 1989) was beginning to fade until President Bush called for a constitutional amendment banning flag desecration. This was followed by congressional debate and ongoing political posturing that the media covered. Thus, they conclude that "elites can keep some Court decisions on the media's agenda if they sustain a reaction" (Franklin and Kosaki 1995, 360). Given the extraordinary efforts of same-sex marriage opponents to change laws and amend constitutions to prohibit same-sex marriage, this work suggests that coverage of same-sex marriage in the media may be driven more by opponents than supporters.

In order to understand how the media are portraying same-sex marriage, a research assistant and I undertook a content analysis of entries in the *New York Times* over the twenty-five-year period from 1980 to 2004. Because there were 1,905 entries, we randomly selected a set number of entries for each year and independently read and coded them, which we did to try to minimize any bias either of us might bring to the analysis. In about half of the years the entries included a few false hits such as corrections, index summaries, etc. They were excluded from the analysis. In total, we coded 317 entries. For each entry we looked to determine how same-sex marriage was being covered. Did the entry treat it in a negative or positive way? Did it do both? Table 13.5 (p. 392) presents the results and appendix 8 explains the methodology and coding rules.

Before discussing the data, it is important to state the obvious point that coding decisions are subjective. Although my research assistant and I did all initial coding independently and had a high agreement rate, it is possible that we were unconsciously biased towards a particular outcome. This risk is inherent in all content coding. That being said, I take some solace in the findings of a clear and consistent pattern of coverage.

Turning to the data, there is a lot going on in table 13.5. The first four columns on the left indicate the year, the number of entries produced in the search, the number of entries read, and the number coded. For example, in 1996 there were 204 entries. We read thirty-one of them and, after excluding false hits, coded twenty-eight. The next three columns (Positive, Negative, Mixed & Tangential) indicate how the entry was coded. The last two columns calculate the percentage of stories coded positive and negative in each year. In addition, asterisks appear in some of the columns. These represent an entry about a country other than the United States. So, for example, of the eleven entries coded as positive in 2003, five involved activities in a foreign country and the remaining six were entries about the United States.

There were not many entries in the years 1980–91. This means that the percentages of positive and negative coverage have little meaning. To find, for example, that 100 percent of all entries in 1988 portrayed same-sex marriage in a positive light, or that 100 percent of all entries in 1982 portrayed same-sex marriage in a negative light, is virtually meaningless when there were only one and three entries in those years, respectively. It is in the years starting with 1996 that there are sufficiently large numbers of both entries and coded entries for analysis to be meaningful.

Careful examination of the years 1996–2004 reveals a consistent pattern. In every year but one (2003), the percentage of negative stories is substantially greater than the percentage of positive stories. Focusing on the years with the largest number of entries and thus the largest number of coded entries is revealing. Starting with the year 1996, fully half of the entries were negative, compared to only 14 percent that were positive. Although 1996 was the year in which a Hawaii court ordered the issuance of same-sex marriage licenses, it was also the year that the federal Defense of Marriage Act was enacted. And, of course, it was a presidential election year. This suggests that it was the negative elite reaction to the Hawaii decision that received sustained coverage, not the positive nature of the decision itself.

A similar result is apparent in the data for 2000 and 2004. In 2000, the percentage of negative entries outweighs positive ones by a ratio of better than five to one! This might be particularly surprising since 2000 was the year that Vermont enacted its civil unions law. However, it was also a presidential election year, which again suggests that *New York Times* coverage of same-sex marriage was driven more by elite opposition to it than by supportive litigation. Similarly, in 2004, the year with the largest number of coded entries, there are more than two and one-half times as many negative entries as positive ones.

Table 13.5   *New York Times* Entries Mentioning "Same-Sex Marriage, Gay Marriage,
              or Homosexual Marriage," by Year and Content, 1980–2004

Year	Entries	Read	Coded	Positive	Negative	Mixed & Tangential	%Pos.	%Neg.
1980	1	1	1			1	-	-
1981	2	2	2		1	1	0	50
1982	3	3	3		3		0	100
1983	2	2	2		1	1	0	50
1984	6	6	6	3	3		50	50
1985	3	3	3		2	1	0	67
1986	7	7	6	1	5		17	83
1987	2	2	1	1			100	0
1988	1	1	1	1			100	0
1989	6	6	6	3		3	50	0
1990	2	2	2	2			100	0
1991	5	5	4		3	1	0	75
1992	19	10	10	3	6	1	30	60
1993	19	10	8		1	7	0	13
1994	28	10	8	2	2	4*	25	25
1995	20	10	9	2	1	6*	22	11
1996	204	31	28	4	14	10	14	50
1997	61	16	14		4	10**	0	29
1998	56	14	14	1	8	5	7	57
1999	63	16	15	2*	5	8	13	33
2000	108	22	20	2*	11	7	10	55
2001	36	12	12	1*	3	8***	8	25
2002	34	12	10	2	5**	3	20	50
2003	224	34	31	11*****	10	10*	36	32
2004	993	114	101	16	43	42*	16	42
Totals:	1,905	351	317	57	131	129	18	41

"Mixed" = Both positive and negative positions taken, or no position taken.
"Tangential" = Tangential mention of search term.
* = 1 story on same-sex marriage in a foreign country.
SOURCE: See Appendix 8.

Given the presidential election campaign and the mobilization by same-sex marriage opponents around constitutional amendments banning same-sex marriage that appeared on ballots in eleven states, this makes sense.

As noted above, the data for 2003 don't fit the pattern. As presented in the table, slightly more entries were coded positive (36 percent) than were coded negative (32 percent). Since *Goodridge* was decided in November, 2003, perhaps it created a surge of positive *New York Times* entries about same-sex marriage. While this is possible, the data also reveal that five of the eleven entries coded as positive dealt with foreign countries. There were four entries dealing with Canada and its provinces and one dealing with Belgium. It is likely that the appearance of these stories in the *New York Times* had nothing to do with the *Goodridge* decision. Rather, they reflected same-sex marriage activities occurring outside the United States and independently of any same-sex litigation in the United States. They would have appeared regardless of who won *Goodridge* or even whether the case was brought. Removing these five foreign entries from the positive count (and one from the "Mixed & Tangential" count) reduces the percentage of positive entries from 36 percent to 20 percent, substantially fewer than the 40 percent of entries coded negative (when the foreign entries are removed) and in keeping with results from other years.

Supporters of same-sex marriage might respond to these data by claiming that any coverage is better than no coverage. Even negative coverage of same-sex marriage presents it as a possibility, in some sense validating it as a serious policy. But this argument assumes that readers look past critical comments to evaluate the underlying issue itself. While this is most likely the case for supporters of same-sex marriage, there is no reason to believe critical news stories about same-sex marriage have this effect on the undecided or uninformed reader. It is far more likely that negative coverage of same-sex marriage associates it with a bad idea.

Overall, analysis of the *Reader's Guide to Periodical Literature* and the *New York Times* shows that over the period 1980–2004 the issue of same-sex marriage has received increasing media attention. However, the temporal distribution of that attention suggests that it is largely driven by opposition to same-sex marriage, not litigation in support of it. This conclusion is corroborated by content analysis of *New York Times* entries that shows that the coverage is substantially more negative than positive. The hoped-for silver lining has tarnished.

There is, however, one more location where litigation may have influenced media coverage—editorials and signed op-ed articles. Although news coverage may not be supportive of same-sex marriage, perhaps there was a change in editorials and elite opinion as expressed in op-ed articles. Perhaps litigation for same-sex marriage influenced the way in which editorial writers thought about the issue and the kinds of opinions expressed in op-ed articles. In order to test this hypothesis, I read and analyzed all editorials and signed op-ed articles dealing with same-sex marriage, gay marriage, homosexual marriage, domestic partnership, or civil union in two major newspapers, the *New York Times* (1980–2004) and the *Chicago Tribune* (1986–2004). I included the *Tribune* because it is generally thought to be a more conservative paper.[29]

29. However, the *Tribune*, published in the third largest city in the country, may not be fully representative of conservative viewpoints. Consider, for example, the condemnation of the 1996 *Baehr* decision in the *Boston Herald*: "It is folly to devalue [marriage] with an arrangement shunned for thousands of years" ("Marriage in a Democracy" 1996). See also the reaction in the *Indianapolis Star*: "[M]arriage is inherently a union of a man and a woman, recognized by virtually every culture through history and ordained by God" ("Cheapening Marriage" 1996). Many other similar reactions could easily be presented.

The data are presented in tables 13.6 and 13.7. Overall, the *Times* published 40 editorials and 125 op-eds over the twenty-five-year period 1980–2004 while the *Tribune* published 27 editorials and 133 op-eds over the twenty-year period 1985–2004.

Examining results for the *Times* in table 13.6, in only eleven of the twenty-five years I surveyed was there any editorial on the subject. With the exception of 2004, when a full half of all editorials over the twenty-five-year period were published (twenty), the largest number of editorials on this issue in any one year was six in 2003, followed by four in 1996 and two in 1999 and 2000. As for op-eds, in barely half of the years surveyed (thirteen) was there any op-ed concerning the issue. In only three years (1996, 2003, and 2004) were there more than five op-eds and, in the remaining ten years, eight of them had only one or two op-eds. Just about half of all op-eds in the *Times* appeared in one year, 2004.

The pattern in the *Tribune* is similar (see table 13.7, p. 399). Editorials appeared in only nine of the twenty years surveyed and in only one year, 2004, were there more than four editorials, when there were eleven. As for op-eds, they appeared in fourteen of the twenty years. In ten of those fourteen years there were four or fewer op-eds. The three years of 1996, 2003, and 2004 account for 105 op-eds, a whopping 79 percent of the total.

There is an interesting pattern in both newspapers. Approximately two-thirds of all editorials and op-eds over the period surveyed appeared in the presidential election years of 1996, 2000, and 2004.[30] With the *Times*, 26 of 40 editorials (65 percent) and 89 of 125 op-eds (71 percent) appeared in those three years. The percentages are similar with the *Tribune*, with 16 of the 27 editorials (59 percent) appearing in those three years as well as 88 of 133 op-eds (66 percent). More poignantly, fully half of the *Times* editorials and op-eds appeared in one year, 2004 (the corresponding figures for the *Tribune* were 41 percent of all editorials and 42 percent of all op-eds). That year, of course, witnessed eleven ballot measures banning same-sex marriage.

This pattern of editorials and op-eds suggests two points. First, much of the interest in the issue by editorial and op-ed page writers appears driven by electoral politics. Second, outside of election years, only a keen and vigilant reader of the *Times* and *Tribune* editorial pages would have seen any piece on same-sex marriage, gay marriage, homosexual marriage, domestic partnership, or civil union. Even in 2004, with the largest number of editorials by far, the *Times's* and *Tribune's* readers only would have come across an editorial approximately once every three and five weeks, respectively. While there were more op-eds, as the content analysis reported below shows, most of them only touched on the issue tangentially or didn't take clear positions. These small

30. Note, too, that DOMA was enacted in 1996.

Table 13.6   *New York Times* Editorials and Op-Eds Mentioning "Same-Sex Marriage, Gay Marriage, Homosexual Marriage, Domestic Partnership, or Civil Union," 1980–2004

Year	Editorials				Op-Eds			
	Number	Positive	Negative	Mixed & Tangential	Number	Positive	Negative	Mixed & Tangential
1980	0	0	0	0	0	0	0	0
1981	0	0	0	0	0	0	0	0
1982	1	0	0	1	0	0	0	0
1983	0	0	0	0	1	0	0	1
1984	1	0	0	1	0	0	0	0
1985	0	0	0	0	0	0	0	0
1986	0	0	0	0	0	0	0	0
1987	0	0	0	0	0	0	0	0
1988	0	0	0	0	0	0	0	0
1989	0	0	0	0	0	0	0	0
1990	0	0	0	0	0	0	0	0
1991	0	0	0	0	0	0	0	0
1992	0	0	0	0	1	1	0	0
1993	0	0	0	0	2	0	0	2
1994	0	0	0	0	0	0	0	0
1995	1	0	0	1	2	0	0	2*
1996	4	4	0	0	22	5	4	13
1997	1	0	0	1	3	0	0	3
1998	1	1	0	0	2	0	0	2
1999	2	2	0	0	2	2*	0	0
2000	2	2	0	0	5	0	2	3
2001	0	0	0	0	1	1	0	0
2002	1	0	0	1	2	0	0	2
2003	6	3*	0	3	20	5	0	15
2004	20	8	0	12	62	10	2	50
Totals:	40	20	0	20	125	24	8	93

"Mixed" = Both positive and negative positions taken, or no position taken.
"Tangential" = Tangential mention of search term.
* = 1 story on same-sex marriage in a foreign country.

SOURCE: See Appendix 8.

numbers of editorials and op-eds, easily missed or tangential, seem unlikely to significantly influence opinion.

As small as the numbers are, though, it is still important to determine the content of the coverage. Changes in elite opinions as measured by editorials and op-eds may be a precursor of broader societal change. In order to assess this possibility, my research assistant and I independently read and coded all editorials and op-eds mentioning the search terms in the two newspapers.

The *Times* editorial board has been supportive of same-sex marriage since at least the spring of 1996. As early as April, 1996, a *Times* editorial criticized "the fundamental unfairness of government denying a whole class of citizens the important benefits that flow from civil marriages" ("The Freedom to Marry" 1996). After the decision in *Baehr v. Miike* (1996) in December, the *Times* editorialized that the decision was "a breakthrough for fairness." The editorial went on to write of the "unfairness of denying gay people the right to marry" ("The Message From Hawaii" 1996).

The *Times* also editorialized in support of domestic partnerships in New York and civil unions in Vermont. New York City Mayor Rudolph Giuliani was praised for offering "enlightened legislation to make registered domestic partners, whether heterosexual or homosexual, equal to married spouses under all New York City government rules and policies" ("Equality for Domestic Partners" 1998). In an editorial in late December, 1999, the *Times* called the Vermont Supreme Court's *Baker v. Vermont* decision "a breakthrough for fairness," using the same language it had used to characterize the Hawaii decision ("Vermont's Momentous Ruling" 1999). A few months later the *Times* wrote that "Vermonters should be proud that they are leading the way toward a society that values stable gay relationships." The editorial also noted that "in time, Vermont's example will show the rest of the country that same-sex unions are not a threat to traditional marriage and deserve the name of marriage as well as the law's full protection" ("Legal Unions for Gays in Vermont" 2000). Finally, on February 18, 2004, an editorial stated, "this page fully supports the right of gay men and lesbians to marry" ("Gay Marriage in the States" 2004). Overall, as table 13.6 shows, fully half of the *Times's* editorials have been positive and none can fairly be categorized as negative.

But what was the *Times's* editorial position on same-sex marriage *before* the *Baehr* litigation? This is not entirely clear because the *Times* did not address the issue before *Baehr*. The closest it came to discussing the issue was in editorials in 1989 and 1993 dealing with extending domestic partnership benefits to gay city workers in New York (not included in table 13.6). The *Times* was critical of proposed rules extending rent control to unrelated adults in a 1989 editorial, but the opposition seems based on the rules rather than the concept ("We Now Pronounce You a Family" 1989). A clearer statement of the *Times's* position came in a 1993 editorial criticizing New York City Mayor David Dinkins for not going far enough in granting benefits to domestic partners. The *Times* wrote that "in moving to grant them some of the benefits enjoyed by married couples, Mayor David Dinkins makes a welcome gesture of recognition and respect to the non-marital relationships that constitute 'family' for millions of New Yorkers" ("Not Enough for Domestic Partners" 1993). This suggests that the *Times* was supportive of same-sex marriage before the *Baehr* litigation, although the issue was not discussed. However, this also suggests that it was the Hawaii litigation that led the *Times* to take a pro-same-sex marriage position. The *Times* position evolved from support for domestic partnership benefits to full equality of civil marriage. It may well be that litigation played a key role for the *Times*.

The *Tribune*, in contrast, has evolved more slowly. In 1996, for example, the paper called on the Illinois governor to sign a so-called defense of marriage act bill refusing recognition of out-of-state same-sex marriages. At the same, time, however, it supported "some sort of domestic partnership legislation." The last line of the editorial underscored the *Tribune*'s opposition to same-sex marriage: "but don't call it marriage" ("The Meaning of Marriage" 1996). This dual position of condemnation of same-sex marriage along with support for some sort of legal protections for same-sex couples has marked the *Tribune*'s position. For example, in response to the Hawaii decision in December, 1996, the *Tribune* suggested enacting a "legal framework for homosexuals who want more or less permanent partnerships, and give it some name other than marriage" ("The Challenge that Hawaii Poses" 1996). In 1997 the paper editorialized in support of a Chicago City Council ordinance to extend "benefits to the domestic partners of homosexual city employees" ("Yes to Domestic Partner Benefits" 1997). Yet in response to the enactment of civil unions in Vermont the *Tribune* warned, "to try to retrofit that institution [marriage] to accommodate gays is neither wise nor politically feasible" ("Vermont's 'Civil Unions' Experiment" 2000). In a later editorial the paper found civil unions "a reasonable compromise" and characterized their enactment "as sensible as it is fair" ("Vermont's 'Civil Unions' Option" 2000).

The *Tribune*'s strongest editorial statement on same-sex marriage came in response to the U.S. Supreme Court's *Lawrence* decision in 2003. The *Tribune* maintained its support of civil unions, editorializing that "the best prospect for guaranteeing such rights is to press for government recognition of same-sex civil unions without getting embroiled in the debate on redefining marriage" ("On Gay Rights and Commitments" 2003). However, the editorial board noted that it was moving toward supporting same sex-marriage:

> Seven years ago this page supported Illinois' defense of marriage act, which withheld recognition of same-sex marriages granted in other states. That view has changed. Traditions evolve. For eons, women were relegated to second-class status. Until relatively recently, many states banned mixed-race marriage. Over time, the legal and cultural barriers to same-sex marriage will properly dissolve. ("On Gay Rights and Commitments" 2003)

Despite these brave words, the *Tribune*'s response to the *Goodridge* decision in November, 2003, was to again call for civil unions ("Marriage in Massachusetts" 2003). Throughout the period studied, the *Tribune* did not move from this position.

Overall, as table 13.7 shows, only two of twenty-seven editorials could be fairly categorized as supportive, while five were categorized as negative. The

bulk of the *Tribune*'s editorials dealing with these issues avoided clear positions. These findings suggest that the *Tribune* was less influenced by litigation
and certainly less supportive of same-sex marriage than the *Times*.

It's not obvious what to make of the op-eds in both papers. Op-eds are
opinion pieces and are typically written by people with strong feelings. Thus,
it's not clear that they have much persuasive power. On the other hand, focus
on the issue might give it a kind of credibility. A reader might reason that if
same-sex marriage is important enough to garner attention from op-ed page
editors, then perhaps it is deserving of further attention.

In both papers the large majority of op-ed pieces mentioning the search
terms did so either in passing or without taking a clear position. But among the
roughly one quarter of the *Times's* op-eds that could be characterized as either
positive or negative, positive pieces outnumbered negative ones by three to one.
With the *Tribune*, where nearly 40 percent of the op-eds could be characterized,
positive pieces outnumbered negative ones by better than two to one. Some of
the criticism, however, was quite strident. Writing in the *Tribune* in 1996 in
reaction to the Hawaii litigation, Linda Bowles called "homosexual marriage"
a "monstrously stupid idea" (Bowles 1996B). In the *Times*, Lisa Schiffren more
calmly, but no less powerfully, wrote that same-sex marriage is "inherently in-
compatible with our culture's understanding of the institution [of marriage]"
(Schiffren 1996). Both authors criticized the courts, with Bowles claiming in another *Tribune* op-ed piece that "the greatest enemy in America to a government
of, by and for the people is the third rail of government, the judiciary" (Bowles
1996A) and Schiffren echoed the theme in the *Times*: "for a court in Hawaii to
assume that it has the power to radically redefine marriage is a stunning abuse of
power" (Schiffren 1996). Other negative pieces took a more disparaging tone,
with one piece quoting a jilted man who applied for a marriage license to marry
his 1966 Mustang GT: "Well, in California they are doing same-sex marriages.
So we are here in Tennessee. Why can't we do the good ol' boy thing and marry
our cars and trucks?" ("Commentary" 1999).

On the supportive side, there was a great deal of emphasis on fairness and
equality. In the *Tribune*, supportive arguments ran from equating opposition to
same-sex marriage with homophobia (opponents "abhor gay marriage because
they abhor gays"[Chapman 1996]) to equating it with racism and the sad history of antimiscegenation laws (Jackson 2004) to a moving piece about the
pain that the denial of marriage imposes on loving same-sex couples (Murphy
1996). The view of supporters was well captured in a 2003 piece:

> There was a time in this country when we thought women were too silly to vote,
> that segregation was a good idea, that blacks and whites could not fight alongside
> each other in the military. We cringe to remember our folly at these beliefs. In 20
> years, we will look back with equal horror on people who thought there should
> be a law against gay marriage. (Lobley 2003)

Table 13.7   *Chicago Tribune* **Editorials and Op-Eds Mentioning "Same-Sex Marriage, Gay Marriage, Homosexual Marriage, Domestic Partnership, or Civil Union," 1985–2004**

	Editorials				Op-Eds			
Year	Number	Positive	Negative	Mixed & Tangential	Number	Positive	Negative	Mixed & Tangential
1985	0	0	0	0	0	0	0	0
1986	0	0	0	0	0	0	0	0
1987	0	0	0	0	1	0	0	1
1988	0	0	0	0	0	0	0	0
1989	0	0	0	0	2	2	0	0
1990	0	0	0	0	0	0	0	0
1991	0	0	0	0	0	0	0	0
1992	0	0	0	0	1	1	0	0
1993	0	0	0	0	6	1	0	5
1994	1	0	0	1	4	2	0	2
1995	1	0	0	1*	0	0	0	0
1996	2	0	2	0	30	8	9	13
1997	3	0	0	3	4	2	0	2
1998	0	0	0	0	1	1	0	0
1999	1	0	1	0	3	1	1	1
2000	3	0	2	1	2	0	0	2
2001	0	0	0	0	3	1	0	2
2002	1	0	0	1	1	0	0	1
2003	4	2	0	2	19	10	2	7
2004	11	0	0	11	56	7	3	46
Totals:	27	2	5	20	133	36	15	82

"Mixed" = Both positive and negative positions taken, or no position taken.
"Tangential" = Tangential mention of search term.
* = 1 story on same-sex marriage in a foreign country.

SOURCE: See Appendix 8.

Supportive op-eds in the *Times* made similar arguments. Nicholas Kristof powerfully compared the federal marriage amendment with attempts in the early twentieth century to ban interracial marriage by constitutional amendment (Kristof 2004). Other writers praised the *Goodridge* decision as "path-breaking" (Rubenstein and Sears 2003). Perhaps most powerfully, David Brooks, the *Times's* resident conservative op-ed columnist, urged conservatives to support same-sex marriage: "We shouldn't just allow gay marriage. We should insist on gay marriage. We should regard it as scandalous that two people could claim to love each other and not want to sanctify their love with marriage and fidelity" (Brooks 2003).

Although elite opinion remains split on the propriety of same-sex marriage, examination of editorials and op-eds in the *Times* and *Tribune* reveals a growing convergence toward a more liberal position, beginning in the early 1990s. This leads to the question of the impact of the litigation on public opinion, to which I now turn.

Public Opinion

One of the most important claims that is made on behalf of litigation to produce significant social reform is that it can increase public support for it. Throughout the book I have examined this claim in the context of several of the great symbolic cases that are repeatedly pointed to as examples of judicial efficacy, and found the evidence lacking. What about with same-sex marriage? Did the litigation strategy, and judicial victories in Hawaii, Vermont, and Massachusetts, increase support for same-sex marriage? If so, then it is important to know how this issue differs from others previously considered. If not, then perhaps the litigation increased public support for other gay-rights issues, ranging from civil unions to workplace discrimination to general acceptance of gays and lesbians. In order to test these hypotheses, I examined polling data to determine if and when any movement in public opinion toward support for same-sex marriage and gay rights more generally occurred.

Examining the influence of litigation on support for same-sex marriage is more challenging than one might suspect. The first challenge is that few polls were taken on the issue prior to the litigation campaign. This makes it difficult to know with much certainty the state of public opinion prior to the litigation. Second, as with abortion, question ordering influences results. That is, responses to questions measuring support for same-sex marriage vary by whether they are asked before or after questions about civil unions. Third, poll results must be interpreted in context. The challenge is to disentangle the effects of litigation from the effects of other actions that could plausibly produce changes in public opinion. In the end, this is an impossible task. But all is not lost because if the litigation played an important role in changing public attitudes then I should see public opinion shift substantially in support of same-sex marriage after the decisions. Likewise, I should find substantial shifts in public opinion toward support for civil rights protections for gays and lesbians after the judicial victories. If the data don't show substantial changes in public opinion, then at the very least I can conclude that the case for litigation is unsupported in a critical area.

Turning to the data, surprisingly they don't support the claim that litigation to win the right to same-sex marriage has substantially increased support for it among the general public (see table 13.8, p. 402). The earliest poll on the issue was asked in 1988 by the National Opinion Research Center. In response to the question of whether respondents agreed or disagreed that "homosexual couples should have the right to marry one another," 12 percent agreed and

73 percent disagreed (Bowman and O'Keefe 2004, 22).[31] In 1989, however, a poll by Yankelovich, CNN, and *Time* magazine (table 13.8A), and a Gallup poll (table 13.8D), each found support for same-sex marriage from 23 percent of respondents and opposition from 69 percent. In 1991 and 1992, polls done by Princeton Survey Research Associates for *Newsweek* magazine found support for same-sex marriage at 30 percent and 35 percent, respectively (table 13.8B). And in January, 1993, five months before the Hawaii Supreme Court decision in *Baehr v. Lewin* (1993), Yankelovich, CNN, and *Time* magazine found 27 percent of respondents supporting same-sex marriage and 65 percent opposing it. Thus, on the eve of the first successful litigation, support for same-sex marriage ranged from above one-quarter of respondents to more than one-third.

Litigation to win the right to same-sex marriage doesn't appear to have substantially increased support for same-sex marriage. Consider, for example, the results from *Newsweek* magazine polls over the years since 1992 (table 13.8B). As noted above, in August, 1992, nearly a year before the Hawaii Supreme Court decision, 35 percent of respondents answered positively to the question, "thinking about what might be done to protect the rights of gays and lesbians, do you think that there should or should not be legally sanctioned gay marriages?" Over the next twelve years, the identical question was asked seven times. In no poll did support exceed the 35 percent recorded in 1992 and in only two of the five polls were the results matched. Thus, despite the Hawaii, Vermont, and Massachusetts decisions, public opinion was no more supportive of same-sex marriage after the decisions than before them.

Similar results are found in the polls done by Yankelovich, CNN, and *Time* magazine (table 13.8A). In August 1992, the year before the Hawaii decision, 27 percent of respondents answered yes to the question, "do you think marriages between homosexual men or homosexual women should be recognized as legal by the law or not?" (67 percent answered no). Over the next twelve years, the identical question was asked on eight different occasions. In all those years opposition never dropped below 60 percent and support never rose above 33 percent. In the May, 2004, poll, 32 percent of respondents supported the legal recognition of same-sex marriage while 60 percent opposed it. Although twelve years, and three important court decisions, had intervened since the 1992 poll, the responses differed by only a few percentage points.

Polls taken by the Pew Research Center (table 13.8C) report the same trend. While there was a jump in support from May 1996 to March 2001, this occurred before *Goodridge* in November, 2003. There has been no sustained increase since then. Indeed in June and July of 2006, Pew reports support for

---

31. Brewer and Wilcox (2005, 607) report the poll results slightly differently, with 11 percent agreeing and 69 percent disagreeing.

Table 13.8a-b   Should Same-Sex Marriages be Recognized
                 by Law? 1989–2005 (percentages)

A Yankelovich, CNN, *Time* (1989–2004)*

Date	Yes	No
October, 1989	23	69
August, 1992	27	67
January, 1993	27	65
June, 1994	31	64
September, 1996	26	65
October, 1998	29	64
July, 2003^	33	60
November, 2003^	32	62
February, 2004^	30	62
May, 2004	32	60

*The actual question wording is, "do you think marriages between homo-
sexual men or homosexual women should be recognized as legal by the law
or not?"
^Poll taken by Harris, CNN, and *Time*.

B. PSRA and *Newsweek* (1991–2004)*

Date	Should	Should Not
February, 1991^**	30	62
August, 1992	35	58
February, 1994	29	62
May, 1996	33	58
June, 1997	35	56
July, 1998	33	61
March, 2000	34	57
April, 2002	35	57
February, 2004	33	58

*The actual question wording is, "thinking about what might be done to
protect the rights of gays and lesbians, do you think that there should or
should not be legally sanctioned gay marriages?"
**The actual question wording is, "do you think that homosexual couples
should be allowed to get legally married or not?"
^Poll taken by PSRA.

same-sex marriage from 33 percent and 35 percent of respondents, respectively, virtually unchanged from March 2001 when 35 percent of respondents
supported same-sex marriage.

The Gallup organization has also polled on same-sex marriage (table
13.8D) and its results provide the best case for the positive effect of litigation
on support for same-sex marriage. Between March, 1996, and May, 2006, support for same-sex marriage increased 12 percentage points. However, almost
all of that change occurred by February, 1999, prior to either the Vermont or
Massachusetts litigation. While responses bounced around a fair bit in 2004
and 2005, with support as low as 28 percent in March, 2005, and as high as 39
percent the next month (opposition correspondingly ranging from 68 percent in

Table 13.8c-d   Should Same-Sex Marriages be Recognized by Law? 1989–2005 (percentages)

C. Pew Research Center (1996–2006)*			
Date	Favor	Oppose	Unsure
May, 1996	27	65	8
March, 2001	35	57	8
October, 2003^	32	59	9
November, 2003	30	62	8
February, 2004	30	63	7
March, 2004	32	59	9
July, 2004	32	56	12
August, 2004	29	60	11
December, 2004	32	61	7
July, 2005	36	53	11
March, 2006	39	51	10
June, 2006	33	55	12
July, 2006	35	56	9

*The actual question wording is, "do you strongly favor, favor, oppose, or strongly oppose allowing gays and lesbians to marry legally?"
^PollingReport.com reports results slightly different results, with 30 percent agreeing and 58 percent disagreeing.

D. Gallup (1989–2006)*		
Date	Should Be Valid	Should Not Be Recognized
October, 1989**	23	69
March, 1996	27	68
February, 1999	35	62
January, 2000	34	62
June, 2003	39	55
October, 2003	35	61
December, 2003	31	65
February, 2004^	34	62
March, 2004	33	61
May, 2004^	39	59
July, 2004	32	62
March, 2005	28	68
April-May, 2005	39	56
August, 2005	37	59
May, 2006	39	58

^Average of two different polls.
*The actual question wording is, "do you think marriages between homosexuals should or should not be recognized by the law as valid, with the same rights as traditional marriages?"
**The actual question wording is, "should homosexual couples have the same rights as married couples?"
SOURCES: Bowman and O'Keefe (2004, 22, 24, 25); Brewer and Wilcox (2005); "Law and Civil Rights"; Newport (2004); Newport (2005); Saad (2005); Saad (2006); Yang (1997, 501 Table 54).

March to 56 percent in April–May, 2005), overall there has been only a small change since 1999. Writing in 2001, Frank Newport reported for Gallup that "polling consistently shows that at least six out of ten Americans are opposed to the recognition of marriages between homosexuals as legally valid unions, with the same rights as traditional marriages" (Newport, 2001). In March, 2004, after *Goodridge*, Newport sounded the same theme, writing that "the current level of opposition to legalized same-sex marriage [61 percent] is little changed from responses to surveys that stretch back to 1999" (Newport 2004, 1). While poll results in the spring of both 2005 and 2006 report 39 percent of respondents supporting same-sex marriage, that represents a gain of only 4 percentage points since 1999 (although a larger gain since 1996). Reviewing these data, Persily, Eagan, and Wallsten conclude, "support for the legalization of gay marriage has risen only slightly since 1996, the first year Gallup asked Americans their opinion on this issue [in a regular manner]" (Persily, Eagan, and Wallsten 2006, 14).

A host of other polls show little change over the last few years, and less support than Gallup has reported. For example, a Quinnipiac University poll of November, 2006, found 34 percent of respondents supporting same-sex marriage, virtually identical to the 35 percent supporting it in December, 2003. Similarly, ABC News, in late May and early June, 2006, found support for same-sex marriage from 36 percent of respondents, also virtually identical to the 37 percent supporting it in September, 2003. And an April 2006 poll from FOX News/Opinion Dynamics found support from 33 percent of respondents ("Law and Civil Rights" 2006).

Overall, public opinion data don't support the claim that litigation on behalf of same-sex marriage substantially increased public support for it. Reviewing poll trends over several decades, Brewer and Wilcox (2005, 601) conclude that "the overall picture that emerges is one of striking stability." There is only somewhat more support for same-sex marriage, and somewhat less opposition to it, in 2006 as there was in 1992, the year before the current round of litigation started. Throughout this time period, roughly one-third of the public has supported same-sex marriage while 60 percent or so has opposed it. Perhaps most importantly, the one judicial opinion requiring same-sex marriage, the *Goodridge* decision in Massachusetts in 2003, seems not to have increased public support for it. As Brewer and Wilcox (2005, 602) conclude, looking "at the entire set of polls measuring public support for same-sex marriage, no durable trend in public support over the past few years emerges." If this claim is too strong, the data do suggest that there has been no surge in support for same-sex marriage as proponents of the dynamic court would predict.

If the litigation hasn't substantially increased public support for same-sex marriage, perhaps it has contributed to increasing support for gays in other areas. In particular, perhaps the legal claim for same-sex marriage has made civil unions appear more acceptable. Although civil unions were initially seen as a radical change, perhaps same-sex marriage litigation led civil unions to be seen as a moderate, compromise position that extended benefits to gay men and lesbians without calling those benefits "marriage."

Unfortunately, time-series data on support for civil unions starting before same-sex marriage litigation don't exist. For the most part pollsters didn't ask questions about civil unions until after Vermont adopted them at the end of the twentieth century. However, there are some earlier questions that were asked that shed some light. In 1989, when Gallup asked, "should homosexual couples have the same legal rights as married couples?," 23 percent agreed and 69 percent disagreed (Bowman and O'Keefe 2004, 30). In 1991, 39 percent of respondents answered yes to a question from PSRA, "do you think a homosexual couple who live together in a long-term relationship should be able to get the same job benefits as a married couple, or not?" (Bowman and O'Keefe 2004, 31). Two years later, in 1993, 38 percent agreed and 57 percent disagreed with the statement that "homosexual couples should be able to enjoy the full rights granted to married heterosexual couples" asked by NBC and the *Wall Street Journal* (Bowman and O'Keefe 2004, 31). Similarly, 37 percent in a 1996 poll supported "allowing homosexual couples to have the same benefits as married heterosexual couples, such as health benefits, inheritance rights and Social Security survivor benefits" (Bowman and O'Keefe 2004, 32). While the wording of these questions differs, and they emphasize different points, these polls suggest that in the years prior to the litigation success in support of same-sex marriage there was moderate and growing support for civil unions, which was noticeably more robust than support for same-sex marriage. Indeed, it may well be that this support, expressed prior to the litigation in Vermont, both made the Vermont decision possible and protected it from successful backlash. The background of this support for civil unions will be explored in the next section.

In the first decade of the twenty-first century there has been an "unmistakable rise in support for civil unions" (Persily, Eagan, and Wallsten 2006, 40). Table 13.9 reports data from Gallup. It shows that by May, 2004, approximately one-half of Americans supported civil unions. Other polls report similar data. For example, in May, 2000, the Associated Press reported that 42 percent of respondents responded positively to the question of whether "gays and lesbians should or should not be allowed to form a domestic partnership that would give the same-sex couple the same rights and benefits as opposite-sex marriages" (Bowman and O'Keefe 2004, 31; "Law and Civil Rights (p. 2)" 2006). In July, 2003, 53 percent of respondents told NBC and the *Wall Street Journal* that they would favor "allowing gay and lesbian couples to enter into legal agreements with each other that are not marriages, but that would give them many of the same legal and financial relationships as married couples" (Bowman and O'Keefe 2004, 31; "Law and Civil Rights (p. 2)" 2006). In September, 2003, 40 percent of respondents answered positively to an ABC

Table 13.9   Should Civil Unions be Recognized by Law?
                  Gallup, 2000–2004 (percentages)*

Date	Favor	Oppose
January, 2000**	40	53
October, 2000***	42	54
May, 2001	44	52
February, 2002	41	53
May, 2002	46	51
May, 2003	49	49
July, 2003	40	57
March, 2004	54	42
May, 2004	49	48

*The actual question wording is, "would you favor or oppose a law that would allow homosexual couples to legally form civil unions, giving them some of the legal rights of married couples?"

**The actual question wording is, "do you think gay partners who make a legal commitment to each other should or should not be entitled to the same rights and benefits as couples in traditional marriages?"

***The actual question wording is, "would you vote for or against a law that would allow homosexual couples to legally form civil unions, giving them some of the legal rights of married couples?"

SOURCES: Bowman and O'Keefe 2004, 32; Brewer and Wilcox 2005, 610; "Law and Civil Rights (p. 2)."

News poll question asking whether "homosexual couples should or should not be allowed to form legally recognized civil unions, giving them the legal rights of married couples in areas such as health insurance, inheritance and pension coverage" ("Law and Civil Rights" 2006). Similarly, in October, 2003, 45 percent of respondents told Pew that they favored "allowing gay and lesbian couples to enter into legal agreements with each other that would give them many of the same rights as married couples" ("Law and Civil Rights" 2006). Importantly, all of these responses came before the Massachusetts Court issued its *Goodridge* decision supporting same-sex marriage. Also, as Brewer and Wilcox (2005, 602) note, support for civil unions "appears to be substantially greater than public support for same-sex marriage." And in the 2000 presidential election, the Democratic Party platform came close to explicitly supporting civil unions, stating "we support the full inclusion of gay and lesbian families in the life of the nation. This would include an equitable alignment of benefits" ("Prosperity, Progress, and Peace" 2000).

The growth in support for civil unions appears to be continuing in the years after *Goodridge*. In polls done in July of 2005 and 2006 for the Pew Research Center for the People & the Press and the Pew Forum on Religion & Public Life, 53 percent and 54 percent of respondents, respectively, favored allowing "gay and lesbian couples to enter into legal agreements with each other that would give them many of the same rights as married couples" ("Law and Civil Rights" 2006). In the 2004 presidential election campaign both President Bush and his Democratic challenger, Senator John Kerry, supported civil unions. While in the 1990s this would have been seen as a radical position, by 2004 support for civil unions was seen as a moderate compromise.

There is an important caveat to interpreting these data—question ordering has a large impact on the results. Survey researchers have discovered that support for civil unions is higher when the question is asked after a question about same-sex marriage. Reviewing the data in 2005, Brewer and Wilcox note that "support for civil unions is greater when respondents are primed to consider same-sex marriage in an earlier question in the interview" (Brewer and Wilcox 2005, 600). Put another way, "people appear to be more likely to express support for civil unions when they are first allowed to express opposition to same-sex marriage" (Brewer and Wilcox 2005, 603). For example, in a May, 2004, Gallup Poll, respondents were 7 percentage points more supportive of civil unions when the civil unions question was asked following the marriage question than when the civil unions question was asked first (Gallup Poll 2004).[32] When both options are posed in the same question, respondents virtually always prefer civil unions to marriage. For example, when asked in late 2006 to choose between civil unions and marriage, 44 percent of respondents to a Quinnipiac University poll chose civil unions compared to 24 percent who chose marriage ("Law and Civil Rights" 2006). While other polls have reported smaller gaps, in virtually all of them civil unions are preferred to marriage.

In sum, it is hard to make a strong case that litigation in support of same-sex marriage has substantially increased support for it. For the most part, support for same-sex marriage has been increasing slowly with much of the change occurring before the *Goodridge* decision. As for civil unions, in the years following *Goodridge* approximately one-half of the American public was in support. This represents an increase of about 10 percentage points since 2000 and somewhat more since the mid-1990s. Support for civil unions is higher than support for same-sex marriage and civil unions are almost always the preferred position when respondents are asked to chose between them. These findings raise the question of what led to the growth in support for civil unions (and perhaps the slower growth in support for same-sex marriage), and what role litigation played. The next section suggests an answer.

The Times They Are A-Changing

Court cases don't appear in a vacuum. As I have stressed throughout the book, to fully understand the contribution of a judicial decision to significant social reform one must examine the broader setting in which the decision is is-

---

32. Interestingly, the reverse pattern occurs with support for same-sex marriage: support for it drops if the question is posed after a question on civil unions compared to when it's asked first or alone.

sued. This is as true for same-sex marriage as it is for civil rights, abortion and women's rights, and the other issues I have examined.

Opportunities for, and acceptance of, gay men and lesbians have improved dramatically in the United States over the last few decades, with one scholar of gay rights characterizing the change as "rapid and extraordinary" (D'Emilio 2007, 45). While discrimination still exists, it has lessened. For example, while it wasn't until 1973 that the American Psychiatric Association removed homosexuality from its Diagnostic and Statistical Manual of Mental Disorders (Ricci and Biederman 2004), in 2000 it endorsed the concept of civil unions and in 2005 it supported legal recognition of same-sex civil marriage. A year earlier, the American Psychological Association also endorsed same-sex marriage. The breadth of change that has occurred can be seen in any number of areas ranging from public opinion surveys to both public and private employment, to benefit and nondiscrimination polices to television and movie treatment to societal understandings more broadly. Taken together, these changes suggest that support for same-sex marriage would grow over time.

Starting with public opinion, Karlyn Bowman, the author of a major compilation of survey data on gay men and lesbians in 2004, noted that there's been an "enormous increase in tolerance" over the last several decades (quoted in Ricci and Biederman 2004). One area in which this can be seen is in the willingness of Americans to hire gay men and lesbians for a variety of jobs. Table 13.10 presents the data. It shows that majorities of Americans support hiring gay men and lesbians in every category about which pollsters have asked, including such sensitive ones as elementary school teacher and clergy. Importantly, the 50 percent support level was reached in all the categories before litigation for same-sex marriage produced victories. For example, more than two-thirds of the increase in support for gay men and lesbians serving as elementary school teachers occurred by 1992.

A closer examination of the data reveals that from 1977 to 2005 the percentage of Americans believing that gay men and lesbians should be hired as salespersons increased by 24 percentage points. Even larger increases were recorded in support for gay men and lesbians working as doctors (36 percentage points), serving in the armed forces (27 percentage points), and, perhaps surprisingly, working as elementary school teachers (32 percentage points). And the high level of public support for gay men and lesbians serving in the military was held despite the unwillingness of the federal government to allow gays to serve openly. Overall, while 56 percent of respondents in 1977 answered yes to a Gallup question about whether "homosexuals should or should not have equal rights in terms of job opportunities," by 1993 80 percent agreed and by 2007 that percentage had reached 89 percent, an increase of 33 percentage points over the 1977 result (Saad 2007)!

There has been an increase in support as well for more sensitive areas such as sexual behavior and acceptance of a gay and lesbian lifestyle. Gallup has re-

Table 13.10 Percentage of Americans Willing to Hire Gay Men and
Lesbians for Various Occupations, 1977 and 2005

Position	% Supporting (1977)	First Year with 50+% Support	% Supporting* (2005)
Salesperson	68%	1977	92%
Armed Forces	51%	1977	78%
Doctors	44%	1992	80%
Clergy	36%	1996	51%
Elementary School Teachers	27%	1992	59%
High School Teachers	47%^	1992	67%

*The percentages reported for 2005 are the average of two sub-samples of a May, 2005, Gallup Poll.
^The reported percentage is from 1989.
SOURCES: Bowman and O'Keefe (2004, 13–14); Gallup Poll (2005).

peatedly asked the public whether "homosexual relations between consenting adults should or should not be legal." In 1977, the public was evenly divided, with 43 percent supporting legalization and 43 percent opposing it. In the mid and late 1980s support dropped precipitously, no doubt in reaction to the AIDS crisis. But by 1992, 48 percent supported legalization and 44 percent opposed it. In 1999, for the first time, half of all respondents supported legalization and by May, 2003, Gallup reported 60 percent of respondents supporting legalization versus only 35 percent opposing it. While support dropped later that year to about 50 percent and remained in that range through 2005, by 2007 it had returned to near 60 percent (Saad 2007).

A similar trend can be seen in responses to a Gallup question on whether "homosexuality should be considered an acceptable alternative lifestyle." In 1982 only 34 percent of respondents thought so, versus 51 percent who were opposed. By 1999, however, 50 percent considered homosexuality an acceptable alternative life style and that percentage has continued to rise, reaching 57 percent in May, 2007 (Saad 2007). Overall, in 1998, 82 percent of respondents to a CNN/*Time* poll agreed that as "a matter of principle, the federal government should treat homosexuals and heterosexuals equally" ("Law and Civil Rights (p. 2)" 2006). And in July, 2003, when respondents were asked whether their "attitudes toward gays and lesbians might have changed in the past few years," a whopping 32 percent said they had become more accepting, four times as many respondents as said they had become less accepting (8 percent) (CNN/USA Today/Gallup Poll in "Law and Civil Rights (p. 2)" 2006).

Taken together, these data strongly suggest that since the 1970s public opinion has become increasingly more accepting of the participation of gay men and lesbians throughout society. Importantly, the data also suggest that this trend is likely to continue. This is because the strongest supporters of equality for gay men and lesbians are young people. For example, in 1997, before the Vermont and Massachusetts litigation, 50 percent of college freshman supported same-sex marriage, rising to 59 percent by 2002 (Bowman and O'Keefe 2004, 29). A national survey of one thousand high school seniors in 2001 found even greater support (66 percent) for same-sex marriage (Ricci and Biederman 2004). In terms of sexual relations, Gallup reported that in May, 2003, 69 percent of eighteen to twenty-nine-year-olds supported legalization compared to only 39 percent of those sixty-five and older (Bowman and O'Keefe 2004, 5). And in May, 2007, Gallup found that 75 percent of those eighteen to thirty-four believed that "homosexuality should be considered an acceptable alternative lifestyle," compared to 45 percent of those fifty-five and older. Unless these younger respondents change their views as they age, support for equal treatment for gay men and lesbians should only become stronger (Saad 2007). As Evan Wolfson, executive director of Freedom to Marry, somewhat mischievously put it, "we have a secret weapon: death" (Wolfson 2004).

A final piece of public opinion data may help further explain the increase in supportive responses. Since 1985, *Newsweek* has asked whether respondents "have a friend or close acquaintance who is gay or lesbian." In 1985, only 22 percent responded yes. By 1996, however, that percentage reached over half, at 56 percent (Bowman and O'Keefe 2004, 17). Whether this a result of gay men and lesbians "coming out of the closet" or heterosexuals becoming comfortable enough to admit to having gay friends and acquaintances, it suggests that discrimination and denial of rights may continue to lessen.

As the public opinion data on employment discrimination suggest, the treatment of gay men and lesbians in the workplace has improved dramatically. Starting in 2000, the Human Rights Campaign (HRC) has published annual studies of the treatment of gay men and lesbians in the workplace.[33] Reviewing the changes over the 1990s, HRC concludes that the 1990s were a "landmark decade for gay, lesbian, bisexual and transgendered workers as thousands of employers began to recognize the value of treating these employees equitably" (Mills 2000, 9).

According to the HRC, one of the "most stunning gains" in the 1990s was the "rapid spread of domestic partner benefits" (Mills 2000, 5). At the start of the decade fewer than two dozen U.S. employers offered domestic partner benefits. In 1991, Lotus raised the stakes in the software industry when it became the first publicly held corporation to offer health insurance coverage to the domestic partners of its employees. By the end of the decade HRC had identified 2,856 private companies, colleges and universities, and state and local governments that offered domestic partner health coverage (Mills 2000, 5). And as of August, 2000, that number jumped more than 25 percent, to 3,572 ("The State of the Workplace" 2000, 8).

The list of large companies that provided health care benefits to domes-

33. The studies are available on the Internet at http://www.hrc.org/issues/marriage/domestic_partners/2945.htm.

tic partners by the end of the 1990s was impressive. In response to an ordinance in San Francisco noted below, in July, 1999, United Airlines became the first major U.S. airline to offer domestic partner benefits to its gay and lesbian employees. United was quickly followed by American Airlines and U.S. Airways (Mills 2000, 19–20). In March, 2000, Cummins Engine Company, a maker of large diesel engines based in Columbus, Indiana, announced domestic partner benefits for its employees. Subaru followed in May ("The State of the Workplace" 2000, 27) and then on June 8 the big three automakers, DaimlerChrysler, General Motors, and Ford, along with the United Auto Workers, jointly announced domestic partner benefits for their four hundred thousand plus employees ("The State of the Workplace" 2000, 8). Overall, a 1999 national survey of employers found that 18 percent offered health coverage to "nontraditional" partners, an increase of 5 percentage points in just two years ("The State of the Workplace" 2000, 25). By the end of the decade, employers that offered domestic partner health benefits operated in all fifty states ("The State of the Workplace" 2000, 26). Since 2000 the trend has continued and as of June 1, 2006, a majority of *Fortune* magazine's annual list of the five hundred largest public corporations in the United States provided health insurance benefits to employees' same-sex domestic partners ("The State of the Workplace" 2006, 3, 7).

Similar change occurred on college campuses and in state and local governments. At the end of the 1990s HRC identified 118 colleges and universities that provided domestic partner benefits. These included thirty-five of the nation's top fifty universities and twenty-four of the nation's top forty liberal arts colleges according to the 2000 *U.S. News and World Report* college rankings ("The State of the Workplace" 2000, 27). And that trend has continued with 92 percent of *U.S. News and World Report's* top twenty-five four-year colleges and universities providing health coverage to domestic partners by 2006 ("The State of the Workplace" 2006, 9).

Government at all levels also began offering domestic partner health care benefits in the 1990s. A key event was the enactment of the San Francisco Equal Benefits Ordinance in November, 1996. The ordinance prohibits San Francisco from entering into contracts that discriminate in the provision of benefits between married employees and those with domestic partners. Because San Francisco contracts with many national corporations, HRC found that the ordinance played a "major role in effecting change in workplaces across the nation" (Mills 2000, 5). Later in the decade, in 1998, at least eight city or local governments instituted domestic partner benefits for public employees including New York City and Philadelphia. In 1999 at least another eight did so including Cook County, Illinois, and Pittsburgh (Mills 2000, 9). By the end of the decade, seventy-four city and county governments had enacted such laws ("The State of the Workplace" 2000, 28).

Overall, by 2000 there was a major increase in the provision of domestic partner benefits across private, educational, and governmental institutions from just a handful in 1990 to over three thousand five hundred in 2000. Here, too, the trend has continued. As of December 31, 2005, HRC identified 9,370 private employers, governments and government agencies, and colleges and universities that provided health insurance coverage to employees' domestic partners, a 14 percent increase over 2004 and roughly a tripling of the number in 2000 ("The State of the Workplace" 2006, 9).

Gains have been equally impressive in the adoption of nondiscrimination policies. As of August 2000, HRC identified 1,708 companies, colleges and universities, state and local governments, and federal agencies that had written policies prohibiting discrimination based on sexual orientation ("The State of the Workplace" 2000, 8). In the private sector, in the 1980s, numerous employers adopted such policies, including IBM, AT&T, Eastman Kodak, Harley-Davidson, Microsoft, Apple, and McDonalds (Mills 2000, 10, 22). By 1996 a majority of Fortune 500 companies had included sexual orientation in their nondiscrimination policies ("The State of the Workplace" 2000, 8). And by June 1, 2006, 430 of the Fortune 500 companies, a "whopping" 86 percent, include sexual orientation in their nondiscrimination policies ("The State of the Workplace" 2006, 1, 8).

Similar growth was seen in the adoption of nondiscrimination polices on college and university campuses. By the end of the decade at least 308 colleges and universities included sexual orientation in their nondiscrimination policies. These included forty-four of the top fifty national universities and twenty-eight of the nation's top forty liberal arts colleges, according to the 2000 *U.S. News and World Report* college rankings ("The State of the Workplace" 2000, 24). Here, too, change has continued. As of June 1, 2006, 562 colleges and universities had written nondiscrimination policies that included "sexual orientation" ("The State of the Workplace" 2006, 9).

On the state level, Wisconsin was the first state to prohibit antigay employment discrimination in 1982, followed by Massachusetts in 1989. Nine other states followed in the 1990s. By the end of the decade eleven states and at least 116 cities and counties and the District of Columbia had enacted provisions outlawing job discrimination based on sexual orientation in the private sector ("The State of the Workplace" 2000, 16). In the public sector, by the end of the decade twenty states prohibited discrimination against gays and lesbians in their public workforces, and 180 local governments and agencies offered some protection based on sexual orientation (Mills 2000, 17).

There was action on the federal level as well. In May, 1998, President Clinton issued an executive order prohibiting discrimination based on sexual orientation in the federal civilian work force. A nearly successful effort was made to enact the Employment Non-Discrimination Act (ENDA), which makes it illegal to discriminate based on sexual orientation. In September, 1996, ENDA came within one vote of passing in the Senate (Dupuis 2002, 92).

Overall, by the end of 2005, HRC identified 2,958 private employers, state and local governments, government agencies, and colleges and universities that included "sexual orientation" in their nondiscrimination policies. This number was 3 percent higher than in the preceding year ("The State of the Workplace" 2006, 9). While discrimination against gay men and lesbians remains, change has been dramatic. And this change has been powered by political and market forces, without major backlash.

Another measure of the public's changing views can be found in the appearance of gay and lesbian characters on television shows and in movies. Prime-time television shows are designed to bring in large viewing audiences, allowing the networks to charge top dollar for advertisements. Thus, networks are highly unlikely to produce and air shows that will offend a potential audience. But this has not precluded prime-time television shows from presenting gay and lesbian characters in important roles. Starting in 1996 the Gay & Lesbian Alliance Against Defamation (GLAAD) has tracked the number of such characters. In its report on the 1996–97 television season it identified thirty-four gay, lesbian, bisexual, and transgender characters, "more . . . than any season before" ("TV Scoreboard 1996–1997 Season"). The year 1997 also witnessed a "groundbreaking moment on network television" ("Gays on TV" 2003). On April 30, 1997, Ellen DeGeneres, the star of the prime-time *Ellen* show on ABC, announced that she was gay both in person and in character, becoming the first title character of a television show to be openly gay or lesbian (Dupuis 2002, 61). The show was hyped with DeGeneres appearing on the cover of the April 14, 1997, issue of *Time* Magazine with the caption, "Yep, I'm Gay." There was also a long story about her coming out (Handy 1997).

A second breakthrough occurred in the 1988–89 season with the introduction of the first gay male lead character on national network television (NBC) on a new sitcom, *Will & Grace* ("TV Scoreboard 1998–1999 Season"). Then, in the 2000–2001 season, the cable network Showtime premiered *Queer as Folk,* which GLAAD described as a "ground-breaking drama" about an "extended family of gay and lesbian characters" ("The 2000–2001 Television Season: Leading Roles"). Others have described it as a "provocative series about gay and lesbian characters [which] deals with sensitive issues such as AIDS, promiscuous sex and drug use" ("Gays on TV" 2003). *Queer as Folk* became "one of the top-rated series" on Showtime ("Gays on TV" 2003).

Gay men and lesbians are also increasingly appearing in the movies. While there were various negative portrayals as early as the 1960s, more positive depictions began appearing in the 1980s. For example, *Personal Best* (1982), starring Mariel Hemingway, presented a lesbian relationship in a supportive way (though the Hemingway character leaves her lesbian lover for a man). In 1988, *Torch Song Trilogy* told the story of three periods in a gay man's life. Tom Hanks won an Oscar for his portrayal of a gay man with AIDS who sues his employer for discrimination in *Philadelphia* in 1993. In 1996, Robin

Williams starred in *The Birdcage,* a remake of the classic French film, *La Cage aux Folles.* The farcical plot revolved around a gay male couple whose son is engaged to the daughter of a conservative politician. It was the first movie starring gay characters in positive roles to gross more than $100 million ("Gays in the Movies: A Timeline"). Then, in 2005, *Brokeback Mountain* told the romantic and tragic story of two gay men. It received eight Oscar nominations, more than any other film in 2005, and was a commercial and critical success ("Gays in the Movies: A Timeline").

The increasing appearance of gay men and lesbians on television and in movies is further evidence that Americans are becoming more tolerant and accepting. Suzanna Walters sees a "sea change in our culture, where gays and lesbians have entered into the sort of popular imagination in mainstream television, network and cable televisions, films, advertising" ("Gays on TV" 2003).[34] As with changes in public opinion, these cultural changes also point to greater acceptance.

Another indication of growing acceptance is the publication of same-sex union announcements in daily newspapers. Prior to 1990, no mainstream newspaper accepted them. However, on August 18, 2002, the *New York Times*, the nation's paper of record, announced that it would "publish reports of same-sex commitment ceremonies and of some types of formal registration of gay and lesbian partnerships" ("*Times* Will Begin Reporting Gay Couples' Ceremonies" 2002). GLAAD has tracked newspaper policies since then. Two years later, in August, 2004, GLAAD reported that the number of newspapers publishing same-sex union announcements had risen from 69 in August, 2002, to 504, about one-third of the daily newspapers in the United States. This included newspapers in all of the nation's top twenty-five media markets, forty-four of the top fifty, and seventy-seven of the top one hundred. It included newspapers in all states except Mississippi ("GLAAD's Announcing Equality" 2004).

A final example of how dramatic the change has been occurs every year at Walt Disney World in Orlando, Florida. Since 1991, gay men and lesbians from around the United States and the world have traveled to Orlando for Gay Days, a weekend of events centered around the Disney theme parks.[35] Attendance at Gay Days has grown considerably, attracting substantially more than one hundred thousand gay men, lesbians, bisexuals, and family and friends. Major national businesses like Bud Light, Saturn (the "official vehicle of gay days"), Delta Airlines (the "official airline of gay days") and others sponsor the event. Mainstream guidebooks feature it. For example, the online edition of the travel

34. But note that Walters (2003) views the effects of this heightened visibility on discrimination as nuanced, with both positive and negative implications.
35. For more information see the official Web site of Gay Days, http://www.gaydays.com/.

guide *Frommers* not only describes the event but does so in an upbeat way: "for a few days each year the global spell of Disney magic is cast upon gays, lesbians and their families as the theme park itself, Universal Studios, Sea World and Busch Gardens open their doors for rides, movie mania and lots of parties" ("Gay Days at Walt Disney World"). How much more mainstream can one be?

The United States is not the only country in the world with gay men and lesbians who seek the right to equal treatment, including marriage. There is a worldwide movement for change. Outside the United States, same-sex marriage is gaining ground. The Netherlands legalized same-sex marriage in 2001, followed by Belgium in 2003, most Canadian provinces between 2003 and 2005, Spain and Canada as a whole in 2005, and South Africa in 2006. As of 2006 nearly twenty countries have legalized same-sex civil unions including all the Scandinavian countries starting with Denmark in 1989, as well as France (1999), Germany (2001), the United Kingdom (2005), and New Zealand (2005). In addition, various cities and regions, including Buenos Aires, Argentina (2003) and Mexico City, Mexico (2007) have adopted civil unions. While the provisions of these acts differ, and not all include the identical rights granted to married couples, they demonstrate that the quest for marriage equality is a worldwide phenomenon.

As the heading of this section proclaims, times are changing. Public opinion data, employment benefits, nondiscrimination policies, television and movie portrayals, and worldwide trends all demonstrate a consistent pattern; since the 1970s, opportunities for gay men and lesbians have increased dramatically and discrimination has decreased. Importantly, these changes are not primarily the result of litigation. Rather, they are the result of a changing culture. They provide the context and background for claims for marriage equality. It is likely that these cultural understandings have provided much of the support for civil unions and same-sex marriage. And if these trends continue, as the data suggest they will, it is possible, if not likely, that over time support will grow for same-sex marriage so that it will become politically feasible to enact it.

Conclusion: When Will They Ever Learn?

The foregoing analysis shows that litigation as a means of obtaining the right to same-sex marriage has not succeeded. While seven states have enacted laws that extend state marriage benefits to same-sex couples, only in Massachusetts may same-sex couples legally be "married" under state law. Because of the denial of federal benefits, nowhere in the United States are same-sex couples treated equally with married heterosexual couples. Since that was the goal of litigation, clearly it has not succeeded. Further, one result of litigation for same-sex marriage has been to create legal and constitutional barriers to its achievement. Unintended though it was, there has been a tremendous backlash against same-sex marriage. From the federal Defense of Marriage Act to the forty-five states that have adopted measures designed to prevent the recognition of same-sex marriages to the twenty-seven states that have constitutional provisions limiting marriage to heterosexuals, there exist more legal barriers to same-sex marriage after the litigation than there were before it. As a result of the litigation effort, not only must same-sex marriage proponents convince the public that their cause is just, but also they must overturn laws and amend constitutions. In addition, there is little evidence that public opinion has substantially moved in favor of same-sex marriage as a result of the litigation. And while there has been increased media attention to the issue, that attention, at least as far as coverage in the *New York Times*, is more negative than positive. In sum, while some progress has been made in extending marriage rights to gay men and lesbians, substantial barriers have been created. Indeed, one could argue that given the federal Defense of Marriage Act and the legal barriers in forty-five states, proponents of same-sex marriage would have been better off never having litigated in the first place.

The problem is that activists for same-sex marriage turned to courts too soon in the reform process. As I wrote in the introduction, "Perhaps only when political, social, and economic forces have already pushed society far along the road to reform will courts have any independent effect. And even then their decisions may be more a reflection of significant social reform already occurring than an independent, important contribution to it" (pp. 5–6). That change has yet to occur with same-sex marriage, so litigation as a method of social reform is premature. The executive director of the National Gay and Lesbian Task Force, Matt Foreman, acknowledged this in the aftermath of the 2004 election, noting, "there is no putting lipstick on this pig . . . Our legal strategy is at least 10 years ahead of our political and legislative strategy" (quoted in Liptak 2004). The result of litigation under such conditions may be to set back the movement rather than to produce positive change.

In the introduction to the chapters on same-sex marriage I quoted same-sex marriage litigator Evan Wolfson's exuberant claim that the Hawaiian case, *Baehr v. Lewin*, was "a breakthrough case that most might see as gay people's *Loving v. Virginia*" (Wolfson 1994, 612 n.196). A comparison of the conditions when the U.S. Supreme Court struck down antimiscegenation laws in *Loving* in 1967 to the conditions when Hawaiian, Vermont, and Massachusetts courts struck down denials of marriage licenses to same-sex couples underscores my point. First, of course, *Loving* was a decision of the U.S. Supreme Court while *Baehr* and *Baker* came from two of the smallest and least representative states of the union and *Goodridge* came from one of the most liberal ones. But more importantly, at the time of *Loving* only sixteen states banned interracial marriages while at the time of *Baehr*, *Baker*, and *Goodridge no state permitted* same-sex marriages. Further, the decision in *Loving* came three years after the passage of the 1964 Civil Rights Act, one of the nation's most important legislative acts prohibiting race-based discrimination in employment and accommodations. There has been no such major national legislation prohibiting discrimination against gays and lesbians. Similarly, *Loving* came in the wake of a powerful civil rights movement with widespread support. Gay-rights activists have not successfully built such a movement. Finally, President Johnson spoke eloquently and forcefully in favor of civil rights, including to a joint session of Congress; there has been no such major support for gay rights from any U.S. president. The comparison with *Loving* shows how dramatically different the conditions are between *Loving* and *Baehr*, *Baker*, and *Goodridge*.

Given these differences, it is not surprising that the results of litigation in *Loving* and *Baehr*, *Baker*, and *Goodridge* differ so markedly. Indeed, one of the most fascinating results of the litigation has been the stunningly successful countermobilization against same-sex marriage. Although the decisions may have encouraged a movement around the country in support of same-sex marriage, the litigation more powerfully mobilized opponents. I have found such a pattern before in cases like *Brown* and *Roe* where the losers in court mobilized and effectively stymied change. One of the most important lessons, then, that comes from litigation for marriage equality is that litigation on behalf of the relatively disadvantaged, if successful, is likely to be met with powerful political resistance. Thus, the political insulation of the judiciary, the very attribute that allows the relatively disadvantaged to have their day in court, also limits the efficacy of judicial victories. It is a sad catch-22 situation that proponents of issues like same-sex marriage face.

What, then, should proponents of same-sex marriage have done? While hindsight is twenty-twenty, a legislative strategy would have been less likely to produce backlash. However, if proponents insisted on litigation, a more incremental strategy would have been less likely to arouse intense opposition and more likely to succeed. Same-sex marriage proponents might have adopted the initial strategy of the NAACP, noted in chapter 3. Rather than challenging the separate-but-equal standard head-on, NAACP litigators accepted the standard and argued that defendants weren't providing equality. Even though the standard was anathema to the NAACP, it understood that neither the courts nor the country were ready to dismantle segregation. It took several decades of litigation, and victory in a slew of cases, before the NAACP was ready to challenge the separate-but-equal doctrine itself. By analogy, if same-sex marriage proponents had asked only for civil unions rather than marriage, they might have achieved more.

There are several reasons to believe such an incremental strategy would have worked. First, public opinion data as well as changes in employment policies and broader cultural behavior show that majorities of Americans support extending equal rights to gay men and lesbians across many issues. However, they are hesitant to use the word "marriage." As has been discussed, polls show that there is substantially more support for civil unions than for marriage. By litigating for civil unions, same-sex marriage proponents could have built upon this foundation. Second, the experience of states like Vermont shows that the adoption of civil unions, even when court ordered, doesn't arouse the same level of opposition as does same-sex marriage. After all, even President George W. Bush supported civil unions! Civil union victories in courts might not have led to the Defense of Marriage Act and the state laws and constitutional amendments banning same-sex marriage. Third, a proliferation of civil unions might soften up opposition to same-sex marriage. If and when a majority of states offered civil unions or domestic partnerships, then it might be time to litigate for same-sex marriage. As an editorial in the *New York Times* in 2004 correctly noted, the judiciary is "only one part of a much larger story. Gay rights and gay marriages are being driven by an array of social forces and institutions" ("The Road to Gay Marriage" 2004). Building on those forces offers the best hope for achieving equality.

Many supporters of same-sex marriage would no doubt be frustrated by this strategy. "How can you ask us," they might say, "to litigate for a second-class status like civil unions when gay men and lesbians are entitled to equal treatment and benefits?" The response is that the battle for same-sex marriage is not only about the rhetoric of rights but also about the reality of political power. The most poignant and powerful rights' claims will fail without political support. And until that political support is present, litigation is likely to produce backlash.

Critics of this argument may claim that I have underestimated the amount of change that has occurred through litigation. Before the litigation campaign there was little or no serious discussion of civil unions or same-sex marriage. After judicial victories and the enactment of civil unions in Vermont and marriages in Massachusetts, neither status seems outlandish. Clearly, this is correct. However, this progress has not been cost free. It has come with the legislative and constitutional barriers limiting same-sex marriage I have discussed. If the cause of same-sex marriage has taken a step forward, it has also taken two steps back.

A final argument in favor of continued litigation might be that regardless of how powerful the backlash to same-sex marriage litigation was, it is now a spent force. Virtually all of the states likely to adopt constitutional amendments, as this argument goes, have already done so. Thus, there is little to lose in continued litigation, particularly in states where the constraints on courts are weak. While this is plausible, there are several caveats. First, same-sex marriage proponents need to carefully measure the amount of support they have, both from political elites and the public. It seems virtually certain that any same-sex marriage litigation victory will be opposed by the hierarchy of the Catholic Church as well as conservative Christian denominations in the state and many Republicans. Same-sex marriage proponents must be reasonably certain they can defeat moves to overturn any supportive judicial decision. Second, politically, no state is an island. That is, what happens in one state can affect what happens in other states as well as what happens nationally. This is a particular concern in presidential election years.

An example of national concern about state action comes from Massachusetts where the Constitutional Convention met on June 14, 2007, to decide whether to place a constitutional amendment banning same-sex marriage on the November, 2008, ballot. With an open presidential race in 2008, it appears that many Democrats were concerned that having a constitutional amendment on the ballot in Massachusetts would hurt the national campaign. Senator Kennedy lobbied legislators to turn down the amendment as did Nancy Pelosi, the Speaker of the U.S. House of Representatives (Phillips 2007; LeBlanc 2007). Some political leaders in Massachusetts said that one reason for opposing the amendment was to allow Democratic presidential candidates to "potentially sidestep the controversial subject" (Mishra 2007). Others noted that having the amendment on the ballot would hurt Democrats' chances of "winning the White House and retaining control of Congress" (Phillips and Estes 2007). To the surprise of many people involved in the same-sex marriage battle, the Constitutional Convention turned the amendment down. The point, however, is that local state action can have important, and detrimental, national implications for gay-rights supporters.

Ultimately, the use of litigation to win the right to same-sex marriage lends further support to the argument that courts are severely limited in their capacity to further the interests of the relatively disadvantaged. While I can understand the frustration felt by advocates of same-sex marriage, succumbing to the "lure of litigation" appears to have been the wrong move. While it is conceivable that few people could have foreseen the negative reaction to the Hawaii litigation (other than readers of this book!), after 1996 it was clear that any further litigation victories would produce continued backlash. To continue to litigate in the light of these events confused the rhetoric of rights with the reality of reaction. By litigating when they did, proponents of same-sex marriage moved too far and too fast ahead of the curve, leaping beyond what the American public could bear. The lesson here is a simple one: those who rely on the courts absent significant public and political support will fail to achieve meaningful social change, and may set their cause back.

14

Conclusion:
The Fly-Paper Court

This study has examined whether, and under what conditions, courts can produce significant social reform. Contrasting two functional and historically derived views of the courts, three constraints and four conditions were developed. They were successful in understanding the mostly disappointing results of attempts to use the courts to produce significant social reform in civil rights, abortion, women's rights, the environment, reapportionment, criminal rights, and same-sex marriage. Their success, particularly in the paradigmatic cases of *Brown* and *Roe*, suggests general applicability.

The findings show that, with the addition of the four conditions, the constraints derived from the Constrained Court view best capture the capacity of the courts to produce significant social reform. This is the case because, on the most fundamental level, courts depend on political support to produce such reform (Constraint II). For example, since the success of civil rights in fields such as voting and education depended on political action, political hostility doomed court contributions. With same-sex marriage, lack of support led to the enactment of legal barriers. With women's rights, lack of enforcement of existing laws, in addition to an unwillingness to extend legal protection, had a similar dampening effect. And with abortion and the environment, hostility from many political leaders created barriers to implementation. This finding appears clearly applicable to other fields.

Courts will also be ineffective in producing change given any serious resistance because of their lack of implementation powers (Constraint III). The structural constraints of the Constrained Court view, built into the American judicial system, make courts virtually powerless to produce change. They must depend on the actions of others for their decisions to be implemented. With civil rights, little changed until the federal government became involved. With women's rights, we still lack a serious government effort, and stereotypes that constrain women's opportunities remain powerful. Similarly, the uneven availability of access to legal abortion demonstrates the point, as does the backlash against same-sex marriage. Where there is local hostility to change, court orders will be ignored. Community pressure, violence or threats of violence, and lack of market response all serve to curtail actions to implement court decisions. This finding, too, appears applicable across fields.

Despite these constraints on change, in at least several of the movements examined major legal cases were won. The chief reason is that the remaining constraint, the lack of established legal precedents, was weak (Constraint I). That is, there were precedents for change and supportive movements within the broader legal culture. In civil rights, litigation in the 1930s and 1940s progressively battered the separate-but-equal standard, setting up the argument and decision in *Brown*. In women's rights, the progress of civil rights litigation, particularly in the expansion of the Fourteenth Amendment, laid the groundwork. In the area of abortion, notions of a sphere of privacy in sexual matters were first developed by the Supreme Court in 1965, broadened in 1972, and forcefully presented in several widely read law-review articles. And, by the date of the Supreme Court's abortion decisions, numerous lower courts had invalidated state abortion statutes on grounds that the Supreme Court came to enunciate. Without these precedents, which took decades to develop, it would have been years before even a legal victory could have been obtained. But legal victories do not automatically or even necessarily produce the desired change.

A quick comparison between civil rights and abortion illustrates these points. While both had legal precedents on which to construct a winning legal argument, little else was similar. With civil rights, there was a great deal of white hostility to blacks, especially in the South. On the whole, political leaders, particularly Southerners, were either supportive of segregation or unwilling to confront it as an important issue. In addition, court decisions required individuals and institutions hostile to civil rights to implement the changes. Until Congress acted a decade later, these two constraints remained and none of the conditions necessary for change were present. After congressional and executive actions were taken, the constraints were overcome and conditions for change were created, including the creation of incentives, costs, and the context in which courts could be used as cover. Only then did change occur. In contrast, at the time of the abortion decisions there was much public and elite support for abortion. There was an active reform movement in the states, and Congress was quiet, with no indication of the opposition that many of its members would later provide.[1] Also, the presence of the market condition partially overcame the implementation constraint. To the extent that the abortion decisions had judicial effects, it is precisely because the constraints

---

1. Comparing the aftermath of the abortion and civil rights decisions, it seems clear that there was substantially less turmoil over abortion than over civil rights. See Friedman (1983, 23); Tatalovich and Daynes (1981, 6–7).

were weak and a condition necessary for change was present. Civil rights and abortion litigation, then, highlight the existence and force of the constraints and conditions.

Turning to the question of extra-judicial or indirect effects, courts are in a weak position to produce change. Only a minority of Americans know what the courts have done on important issues. Fewer still combine that knowledge with the belief in the Supreme Court's constitutional role, a combination that would enable the Court, and the lower courts, to legitimate behavior. This makes courts a particularly poor tool for changing opinions or for mobilization. As Peltason puts it, "litigation, by its complexity and technical nature and by its lack of dramatic moments, furnishes an ineffective peg around which to build a mass movement" (Peltason 1971, 103). Rally round the flag is one thing but rally round the brief (or opinion) is quite another! The evidence from the movements examined makes dubious any claim for important extra-judicial effects of court action. It strikes at the heart of the Dynamic Court view.

The cases examined show that when the constraints are overcome, and one of the four conditions is present, courts can help produce significant social reform. However, this means, by definition, that institutional, structural, and ideological barriers to change are weak. A court's contribution, then, is akin to officially recognizing the evolving state of affairs, more like the cutting of the ribbon on a new project than its construction. Without such change, the constraints reign. When Justice Jackson commented during oral argument in *Brown*, "I suppose that realistically this case is here for the reason that action couldn't be obtained from Congress" (quoted in Friedman 1969, 244),[2] he identified a fundamental reason why the Court's action in the case would have little effect.

Given the constraints and the conditions, the Constrained Court view is the more accurate: U.S. courts can almost never be effective producers of significant social reform. At best, they can second the social reform acts of the other branches of government. Problems that are unsolvable in the political context can rarely be solved by courts. As Scheingold puts it, the "law can hardly transcend the conflicts of the political system in which it is embedded" (Scheingold 1974, 145). Turning to courts to produce significant social reform substitutes the myth of America for its reality. It credits courts and judicial decisions with a power that they do not have.

In contrast to this conclusion, it might be suggested that throughout this book I have asked too much of courts. After all, in all the cases examined, court decisions produced some change, however small. Given that political action appeared impossible in many instances, such as with civil rights in the 1950s, same-sex marriage in the 1990s, and reform of the criminal justice sys-

---

2. On this point, John Hart Ely's (1980) legislative-failure defense of judicial activism frees the Court to act in precisely those instances where it is most unlikely to be of any help.

tem more generally, isn't some positive change better than none? In a world of unlimited resources, this would be the case. In the world in which those seeking significant social reform live, however, strategic choices have costs, and a strategy that produces little or no change and induces backlash drains resources that could be more effectively employed in other strategies. In addition, vindication of constitutional principles accompanied by small change may be mistaken for widespread significant social reform, inducing reformers to relax their efforts.

In general, then, not only does litigation steer activists to an institution that is constrained from helping them, but also it siphons off crucial resources and talent, and runs the risk of weakening political efforts. In terms of financial resources, social reform groups don't have a lot of money. Funding a litigation campaign means that other strategic options are starved of funds. In civil rights, while *Brown* was pending in June 1953, Thurgood Marshall and Walter White sent out a telegram to supporters of the National Association for the Advancement of Colored People asking for money, stating "funds entirely spent" (quoted in Kluger 1976, 617). Compare this to the half-million-dollar estimates of the cost of the freedom rides, largely due to fines and bail (Sarratt 1966, 337). Further, the legal strategy drained off the talents of people such as Thurgood Marshall and Jack Greenberg. As Martin Luther King, Jr., complained: "to accumulate resources for legal actions imposes intolerable hardships on the already overburdened" (King 1963, 157).

In the abortion field, reliance on the Court seriously weakened the political efficacy of pro-choice forces. After the 1973 decisions, many pro-choice activists simply assumed they had won and stopped their pro-choice activity. According to J. Hugh Anwyl, at one time executive director of Planned Parenthood of Los Angeles, pro-choice activists went "on a long siesta" after the abortion decisions (quoted in Johnston 1977, 1). This view was concurred in by a National Abortion Rights Action League activist, Janet Beals: "Everyone assumed that when the Supreme Court made its decision in 1973 that we'd got what we wanted and the battle was over. The movement afterwards lost steam" (quoted in Phillips 1980, 3).[3] Jackson and Vinovskis found that, after the decisions, "state-level pro-choice groups disbanded, victory seemingly achieved" (Jackson and Vinovskis 1983, 73). By 1977, a survey of pro-choice and anti-abortion activity in thirteen states nationwide found that abortion rights advocates had failed to match the activity of their opponents (Johnston 1977, 24). The political organization and momentum that had changed laws nationwide dissipated in celebration of Court victory.

The pro-choice movement was harmed in a second way by its reliance on Court action. The most restrictive version of the Hyde Amendment, banning

3. Others in agreement with this analysis include Tatalovich and Daynes (1981, 101, 164), and participants in a symposium at the Brookings Institution, noted in Steiner (1983, 84).

federal funding even for most medically necessary abortions, was passed with the help of a parliamentary maneuver by pro-choice legislators. Their strategy, as reported the following day on the front pages of the *New York Times* and *Washington Post*, was to pass such a conservative bill that the Court would have "no choice" but to overturn it (Tolchin 1977; Russell 1977).[4] This reliance on the Court was totally unfounded. With hindsight, Karen Mulhauser, former director of NARAL, suggested that "had we made more gains through the legislative and referendum processes, and taken a little longer at it, the public would have moved with us" (quoted in Williams 1979, 12). By winning a Court case "without the organization needed to cope with a powerful opposition" (Rubin 1982, 169), pro-choice forces vastly overestimated the power and influence of the Court.

A further danger of litigation as a strategy for significant social reform is that symbolic victories may be mistaken for substantive ones, covering a reality that is distasteful. Rather than working to change that reality, reformers relying on a litigation strategy for reform may be misled (or content?) to celebrate the illusion of change. Throughout this book, the reader has encountered numerous claims about the symbolic importance of judicial decisions. Yet none of them has withstood empirical analysis. In criminal rights, for example, the contribution of the Court's decisions seems more symbolic than substantive, having "more significance as a declaration of intent than as a working instrument of law" (Elsen and Rosett 1967, 645). For some, however, this is meaningful. As Schulhofer puts it, "the symbolic effects of criminal procedural guarantees are important; they underscore our societal commitment to restraint in an area in which emotions easily run uncontrolled" (Schulhofer 1987, 460).[5] Yet, chapter 11 has shown that these "societal commitments" are not always shared by those responsible for implementing them. There is a danger that symbolic gains cover for actual failings. In strong but colorful language, Tigar sums up this view of the criminal rights revolution, and the dangers of substituting symbolic gain for substantive change more generally: "the constitutional revolution in criminal procedure has amounted to little more than an ornament, or golden cupola, built upon the roof of a structure found rotting and infested, assuring the gentlefolk who only pass by without entering that all is well inside" (Tigar 1970, 7).

Brown, too, illustrates the point. Although it is perhaps the nation's most widely celebrated Supreme Court decision, by the early years of the twenty-first century it has come to sit alongside growing de facto racial segregation (Orfield and Lee 2004, 2006). Thus the celebration of *Brown* may serve an ideological function of assuring Americans that they have lived up to their constitutional principles of equality without actually requiring them to do so.

4. See also Gelb and Palley (1979, 376–77) and Jaffe et al. (1981, 129).
5. See also Schulhofer (1981, 883, 892–93).

Celebration of *Brown* relieves Americans of the obligation to confront the systematic racial biases that permeate society. It encourages them to look to legal solutions for political and cultural problems. In this way, *Brown* serves a deeply conservative function of diverting resources away from substantive political battles, where success is possible, to symbolic legal ones, where it is not.

Successful litigation for significant social reform runs the risk of instigating countermobilization. While I have found little evidence that court decisions mobilize supporters of significant social reform, the data suggest that they can mobilize opponents. With civil rights, there was growth in the membership and activities of pro-segregation groups such as the White Citizens Councils and the Ku Klux Klan in the years after *Brown*. With abortion, the Right to Life movement expanded rapidly after 1973. While both types of groups existed before Court action, they appeared reinvigorated after it. In addition, in the wake of the Supreme Court's 1989 *Webster* decision, seen by many as a threat to continuing access to safe and legal abortion, pro-choice forces seemed to gain renewed vigor. With same-sex marriage, there was a massive and effective countermobilization in response to the Hawaii, Vermont, and Massachusetts decisions. These examples suggest that one result of litigation to produce significant social reform is to strengthen the opponents of such change. And that, of course, is far from the aim of those who litigate.

Why do judicial decisions appear to effectively mobilize opponents? With same-sex marriage, why was there a ferocious backlash after the Hawaii and Massachusetts decisions but not after the Connecticut or New Hampshire legislative enactments of civil unions? In the particular case, part of the answer likely has to do with timing (Connecticut and New Hampshire acted later) and with the greater public support for civil unions compared to marriage. More generally, legislators are unlikely to enact highly controversial legislation they believe that most of their constituents oppose while judges sometimes will act without political support. Thus, judicial decisions can appear to come out of the blue. They can be unexpected and shocking. Along the same lines, legislative acts require the support of majorities of relatively large legislatures, typically numbering in the hundreds, in two separate chambers, and the concurrence of the governor, while judicial opinions are the work of a handful of judges. Thus, in contrast to legislative acts, it is easy to characterize a judicial decision as the result of a few "activist" judges who don't share the public's beliefs and attitudes. Throughout the book I quoted opponents of judicial decisions furthering significant social reform criticizing the decisions as illegitimate because they came from the courts. Consider, for example, the remarks of President Bush in his State of the Union address on January 20, 2004, at the start of the presidential election year, in support of a constitutional amendment banning same-sex marriage. Bush underscored this concern with judicial action, saying, in part:

Activist judges . . . have begun redefining marriage by court order, without
regard for the will of the people and their elected representatives. On an issue
of such great consequence, the people's voice must be heard. If judges insist on
forcing their arbitrary will upon the people, the only alternative left to the people
would be the constitutional process. Our nation must defend the sanctity of marriage. (Bush 2004)

This concern may be more than rhetorical. Legislators face frequent elections
while judges either have life tenure or infrequently face the electorate. When
judges make unpopular decisions, people may feel that their lives are being
reordered without their input. Thus, the judiciary may be institutionally structured to be susceptible to backlash.

A final reason why judicial decisions on controversial issues may spark
backlash is that while legislative enactments are about preferences, judicial
decisions are about principle. It is possible to compromise preferences but
principles, by definition, can't be compromised. To be told by an electorally
unaccountable judge that deeply-held principles are wrong may outrage those
who hold competing principles. In contrast, when a legislature extends a benefit or enacts an entitlement program, one's disagreement may be less intense.
After all, what one legislature has done another can undo and the next election
is likely only a few years away. Again, the reasons that make litigation attractive to the relatively disadvantaged are the very reasons that judicial victories
are susceptible to backlash.[6]

It is important to note here that there were options other than litigation
in all the cases discussed. With civil rights, massive voter-registration drives
could have been started in the urban North and in some major Southern cities.
Marches, demonstrations, and sit-ins could have been organized and funded
years before they broke out, based on the example of labor unions and the
readiness of groups like the Congress of Racial Equality. Money could have
been invested in public relations. Amazingly, in 1957 the NAACP spent just
$7,814 for its Washington Bureau operations. Its entire "public relations and
informational activities" spending for 1957 was $17,216. NAACP lobbyists
did not even try to cultivate the black press or the black church, let alone their
white counterparts. And even in 1959 the public relations budget was only
$10,135 (Ware 1962, 188–89, 189, 190, 13). When activists succumbed to the
"lawyers' vision of change without pain" (Scheingold 1974, 145), a "massive
social revolution" was sidetracked into "legal channels" (Horwitz 1979, 184).
Because the NAACP failed to understand the limits on U.S. courts, its strategy
was bound to fail.[7]

---

6. For a somewhat different view, see Klarman (2005).

7. A similar case can be made with significant social reform of the environment, where
continuing and strengthening the movement could have been emphasized. With reform of the
criminal justice system, organizations such as those that evolved out of the civil rights movement

With women's groups, the kinds of political activities and grassroots organizing that started in the 1980s could have been organized earlier. Organizing around issues such as the earning gap and comparable worth could have been funded. Political activity on behalf of abortion at the state level could have been given greater emphasis. And coalition building, crucial in any ongoing political movement, could have been supported. Only belatedly, after June 1977, did pro-choice forces begin to work together to influence the legislative process (Gelb and Palley 1979, 378). As with civil rights, there was no lack of alternatives for social reform action.[8]

Similarly, same-sex marriage proponents could have focused on the extension of benefits to domestic partners. Polls have repeatedly shown both growing and majority support for such action. By not arguing for marriage, they could have avoided the explosive response that the quest for same-sex marriage engenders.

If this is the case, then there is another important way in which courts affect social change. It is, to put it simply, that courts act as "fly-paper" for social reformers who succumb to the "lure of litigation." If the constraints of the Constrained Court view are correct, then courts can seldom produce significant social reform. Yet if groups advocating such reform continue to look to the courts for aid, and spend precious resources in litigation, then the courts also limit change by deflecting claims from substantive political battles, where success is possible, to harmless legal ones where it is not. Even when major cases are won, the achievement is often more symbolic that real. Thus, courts may serve an ideological function of luring movements for social reform to an institution that is structurally constrained from serving their needs, providing only an illusion of change.[9]

This conclusion does not deny that courts can sometimes help social reform movements. Occasionally, though rarely, when the constraints are overcome, and one of the conditions is present, courts can make a difference. Sometimes, too, litigation can remove minor but lingering obstacles. But here litigation is often a mopping-up operation, and it is often defensive. In civil rights, for example, when opponents of the 1964 and 1965 acts went to court to invalidate them, the courts' refusal to do so allowed change to proceed. Similarly, if there had never been a *Brown* decision, a Southern school board or state wanting to

---

could have been reinvigorated (see chapter 11). And even with reapportionment, building political organizations and lobbying for substantive reform could have created pressure (and did in the late 1960s) for significant social reform.

8. For an argument that only through violence or its threat can minority groups achieve benefits, see Piven and Cloward (1979).

9. This point was not lost on the nineteenth-century founders of the Legal Aid Society. Their aim was not merely to help the poor but, paraphrasing Arthur Von Briesen, an early force in the legal aid movement, to "deflect them from anarchy, socialism, and bolshevism." Legal aid was also popular with Vice-President Theodore Roosevelt, who saw it as a "necessary bulwark against 'chaos' and 'violent revolution'" (quotes from Auerbach 1976, 53–55).

avoid a federal fund cutoff in the late 1960s might have challenged its state law requiring segregation. An obliging court decision would have removed the obstacle without causing much of a stir, or wasting the scarce resources of civil rights groups. This is a very different approach to the courts than one based on using them to produce significant social reform.

Litigation can also help reform movements by providing defense services to keep the movement afloat. In civil rights, the NAACP Legal Defense and Educational Fund, Inc. (Inc. Fund) provided crucial legal service that prevented the repressive legal structures of the Southern states from totally incapacitating the movement. In springing demonstrators from jail, providing bail money, and forcing at least a semblance of due process, Inc. Fund lawyers performed crucial tasks. But again, this is a far cry from a litigation strategy for significant social reform.

The findings of this study also suggest that a great deal of writing about courts is fundamentally flawed. Treating courts and judges as either philosophers on high or as existing solely within a self-contained legal community ignores what they actually do. This does not mean that philosophical thinking and legal analysis should be abandoned. It emphatically does mean that the broad and untested generalizations offered by constitutional scholars about the role, impact, importance, and legitimacy of courts and court opinions that pepper this book must be rejected. When asking those sorts of questions about courts, they must be treated as political institutions and studied as such. To ignore social science literature and eschew empirical evidence, as much court writing does, makes it impossible to understand courts as they are.

American courts, with their power of judicial review, are an important part of the notion of American exceptionalism. Unlike the courts of many other countries, American courts are vested with the power to declare invalid acts of democratically accountable political actors. From time to time in American history, great debates have flourished about the role of the courts about whether the exercise of judicial review is consistent with a self-governing democracy. Since the 1950s, the debate has raged anew, with its most recent manifestation the debate over "strict construction" of the Constitution and "judicial activism." Its focus has been on the movements I have examined. Yet, while such concerns are of intellectual importance, the analysis presented here has shown that they may be of little practical value. Normative and constitutional concerns about whether courts ought to be used to further social reform are misplaced if the conditions under which they can do so are so rare as to make the production of that change unlikely. Of greater concern are the implications of seeking significant social reform through the courts for political participation, mobilization, and reform. Social reformers, with limited resources, forgo other options when they elect to litigate. Those options are mainly political and involve mobilizing citizens to participate more effectively. The analysis in this book has shown that in assuming that courts can overcome political obstacles and produce change without mobilization and participation, reformers both reified and removed courts from the political and economic system in which they operate. And while such exercises may make for fine reading in constitutional-law textbooks, they seldom bring reform any closer.

American courts are not all-powerful institutions. They were designed with severe limitations and placed in a political system of divided powers. To ask them to produce significant social reform is to forget their history and ignore their constraints. It is to cloud our vision with a naive and romantic belief in the triumph of rights over politics. And while romance and even naiveté have their charms, they are not best exhibited in courtrooms.

Epilogue

The first edition of *The Hollow Hope* hit a raw nerve. The argument presented in the preceding chapters did not sit easily with many readers. And they have not been reticent in voicing their criticisms and concerns. Indeed, there have been dozens of reviews of the first edition, an edited collection of essays evaluating and testing the argument (Schultz 1998), follow-up studies, and countless course papers. I have responded to some criticisms in an article (Rosenberg 1992) and a book chapter (Rosenberg 1998). For the benefit of the reader, I have posted a response to critics as well as a list of reviews on a permanent Web page maintained by the University of Chicago Press. It can be found at http://www.press.uchicago.edu/books/rosenberg/.

I have little doubt that the material contained in this second edition will also be controversial to many people. It will be seen as a radical assault on the importance of rights in the United States. But the argument of *The Hollow Hope* isn't radical. What is radical is the belief that litigation can produce significant social reform, that rights triumph over politics. This is a historically odd idea. Until the mid-twentieth century, proponents of significant social reform mostly understood that change would only come through the building and nurturing of social movements and subsequent legislative victories. However, since roughly the mid-twentieth century, particularly during the Warren and Burger Courts, this was forgotten. Liberals increasingly turned to litigation. Forgetting the lessons of history, the liberal agenda was hijacked by a group of elite, well-educated and comparatively wealthy lawyers who uncritically believed that rights trump politics and that successfully arguing before judges is equivalent to building and sustaining political movements. As I have argued, absent specific conditions, this flirtation with litigation is fundamentally flawed.

In the waning decades of the twentieth century and the early years of the twenty-first century there appears to be a growing realization that courts may be limited in their ability to produce significant social reform. Although the argument of *The Hollow Hope* still has many critics, it is now seen as less controversial than it used to be. For example, in a 2005 op-ed article in the *Los Angeles Times*, Rosa Brooks wrote that "although Rosenberg was at first roundly attacked by legal scholars (who have something of a professional stake in believing that Supreme Court decisions matter), today many constitutional experts accept that Rosenberg was correct" (Brooks 2005). Brooks may be right, but I doubt the conversion is genuine. The heavy reliance on litigation to win marriage equality belies her claim. Rather, I suspect that given the hostility to significant social reform by the Rehnquist and Roberts' Courts, many supporters of the relatively disadvantaged are looking elsewhere. If and when the Court becomes more amenable to significant social reform, they will come running back, briefs in hand.

If reformers are turning away from the courts because of judicial hostility to significant social reform, and if the argument of *The Hollow Hope* is correct, then are conservative courts a good thing for proponents of significant social reform? The answer, alas, is no. Courts are not symmetrically constrained from furthering both liberal and conservative change. Courts can easily do damage to significant reform. This is because typically significant social reform litigators are asking courts to require change while conservatives are supporting the status quo. Further, it is easier to dismantle reform programs than to create them. For example, dismantling school desegregation or affirmative action programs is much easier than requiring them. Conservative courts not only are unlikely to further significant social reform, but also they are likely to roll it back. It is another sad irony for liberal reformers that courts can do more harm than good.

None of this means that law is irrelevant or that courts can never further the goals of the relatively disadvantaged. For the civil rights movement, for example, courts played an important role in keeping the sit-in movement going, ending the Montgomery bus boycott by providing the boycotters with leverage they could use, furthering school desegregation by threatening to cutoff federal funds under Title VI, and upholding affirmative action programs. With abortion, courts allowed the market to meet demand. But in each case courts were effective because a political movement was supporting change. The analysis does mean that courts acting alone, as in *Brown* or *Goodridge*, are structurally constrained from furthering the goals of the relatively disadvantaged.

In the end, there is no substitute for political action. As long as many of the brightest and most idealistic young people embark on legal careers and look to legal strategies to produce significant social reform, that reform is unlikely to be achieved. Political organizing, political mobilization, and voter registration may not be glamorous, or pay six-figure salaries, but they are the best if not the only hope to produce change—not as a fallback position, not as a complement to a legal strategy, but as the strategy itself. Unless and until this occurs, there is little hope for change. If it occurs, if those seeking significant social reform build a mass political base, then the hope for reform will not be hollow.

APPENDIX 1

Black Children in Elementary and Secondary School with Whites: State-by-State Breakdown, 1954–1972

YEAR	Alabama		Arkansas		Florida	
	%	#	%	#	%	#
1954–55	0	0	.02	20*	0	0
1955–56	0	0	.05	47	0	0
1956–57	0	0	.03	34	0	0
1957–58	0	0	.09	98	0	0
1958–59	0	0	.08	80	0	0
1959–60	0	0	.09	98	.26	512
1960–61	0	0	.10	113	.01	28
1961–62	0	0	.14	151	.27	648
1962–63	0	0	.22	247	.68	1,551
1963–64	.0007	21	.32	362	1.5	3,650
1964–65	.03	101	.81	930	2.7	6,612
1965–66	.43	1,250*	6.0	6,671*	9.8	25,000*
1966–67	4.7	12,900	16.6	19,500	20.8	58,150
1968–69	14.4	38,800	28.8	30,700	40.8	127,400
1970–71	80.0	216,000	91.4	97,000	90.1	299,500
1972–73	83.5	210,300	98.1	98,400	96.4	332,800

YEAR	Georgia		Louisiana		Mississippi	
	%	#	%	#	%	#
1954–55	0	0	0	0	0	0
1955–56	0	0	0	0	0	0
1956–57	0	0	0	0	0	0
1957–58	0	0	0	0	0	0
1958–59	0	0	0	0	0	0
1959–60	0	0	0	0	0	0
1960–61	0	0	.0004	1	0	0
1961–62	.003	8	.004	12	0	0
1962–63	.01	44	.04	107	0	0
1963–64	.05	177	.60	1,184	0	0
1964–65	.40	1,337	1.1	3,581	.02	57
1965–66	2.7	9,465*	.85	2,700*	.59	1,750*
1966–67	9.9	34,050	3.5	9,350	3.2	8,500
1968–69	23.6	74,400	18.0	57,400	11.7	26,400
1970–71	83.1	303,700	75.9	258,800	89.1	242,600
1972–73	86.8	322,100	82.9	287,100	91.5	242,600

YEAR	North Carolina		South Carolina		Tennessee	
	%	#	%	#	%	#
1954–55	0	0	0	0	0	0
1955–56	0	0	0	0	.07	85
1956–57	0	0	0	0	.08	100*
1957–58	.003	11	0	0	.09	120*
1958–59	.004	14	0	0	.06	82
1959–60	.01	34	0	0	.12	169
1960–61	.03	82	0	0	.25	376
1961–62	.06	203	0	0	.75	1,167
1962–63	.26	879	0	0	1.1	1,810
1963–64	.54	1,865	.003	9	2.7	4,486
1964–65	1.4	4,963	.10	265	5.4	9,289
1965–66	5.2	18,000*	1.7	4,731	16.3	28,801
1966–67	15.6	54,750	6.0	14,750	31.7	58,850
1968–69	41.0	144,500	20.7	49,300	41.3	76,300
1970–71	93.1	327,700	92.9	242,600	74.1	140,500
1972–73	99.4	345,900	93.9	245,400	80.0	154,000

YEAR	Texas		Virginia		Delaware	
	%	#	%	#	%	#
1954–55	.001	3	0	0	1.9	200*
1955–56	1.1	2,650	0	0	11.0	1,230
1956–57	1.4	3,380*	0	0	28.5	3,248
1957–58	1.4	3,600*	0	0	36.2	4,497
1958–59	1.2	3,250*	.02	30	43.7	5,727
1959–60	1.2	3,300*	.05	103	44.1	6,196
1960–61	1.2	3,500*	.10	208	45.0	6,738
1961–62	1.3	4,000*	.24	536	53.7	8,540
1962–63	2.3	7,000*	.54	1,230*	55.9	9,498
1963–64	5.5	18,000*	1.6	3,721	56.5	10,209
1964–65	7.8	27,000*	5.2	12,000*	62.2	12,051
1965–66	17.2	60,000*	11.0	26,300	83.2	17,069
1966–67	47.3	160,050	24.8	59,000	100	24,100
1968–69	56.5	214,600	41.9	102,800	100	24,000
1970–71	85.9	346,100	89.6	232,500	100	27,000
1972–73	92.8	388,400	99.3	259,300	98.9	27,800

YEAR	D.C.		Kentucky		Maryland	
	%	#	%	#	%	#
1954–55	NA	NA	0	0	5.1	4,332*
1955–56	NA	NA	.85	313	15.9	13,479*
1956–57	97.0	71,500	20.9	8,017	19.1	20,936*
1957–58	88.5	70,000*	28.4	10,897	22.1	25,650
1958–59	81.5	69,007	27.5	11,492	32.4	37,775
1959–60	81.9	73,290	38.9	16,329	29.3	38,053
1960–61	84.1	81,392	47.7	20,000*	33.6	45,943
1961–62	85.6	88,881	51.2	22,021	41.5	59,729
1962–63	79.2	87,749	54.1	24,346	45.1	69,147
1963–64	83.8	98,813	54.4	29,855	47.8	76,906
1964–65	86.0	106,578	68.1	37,585	50.9	86,205
1965–66	84.8	109,270	78.1	46,861	55.6	99,442
1966–67	84.6	116,400	88.5	38,220	64.0	140,550
1968–69	72.1	100,300	94.8	60,700	68.7	138,500
1970–71	66.4	91,400	96.6	64,000	74.2	163,500
1972–73	64.2	85,900	92.6	58,000	75.9	176,300

YEAR	Missouri		Oklahoma		West Virginia	
	%	#	%	#	%	#
1954–55	NA	NA	0	0	4.3	1,100
1955–56	NA	NA	NA	NA	NA	NA
1956–57	NA	NA	8.7	3,177	NA	NA
1957–58	0	NA	18.2	6,633	38.7	10,000*
1958–59	NA	NA	21.2	8,351	39.8	10,000*
1959–60	42.7	35,000*	26.0	10,246*	50.0	12,000*
1960–61	41.7	35,000*	24.0	9,822	66.6	14,000*
1961–62	41.4	35,000*	25.6	10,555	62.0	15,500*
1962–63	38.9	35,000*	23.6	10,557*	61.4	15,500*
1963–64	42.1	40,000*	28.0	12,289*	58.2	13,659*
1964–65	42.3	44,000*	31.1	14,000*	63.4	13,500*
1965–66	75.1	79,000*	38.3	17,500*	79.9	15,850*
1966–67	64.2	83,460	55.7	34,310	84.3	19,220
1968–69	66.5	92,100	82.8	40,500	96.0	19,600
1970–71	69.7	100,900	89.3	47,000	98.9	18,800
1972–73	69.4	103,500	100	55,300	98.9	18,000

SOURCES: Southern Education Reporting Service (1967, 40–44); USCCR (1967, 7); U.S. Department of HEW (*Directory*, 1968, 1970, 1972).

*Estimate.

Blacks at Predominantly White Public Colleges and Universities: State-by-State Breakdown

	1960	1963	1965	1966
Southern States				
Alabama	0	6	200	295*
Arkansas	very low†	46	160	303
Florida	6*	1,000	6,500*	9,928*
Georgia	0	35	200*	475*
Louisiana	several hundred	850	NA	1,000*
Mississippi	0	0	16	131
North Carolina	very small	250	NA	860
South Carolina	0	6	64	169*
Tennessee	several hundred	400	1,399*	1,128*
Texas	several hundred	2,000	3,256*	5,915
Virginia	41‡	46	259	584
Total	—	4,639	12,054 (1.9%)	20,788 (2.6%)
Total without Texas and Florida	—	—	2,298 (0.6%)	4,945(1.2%)
Border States				
Delaware	no great influx	20	50	50*
Kentucky	80 (1959)	—	859*	1,583
Maryland	150 (College Park 1959)	848	955	1,109
Missouri	over 100 (U of MO 1959)	—	2,481	7,938*
Oklahoma	several hundred	—	1,120	2,094
West Virginia	very low	—	1,142	1,328
Total	—	—	6,607 (2.5%)	14,102 (4.9%)

SOURCES: Sarratt (1966, chap. 5); Southern Education Reporting Service (1965, 3–25; 1967, 3); USCCR (1961a, 52–96).

NOTES:
* estimate
† admitted only for courses not otherwise available at black colleges
‡ admitted as above but only to graduate and professional schools
% percent of black enrollment at predominantly white institutions

APPENDIX 3

Black Voter Registration in the Southern States, Pre-and Post-Voting Rights Act, State-by-State Breakdown

State	Pre-Act			Post-Act		
	Registration	%*	Gap†	Registration	%*	Gap†
Alabama	92,737[1]	19.3	49.9	248,432[a]	51.6	38.0
Arkansas	77,714[2]	40.4	25.1	121,000[b]	62.8	9.6
Florida	240,616[1]	51.2	23.6	299,033[c]	63.6	17.8
Georgia	268,000[3]	27.4	35.2	332,496[c]	52.6	27.7
Louisiana	164,601[4]	31.6	48.9	303,148[a]	58.9	34.2
Mississippi	28,500[5]	6.7	63.2	263,754[d]	59.8	31.7
North Carolina	258,000[6]	46.8	50.0	277,404[c]	51.3	31.7
South Carolina	138,544[5]	37.3	38.4	190,017[e]	51.2	30.5
Tennessee	218,000[5]	69.5	3.4	225,000[c]	71.7	8.9
Texas	375,000[6]	57.7	−5.2	400,000[c]	61.6	−8.3
Virginia	144,259[4]	38.3	22.8	243,000[c]	55.6	7.8
Total	2,005,971	40.0	33.4	2,903,284	57.6	18.9

Sources: Lawson (1976, 285); USCCR (1968, 12, 13, 222, 223).

Notes:
* percent of registered black voters out of all eligible black voters
† percent of registered white voters minus percent of registered black voters

Key: [1]May 1964; [2]October 1963; [3]December 1962; [4]October 1964; [5]November 1964; [6]1964; [a]October 1967 [b]August 1967; [c]Summer 1966; [d]September 1967; [e]July 1967

Laws and Actions Designed to Preserve Segregation

	Southern States										
	A L	A K	F L	G A	L A	M S	N C	S C	T N	T X	V A
Politics:											
Anti-NAACP laws	x	x	x	x	x	x		x	x	x	x
Emergency power to officials			x	x	x	x					
Interposition/protest	x	x	x	x	x	x		x			x
Segregation committees	x	x	x	x	x	x	x	x	x	x	x
Sovereignty commissions	x	x		x	x	x					x
State-federal protests	x	x	x	x	x	x		x	x	x	
Schools:											
Compulsory attendance: amended/repealed	x	x	x	x	x	x	x	x	x	x	x
Private schools: authorized/encouraged	x	x		x	x	x		x			x
Pupil assignment	x	x	x	x	x	x	x	x	x	x	x
School closure permitted	x	x	x	x	x	x	x	x		x	x
Scholarships out-of-state	x	x	x	x	x	x	x	x		x	x
Teacher removal	x		x		x		x	x			x
Tuition grants	x	x		x	x	x	x	x			x
Withheld aid to desegregated schools	x	x		x	x			x		x	x

SOURCE: Adapted from Sarratt (1966, 363).

	Border States					
D	D	K	M	M	O	W
E	C	Y	D	O	K	V

| x | x | x | x | x | x | x |

APPENDIX 5

Method for Obtaining Information for Table 4.1 and Figure 4.1

The figure, table, and discussion of magazine coverage of civil rights are based on my examination of the *Reader's Guide To Periodical Literature* from 1940 to 1965. In each volume I turned to the index category entitled "Negroes In The United States" and counted entries, both in general and for the specific magazines listed. Since the number of magazines indexed varied over time, I noted the variation as well. However, the variation was not great enough to affect the trend in the changes of coverage.

There was a problem of repetitions. That is, within the larger category, entries were sometimes repeated under different subheadings. Since the number of entries in each year was large, purging repetitions would have been an onerous and time-consuming task. By counting each entry I have inflated the *actual* number of articles about Negroes in the U.S. However, since my purpose is only to *compare* coverage, and since my treatment of the entries was consistent, this should not cause a problem.

With *TV Guide*, I used an index issued by the magazine itself.[1] Here I used the index entries entitled "Civil Rights," "Blacks," "Minorities," "Minorities—Programming," "Protest Movements," and "Race Relations."

Reader's Digest, Ladies Home Journal, Life, Saturday Evening Post, and *TV Guide* were selected because they had the largest circulation of any American magazines (Sunday news magazines excluded) over the period in question.[2] The *New York Times Sunday Magazine, New Republic, Newsweek*, and *Time* were selected as magazines that political elites would read.

Finally, although I used great care in counting, the combination of small print and thousands of entries may have lead to errors. I am confident, however, that any errors are small, given the number of entries and the care I used.

The figures from the *New York Times Index* were kindly provided by Paul Burstein, currently at the University of Washington.

1. Johnson and Post (1979).
2. See, for the relevant years, N.W. Ayer and Son's.

APPENDIX 6

Illegal Abortions

Abortion is not new; women have been having abortions for thousands of years. Abortion before "quickening" (about five months) was allowed under the British common law and was permitted in most of the United States until the mid and late 1800s (Lader 1966, 85–87). The Catholic church originally allowed abortion in the first few months of pregnancy and it was not until 1869 that Pope Pius IX forbade it (U.S. Congress, Senate 1974, 3: 403). World-wide, abortion is the "most common form of birth control," with more women using it to control fertility than either the pill and IUD combined, or sterilization (U.S. Congress, Senate 1974, 2: 570).

The challenge this presents for the analysis of Court efficacy in producing change is that the number of *legal* abortions is not equivalent to the number of abortions. In assessing the Court's contribution to abortion, then, both legal and illegal abortions must be included. And since illegal abortions are impossible to count accurately, the best that can be done is to rely on a range of estimates. These estimates are presented in table A1.

Table A1 makes clear that while most students of illegal abortion agree that the number was substantial, they have differed markedly on the figures. By the mid-1960s, however, the range seemed to be settling around 1 million. For obvious reasons of partisanship and lack of hard data, these figures can only be taken as very rough estimates. More subtly, however, there are two factors that suggest that the estimates are too low. One is that they are derived, in part, from reported maternal deaths due to illegal abortions, deaths that are notoriously under-reported. Such deaths have been high. In 1930, abortion was the "certified cause of death for almost 2,700 women" (U.S. Cong., Senate 1974, 2: 126), and by the 1950s "researchers found that botched abortions were the largest single cause of maternal deaths in the United States" (Monroe 1968, 10). Deaths from illegal abortions accounted for 18 percent of all maternal deaths in 1930, nearly 21 percent in 1962, and 16 percent in 1969 (U.S. Cong., Senate 1974, 2: 129). Whatever the figure,[1] as an official

1. Leavy and Kummer (1962, 124) suggest 5,000 in 1962. In Senate testimony, Congresswoman Bella Abzug (D., N.Y.) cited estimates that illegal abortions were the third largest source of illegal income in the United States, after narcotics and gambling (U.S. Cong., Senate 1974, 1: 102). The same figure can also be found in Sarvis and Rodman (1973, 65).

Table A1   Estimates of Illegal Abortions

Year	Estimate	Estimator
1936	681,600	Taussig
1937	200,000	Wiehl and Berry
late 1930s	50,000	Pearl
1941–42	under 100,000	Whelpton and Kiser
1947	nearly 2 million	McPartland
1951	minimum 330,000	Fisher
1950s	600,000	Kinsey
1955	200,000–1.2 million	Planned Parenthood
1957	1,200,000	Tietze
1962	more than 1 million	Leavy and Kummer
1963	200,000–1 million	*New Republic*
	100,000 in New York City	*New Republic*
1965	1.5 million	*Time*
1966	1 million	*Newsweek*
1967	A million or more	Rosen
1967	minimum 300,000	Fisher
1967	more than a million	*New York Times*
1968	100,000 in California	Clark
1968	250,000–2 million	Lucas
1970	800,000	Guttmacher
1970	1 million	Senator Packwood
1970	1 million	Rossi
1972	750,000–1 million	Lader

SOURCES: Callahan (1970, 132, 133); Clark (1969, 1, 3); Packwood, (1970, 12673); "Gynecology" (1965, 82); Lader (1966, 2; 1973, 22, 29 n.2); Leavy and Kummer (1962, 124); Lucas (1968, 730); Ridgeway (1963, 14); Rosen (1967, xvii, 6); "Start on Abortion Reform" (1967, 34); "The Abortion Epidemic" (1966, 92).

of the Center for Disease Control testifying in 1974 commented, "official reports undoubtedly give a minimum estimate" of such deaths.[2]

The second reason for thinking that the estimates are low is that they are often based on samplings of married women (Kinsey's estimates for example). Whether this was done for political reasons or for moral ones, it excluded from the sample those women most likely to seek abortions, single women. Studies of women obtaining legal abortions show that, in the years before the Court acted, approximately two-thirds to three-quarters were single.[3] By the mid-1980s, the figure had reached just over 81 percent (Hen-

2. U.S. Cong., Senate (1974, 2: 176); cf. Callahan (1970, 135–36).
3. Center for Disease Control (1974, n.p., table 10) (U.S., 1972: 69.6 percent unmarried); Fujita and Wagner (1973, 237) (Washington state, 1969–70: 65 percent never married, 12 percent separated, widowed, or divorced); Steinhoff (1973, 219) (New York, 1970–71: 55.9 percent never married, 14.2 percent separated, widowed, or divorced); Tietze and Dawson (1973) (U.S., 1970–72: average 69.1 percent never married or not married at time of abortion); U.S. Cong., Senate (1974, 1: 439–43) (California, 1968–71: average 54 percent never married, 19 percent other and not reported, 27 percent married); U.S. Cong., Senate (1974, 2: 131) (U.S., 1974: two-thirds not married).

shaw and Silverman 1988, 159). Thus, while one should approach estimates of the number of illegal abortions with care, the 1 million figure is probably not a grossly unreasonable estimate.

The question that needs to be faced now is the relationship between illegal and legal abortions. The leading study was made by Christopher Tietze, senior consultant at the Population Council in New York. Using figures from New York, Tietze concluded that about 70 percent of legal abortions replace illegal ones (Tietze 1973). That is, Tietze estimated that about 70 percent of women undergoing legal abortions would have had illegal ones if legal abortions weren't available.[4] Another study, based on nationwide data in 1971, concluded that "well over half—most likely between two-thirds and three-fourths—of all legal abortions in the United States in 1971 were replacements for illegal abortions" (Sklar and Berkov, 1974). In 1975, Harriet Pilpel, a legal activist involved in abortion litigation, testified that "at the very least, 70 percent of today's abortions . . . would have been performed anyway" (U.S. Cong., Senate 1976, 4: 244). Writing in 1977 Judith Blake was able to conclude that "most legal abortions replaced abortions that would have occurred anyway on an illegal basis" (Blake 1977b, 46).

The point of this discussion is twofold: 1) in all likelihood the total abortion rate did not change a great deal, despite legislative and Supreme Court action; 2) the replacement of illegal abortions by legal abortions removed a serious health hazard to women. To the extent, then, that the Court contributed to the ease of abortion, the Court produced change by removing the need for women to seek dangerous, illegal abortions.

4. The same figure and analysis were presented by Tietze in 1974 in Senate testimony. See U.S. Cong., Senate (1974, 2: 3–6).

APPENDIX 7

Method for Obtaining Information for Tables 8.1A, 8.1B, 8.2A, and 8.2B, and for Figures 8.1 and 8.2

The figures, tables, and discussion of magazine coverage of abortion and women's rights are based on my examination of the *Reader's Guide To Periodical Literature* from 1940 to 1976. As with civil rights, in each volume I turned to specific index categories and counted entries, both in general and for the specific magazines listed. Since the number of magazines indexed varied over time, I noted the variation as well. However, the variation was not great enough to affect the trend in the changes of coverage.

The index category for table 8.1A was simply "Abortion." For table 8.1B, the category was "United States Supreme Court Decisions" and the sub-heading was "Abortion Decision." To compile table 8.2A, I examined entries under the sub-heading "Equal Rights" of the main heading "Woman." The category "Feminism" had virtually no entries and was not even listed in the index for about one-fourth of the years. In table 8.2B, I reported entries under the headings "Women's Liberation Movements" and "National Organization For Women," first appearing in 1969. I am confident that the categories presented in tables 8.2A and 8.2B present an accurate picture.

There may be a problem of repetitions. That is, within the larger category, entries were sometimes repeated under different sub-headings. Since the number of entries in each year was large, purging repetitions would have been an onerous and time-consuming task. By counting each entry I have inflated the *actual* number of articles in the relevant category. However, since my purpose is only to *compare* coverage, and since my treatment of the entries was consistent, this should not cause a problem.

Reader's Digest, Ladies Home Journal, Life, and the *Saturday Evening Post* were selected because they had among the largest circulations of any American magazines (Sunday news magazines excluded) over the period in question.[1] The *New York Times Sunday Magazine, Newsweek, New Republic*, and *Time* were selected as magazines that political elites would read.

Finally, although I used great care in counting, the combination of small

---

1. See, for the relevant years, N.W. Ayer and Son's.

print and hundreds of entries may have lead to errors. With the *New York Times*, the numbers are based on rather crude estimates generated with a ruler. They should be used only as a general indication of the trend of coverage. All in all, I am confident that any errors are small, given the number of entries and the care I used.

APPENDIX 8

Coding Rules and Method for Obtaining Information for Tables 13.3, 13.4, 13.5, 13.6, and 13.7.

I used Lexis to compile and analyze data from the *New York Times* and the *Chicago Tribune*.

For table 13.3, I searched the *New York Times* for "Same-Sex Marriage, Gay Marriage or Homosexual Marriage" from 1980–2004. Table 13.4 is simply a monthly breakdown for selected years of the data contained in table 13.3.

Table 13.5 reports the content analysis of the *Times* entries. In order to minimize subjectivity, I hired a third-year law student at the University of Chicago as a research assistant to independently read and code entries. We read all entries in years with fewer than ten. As the number of entries increased, we sampled. In order to balance the sample, we spaced out the reading numerically, starting with the last entry for the year. For example, in years where there were more than ten but fewer than twenty entries, we read every other entry, or approximately one-half. In years with more than twenty but fewer than fifty entries, we read every third. In years with more than fifty entries, we read anywhere from 26 percent of the entries (1997) to 11.5 percent (2004). Table 13.5 reports the number of entries produced for each year, the number read, and the number coded.

Entries that fell into four categories were not coded. These included those contained in the "News Summary" (the index to the *Times* found on page 2), noted in the "Corrections," listed in "Inside" (an index to the Metropolitan Desk section of the paper), and three false hits where the words in the search terms appeared but didn't refer to the subjects of same-sex marriage, gay marriage, or homosexual marriage. For example, Dennis Hevesi (1986) wrote an article about a minister who had been stripped of his authority to offer "ministry to homosexuals, marriage annulments," etc.

We independently coded entries as positive, negative, or mixed and tangential. Our agreement rate was over 90 percent. Where we initially had different coding, we discussed the issue and reached a joint decision.

An entry was coded as *positive* when it reported support for same-sex marriage, gay marriage, or homosexual marriage or compared the cause favorably to past civil rights struggles. Entries coded as positive include a story on an elderly gay couple in New York City celebrating their forty-third anniversary (Kaufman 1992), reports of support for same-sex marriage by the Unitarian

Church (UPI 1984), the ACLU (UPI 1986), and the California Bar Association (Gutis 1989), a story on businesses "eagerly wooing the affluent gay market" for wedding products (Flaherty 2004), and interviews with children of gay parents marrying in San Francisco (Brown 2004).

Negative coding occurred when an entry reported efforts to prohibit same-sex marriage, gay marriage, or homosexual marriage, disparaged or rejected it, or proclaimed heterosexual marriage to be virtuous and immutable. Entries coded negative included many statements by elected officials and candidates opposing same-sex marriage as well as reports of legislative action on both the state and federal level opposing same-sex marriage. Other entries reported opposition to same-sex marriage from religious groups (Associated Press 1999; Goodstein 2003), from conservative activists (Dunlap 1996; Kirkpatrick 2004A), and from courts (Associated Press 1997).

Entries were coded *mixed and tangential* when they reported both support and opposition, discussed the issue without reporting a point of view, or mentioned the issue tangentially. For example, tangential entries include a 1983 discussion of qualifications for rent control in New York City (Schanberg 1983), an article on how the end of the Cold War has put Eastern European ethnic voters up for grabs (Friedman 1992), and an article on attempts to encourage young people to vote (Elliott 2000). Mixed entries included a story on a Texas county voting against a real estate tax abatement to Apple Computer because it grants benefits to same-sex partners (Associated Press 1993), a story on support and opposition for a constitutional amendment banning same-sex marriage (Hulse 2004), and a piece on whether Grinnell College's housing policy for married students applies to same-sex relationships ("Campus Life" 1989).

Compiling the raw data for editorials and op-eds reported in tables 13.6 and 13.7 proved more challenging. We searched the *New York Times* from 1980–2004 and the *Chicago Tribune* from 1985–2004 for "same-sex marriage, gay marriage, homosexual marriage, domestic partnership or civil union." Using the words "editorial" or "op-ed" as key terms was not fully effective for a variety of reasons. First, the *Times* includes editorials, op-eds, and letters to the editor in Lexis searches so we had to read each "hit" to place it appropriately. Second, the *Chicago Tribune*'s op-ed section as compiled by Lexis has had several names over the years including "Perspective" and "Commentary." Thus, the data presented are the results of some trial and error and much cross-checking, including numerous phone calls to helpful research assistants at Lexis. I am confident that the data, at the very least, are reasonably complete and don't systematically exclude editorials and op-eds.

Four types of entries were excluded: corrections, letters to the editor (they were included in the data reported and analyzed in tables 13.3–13.5), false hits, and pieces that were clearly not relevant. Examples of false hits include a 1981 *Times* editorial about restoring civil and union rights in Poland

("The Cry From Poland" 1981) and a 1983 op-ed that identified Raul Afonsin of Argentina as the "leader of the radical Civil Union" (Cox 1983). Pieces that were excluded as not relevant include a *Tribune* op-ed by Ellen Goodman complaining that "many of us are living in domestic partnership with machines whose primary feature is to make us feel dumb" (Goodman 1995).

We followed the same coding rules for editorials and op-eds as with the initial search reported in tables 13.3–13.5, with one exception. Since in coding editorials and op-eds we focused on the view of the author, positions of candidates and elected officials noted in the piece were not determinative.

Case References

Adele v. *Markle*, 342 F. Supp. 800 (D. Ct. 1972).

Adams v. *Howerton*, 486 F. Supp. 1119 (C.D. Cal. 1980).

Adams v. *Richardson*, 356 F. Supp. 92 (D.D.C. 1973), *modified & aff'd*, 480 F.2d 1159 (D.C. Cir. 1973).

AFSCME v. *State of Washington*, 578 F. Supp., 846 (W.D. Wash. 1983), *reversed*, 770 F.2d 1401 (9th Cir. 1985).

Aguilar v. *Texas*, 378 U.S. 108 (1964).

Alabama v. *U.S.*, 304 F.2d 583 (5th Cir. 1962).

Alexander v. *Holmes County*, 396 U.S. 19 (1969).

Argersinger v. *Hamlin*, 407 U.S. 25 (1972).

Babbitz v. *McCann*, 310 F. Supp. 293 (E.D. Wis. 1970).

Baehr v. *Lewin*, 74 Haw. 530, 852 P.2d 44, *clarified on grant of reconsideration in part*, 74 Haw. 645, 852 P.2d 74 (Haw. 1993).

Baehr v. *Miike*, No. 91–1394–05 (Haw. First Cir. Ct. 1996).

Bailey v. *Patterson*, 369 U.S. 31 (1962) (*per curiam*).

Baker v. *Carr*, 179 F. Supp. 824 (M.D. Tenn. 1959).

Baker v. *Carr*, 369 U.S. 186 (1962).

Baker v. *Nelson*, 191 N.W.2d 185 (Minn. 1971).

Baker v. *Vermont*, 744 A.2d 864 (Vt. 1999).

Baltimore Gas & Electric Co. v. *NRDC*, 462 U.S. 87 (1983).

Barenblatt v. *U.S.*, 360 U.S. 109 (1959).

Barnes v. *City of Gadsden*, 361 U.S. 915 (1959).

Barrows v. *Jackson*, 346 U.S. 249 (1953).

Beal v. *Doe*, 432 U.S. 438 (1977).

Beilan v. *Board of Education*, 357 U.S. 399 (1958).

Bell v. *Wolfish*, 441 U.S. 520 (1979).

Bellotti v. *Baird*, 443 U.S. 622 (1979).

Bivens v. *Six Unknown Federal Narcotics Agents*, 403 U.S. 388 (1971).

Board of Trustees v. *Frazier*, 350 U.S. 979 (1956).

Bolling v. *Sharpe*, 347 U.S. 497 (1954).

Boynton v. *Virginia*, 364 U.S. 454 (1960).

Bradwell v. *The State*, 83 U.S. (16 Wallace) 130 (1872).

Brief for the United States as *Amicus Curiae, Brown* v. *Board of Education*, 347 U.S. 483 (1954).

Brief for Appellants, *Baker* v. *Carr*, 369 U.S. 186 (1962).

Brief of Governor J. Howard Edmondson, Governor of the State of Oklahoma as *Amicus Curiae, Baker* v. *Carr*, 369 U.S. 186 (1962).

Brief of the National Institute of Municipal Law Officers as *Amicus Curiae, Baker* v. *Carr*, 369 U.S. 186 (1962).

Brief for the United States as *Amicus Curiae, Baker* v. *Carr*, 369 U.S. 186 (1962).

Brief for the American College of Obstetricians and Gynecologists, American Medical Women's Association, American Psychiatric Association, New York Academy of Medicine, Medical School Deans and Professors and Certain Individual Physicians as *Amicus Curiae, Doe* v. *Bolton*, 410 U.S. 179 (1973).

Brief of the American Ethical Union, American Friends Service Committee, American Humanist Association, American Jewish Congress, Episcopal Diocese of New York, New York State Council of Churches, Union of American Hebrew Congregations, Unitarian Universalist Association, United Church of Christ and the Board of Christian Social Concerns of the United Methodist Church as *Amicus Curiae, Doe*, v. *Bolton*, 410 U.S. 179 (1973).

Brief for Appellants, *Doe* v. *Bolton*, 410 U.S. 179 (1973).

Brief of Representative Jim Wright et al. as *Amicus Curiae, Harris* v. *McRae*, 448 U.S. 297 (1980).

Brief for Appellants, *Roe* v. *Wade*, 410 U.S. 113 (1973).

Brief for Planned Parenthood Federation of America, Inc., and Association of American Planned Parenthood Physicians as *Amicus Curiae, Roe* v. *Wade*, 410 U.S. 113 (1973).

Brief for the United States as *Amicus Curiae, Shelley* v. *Kraemer*, 334 U.S. 1 (1948).

Briggs v. *Elliott*, 103 F. Supp. 920 (E.D.S.C. 1952).

Briggs v. *Elliott*, 132 F. Supp. 776 (E.D.S.C. 1955).

Browder v. *Gayle*, 142 F. Supp. 707 (M.D. Al. 1956).

Brown v. *Board of Education*, 98 F. Supp. 797 (D. Kan. 1951).

Brown v. *Board of Education*, 347 U.S. 483 (1954) (*Brown I*).

Brown v. *Board of Education*, 349 U.S. 294 (1955) (*Brown II*).

Brown v. *Louisiana*, 383 U.S. 131 (1966).

Burton v. *Wilmington Parking Authority*, 365 U.S. 715 (1961).

Califano v. *Goldfarb*, 430 U.S. 199 (1977).

Califano v. *Webster*, 430 U.S. 313 (1977).

Califano v. *Westcott*, 443 U.S. 76 (1979).

Calvert Cliffs' Coordinating Committee v. *AEC*, 449 F.2d 1109 (D.C. Cir. 1971).

Cannon v. *University of Chicago*, 441 U.S. 677 (1979).

Chevron U.S.A. v. *NRDC*, 467 U.S. 837 (1984).

Citizens to Preserve Overton Park v. *Volpe*, 401 U.S. 402 (1971).

City of Akron v. *Akron Center for Reproductive Health*, 462 U.S. 416 (1983).

Cleveland Board of Education v. *LaFleur*, 414 U.S. 632 (1974).

Cohen v. *Public Housing Authority*, 358 U.S. 928 (1959).

Colautti v. *Franklin* 439 U.S. 379 (1979).

Colegrove v. *Green*, 328 U.S. 549 (1946).

Connecticut Fund for the Environment v. *EPA*, 696 F.2d 169 (2nd Cir. 1982).

Conservation Society of Southern Vermont v. *Secretary of Transportation*, 362 F. Supp. 627 (D. Vt. 1973), *aff'd*, 508 F.2d 927 (2nd Cir. 1974), *affirmance vacated and remanded*, 423 U.S. 809 (1975), *rev'd*, 531 F.2d 637 (2nd Cir. 1976).

Cooper v. *Aaron*, 358 U.S. 1 (1958).

Cooper v. *Fitzharris*, 551 F.2d 1162 (9th Cir. 1977).

Cooper v. *Pate*, 378 U.S. 546 (1964) (*per curiam*).

Corning Glass v. *Brennan*, 417 U.S. 188 (1974).

County of Washington v. *Gunther*, 452 U.S. 161 (1981).

Craig v. *Boren*, 429 U.S. 190 (1976).

Cruz v. *Beto*, 405 U.S. 319 (1972) (*per curiam*).

Davis v. *County School Board of Prince Edward County, Virginia*, 103 F. Supp. 337 (E.D. Va. 1952).

Dawley v. *City of Norfolk, Virginia*, 359 U.S. 935 (1959).

De Santo v. *Barnsley*, 476 A.2d 952 (Pa. Super. 1984).

Dean v. *District of Columbia*, 653 A.2d 307 (D.C. App. 1995).

Dekosenko v. *Brandt*, 313 N.Y.S.2d 827 (Sup. Ct. 1970).

Derrington v. *Plummer*, 240 F.2d 922 (5th Cir. 1956), *cert. denied*, 353 U.S. 924 (1957).

Doe v. *Bolton*, 319 F. Supp. 1048 (N.D. Ga. 1970).

Doe v. *Bolton*, 410 U.S. 179 (1973).

Doe v. *General Hospital of the District of Columbia*, 313 F. Supp. 1170 (D.D.C. 1970).

Doe v. *Poelker*, 515 F.2d 541 (8th Cir. 1975).

Doe v. *Randall*, 314 F. Supp. 32 (D. Minn. 1970).

Doe v. *Scott*, 321 F. Supp. 1385 (N.D. Ill. 1971).

Dothard v. *Rawlinson*, 433 U.S. 321 (1977).

Duren v. *Missouri*, 439 U.S. 357 (1979).

EDF v. *Corps of Engineers*, 325 F. Supp. 728 (E.D. Ark. 1971).

EDF v. *Corps of Engineers*, 470 F.2d 289 (8th Cir. 1972).

EDF v. *Ruckelshaus*, 439 F.2d 584 (D.C. Cir. 1971).

EDF v. *Ruckelshaus*, 3 *ELR* 20173 (D.D.C. Jan. 29, 1973).

Edwards v. *California*, 314 U.S. 160 (1941).

Eisenstadt v. *Baird*, 405 U.S. 438 (1972).

Elkins v. *United States*, 364 U.S. 206 (1960).

Ely v. *Velde*, 451 F.2d 1130 (4th Cir. 1971).

Escobedo v. *Illinois*, 378 U.S. 478 (1964).

Estelle v. *Gamble*, 429 U.S. 97 (1976).

Ethyl Corp. v. *EPA*, 541 F.2d 1 (D.C. Cir. 1976).

Evers v. *Dwyer*, 358 U.S. 202 (1958).

Ex Parte Siebold, 100 U.S. 371 (1880).

Ex Parte Yarbrough, 110 U.S. 651 (1884).

Florida v. *Barquet*, 262 So.2d 431 (Sup. Ct. Fl. 1972).

Frontiero v. *Richardson*, 411 U.S. 677 (1973).

Furman v. *Georgia*, 408 U.S. 238 (1972).

Gayle v. *Browder*, 352 U.S. 903 (1956).

Gebhardt v. *Belton*, 33 Del. 145, 91 A.2d 137 (1952).

Gedulding v. *Aiello*, 417 U.S. 484 (1974).

General Electric v. *Gilbert*, 429 U.S. 125 (1976).

Gideon v. *Wainwright*, 372 U.S. 335 (1963).

Goesaert v. *Cleary*, 335 U.S. 464 (1948).

Gomillion v. *Lightfoot*, 364 U.S. 339 (1960).

Goodridge v. *Department of Public Health*, 440 Mass. 309; 798 N.E.2d 941 (2003).

Goss v. *Board of Education of Knoxville*, 373 U.S. 683 (1963).

Gray v. *Sanders*, 372 U.S. 368 (1963).

Green v. *County School Board of New Kent County, Virginia*, 391 U.S. 430 (1968).

Gregg v. *Georgia*, 428 U.S. 153 (1976).

Griffin v. *Prince Edward County*, 375 U.S. 391 (1964).

Griswold v. *Connecticut*, 381 U.S. 479 (1965).

Grove City College v. *Bell*, 465 U.S. 555 (1984).

Grovey v. *Townsend*, 295 U.S. 45 (1935).

Guinn & Beal v. *U.S.*, 347 (1915).

H.L. v. *Matheson*, 450 U.S. 398 (1981).

Haines v. *Kerner*, 404 U.S. 519 (1972).

Harper v. *Virginia Board of Elections*, 383 U.S. 663 (1966).

Harris v. *McRae*, 448 U.S. 297 (1980).

Hawkins v. *Board of Control*, 350 U.S. 413 (1956).

Heart of Atlanta Motel v. *U.S.*, 379 U.S. 241 (1964).

Henderson v. *U.S.*, 339 U.S. 816 (1950).

Hodgson v. *Minnesota*, 110 S.Ct. 2926 (1990).

Holt v. *Sarver*, 309 F. Supp. 362 (E.D. Ark. 1970), *aff'd*, 442 F.2d 304 (8th Cir. 1971).

Hoyt v. *Florida*, 368 U.S. 57 (1961).

Hurd v. *Hodge*, 334 U.S. 24 (1948).

In re Gault, 387 U.S. 1 (1967).

In re George Anastaplo, 366 U.S. 82 (1961).

In re Girard College Trusteeship, 357 U.S. 570 (1958).

Irvine v. *California*, 347 U.S. 128 (1954).

Jacqueline R. and Beecham v. *Leahy*, 130 Vt. 164, 287 A.2d 836 (Sup. Ct. Vt. 1972).

Jencks v. *U.S.*, 353 U.S. 657 (1957).

Johnson v. *Avery*, 393 U.S. 483 (1969).

Johnson v. *Transportation Agency, Santa Clara County*, 480 U.S. 616 (1987).

Johnson v. *Zerbst*, 304 U.S. 458 (1938).

Jones v. *Hallahan*, 501 S.W.2d 588 (Ky. Ct. App. 1973).

Jones v. *Mayer Co.*, 392 U.S. 409 (1968).

Kahn v. *Shevin*, 416 U.S. 351 (1974).

Katzenbach v. *McClung*, 379 U.S. 294 (1964).

Ker v. *California*, 374 U.S. 23 (1963).

Klein v. *Nassau County Medical Center*, 347 F. Supp. 496 (E.D.N.Y. 1972).

Kleppe v. *Sierra Club*, 427 U.S. 390 (1976).

Konigsberg v. *California*, 366 U.S. 36 (1961).

Lane v. *Wilson*, 307 U.S. 268 (1939).

Lawrence v. *Texas*, 539 U.S. 558 (2003).

Lead Industries Association v. *EPA*, 647 F.2d 1130 (D.C. Cir. 1980).

Leighton v. *Goodman*, 311 F. Supp. 1181 (S.D.N.Y. 1970).

Lerner v. *Casey*, 357 U.S. 468 (1958).

Levitt and Sons, Inc. v. *Division against Discrimination*, 31 N.J. 514, 158 A.2d 177 (Sup. Ct. N.J. 1960), *cert. denied*, 363 U.S. 418 (1960).

Lewis v. *Harris*, 188 N.J. 415; 908 A.2d 196 (2006).

Li v. *State*, 338 Or. 376; 110 P.3d 91 (2005).

Linkletter v. *Walker*, 381 U.S. 618 (1965).

Lockyer v. *City and County of San Francisco*, 33 Cal. 4th 1055; 95 P.3d 459 (2004).

Los Angeles v. *Manhart*, 435 U.S. 702 (1978).

Loving v. *Virginia*, 388 U.S. 1 (1967).

Lucy v. *Adams*, 350 U.S. 1 (1955).

McLaughlin v. *Florida*, 379 U.S. 184 (1964).

McLaurin v. *Oklahoma Board of Regents*, 339 U.S. 637 (1950).

McMann v. *Richardson*, 397 U.S. 759 (1970).

Maher v. *Roe*, 432 U.S. 464 (1977).

Mapp v. *Ohio*, 367 U.S. 643 (1961).

Marbury v. *Madison*, 5 U.S. (1 Cranch) 137 (1803).

Meachum v. *Fano*, 427 U.S. 215 (1976).

Meritor Savings Bank v. *Vinson*, 477 U.S. 57 (1986).

Michael M. v. *Superior Court*, 450 U.S. 464 (1981).

Milliken v. *Bradley*, 433 U.S. 267 (1977).

Minor v. *Happersett*, 88 U.S. (21 Wallace) 162 (1879).

Miranda v. *Arizona*, 384 U.S. 436 (1966).

Missouri ex. rel. Gaines v. *Canada*, 305 U.S. 337 (1938).

Mitchell v. *U.S.*, 313 U.S. 80 (1941).

Morgan v. *Virginia*, 328 U.S. 373 (1946).

Naim v. *Naim*, 350 U.S. 891 (1955) (*per curiam*), 350 U.S. 985 (1956).

Nashville Gas Co. v. *Satty*, 434 U.S. 136 (1976).

Nixon v. *Condon*, 286 U.S. 73 (1932).

Nixon v. *Herndon*, 273 U.S. 536 (1927).

NRDC v. *EPA*, No. 72-2233 (D.C. Cir. Oct. 28, 1973).

NRDC v. *EPA*, 489 F.2d 390 (5th Cir. 1974).

NRDC v. *Morton*, 458 F.2d 827 (D.C. Cir. 1972).

NRDC v. *Train*, 545 F.2d 320 (2nd Cir. 1976).

Ohio v. *Akron Center for Reproductive Health*, 110 S.Ct. 2972 (1990).

Ohio v. *Wyandotte Chemicals Corp.*, 401 U.S. 493 (1971).

Orr v. *Orr*, 440 U.S. 268 (1979).

Planned Parenthood v. *Ashcroft*, 462 U.S. 476 (1983).

Planned Parenthood v. *Danforth*, 428 U.S. 52 (1976).

Plessy v. *Ferguson*, 163 U.S. 537 (1896).

People v. *Barksdale*, 8 Cal.3d 320, 503 P.2d 257 (1972).

People v. *Belous*, 71 Cal.2d 954, 458 P.2d 194 (Sup. Ct. Cal. 1969).

Phillips v. *Martin Marietta Corp.*, 400 U.S. 542 (1971).

Pinkney v. *Ohio EPA*, 375 F. Supp. 305 (N.D. Ohio 1974).

Pittsburgh Press v. *Pittsburgh Commission on Human Relations*, 413 U.S. 376
    (1973).

Poe v. *Menghini*, 339 F. Supp. 986 (D. Kan. 1972).

Poelker v. *Doe*, 432 U.S. 519 (1977).

Powell v. *Alabama*, 287 U.S. 45 (1932).

Price v. *Dennison Independent School District*, 348 F.2d 1010 (5th Cir. 1965).

Procunier v. *Martinez*, 416 U.S. 396 (1974).

Reed v. *Reed*, 404 U.S. 71 (1971).

Reitman v. *Mulkey*, 387 U.S. 369 (1967).

Reynolds v. *Sims*, 377 U.S. 533 (1964).

Rhodes v. *Chapman*, 452 U.S. 337 (1981).

Rice v. *Sioux City Memorial Park Cemetery*, 348 U.S. 880 (1954).

Roe v. *Wade*, 314 F. Supp. 1217 (N.D. Tx. 1970).
Roe v. *Wade*, 410 U.S. 113 (1973).
Rostker v. *Goldberg*, 453 U.S. 57 (1981).
Scenic Hudson Preservation Conference v. *FPC*, 354 F.2d 608 (2nd Cir. 1965).
Scenic Hudson Preservation Conference v. *FPC*, 453 F.2d 463 (2nd Cir. 1971).
Schlesinger v. *Ballard*, 419 U.S. 498 (1975).
Scott v. *Illinois*, 440 U.S. 367 (1979).
Shelley v. *Kraemer*, 334 U.S. 1 (1948).
Sierra Club v. *EPA*, 540 F.2d 1114 (D.C. Cir. 1976).
Sierra Club v. *Morton*, 405 U.S. 727 (1972).
Sierra Club v. *Ruckelshaus*, 344 F. Supp. 253 (D.D.C. 1972), *aff'd by an equally divided Court sub nom. Fri* v. *Sierra Club*, 412 U.S. 541 (1973).
Singer v. *Hara*, 11 Wash. App. 247; 522 P.2d 1187 (1974).
Singleton v. *Jackson Municipal Separate School District*, 348 F.2d 729 (5th Cir. 1965).
Sipuel v. *Oklahoma Board of Regents*, 332 U.S. 631 (1948).
Smith v. *Allwright*, 321 U.S. 649 (1944).
State v. *Louden*, 15 Utah 2d 64, 387 P.2d 240 (1963).
Stell v. *Board of Education for City of Savannah*, 387 F.2d 486 (5th Cir. 1967).
Strauder v. *West Virginia*, 100 U.S. 303 (1879).
Strycker's Bay Neighborhood Council v. *Karlen*, 444 U.S. 223 (1980).
Supplemental Brief for Planned Parenthood Federation of America, Inc., and American Association of Planned Parenthood Physicians as *Amicus Curiae, Roe* v. *Wade*, 410 U.S. 113 (1973).
Supplementary Appendix to Brief as *Amicus Curiae* for the American College of Obstetricians and Gynecologists, American Medical Women's Association, American Psychiatric Association, New York Academy of Medicine, Medical School Deans and Professors, and Certain Individual Physicians: Legal, Medical and Social Science Materials Regarding Abortion Law Restrictions, *Doe* v. *Bolton*, 410 U.S. 179 (1973).
Swann v. *Charlotte-Mecklenburg Board of Education*, 402 U.S. 1 (1971).
Sweatt v. *Painter*, 339 U.S. 629 (1950).
Tanner v. *Armco Steel Corp.*, 340 F. Supp. 532 (S.D. Tx. 1972).
Taylor v. *Louisiana*, 419 U.S. 522 (1975).
Tehan v. *Shott*, 382 U.S. 406 (1966).
Tennessee Valley Authority v. *Hill*, 437 U.S. 153 (1978).
Terry v. *Adams*, 345 U.S. 461 (1953).
Terry v. *Ohio*, 392 U.S. 1 (1968).
Texas v. *Johnson*, 491 U.S. 397 (1989).
Turner v. *Utah*, 423 U.S. 44 (1975).
United States v. *Anthony*, 24 F. Cas. 829 (N.D.N.Y. 1873).
United States v. *Classic*, 313 U.S. 299 (1941).

United States v. *Cronic*, 466 U.S. 648 (1984).

United States v. *Mosley*, 238 U.S. 383 (1915).

United States v. *Saylor*, 322 U.S. 385 (1944).

United States v. *Vuitch*, 402 U.S. 62 (1971).

United States v. *Yazell*, 382 U.S. 341 (1966).

U.S. v. *Alabama*, 628 F. Supp. 1137 (N.D. Al. 1985).

U.S. v. *Montgomery County Board of Education*, 395 U.S. 225 (1969).

U.S. v. *Jefferson County Board of Education*, 372 F.2d 836 (5th Cir. 1966), *affirmed en banc*, 380 F.2d 385 (5th Cir. 1967).

U.S. v. *St. Clair*, 291 F. Supp. 122 (S.D.N.Y. 1968).

University of California v. *Bakke*, 438 U.S. 265 (1978).

Uphaus v. *Wyman*, 360 U.S. 72 (1959).

Vermont Yankee Nuclear Power Corp. v. *NRDC*, 435 U.S. 519 (1978).

Walsingham v. *Florida*, 250 So.2d 857 (Sup. Ct. Fl. 1971).

Washington v. *Watkins*, 655 F.2d 1346 (5th Cir. 1981), *cert. denied*, 456 U.S. 949 (1982).

Watson v. *Memphis*, 373 U.S. 526 (1963).

Webster v. *Reproductive Health Services*, 109 S.Ct. 3040 (1989).

Weeks v. *United States*, 232 U.S. 383 (1914).

Weinberger v. *Wiesenfeld*, 420 U.S. 636 (1975).

Wesberry v. *Sanders*, 376 U.S. 1 (1964).

Wilderness Society v. *Morton*, 479 F.2d 842 (D.C. Cir. 1973).

Williams v. *Zbaraz*, 448 U.S. 358 (1980).

Wolf v. *Colorado*, 338 U.S. 25 (1949).

Wolff v. *McDonnell*, 418 U.S. 539 (1974).

Wright v. *Georgia*, 373 U.S. 284 (1963).

Worcester v. *Georgia*, 31 U.S. (6 Peters) 515 (1832).

Wyatt v. *Stickney*, 344 F. Supp. 373, 344 F. Supp. 387 (M.D. Ala. 1972), *enforcing* 325 F. Supp. 781, 334 F. Supp. 1341 (M.D. Ala. 1971), *affirmed in part, remanded in part, decision reversed in part sub nom. Wyatt* v. *Aderholt*, 503 F.2d 1305 (5th Cir. 1974).

YWCA Of Princeton, N.J. v. *Kugler*, 342 F. Supp. 1048 (D. N.J. 1972).

References

"A Safer World and a More Hopeful America." 2004 Republican Party Platform. http://www.gop.com/media/2004platform.pdf.

"A Woman's Right." 1973. Editorial. *Evening Star* (Washington, D.C.) 27 Jan.: A4.

Abernathy, Ralph David. 1989. *And the Walls Came Tumbling Down.* New York: Harper & Row.

"Abortion and Privacy." 1973. Editorial. *Wall Street Journal* 26 Jan.: 12.

"Abortions Legal for Year, Performed for Thousands." 1973. *New York Times* 31 Dec.: 14.

Abraham, Yvonne, and Rick Klein. 2004. "Free to Marry Historic Date Arrives for Same-Sex Couples in Massachusetts." *Boston Globe* 17 May: 1.

———, and Michael Paulson. 2004. "Wedding Day First Gays Marry, Many Seek Licenses." *Boston Globe* 18 May: 1.

Adamany, David. 1973. "Law and Society: Legitimacy, Realigning Elections, and the Supreme Court." *1973 Wis. L. Rev.* 791.

Alan Guttmacher Institute. 1976. *Abortion 1974–1975: Need and Services in the United States, Each State and Metropolitan Area.* New York: Planned Parenthood Federation of America.

———. 1979. *Abortions and the Poor: Private Morality, Public Responsibility.* New York: Alan Guttmacher Institute.

Aleinikoff, Alexander T. 1982. "The Limits of Litigation: Putting the Education Back into *Brown* v. *Board of Education.*" 80 *Mich. L. Rev.* 896.

"All God's Chillun." 1954. Editorial. *New York Times* 18 May: 28.

Alpert, Geoffrey P., Ben M. Crouch, and C. Ronald Huff. 1984. "Prison Reform by Judicial Decree: The Unintended Consequences of Ruiz v. Estelle." 9 *Justice Systems J.* 291.

American Council on Education. 1949. *Intergroup Relations in Teaching Mate-*

rials: A Survey and Appraisal. Washington, D.C.: American Council on Education.

American Jewish Congress. Commission on Law and Social Action. 1957. *Assault upon Freedom of Association: A Study of the Southern Attack on the National Association for the Advancement of Colored People.* New York: The Congress.

"Americans Evaluate the Court System." 1982. *Public Opinion* 5 (Aug./Sept.): 24–27.

"An Appeal for Human Rights." 1960. *Atlanta Constitution* 9 March: 13.

Andersen, Ellen Ann. 2006. *Out of the Closets and into the Courts: Legal Opportunity Structure and Gay Rights Litigation.* Revised paperback edition. Ann Arbor: University of Michigan Press.

Anderson, Frederick. 1973. *NEPA in the Courts: A Legal Analysis of the National Environmental Policy Act.* Baltimore: Johns Hopkins University Press for Resources for the Future.

Anderson, J. W. 1964. *Eisenhower, Brownell, and the Congress: The Tangled Origins of the Civil Rights Bill of 1956–1957.* University, Ala: University of Alabama Press.

Anderson, Robert E., Jr. 1971. "Mobile, Alabama: The Essence of Survival." In *The South and Her Children: School Desegregation, 1970–1971.* Southern Regional Council. Atlanta: Southern Regional Council. 38–49.

Angelos, Claudia, and James B. Jacobs. 1985. "Prison Overcrowding and the Law." In "Our Crowded Prisons." *Annals of the American Academy of Political and Social Science* 478 (March): 100–112.

An Imperial Judiciary: Fact or Myth? 1979. Washington, D.C.: American Enterprise Institute.

Anthony, Paul. 1957. "Pro-Segregation Groups' History and Trends." *New South* 12.1: 4–10.

Aptheker, Herbert. 1964. *Soul of the Republic: The Negro Today.* New York: Marzani and Munsell.

Arney, William Ray, and William H. Trescher. 1976. "Trends in Attitudes Toward Abortion, 1972–1975." *Family Planning Perspectives* 8: 117–24.

Aronow, Geoffrey F. 1980. "The Special Master in School Desegregation Cases: The Evolution of Roles in the Reformation of Public Institutions through Litigation." 7 *Hastings Const. L. Q.* 739.

Associated Press. 1993. "Apple Denied a Tax Break." *New York Times* 1 Dec., sec. D: 7.

———. 1997. "National News Briefs; Court Says a Lesbian Can Be Denied a Job." *New York Times* 1 June: 27.

———. 1999. "Pastor Defrocked for Holding Gay Marriage." *New York Times* 18 Nov.: 14.

————. 2004. "Some Important Dates in the Gay Marriage Debate in Massachusetts." *Boston Herald* 14 May.

Auerbach, Carl A. Commentary. 1971. In *Reapportionment in the 1970s.* Ed. Nelson W. Polsby. Berkeley: University of California Press. 74–90.

Auerbach, Jerold S. 1976. *Unequal Justice.* New York: Oxford University Press.

"Average of 63% Approve of Legal Abortions: No Change Over 15 Years." 1987. *Family Planning Perspectives* 19: 221.

Ayres, Whitfield Q. 1984. "Racial Desegregation in Higher Education." In *Implementation of Civil Rights Policy.* Ed. Charles S. Bullock, III, and Charles M. Lamb. Monterey, Calif: Brooks/Cole. 118–47.

Bai, Matt. 2004. "Who Lost Ohio?" *New York Times Sunday Magazine* 21 Nov.: 67–74.

Bailey, Stephen K., and Edith K. Mosher. 1968. *ESEA: The Office of Education Administers a Law.* Syracuse, N.Y.: Syracuse University Press.

Baldwin, Malcolm F., and James K. Page, Jr. 1970. *Law and the Environment.* New York: Walker & Co. for the Conservation Foundation.

Barclay, Scott, and Shauna F. Fisher. 2006. "Said and Unsaid: State Legislative Signaling to State Courts over Same Sex Marriage 1990–2004." Paper presented at the Law and Society Association Annual Meeting, Baltimore, Md., 7 July.

Bardach, Eugene, and Lucian Pugliaresi. 1977. "The Environmental Impact Statement vs. the Real World." *The Public Interest* 49 (Autumn): 22–38.

Barnes, Catherine A. 1983. *Journey from Jim Crow: The Desegregation of Southern Transit.* New York: Columbia University Press.

Bazelon, David L. 1969. Foreword. In "A Symposium: The Right to Treatment." 57 *Geo. L. J.* 676.

————. 1977. "Coping with Technology through the Legal Process." 62 *Cornell L. Rev.* 817.

————. 1981. "Science and Uncertainty: A Jurist's View." 5 *HELR* 209.

Beatty, Jerry K. 1972. "State Court Evasion of United States Supreme Court Mandates During the Last Decade of the Warren Court." 6 *Val. U. L. Rev.* 260.

Beaumont, Thomas. 2004. "President's Focus in Iowa, U.S.: Rev Up GOP's Base." *Des Moines Register* 4 Nov.: 1.

"'Beautiful Bogalusa'." *South Today* 1.7 (February): 8.

Becker, Mary E. 1987. "Prince Charming: Abstract Equality." *1987 Supreme Court Review* 201.

————. 1989. "Commentary—Obscuring the Struggle: Sex Discrimination, Social Security, and Stone, Seidman, Sunstein, and Tushnet's *Constitutional Law.*" 89 *Colum. L. Rev.* 264.

Becker, Theodore L., and Malcolm M. Feeley, eds. 1973. *The Impact of Supreme Court Decisions.* 2nd ed. New York: Oxford University Press.

Belkin, Lisa. 1989. "Women in Rural Areas Face Many Barriers to Abortions." *New York Times* 11 July: 1 + .

Bell, Derrick. 1980. *"Brown* and the Interest-Convergence Dilemma." In *Shades of Brown: New Perspectives on School Desegregation.* Ed. Derrick Bell. New York: Teachers College Press. 91–106.

————, ed. 1980. *Shades of Brown: New Perspectives on School Desegregation.* New York: Teachers College Press.

Beller, Andrea H. 1983. "The Effects of Title VII of the Civil Rights Act of 1964 on Women's Entry into Nontraditional Occupations: An Economic Analysis." 1 *Law & Inequality* 73.

Belluck, Pam. 2000. "Nebraskans to Vote on Most Sweeping Ban on Gay Unions." *New York Times* 21 Oct.: A9.

————. 2004. "Hundreds of Same-Sex Couples Wed in Massachusetts." *New York Times* 18 May: 1.

Bendiner, Robert. 1956. "The Negro Vote and the Democrats." *Reporter* 31 (May): 8–12.

————. 1964. *Obstacle Course on Capital Hill.* New York: McGraw-Hill.

Benton, F. Warren, and Judith A. Silberstein. 1983. "State Prison Expansion: An Explanatory Model." 11 *J. Crim. Justice.* 121.

Berger, Caruthers Gholson. 1971. "Equal Pay, Equal Employment Opportunity and Equal Enforcement of the Law for Women." In Symposium Issue: "Women and the Law" 5 *Val. U. L. Rev.* 203.

Berger, Margaret A. 1980. *Litigation on Behalf of Women.* New York: Ford Foundation.

Bergmann, Barbara R. 1986. *The Economic Emergence of Women.* New York: Basic.

Berman, Daniel M. 1962. *A Bill Becomes a Law: The Civil Rights Act of 1960.* New York: Macmillan.

————. 1966. *A Bill Becomes a Law: Congress Enacts Civil Rights Legislation.* 2nd ed. New York: Macmillan.

Berman, William C. 1970. *The Politics of Civil Rights in the Truman Administration.* N.p.: Ohio State University Press.

Bernstein, Barton J. 1972. "The Ambiguous Legacy: The Truman Administration and Civil Rights." In *Politics and Policies of the Truman Administration.* Ed. Barton J. Bernstein. Chicago: Quadrangle. 269–314.

Bickel, Alexander M. 1962, 1986. *The Least Dangerous Branch: The Supreme Court at the Bar of Politics.* 2nd ed. New Haven: Yale University Press.

————. 1971. "The Supreme Court and Reapportionment." In *Reapportionment in the 1970s.* Ed. Nelson W. Polsby. Berkeley: University of California Press. 57–74.

————. 1972. *The Supreme Court and the Idea of Progress*. New Haven: Yale University Press.

Bicker, William E. 1971. "The Effects of Malapportionment in the States—A Mistrial." In *Reapportionment in the 1970s*. Ed. Nelson W. Polsby. Berkeley: University of California Press. 151–201.

Bird, Caroline. 1968. *Born Female: The High Cost of Keeping Women Down*. New York: David McKay.

Birkby, Robert H., and Walter F. Murphy. 1964. "Interest Group Conflict in the Judicial Arena: The First Amendment and Group Access to the Courts." 42 *Tex. L. Rev.* 1018.

Black, Earl. 1976. *Southern Governors and Civil Rights: Racial Segregation as a Campaign Issue in the Second Reconstruction*. Cambridge: Harvard University Press.

"Black Game." 1936. *Time* 17 Aug.: 10–11.

Blake, Judith. 1971. "Abortion and Public Opinion: The 1960–1970 Decade." *Science* 12 Feb.: 540–49.

————. 1973. "Elective Abortion and our Reluctant Citizenry: Research on Public Opinion in the United States." In *The Abortion Experience*. Ed. Howard J. Osofsky and Joy D. Osofsky. New York: Harper. 447–67.

————. 1977a. "The Abortion Decisions: Judicial Review and Public Opinion." In *Abortion: New Directions for Policy Studies*. Ed. Edward Manier, William Liu, and David Solomon. Notre Dame: University of Notre Dame Press. 51–82.

————. 1977b. "The Supreme Court's Abortion Decisions and Public Opinion in the United States." *Population and Development Review* 3: 45–62.

Blank, Rebecca M. 1988. "Women's Paid Work, Household Work, Household Income, and Household Well-Being." In *The American Woman 1988–89: A Status Report*. Ed. Sara E. Rix. New York: Norton. 123–61.

Blau, Francine D. 1984. "Occupational Segregation and Labor Market Discrimination." In *Sex Segregation in the Workplace: Trends, Explanations, Remedies*. Ed. Barbara F. Reskin. Washington, D.C.: National Academy Press. 117–43.

Blaustein, Albert P., and Robert L. Zangrando. 1968. *Civil Rights and the American Negro*. New York: Washington Square.

Blumrosen, Ruth Gerber. 1984. "Update: Wage Discrimination Revisited." In "Special Issue: Comparable Worth." *Women's Rights L. Rptr.* 8.1&2: 109.

Boer, Connie De. 1977. "The Polls: Women at Work." *Public Opinion Quarterly* 41: 268–77.

Bowler, Mike. 1970. "North or South: Who Will Show the Way to School Integration?" *South Today* 2.5 (December): 5–8.

Bowles, Linda. 1996a. "What Constitution?" *Chicago Tribune* 11 Dec.: 27.

————. 1996b. "Tolerating Ourselves to Death." *Chicago Tribune* 15 May: 19.

Bowman, James S. 1976. "The Environmental Movement: An Assessment of Ecological Politics." 5 *Env. Aff.* 649.

Bowman, Karlyn, and Bryan O'Keefe. 2004 (July 6). "Attitudes about Homosexuality & Gay Marriage." Washington, D.C.: American Enterprise Institute.

Boylan, Ann Marie. 1971. "Ida Phillips vs. Martin Marietta Corporation." *Women's Rights Law Reporter* 1.1: 11–21.

Brakel, Jan. 1986. "Prison Reform Litigation: Has the Revolution Gone Too Far?" 70 *Judicature* 5.

Branch, Taylor. 1988. *Parting the Waters: America in the King Years 1954–1963.* New York: Simon & Schuster.

Brewer, Paul R., and Clyde Wilcox. 2005. "The Polls—Trends: Same-Sex Marriage and Civil Unions." *Public Opinion Quarterly* 69.4 (Winter): 599–616.

Brink, William, and Louis Harris. 1963. *The Negro Revolution in America.* New York: Simon.

Brody, Jane E. 1973. "States and Doctors Wary on Eased Abortion Ruling." *New York Times* 16 Feb.: 1 + .

————. 1981. "Abortion Curbs Found to Have Little Impact." *New York Times* 4 Sept.: 1 + .

Bronstein, Alvin. J. 1977. "Reform without Change: The Future of Prisoners' Rights." 4 *Civil Liberties Rev.* 27.

————. 1984a. Discussion. In colloquium, "The Prison Overcrowding Crisis." 12 *N.Y.U. Rev. L. & Soc. Change* 346.

————. 1984b. Responses. In colloquium, "The Prison Overcrowding Crisis." 12 *N.Y.U. Rev. L. & Soc. Change* 324.

Brooks, David. 2003. "The Power of Marriage." *New York Times* 22 Nov.: 15.

Brooks, Rosa. 2005. "A Court that Nudges More than it Leads." *Los Angeles Times* 20 July, sec. B: 13.

Brown, Clair, and Joseph A. Pechman. 1987. *Gender in the Workplace.* Washington, D.C.: Brookings.

Brown, Patricia Leigh. 2004. "For Children of Gays, Marriage Brings Joy." *New York Times* 19 March: 14.

Brown, Ralph S., Jr. 1970. "Comment: On the Environment." *Civil Liberties* (May): 2.

Browne, Angela. 1987. *When Battered Women Kill.* New York: The Free Press.

Bryant, Barbara Everitt. 1977. *American Women Today and Tomorrow.* Washington, D.C.: National Commission on the Observance of International Women's Year.

Bullock, Charles S., III, and Charles M. Lamb, eds. 1984. *Implementation of Civil Rights Policy.* Monterey: Brooks/Cole.

Bureau of National Affairs. 1987. *Sexual Harassment: Employer Policies and Problems.* Washington, D.C.: Bureau of National Affairs.

Burger, Warren E. 1964. "Who Will Watch the Watchman?" 14 *Am. U. L. Rev.* 1.
———. 1985. Foreword. In "Our Crowded Prisons." *Annals of the American Academy of Political and Social Science* 478 (March): 9.
Burgess, Elaine, M. 1969. "Race Relations and Social Change." In *Comparative Perspectives on Race Relations.* Ed. Melvin M. Tumin. Boston: Little, Brown. 258–76.
Burk, Robert Fredrick. 1984. *The Eisenhower Administration and Black Civil Rights.* Knoxville: University of Tennessee Press.
Burkey, Richard M. 1971. *Racial Discrimination and Public Policy in the United States.* Lexington: Heath.
Burns, Haywood. 1965. "The Federal Government and Civil Rights." In *Southern Justice.* Ed. Leon Friedman. New York: Pantheon. 228–54.
Burstein, Paul. 1979. "Public Opinion, Demonstrations, and the Passage of Antidiscrimination Legislation." *Public Opinion Quarterly* 43: 157–72.
———, and Margo MacLeod. 1979. "Prohibiting Employment Discrimination: Ideas and Politics in the Congressional Debate Over Equal Opportunity Legislation." MS. Yale University, Department of Sociology.
———, and Kathleen Monaghan. 1986. "Equal Employment Opportunity and the Mobilization of Law." 20 *Law & Soc'y Rev.* 355.
Bush, George W. 2004. "State of the Union." http://www.whitehouse.gov/news /releases/2004/01/20040120-7.html.
Caldwell, Lynton K. 1985. "NEPA's Unfulfilled Promise." *The Environmental Forum* 3 (Jan.): 38 + .
Caldwell, Wallace F. 1965. "State Public Accommodations Laws, Fundamental Liberties and Enforcement Programs." 40 *Wash. L. Rev.* 841.
Callahan, Daniel. 1970. *Abortion: Law, Choice and Morality.* New York: Macmillan.
Cameron, Roderick A. 1970. "Demonstrate." In *Earth Day—The Beginning: A Guide For Survival.* Compiled and edited by the National Staff of Environmental Action. New York: Arno. 173–78.
Campbell, Angus. 1971. *White Attitudes Toward Black People.* Ann Arbor: Institute for Social Research.
Campbell, David E., and J. Quin Monson. 2007. "The Case of Bush's Re-Election: Did Gay Marriage Do It?" In *A Matter of Faith? Religion in the 2004 Presidential Election.* Ed. David E. Campbell. Washington, D.C.: Brookings Institution Press. 120–41.
"Campus Life: Grinnell; Campus Housing for Gay Students Being Considered." 1989. *New York Times* 17 Sept., sec. 1, part 2: 60.
Canon, Bradley C. 1973a. "Is the Exclusionary Rule in Failing Health? Some New Data and a Plea Against a Precipitous Conclusion." 62 *Ky. L. Rev.* 681.
———. 1973b. "Reactions of State Supreme Courts to a U.S. Supreme Court Civil Liberties Decision." 8 *Law & Soc'y Rev.* 109.

————. 1974. "Organizational Contumacy in the Transmission of Judicial Policies: The *Mapp, Escobedo, Miranda,* and *Gault* Cases." 20 *Vill. L. Rev.* 50.

————. 1977. "Testing the Effectiveness of Civil Liberties Policies at the State
and Federal Levels: The Case of the Exclusionary Rule." *American Politics
Quarterly* 5: 57–82.

————, and Kenneth Kolson. 1971. "Rural Compliance with Gault: Kentucky,
A Case Study." 10 *J. Family L.* 300.

Cantrall, William R., and Stuart S. Nagel. 1973. "The Effects of Reapportionment on the Passage of Nonexpenditure Legislation." In "Democratic Representation and Apportionment: Quantitative Methods, Measures, and Criteria." *Annals of the New York Academy of Sciences* 29: 269–79.

Caplan, Gerald M. 1985. "Questioning *Miranda.*" 38 *Vand. L. Rev.* 1417.

Carden, Maren Lockwood. 1974. *The New Feminist Movement.* New York:
Sage.

————. 1977. *Feminism in the Mid-1970's.* New York: Ford Foundation.

Carpenter, Marie Elizabeth. 1941. "The Treatment of the Negro in American
History School Textbooks." Ph.D. Diss. Columbia University.

Carson, Clayborne. 1981. *In Struggle.* Cambridge: Harvard University Press.

Carson, Rachel. 1962. *Silent Spring.* Boston: Houghton Mifflin.

Carter, Robert L. 1968. "The Warren Court and Desegregation." 67 *Mich. L.
Rev.* 237.

————. 1980. "A Reassessment of *Brown* v. *Board.*" In *Shades of Brown: New
Perspectives on School Desegregation.* Ed. Derrick Bell. New York:
Teachers College Press. 21–28.

Carter, Roy E., Jr. 1957. "Segregation and the News: A Regional Content
Study." *Journalism Quarterly* 34: 3–18.

Cavanagh, Ralph, and Austin Sarat. 1980. "Thinking about Courts: Toward and
Beyond a Jurisprudence of Judicial Competence." 14 *Law & Soc'y Rev.*
371.

Center For Disease Control. 1974. *Abortion Surveillance: 1972.* Atlanta: U.S.
Dept. of HEW.

Chafe, William H. 1972. *The American Woman.* New York: Oxford University
Press.

————. 1980. *Civilities and Civil Rights: Greensboro, North Carolina, and the
Black Struggle for Freedom.* New York: Oxford University Press.

————. 1982. "Greensboro, North Carolina." In *Southern Businessmen and
Desegregation.* Ed. Elizabeth Jacoway and David R. Colburn. Baton Rouge:
Louisiana State University Press. 42–69.

Chapman, Stephen. 1996. "Unspeakable Unions?; The Flimsy Case against
Gay Marriage." *Chicago Tribune* 25 Jan.: 27.

Chase, Harold W. 1972. *Federal Judges: The Appointing Process.* Minneapolis:
University of Minnesota Press.

Chayes, Abram. 1976. "The Role of the Judge in Public Law Litigation." 89 *Harv. L. Rev.* 1281.

"Cheapening Marriage." 1996. Editorial. *Indianapolis Star* 5 Dec.: A18.

Chilton, Bradley S. 1989. "The Role of the Judge as Catalyst in Prison Reform Litigation: Resources, Remedies, and Rights." Paper presented at the Annual Meeting of the American Political Science Association, Atlanta, Ga., Aug. 31–Sept. 3.

Cho, Yong Hyo, and George H. Frederickson. 1973. "Apportionment and Legislative Responsiveness to Policy Preferences in the American States." In "Democratic Representation and Apportionment: Quantitative Methods, Measures, and Criteria." *Annals of the New York Academy of Sciences* 29: 248–68.

Choper, Jesse. 1980. *Judicial Review and the National Political Process.* Chicago: University of Chicago Press.

"Civil Rights at First Base." 1956. Editorial. *New York Times* 27 April: 26.

"Civil Rights Reports." 1956. Editorial. *New York Times* 23 May: 30.

"Civil Unions are Discriminatory." Lambda Legal. http://www.lambdalegal.org /our-work/publications/facts-backgrounds/civil-unions-discriminatory .html.

Clark, Tom C. 1969. "Religion, Morality, and Abortion: A Constitutional Appraisal." 2 *Loyola U. of L.A. L. Rev.* 1.

Clauss, Carin Ann. 1986. "Comparable Worth—The Theory, Its Legal Foundation, and the Feasibility of Implementation." In "Symposium: Comparable Worth." 20 *U. Mich. J. L. Ref.* 7.

Cleaver, Eldridge. 1968. *Soul on Ice.* New York: McGraw-Hill.

Clift, Eleanor. 1971. "All's Quiet in Jackson: A City Strives for Quality Education." *South Today* 3.5 (December): 1 + .

Clines, Francis C. 1964. "U.S. Court Edicts Irk Prosecutors." *New York Times* 22 Aug.: 23.

Cobb, Alonzo, Jr. 1985. "Home Truths about Prison Crowding." In "Our Crowded Prisons." *Annals of the American Academy of Political and Social Science* 478 (March): 73–85.

Cohn, Jules. 1970. "Is Business Meeting the Challenge of Urban Affairs?" *Harvard Business Review* 48.2 (March–April): 68–82.

Cole, David. 1984. "Strategies of Difference: Litigating for Women's Rights in a Man's World." 2 *Law & Inequality* 33.

Collier, Bert. 1957. "Segregation and Politics." In *With All Deliberate Speed.* Ed. Don Shoemaker. New York: Harper. 110–29.

Collins, William C. 1984. Responses. In colloquium, "The Prison Overcrowding Crisis." 12 *N.Y.U. Rev. L. & Soc. Change* 339.

Comment. 1952. "Search and Seizure in Illinois: Enforcement of the Constitutional Right of Privacy." 47 *Nw. U. L. Rev.* 493.

Comment. 1963. "Beyond the Ken of the Courts: A Critique of Judicial Refusal to Review the Complaints of Convicts." 72 *Yale L. J.* 506.

Comment. 1977. "Confronting the Conditions of Confinement: An Expanded Role for Courts in Prison Reform." 12 *Harv. C.R.—C.L. L. Rev.* 367.

"Commentary." 1999. *Chicago Tribune* 7 March: 21.

Committee on Reapportionment of the American Political Science Association. 1951. "The Reapportionment of Congress." *American Political Science Review* 45: 153–57.

Commoner, Barry. 1988. "Failure of the Environmental Effort." 18 *ELR* 10195.

Conservation Foundation. 1987. *State of the Environment: A View Toward the Nineties.* Washington, D.C.: The Conservation Foundation.

Cooper, Phillip J. 1988. *Hard Judicial Choices: Federal District Court Judges and State and Local Officials.* New York: Oxford University Press.

Cooperman, Alan. 2004. "Same-Sex Bans Fuel Conservative Agenda." *Washington Post* 4 Nov.: A39.

Council for Public Interest Law. 1976. *Balancing the Scales of Justice: Financing Public Interest Law in America.* N.P.: The Council for Public Interest Law.

Council on Environmental Quality. 1970. *Environmental Quality: The First Report of the Council on Environmental Quality.* Washington, D.C.: GPO.

Cover, Robert M. 1982. "The Origins of Judicial Activism in the Protection of Minorities." 91 *Yale L. J.* 1287.

Cowan, Alison Leigh. 1989. "Poll Finds Women's Gains Have Taken Personal Toll." *New York Times* 21 Aug.: 1 + .

Cowan, Ruth B. 1976. "Women's Rights through Litigation: An Examination of the American Civil Liberties Union Women's Rights Project, 1971–1976." 8 *Colum. Human Rights L. Rev.* 373.

Cox, Robert. 1983. "New Argentine Chief Needs Reagan's Help." *New York Times* 3 Nov.: 31.

Crandall, Robert W. 1987. "Learning the Lessons." In "The Politics of the Environment, 1970–1987." *Wilson Quarterly* 11 (Autumn): 69–80.

Critique. 1974. "On the Limitations of Empirical Evaluations of the Exclusionary Rule: A Critique of the Spiotto Research and United States v. Calandra." 69 *Nw. U. L. Rev.* 740.

Currivan, Gene. 1970. "Poll Finds Shift to Left Among College Freshmen." *New York Times* 20 Dec.: 42.

Dahl, Robert A. 1957. "Decision-Making in a Democracy: The Supreme Court as a National Policy Maker." 6 *J. Pub. L.* 279.

Dalfiume, Richard M. 1970. "Stirrings of Revolt." In *The Segregation Era 1863–1954.* Ed. Allen Weinstein and Frank Otto Gatell. New York: Oxford University Press. 235–47.

Daniels, Lee A. 1989. "The Winning Way to Desegregate the Schools." *New York Times* 17 Dec., sec. 4: 4.

Daniels, William J. 1973. "The Supreme Court and Its Public." 37 *Alb. L. Rev.* 632.

Dao, James. 2004. "Same-Sex Marriage Issue Key to Some G.O.P. Races." *New York Times* 4 Nov., sec. P ("The Elections"): 4.

Darney, Philip D., Uta Landy, Sara MacPherson, and Richard L. Sweet. 1987. "Abortion Training in U.S. Obstetrics and Gynecology Residency Programs." *Family Planning Perspectives* 19: 158–62.

Davidson, Roger H. 1983. "Procedures and Politics in Congress." In *The Abortion Dispute and the American System.* Ed. Gilbert Y. Steiner. Washington, D.C.: Brookings. 30–46.

Deckard, Barbara S. 1983. *The Women's Movement.* 3d ed. New York: Harper.

DeCrow, Karen. 1974. *Sexist Justice.* New York: Random House.

D'Emilio, John. 2007. "Will the Courts Set Us Free?: Reflections on the Campaign for Same-Sex Marriage." In *The Politics of Same Sex Marriage.* Eds. Craig A. Rimmerman and Clyde Wilcox. Chicago: The University of Chicago Press. 39–64.

DeMott, Benjamin. 1970. "In and Out of Women's Lib." *Atlantic Monthly* (March): 110–17.

"De-Sexing the Job Market." 1965. Editorial. *New York Times* 20 Aug.: 20.

Diehm, Cynthia, and Margo Ross. 1988. "Battered Women." In *The American Woman 1988–89: A Status Report.* Ed. Sara E. Rix. New York: Norton. 292–302.

Dionne, E. J., Jr. 1989. "Poll on Abortion Finds the Nation Is Sharply Divided." *New York Times* 26 Ap.: 1 +.

Diver, Colin S. 1979. "The Judge as Political Powerbroker: Superintending Structural Change in Public Institutions." 65 *Va. L. Rev.* 43.

Dixon, Robert G., Jr. 1962a. "Civil Rights in Transportation and the I.C.C." 31 *Geo. Wash. L. Rev.* 198.

———. 1962b. "Legislative Apportionment and the Federal Constitution." 27 *Law & Contemporary Problems* 329.

———. 1968. *Democratic Representation: Reapportionment in Law and Politics.* New York: Oxford University Press.

Dolbeare, Kenneth M. 1967. "The Public Views the Supreme Court." In *Law, Politics, and the Federal Courts.* Ed. Herbert Jacob. Boston: Little, Brown. 194–212.

"Domestic Violence Intervention Calls for More Than Treating Injuries." 1990. *Journal of the American Medical Association.* 264. 8: 939–40.

Du Bois. W. E. B. 1947. "Three Centuries of Discrimination." *Crisis* 54: 362 +.

Ducat, Craig, and Robert Dudley. 1985. "Presidential Power in the Federal

Courts During the Post-War Era." Paper presented at the Annual Meeting of the American Political Science Association, New Orleans. Aug. 29– Sept. 1.

Dudley, Robert, and Craig Ducat. 1986. "Federal District Judges and Presidential Power: A Multivariate Analysis." Paper presented at the Annual Meeting of the American Political Science Association, Washington, D.C., Aug.

Dudziak, Mary L. 1988. "Desegregation as a Cold War Imperative." 41 *Stanford L. Rev.* 61.

Dunlap, David W. 1996. "Fearing a Toehold for Gay Marriages, Conservatives Rush to Bar the Door." *New York Times* 6 March: 13.

Dunne, Finley Peter. 1901. "The Supreme Court's Decisions." In *Mr. Dooley's Opinions.* Finley Peter Dunne. New York: R. H. Russell. 21–26.

Dupuis, Martin. 2002. *Same-Sex Marriage, Legal Mobilization, and the Politics of Rights.* New York: Peter Lang.

Dutton, Donald. 1988. *The Domestic Assault of Women.* Boston: Allyn and Bacon.

Eagles, Charles W., ed. 1986. *The Civil Rights Movement in America.* Jackson: University of Mississippi Press.

Ebaugh, Helen Rose Fuchs, and C. Allen Haney. 1980. "Shifts in Abortion Attitudes: 1972–1978. *Journal of Marriage and the Family* 42: 491–99.

Echols, Alice. 1989. *Daring to be Bad: Radical Feminism in America 1967– 1975.* Minneapolis: University of Minnesota Press.

Edelman, Marian Wright. 1973. "Southern School Desegregation, 1954–1973: A Judicial-Political Overview." *Annals of the American Academy of Political and Social Science* 407: 32–41.

Ehrlich, Paul. 1968. *The Population Bomb.* New York: Ballantine.

Eich, William. 1986. "Gender Bias in the Courtroom: Some Participants Are More Equal than Others." 69 *Judicature* 339.

Eisenberg, Theodore, and Stephen C. Yeazell. 1980. "The Ordinary and the Extraordinary in Institutional Litigation." 93 *Harv. L. Rev.* 465.

Ekland-Olson, Sheldon, and Steve J. Martin. 1988. "Organizational Compliance with Court-Ordered Reform." 22 *Law & Soc'y Rev.* 359.

Elliott, Stuart. 2000. "The Media Business: Advertising—Addenda; Campaign to Use E-Mail to Promote Youth Vote." *New York Times* 25 Sept., sec. C: 19.

Elliott, Ward. 1970. "Prometheus, Proteus, Pandora, and Procrustes Unbound: The Political Consequences of Reapportionment." 37 *U. Chic. L. Rev.* 474.

Elman, Philip, interviewed by Norman Silber. 1987. "The Solicitor General's Office, Justice Frankfurter, and Civil Rights Litigation, 1946–1960: An Oral History." 100 *Harv. L. Rev.* 817.

Elsen, Sheldon, and Arthur Rosett. 1967. "Protections for the Suspect Under Miranda v. Arizona." 67 *Colum. L. Rev.* 645.

Ely, John Hart. 1980. *Democracy and Distrust.* Cambridge: Harvard University Press.

Encyclopedia of Associations. Various Years. Detroit: Gale Research.

Epstein, Cynthia Fuchs. 1975. "Ten Years Later: Perspectives on the Woman's Movement." *Dissent* 22: 169–76.

"Equality for Domestic Partners." 1998. Editorial. *New York Times* 13 May: 22.

Erikson, Robert S. 1971. "The Partisan Impact of State Legislative Reapportionment." *Midwest Journal of Political Science* 15: 57–71.

———. 1973. "Reapportionment and Policy: A Further Look at Some Intervening Variables." In "Democratic Representation and Apportionment: Quantitative Methods, Measures, and Criteria." *Annals of the New York Academy of Sciences* 29: 280–90.

Erskine, Hazel Gaudet. 1962. "The Polls: Race Relations." *Public Opinion Quarterly* 26: 137–48.

———. 1971. "The Polls: Women's Role." *Public Opinion Quarterly* 35: 275–90.

———. 1972. "The Polls: Pollution and Its Costs." *Public Opinion Quarterly* 36: 120–35.

Ervin, Sam J. 1967. "Miranda v. Arizona: A Decision Based on Excessive and Visionary Solicitude for the Accused." 5 *Am. Crim. L. Q.* 125.

Espenshade, Thomas J. 1979. "The Economic Consequences of Divorce." *Journal of Marriage and the Family* 41: 615–25.

Esposito, John C. 1970. "Air and Water Pollution: What to Do While Waiting for Washington." 5 *Harv. Civil Rights—Civil Liberties L. Rev.* 32.

Ethridge, Mark III. 1973. "The Greensboro Four." *South Today* 4.7 (April): 4.

"Exit Polls." 2004. CNN exit poll. http://www.cnn.com/ELECTION/2004/pages/results/epolls/.

"F.B.I. Kept Secret File on the Supreme Court." 1988. *New York Times* 21 Aug.: 14.

Faculty Note. 1967. "A Postscript to the Miranda Project: Interrogation of Draft Protesters." 77 *Yale L. J.* 300.

Fair, Daryl R. 1981. "Prison Reform by the Courts." In *Governing Through Courts.* Ed. Richard A. L. Gambitta, Marilyn L. May, and James C. Foster. Beverly Hills: Sage. 149–59.

Fairclough, Adam. 1987. *To Redeem the Soul of America: The Southern Christian Leadership Conference and Martin Luther King, Jr.* Athens, Ga.: University of Georgia Press.

Farhi, Paul, and James V. Grimaldi. 2004. "GOP Won with Accent on Rural and Traditional." *Washington Post* 4 Nov.: 1.

Farmer, James. 1985. *Lay Bare the Heart: An Autobiography of the Civil Rights Movement.* New York: Plume.

Farrell, William E. 1973. "Ruling Seems to Forestall Abortion Debate in Albany." *New York Times* 23 Jan.: 1 + .

Feeley, Malcolm M. 1979. *The Process Is the Punishment.* New York: Russell Sage.

————. 1989. "The Significance of Prison Conditions Cases: Budgets and Reasons." 23 *Law & Soc'y Rev.* 273.

Feld, Barry C. 1988. "*In re Gault* Revisited: A Cross-State Comparison of the Right to Counsel in Juvenile Court." 34 *Crime & Delinquency* 393.

————. 1989. "The Right to Counsel in Juvenile Court: An Empirical Study of When Lawyers Appear and the Difference They Make." 79 *J. Crim. L. & Criminology* 1185.

Fenton, John H., and Kenneth N. Vines. 1957. "Negro Registration in Louisiana." *American Political Science Review* 51: 704–13.

Fenton, John M. 1960. *In Your Opinion.* Boston: Little, Brown.

Ferree, Myra Marx. 1974. "A Woman for President? Changing Responses: 1958–1972." *Public Opinion Quarterly* 38: 390–99.

Ferster, Elyce Zenoff, and Thomas F. Courtless. 1972. "Pre-Dispositional Data, Role of Counsel and Decisions in a Juvenile Court." 7 *Law & Soc'y Rev.* 195.

Finch, Minnie. 1981. *The NAACP: Its Fight for Justice.* Metuchen, N.J.: Scarecrow.

Finn, Peter. 1984. "Judicial Responses to Prison Crowding." 67 *Judicature* 318.

Fiske, Edward B. 1967. "Clergymen Offer Abortion Advice." *New York Times* 22 May: 1 + .

Fiss, Owen M. 1979. "The Supreme Court, 1978 Term—Foreword: The Forms of Justice." 93 *Harv. L. Rev.* 1.

Flaherty, Julie. 2004. "Freedom to Marry, and to Spend on it." *New York Times* 6 May, sec. 9: 2.

Fleming, Harold C. 1965. "The Federal Executive and Civil Rights: 1961–1965." *Daedalus* (Fall): 921–48.

"For Whom Did Negroes Vote in 1956?" 1957. *Congressional Quarterly Weekly Report* 7 June: 704–05.

Ford Foundation. 1974. *Law and Justice.* New York: Ford Foundation.

————, and American Bar Association Committee on Public Interest Practice. 1976. *Public Interest Law: Five Years Later.* New York: Ford Foundation; Chicago: American Bar Association.

Forman, James. 1972. *The Making of Black Revolutionaries.* New York: Macmillan.

Forrest, Jacqueline Darroch, and Stanley K. Henshaw. 1987. "The Harassment of U.S. Abortion Providers." *Family Planning Perspectives* 19: 9–13.

Forrest, Jacqueline Darroch, Ellen Sullivan, and Christopher Tietze. 1978. "Abortion in the United States, 1976–1977." *Family Planning Perspectives* 10: 271–79.

————, 1979a. *Abortion 1976–1977: Need and Services in the United States, Each State and Metropolitan Area.* New York: Alan Guttmacher Institute.

————, 1979b. "Abortions in the United States, 1977–1978." *Family Planning Perspectives* 11: 329–41.

Frank, Robert P. 1985. "Delegation of Environmental Impact Statement Preparation: A Critique of NEPA's Enforcement." 13 *B.C. Envtl. Aff. L. Rev.* 79.

Franklin, Charles H., and Liane C. Kosaki. 1989. "Republican Schoolmaster: The U.S. Supreme Court, Public Opinion, and Abortion." *American Political Science Review* 83: 751–71.

————. 1995. "Media, Knowledge, and Public Evaluations of the Supreme Court." In *Contemplating Courts.* Ed. Lee Epstein. Washington, D.C.: Congressional Quarterly Press. 352–75.

Frederickson, George H., and Yong Hyo Cho. 1974. "Legislative Apportionment and Fiscal Policy in the American States." *Western Political Quarterly* 27: 5–37.

Free, Lloyd, and Hadley Cantril. 1967. *The Political Beliefs of Americans.* New Brunswick, N.J.: Rutgers University Press.

Freeman, Jo. 1971. "The Legal Basis of the Sexual Caste System." In Symposium Issue: "Women and the Law." 5 *Val. U. L. Rev.* 203.

————. 1973. "The Origins of the Women's Liberation Movement." *American Journal of Sociology* 78: 792–811.

————. 1975. *The Politics of Women's Liberation.* New York: David McKay.

Freeman, Michael D. A. 1981. "'But If You Can't Rape Your Wife, Who[m] Can You Rape?': The Marital Rape Exception Re-examined." 15 *Family L. Q.* 1.

Friedman, Lawrence M. 1967. "Legal Rules and the Process of Social Change." 19 *Stan. L. Rev.* 786.

————. 1983. "The Conflict Over Constitutional Legitimacy." In *The Abortion Dispute and the American System.* Ed. Gilbert Y. Steiner. Washington, D.C.: Brookings. 13–29.

Friedman, Leon, ed. 1965. *Southern Justice.* New York: Pantheon.

————, ed. 1969. *Argument: The Oral Argument Before the Supreme Court in Brown v. Board of Education of Topeka, 1952–1955.* New York: Chelsea House.

Friedman, Leon. 1973. "'Fathers Don't Make Good Mothers,' Said the Judge." *New York Times* 28 Jan., sec. 4: 12.

Friedman, Thomas L. 1992. "The 1992 Campaign: Ethnic Voters; Cold War's End Opens Battle on Domestic Issues." *New York Times* 18 Sept.: 20.

Friendly, Henry J. 1963. "The Gap in Lawmaking—Judges Who Can't and Legislators Who Won't." 63 *Colum. L. Rev.* 787.

Froomkin, Dan. 2004. "How Did He Do It?" *Washington Post* 3 Nov. http://www.lexis-nexis.com/.

Frug, Gerald E. 1978. "The Judicial Power of the Purse." 126 *U. Pa. L. Rev.* 715.

Fuentes, Sonia Pressman. 1971. "Federal Remedial Sanctions: Focus on Title VII." In Symposium Issue: "Women and the Law." 5 *Val. U. L. Rev.* 203.

Fujita, Byron N., and Nathaniel N. Wagner. 1973. "Referendum 20—Abortion Reform in Washington State." In *The Abortion Experience.* Ed. Howard J. Osofsky and Joy D. Osofsky. New York: Harper. 232–60.

Gaither, Thomas. 1960. "Orangeburg: Behind the Carolina Stockade." In *Sit-Ins: The Students Report.* Ed. Jim Peck. New York: Congress of Racial Equality. N.p.

Galanter, Marc. 1974. "Why the 'Haves' Come Out Ahead: Speculations on the Limits of Legal Change." 9 *Law & Soc'y Rev.* 95.

Gallup, George H. 1972. *The Gallup Poll: Public Opinion 1935–1971.* 3 vols. New York: Random House.

Gallup Poll. 2004 (May 2–4). http://nationaljournal.com/members/polltrack/2004/issues/04homosexuality.htm#12.

———. 2005 (May 2–5). http://nationaljournal.com/members/polltrack/2005/issues/05homosexuality.htm.

Gambitta, Richard A. L., Marilyn L. May, and James C. Foster, eds. 1981. *Governing Through Courts.* Beverly Hills: Sage.

Garrett, Theodore L. 1986. "Citizen Suits: A Defense Perspective." 16 *ELR* 10162.

Garrison, Lloyd. 1961. "Maryland to Assist Envoys." *New York Times* 14 Sept.: 1+.

Garrow, David J. 1978. *Protest at Selma.* New Haven: Yale University Press.

———. 1981. *The FBI and Martin Luther King, Jr.* New York: Penguin.

———. 1985. "The Origins of the Montgomery Bus Boycott." *Southern Changes* 7.5&6 (Oct./Dec.): 21–27.

———. 1986. *Bearing the Cross: Martin Luther King, Jr., and the Southern Christian Leadership Conference.* New York: Morrow.

Gates, Robin L. 1962. *The Making of Massive Resistance.* Chapel Hill: University of North Carolina Press.

"Gay Days at Walt Disney World." *Frommer's.* http://events.frommers.com/sisp/index.htm?fx=event&event_id=28941.

"Gay Marriage in the States." 2004. Editorial. *New York Times* 18 Feb.: 18.

"Gays in the Movies: A Timeline." http://abcnews.go.com/WNT/popup?id=1386791&contentIndex=1&page=1.

"Gays on TV." 2003. Online News Hour, 19 Nov. http://www.pbs.org/newshour/bb/media/july-dec03/gaysinmedia_11–19.html.

Gelb, Joyce, and Marian Lief Palley. 1979. "Women and Interest Group Politics: A Comparative Analysis of Federal Decision-Making." *Journal of Politics* 41: 362–92.

———. 1982. *Women and Public Policies.* Princeton: Princeton University Press.

————. 1987. *Women and Public Policies.* Rev. ed. Princeton: Princeton University Press.

Gelder, Lawrence Van. 1973. "Cardinals Shocked—Reaction Mixed." *New York Times* 23 Jan.: 1 + .

Gelpi, Barbara C., Nancy C. M. Hartsock, Clare C. Novak, and Myra H. Strober, eds. 1986. *Women and Poverty.* Chicago: University of Chicago Press.

Gertner, Nancy. 1986. "Thoughts on Comparable Worth Litigation and Organizational Strategies." In "Symposium: Comparable Worth." 20 *U. Mich. J. L. Ref.* 163.

Giari, Maygene. 1979. "In Oklahoma, Building More Prisons Has Solved No Problems." 25 *Crime & Delinquency* 450.

Gibbons, Tom, and Jim Casey. 1987. "Ed Meese's War on Miranda Draws Scant Support." *Chicago Sun-Times* 17 Feb.: 41.

Giles, Michael W. 1975. "H.E.W. Versus the Federal Courts: A Comparison of School Desegregation Enforcement." *American Politics Quarterly* 3: 81–90.

Gillroy, John M., and Robert Y. Shapiro. 1986. "The Polls: Environmental Protection." *Public Opinion Quarterly* 50: 270–79.

"GLAAD's Announcing Equality Project Marks Two-Year Anniversary with 504 Inclusive Newspapers." 2004. Gay & Lesbian Alliance Against Defamation. http://www.glaad.org/media/archive_detail.php?id=3704&.

Glaberson, William. 1990. "Confronting Assembly-Line Justice: Tumult in New York's Courtrooms." *New York Times* 16 Jan.: 12.

Glantz, Oscar. 1970. "The Black Vote." In *The Segregation Era 1863–1954.* Ed. Allen Weinstein and Frank Otto Gatell. New York: Oxford University Press. 248–61.

Glazer, Nathan. 1975. "Towards an Imperial Judiciary?" *The Public Interest* (Fall): 104–23.

Golann, Stuart, and William J. Fremouw, eds. 1976. *The Right to Treatment for Mental Patients.* New York: Irvington.

Goldberg, Carey. 2000a. "In Vermont, Gay Couples Head for the Almost-Altar." *New York Times* 2 July: 10.

————. 2000b. "Vermont Senate Votes for Gay Civil Unions." *New York Times* 20 April: 12.

Goldman, Eric F. 1961. "Progress—By Moderation *And* Agitation." *New York Times Magazine* 18 June: 5 + .

Goldman, Sheldon, and Thomas P. Jahnige. 1976. *The Federal Courts as a Political System.* 2nd ed. New York: Harper & Row.

Goldsmith, Richard I., and William C. Banks. 1983. "Environmental Values: Institutional Responsibility and the Supreme Court." 7 *HELR* 1.

Good, Paul. 1967. "Odyssey of a Man—And a Movement." *New York Times Magazine* 25 June: 5 + .

Goodman, Ellen. 1995. "What's Wrong with a Simple On/Off Switch?" *Chicago Tribune* 5 Dec.: 25.

Goodman, Janice, Rhonda Copelon Schoenbrod, and Nancy Stearns. 1973. "Doe and Roe: Where Do We Go From Here?" *Women's Rights Law Reporter* 1.4: 20–38.

Goodpaster, Gary. 1986. "The Adversary System, Advocacy, and Effective Assistance of Counsel in Criminal Cases." In colloquium, "Effective Assistance of Counsel for the Indigent Criminal Defendant: Has the Promise Been Fulfilled?" 14 *N.Y.U. Rev. L. & Soc. Change* 90.

Goodstein, Laurie. 2003. "National Briefing Religion: Bishops Turn to Constitution to Bar Gay Marriage." *New York Times* 11 Sept.: 12.

Gordon, Robert W. 1984. "Critical Legal Histories." 36 *Stan. L. Rev.* 57.

Gorski, Eric. 2004. "Dobson Shifts Power to Focus on Politics." *Denver Post* 14 Nov.: 1.

Graham, Fred P. 1966a. "Survey Shows Court Rule Curbs Police Questioning: Free Counsel a Problem." *New York Times* 20 June: 1 + .

———. 1966b. "U.S. Judge, Chiding High Court, Backs Legalization of Wiretapping." *New York Times* 6 Aug.: 9.

Graham, Hugh Davis. 1990. *The Civil Rights Era*. Oxford: Oxford University Press.

Granberg, Donald, and Beth Wellman Granberg. 1980. "Abortion Attitudes, 1965–1980: Trends and Determinants." *Family Planning Perspectives* 12: 250–61.

Grant, W. Vance, and Thomas D. Snyder. N.d. Digest of Education Statistics 1983–84. Washington, D.C.: GPO.

Greeley, Andrew M., and Paul B. Sheatsley. 1971. "Attitudes Toward Racial Integration" *Scientific American* (Dec.): 13–19.

Green, John C., Corwin E. Smidt, James L. Guth, and Lyman A. Kellstedt. 2004. "The American Religious Landscape and the 2004 Presidential Vote: Increased Polarization." http://pewforum.org/publications/surveys/postelection.pdf.

Green, Wayne E. 1966. "Police vs. 'Miranda'—Has the Supreme Court Really Hampered Law Enforcement?" *Wall St. J.* Midwest ed. 15 Dec.: 14.

Greenberg, Jack. 1968. "The Supreme Court, Civil Rights and Civil Dissonance." 77 *Yale L. J.* 1520.

———. 1973. Preface. "Blacks and the Law." *Annals of the American Academy of Political and Social Science* 47: ix–x.

———. 1974. "Litigation for Social Change: Methods, Limits and Role In Democracy." *Record of the Association of the Bar of the City of New York* 29: 320–75.

———. 1977. *Judicial Process and Social Change*. St. Paul: West.

Greenberg, Quinlan, Rosner Research. 2004. Survey, Nov. 2–3. http://national journal.com/members/polltrack/2004/todays/11/1110greenberg.htm.

Greenberger, Scott S. 2004. "Gay-Marriage Ruling Pushed Voters, Mobilized Bush, Left Kerry Wary." *Boston Globe* 7 Nov., sec. B: 1.

Greenhouse, Linda. 1983. "Paper Siege by Prisoner Provokes Ire." *New York Times* 7 April, sec. 2: 10.

Griffiths, Martha. 1966. "Women are Being Deprived of Legal Rights by the Equal Employment Opportunity Commission." *Cong. Rec.,* 20 June: 13689–94.

Grisso, Thomas. 1980. "Juveniles' Capacities to Waive *Miranda* Rights: An Empirical Analysis." 68 *Calif. L. Rev.* 1134.

Grossman, Joel B. 1967. "A Model for Judicial Policy Analysis: The Supreme Court and the Sit-In Cases." In *Frontiers of Judicial Research.* Ed. Joel B. Grossman and Joseph Tanenhaus. New York: Wiley. 405–60.

———. 1970. "The Supreme Court and Social Change." *American Behavioral Scientist* 13: 535–51.

———, and Austin Sarat. 1981. "Access to Justice and the Limits of Law." In *Governing Through Courts.* Ed. Richard A. L. Gambitta, Marilyn L. May, and James C. Foster. Beverly Hills: Sage. 77–92.

Gryski, Gerard S., and Eleanor C. Main. 1983. "The Implementation of U.S. Supreme Court Decisions by State Courts of Last Resort: The Case of Sex Discrimination." Paper presented at the Annual Meeting of the American Political Science Association, Chicago, Sept. 1–4.

Guarino, David. R. 2003. "Poll finds Massive Backing for Gay Unions; Narrow Marriage Support." *The Boston Herald* 23 Nov.: 7.

Guggenheim, Martin. 1986. "Divided Loyalties: Musings on Some Ethical Dilemmas for the Institutional Criminal Defense Attorney." In colloquium, "Effective Assistance of Counsel for the Indigent Criminal Defendant: Has the Promise Been Fulfilled?" 14 *N.Y.U. Rev. L. & Soc. Change* 14.

Gutis, Philip S. 1989. "Ideas and Trends; Small Steps toward Acceptance Renew Debate on Gay Marriage." *New York Times* 5 Nov., sec. 4: 24.

"Gynecology—More Abortion: The Reasons Why." 1965. *Time* 17 Sept.: 82.

Haines, Charles Grove. 1922. "General Observations on the Effects of Personal, Political, and Economic Influences in the Decisions of Judges." 17 *Ill. L. Rev.* 96.

Haines, Herbert H. 1988. *Black Radicals and the Civil Rights Mainstream, 1954–1970.* Knoxville: University of Tennessee Press.

Hakman, Nathan. 1966. "Lobbying the Supreme Court—An Appraisal of 'Political Science Folklore'." 35 *Fordham L. Rev.* 15.

Halpern, Charles R. 1976. "The Right to Habilitation: Litigation as a Strategy for Social Change." In *The Right to Treatment for Mental Patients*. Ed. Stuart Golann, and William J. Fremouw. New York: Irvington. 73–98.

Hamilton, Charles V. 1965. "Southern Judges and Negro Voting Rights: The Judicial Approach to the Solution of Controversial Social Problems." *1965 Wis. L. Rev.* 72.

Hampton, Henry, and Steve Fayer. 1990. *Voices of Freedom: An Oral History of the Civil Rights Movement from the 1950s through the 1980s*. New York: Bantam.

Handler, Joel F. 1978. *Social Movements and the Legal System: A Theory of Law Reform and Social Change*. New York: Academic Press.

Handy, Bruce. 1997. "Roll Over, Ward Cleaver; and Tell Ozzie Nelson the News. Ellen DeGeneres is Poised to Become TV's First Openly Gay Star. Is America Ready or Not?" *Time* 14 April: 78+.

Hanks, Eva H., and John L. Hanks. 1970. "A Environmental Bill of Rights: The Citizen Suit and the National Environmental Policy Act of 1969." 24 *Rutgers L. Rev.* 230.

Hansen, John Mark. 1987. "Creating a New Politics: The Evolution of an Agricultural Policy Network in Congress, 1919–1980." Ph.D. Diss. Yale University.

Hansen, Susan B. 1980. "State Implementation of Supreme Court Decisions: Abortion Rates Since *Roe* v. *Wade*." *Journal of Politics* 42:372–95.

Hanson, Roger A., and Robert E. Crew, Jr. 1973. "The Policy Impact of Reapportionment." 8 *Law & Soc'y Rev.* 69.

Harding, Vincent. 1979. "So Much History, So Much Future: Martin Luther King, Jr., and the Second Coming of America." In *Have We Overcome? Race Relations Since Brown*. Ed. Michael V. Namorato. Jackson: University of Mississippi Press. 31–78.

Harriman, Linda, and Jeffrey D. Straussman. 1983. "Do Judges Determine Budget Decisions? Federal Court Decisions in Prison Reform and State Spending for Corrections." *Public Administration Review* 43: 343–51.

Harris, Louis, and Associates, Inc. N.d. *The 1972 Virginia Slims American Women's Opinion Poll*. N.p.: n.p.

Harris, M. Kay. 1976. *After Decision: Implementation of Judicial Decrees in Correctional Settings: A Case Study of Collins v. Schoonfield*. Washington, D.C.: American Bar Association.

———, and Dudley P. Spiller, Jr. 1976. *After Decision: Implementation of Judicial Decrees in Correctional Settings*. Washington, D.C.: American Bar Association.

Hassler, Gregory L., and Karen O'Connor. 1986. "Woodsy Witchdoctors Versus Judicial Guerrillas: The Role and Impact of Competing Interest Groups in Environmental Litigation." 13 *B.C. Envtl. Aff. L. Rev.* 487.

Hay, Douglas, Peter Linebaugh, Joh G. Rule, E. P. Thompson, and Cal Winslow.

1975. *Albion's Fatal Tree: Crime and Society in Eighteenth Century England.* London: Allen Lane.

Hayden, Casey, and Mary King. 1966. "Sex and Caste." *Liberation* 11.2: 45–46.

Hays, Samuel P. 1986. "Environmental Litigation in Historical Perspective." 19 *U. Mich. J. L. Ref.* 969.

Hazel, David William. 1957. "The National Association for the Advancement of Colored People and the National Legislative Process: 1940–1954." Ph.D. Diss. University of Michigan.

Henry, Charles P. 1979. "Big Philanthropy and the Funding of Black Organizations." *The Review of Black Political Economy* 9: 174–90.

Henshaw, Stanley K. 1986. "Induced Abortion: A Worldwide Perspective." *Family Planning Perspective* 18: 250–54.

———, Nancy J. Binkin, Ellen Blaine, and Jack C. Smith. 1985. "A Portrait of American Women Who Obtain Abortions." *Family Planning Perspectives.* 17: 90–96.

———, Jacqueline Darroch Forrest, and Ellen Blaine. 1984. "Abortion Services in the United States, 1981 and 1982." *Family Planning Perspectives* 16: 119–27.

———, and Jacqueline Darroch Forrest, Ellen Sullivan, and Christopher Tietze. 1982. "Abortion Services in the United States, 1979 and 1980." *Family Planning Perspectives* 14: 5–15.

———, Jacqueline Darroch Forrest, and Jennifer Van Vort. 1987. "Abortion Services in the United States, 1984 and 1985." *Family Planning Perspectives* 19: 63–70.

———, and Kevin O'Reilly. 1983. "Characteristics of Abortion Patients in the United States, 1979 and 1980." *Family Planning Perspectives* 15: 5 + .

———, and Jane Silverman. 1988. "The Characteristics and Prior Contraceptive Use of U.S. Abortion Patients." *Family Planning Perspectives* 20: 158 + .

———, and Lynn S. Wallisch. 1984. "The Medicaid Cutoff and Abortion Services for the Poor." *Family Planning Perspectives* 16: 170 + .

Herbers, John. 1983. "Income Gap Between Races Wide as in 1960, Study Shows." *New York Times* 18 July: 1 + .

Herman, Susan. 1984. "Institutional Litigation in the Post-*Chapman* World." In colloquium, "The Prison Overcrowding Crisis." 12 *N.Y.U. Rev. L. & Soc. Change* 308.

Hevesi, Dennis. 1986. "Episcopal Resolution Assails Vatican Coercion." *New York Times* 23 Oct.: 17.

Hill, James P. 1985. "The Politics of Environmental Law." 64 *Mich. B. J.* 164.

Hillygus, D. Sunshine, and Todd G. Shields. 2005. "Moral Issues and Voter Decision Making in the 2004 Presidential Election." *PS: Political Science and Politics* 38 (April): 201–9.

Hinds, Michael deCourcy. 1989. "Rioters Destroy Nearly Half of the Buildings in a Pennsylvania Prison." *New York Times* 28 Oct.: 9.

Hoban, Thomas More, and Richard Oliver Brooks. 1987. *Green Justice: The Environment and the Courts.* Boulder: Westview Press.

Hochschild, Arlie. 1989. *The Second Shift: Working Parents and the Revolution at Home.* New York: Viking Penguin.

Hochschild, Jennifer L. 1984. *The New American Dilemma.* New Haven: Yale University Press.

Hole, Judith, and Ellen Levine. 1971. *Rebirth of Feminism.* New York: Quadrangle.

Holland, Maria C. 1985. "Judicial Review of Compliance with the Environmental Policy Act: An Opportunity for the Rule of Reason." 12 *B.C. Envtl. Aff. L. Rev.* 743.

Hooker, Robert. 1971. "Race and the Mississippi Press." *New South* 26.1: 55–62.

Hopper, Columbus B. 1985. "The Impact of Litigation on Mississippi's Prison System." 65 *Prison J.* 54.

Horowitz, Donald L. 1977. *The Courts and Social Policy.* Washington, D.C.: Brookings.

Horwitz, Morton J. 1979. "The Jurisprudence of *Brown* and the Dilemmas of Liberalism." In *Have We Overcome? Race Relations Since Brown.* Ed. Michael V. Namorato. Jackson: University of Mississippi Press. 173–87.

Hoyman, Michelle, and Lamont Stallworth. 1986. "Suit Filing by Women: An Empirical Analysis." 62 *Note Dame L. Rev.* 61.

Hughes, Langston. 1962. *Fight for Freedom.* New York: Norton.

Hulse, Carl. 2004. "Gay Official Denounces Amendment." *New York Times* 24 March: 18.

Hyman, Herbert H., and Paul B. Sheatsley. 1956. "Attitudes Toward Desegregation." *Scientific American* Dec.: 35–39.

———. 1964. "Attitudes Toward Desegregation." *Scientific American* July: 16–23.

Inbau, Fred E. 1966. "Democratic Restraints upon Police." 57 *J. Crim. L., C. & P.S.* 265.

Ingram, Helen M., and Dean E. Mann. 1984. "Preserving the Clean Water Act: The Appearance of Environmental Victory." In *Environmental Policy in the 1980s: Reagan's New Agenda.* Ed. Norman J. Vig and Michael E. Kraft. Washington, D.C.: Congressional Quarterly Press. 251–71.

"Interrogations in New Haven: The Impact of *Miranda.*" 1967. 76 *Yale L. J.* 1519.

"Issue of the Year: The Environment." 1971. *Time* 4 Jan.: 21–22.

"It's 4 Million Negro Votes That the Fight's All About." 1957. *U.S. News & World Report* 16 Aug.: 40–41.

Iyengar, Shanto, and Donald R. Kinder. 1987. *News That Matters.* Chicago: University of Chicago Press.

Jackson, Derrick Z. 2004. "Racism Echoes in Gay Marriage Ban." *Chicago Tribune* 5 April: 17.

Jackson, John E., and Maris A. Vinovskis. 1983. "Public Opinion, Elections, and the 'Single-Issue' Issue." In *The Abortion Dispute and the American System.* Ed. Gilbert Y. Steiner. Washington, D.C.: Brookings. 64–81.

Jacobs, James B. 1980. "The Prisoners' Rights Movement and its Impacts, 1960–1980." In *Crime and Justice: An Annual Review of Research.* Vol. 2. Ed. Norval Morris and Michael Tonry. Chicago: University of Chicago Press. 429–70.

———. 1984. "The Politics of Prison Expansion." In colloquium, "The Prison Overcrowding Crisis." 12 *N.Y.U. Rev. L. & Soc. Change* 209.

Jacoway, Elizabeth. 1982. "An Introduction." In *Southern Businessmen and Desegregation.* Ed. Elizabeth Jacoway and David R. Colburn. Baton Rouge: Louisiana State University Press. 1–14.

———, and David R. Colburn, eds. 1982. *Southern Businessmen and Desegregation.* Baton Rouge: Louisiana State University Press.

Jaffe, Frederick S., Barbara L. Lindheim, and Philip R. Lee. 1981. *Abortion Politics.* New York: McGraw-Hill.

Jaynes, Gerald David, and Robin M. Williams, Jr. 1989. *A Common Destiny: Blacks and American Society.* Washington, D.C.: National Academy Press.

Jennings, Dennis L., Teresa M. Amabile, and Lee Ross. 1982. "Informal Co-variation Assessment: Data-Based Versus Theory Based Judgments." In *Judgement Under Uncertainty: Heuristics and Biases.* Ed. Daniel Kahneman, Paul Slovic, and Amos Tversky. Cambridge: Cambridge University Press. 211–30.

Johnson, Catherine E., ed., and Joyce Post (indexer). 1979. *TV Guide 25 Year Index.* Kemp, Texas: Triangle.

Johnson, Charles A. 1979. "Lower Court Reactions to Supreme Court Decisions: A Quantitative Examination." *American Journal of Political Science* 23: 792–804.

———, and Bradley C. Canon. 1984. *Judicial Policies: Implementation and Impact.* Washington, D.C.: Congressional Quarterly Press.

Johnson, Dirk, and Debra Rosenberg. 2004. "The Gay War Rolls On." *Newsweek* 26 July: 34.

Johnson, Frank M., Jr. 1981. "The Role of the Federal Courts in Institutional Litigation." In "Symposium, Judicially Managed Institutional Reform." 32 *Alabama L. Rev.* 271.

Johnson, George E., and Gary R. Solon. 1986. "The Attainment of Pay Equity Between the Sexes by Legal Means: An Economic Analysis." In "Symposium: Comparable Worth." 20 *U. Mich. J. L. Ref.* 183.

Johnston, John D., Jr., and Charles L. Knapp. 1971. "Sex Discrimination by Law: A Study in Judicial Perspective." 46 *N.Y.U L. Rev.* 675.

Johnston, Laurie. 1977. "Abortion Foes Gain Support as They Intensify Campaign." *New York Times* 23 Oct., sec. 1: 1 + .

Jones, Elise F., and Charles F. Westoff. 1972. "Attitudes Toward Abortion in the United States in 1970 and the Trend Since 1965." In *Demographic and Social Aspects of Population Growth.* Ed. Charles F. Westoff and Robert Parke, Jr. Washington, D.C.: GPO. 569–78.

Jones, Jeffrey M. 2004. "Different Influences Found for Bush, Kerry Voters." Gallup News Service, 16 Dec.

Jost, Kenneth. 1989. "The Women at Justice." 75 *American Bar Association Journal* 75 (Aug.): 54 + .

"Judge Rejects Suit to Halt Abortions by Air Force." 1971. *New York Times* 21 Jan.: 37.

Kahneman, Daniel, Paul Slovic, and Amos Tversky, eds. 1982. *Judgment Under Uncertainty: Heuristics and Biases.* Cambridge: Cambridge University Press.

Kalodner, Howard I. 1978. Introduction. In *Limits to Justice.* Ed. Howard I. Kalodner, and James J. Fishman. Cambridge, Mass.: Ballinger. 1–24.

———, and James J. Fishman, eds. 1978. *Limits to Justice.* Cambridge, Mass.: Ballinger.

Kaufman, Michael T. 1992. "About New York; 43 Years Later, a Love Still Thrives." *New York Times* 23 Dec., sec. B: 3.

Kemp, Kathleen A., Robert A. Carp, and David W. Brady. 1978. "The Supreme Court and Social Change: The Case of Abortion." *Western Political Quarterly* 31: 19–31.

Kennedy, Robert F., Jr. 1978. *Judge Frank M. Johnson, Jr.: A Biography.* New York: G. P. Putnam.

Kessel, John N. 1966. "Public Perceptions of the Supreme Court." *Midwest Journal of Political Science* 10: 167–91.

Killian, Lewis M., and Charles U. Smith. 1960. "Negro Protest Leaders in a Southern Community." *Social Forces* 38: 253–57.

King, Martin Luther, Jr. 1958. *Stride Toward Freedom: The Montgomery Story.* New York: Harper.

———. 1963. *Why We Can't Wait.* New York: Harper.

———. [1963] 1968. *Letter from Birmingham Jail.* Stamford: Overbrook Press.

King, Mary. 1987. *Freedom Song: A Personal Story of the 1960s Civil Rights Movement.* New York: Morrow.

King, Wayne. 1973. "Despite Court Ruling, Problems Persist in Gaining Abortions." *New York Times* 20 May: 35.

Kingdon, John W. *Congressmen's Voting Decision*. 1981. 2nd ed. New York: Harper.

———. 1984. *Agendas, Alternatives, and Public Policies*. Boston: Little, Brown.

Kirchick, William D. 1975. "The Continuing Search for a Constitutionally Protected Environment." 4 *Env. Aff.* 515.

Kirkpatrick, David D. 2004a. "Rally against Gay Marriage Draws Thousands to Capital." *New York Times* 16 Oct.: 12.

———. 2004b. "Marriage between Gays Becomes Issue in Campaigns." *New York Times* 30 Oct.: 16.

Kirp, David L., and Gary Babcock. 1981. "Judge and Company: Court Appointed Masters, School Desegregation, and Institutional Reform. In "Symposium, Judicially Managed Institutional Reform." 32 *Alabama L. Rev.* 317.

Klarman, Michael J. 2005. "*Brown* and *Lawrence* (and *Goodridge*)." *Michigan Law Review* 104: 431–89.

Klein, Rick. 2004. "Behind the Scenes: House Speaker's Gambit Sparked Anger, Furious Maneuvering." *Boston Globe* 12 Feb., sec. B: 7.

Kluger, Richard. 1976. *Simple Justice*. New York: Knopf.

Kolata, Gina. 1990. "Under Pressure and Stigma, More Doctors Shun Abortions." *New York Times* 8 Jan.: 1 + .

Kolbert, Elizabeth. 1989. "State Court Awards $1.3 Million for 7 Attica Inmates' Injuries." *New York Times* 26 Oct., sec. B: 1.

"Koota Says New Court Rulings Have 'Shackled' Police Officials: Change in Positions." 1966. *New York Times* 13 Aug.: 1 + .

Koppelman, Andrew. 2006. *Same Sex, Different States: When Same-Sex Marriages Cross State Lines*. New Haven: Yale University Press.

Kousser, Morgan. 1974. *The Shaping of Southern Politics*. New Haven: Yale University Press.

Kraar, Louis. 1958. "NAACP Setbacks." *Wall Street Journal* 30 Jan.: 1 + .

Krislov, Samuel. 1959. "Constituency versus Constitutionalism: The Desegregation Issue and Tensions and Aspirations of Southern Attorneys General." *Midwest Journal of Political Science* 3: 75–92.

———. 1973. "The OEO Lawyers Fail to Constitutionalize a Right to Welfare: A Study in the Uses and Limits of the Judicial Process." 58 *Minn. L. Rev.* 211.

Kristof, Nicholas D. 2004. "Marriage: Mix and Match." *New York Times* 3 March: 23.

Kurland, Philip B., and Gerhard Casper, eds. 1975. *Landmark Briefs and Arguments of the Supreme Court of the United States: Constitutional Law*. Arlington: University Publications of America.

Lader, Lawrence. 1966. *Abortion.* New York: Bobbs-Merrill.

———. 1973. *Abortion II: Making the Revolution.* Boston: Beacon.

LaFave, Wayne R. 1965a. "Improving Police Performance Through the Exclusionary Rule—Part I: Current Police and Local Court Practices." 30 *Mo. L. Rev.* 391.

———. 1965b. "Improving Police Performance Through the Exclusionary Rule—Part II: Defining the Norms and Training the Police." 30 *Mo. L. Rev.* 566.

Langan, Patrick A., and Christopher A. Innes. 1986. *Preventing Domestic Violence Against Women.* Washington, D.C.: U.S. Department of Justice, Bureau of Justice Statistics Special Report (August).

Langer, Gary. 2004. "Poll: Ohio Reflects Divisions across the Nation—Economy and Terrorism Are Big Concerns for Ohio—Voters Analysis." ABC News, 3 Nov. http://abcnews.go.com/Politics/story?id=222327&page=1.

———, and Jon Cohen. 2005. "Voters and Values in the 2004 Election." *Public Opinion Quarterly* 69 (5): 744–59.

Lasch, Robert. "Along the Border." 1957. In *With All Deliberate Speed.* Ed. Don Shoemaker. New York: Harper. 56–70.

Lasser, William. 1988. *The Limits of Judicial Power: The Supreme Court in American Politics.* Chapel Hill: University of North Carolina Press.

"Law and Civil Rights." 2006. PollingReport.com. http://pollingreport.com/civil.htm.

"Law and Civil Rights (p. 2)." 2006. PollingReport.com. http://pollingreport.com/civil2.htm.

Lawrence, Charles. 1980. "'One More River to Cross'—Recognizing the Real Injury in *Brown:* A Prerequisite to Shaping New Remedies." In *Shades of Brown: New Perspectives on School Desegregation.* Ed. Derrick Bell. New York: Teachers College Press. 49–68.

Lawson, Steven F. 1976. *Black Ballots: Voting Rights in the South, 1944–1969.* New York: Columbia University Press.

"Lawyer Re-elected President of NOW." 1975. *New York Times.* 27 Oct.: 8.

Leavy, Zad, and Jerome M. Kummer. 1962. "Criminal Abortion: Human Hardship and Unyielding Laws." 35 *So. Cal. L. Rev.* 123.

LeBlanc, Steve. 2007. "Massachusetts Same-Sex Marriage Faces Test this Week." Associated Press, 13 June. http://www.advocate.com/news_detail_ektid46126.asp.

Lefstein, Norman. 1986. "Keynote Address." In colloquium, "Effective Assistance of Counsel for the Indigent Criminal Defendant: Has the Promise Been Fulfilled?" 14 *N.Y.U. Rev. L. & Soc. Change* 1.

———, Vaughn Stapleton, and Lee Teitelbaum. 1969. "In Search of Juvenile Justice: *Gault* and its Implementation." 3 *Law & Soc'y Rev.* 491.

"Legal Unions for Gays in Vermont." 2000. Editorial. *New York Times* 18 March: 14.

Lehne, Richard. 1978. *The Quest for Justice.* New York: Longman.

———, and John Reynolds. 1978. "The Impact of Judicial Activism on Public Opinion." *Am. J. of Pol. Sci.* 22: 896–904.

Leiken, Lawrence S. 1970. "Police Interrogation in Colorado: The Implementation of *Miranda.*" 47 *Denver L. J.* 1.

Lerner, Benjamin. 1986a. Discussion. In colloquium, "Effective Assistance of Counsel for the Indigent Criminal Defendant: Has the Promise Been Fulfilled?" 14 *N.Y.U. Rev. L. & Soc. Change* 105.

———. 1986b. Response. In colloquium, "Effective Assistance of Counsel for the Indigent Criminal Defendant: Has the Promise Been Fulfilled?" 14 *N.Y.U. Rev. L. & Soc. Change* 101.

Lester, Will. 2004. "Survey: Format Influenced Voter Priorities." Associated Press, 11 Nov.

Leuchtenburg, William E. 1979. "The White House and Black America: From Eisenhower to Carter." In *Have We Overcome? Race Relations Since Brown.* Ed. Michael V. Namorato. Jackson: University of Mississippi Press. 121–45.

Leventhal, Harold. 1974. "Environmental Decisionmaking and the Role of the Courts." 122 *U. Pa. L. Rev.* 509.

Levin, Henry M. 1979. "Education and Earnings of Blacks and the *Brown* Decision." In *Have We Overcome? Race Relations Since Brown.* Ed. Michael V. Namorato. Jackson: University of Mississippi Press. 79–119.

Lewin, Tamar. 1989. "Views on Abortion Remain Divided." *New York Times* 22 Jan.: 17.

———. 1990. "Abortions Harder to Get In Rural Areas of Nation." *New York Times* 28 June: A9.

Lewis, Anthony. 1960a. "Congress Sends Civil Rights Bill to White House." *New York Times* 22 April: 1.

———. 1960b. "Negro Vote Held Vital to Kennedy." *New York Times* 27 Nov.: 51.

———. 1961. "Bus Segregation Assailed by Rusk." *New York Times* 2 June: 21.

Lewis, David Levering. 1970. *King: A Biography.* Urbana: University of Illinois Press.

———. 1986. "The Origins and Course of the Civil Rights Movement." In *The Civil Rights Movement in America.* Ed. Charles W. Eagles. Jackson: University of Mississippi Press. 3–17.

Lewis, Gregory B. 2005. "Same-Sex Marriage and the 2004 Presidential Election." *PS: Political Science and Politics* 38 (April): 195–99.

————, and Seong Soo Oh. Forthcoming. "Public Opinion and State Action on Same-Sex Marriage." *State and Local Government Review.*

Lewis, Raphael. 2004. "Same-Sex Marriage Ban Loses Ground." *Boston Globe* 5 Nov., sec. B: 1.

Lieberman, Jethro K. 1976. *Milestones! 200 Years of American Law.* St. Paul: West.

Lightfoot, Sara Lawrence. 1980. "Families as Educators: The Forgotten People of *Brown.*" In *Shades of Brown: New Perspectives on School Desegregation.* Ed. Derrick Bell. New York: Teachers College Press. 3–19.

Lipinski, Ann Marie. 1989. "Abortion Clinics Face Must-Win Case." *Chicago Tribune* 6 Aug.: 1 + .

Liptak, Adam. 2004. "Caution in Court for Gay Rights Groups." *New York Times* 12 Nov.: 16.

Liroff, Richard. 1976. *A National Policy for the Environment: NEPA and its Aftermath.* Bloomington: Indiana University Press.

————. 1980. *Judicial Review Under NEPA—Lessons for Users of Various Approaches to Environmental Impact Assessment.* Springfield, Va.: U.S. Department of Commerce.

Lobley, Pam. 2003. "We'll Recoil in Shame 20 Years from Now." *Chicago Tribune* 19 Aug.: 19.

Lochhead, Carolyn. 2004. "Gay Marriage: Did Issue Help Re-Elect Bush?" *San Francisco Chronicle* 4 Nov.: 1.

Lofton, Paul S., Jr. 1982. "Calm and Exemplary: Desegregation in Columbia, South Carolina." In *Southern Businessmen and Desegregation.* Ed. Elizabeth Jacoway and David R. Colburn. Baton Rouge: Louisiana State University Press. 70–81.

Lomax, Louis E. 1960. "The Negro Revolt Against 'The Negro Leaders'," *Harper's* June: 41–48.

————. 1963. *The Negro Revolt.* New York: Signet.

————. 1964. "The Unpredictable Negro." In *Freedom Now!* Ed. Alan F. Westin. New York: Basic. 22–25.

Lucas, Roy. 1968. "Federal Constitutional Limitations on the Enforcement and Administration of State Abortion Statutes." 46 *N.C.L. Rev.* 730.

Luker, Kristin. 1984. *Abortion and the Politics of Motherhood.* Berkeley: University of California Press.

Lusky, Louis. 1963. "Racial Discrimination and the Federal Law: A Problem in Nullification." 63 *Colum. L. Rev.* 1163.

McAdam, Doug. 1982. *Political Process and the Development of Black Insurgency, 1930–1970.* Chicago: University of Chicago Press.

————. 1988. *Freedom Summer.* New York: Oxford University Press.

Macbeth, Angus. 1975. "The National Environmental Policy Act After Five Years." 2 *Colum. J. Envtl. L.* 1.

"Marriage in a Democracy." 1996. Editorial. *Boston Herald* 5 Dec.: 44.

"Marriage in Massachusetts." 2003. Editorial. *Chicago Tribune* 20 Nov.: 30.

McCann, Michael. 1986. *Taking Reform Seriously: Perspectives on Public Interest Liberalism.* Ithaca: Cornell University Press.

————. 1994. *Rights at Work: Pay Equity Reform and the Politics of Legal Mobilization.* Chicago: University of Chicago Press.

McCloskey, Robert G. 1960. *The American Supreme Court.* Chicago: University of Chicago Press.

McConville, Michael, and Chester L. Mirsky. 1987. "Criminal Defense of the Poor in New York City." 15 *N.Y.U. Rev. L. & Soc. Change* 581.

McCubbins, Mathew D., and Thomas Schwartz. 1988. "Congress, the Courts, and Public Policy: Consequences of the One Man, One Vote Rule." *American Journal of Political Science* 32: 388–415.

McGlen, Nancy E., and Karen O'Connor. 1983. *Women's Rights.* New York: Praeger.

McGraw, Robert E., Gloria J. Sterin, and Joseph M. Davis. 1982. "A Case Study of Divorce Law Reform and Its Aftermath." 20 *Journal of Family Law* 443.

McKay, Robert B. 1956. "'With All Deliberate Speed': A Study of School Desegregation." 31 *N.Y.U. L. Rev.* 991.

————. 1963. "Political Thickets and Crazy Quilts." 61 *Mich. L. Rev.* 645.

————. 1977. *Nine for Equality Under Law: Civil Rights Litigation.* New York: Ford Foundation.

MacKinnon, Catherine A. 1979. *Sexual Harassment of Working Women: A Case of Sex Discrimination.* New Haven: Yale University Press.

————. 1987. *Feminism Unmodified: Discourses on Life and Law.* Cambridge: Harvard University Press.

McLaughlin, Steven D., Barbara D. Melber, John O. G. Billy, Denise M. Zimmerle, Linda D. Winges, and Terry R. Johnson. 1988. *The Changing Lives of American Women.* Chapel Hill: University of North Carolina Press.

McLaurin, Melton. 1970. "State Textbooks: Distorted Image of Negroes Presented in Some Histories." *New South* 2.3 (Oct.): 8.

McLindon, James B. 1987. "Separate But Unequal: The Economic Disaster of Divorce for Women and Children." 21 *Family L. Q.* 351.

Malcolm, Andrew H. 1973. "Violent Drug Raids Against the Innocent Found Widespread." *New York Times* 25 June: 1 + .

————. 1989. "More and More, Prison is America's Answer to Crime." *New York Times* 26 Nov., sec. 4: 1.

————. 1990. "States' Prisons Continue to Bulge, Overwhelming Efforts at Reform." *New York Times* 20 May, sec. 1: 1.

————. 1991. "More Cells for More Prisoners, but to What End?" *New York Times* 18 Jan.: B10.

Manwaring, David R. 1968. "The Impact of Mapp v. Ohio." In *The Supreme Court as a Policy-Maker: Three Studies on the Impact of Judicial Decisions*. Carbondale, Ill.: Public Affairs Research Bureau and Southern Illinois University Press.

Marcus, Lloyd. 1961. *The Treatment of Minorities in Secondary School Textbooks*. New York: Anti-Defamation League of B'nai B'rith.

Marquart, James W., and Ben M. Crouch. 1985. "Judicial Reform and Prisoner Control: The Impact of *Ruiz* v. *Estelle* on a Texas Penitentiary." 19 *Law & Soc'y Rev.* 557.

Marshall, Ray. 1975. "Black Employment in the South Since 1954." In *Two Decades of Change*. Ed. Ernest M. Lander, Jr., and Richard J. Calhoun. Columbia: University of South Carolina Press. 27–46.

Marshall, Tom. 1985. "Public Opinion and the Supreme Court: Half a Century of Representation." Paper presented at the Annual Meeting of the American Political Science Association, New Orleans, Aug. 29–Sept. 1.

———. 1989. *Public Opinion and the Supreme Court*. Boston: Unwin Hyman.

Martin, Del. 1981. Foreword. In *Woman-Battering*. Mildred Daley Pagelow. Beverly Hills: Sage. 7–8.

Martin, Joanna Foley. 1971. "Confessions of a Non-Bra-Burner." *Chicago Journalism Review* 4.7: 11 + .

Mason, Karen Oppenheim, John L. Czajka, and Sara Arber. 1976. "Change in U.S. Women's Sex-Role Attitudes. 1964–1974." *American Sociological Review* 41: 573–96.

Matthews, Donald R., and James W. Prothro. 1963a. "Social and Economic Factors and Negro Voter Registration in the South." *American Political Science Review* 57: 24–44.

———. 1963b. "Political Factors and Negro Voter Registration in the South." *American Political Science Review* 57: 355–67.

———. 1966. *Negroes and the New Southern Politics*. New York: Harcourt.

Mays, Larry, and William A. Taggart. 1985. "The Impact of Litigation on Changing New Mexico Prison Conditions." 65 *Prison J.* 38.

Meadows, Donnella H., Dennis L. Meadows, Jorgen Randers, and William W. Behrens III. 1972. *The Limits to Growth: A Report for the Club of Rome's Project on the Predicament of Mankind*. New York: Universe.

Means, Cyril C., Jr. 1968. "The Law of New York Concerning Abortion and the Status of the Foetus, 1964–1968: A Case of Cessation of Constitutionality." 14 *New York Law Forum* 411.

———. 1971. "The Phoenix of Abortion Freedom: Is a Penumbral or Ninth-Amendment Right About to Arise from the Nineteenth-Century Legislative Ashes of a Fourteenth-Century Common-Law Liberty?" 17 *New York Law Forum* 335.

Medalie, Richard J., Leonard Zeitz, and Paul Alexander. 1968. "Custodial Police Interrogation in Our Nation's Capital: The Attempt to Implement Miranda." 66 *Mich. L. Rev.* 1347.

Meier, August, and Elliott Rudwick, eds. 1970. *Black Protest in the Sixties.* Chicago: Quadrangle.

————. 1973. *Core: A Study in the Civil Rights Movement 1942–1968.* New York: Oxford University Press.

Melnick, R. Shep. 1983. *Regulation and the Courts: The Case of the Clean Air Act.* Washington, D.C.: Brookings.

Mertz, Cadence. 2001. "The Business of Civil Unions." *Burlington Free Press* 24 June, sec. E: 1.

Meyer, Sylvan. 1960. "The Press and the Schools." In *Racial Crisis and the Press.* Walter Spearman and Sylvan Meyer. Atlanta: Southern Regional Council. 30–54.

Miles, Rufus E., Jr. 1974. *The Department of Health, Education, and Welfare.* New York: Praeger.

Miller, Arthur S. 1968. *The Supreme Court and American Capitalism.* New York: The Free Press.

Miller, Jeffrey G. 1984. "Private Enforcement of Federal Pollution Control Laws Part III." 14 *ELR* 10407.

Miller, Loren. 1970. "Very Deliberate Speed." In *The Segregation Era 1863–1954.* Ed. Allen Weinstein and Frank Otto Gatell. New York: Oxford University Press. 280–93.

Mills, Kim I (with Daryl Herrschaft). 2000. "The State of the Workplace for Gay, Lesbian, Bisexual and Transgender Americans 1999." Washington, D.C.: Human Rights Campaign Foundation. http://www.hrc.org/documents/sotw1999.pdf.

Milner, Neal A. 1971a. "Supreme Court Effectiveness and the Police Organization." In "Police Practices." 36 *Law & Contemporary Problems* 445.

————. 1971b. *The Court and Local Law Enforcement: The Impact of Miranda.* Beverly Hills: Sage.

Minor, F. W. 1970. "Mississippi Schools in Crisis." *New South* 25.1 (Winter): 31–36.

Mishra, Raja. 2007. "Mass. May Inspire Advocates in Other States to Action." *Boston Globe* 15 June: B6.

Mitchell, Robert Cameron. 1984. "Public Opinion and Environmental Politics in the late 1970s and 1980s." In *Environmental Policy in the 1980s: Reagan's New Agenda.* Ed. Norman J. Vig and Michael E. Kraft. Washington, D.C.: Congressional Quarterly Press. 51–74.

Mohr, James C. 1978. *Abortion in America: The Origins and Evolution of National Policy, 1800–1900.* New York: Oxford University Press.

Monroe, Keith. 1968. "How California's Abortion Law Isn't Working." *New York Times Magazine* 29 Dec.: 10 + .

Monti, Daniel J. 1980. "Administrative Foxes in Educational Chicken Coops." 2 *Law & Policy Q.* 233.

Moody, Anne. 1968. *Coming of Age in Mississippi.* New York: Dial.

Moon, Henry Lee. 1956. "The Negro Break-Away from the Democrats." *New Republic* 3 Dec.: 17.

———. 1957a. "The Negro Vote in the Presidential Election of 1956." *Journal of Negro Education* 26: 219–30.

———. 1957b. "Purists and Progress." *New Republic* 12 Aug.: 3–4.

Morris, Aldon D. 1984. *The Origins of the Civil Rights Movement: Black Communities Organizing for Change.* New York: The Free Press.

Mucciaroni, Gary. Forthcoming. *Same Sex, Different Politics: Issues and Institutions in the Struggle for Gay and Lesbian Rights.* Chicago: The University of Chicago Press.

Mulhauser, Dana. 2004. "Dispatch from the Massachusetts Constitutional Convention: The Tragic Lives of State Legislators." http://www.slate.com/id/2095452.

Mullen, Joan. 1985. "Prison Crowding and the Evolution of Public Policy." In "Our Crowded Prisons." *Annals of the American Academy of Political and Social Science* 478 (March): 31–46.

Munger, Frank J., and Richard F. Fenno, Jr. 1962. *National Politics and Federal Aid to Education.* Syracuse: Syracuse University Press.

Murphy, Dean E. 2004. "Some Democrats Blame One of Their Own." *New York Times* 5 Nov.: 18.

Murphy, Michael J. 1966. "Judicial Review of Police Methods in Law Enforcement—The Problem of Compliance by Police Departments." 44 *Tx. L. Rev.* 939.

Murphy, Patrick T. 1996. "Why Should Government Stand in the Way of Gay Marriages?" *Chicago Tribune* 24 Nov.: 23.

Murphy, Walter F. 1959a. "Lower Court Checks on Supreme Court Power." *American Political Science Review* 53: 1017–31.

———. 1959b. "The South Counterattacks: The Anti-NAACP Laws." Western Political Quarterly 12: 371–90.

———. 1962. *Congress and the Court.* Chicago: University of Chicago Press.

———, and Joseph Tanenhaus. 1968a. "Public Opinion and the Supreme Court: A Preliminary Mapping of Some Prerequisites for Court Legitimation of Regime Change." 2 *L. & Soc'y Rev.* 357.

———. 1968b. "Public Opinion and Supreme Court: The Goldwater Campaign." *Public Opinion Quarterly* 32: 31–50.

———, and Daniel L. Kastner. 1973. *Public Evaluations of Constitutional Courts: Alternative Explanations.* Beverly Hills: Sage.

Murray, Pauli. 1971. "Economic and Educational Inequality Based on Sex: An

Overview." In Symposium Issue: "Women and the Law." 5 *Val. U. L. Rev.* 203.

Muse, Benjamin. 1961. *Virginia's Massive Resistance.* Bloomington: Indiana University Press.

Muskie, Edmund S. 1988. "Reflections on a Quarter Century of Environmental Activism: On Postponing Deadlines, Second-Guessing the Congress, and Ignoring Problems Until it is Too Late." 18 *ELR* 10081.

Myrdal, Gunnar. 1962. *An American Dilemma: The Negro Problem and Modern Democracy.* New York: Harper.

"N.A.A.C.P. Sets Advanced Goals." 1954. *New York Times* 18 May: 16.

Nagel, Stuart S. 1965. "Court-Curbing Proposals in American History." 18 *Vand. L. Rev.* 925.

Nagourney, Adam. 2004. "'Moral Values' Carried Bush, Rove Says." *New York Times* 10 Nov.: 20.

Namorato, Michael V., ed. 1979. *Have We Overcome? Race Relations Since Brown.* Jackson: University of Mississippi Press.

National Association for the Advancement of Colored People. 1939–41, 1947–61, 1964–66. *Annual Reports.* New York: The Association.

Navasky, Victor S. 1977. *Kennedy Justice.* New York: Atheneum.

Neely, Richard. 1981. *How Courts Govern America.* New Haven: Yale University Press.

Neier, Aryeh. 1982. *Only Judgment: The Limits of Litigation in Social Change.* Middletown: Wesleyan University Press.

Neubauer, David W. 1974. "Confessions in Prairie City: Some Causes and Effects." 65 *J. Crim. L. & Criminology* 103.

Newland, Chester A. 1964. "Press Coverage of the United States Supreme Court." *Western Political Quarterly* 17: 15–36.

Newport, Frank. 2001. "American Attitudes toward Homosexuality Continue to Become More Tolerant." Gallup Poll News Service, 4 June.

———. 2004. "Opposition to Legalized Same-Sex Marriage Steady." Gallup Poll News Service, 11 March.

———. 2005. "Americans Turn More Negative toward Same-Sex Marriage." Gallup Poll News Service, 19 April.

———, and David W. Moore. 2004. "Key Insights from Election 2004." Gallup News Service, 8 Nov.

Newton, Margaret W. 1988. "Women and Pension Coverage." In *The American Woman 1988–89: A Status Report.* Ed. Sara E. Rix. New York: Norton. 264–70.

New York State Advisory Committee to the U.S. Commission on Civil Rights. 1974. *Warehousing Human Beings: A Review of the New York State Correctional System.* N.p.

Nisbett, Richard, and Lee Ross. 1980. *Human Inference: Strategies and Short-comings of Social Judgment.* Englewood Cliffs: Prentice-Hall.

"No Shackles on the Law." 1966. Editorial. *New York Times* 15 Aug.: 26.

Noonan, John T., Jr. 1973. "Raw Judicial Power." *National Review* 22 March: 260–64.

North, Sandie. 1970. "Reporting the Movement." *Atlantic Monthly* March: 105–6.

"Not Enough for Domestic Partners." 1993. Editorial. *New York Times* 6 Feb.: 20.

Note. 1963. "Judicial Performance in the Fifth Circuit." 73 *Yale L. J.* 90.

———. 1966. "The Congress, the Court and Jury Selection: A Critique of Titles I and II of the Civil Rights Bill of 1966." 52 *Va. L. Rev.* 1069.

———. 1967. "The Courts, HEW, and Southern School Desegregation." 71 *Yale L. J.* 321.

———. 1968. "Effect of Mapp v. Ohio on Police Search-and-Seizure Practices in Narcotics Cases." 4 *Colum. J. L. & Soc. Probs.* 87.

———. 1969. "Government Litigation in the Supreme Court: The Roles of the Solicitor General." 78 *Yale L. J.* 1442.

———. 1970. "Toward a Constitutionally Protected Environment." 56 *U. Va. L. Rev.* 458.

———. 1975. "The *Wyatt* Case: Implementation of a Judicial Decree Ordering Institutional Change." 84 *Yale L. J.* 1338.

———. 1977. "Implementation Problems in Institutional Reform Litigation." 91 *Harv. L. Rev.* 428.

———. 1979. "'Mastering' Intervention in Prisons." 88 *Yale L. J.* 1062.

———. 1980. "Judicial Intervention and Organization Theory: Changing Bureaucratic Behavior and Policy." 89 *Yale L. J.* 513.

———. 1987. "The Exclusionary Rule and Deterrence: An Empirical Study of Chicago Narcotics Officers." 54 *U. Chi. L. Rev.* 1016.

"NOW Still Growing—But It's Still White and Middle-Class." 1976. *New York Times* 24 Jan.: 20.

N. W. Ayer & Son's. Various Years. *Directory of Newspapers And Periodicals.* Philadelphia: N. W. Ayer & Son.

Oaks, Dallin. 1970. "Studying the Exclusionary Rule in Search and Seizure." 37 *U. Chi. L. Rev.* 665.

O'Brien, David M. 1985. "'The Imperial Judiciary': Of Paper Tigers and Socio-Legal Indicators." 2 *J. L. & Pol.* 1.

O'Connor, Karen. 1980. *Women's Organizations' Use of the Courts.* Lexington: Heath.

———, and Lee Epstein. 1982. "A Research Note: Amicus Curiae Participation in U. S. Supreme Court Litigation: An Appraisal of Hakman's 'Folklore.'" 16 *Law & Soc'y Rev.* 311.

————. 1984. "Institutional and External Responses to Supreme Court Policies: The Case of Abortion." Paper presented at the Annual Meeting of the American Political Science Association, Washington, D.C., Aug. 29–Sept. 2.

O'Farrell, Brigid, and Sharon L. Harlan. 1984. "Job Integration Strategies: Today's Programs and Tomorrow's Needs." In *Sex Segregation in the Workplace: Trends, Explanations, Remedies*. Ed. Barbara F. Reskin. Washington, D.C.: National Academy Press. 267–91.

O'Leary, Rosemary. 1989. "Judges and Bureaucrats: The Case of the U.S. Environmental Protection Agency." Paper presented at the Annual Meeting of the American Political Science Association, Atlanta, Ga., Aug. 31–Sept. 3.

O'Rourke, Timothy G. 1980. *The Impact of Reapportionment*. New Brunswick, N.J.: Transaction Books.

"On Gay Rights and Commitments." 2003. Editorial. *Chicago Tribune* 3 July: 24.

Oppenheimer, Martin. 1963. "The Genesis of the Southern Negro Student Movement (Sit-In Movement): A Study in Contemporary Negro Protest." Ph.D. Diss. University of Pennsylvania.

Orfield, Gary. 1969. *The Reconstruction of Southern Education*. New York: Wiley.

————. 2006. "Racial Transformation and the Changing Nature of Segregation." Cambridge, MA: The Civil Rights Project at Harvard University.

————, and Chengmei Lee. 2004. "*Brown* at 50: King's dream or *Plessy*'s Nightmare?" Cambridge, MA: The Civil Rights Project at Harvard University.

Orland, Leonard. 1975. *Prisons: Houses of Darkness*. New York: The Free Press.

Osofsky, Howard J., and Joy D., eds. 1973. *The Abortion Experience*. New York: Harper.

Ostling, Richard N. 2004. "Election Reinforces U.S. Religious Divide." Associated Press, 4 Nov.

Otten, Alan L. 1956. "The Negro Vote." *Wall Street Journal* 13 Ap.: 1 + .

Packwood, Robert. 1970. "S. 3746—Introduction of National Abortion Act." *Cong. Rec.,* 23 April 1970: 12672–73.

Page, Benjamin I., and Robert Y. Shapiro. 1982. "Changes in Americans' Policy Preferences, 1935–1979." *Public Opinion Quarterly* 46: 24–42.

————. 1983. "Effects of Public Opinion on Policy." *American Political Science Review* 77: 175–90.

Page, Clarence. 2004. "Bush's 'Values' Got More Black Voters in His Camp than in 2000, But All is Not Lost for Democrats." *Chicago Tribune* 7 Nov.: 9.

Pagelow, Mildred Daley. 1981. *Woman-Battering*. Beverly Hills: Sage.

Parham, Joseph B. 1957. "Halls of Ivy—Southern Exposure." In *With All Deliberate Speed*. Ed. Don Shoemaker. New York: Harper. 163–82.

Patterson, Jack. 1966. "Business Response to the Negro Movement." *New South* 24.1 (Winter): 67–74.

Paul, Arnold M. 1960. *Conservative Crisis and the Rule of Law: Attitudes of Bar and Bench 1887–95.* Ithaca: Cornell University Press.

Paul, Faith G. 1988. "Judicial Capacity in Public Higher Education and Social Policy: An Investigation of Compliance with Court Ordered Desegregation of Undergraduate Enrollment in Higher Education." MS, University of Chicago Department of Political Science.

Pear, Robert. 1984. "Wage Lag is Found for White Women." *New York Times* 16 Jan.: 1 + .

Pearce, Diana M. 1986. "Toil and Trouble: Women Workers and Unemployment Compensation." In *Women and Poverty.* Ed. Barbara C. Gelpi, Nancy C. M. Hartsock, Clare C. Novak, and Myra H. Strober. Chicago: University of Chicago Press. 141–61.

Peck, Jim, ed. 1960. *Sit-Ins: The Students Report.* New York: Congress of Racial Equality.

Peirce, Neal R. 1987. "Prisons: Budget Rathole for the States." 10 *Public Administration Times* 2.

Peltason, Jack W. 1971. *Fifty-Eight Lonely Men.* Urbana: University of Illinois Press.

"Pentagon Expands Rules on Abortions." 1971. *New York Times* 17 Jan.: 43.

Persily, Nate, Patrick Eagan, and Kevin Wallsten. 2006. "Gay Marriage, Public Opinion and the Courts." University of Pennsylvania Law School, Public Law and Legal Theory Research Paper Series, Research Paper No. 06–17.

———. 2008. "Gay Rights." In *Public Opinion and Constitutional Controversy.* Eds. Nathaniel Persily, Jack Citrin, and Patrick J. Egan. New York: Oxford University Press. 234–66.

Pew Research Center Survey. 2004 (Nov. 5–8). http://nationaljournal.com/members/polltrack/2004/todays/11/1112pew.htm#.

Phillips, Frank. 2003. "Support for Gay Marriage." *The Boston Globe* 8 April: 1.

———. 2007. "Tight Vote Looms on Same-Sex Marriage Lobbying Intense on Both Sides." *Boston Globe* 14 June: 1.

———, and Andrea Estes. 2007. "Right of Gays to Marry Set for Years to Come—Vote Keeps Proposed Ban off 2008 State Ballot." *Boston Globe* 15 June: 1.

———, and Rick Klein. 2003. "50% in Poll Back SJC Ruling on Gay Marriage." *Boston Globe* 23 Nov.: 1.

Phillips, Richard. 1980. "The Shooting War Over 'Choice' or 'Life' Is Beginning Again." *Chicago Tribune* 20 Ap., sec. 12: 3.

Pinard, Maurice, Jerome Kirk, and Donald von Eschen. 1969. "Processes of Recruitment in the Sit-In Movement." *Public Opinion Quarterly* 33: 355–69.

Pinello, Daniel R. 2006. *America's Struggle for Same-Sex Marriage.* Cambridge: Cambridge University Press.

Piven, Frances Fox, and Richard Cloward. 1979. *Poor People's Movements.* New York: Vintage.

Pollack, Harriet. 1989. "Comments." In "Symposium: The Future of Criminal Justice Under the Constitution." 25 *Crim L. Bull.* 3 (Jan./Feb.): 24–27.

Pollak, Louis H. 1957. "The Supreme Court Under Fire." 6 *J. Pub. L.* 428.

Pollitt, Daniel H. 1960. "Dime Store Demonstrations: Events and Legal Problems of First Sixty Days." *1960 Duke L. J.* 315.

Polsby, Nelson W., ed. 1971. *Reapportionment in the 1970s.* Berkeley: University of California Press.

Pomeroy, Richard, and Lynn C. Landman. 1972. "Public Opinion Trends: Elective Abortion and Birth Control Services to Teenagers." *Family Planning Perspectives* 4: 44–55.

Posey, Barbara Ann. 1961. "Why I Sit-In." *Social Progress* 51 (Feb.): 8–10.

Powell, Adam Clayton, Jr. 1971. *Adam by Adam.* New York: Dial.

Preface. 1986. In colloquium, "Effective Assistance of Counsel for the Indigent Criminal Defendant: Has the Promise Been Fulfilled?" 14 *N.Y.U. Rev. L. & Soc. Change* 1.

"President Calls for Constitutional Amendment Protecting Marriage." 2004 (Feb. 24). http://www.whitehouse.gov/news/releases/2004/02/20040224 –2.html.

President's Committee on Civil Rights. 1947. *To Secure These Rights.* Washington, D.C.: GPO; New York: Simon.

Pritchett, C. Herman. 1964. "Equal Protection and the Urban Majority." *American Political Science Review* 58: 869–75.

Project. 1973. "Judicial Intervention in Corrections: The California Experience—An Empirical Study." 20 *U.C.L.A. L. Rev.* 452.

"Prosperity, Progress, and Peace." 2000. The 2000 Democratic National Platform. http://www.democrats.org/pdfs/2000platform.pdf.

Purdum, Todd S. 1996. "Gay Rights Groups Attack Clinton on Midnight Signing." *New York Times* 22 Sept.: 22.

Puro, Steven. 1981. "The United States as Amicus Curiae." In *Courts, Law, and Judicial Processes.* Ed. S. Sidney Ulmer. New York: The Free Press. 220–29.

Rabin, Robert L. 1976. "Lawyers For Social Change: Perspectives on Public Interest Law." 28 *Stan. L. Rev.* 207.

Rabkin, Jeremy. 1983. "The Judiciary in the Administrative State." *The Public Interest* (Spring): 62–84.

Raines, Howell. 1983. *My Soul Is Rested: Movement Days in the Deep South Remembered.* New York: Penguin.

Randolph, A. Philip. 1964. "The March On Washington Movement During

World War II." In *Freedom Now!* Ed. Alan F. Westin. New York: Basic. 75–78.

Rankin, Deborah. 1986. "Splitting the Assets Fairly in Divorce." *New York Times* 30 March, sec. 3: 11.

Rawls, John. 1971. *A Theory of Justice.* Cambridge: Harvard University Press.

Rebell, Michael, and Arthur R. Block. 1982. *Educational Policy Making and the Courts: An Empirical Study of Judicial Activism.* Chicago: University of Chicago Press.

Reedy, Cheryl D. 1982. "The Supreme Court and Congress on Abortion: An Analysis of Contemporary Institutional Capacity." Paper presented at the Annual Meeting of the American Political Science Association, Denver, Sept. 2–5.

Rees, Robert M. 2004. "Same Sex Marriage: From Frontline to Footnote." *Honolulu Weekly* 7 April. http://honoluluweekly.com/cover/detail.php?id=7.

Remsen, Nancy. 2000. "Statehouse Sees Shift in Power." *Burlington Free Press* 9 Nov: 1.

"Report of the New York Task Force on Women in the Courts." 1986. 15 *Fordham Urban L. J.* 1.

Representation and Apportionment. 1966. Washington, D.C.: Congressional Quarterly Press.

Reskin, Barbara F., ed. 1984. *Sex Segregation in the Workplace: Trends, Explanations, Remedies.* Washington, D.C.: National Academy Press.

———, and Heidi I. Hartmann, eds. 1986. *Women's Work, Men's Work: Sex Segregation on the Job.* Washington, D.C.: National Academy Press.

Resnick, Judith. 1984. "Commentaries on Prison Litigation." 9 *Justice System J.* 347.

"Respect for Privacy." 1973. Editorial. *New York Times* 24 Jan.: 40.

Rhode, Deborah L. 1989. *Justice and Gender: Sex Discrimination and the Law.* Cambridge: Harvard University Press.

"Rhode Island Abortion Law Is Declared Unconstitutional." 1973. *New York Times* 17 May: 22.

Ricci, James, and Patricia Ward Biederman. 2004. "Acceptance of Gays on Rise, Polls Show." *Los Angeles Times* 30 March, sec. B: 1.

Ridgeway, James. 1963. "One Million Abortions." *New Republic* 9 Feb.: 14–17.

Ring, Dan. 2004. "No Backlash in Mass.: Official May End Effort to Ban Gay Marriages." *The Republican* (Springfield, Mass.) 5 Nov.

Roberts, E. F. 1970a. "The Right to a Decent Environment; E = MC²: Environment Equals Man Times Courts Redoubling their Efforts." In "Symposium—Law and the Environment." 55 *Cornell L. Rev.* 663.

———. 1970b. "The Right to a Decent Environment: Progress Along a Constitutional Avenue." In *Law and the Environment.* Ed. Malcolm F. Baldwin and James K. Page, Jr. New York: Walker & Co. for the Conservation Foundation. 134–65.

Roberts, Gene. 1966. "The Story of Snick: From 'Freedom High' to 'Black Power'." *New York Times Magazine* 25 Sept.: 27 + .

Robertson, Nan. 1966. "Ervin Protests Curbs on Police." *New York Times* 23 July: 54.

Robinson, Glen. 1957. "Man in No Man's Land." In *With All Deliberate Speed*. Ed. Don Shoemaker. New York: Harper. 183–201.

Robinson, Jo Ann Gibson. 1987. *The Montgomery Bus Boycott and the Women Who Started It: The Memoir of Jo Ann Gibson Robinson*. Ed. David J. Garrow. Knoxville: University of Tennessee Press.

Rodgers, Harrell R., Jr., and Charles S. Bullock III. 1972. *Law and Social Change: Civil Rights Laws and Their Consequences*. New York: McGraw-Hill.

———. 1976. "School Desegregation: A Multivariate Test of the Role of Law in Effectuating Social Change." *American Politics Quarterly* 4: 153–76.

Roisman, Anthony Z. 1986. "The Role of the Citizen in Enforcing Environmental Laws." 16 *ELR* 10163.

Roos, Patricia, and Barbara F. Reskin. 1984. "Institutional Factors Contributing to Sex Segregation in the Workplace." In *Sex Segregation in the Workplace: Trends, Explanations, Remedies*. Ed. Barbara F. Reskin. Washington, D.C.: National Academy Press. 235–60.

Rosen, Harold, ed. 1967. *Abortion in America*. Boston: Beacon.

Rosen, R. A. Hudson, H. W. Werley, Jr., J. W. Ager, and F. P. Shea. 1974. "Health Professionals' Attitudes Toward Abortion." *Public Opinion Quarterly* 38: 159–73.

Rosenbaum, Walter A. 1974. "The End of Illusion: NEPA and the Limits of Judicial Review." In *Environmental Politics*. Ed. Stuart S. Nagel. New York: Praeger. 260–77.

Rosenberg, Debra, and Karen Breslau. 2004. "Winning the 'Values' Vote." *Newsweek* 15 Nov.: 23.

Rosenberg, Gerald N. 1985. "Judicial Independence and the Reality of Political Power." Paper presented at the Annual Meeting of the American Political Science Association, New Orleans, Aug. 29–Sept. 1.

———. 1992. "Hollow Hopes and Other Aspirations: A Reply to Feeley and McCann." In "Symposium: The Supreme Court and Social Change." 17 *Law & Social Inquiry* 761.

———. 1998. "Knowledge and Desire: Thinking about Courts and Social Change." In *Leveraging the Law: Using Courts to Achieve Social Change*. Ed. David Schultz. New York: Peter Lang. 251–91.

Rosenthal, Alan. 1974. "Turnover in State Legislatures." *American Journal of Political Science* 18: 609–16.

Rosenthal, Jack. 1971. "Survey Finds 50% Back Liberalization of Abortion Policy." *New York Times* 28 Oct.: 1 +.

Rosenthal, Steve. 2004. "Okay, We Lost Ohio. The Question is, Why?" *Washington Post* 5 Dec., sec. B: 3.

Rosoff, Jeannie I. 1975. "Is Support for Abortion Political Suicide?" *Family Planning Perspectives* 7: 13–22.

Ross, Susan Deller, and Ann Barcher. 1983. *The Rights of Women.* Rev. Ed. New York: Bantam.

Rostow, Eugene V. 1952. "The Democratic Character of Judicial Review." 66 *Harv. L. Rev.* 193.

Rothchild, Nina. 1984. "Overview of Pay Initiatives, 1974–1984." In U.S. Commission on Civil Rights, *Comparable Worth: Issues for the 80's.* N.p. 119–28.

Rothwax, Harold J. 1969. "The Law as an Instrument of Social Change." In *Justice and the Law in the Mobilization for Youth Experience.* Ed. Harold H. Weissman. New York: Association Press. 137–44.

Rowan, Carl. 1956. "Who Gets the Negro Vote?" *Look* 13 Nov.: 37–9.

Rubenstein, William B., and R. Bradley Sears. 2003. "Toward More Perfect Unions." *New York Times* 20 Nov.: 31.

Rubin, Eva R. 1982. *Abortion, Politics, and the Courts.* Westport: Greenwood.

Russell, Mary. 1977. "House Bars Use of U.S. Funds in Abortion Cases." *Washington Post* 18 June: 1 +.

Rutenberg, Jim. 2004. "The Polling: Poll Question Stirs Debate on Meaning of 'Values.'" *New York Times* 6 Nov.: 13.

Saad, Lydia. 2005. "Gay Rights Attitudes a Mixed Bag." Gallup Poll News Service, 20 May.

———. 2006. "Americans Still Oppose Gay Marriage But only Half Favor a Constitutional Amendment to Bar It." Gallup Poll News Service, 22 May.

———. 2007. "Tolerance for Gay Rights at High Ebb." Gallup News Service, 29 May.

Sarratt, Reed. 1966. *The Ordeal of Desegregation.* New York: Harper.

Sarvis, Betty, and Hyman Rodman. 1973. *The Abortion Controversy.* New York: Columbia University Press.

Sassower, Doris L. 1971. "The Role of Lawyers in Women's Liberation." *Case and Comment* 76.2: 9–15.

Sax, Joseph L. 1971. *Defending the Environment: A Strategy for Citizen Action.* New York: Knopf.

Schafran, Lynn Hecht. 1987. "Documenting Gender Bias in the Courts: The Task Force Approach." 70 *Judicature* 280.

Schanberg, Sidney H. 1968. "Rockefeller Asks Abortion Reform." *New York Times* 10 Jan: 1 +.

———. 1969. "Albany Action on Abortion Reform Seen as Likely." *New York Times* 30 Jan.: 22.

————. 1983. "New York; The Toothbrush Test." *New York Times* 14 May: 23.

Scheingold, Stuart A. 1974. *The Politics of Rights: Lawyers, Public Policy, and Political Change.* New Haven: Yale University Press.

————. 1989. "Constitutional Rights and Social Change: Civil Rights in Perspective." In *Judging the Constitution: Critical Essays on Judicial Lawmaking.* Ed. Michael W. McCann and Gerald L. Houseman. Glenview, Ill.: Scott, Foresman.

Schiffren, Lisa. 1996. "Gay Marriage, an Oxymoron." *New York Times* 23 March: 21.

Schmeck, Harold M., Jr. 1967. "Doctors Critical of Abortion Laws." *New York Times* 30 April: 82.

"School Report Says Many Southern Cities are Lagging." 1972. *South Today* 3.11 (June): 1 + .

"School Support." 1969. *South Today* 1.2 (August): 2.

Schulder, Diane, and Florynce Kennedy. 1971. *Abortion Rap.* New York: McGraw-Hill.

Schulhofer, Stephen J. 1981. "Confessions and the Constitution." 79 *Mich. L. Rev.* 865.

————. 1986. "Effective Assistance on the Assembly Line." 14 *N.Y.U. Rev. L. & Soc. Change* 137.

————. 1987. "Reconsidering *Miranda.*" 54 *U. Chi. L. Rev.* 435.

Schultz, David A., ed. 1998. *Leveraging the Law: Using Courts to Achieve Social Change.* New York: Peter Lang.

Schultz, Terri. 1977. "Though Legal, Abortions Are Not Always Available." *New York Times* 2 Jan., sec. 4: 8.

Scigliano, Robert. 1971. *The Supreme Court and the Presidency.* New York: The Free Press.

Searles, Ruth, and J. Allen Williams, Jr. 1962. "Negro College Students' Participation in Sit-Ins." *Social Forces* 40: 215–20.

Seeburger, Richard H., and R. Stanton Wettick, Jr. 1967. "*Miranda* in Pittsburgh—A Statistical Study." 29 *U. Pitt. L. Rev.* 1.

Seeger, Pete, and Bob Reiser. 1989. *Everybody Says Freedom: A History of the Civil Rights Movement in Songs and Pictures.* New York: W. W. Norton.

Seelye, Katharine. "Abortions in Pa. Keep Declining." *Philadelphia Inquirer* 20 July: 1-A.

————. 2004. "Moral Values Cited as a Defining Issue of the Election." *New York Times* 4 Nov., sec. P ("The Elections"): 4.

Segal, Jeffrey A., and Reedy, Cheryl D. 1988. "The Supreme Court and Sex Discrimination: The Role of the Solicitor General." *Western Political Quarterly* 41: 553–68.

Segers, Mary C. "Governing Abortion Policy." 1981. In *Governing Through*

Courts. Ed. Richard A. L. Gambitta, Marilyn L. May, and James C. Foster. Beverly Hills: Sage. 283–300.

"'Segregation Academies' Flourish in South." 1969. *South Today* 1.4 (October): 1 + .

"Segregation Reported in Federal Housing Projects." 1985. *New York Times* 11 Feb.: 15.

Seims, Sara. 1980. "Abortion Availability in the United States." *Family Planning Perspectives* 12: 88 + .

Selke, William L. 1985. "Judicial Management of Prisons? Responses to Prison Litigation." 65 *Prison J.* 26.

Sellers, Cleveland. 1973. *The River of No Return.* New York: Morrow.

"Sex and Caste." 1966. *Liberation* 11.2: 35–6.

Shapiro, Martin. 1964. *Law and Politics in the Supreme Court: New Approaches to Political Jurisprudence.* Glencoe: The Free Press.

———. 1981. *Courts: A Comparative and Political Analysis.* Chicago: University of Chicago Press.

Shoemaker, Don., ed. 1957. *With All Deliberate Speed.* New York: Harper.

Shouse, Ben. 2004. "Advocate Promotes Religious Stance." *Argus Leader* 5 Oct., sec. B: 1.

Siepmann, Charles A., and Sidney Reisberg. 1949. "'To Secure These Rights': Coverage of a Radio Documentary." *Public Opinion Quarterly* 12: 649–58.

Sindler, Allan P. 1971. Commentary. In *Reapportionment in the 1970s.* Ed. Nelson W. Polsby. Berkeley: University of California Press. 285–90.

Sive, David. 1970a. Discussion. In *Law and the Environment.* Ed. Malcolm F. Baldwin and James K. Page, Jr. New York: Walker & Co. for the Conservation Foundation. 67–102.

———. 1970b. "The Environment: Is it Protected by the Bill of Rights?" *Civil Liberties* April: 3 + .

———. 1970c. "Some Thoughts of an Environmental Lawyer in the Wilderness of Administrative Law." 70 *Colum. L. Rev.* 612.

———. 1978. "Environmental Decision-making: Judicial and Political Review." 28 *Case Western Reserve L. Rev.* 827.

Sklar, June, and Beth Berkov. 1974. "Abortion, Illegitimacy, and the American Birth Rate." *Science* 13 Sept.: 909–15.

Skolnick, Jerome H. 1975. *Justice Without Trial: Law Enforcement in Democratic Society.* 2nd ed. New York: Wiley.

Smallwood, James. 1983. "Texas." In *The Black Press in the South, 1865–1979.* Ed. Henry Lewis Suggs. Westport: Greenwood. 357–77.

Smith, Daniel A., Matthew DeSantis, and Jason Kassel. 2006. "Same-Sex Marriage Ballot Measures and the 2004 Presidential Election." *State and Local Government Review* 38 (2): 78–91.

Smith, George P. III. 1974. "The Environment and the Judiciary: A Need for Co-operation or Reform?" 3 *Env. Aff.* 627.

Smith, Tom W. 1985. "The Polls: America's Most Important Problems, Part II: Regional, Community, and Personal." *Public Opinion Quarterly* 49: 403–10.

Snyed, Ross. 2000. "Vermonters Have Say on Gay Marriage." Associated Press, 25 Jan.

Sokolow, Alvin D. 1973. "Legislative Pluralism, Committee Assignments, and Internal Norms: The Delayed Impact of Reapportionment in California." In "Democratic Representation and Apportionment: Quantitative Methods, Measures, and Criteria." *Annals of the New York Academy of Sciences* 29: 291–313.

Sollom, Terry, and Patricia Donovan. 1985. "State Laws and the Provision of Family Planning and Abortion Services in 1985." *Family Planning Perspectives* 12: 262–66.

"'Someone Has to Translate Rights in Realities': Conversation with Civil Rights Lawyer Jack Greenberg." 1975. 2 (Fall) *Civil Liberties Rev.* 104.

Sorensen, Theodore. 1965. *Kennedy.* New York: Harper.

Souris, Theodore. 1966. "Stop and Frisk or Arrest and Search—The Use and Misuse of Euphemisms." 57 *J. Crim L., C. & P.S.* 251.

Southern Education Reporting Service. 1965. *Statistical Summary of School Segregation—Desegregation in the Southern and Border States.* Nashville: Southern Education Reporting Service.

———. 1967. *A Statistical Summary of School Segregation—Desegregation in the Southern and Border States.* Nashville: Southern Education Reporting Service.

Southern Regional Council. N.d. *Race in the News.* Atlanta: Southern Regional Council.

———. 1960a. *The Student Protest Movement: A Recapitulation.* N.p.: The Southern Regional Council.

———. 1960b. *The Student Protest Movement Winter 1960.* Revised. Atlanta: The Southern Regional Council (April 1).

———. 1961. *The Freedom Ride May 1961.* Atlanta: The Southern Regional Council.

———. 1962. "A Statement on the 'Economic Costs of Racial Discrimination in Employment' Presented to the Joint Committee of Congress in September 1962 by the Council of Economic Advisers." Southern Regional Council Report L-37, Oct. 15.

———. 1964. *Law Enforcement in Mississippi.* Atlanta: Southern Regional Council.

———. 1969. *The Federal Retreat in School Desegregation.* Atlanta: Southern Regional Council.

————. 1971. *The South and Her Children: School Desegregation 1970–1971*. Atlanta: Southern Regional Council.

Spearman, Walter, and Sylvan Meyer. 1960. *Racial Crisis and the Press*. Atlanta: Southern Regional Council.

Special Issue. 1984. "Comparable Worth." 8 *Women's Right Law Reporter* 7.

Special Project. 1978. "The Remedial Process in Institutional Reform Litigation." 78 *Colum. L. Rev.* 784.

Specter, Arlen. 1962. "*Mapp* v. *Ohio:* Pandora's Box for the Prosecutor." 111 *U. Pa. L. Rev.* 4.

Spencer, Rich. 1979. "New Curbs Cut Medicaid—Funded Abortions 99%, HEW Reports." *Washington Post* 8 March: 1 + .

Spicer, George W. 1964. "The Federal Judiciary and Political Change in the South." *Journal of Politics* 26: 154–76.

Spiotto, James E. 1973. "Search and Seizure: An Empirical Study of the Exclusionary Rule and Its Alternatives." 2 *J. Legal Studies* 243.

"Start on Abortion Reform." 1967. Editorial. *New York Times* 29 April: 34.

State of Vermont 2000 Vital Statistics. http://www.healthvermont.gov/research /stats/2000/2000vital.aspx#dvrc.

Steamer, Robert J. 1960. "The Role of the Federal District Courts in the Segregation Controversy." *Journal of Politics* 22: 417–38.

Steiner, Gilbert Y., ed. 1983. *The Abortion Dispute and the American System*. Washington, D.C.: Brookings.

Steinhoff, Patricia G. 1973. "Background Characteristics of Abortion Patients," In *The Abortion Experience*. Ed. Howard J. Osofsky and Joy D. Osofsky. New York: Harper. 206–31.

————, and Milton Diamond. 1977. *Abortion Politics: The Hawaii Experience*. Honolulu: University Press of Hawaii.

Stickney, Stonewall B. 1976. "*Wyatt* v. *Stickney:* Background and Postscript." In *The Right to Treatment for Mental Patients*. Ed. Stuart Golann, and William J. Fremouw. New York: Irvington. 29–46.

Stolberg, Sheryl Gay. 2004. "Same-Sex Marriage Amendment Fails in House." *New York Times* 1 October: 14.

Stone, Christopher D. 1974. *Should Trees Have Standing? Toward Legal Rights for Natural Objects*. Los Angeles: William Kaufmann.

Stone, Geoffrey, R., Louis M. Seidman, Cass R. Sunstein, and Mark V. Tushnet. 1986. *Constitutional Law*. Boston: Little, Brown.

Streator, George. 1946. "Negro Congress Appeals to U.N." *New York Times* 2 June, sec. 1: 33.

————. 1947. "U.N. Gets Charge of Wide Bias in U.S." *New York Times* 24 Oct.: 9.

Strober, Myra H. 1984. "Toward a General Theory of Occupational Sex Segregation: The Case of Public School Teaching." In *Sex Segregation in the*

Workplace: Trends, Explanations, Remedies. Ed. Barbara F. Reskin. Washington, D.C.: National Academy Press. 144–56.

———, and Carolyn L. Arnold. 1987. "The Dynamics of Occupational Segregation Among Bank Tellers." In *Gender in the Workplace.* Ed. Clair Brown and Joseph A. Pechman. Washington, D.C.: Brookings. 107–48.

Stroman, Carolyn A. 1978. "Race, Public Opinion, and Print Media Coverage." Ph.D. Diss. Syracuse University.

"Strong at Home, Respected in the World." The 2004 Democratic National Platform for America. http://www.democrats.org/pdfs/2004platform.pdf.

Strunk, Mildred, ed. 1947. "The Quarter's Polls." *Public Opinion Quarterly* 11: 639–83.

———. 1950. "The Quarter's Polls." *Public Opinion Quarterly* 14: 173–92.

Suggs, Henry Lewis, ed. 1983. *The Black Press in the South, 1865–1979.* Westport: Greenwood.

Sullivan, Andrew. 2000. "State of the Union: Why 'Civil Union' Isn't Marriage." *The New Republic* 8 May: 18–23.

Sullivan, Ellen, Christopher Tietze, and Joy G. Dryfoos. 1977. "Legal Abortion in the United States, 1975–1976." *Family Planning Perspectives* 9: 116 + .

Sundquist, James L. 1968. *Politics and Policy: The Eisenhower, Kennedy, and Johnson Years.* Washington, D.C.: Brookings.

Sutherland, Elizabeth, ed. 1965. *Letters from Mississippi.* New York: McGraw-Hill.

Symposium. "Comparable Worth." 1986. 20 *U. Mich. J. L. Ref.* 1.

Taggart, William A. 1989. "Redefining the Power of the Federal Judiciary: The Impact of Court-Ordered Prison Reform on State Expenditures for Corrections." 23 *Law & Soc'y Rev.* 241.

Tapper, Jake, and Jody Hassett. 2004. "Was Same-Sex Marriage Partly to Blame for Kerry Loss? Conservative Backlash May Have Cost Kerry Crucial Ohio." ABC News 5 Nov. http://abcnews.go.com/wnt/story?id= 230634&page=1.

Tarr-Whelan, Linda., ed. 1984. *A Women's Rights Agenda for the States.* N.p.: Conference on Alternative State and Local Policies.

Tatalovich, Raymond. 1988. "Abortion: Prochoice Versus Prolife." In *Social Regulatory Policy.* Ed. Raymond Tatalovich and Byron W. Daynes. Boulder: Westview. 177–209.

———, and Byron W. Daynes. 1981. *The Politics of Abortion.* New York: Praeger.

———. 1989. "The Geographic Distribution of U.S. Hospitals with Abortion Facilities." *Family Planning Perspectives* 21: 81–84.

Taylor, Stuart, Jr. 1987. "Backstage Drama Marked '54 Bias Case." *New York Times* 22 March: 1 + .

Teachout, Peter R. 1965. "Louisiana Underlaw." In *Southern Justice.* Ed. Leon Friedman. New York: Pantheon. 57–79.

Tedrow, Lucky M., and E. R. Mahoney. 1979. "Trends in Attitudes Toward Abortion: 1972–1976." *Public Opinion Quarterly* 43: 181–89.

Terjen, Kitty. 1972. "Close-Up on Segregation Academies." *New South* 27.4 (Fall): 50–58.

———. 1973. "Cradle of Resistance: Prince Edward County Today." *New South* 28.3 (Summer): 18–27.

"Text of Nixon Speech." 1970. *New York Times* 2 Jan.: 12.

Thayer, James Bradley. 1901. *John Marshall.* Boston: Houghton, Mifflin.,

"The Abortion Epidemic." 1966. *Newsweek* 14 Nov.: 92.

The American Woman 1988–89: A Status Report. 1988. Ed. Sara E. Rix. New York: Norton.

"The Challenge that Hawaii Poses." 1996. Editorial. *Chicago Tribune* 8 Dec.: 22.

"The Cry from Poland." 1981. Editorial. *New York Times* 18 Dec.: 34.

"The Decision Blow by Blow." 1973. *Time* 5 Feb.: 51.

The Federalist Papers. 1961. Ed. Clinton Rossiter. New York: Mentor.

"The First Year Report of the New Jersey Supreme Court Task Force on Women in the Courts—June 1984." 1986. *Women's Rts. L. Rptr.* 9.2: 129.

"The Freedom to Marry." 1996. Editorial. *New York Times* 7 April, sec. 4: 10.

"The Law—Criminal Justice Concerns about Confessions." 1966. *Time* 29 April: 52.

"The Meaning of Marriage. 1996. Editorial. *Chicago Tribune* 30 April: 16.

"The Message from Hawaii." 1996. Editorial. *New York Times* 6 Dec.: 38.

"The Press—Dilemma in Dixie." 1956. *Time* 20 February: 76 + .

"The Road to Gay Marriage." 2004. Editorial. *New York Times* 7 March: 12.

"The State of the Workplace for Gay, Lesbian, Bisexual and Transgender Americans 2000." 2000. Washington, D.C.: Human Rights Campaign Foundation. http://www.hrc.org/documents/sow2000.pdf.

"The State of the Workplace for Gay, Lesbian, Bisexual and Transgender Americans 2005–2006." 2006. Washington, D.C.: Human Rights Campaign Foundation. http://www.hrc.org/documents/sotw20052006.pdf.

"The Supreme Court and Abortion." 1973. Editorial. *Christian Science Monitor* 29 Jan.: 14.

"The 2000–2001 Television Season: Leading Roles." Gay & Lesbian Alliance Against Defamation. http://www.glaad.org/eye/ontv/00–01/leading.php?.

"13 More Gay Couples Wed in New Paltz." *Poughkeepsie Journal* 6 June, sec. B: 1.

Thomas, Jim, Devin Keeler, and Kathy Harris. 1986. "Issues and Misconceptions in Prisoner Litigation: A Critical View.: 24 *Criminology* 775.

Thompson, Edward P. 1975. *Whigs and Hunters: The Origins of the Black Acts.* London: Allen Lane.

Thompson, Julius Eric. 1983. "Mississippi." In *The Black Press in the South, 1865–1979.* Ed. Henry Lewis Suggs. Westport: Greenwood. 177–210.

Thornton, J. Miles III. 1980. "Challenge and Response in the Montgomery Bus Boycott of 1955–1956." *Alabama Review* 33 (July): 163–235.

Tietze, Christopher. 1970. "United States: Therapeutic Abortions, 1963 to 1968." *Studies in Family Planning* 1.59: 5–7.

————. 1973. "Two Years' Experience with a Liberal Abortion Law: Its Impact in New York City." *Family Planning Perspectives* 5: 36–41.

————, and Deborah A. Dawson. 1973. "Induced Abortion: A Factbook." *Reports on Population/Family Planning* 14: 1–56.

Tigar, Michael E. 1970. "Foreword—Waiver of Constitutional Rights: Disquiet in the Citadel." 84 *Harv. L. Rev.* 1.

"*Time* 100/Heroes & Icons." 2004. *Time* April 26: 120.

"*Times* Will Begin Reporting Gay Couples' Ceremonies." 2002. *New York Times* 18 Aug.: 30.

Toch, Hans. 1985. "Warehouses for People?" In "Our Crowded Prisons." *Annals of the American Academy of Political and Social Science* 478 (March): 58–72.

Tolchin, Martin. 1967. "Defiance Pledged on Abortion Law." *New York Times* 12 March: 81.

————. 1977. "House Bars Medicaid Abortions and Funds for Enforcing Quotas." *New York Times* 18 June: 1 + .

"Topeka Has Failed to Do Enough to Integrate Schools, Court Says." 1989. *New York Times* 14 Dec.: 17.

Traynor, Roger J. 1962. "Mapp v. Ohio at Large in the Fifty States." *1962 Duke L. J.* 319.

————. 1977. "The Limits of Judicial Creativity." 63 *Iowa L. Rev.* 1.

T.R.B. 1957. "Washington Wire." *New Republic* 15 July: 2.

Trubek, David M. 1978. "Environmental Defense I: Introduction to Interest Group Advocacy in Complex Disputes." In *Public Interest Law.* Ed. Burton A. Weisbrod, Joel F. Handler, and Neil K. Komesar. Berkeley: University of California Press. 151–94.

————, and William J. Gillen. 1978. "Environmental Defense, II: Examining the Limits of Interest Group Advocacy in Complex Disputes." In *Public Interest Law.* Ed. Burton A. Weisbrod, Joel F. Handler, and Neil K. Komesar. Berkeley: University of California Press. 195–217.

Turner, Tom. 1988. "Trends: Legal Eagles." *The Amicus Journal.* 10.1 (Winter): 25–37.

Turner, William Bennett. 1979. "When Prisoners Sue: A Study of Prisoner Section 1983 Suits in the Federal Courts." 92 *Harv. L. Rev.* 610.

————. 1984a. Discussion. In colloquium, "The Prison Overcrowding Crisis." 12 *N.Y.U. Rev. L. & Soc. Change* 347.

————. 1984b. Responses. In colloquium, "The Prison Overcrowding Crisis." 12 *N.Y.U. Rev. L. & Soc. Change* 331.

Tushnet, Mark V. 1987. *The NAACP's Legal Strategy Against Segregated Education, 1925–1950.* Chapel Hill: University of North Carolina Press.

"TV Scoreboard 1996–1997 Season." Gay & Lesbian Alliance Against Defamation. http://www.glaad.org/eye/ontv/past/1996_1997.php?.

"TV Scoreboard 1998–1999 Season." Gay & Lesbian Alliance Against Defamation. http://www.glaad.org/eye/ontv/past/1998_1999.php?.

Tversky, Amos, and Daniel Kahneman. 1982a. "Causal Schemas in Judgments Under Uncertainty." In *Judgment Under Uncertainty: Heuristics and Biases.* Ed. Daniel Kahneman, Paul Slovic, and Amos Tversky. Cambridge: Cambridge University Press. 117–28.

————. 1982b. "Judgment Under Uncertainty: Heuristics and Biases." In *Judgment Under Uncertainty: Heuristics and Biases.* Ed. Daniel Kahneman, Paul Slovic, and Amos Tversky. Cambridge: Cambridge University Press. 3–20.

"25 New Gay Marriages Conducted in N.Y." 2004. Associated Press, 20 March.

Tybor, Joseph R., and Mark Eissman. 1986. "Illegal Evidence Destroys Few Cases." *Chicago Tribune* 5 Jan.: 1 + .

Tyler, Joseph R., and Mark Eissman. 1986. "Illegal Evidence Destroys Few Cases." *Chicago Tribune* 5 Jan.: 1 + .

Tyler, Gus. 1962. "Court Versus Legislature: (The Socio-Politics of Malapportionment)." 27 *Law and Contemporary Problems* 390.

Ulmer, S. Sidney. 1971. "Earl Warren and the *Brown* Decision." *Journal of Politics* 33: 689–702.

————, and David Willison. 1985. "The Solicitor General of the United States as *Amicus Curiae* in the United States Supreme Court, 1969–1983 Terms." Paper presented at the Annual Meeting of the American Political Science Association, New Orleans, Aug. 29–Sept. 1.

UPI. 1984. "Around The Nation; Unitarians Endorse Homosexual Marriages." *New York Times* 29 June: 10.

————. 1986. "Around the Nation; Rights Group Backs Homosexual Marriages." *New York Times* 28 Oct.: 20.

U.S. Bureau of the Census. Various Years. *Abstract of the United States.* Washington, D.C.: GPO.

————. Current Population Reports. Series P-23, No. 154. 1989a. *Child Support and Alimony: 1985.* supplemental report. Washington, D.C.: GPO.

————. Current Population Reports. Series P-23, No. 163. 1989b. *Changes in American Family Life.* Washington, D.C.: GPO.

————. Current Population Reports. Series P-60, No. 161. 1984. *Money Income of Households, Families, and Persons in the United States: 1982.* Washington, D.C.: GPO.

———. Current Population Reports. Series P-60, No. 161. 1988. *Money Income and Poverty Status in the United States: 1987.* Advance Data from the March 1988 Current Population Survey. Washington, D.C.: GPO.

———. Current Population Reports. Series P-60, No. 163. 1989. *Poverty in the United States: 1987.* Washington, D.C.: GPO.

U.S. Census Bureau. 2006. Population and Household Economic Topics, Population Finder. http://www.census.gov/population/www/.

U.S. Commission on Civil Rights. 1959. *Report of the U.S. Commission on Civil Rights 1959.* Washington, D.C.: GPO.

———. 1961a. *Equal Protection of the Laws in Higher Public Education, 1960.* Washington, D.C.: GPO.

———. 1961b. *1961 U.S. Commission on Civil Rights Report.* 5 vols. Washington, D.C.: GPO.

———. 1963a. *Civil Rights '63: 1963 Report of the U.S. Commission on Civil Rights.* Washington D.C.: GPO.

———. 1963b. *Freedom to the Free.* Washington, D.C.: GPO.

———. 1963c. *1963 Staff Report: Public Education.* Washington, D.C.: GPO.

———. 1965. *The Voting Rights Act . . . The First Months.* Washington, D.C.: N.p.

———. 1967. *Southern School Desegregation, 1966–67.* Washington, D.C.: GPO.

———. 1968. *Political Participation.* Washington, D.C.: GPO.

———. 1969. *Federal Enforcement of School Desegregation.* Washington, D.C.: The Commission.

———. 1970. *HEW and Title VI.* Washington, D.C.: GPO.

———. 1974a. *Mortgage Money: Who Gets It?* Washington, D.C.: The Commission.

———. 1974b. *The Federal Civil Rights Enforcement Effort—1974.* 7 vols. Washington, D.C.: GPO.

———. 1974c. *Women and Poverty.* Washington, D.C.: The Commission.

———. 1975a. *Constitutional Aspects of the Right to Limit Childbearing.* Washington, D.C.: The Commission.

———. 1975b. *School Desegregation: The Courts and Suburban Migration.* Washington, D.C.: The Commission.

———. 1975c. *The Voting Rights Act: Ten Years After.* Washington, D.C.: GPO.

———. 1975d. *Twenty Years After Brown: Equal Opportunity in Housing.* Washington, D.C.: GPO.

———. 1976a. *A Guide to Federal Laws and Regulations, Prohibiting Sex Discrimination.* Rev. ed. Washington, D.C.: GPO.

———. 1976b. *Fulfilling the Letter and Spirit of the Law: Desegregation of the Nation's Public Schools.* N.p.

————. 1977a. *Reviewing a Decade of School Desegregation 1966–1975: Report of a National Survey of School Superintendents.* Washington, D.C.: GPO.

————. 1977b. *Sex Bias in the U.S. Code.* Washington, D.C.: The Commission.

————. 1977c. *Twenty Years After Brown.* Washington, D.C.: GPO.

————. 1978. *Statement on the Equal Rights Amendment.* Washington, D.C.: GPO.

————. 1979a. *Desegregation of the Nation's Schools: A Status Report.* Washington, D.C.: GPO.

————. 1979b. *Women Still in Poverty.* Washington, D.C.: The Commission.

————. 1979c. *Women's Rights in the United States of America.* Washington, D.C.: The Commission.

————. 1981. *With All Deliberate Speed: 1954–19?* N.p.

————. 1982. *Statement of the U.S. Commission on Civil Rights on School Desegregation.* N.p.

————. 1984. *Comparable Worth: Issue for the 80's.* N.p.

U.S. Commission on Civil Rights. State Advisory Commissions to the Commission on Civil Rights. 1961. *The 50 States Report.* Washington, D.C.: GPO.

U.S. Cong. House. Committee on the Judiciary, Subcommittee No. 5. 1957. *Hearings.* 85th Cong., 1st sess. Washington, D.C.: GPO.

————. Senate. Committee on the Judiciary, Subcommittee on Constitutional Rights. 1957. *Hearings.* 85th Cong., 1st sess. Washington, D.C.: GPO.

————. Senate. Committee on the Judiciary, Subcommittee on Constitutional Amendments. 1962. *Hearings.* 87th Cong., 2nd sess. Washington, D.C.: GPO.

————. Senate. Committee on the Judiciary. 1970a. "Equal Rights 1970." *Hearings.* 91st Cong. 2nd sess. Washington, D.C.: GPO.

————. Senate. Committee on the Judiciary, Subcommittee on Constitutional Amendments. 1970b. *Hearings.* 91st Cong., 2nd sess. Washington, D.C.: GPO.

————. Senate. 1972. *Equal Rights for Men and Women.* 92nd Cong., 2nd sess. S. Rept. 92–689. Washington, D.C.: GPO.

————. Senate. Committee on the Judiciary, Subcommittee on Constitutional Amendments. 1974, 1976. *Hearings.* 93rd Cong. 2nd sess., 94th Cong., 1st sess., 4 vols. Washington, D.C.: GPO.

U.S. Department of Health, Education, and Welfare. National Center for Education Statistics. Various Years. *Statistics of Local Public School Systems: Finances.* Washington, D.C.: HEW.

————. Office of Civil Rights. Various years. *The Directory of Public Elementary and Secretary Schools in Selected Districts: Enrollment and Staff by Racial/Ethnic Group.* Washington, D.C.: GPO.

———. Office of Education. 1973. *Expenditures and Revenues for Public Elementary and Secondary Education 1970–1971.* Washington, D.C.: GPO.

———. Office of Education. Various years. *Revenues and Expenditures for Public Elementary and Secondary Education.* Washington, D.C.: GPO.

———. Office of Education. Various Years. *Statistics of State School Systems.* Washington, D.C.: GPO.

U.S. Department of Justice. Bureau of Justice Statistics. 1984. *Special Report: The Prevalence of Guilty Pleas.* Washington, D.C.: Bureau of Justice Statistics.

———. Bureau of Justice Statistics. 1989a. *Sourcebook of Criminal Justice Statistics—1989.* Washington, D.C.: GPO.

U.S. Department of Justice. Federal Bureau of Investigation. 1989b. *Uniform Crime Reports—Crime in the United States 1988.* Washington, D.C.: GPO.

U.S. Dept. of Labor. Bureau of Labor Statistics. 1977. *U.S. Working Woman: A Databook.* Washington, D.C.: GPO.

———. Bureau of Labor Statistics. 1982. *Labor Force Statistics Derived from the Current Population Survey: A Databook.* Washington, D.C.: GPO.

———. Bureau of Labor Statistics. 1988. *Labor Force Statistics Derived from the Current Population Survey: 1948–1987.* Washington, D.C.: GPO.

U.S. Dept. of Labor, Employment Standards Administration. Women's Bureau. 1971. *American Women at the Crossroads: Directions for the Future.* Washington, D.C.: n.p.

———. Employment Standards Administration. Women's Bureau. 1976a. *Mature Women Workers: A Profile.* Washington, D.C.: GPO..

———. Employment Standards Administration. Women's Bureau. 1976b. *The Earnings Gap Between Women and Men.* Washington, D.C.: GPO.

———. Employment Standards Administration. Women's Bureau. 1976c. *Women Workers Today.* Washington, D.C.: n.p.

———. Employment Standards Administration. Women's Bureau. 1979. *The Earnings Gap Between Women and Men.* Washington, D.C.: GPO.

U.S. General Accounting Office. 1997. Defense of Marriage Act, GAO/OGC-97–16 (Washington, D.C.: 31 January, 1997). http://www.gao.gov/archive/1997/og97016.pdf.

———. 2004. Defense of Marriage Act, GAO-04–353R (Washington, D.C.: January 23, 2004). http://www.gao.gov/new.items/d04353r.pdf.

U.S. Merit Systems Protection Board. 1988. *Sexual Harassment in the Federal Government: An Update.* Washington, D.C.: GPO.

Uslaner, Eric M. 1978. "Comparative Policy Formation, Interparty Competition, and Malapportionment: A New Look at 'V. O. Key's Hypotheses'." *Journal of Politics* 40: 409–32.

"Vermont Governor Signs Gay Union Bill." 2000. Associated Press, 26 April.

"Vermont's 'Civil Unions' Experiment." 2000. Editorial. *Chicago Tribune* 10 April: 14.

"Vermont's 'Civil Unions' Option." 2000. Editorial. *Chicago Tribune* 26 April: 14.

"Vermont's Momentous Ruling." 1999. Editorial. *New York Times* 22 Dec.: 26.

Vestal, Christine. 2007a. "Civil Unions Spread, but Gays Want to Wed." State line.org, 31 May. http://www.stateline.org/live/details/story?contentId=212354.

———. 2007b. "Gay Marriage Ripe for Decision in 3 Courts." Stateline.org, 1 March. http://www.stateline.org/live/ViewPage.action?siteNodeId=136&languageId=1&contentId=20695.

Vig, Norman J., and Michael E. Kraft, eds. 1984a. *Environmental Policy in the 1980s: Reagan's New Agenda.* Washington, D.C.: Congressional Quarterly Press.

———. 1984b. "Environmental Policy from the Seventies to the Eighties." In *Environmental Policy in the 1980s: Reagan's New Agenda.* Ed. Norman J. Vig and Michael E. Kraft. Washington, D.C.: Congressional Quarterly Press. 3–26.

Vines, Kenneth N. 1964. "Federal District Judges and Race Relations Cases in the South." *Journal of Politics* 26: 337–57.

Virtanen, Michael. 2004. "NY Judge Refuses to Void Gay Marriages." Associated Press, 16 September. http://legalminds.lp.findlaw.com/list/queerlaw/msg05805.html.

Vogel, David. 1987. "A Big Agenda." In "The Politics of the Environment, 1970–1987." *Wilson Quarterly* 11 (Autumn): 51–68.

Vose, Clement E. 1967. *Caucasians Only.* Berkeley: University of California Press.

VoteOnMarriage.org. http://www.voteonmarriage.org.

Voter Education Project, and Southern Regional Council, Inc. 1966. *Voter Registration in the South.* Atlanta: Southern Regional Council.

Wald, Patricia M. 1985. "Negotiation of Environmental Disputes: A New Role for the Courts?" 10 *Colum. J. Envtl. L.* 1.

Walker, Adrian. 2005. "Calm after the Storm." *Boston Globe* 16 May, sec. B: 1.

Walters, Suzanna Danuta. 2003. *All the Rage: The Story of Gay Visibility in America.* Chicago: University of Chicago Press.

Ware, Gilbert. 1962. "The National Association for the Advancement of Colored People and the Civil Rights Act of 1957." Ph.D. Diss. Princeton University.

"Warren Calls Vote Rulings Most Vital." 1969. *New York Times* 27 June: 1 + .

Wasby, Stephen L. 1970. *The Impact of the United States Supreme Court: Some Perspectives.* Homewood, Ill.: Dorsey.

———. 1973. "The Communication of the Supreme Court's Criminal Procedure Decisions: A Preliminary Mapping." 18 *Vill. L. Rev.* 1086.

———. 1976. *Small Town Police and the Supreme Court*. Lexington: D. C. Heath.

———. 1978a. Book Review. 31 *Vand. L. Rev.* 727.

———. 1978b. *The Supreme Court in the Federal Judicial System*. New York: Holt.

———. 1983. "Is 'Planned Litigation' Planned?" Paper presented at the Annual Meeting of the American Political Science Association, Chicago, Sept. 1–4.

———. 1985. "Civil Rights Litigation by Organizations: Constraints and Choices." 68 *Judicature* 337.

———, Anthony A. D'Amato, and Rosemary Metrailer. 1977. *Desegregation from Brown to Alexander*. Carbondale, Ill.: Southern Illinois University Press.

Wasserman, Gabriel J. 2004. "West Barred from Gay Vows." *Poughkeepsie Journal* 8 June: 1.

Watters, Pat. 1965. "Why the Negro Children March." *New York Times Magazine* 21 March: 29 + .

———, and Reese Cleghorn. 1967. *Climbing Jacob's Ladder*. New York: Harcourt.

Wayne, Stephen J. 1980. *The Road to the White House*. New York: St. Martin's.

"We Now Pronounce You a Family." 1989. Editorial. *New York Times* 15 Dec.: 42.

Weaver, Bill, and Oscar C. Page. 1982. "The Black Press and the Drive for Integrated Graduate and Professional Schools." *Phylon* 43: 15–28.

Wehrwein, Austin C. 1966a. "Chicago Police Head Assails Courts for Rulings on Crime." *New York Times* 24 Jan.: 35.

———. 1966b. "Desmond Asserts High Court Ruling Foils Police." *New York Times* 30 April: 13.

Weinstein, Jack B. 1962. "Local Responsibility for Improvement of Search and Seizure Practices." 34 *Rocky Mt. L. Rev.* 150.

Weinstock, Edward, Christopher Tietze, Frederick S. Jaffe, and Joy G. Dryfoos. 1975. "Legal Abortions in the United States Since the 1973 Supreme Court Decisions." *Family Planning Perspectives* 7: 23–31.

Weisbrod, Burton A., Joel F. Handler, and Neil K. Komesar. 1978. *Public Interest Law*. Berkeley: University of California Press.

Weiss, Nancy J. 1989. *Whitney M. Young, Jr., and the Struggle for Civil Rights*. Princeton: Princeton University Press.

Weitzman, Lenore J. 1981. "The Economics of Divorce: Social and Economic Consequences of Property, Alimony and Child Support Awards." 28 *U.C.L.A. L. Rev.* 1181.

———. 1985. *The Divorce Revolution*. New York: The Free Press.

Wenner, Lettie M. 1982. *The Environmental Decade in Court.* Bloomington: Indiana University Press.

———. 1988. "The Reagan Era in Environmental Litigation." Paper presented at the Annual Meeting of the American Political Science Association, Washington, D.C., Sept. 1–4.

———. Forthcoming. "Environmental Policy in the Courts." In *Environmental Policy in the 1990s.* Ed. Norman J. Vig and Michael E. Kraft. Congressional Quarterly Press.

Westin, Alan F., ed. 1964. *Freedom Now!* New York: Basic.

Whalen, Charles and Barbara. 1985. *The Longest Debate: A Legislative History of the 1964 Civil Rights Act.* Cabin John, Md.: Seven Locks.

Where Does Negro Voter Strength Lie?" 1956. *Congressional Quarterly Weekly Report* 4 May: 491–96.

White, Welsh S. 1986. "Defending *Miranda:* A Reply to Professor Caplan." 39 *Vand. L. Rev.* 1.

Wiebe, Robert H. 1979. "White Attitudes and Black Rights from *Brown* to *Bakke.*" In *Have We Overcome? Race Relations Since Brown.* Ed. Michael V. Namorato. Jackson: University of Mississippi Press. 147–71.

Wilke, Michael. 2005. "Same-Sex Marriage Ads Dominate 2004." Commercial closet.org, 31 Jan. http://www.commercialcloset.org/cgi-bin/iowa/index.html?page=column&record=92.

Wilkerson, Isabel. 1990. "In North Dakota, Option of Abortion is Limited." *New York Times* 6 May, sec. 1: 33.

Wilkins, Roy, with Tom Mathews. 1984. *Standing Fast: The Autobiography of Roy Wilkins.* New York: Penguin.

Wilkinson, Harvie J., III. 1979. *From Brown to Alexander: The Supreme Court and School Integration, 1954–1978.* New York: Oxford University Press.

Willhelm, Sidney. 1981. "The Supreme Court: A Citadel for White Supremacy." 79 *Mich. L. Rev.* 847.

Williams, Juan. 1988. *Eyes on the Prize: America's Civil Rights Years, 1954–1965.* New York: Penguin.

Williams, Lena. 1987. "Laxity Charged in College Integration Enforcement." *New York Times* 4 Oct.: 11.

Williams, Robin M., Jr. 1965. "Social Change and Social Conflict: Race Relations in the United States, 1944–1964." *Sociological Inquiry* 35: 8–25.

Williams, Roger M. 1979. "The Power of Fetal Politics." *Saturday Review* 9 June: 12–15.

Wilson, James B. 1965. "Municipal Ordinance, Mississippi Style." In *Southern Justice.* Ed. Leon Friedman. New York: Pantheon. 35–42.

Wilson, James Q. 1968. *Variations of Police Behavior.* Cambridge: Harvard University Press.

Winn, William. 1970a. "Atlanta: Schools Order Reveals a Crisis of Leadership." *South Today* 1.7 (February): 4–5.

———. 1970b. "School Integration: What Worked in Recent Weeks Across the South." *South Today* 1.8 (March): 4–5.

Winter, James P. 1981. "Media-Public Agenda-Setting for Five Issues, 1948–1976." Paper presented at the Annual Meeting of the Midwest Political Science Association, Cincinnati, April.

———, and Chaim H. Eyal. 1981. "Agenda-Setting for the Civil Rights Issue." *Public Opinion Quarterly* 45: 376–83.

Wisdom, John Minor. 1967. "The Frictionmaking, Exacerbating Political Role of Federal Courts." 21 *Sw. L. Rev.* 411.

Wise, Michael. 1973. "Congress, Busing, and Federal Law." *Civil Rights Digest* 5.5: 28–35.

Wishik, Heather Ruth. 1986. "Economics of Divorce: An Exploratory Study." 20 *Family L. Q.* 79.

Witt, James W. 1973. "Non-Coercive Interrogation and the Administration of Criminal Justice: The Impact of Miranda on Police Effectuality." 64 *J. Crim. L. & Criminology* 320.

Wolff, Miles. 1970. *Lunch at the Five and Ten.* New York: Stein and Day.

Wolfson, Evan. 1994. "Crossing the Threshold: Equal Marriage Rights For Lesbians and Gay Men and the Intra-Community Critique." 21 *N.Y.U. Rev. of Law & Soc. Change* 567.

———. 2004. "Marriage Equality and Some Lessons for the Scary Work of Winning." Speech delivered to the National Lesbian & Gay Law Associations' 'Lavender Law' Conference, 30 Sept. http://www.freedomtomarry .org/document.asp?doc_id=1937.

"Women's Movement at Age 11: Larger, More Diffuse, Still Battling." 1977. *New York Times* 15 Nov.: 46.

"Women's Pay Seen as Rising but Still Behind Men's in 2,000." 1984. *New York Times* 31 Oct.: 16.

Woodward, C. Vann. 1974. *The Strange Career of Jim Crow.* Rev. ed. New York: Oxford University Press.

Worthington, Rogers. 1990. "Public Defenders Buried under Burden of Justice." *Chicago Tribune* 20 Oct.: 1 + .

Wynn, Daniel Webster. 1955. *The NAACP versus Negro Revolutionary Protest.* New York: Exposition.

———. 1974. *The Black Protest Movement.* New York: Philosophical Library.

Yang, Alan S. 1997. "The Polls—Trends: Attitudes toward Homosexuality." *Public Opinion Quarterly* 61 (3): 477–507.

Yannacone, Victor J. 1970a. Discussion. In *Law and the Environment.* Ed. Malcolm F. Baldwin and James K. Page, Jr. New York: Walter & Co. for the Conservation Foundation. 67–102.

————. 1970b. Sue the Bastards. In *Earth Day—The Beginning: A Guide for Survival.* Compiled and edited by the National Staff of Environmental Action. New York: Arno. 179–95.

Yarbrough, Tinsley E. 1981. *Judge Frank Johnson and Human Rights In Alabama.* University, Ala: University of Alabama Press.

————. 1984. "The Alabama Prison Litigation." 9 *Justice System J.* 276.

Yeates, John W. 1970. "Private Schools and Public Confusion." *New South* 25.4 (Fall): 83–85.

"Yes to Domestic Partner Benefits." 1997. Editorial. *Chicago Tribune* 28 Feb.: 22.

Youngblood, J. Craig, and Parker C. Folse III. 1981. "Can Courts Govern? An Inquiry Into Capacity and Purpose." In *Governing Through Courts.* Ed. Richard A. L. Gambitta, Marilyn L. May, and James C. Foster. Beverly Hills: Sage. 23–65.

Younger, Evelle J. 1966. "Results of a Survey Conducted in the District Attorney's Office of Los Angeles County Regarding the Effect of the Miranda Decision Upon the Prosecution of Felony Cases." 5 *Am. Crim. L. Q.* 32.

————. 1967. "Interrogation of Criminal Defendants—Some Views on *Miranda* v. *Arizona.*" 35 *Ford. L. Rev.* 255.

Yudof, Mark G. 1981. "Implementation Theories & Desegregation." In "Symposium, Judicially Managed Institutional Reform." 32 *Alabama L. Rev.* 441.

Zanden, James W. Vander. 1963. "The Non-Violent Resistance Movement Against Segregation." *American Journal of Sociology* 68: 544–50.

Zeleny, Jeff. 2004. "Rove: Marriage Issue and Role of Money were Big." *Chicago Tribune* 10 Nov.: 12.

Zernike, Kate. 2004. "Groups Vow Not to Let Losses Dash Gay Rights." *New York Times* 14 Nov.: 30.

Zinn, Howard. 1962. *Albany: A Study in National Responsibility.* Atlanta: Southern Regional Council.

————. 1964. *SNCC: The New Abolitionists.* Boston: Beacon.

Zion, Sidney E. 1965. "High Court Scored on Crime Rulings." *New York Times* 14 May: 39.

————. 1966. "Koota Says New Court Rulings Have 'Shackled Police Officials—A Detective's View." *New York Times* 13 Aug.: 1 + .

Index

Abernathy, Ralph, 132, 137
abortion, 6–7; clinics, 195–98; illegal, 180n7; legal, 178–80, 184, 189–95; referral services, 259–60; reform, 184, 258–64; rights, 173–78, 181–82, 423–24
accommodations and public places, desegregation of, 65–67
ACLU (American Civil Liberties Union): National Prison Project, 306–7, 314; Women's Rights Project, 224–25
Adamany, David, 126
Adams v. Richardson (1973), 55, 57
affirmative action, 226
African Americans. *See* black: Americans
Air Quality Act (1967), 290
Alabama: anti-NAACP actions, 80, 88, 91; and prison reform, 309
Alan Guttmacher Institute, 178, 178n6, 191, 195
Alaska: and abortion law, 263; Constitution of, 363
Alexander v. Holmes County (1969), 45–46, 49n11
Allard, Wayne, 365
Alliance for Marriage, 361–62
Alternatives to Marriage Project, 358
America Coming Together, 378
American Bar Association, 84; Commission on Correctional Facilities and Services, 308–9; Committee on Judicial Selection, 211
American Family Association, 361
American Law Institute, model penal code on abortion, 184, 259

American Medical Association, 184
American Political Science Association, 293
American Psychiatric Association, 408
American Psychological Association, 408
Americans United to Preserve Marriage, 375
Anderson, J. W., 118–19
Anthony, Daniel, 257
anti-abortion movement, 188
Anwyl, J. Hugh, 423
Argersinger v. Hamlin (1972), 330
Arizona, and ban on same-sex marriages, 364
Arney, William, 237
Aronow, Geoffrey, 23, 27
arrests, 318
Atlanta, Georgia, and desegregation, 95
Attica prison, New York, 309
attorney general: and access to voting records, 59; empowered to bring desegregation suits on behalf of individuals, 47, 47n7
attribution, and assessment of influence, 109
Auerbach, Carl, 300
Ayres, Whitfield, 105

Babcock, Gary, 29
Baehr v. Lewin (1993), 339, 343–44
Baehr v. Miike (1996), 343–44
Bailey v. Patterson (1962), 64
Baker, Ella, 143
Baker v. Carr (1962), 294–95
Baker v. Vermont (1999), 341, 344–47
Barenblatt v. U.S. (1959), 74n4
Barnes, Catherine, 64, 155
Barnett, Ross, 78
Barr, Bob, 365

Barron, Christopher, 377
Barrows v. Jackson (1953), 68
basic goods, 4
Baton Rouge, Louisiana, bus boycott, 137,
    138n26
Bauer, Gary, 375
Bay of Pigs invasion, 163–64
Bazelon, David, 18, 280
Beals, Janet, 423
Beal v. Doe (1977), 176
Beatty, Jerry, 88
Becker, Mary, 207, 213, 219
Beilan v. Board of Education (1958), 74n4
Beller, Andrea, 226
Bellotti v. Baird (1979), 176
Bell v. Wolfish (1979), 305n3
Bendiner, Robert, 161
Bennett, Robert T., 380
Berger, Margaret, 174, 210–11, 221
Bergmann, Barbara, 225–26, 249
Berman, Daniel, 123
bias: courts and, 17, 89–91, 219–22; in state
    and federal laws, 218–19
Bickel, Alexander, 25, 297
Birmingham, Alabama, 64
*Bivens v. Six Unknown Federal Narcotics
    Agents* (1971), 318n26
black: Americans, 61–62, 110, 131–55, 158,
    168–69 (*see also* civil rights); churches,
    159; colleges, 159; groups, and civil
    rights, 142–50, 159–60 (*see also names
    of specific organizations and leaders*);
    migration, 62, 159–60; press, 133
Black, Earl, 95
Blackwell, J. Kenneth, 380
Blaine, Ellen, 195
Blake, Judith, 187, 236–37, 260–61
Block, Arthur, 27–29, 29n19, 32
Blumrosen, Ruth, 208
Bob Jones University, 55
Bogalusa, Louisiana, 97
Bolling v. Sharpe (1954), 42, 42n1
Bonauto, Mary, 371, 377
border states, and desegregation of education,
    50–51, 56, 103–4
Bositis, David, 381
Boston Bar Association, 350
Bowles, Linda, 398
Bowman, Karlyn, 408
Boynton v. Virginia (1960), 63, 65–66, 142n33
Bradwell v. The State (1872), 219–20

Brakel, Jan, 307
Brennan, Justice William, 22, 45, 294, 307,
    313
Briggs v. Elliott, 88–89
Bronstein, Alvin, 307, 309
Brooks, David, 399
Brooks, Rosa, 431
Brown, Judge, 49, 86
Brown, Ralph, Jr., 278
Brownell, Attorney General, 118, 155–56
Brown II (1955), 43–45
Brown v. Board of Education (1954), 6, 39–43,
    45, 71, 73, 76, 93, 127, 166–67, 424–25
*Brown v. Board of Education of Topeka,
    Kansas* (1979), 40n2
Buckley, James, 185
Bunning, Jim, 373
bureaucracy, ideal Weberian, 16–17. *See also*
    judicial bureaucracy
bureaucratic reform, 19–21, 23
Burger, Warren, 46, 313, 317, 318n26
Burger Court, 305, 430
Burk, Robert, 76n7, 118–19
Burress, Phil, 379
Burstein, Paul, 168, 225
Burton v. Wilmington Parking Authority
    (1961), 65–66
Bush, George W., 349, 366, 369–71, 406–7,
    425–26
business incentives, and civil rights, 101–2,
    141–42, 153–54
Butler, William F., 23

Caldwell, Lynton, 283
Califano v. Goldfarb (1977), 203
Califano v. Webster (1977), 203n5
California: and abortion law, 200, 263;
    Constitution of, 68; Proposition 22
    ("Knight Initiative"), 351n13; and
    reapportionment, 302; and same-sex
    unions, 351, 360
California Supreme Court, 359
*Calvert Cliffs' Coordinating Committee v.
    AEC* (1971), 274
Cameron, Roderick, 271–72
Canon, Bradley, 317–19
Caplan, Gerald, 326
Carden, Maren, 244, 255
Carig v. Boren (1976), 203
Carson, Brad, 373–74
Carson, Rachel, 290

Carter, Ray, Jr., 112
Carter administration, 185
case selection, control of, 92
Catholic Church, 356
causation, issues of, 7, 107–10
Cavanagh, Ralph, 24, 27–29
Chafe, William, 248
Chayes, Abram, 24
Chicago police, 318, 322–23, 326
Chicago Tribune, coverage of same-sex
    marriage, 394, 397–400
child labor, 5n5
child support, 216–17
Cho, Yong Hyo, 295, 301
Cincinnati police, 322
Citizen's Advisory Council on the Status of
    Women, 205, 207
*City of Akron v. Akron Center for Reproductive
    Health* (1983), 177
civil rights, 6–7, 22, 39–41, 254–55, 308,
    423; and accommodations and public
    places, 65–67; and education, 42–57, 79;
    and housing, 67–70, 84–85; post-1964,
    94–105; resistance to, 155–56; and
    transportation, 63–65; and voting, 57–63,
    80–81
Civil Rights Act (1871), 305
Civil Rights Act (1957), 46, 58–59, 66,
    118–19, 162, 205
Civil Rights Act (1960), 46–47, 59, 66,
    119–20, 162
Civil Rights Act (1964), 40, 46–47, 51–52,
    55, 65, 74–75, 81, 94, 94n30, 97, 109,
    120–21; Title II, 66; Title III, 66–67; Title
    VI, 47–49, 70, 121–23; Title VII, 204,
    204n6, 205–6, 226, 252
Civil Rights Act (1968): Title VIII, 68, 70
civil rights groups, funding of, 150–54. *See
    also names of organizations*
Civil Rights Restoration Act (1988), 14n9
civil unions, 345–47
Clark, Justice Tom, 81, 182
Clean Air Act (1963), 290
Cleaver, Eldridge, 149
Clement, Frank, 164
Cleveland Board of Education v. LaFleur
    (1974), 204
Clinton, Bill, 412
Clinton, Tennessee, 131, 164
Coburn, Dr. Tom, 373–74
Colautti v. Franklin (1979), 177

Cold War, 73, 162–67
Colegrove v. Green (1946), 294, 298
colleges and universities: desegregation of,
    54–57, 80, 104–5; and domestic partner
    benefits, 411; nondiscrimination policies
    of, 412; women's studies programs at, 251
Colorado: and abortion law, 262; Constitution
    of, 364
Columbia, South Carolina, 102n34
Commission on Intergovernmental Relations
    (Kestnbaum Commission), 293–94
Committee on Civil Rights (PCCR), 69, 123,
    159, 164, 168
Commoner, Barry, 276
comparable worth, 204, 208–9
Concerned Women for America, 361
conditions for producing significant social
    reform, 420; costs of compliance
    (condition II), 33; incentives (condition I),
    33, 97–102; leverage and cover (condition
    IV), 33–35, 102–3, 284–85, 311–13;
    market (condition III), 33, 195–201, 285
Conference of State Chief Justices, 84
Congress: anti-abortion activity and, 185–87;
    and civil rights, 46–49, 52, 56–70, 117–21,
    167–68; as constraint on court action, 14,
    14n9, 74–75; and environmental reform,
    274–78, 283; and women's rights, 205–7.
    See also names of specific legislation
Connecticut and same-sex unions, 351, 360
consciousness-raising, 255–56
Conservation Foundation, 275
Constitution, U.S., 339, 349, 362; Fourth
    Amendment, 316; Fifth Amendment,
    273, 324; Sixth Amendment, 324,
    329–30; Ninth Amendment, 273; Tenth
    Amendment, 273; Fourteenth Amendment,
    58, 66–68, 175, 204n7, 273, 314; Fifteenth
    Amendment, 57; Nineteenth Amendment,
    205
constitutional amendments, proposed, 186,
    365–67
constitutional rights: limited nature of, 10–13,
    72–73; new or expanded, 11–12, 271–73,
    278–79
Constrained Court view, 3–7, 9, 30–36, 54,
    86–87, 93, 105–6, 212–13, 313–16,
    420–22; and civil rights, 72–82; logic of,
    10–21; and role of public opinion, 125–26;
    and sociocultural constraints, 82–85
constraints, 420; implementation and

constraints, *(continued)*
  institutional relations (constraint III),
    15–21, 75–82, 94–95, 420–21; limited
    nature of rights (constraint I), 10–13,
    72–73, 94, 181–82, 273, 421; limits on
    judicial independence (constraint II),
    13–15, 73–75, 94–95, 279–80, 332–33;
    overcoming, 30–36; sociocultural, 82–85;
    structural, 85–93
Cooper v. Aaron (1958), 44–45
Cooper v. Pate (1964), 305
CORE (Congress of Racial Equality), 142–44,
  148–50, 152, 154–55
costs: of litigation, 91–93, 281; of segregation,
  158–59
Council for Public Interest Law, 12
Council on Environmental Quality, 276
counsel, right to, 329–34
counter-mobilization against same-sex
  marriage, 343–46, 361–68, 416–17, 425–26
County of Washington v. Gunther (1981), 204
court cases. *See titles of specific cases*
court efficacy: conditions for, 30–36; and
  Dynamic Court view, 21–30
court orders: and local resistance, 189–95;
  and school desegregation, 100, 102; uses
  of, 34–35
courts: as catalysts for change (indirect
  effects), 25; as cover, 102–3; as "fly-
  paper," 427; insulation of, 17; as producers
  of significant social reform, 1–3, 9–10;
  structural constraints of, 85–93
court strategy, coordinated, 92–93
Cover, Robert, 40
Cowan, Ruth, 18, 224
Cox, Judge, 90
criminal defendants, rights of, 304
criminal rights, 304–5
criminal suspects, and *Miranda* warnings,
  326–29
Cross, Al, 373
Cruz v. Beto (1972), 305
cultural barriers, and women's rights, 214–16

Daschle, Tom, 374
Davidson, Judge, 91
Davis v. Prince Edward County, 88
Dawkins, Judge, 91
Dawley v. City of Norfolk, Virginia (1959), 75
Dean, Howard, 345
death penalty cases, 304n1

Defense of Marriage Act (DOMA), 365
"defense of marriage" acts, 363
DeGeneres, Ellen, 413
Delaware: and school desegregation, 103n35;
  Supreme Court of, 104
delay, opportunity for, 18, 87–88
Democratic Party, and civil rights, 57–58, 121
demonstrations: and civil rights, 139–55, 168;
  and women's movement, 257
Department of Defense, U.S., 183
Department of Health, Education, and
  Welfare, U.S., 45, 49; and Civil
  Rights Act, 47–48, 53–54; and school
  desegregation, 77
Department of Interior, U.S., 206
Department of Justice, U.S., 94, 214, 256–57,
  320
Department of Labor, U.S.: Women's Bureau,
  205, 208, 249
Department of State, U.S., 164
discovery process, 24
discriminatory application of non-
  discriminatory laws, 80–81
District of Columbia, and school
  desegregation, 50–51
Diver, Colin, 33–34
divorce, 216–17
Dixon, Robert, 300–301
Dobie, Armistead, 90
Doe v. Bolton (1973), 173–75, 199–200
Doe v. Poelker (1975), 191
domestic partner benefits, 410–12
domestic work, 215–16
Dothard v. Rawlinson (1977), 204
Douglas, Justice William, 295
Drew, Mississippi, 79n14
Dudziak, Mary, 163
Duren v. Missouri (1979), 203
Dynamic Court view, 1–4, 6–9, 30–36, 94,
  125, 174, 313–16; and *Brown,* 39–41; and
  civil rights, 54, 70–72; and environmental
  reform, 272, 286; and extra-judicial
  influence, 107–10, 156; logic of, 21–30;
  and women's rights, 212–13, 228, 245–46

Earth Day (1970), 291
Ebaugh, Helen, 237
economic changes: and civil rights, 157–60;
  and women's rights, 247–50
economic coercion, in support of segregation,
  82–83

economic constraints, and women's rights, 216–18

Edelsberg, Herman, 252–53

Edmondson, J. Howard, 294n27

education, women and, 251–52

Education Amendments Act (1972), 206

EEOC (Equal Employment Opportunity Commission), 206–7, 225–26, 252–53

Ehrlich, Paul, 290

Eisenhower administration, 47, 55, 59, 75–76, 76n6, 76n7, 118–19, 121, 161–62, 165, 298

Eisenstadt v. Baird (1972), 181

electoral changes, and civil rights, 160–62

electoral politics, and same-sex marriage, 369–82

Elementary and Secondary Education Act (1965), 40, 47–49, 52, 94

elites, influence on civil rights, 117–25

Elkins v. United States (1960), 316–17

Elliott, Judge, 90

Elman, Philip, 75, 169

employment discrimination, 203–6, 209–12, 408, 410, 412

Employment Non-Discrimination Act, 412

environmental: groups, 288–89, 291 (*see also names of specific organizations*); movement, 290–92; reform, 18, 271–79, 284–86

Environmental Impact Statements, 276–77, 285

EPA (Environmental Protection Agency), 284, 291

equality standard, used by Court, 213–14

equal pay, 248, 248n1

Equal Pay Act (1963), 204–6, 249n1

Equal Rights Amendment, 174, 206, 235, 244, 257–58

Erikson, Robert, 296–97

Escobedo v. Illinois (1964), 324–25

Esposito, John, 272

Estelle v. Gamble (1976), 305

exceptionalism, American, 428

exclusionary rule, 316–34

executive branch: and civil rights, 46–49, 52, 55–70, 94–95, 117–21; and support for Court, 75–78; and women's rights, 205–7

Executive Orders: No. 9980, 168; No. 9981, 168; No. 11063, 69–70; No. 11375, 206; No. 11478, 206

exit polls, 370–71, 381–82

extra-judicial influence, 7–8, 25–26, 41, 107–10, 107n2, 228, 422

Eyal, Chaim, 126

Fair Employment Practices Committee, 168

Fair Housing Law (1968), 68

Family Research Council, 361

Farmer, James, 141, 143–44, 148–49

Faubus, Orval, 44, 78, 129

FBI (Federal Bureau of Investigation), 77, 77n10

FCC (Federal Communications Commission), 206

federal funding: for abortion, 186–87; and desegregation, 97–100

federal government, influence with Supreme Court, 14

Federal Home Loan Bank Board, 206

Federal Housing Administration, 69

Federalist Papers, No. 78, 15

Federally Employed Women, 254

Federal Marriage Amendment, 365–67

Feeley, Malcolm, 334–35

Feinstein, Diane, 376

Feld, Barry, 315–16

fertility rates, decreasing, 250–51

film industry, portrayal of gay/lesbian characters, 413–14

financial incentives, and desegregation, 97–100

financial resources: courts and, 18–19; leveraging, 33–34

Fiss, Owen, 25

"Flowers from the Heartland," 358–59

Focus on the Family, 361, 367–68

Ford administration, 185

Foreign Assistance Act (1973), 186

Foreman, Matt, 377, 416

Forman, James, 145

Forrest, Jacqueline, 195

Fortas, Justice Abe, 314

foundations: and civil rights, 153; and women's rights, 244–45

Fourth National Survey of Religion and Politics, 371

Frank, Barney, 376–77

Frankfurter, Felix, 13n8, 84n18

Frederickson, George, 295, 301

Freedom Rides, 64, 76–77, 142

Freedom Summer, 144

Freedom to Marry, 358

Human Rights for Women, 254
Humphrey, Hubert, 118
Hyde Amendment, 185–87, 186n16, 235, 423–24
Hyman, Herbert, 128

ICC (Interstate Commerce Commission), 64–65
Illinois, and abortion, 194
implementation, 15–16, 31–32, 75–82, 225–26, 280–82, 299–302, 309–11, 315–16, 332
Inbau, Fred, 325
incremental strategy, for bringing about change, 417–18
Indiana, and prison reform, 312
information gathering, 24, 29, 29n19
Ingram, Helen, 275
In re Gault (1967), 314–15
In re George Anastaplo (1961), 74n4
In re Girard College Trusteeship (1958), 75
Interdepartmental Committee on the Status of Women, 205
interest groups, and litigation strategy, 18
international affairs, and civil rights, 162–67
Iowa, and 2004 elections, 374–75
Irvine v. California (1954), 318n26
issuance of search warrants, 318–19

Jackson, Justice Robert, 1–2, 21, 318n26, 422
Jackson, Mississippi, 45, 101–2
Jackson, President Andrew, 15
Jacobs, James, 306, 310, 313
Jacoway, Elizabeth, 101
Jacques, Cheryl, 375–76
Jaffe, Frederick, 195
Jay, John, 15
Jaybird Democratic Association, 58
Jencks v. U.S. (1957), 74
Johns, Ralph, 141
Johnson, Charles, 43n3
Johnson, Frank M., 20
Johnson, Lyndon B., 119
Johnson administration: and civil rights, 47, 59, 95, 121, 130–31; and women's rights, 206
Johnson v. Avery, 305
Johnson v. Transportation Agency, Santa Clara (1987), 204
Johnson v. Zerbst (1938), 330
Johnston, John, 222

Jones, Elise, 261
Jones, Walter B., 91
Jones v. Mayer Co. (1968), 68
Journey of Reconciliation, 144, 168
judicial activism, 1–3, 2n1
judicial appointment process, 13, 13n6, 14
judicial bureaucracy, 16–21, 86–87
judicial discretion, 10–11, 17, 88–91
judicial independence, 13–15, 22–25, 73–75
judicial misinterpretation, 16–17, 89–91
judicial procedures, evolving, 26–27
judicial selection process, for lower court judges, 18
judicial tenure, 18
jury service, women and, 220–21
juvenile defendants, rights of, 304, 314–16
juvenile justice system, 314–16

Kahn v. Shevin (1974), 203n4, 225
Kalodner, Howard, 29, 103
Katzenbach v. McClung (1964), 94n30
Kennedy, Robert F., 62, 64, 76–77, 120, 149, 165
Kennedy, Ted, 419
Kennedy administration: and civil rights, 47, 55, 59, 64, 76–78, 76n9, 120, 120n8, 121, 123, 165; and reapportionment, 298; and women's rights, 205
Kentucky, and 2004 elections, 373
Keppel, Francis, 97
Kerry, John, 407
King, Martin Luther, Jr., 77, 137–38, 138n25, 139–40, 143, 149, 166, 423
King, Mary, 254–55
Kingdon, John, 111
Kirp, David, 29
Knapp, Charles, 222
Knight, Robert, 380
Konigsberg v. California (1961), 74n4
Kristof, Nicholas, 399

labor unions, support for civil rights, 153
Lader, Lawrence, 259
LaFave, Wayne, 319
Lambda Legal, 353; Marriage Project, 356
Langer, Gary, 371
Lawson, Rev. James, 143, 149
Lawson, Steven, 81, 132
Lefstein, Norman, 330–31
legal argument, technical nature of, 12
legal bureaucracy, 17

legal culture, 11, 17–18
Legal Defense and Education Fund, Inc. (Inc. Fund, NAACP), 55, 91–93, 147, 152, 428
legal profession, attacks on Court, 84
legal representation, for juvenile defendants, 315–16
Legal Services Corporation Act (1974), 186
legal system, 12; access to, 17–18, 23–24, 281
Leiken, Lawrence, 329
Lerner, Benjamin, 331
Lerner v. Casey (1958), 74n4
Leventhal, Judge, 279–80
Levison, Stanley, 143
Lewis, John, 143
Library Services Act (1956), 119
Liroff, Richard, 277, 282
litigation: alternatives to, 426–27; control of, 223–25; cost of, 91–93; environmental, 271–86, 289–90; on job discrimination, 211; by prisoners, 305–6, 313n19; replacing political action, 12; for same-sex marriage, 339–42, 352–54, 368, 415–19
Little Rock, Arkansas, 44, 84, 84n19, 119, 138–39, 158
Livingston, J. Edwin, 91
local governments, resistance to civil rights, 84–85
Log Cabin Republicans, 377
long-term planning, courts and, 20
Los Angeles police, 322
Los Angeles v. Manhart (1978), 203
Lotus Corp., 410
Louisiana, pro-segregation laws and activities, 79, 83
Louisiana Constitution, 364
Loving v. Virginia (1967), 339n1

Macbeth, Angus, 281
MacKinnon, Catherine, 213
Maginnis, Patricia, 259
Maher v. Roe (1977), 176
Mahoney, E. R., 237
Maine, and same-sex unions, 351, 360
Mann, Dean, 275
Mansfield, Texas, 119
Mapp v. Ohio (1961), 316–20
Marbury v. Madison (1803), 15n12, 44
Margold, Nathan, 72–73
Marriage Protection Act of 2004, 367
Marshall, Burke, 131
Marshall, John, 15, 44

Marshall, Margaret, 347
Marshall, Ray, 158
Marshall, Thurgood, 43, 73, 92, 119–20, 146, 149
Marshall, Tom, 13n7
Martin, Joanna, 264
Maryland, and school desegregation, 103
Mason, Karen, 239
Massachusetts: Constitution of, 347–50, 419; prohibition of antigay job discrimination, 412; and same-sex marriage, 347–52, 355–56
Massachusetts Bar Association, 350
Matthews, Donald, 85
Mays, Dr. Benjamin, 145–46
McAdam, Doug, 144
McCann, Michael, 3n2, 12, 20
McConville, Michael, 333
McInturff, Bill, 372
McKay, Robert, 292–93
McLaughlin, Steven, 251
McLaurin v. Oklahoma Board of Regents (1950), 54, 165
McLindon, James, 217
McMann v. Richardson (1970), 330
McNeil, Joseph, 140
Meachum v. Fano (1976), 305n3
Meadows, Donnella, 290
media: and abortion, 229–34; and civil rights, 111–16, 126–27, 130–31, 166–67; coverage of Supreme Court, 112; and environmental reform, 288, 290–91; portrayal of gay/lesbian characters, 413–14; and same-sex marriage, 358–59, 382–400, 416; and women's rights, 242, 256, 264–65. *See also* black: press
Melnick, R. Shep, 278, 280–82
Menino, Thomas M., 348
Meritor Savings Bank v. Vinson (1986), 204
Meyer, Sylvan, 111–12
Michelman, Kate, 195
Michigan, and 2004 elections, 373
Miller, Jeffrey, 281
Milliken v. Bradley (1977), 34
Minnesota, and abortion, 194
Miranda v. Arizona (1966), 324–29
Mirsky, Chester, 333
Mississippi: and pro-segregation laws, 79; and voting rights, 61
Missouri Constitution, 364
Missouri ex. rel. Gaines v. Canada (1938), 54

Mitchell, John, 48
Mitchell v. U.S. (1941), 63–64
Monaghan, Kathleen, 225
Mongiardo, Dr. Daniel, 373
monitoring commissions, 27
Montana, and abortion, 194
Montgomery bus boycott, 134–38, 140, 145
Montgomery County, Alabama, 67
Moon, Henry, 146–47
"moral values," in 2004 elections, 370–72, 376, 381
Morgan v. Virginia (1946), 63–65, 142n33
motion to suppress evidence, 318
Motor Vehicle Air Pollution Control Act (1965), 290
Mulhauser, Karen, 424
Murphy, Walter, 126, 300
Musgrave, Marilyn, 365
music, of civil rights movement, 144

NAACP (National Association for the Advancement of Colored People), 43, 72–73, 79–80, 91–93, 119, 122–23, 122n10, 122n11, 140, 145–55, 160, 166, 426; "Statement on the Denial of Human Rights . . . and an Appeal to the United Nations for Redress," 163
Nabritt III, James, 92
NARAL (National Association for the Repeal of Abortion Laws), 241–42, 244, 260
Nashif, Tim, 362
Nashville Gas Co. v. Satty (1976), 204n7
National Association of Real Estate Brokers, 83
National Association of State Attorneys General, 84
National Centers for Disease Control, 178, 187
National Environmental Policy Act (1970), 273n1, 274, 276–77, 283, 285, 290
National Forest Management Act (1976), 283
National Institute of Corrections, 309
National Institute of Municipal Law Officers, 294
National Judicial Education Program to Promote Equality for Women and Men in the Courts, 221–22, 221n36
National Negro Congress, 163
National Science Foundation Authorization Act (1974), 186
National Urban League (NUL), 152

National War Labor Board, 248
National Women's Political Caucus, 242
Nebraska Constitution, 363
negotiations, facilitating, courts' role in, 26
Neier, Aryeh, 22, 125, 127
Nelson, Terry, 375
Netherlands, and same-sex marriage, 415
Network for Economic Rights, 254
Nevada Constitution, 364
New Hampshire: and abortion law, 262; and same-sex unions, 351, 360
New Jersey: and reapportionment, 301–2; and same-sex unions, 351, 360
New Mexico, and same-sex marriage, 359
New Paltz, New York, 359
Newport, Frank, 404
New York City: justice system of, 331, 334; police, 318–19
New York State, and abortion law, 263
New York Times, coverage of same-sex marriage, 382–400
Nickles, Don, 365
Nixon administration, 55; and abortion, 183; and Civil Rights Act, 48–49; and environmental reform, 274–75, 291–92; and women's rights, 206
Nixon v. Condon (1932), 58
Nixon v. Herndon (1927), 57
nondiscrimination policies, 412–13
North, Sandie, 264
North Carolina, and abortion law, 262
North Dakota, and abortion, 194
NOW (National Organization for Women), 241–45, 253–54; Legal Defense and Education Fund, 242

Oaks, Dallin, 323
O'Connor, Karen, 224, 229
Odell, Rice, 291
Office of Civil Rights, 55
Ohio, and 2004 elections, 377–82
Ohio v. Akron Center for Reproductive Health (1990), 176
Oklahoma, and 2004 elections, 373–74
O'Leary, Rosemary, 280
Oregon, and same-sex unions, 351, 360
Oregon Supreme Court, 360
Orfield, Gary, 85, 100–101
O'Rourke, Timothy, 296–97, 300–302
Orr v. Orr (1979), 203
Otten, Alan, 161

Packwood, Bob, 183, 263
Page, Benjamin, 127–28
Palley, Marian, 217, 244
Parchman Prison, Mississippi, 311–12
Parks, Rosa, 134, 134n18
passage of time, and assessment of influence,
    109, 124–25
Passman, Otto, 89
Patterson, Jack, 101
Paul, Faith, 105
Pelosi, Nancy, 419
Peltason, Jack, 76, 90, 422
People v. Barksdale (1972), 200
*Pittsburgh Press v. Pittsburgh Commission on
    Human Relations* (1973), 204
Planned Parenthood, 190
Planned Parenthood v. Ashcroft (1983), 176–77
Planned Parenthood v. Danforth (1976), 176
Playboy Foundation, 244
Plessy v. Ferguson (1896), 54
Poelker v. Doe (1977), 177, 191
police: brutality, 324, 326; coercion, 324–25;
    and exclusionary rule, 321–23; and
    Miranda warnings, 326–29
political representation, women and, 215–16
political support: and abortion rights,
    182–89, 235; and desegregation,
    94–96; and environmental movement,
    282–84; and prison reform, 308–9; and
    reapportionment, 299–300; and same-sex
    marriage, 356–61; and women's rights,
    235
Pollack, Harriet, 326
polling agencies. *See* public opinion
poll tax, 59
population explosion, 264
Portland, Oregon, and same-sex marriage,
    359–60
poverty, women and, 216
Powell, Adam Clayton, Jr., 122, 137
Powell, Justice Lewis, 34, 177, 221, 313
Powell Amendment, 122–23
Powell v. Alabama (1932), 330
precedent, 11–12, 182; and environmental
    reform, 273, 278–79; and prison reform, 308
Presidential Advisory Council on the Status of
    Women, 183, 263
President's Commission on the Status of
    Women, 174n1, 205
President's Committee on Civil Rights
    (PCCR), 65

prison: conditions, 305–7; reform, 306–7,
    310–11; support groups, 308–9
prison administrators, and prison reform, 310–11
prisoners' rights, 304–14
Pritchett, C. Herman, 107
privacy, right to, 182
private groups, supportive of segregation,
    82–84
private schools, and segregation, 83–84,
    97n32
Procunier v. Martinez (1974), 305
Prothro, James, 85
public defender programs, 330–34
public opinion, 13, 13n7, 16; and abortion,
    188, 235–38, 260–62; and court decisions,
    13, 13n7, 16; and environmental reform,
    286–87; on gays/lesbians, 408–10; and
    reapportionment, 299–300; and same-sex
    marriage, 400–407, 416; and same-sex
    unions, 343–46, 349–50; and 2004 elections,
    370–72; and women's rights, 239–41

Ramspeck Act (1940), 167
Randolph, A. Philip, 168
Rankin, J. Lee, 1–2
Reagan administration, 185
real estate industry, and housing segregation,
    83
reapportionment, 22–23, 292–302
Rebell, Michael, 27–29, 29n19, 32
"reciprocal beneficiaries" law (Hawaii), 344
Reed v. Reed (1971), 173, 203
Rehnquist Court, 431
Reitman v. Mulkey (1967), 68
Republican Party: and civil rights, 118–19,
    121; and same-sex marriage, 367, 375
Reskin, Barbara, 226
restrictive covenant cases, 67–68, 73
retention of jurisdiction, 27
retirement, women and, 217
Reynolds v. Sims, 298, 299n35
Rhodes v. Chapman (1981), 305n3
Rhyne, Charles S., 298
Rice v. Sioux City Memorial Park Cemetery
    (1954), 75
Roberts, E. F., 273
Roberts Court, 431
Robinson, Beth, 346, 355
Robinson, Jo Ann, 136
Roe v. Wade (1973), 6, 173–75, 199
Rogers, S. E., 89

Rogers, William P., 46
Romney, Mitt, 348
Roosevelt, Eleanor, 205
Roosevelt, Franklin D., 168
Rosenthal, Alan, 296
Rostow, Eugene, 25
Rove, Karl, 369–70
Rusk, Dean, 164
Rustin, Bayard, 143

salience: for abortion and women's rights,
    229–34; and extra-judicial influence, 109,
    111; and reapportionment, 300
same-sex marriage, 339–41
same-sex union announcements in
    newspapers, 414
San Francisco: Equal Benefits Ordinance
    (1996), 411; and same-sex marriage, 358–59
Sarachild, Kathie, 255
Sarat, Austin, 24, 27–29
Sarpolus, Ed, 373
Sarratt, Reed, 147
Sassower, Doris, 174
Sax, Joseph, 26
Scarlett, Judge, 89
Scenic Hudson Preservation Conference v.
    FPC (1965), 273
Scheingold, Stuart, 3, 12, 138, 422
Schiffren, Lisa, 398
Schlesinger v. Ballard (1975), 224
school desegregation, 34, 34n23, 42–57, 79,
    83–84, 94–96
Schulhofer, Stephen, 325, 424
SCLC (Southern Christian Leadership
    Conference), 143, 148, 150, 152
SDS (Students for a Democratic Society), 255
search and seizure, 304. *See also* exclusionary
    rule
Sellers, Cleveland, 143, 146, 149
separation of powers, 15–16
sex segregation, 217–18
sexual harassments, 207, 215
Shapiro, Martin, 298
Shapiro, Robert, 127–28
Sheatsley, Paul, 128
Shelley v. Kraemer (1948), 67–70, 73, 75, 165
Sierra Club, 288–89, 291
Sierra Club v. Morton (1972), 273
silver platter doctrine, 316
Sindler, Allan, 302
Singleton v. Jackson Municipal Separate

School District (1965), 45, 48, 88
sit-in cases, 66–67, 92
sit-in movement, 140–42, 145–47, 166
Sive, David, 272, 281–82
Skolnick, Jerome, 321–22
Smith, Woard W., 252, 252n8
Smith v. Allwright (1944), 58, 61
SNCC (Student Non-violent Coordinating
    committee), 142–43, 148, 150, 254–55
social reform, 4–8, 16, 31–32
sociocultural change, and civil rights, 96–97,
    167–69
Sokolow, Alvin, 302
solicitor general, 14, 14n10, 14n11, 293
South Carolina v. Katzenbach (1966), 94n30
South Dakota, and 2004 elections, 374
Southern Education Reporting Service, 49,
    49n13
Southern Manifesto, 74, 78, 78n12
Southern Regional Council, 65, 96, 103, 111
southern states: and anti-NAACP actions, 146;
    and desegregation, 52–54, 56, 95, 97–100;
    and judicial bias, 90–91; and voting rights,
    57–58
special masters, 27, 29–30
Specter, Arlen, 322
Spiotto, James, 318
sponsorship, of civil rights legislation, 124
state abortion laws, 175–78, 183–84, 187–88,
    262–63
state action, violating Fourteenth Amendment,
    66, 68
State and Local Federal Assistance Act (1972),
    206
state constitutions, amendments against same-
    sex unions, 343–44, 347–50, 363–65,
    377–82, 419
state-court judges, opposition to exclusionary
    rule, 320
state courts, and social reform, 340
state leaders, defiance of court orders, 78–81
state/local governments, and domestic partner
    benefits, 411
state/local leaders, and desegregation, 95
states: and antigay job discrimination, 412;
    commissions on status of women, 206;
    and comparable worth policies, 208; and
    gender discrimination, 202–5, 218–19; and
    legal abortions, 190–95; and opposition
    to same-sex unions, 362–65; and pro-
    segregation laws, 79–81

Stearns, Nancy, 198, 236, 241
Stern Foundation, 244
Stewart, Justice Potter, 316–17
Stickney, Dr. Stonewall, 34
Stone, Christopher, 272
Strauder v. West Virginia (1879), 202n1
Strauss, Murray A., 215
Supreme Court, 7; and federal government
    influence, 14; media coverage of, 112;
    public image of, 126, 236. *See also titles
    of specific cases*
Supreme Judicial Court of Massachusetts, 341
Sutherland, Rick, 272, 275
*Swann v. Charlotte-Mecklenburg Board of
    Education* (1971), 46
Sweatt v. Painter (1950), 54–55, 165
symbolic victory, 424

"Take Back Vermont" movement, 345–46
Tanenhaus, Joseph, 126, 300
Taylor, Humphrey, 371
Taylor v. Louisiana (1975), 203
Tedrow, Lucky, 237
Terry v. Adams (1953), 58, 61
Texas: and abortion laws, 175, 175n1; and
    anti-NAACP actions, 79; and prison
    reform, 311
Texas Primary Cases, 57–58, 61
textbooks, coverage of civil rights in, 116–17
Thayer, James Bradley, 12
Third National Conference of Commissions
    on the Status of Women, 253
third-world liberation movements, 145
Thornton III, J. Miles, 137
Thorpe, Roey, 353
Tracy, John, 346
Traditional Values Coalition, 361
"traditional values" groups, 343, 361–62,
    367–68, 375
transportation segregation, 63–65
Traynor, Justice Roger, 11–12, 20
Trescher, William, 237
Trubek, David, 277, 282
Truman administration, 123, 129, 160–61,
    164, 168
Turner, William, 313
Turner v. Utah (1975), 204n7
Tushnet, Mark, 18, 92–93, 93n29
Tuskegee, Alabama, 58

Udall, Stewart, 291

unanimity, in Supreme Court decisions, 43n3
Unemployment Relief Act (1933), 167
United Kingdom, and abortion law, 263
United Nations, 163
United States v. Vuitch (1971), 176n3
United States v. Yazell (1966), 202, 202n2
University of Texas Law School, 80
Uphaus v. Wyman (1959), 74n4
U.S. Army, and Little Rock crisis, 138
U.S. Army Corps of Engineers, 285
U.S. Commission on Civil Rights, 46n6, 47n8,
    49, 52–54, 59, 62, 67, 70, 77, 81, 83, 86,
    88, 92–93, 96, 103, 164, 208, 211, 219
U.S. Conference of Mayors, 293
Uslaner, Eric, 301
U.S. Merit Protection Board, 215
U.S. v. Alabama (1985), 57
U.S. v. Jefferson County Board of Education
    (1966), 45, 52
*U.S. v. Montgomery County Board of
    Education* (1969), 88
Utah, and ban on same-sex marriages, 363

Vermont: Constitution of, 344; and same-sex
    unions, 344–47; Supreme Court of, 341
Veterans Administration, 69
Vines, Kenneth, 85
Vinson, Chief Justice Fred, 55
violence: and civil rights, 123, 153n49;
    in prisons, 307, 309; in support of
    segregation, 82; against women, 214–15
Virginia, and segregation, 79, 159
Vose, Clement, 70
Voter Education Project, 77n11, 153
voting rights, 57–63, 80–81; for women, 205.
    See also reapportionment
Voting Rights Act (1965), 40, 59–61, 81, 94,
    94n30, 109, 121

wage discrimination, 204, 207–8
Wallace, George, 78, 309
Walt Disney World, Gay Days in, 414–15
Walters, Suzanna, 414
War Department, U.S., 248
Warren, Earl, 39, 42, 126, 292, 295, 321, 324
Warren Court, 304–5, 304n2, 308, 430
Wasby, Stephen, 18, 74, 323
Washington, D.C.: and abortion law, 263–64;
    and segregation, 163
Washington State: and abortion law, 263; and
    same-sex unions, 351, 360

Washington v. Watkins (1982), 332n51
Webster v. Reproductive Health Services
(1989), 176, 178n5
Weddington, Sarah, 201
Weeks v. United States (1914), 316
Weinberger v. Wiesenfeld (1975), 203
Weitzman, Lenore, 217
welfare rights, 11
Wenner, Lettie, 18, 281
Wesberry v. Sanders (1964), 295
Westoff, Charles, 261
Weyrich, Paul, 375
White, Justice Byron, 305, 325
White, Welsh, 326
white Americans, and civil rights, 110,
125–31, 144
Wilderness Society, 288, 291
Wilkins, Roy, 76, 145–46, 148–49
Wilkinson, Harvie, 40, 117, 133
Williams, Robert, 163–64
Williams v. Zbaraz (1980), 176n4
Winn, William, 96
Winter, James, 126
Wisconsin, prohibition of antigay job
discrimination, 412
Wisdom, Minor, 52, 86n20, 87, 90–91

Wolff, Miles, 141–42
Wolff v. McDonnell (1974), 305
Wolfson, Evan, 339, 343, 358, 410, 416
Wolf v. Colorado (1949), 316
women, in the workplace, 247–50. *See also*
employment discrimination
Women's Equity Action League, 242, 254
women's groups, 223–25, 241–45, 253–57.
See also names of specific organizations
women's liberation, 254–56
women's movement, 173–74, 221–22,
241–45, 252–65
Women's Political Council (WPC), 135–37
women's rights, 6–7, 202–5, 207–12
Women's Rights Project, 242
Woodward, C. Vann, 163
World War II, 247–49
Worthington, Rogers, 332
Wright, J. Skelly, 166, 274

Yannacone, Victor, 23, 26, 271–72
Yazoo City, Mississippi, 82–83, 101
Young, Whitney M., Jr., 166
Yudof, Mark, 20

Zinn, Howard, 138–39